Contents

Preface		vii
Table of Cases		ix
Table of Statutes and Other Materials		xix
1	Administrative Law	1
2	Civil and Criminal Procedure	24
3	Commercial Law	52
4	Company Law	73
5	Conflict of Laws	93
6	Constitutional Law	103
7	Contract Law	138
8	Conveyancing	148
9	Criminal Law	178
10	Criminology	194
11	Employment Law	218
12	English and European Legal Systems	241
13	Equity and Trusts	266
14	European Union Law	280
15	Evidence	308
16	Family Law	320
17	Jurisprudence	346
18	Land Law	360
19	Law of International Trade	372
20	Public International Law	381
21	Succession	386
22	Tort	393

Preface

Law Update 2003 has been written by an expert team of lawyers, both practitioners and academics, bringing together many years of experience in their different areas of specialisation.

Their research has been collated to provide an annual review and digest of the most recent developments in specific legal subject areas, designed for law students at degree and professional levels and also practitioners seeking a comprehensive update on current legal developments.

The contributors have drawn from a wide range of primary and secondary sources which have been arranged to make the book as user friendly as possible. Materials are reproduced in a concise format with relevant extracts and full source citations, enabling the reader to refer to the source and research in greater depth.

The law is stated as at 1 January 2003.

Table of Cases

A (Children) (Shared Residence), Re [2001]
EWCA Civ 1795   *334*
A v B (A Company) and Another [2002] 2 All
ER 545   *135*
A v L (Jurisdiction: Brussels II) [2002] 1 FLR
1042   *324*
Abbey National Building Society v Cann [1991]
AC 56   *171*
Actionstrength Ltd v International Glass
Engineering IN GL EN SpA and Another
[2002] 1 WLR 566; [2002] 4 All ER 468
55, 138
Adan v Newham London Borough Council
[2001] 1 All ER 930   *10*
Aero Properties Ltd v Citycrest Properties Ltd
[2002] 2 P & CR 21   *169*
Agnew v Inland Revenue Commissioner [2001] 2
AC 710   *78*
AIB Group (UK) plc v Martin and Another
[12002] 1 WLR 94   *66*
Al-Adsani v United Kingdom (No 2) (2002) 34
EHRR 11   *383*
Al Fayed and Others v Commissioner of Police of
the Metropolis (2002) The Times 17 June
29, 30
Al Fayed and Others v Commissioner of Police of
the Metropolis Judgment of 13 August 2002
(nyr)   *35, 36*
Al Khatid v Masry [2002] Fam Law 420   *326*
Aldis v Director of Public Prosecutions (2002)
The Times 6 March   *48*
Alliance and Leicester plc v Slayford [2001] 1 All
ER 1   *176*
Allied Carpets Group plc v Nethercott [2001]
BCC 81   *77*
Allied Dunbar Assurance plc v Homebase Ltd
[2002] 2 EGLR 23   *175*
Amalgamated Investment & Property Co Ltd (In
Liquidation) v Texas Commerce International
Bank Ltd [1982] QB 84   *89*
Andrews v Smith (1835) 2 CM & R 627   *57*
Anglo-Eastern Trust Ltd v Kermanshahchi
[2002] EWCA Civ 198   *30*
Antaios CiaNaviera SA v Salen Rederierana AB,
The Antaios [1984] 3 All ER 229   *380*
Arrest Warrant of 11 April 2000 (Democratic
Republic of the Congo v Belgium) Judgment
of 14 February 2002 (nyr)   *381, 382*
Arthur D Little Ltd (In Administration) v Ableco
Finance LLC [2002] 3 WLR 1387   *78*

Asda Stores Ltd v Thompson and Others [2002]
IRLR 245   *223*
Ashworth Hospital Authority v MGN Ltd [2002]
4 All ER 193   *133*
Associated Provincial Picture Houses Ltd v
Wednesbury Corp [1948] KB 223   *36, 108*
Attorney-General v Able [1984] QB 795   *118, 119*
Attorney-General's Reference (No 7 of 2000)
[2001] 1 WLR 1879   *91*
Attorney-General's Reference (No 2 of 2002)
(2002) The Times 17 October   *316*
Aubergine Enterprises Ltd v Lakewood
International Ltd [2002] 1 WLR 2149   *174*

B (A Child) (Sole Adoption by Unmarried
Father), Re [2002] 1 FLR 196   *337*
B (Interim Care Orders: Directions), Re [2002]
Fam Law 252   *343*
B (Minors) (Termination of Contact: Paramount
Consideration), Re [1993] Fam Law 301
343
B (Non-accidental Injury: Compelling Medical
Evidence), Re [2002] 2 FLR 599   *340*
B v B [2002] Fam Law 173   *325*
B v France [1992] 2 FLR 249   *321*
Badfinger Music v Evans [2001] 2 WTLR 1
271
Bairstow v Queens Moat Houses plc [2001] 2
BCLC 531   *77*
Bank of Credit and Commerce International SA v
Ali (No 2) [2002] 3 All ER 750   *144*
Barclays Bank Ltd v Quistclose Investments Ltd
[1970] AC 567   *268, 269*
Barclays Bank plc v Stuart London Ltd [2001] 2
BCLC 316   *80*
Barder v Barder [1987] 2 All ER 440   *327*
Baumbast v Secretary of State for the Home
Department; R v Secretary of State for the
Home Department Case C–423/99 [2002] 3
CMLR 599   *294, 297*
Bayview Motors Ltd v Mitsui Marine and Fire
Insurance Co Ltd and Others [2002] 1
Lloyd's Rep 652   *378*
Bell v Lever Brothers [1932] AC 161   *54, 55, 141, 142*
Bellinger v Bellinger [2001] 2 FLR 1048   *321, 322*
Bellmex International Ltd (In Liquidation), Re
[2001] 1 BCLC 91   *92*

BHP Petroleum Great Britain Ltd v Chesterfield
    Properties Ltd [2002] 1 All ER 821   *173*
Bircham & Co Nominees (No 2) Ltd v Worrell
    Holdings Ltd [2001] 3 EGLR 83   *164*
Blackburn v Gridquest Ltd (T/A Select
    Employment) [2002] IRLR 604   *238*
Boardman v Phipps [1967] 2 AC 46   *272*
Boehringer Ingelheim KG, Boehringer Ingelheim
    Pharma KG (together Boehringer), Glaxo
    Group Ltd (Glaxo), SmithKline Beecham
    plc, Beecham Group plc and SmithKline &
    French Laboratories Ltd (together
    SmithKline), The Wellcome Foundation Ltd
    (Wellcome) and Eli Lilly and Co (Eli Lilly) v
    Swingward Ltd (Swingward) and Dowelhurst
    Ltd (Dowelhurst) Case C–143/00 [2002]
    ECR I–3759   *303, 304, 305, 307*
Bond van Adverteerders v Netherlands Case
    352/85 [1988] ECR 2085   *283*
Bournemouth Borough Council v Meredith
    Judgment of 24 July 2002 (nyr)   *224*
Boys v Chaplin [1971] AC 356   *99*
Braymist Ltd and Others v Wise Finance Co Ltd
    [2002] 2 WLR 322; [2002] 2 All ER 333
    70, 139
Breeze v John Stacey (1999) The Times 8 July
    30
Brightlife Ltd, Re [1986] BCLC 418   *79*
Bristol & West plc v Bartlett; Paragon Finance
    plc v Banks; Halifax plc v Grant (2002) The
    Times 9 September   *366*
Bristol-Myers Squibb and Others v Paranova
    Cases C–427, 429 and 436/93 [1996] ECR
    I–3457   *305–306, 306*
British Gas Services Ltd v McCaull [2001] IRLR
    60   *230*
Brocklesby v Armitage & Guest [2001] 1 All ER
    172   *410*

C (Application by Mr and Mrs X under s30
    HFEA 1990), Re [2002] Fam Law 351   *344*
C (Intermin Care Order: Residential Assessment),
    Re [1997] 1 FLR 1   *343*
Callery v Gray (No 1) [2001] 1 WLR 2112   *31*
Callery v Gray (No 2) [2001] 1 WLR 2142   *31*
Callery v Gray (Nos 1 and 2) [2002] 1 WLR
    2000; [2002] 3 All ER 417 (HL)   *31, 32,
    143, 247*
Callery v Gray (Costs); Russell v Pal Pak
    Corrugated Ltd [2001] EWCA Civ 246;
    [2001] 4 All ER 1   *256, 258*
Campbell v Edwards [1976] 1 Lloyd's Rep 522
    373

Campbell v MGN Ltd (2002) The Times 29
    March   *131*
Cantor Fitzgerald International v Bird and Others
    [2002] IRLR 867   *221*
Carmine Capolongo v Azienda Agricole Maya
    Case 77/72 [1973] ECR 611   *300*
Caurti v Director of Public Prosecutions [2002]
    Crim LR 131   *185*
Cave v Robinson Jarvis and Rolf [2002] 2 All ER
    641   *409*
Cedarwood Productions Ltd, Re (2001) The
    Times 12 July   *81*
Celulose Beira Industrial SA v Fazenda Pública
    Case C–266/91 [1993] ECR I–4337   *301*
Centros Ltd v Erhvervs-og Selskabsstyrelsen Case
    C–212/97 [1999] ECR I–1459   *283*
Chaplin v Boys [1969] 2 All ER 1085   *410*
Chester v Afshar [2002] 3 All ER 552   *398*
Chillingworth v Esch [1924] 1 Ch 97   *164*
Choitram (T) International SA and Others v
    Pagarani and Others[2001] 1 WLR 1   *266,
    267*
CICB Mortgages v Pitt [1993] 3 WLR 802   *331*
CIL Realisations Ltd, Re [2000] 2 BCLC 361
    79
Ciro Citterio Menswear plc v Thakrar [2002] 1
    WLR 2217   *84*
Clark v Chandler [2002] EWCA Civ 1249   *161*
Clarke v O'Keefe (2000) 80 P & CR 127   *163*
College of North East London, The v Leather
    Judgment of 30 November 2001 (nyr)   *238,
    239*
Commission v Council (Re ERTA) Case 22/70
    [1971] ECR 263   *284, 286, 287, 288*
Commission v Denmark Case 171/78 [1980] ECR
    447   *302*
Commission v Federal Republic of Germany Case
    C–476/98 Judgment of 5 November 2002
    (nyr)   *284*
Commission v Grand Duchy of Luxembourg
    Case C–472/98 Judgment of 5 November
    2002 (nyr)   *284*
Commission v Ireland Case 55/79 [1980] ECR
    481   *302*
Commission v Ireland Case C–151/96 [1997]
    ECR I–3327   *283*
Commission v Italy Case 73/77 [1980] ECR 1533
    302
Commission v Kingdom of Belgium Case
    C–471/98 Judgment of 5 November 2002
    (nyr)   *284*
Commission v Kingdom of Denmark Case
    C–467/98 Judgment of 5 November 2002
    (nyr)   *283*

Commission *v* Kingdom of Sweden Case
C–468/98 Judgment of 5 November 2002
(nyr) *283*

Commission *v* Republic of Austria Case
C–475/98 Judgment of 5 November 2002
(nyr) *284*

Commission *v* Republic of Finland Case
C–469/98 Judgment of 5 November 2002
(nyr) *283*

Commission *v* United Kingdom of Great Britain
and Northern Ireland Case C–466/98
Judgment of 5 November 2002 (nyr) *280,
284, 289*

Commissioner of Police of the Metropolis *v*
Caldwell [1982] AC 341 *178*

Copeland *v* Greenhalf [1952] Ch 488 *362*

Cordle *v* Cordle [2002] 1 FLR 207 *325*

Cornelis Kramer & Others Joined Cases 3,
4–6/76 [1976] ECR 1279 *287*

Costa *v* ENEL [1964] ECR 585 *106*

Council Civil Service Unions *v* Minister for the
Civil Service [1985] AC 374 *108*

Cowl *v* Plymouth City Council (2002) The Times
8 January *19*

Coxall *v* Goodyear Great Britain Ltd (2002) The
Times 5 August *235, 397*

CP Henderson & Co *v* Comptoir d'Escompte de
Paris (1873) LR 5 PC 253 *374*

Crabb *v* Arun District Council [1976] Ch 179
276, 277

Criminal Proceedings against Donatella Calfa
Case C–348/96 [1999] ECR I–11 *283*

Criminal Proceedings against Horst Bickel and
Ulrich Franz Case C–274/96 [1998] ECR
I–7637 *283*

Cruickshank *v* Vaw Motorcast Ltd [2002] IRLR
24 *231*

Curr *v* Marks & Spencer plc [2002] Emp LR 705
226

Currencies Direct Ltd *v* Ellis [2002] 1 BCLC 193
84

D, P and JC *v* United Kingdom [2002] 3 FCR
385 *340*

Day *v* Cook [2002] 1 BCLC 1 *87*

Dawson *v* Wearmouth [1999] 2 AC 308 *333*

Defrenne *v* Sabena (No 2) Case 43/75 [1976]
ECR 455 *230*

Devaynes *v* Noble: Clayton's Case (1816) 1 Mer
572 *279*

Devenney *v* United Kingdom (2002) The Times
11 April *114*

D'Hoop (Marie-Nathalie) *v* Office National de
l'Emploi Case C–224/98 Judgment of 11 July
2002 (nyr) *297*

Diamond *v* Bank of London and Montreal [1979]
QB 333 *99*

Director of Public Prosections *v* Dunn [2001]
Crim LR 130 *186*

D'Jan of London Ltd, Re [1993] BCC 646 *85*

Donoghue *v* Armco Inc and Others [2002] 1 All
ER 748 *96*

Downsview Nominees Ltd *v* First City
Corporation Ltd [1993] AC 295 *366*

Drake (Richard) *v* Agnew and Sons [2002]
EWHC 294 *58*

Dubai Aluminium Co Ltd *v* Salaam [2002]
UKHL 48; (2002) The Times 6 December
274, 395

Dunnett *v* Railtrack plc [2002] 2 All ER 850
25

Ebrahimi *v* Westbourne Galleries Ltd [1973] AC
360 *89*

Edgar *v* Edgar [1980] 1 WLR 1410 *332*

Elkouil *v* Coney Island [2002] IRLR 174 *227*

Elliot *v* C [1983] 1 WLR 939 *178*

Ennstone Building Products Ltd *v* Stanger Ltd
[2002] 1 WLR 3059 *98, 99*

Europa, The [1908] P 84 *378*

Exporteur in Levende Varkens and Others *v*
Commission Cases T–481 and 484/93 [1995]
ECR II–2941 *293*

F, Re [2002] Fam Law 8 *342*

Factortame Ltd *v* Secretary of State for the
Environment, Transport and the Regions
(No 2) [2002] 4 All ER 97 *142*

Fairchild *v* Glenhaven Funeral Services Ltd and
Others [2002] 3 WLR 89; [2002] 3 All ER
305 (HL); [2002] 1 WLR 1052 (CA) *236,
399*

Faulkner *v* Inland Revenue Commissioners [2001]
SRC (SCD) 112 *392*

Fazenda Pública *v* União das Cooperatives
Abastecedoras de Leite de Lisboa, UCRL
(UCAL) Case C–347/95 [1997] ECR I–4911
300

FC Bradley & Sons Ltd *v* Federal Steam
Navigation Co (1926) 24 Ll LR 446 *377*

Ferguson *v* R [1979] 1 WLR 94 *313*

Firma Herbert Schabatke GmbH *v* Federal
Republic of Germany Case C–72/92 [1993]
ECR I–5509 *302*

Foss *v* Harbottle (1843) 2 Hare 461 *88*

Fratelli Cucchi *v* Avez SpA Case 77/76 [1977] ECR 987   *300*

Freeguard *v* Royal Bank of Scotland plc (2002) The Times 25 April   *365*

Freund *v* Charles Scott Developments (South Devon) Ltd [2002] 2 P & CR 31   *165*

Friends' Provident Life Office *v* Hillier Parker May & Rowden [1995] 4 All ER 260   *394*

Frost *v* James Finlay Bank Ltd [2002] Lloyd's Rep IR 503   *176*

Furundzija IT–95–17/1 'Lasva Valley' (1999) 38 ILM 317   *384*

G (Children: Contact), Re [2002] 3 FCR 377   *336*

Galoo Ltd *v* Bright Grahame Murray [1994] 1 WLR 1360   *407*

Germany *v* Commission Joined Cases 281, 283–285 and 287/85 [1987] ECR 3203   *286*

Ghandi *v* Patel [2002] Fam Law 262; [2002] 1 FLR 603   *328, 387*

GIE Groupe Concorde *v* Master of the Vessel Suhadiwarno Panjan [1999] ECR I–6307   *95*

Giles *v* Rhind [2001] 2 BCLC 582   *87, 89*

Gillett *v* Holt [2000] 2 All ER 289   *277*

Gilly (Mr and Mrs) *v* Directeur des Service Fiscaux du Bas-Rhin Case C–336/96 [1998] ECR I–2793   *283*

Golder *v* United Kingdom (1994) 18 EHRR 393   *384*

Goldman *v* Hargrave [1967] 1 AC 645   *401*

Good (Deceased), Re; Carapeto *v* Good and Others (2002) The Times 22 May   *386*

Goode *v* Martin [2002] 1 WLR 620   *27, 28*

Gooden Northamptonshire County Council [2002] 1 EGLR 137   *167*

Goodwin *v* United Kingdom; I *v* United Kingdom [2002] 2 FLR 487   *320, 322*

Gorman *v* Mudd [1992] CA Transcript 1076   *406*

Great Peace Shipping Ltd *v* Tsavliris Salvage (International) Limited, The Great Peace [2002] 4 All ER 689   *52, 141*

Greenpeace Council and Others *v* Commission Case C–321/95P [1998] ECR I–1651   *291*

Gribbon *v* Lutton [2002] QB 902   *163*

Grobbelaar *v* New Group Newspapers Ltd [2002] 4 All ER 732   *404*

Grzelczyk (Rudy) *v* Centre d'aide Sociale d'Ottignies-Louvain-la-Neuve Case C–184/99 [2001] ECR I–6193   *297*

Guidezone Ltd, Re [2000] 2 BCLC 321   *89*

H, Re [1991] 2 All ER 185   *335*

H (Child's Name: First Name), Re [2002] Fam Law 340   *333*

H and A (Paternity: Blood Tests), Re [2002] 1 FLR 1145   *343*

H and R, Re [1996] 1 FLR 80   *340*

HJ *v* HJ (Financial Provision: Equality) [2002] 1 FLR 415   *326*

H *v* S (2002) The Times 3 July   *408*

Hadley *v* Baxendale (1854) 9 Ex 341   *62*

Hagen *v* ICI Chemicals and Polymers Ltd [2002] IRLR 31   *228*

Hallam Land Management Ltd *v* UK Coal Mining Ltd [2002] 2 EGLR 80   *165*

Halloran *v* Delaney [2002] 1 EWCA Civ 1258   *257*

Hammond *v* Osborn [2002] 2 P & CR 20   *176*

Hampton *v* Minns [2002] 1 WLR 1   *68*

Handelswekerij G J Bier BV *v* Mines de Potasse Case 21/76 [1978] QB 708   *96*

Hanson *v* SWEB Property Developments Ltd [2002] 1 P & CR 35   *170*

Harlingdon and Leinster Enterprises Ltd *v* Christopher Hull Fine Art Ltd [1991] 1 QB 564   *59, 60*

Harrison *v* Department of Social Security [1997] COD 220   *40*

Harrods Ltd *v* Harrodian School Ltd [1996] RPC 697   *407*

Hatton *v* Sutherland (2002) The Times 12 February   *397*

Henderson *v* Jauoen and Another [2002] 1 WLR 2971   *95*

Henry Boot Construction (UK) Ltd *v* Malmaison Hotel (Manchester) Ltd [2001] 1 All ER 257   *380*

Hertfordshire Investments Ltd *v* Bubb [2000] 1 WLR 2318   *30–31*

Hewlett Packard Ltd *v* O'Murphy [2002] IRLR 4   *218*

Holaw (470) Ltd *v* Stockton Estates Ltd (2001) 81 P & CR 29   *170*

Hopes (Heathrow) Ltd, Re [2001] 1 BCLC 575   *82*

Hunt *v* Severs [1994] 2 All ER 385   *408*

Hurst *v* Leeming [2002] CP Rep 59   *26*

Ikimi *v* Ikimi [2001] 2 FCR 385   *323*

ILO Case Opinion 2/91 [1993] ECR I–1061   *287*

Industria Gomma Articoli Vari IGAV *v* Ente Nazionale per la Cellulosa e per la Carta (ENCC) Case 94/74 [1975] ECR 699   *301*

Inland Revenue Commissioners *v* Adam &
Partners Ltd [2001] 1 BCLC 222   *90*

Inland Revenue Commissioners *v* Eversden
[2002] STC 1109   *391*

Interbrew SA *v* Financial Times Ltd and Others
[2002] EWCA Civ 274; [2002] EMLR 446
132, 134

Interzuccheri SpA *v* Societa Rezzano e Cavassa
Case 105/76 [1977] ECR 1029   *300*

Investors Compensation Scheme Ltd *v* West
Bromwich Building Society (No 1) [1998] 1
WLR 896   *361*

Irvine *v* Talksport Ltd [2002] 2 All ER 414
406

J A Pye (Oxford) Ltd *v* Graham [2002] 3 WLR
221   *369*

J-S (A Child) (Contact: Parental Responsibility),
Re [2002] 3 FCR 433   *335*

J S Bloor (Measham) Ltd *v* Calcott [2002] 1
EGLR 222   *173*

James *v* Evans [2000] 3 EGLR 1   *162*

Jégo-Quéré *v* Commission Case T–177/01 [2002]
2 CMLR 1137   *290, 291, 294*

Jennings *v* Rice [2002] WTLR 367   *276*

Jewson Ltd *v* Kelly (2002) The Times 3 October
60, 146

Johnson *v* BJW Property Developments Ltd
[2002] 3 All ER 574   *402*

Johnson *v* Gore Wood & Co (No 1) [2002] 2 AC
1   *87, 88*

Johnson *v* Youden [1950] 1 KB 544   *187*

Jones *v* Sherwood Services Ltd [1992] 1 WLR
277   *373*

K *v* K (Ancillary Relief: Pre-nuptial Agreement)
[2002] Fam Law 877   *332*

Kaba (Arben) *v* Secretary of State for the Home
Department Case C–356/98 [2000] ECR
I–2623   *297*

Kajala *v* Noble (1982) 75 Cr App R 149   *317*

Kearns *v* General Council of the Bar [2002] 4 All
ER 1075   *403*

Kiam *v* MGN Ltd [2002] 2 All ER 219   *405*

Kirkton *v* Tetrosyl [2002] IRLR 840   *232*

Krohn *v* Commission Case 175/82 [1986] ECR
753   *293*

Kuwait Airways Corp *v* Iraqi Airways Co (No 1)
[1995] 3 All ER 694   *93*

Kuwait Airways Corp *v* Iraqi Airways Co (No 2)
(1998) The Times 12 May   *93*

Kuwait Airways Corp *v* Iraqi Airways Co (No 3)
[2002] 3 All ER 209   *93, 410*

L *v* L (Financial Provision: Contributions) [2002]
2 FCR 413   *325*

Lafontant *v* Aristide 844 F Supp 128 (East Dist
NY 1994)   *382*

Ladd *v* Marshall [1954] 3 All ER 745   *30*

Lambert *v* Lambert [2002] 3 FCR 673   *326*

Larsen et Kjerulff Case 142/77 [1978] ECR 1543
301

Lawrence *v* Regent Office Care Ltd [2002] IRLR
822   *229*

Le Foe *v* Le Foe and Woolwich plc [2001] 2
FLR 970   *330*

Leakey *v* National Trust [1980] QB 485   *401*

Leander *v* Sweden (1987) 9 EHRR 433   *7*

Les Verts *v* Parliament Case 294/83 [1986] ECR
1339   *292*

Lever (Finance) Ltd *v* Westminster Corp [1971]
1 QB 222   *13*

Lewin *v* Crown Prosecution Service [2002]
EWHC 1049   *185*

Leyland Shipping Co Ltd *v* Norwich Union Fire
Insurance Society Ltd [1918] AC 350   *379*

Lindsay *v* Commissioners of Customs and Excise
(2002) The Times 27 February   *11*

Liverpool Roman Catholic Archdiocese Trustees
Incorporated *v* Goldberg [2001] 1 All ER 182
410

Lloyd *v* Dugdale [2002] 2 P & CR 13   *159*

Lloyds Bank *v* Rosset [1991] AC 107   *330*

London and Blenheim Estates Ltd *v* Ladbroke
Retail Parks Ltd [1993] 4 All ER 157   *363*

Lowe *v* Guise [2002] 3 All ER 454   *407*

M *v* M [2002] Fam Law 177   *326*

Macintyre *v* Phillips (2002) Then Times 30
August   *404*

Marcic *v* Thames Water Utilities Ltd (2002) The
Times 14 February   *401*

Malik *v* Bank of Credit and Commerce
International SA [1997] 3 All ER 1   *144*

Malory Enterprises Ltd *v* Cheshire Homes (UK)
Ltd [2002] Ch 216   *160*

Marcq *v* Christie Manson and Woods Ltd [2002]
4 All ER 1005   *411*

Maronier *v* Larner [2002] 3 WLR 1060   *101*

Matthews *v* Ministry of Defence [2002] 3 All ER
513   *21, 393*

McCulloch *v* May [1947] 2 All ER 845   *407*

McFarlane *v* Tayside Health Board [1999] 4 All
ER 961   *396*

McGhee *v* National Coal Board [1972] 3 All ER
1008   *400*

McManus *v* Beckham [2002] 4 All ER 497   *403*

Medforth v Blake [2000] Ch 86   *366*

Melville v Inland Revenue Commissioners [2001] STC 1271   *390*

Merck, Sharp & Dohme GmbH v Paranova Pharmazeutika Handels GmbH Case C–443/99 [2002] ECR I–3703   *303, 304, 305*

Mesher v Mesher [1980] 1 All ER 126   *325*

Metall und Rohstoff AG v Donaldson Lufkin and Jenrette Inc [1990] 1 QB 391   *99*

Midland Bank v Cooke [1995] 2 FLR 915   *329*

Midwood v Morgan [2001] 3 EGLR 127   *166*

Milasan, The [2002] 2 Lloyd's Rep 458   *379*

Miller v Bain (Director's Breach of Duty) [2002] 1 BCLC 266   *85*

Miller Bros and F P Butler Ltd v Johnston (2002) The Times 18 April   *220*

Milroy v Lord (1862) 4 De GF & J 264   *266, 267*

Mitsui & Co Ltd v Flota Mercante Grancolombiana SA [1988] 2 Lloyd's Rep 208   *376*

Mobil Oil Co Ltd v Birmingham City Council [2002] 3 P & CR 14   *360*

Moran v Director of Public Prosecutions (2002) The Times 6 February   *39*

Morgan v Staffordshire University [2002] IRLR 190   *232*

Morrow v Safeway Stores plc [2002] IRLR 9   *222*

Morton v South Ayrshire Council [2002] IRLR 256   *229*

Moschi v Lep Air Services Ltd [1973] AC 331   *57*

Motemtronic Ltd v Autocar Equipment Ltd (1996) 20 June (unrep)   *57*

Mount v Baker Austin [1998] PNLR 493   *400*

Mousaka Inc v Golden Seagull Maritime Inc and Another [2002] 1 All ER 726   *380*

MPB Structure Ltd Munro [2002] IRLR 601   *238*

Mulox IBC Ltd v Geels Case C–125/92 [1993] ECR I–4075   *95*

Nash v Mash Roe Group plc [1998] IRLR 168   *222*

Nathan v Leonard (2002) The Times 4 June   *389*

National Westminster Bank plc v Amin [2002] 1 FLR 735   *367*

National Westminster Bank plc v Somer International (UK) Ltd [2002] 1 All ER 198   *145*

Needler Financial Services Ltd v Taber [2002] 3 All ER 501   *407*

New Bullas Trading Ltd, Re [1994] 1 BCLC 449   *78, 79*

Newbury District Council v Secretary of State for the Environment; Newbury District Council v International Synthetic Rubber Co Ltd [1981] AC 578   *13*

Newman v Jones (22 March 1982) (unrep)   *363*

North Range Shipping Ltd v Seatrans Shipping Corp [2002] 4 All ER 390   *380*

Norwich Pharmacal Co v Commissioners of Customs and Excise [1974] AC 133   *132, 134*

Nygård (Niels) v Svineafgifsfonden and Ministeriet for Fødevarer, Landbrug og Fiskeri Case C–234/99 [2002] ECR I–3657   *298*

O and N (Children) (Non-accidental Injury: Burden of Proof), Re [2002] 2 FLR 1167   *340, 341*

O'Hara v Chief Constable of the Royal Ulster Constabulary [1997] 2 WLR 1   *36*

O'Hara v United Kingdom (2002) 34 EHRR 32   *36*

O'Neill v Phillips [1999] BCC 600   *90*

Osman v United Kingdom (1998) 5 BHRC 293   *22*

O'Sullivan v Management Agency [1985] 3 All ER 351   *272*

Otis Vehicle Rentals ALS Ltd (Formerly Brandrick Hire (Birimingham) Ltd) v Ciceley Commercials Ltd [2002] EWCA Civ 1064   *64*

OTV Birwelco Ltd v Technical and General Guarantee Co Ltd [2002] 4 All ER 668   *140*

P, C and S v United Kingdom [2002] 2 FLR 631   *339*

Pabst et Richarz KG v Hauptzollamt Oldenburg Case 17/81 [1982] ECR 1331   *302*

Padgham v Rochelle [2002] 99 (38) LSG 36   *176*

Paggetti v Cobb (2002) The Times 12 April   *225*

Papera Traders Co Ltd and Others v Hyundai Merchant Marie Co Ltd and Another, The Eurasian Dream [2002] 1 Lloyd's Rep 719   *377*

Paragon Finance plc v Nash and Another; Paragon Finance plc v Staunton and Another (2001) The Times 25 October   *363*

Parish v Sharman [2001] 2 WTLR 593   *328*
Parkinson v St James and Seacroft University
  Hospital NHS Trust [2001] 3 All ER 97
  396
Parsons Corporation and Others v CV
  Scheepvaartonderneming Happy Ranger, The
  Happy Ranger [2002] 2 All ER (Comm) 24
  (CA); [2002] 1 All ER (Comm) 176   *373,
  374*
Pascoe v Turner [1979] 1 WLR 431   *271*
Peckham v Ellison (1999) 70 P & CR 439   *171*
Pennington v Waine [2002] 4 All ER 214   *266,
  267*
Pepper v Hart [1993] AC 593; [1993] 1 All ER
  42   *105, 241, 242*
Percy v Director of Public Prosecutions (2002)
  The Times 21 January   *126*
Peskin v Anderson [2001] 1 BCLC 372   *86*
Pharmacia & Upjohn SA v Paranova A/S Case
  C–379/97 [1999] ECR I–6927   *306*
Phoenix Finance Ltd v Federation International
  de l'Automobile (2002) The Times 27 June
  27
Phonogram Ltd v Lane [1982] QB 938   *72*
Poplar Housing and Regeneration Community
  Association Ltd v Donoghue [2001] 4 All ER
  604   *17*
Practice Direction (Crime: Life Sentences) [2002]
  1 WLR 1789   *44*
Practice Direction (Crime: Victim Personal
  Statements) [2001] 4 All ER 640   *43*
Practice Direction (Criminal Proceedings:
  Consolidation [2002] 1 WLR 2870   *35*
Practice Direction (Hansard: Citation) [1995] 1
  WLR 192   *242*
Practice Direction (House of Lords: Supporting
  Documents) [1993] 1 WLR 303   *242*
Prestige Properties Ltd v Scottish Provident
  Institution [2002] 3 WLR 1011   *160*

R (A Child), Re [2001] 2 FLR 1358   *333*
R v A (Complainant's Sexual History) [2001] 3
  All ER 1   *28*
R v Adamako [1995] 1 AC 171   *182, 184*
R v Barnett [2002] Crim LR 489   *310*
R v Blenkinsop [1995] 1 Cr App R 7   *317*
R v Bow Street Metropolitan Stipendiary
  Magistrate, ex parte Pinochet Ugarte (No 3)
  [1999] 2 WLR 827   *385*
R v Byrne [2002] Crim LR 487   *308*
R v Caldwell; R v Dixon (1993) 99 Cr App R 73
  317
R v Carass (2001) Judgment of 19 December
  2001 (nyr)   *311*

R v Clare; R v Peach [1995] 2 Cr App R 33
  316, 317
R v Clarke [1995] 2 Cr App R 425   *317*
R v Concannon [2002] Crim LR 213   *190*
R v Dalby [1982] 1 All ER 916; (1982) Cr App R
  348   *180*
R v Dempster [2001] EWCA Crim 571   *314*
R v Dias [2002] Crim LR 490   *180*
R v Dietschmann [2002] Crim LR 132   *181*
R v Director of Public Prosecutions, ex parte
  Kebilene [1999] 3 WLR 175   *118, 119*
R v Dodson; R v Williams [1984] 1 WLR 971
  317
R v Drummond [2002] Crim LR 666   *311*
R v Dyke and Munroe [2002] Crim LR 153
  189
R v East Sussex County Council, ex parte
  Reprotech Ltd [2002] 4 All ER 58   *12*
R v Fenton (1975) 65 Cr App R 261   *182*
R v Forbes [2001] AC 473   *37*
R v Fowden; R v White [1982] Crim LR 588
  317
R v Fowler [2002] Crim LR 521   *49*
R v Gemmell and Richards [2002] Crim LR 926
  178
R v Ghafoor (Imran) (2002) 166 JP 601   *49*
R v Goodfellow [1986] Crim LR 468; (1986) 83
  Cr App R 23   *180*
R v Grimer [1982] Crim LR 674   *317*
R v H (2001) The Times 17 May   *190*
R v Hanratty (James) (Deceased) (2002) The
  Times 16 May   *50*
R v Harmer [2002] Crim LR 401   *191*
R v Heath (1999) The Times 15 October   *191*
R v Hookway [1999] Crim LR 750   *317*
R v Ismail (1991) 92 Cr App R 92   *41*
R v Jackson [1997] 2 Cr App R 297   *41*
R v Jones (Anthony William) and Others [2002] 2
  All ER 113   *41*
R v Kefford (2002) The Times 7 March   *205*
R v Kelly [1998] 3 All ER 741   *188*
R v Kennedy [1999] Crim LR 65   *181*
R v Kidd and Others [1998] 1 WLR 604   *243*
R v Kirk [2002] Crim LR 756   *186*
R v Lambert [2001] 3 WLR 206   *311, 312*
R v Lambert, Ali and Jordan [2001] 2 WLR 211
  312
R v Leeds Crown Court, ex parte Wardle [2001]
  2 WLR 865   *39*
R v Lichniak; R v Pyrah [2002] 4 All ER 1122
  (HL); [2002] QB 296 (CA)   *46*
R v Lucas [1981] QB 720   *310*
R v Marrin (2002) The Times 5 March   *318*

R v Martin [2002] Crim LR 136   *192*
R v Mauricia [2002] Crim LR 655   *313*
R v Metropolitan Police Commissioner, ex parte Blackburn [1968] 2 QB 118   *118*
R v North and East Devon Health Authority, ex parte Coughlan (Secretary of State for Health intervening) [2001] QB 213   *13*
R v Nye (1982) 75 Cr App R 247   *314*
R v Palmer (2002) The Times 18 April   *40*
R v Parks (Sydney Alfred) [1961] 1 WLR 1484   *51*
R v Pendleton (Donald) [2001] UKHL 66; [2002] 1 All ER 524   *50, 263*
R v Powell and English [1991] 1 AC 1   *190*
R v R (Informer: Reduction in Sentence) (2002) The Times 18 February   *44*
R v Secretary of State for Education and Employment [2002] 1 FLR 493   *332*
R v Secretary of State for the Environment, Transport and the Regions, ex parte Spath Holme Ltd [2001] 1 All ER 195   *241*
R v Secretary of State for the Home Department, ex parte Daly [2001] 2 AC 532   *109*
R v Secretary of State for the Home Department, ex parte Ghulam Fatima [1986] AC 527   *324*
R v Secretary of State for Transport, ex parte Factortame (No 1) [1990] 2 AC 85   *104*
R v Secretary of State for Transport, ex parte Factortame Ltd and Others (No 3) Case C–221/89 [1991] ECR I–3905   *283*
R v Secretary of State for Works and Pensions [2002] 2 FLR 1181   *331*
R v Shayler [2002] 2 All ER 477   *127*
R v Singh (Gurphal) [1999] Crim LR 582   *185*
R v Southampton Youth Court, ex parte W; R v Wirral Borough Magistrates' Court, ex parte K Judgment of 23 July 2002 (nyr)   *47*
R v Stephens (2002) The Times 27 June   *312*
R v Stockwell (1993) 92 Cr App R 260   *317*
R v Sullivan and Ballion [2002] Crim LR 758   *188*
R v Summers (1953) 36 Cr App R 14   *313*
R v Tandy (1988) 87 Cr App R 45   *182*
R v Vye [1993] 3 All ER 241   *315*
R v Wacker [2002] Crim LR 839   *182*
R (On the Application of A) v Partnerships in Care Ltd (2002) The Times 11 April   *18*
R (On the Application of Adlard) v Secretary of State for the Environment [2002] EWCA Civ 735   *9*
R (On the Application of Anderson) v Secretary of State for the Home Department [2002] 4 All ER 1089 (HL); [2002] 1 WLR 1143 (CA)   *45, 47*

R (On the Application of Beeson) v Dorset County Council (2002) The Times 21 December   *10*
R (On the Application of Burkett) v Hammersmith and Fulham London Borough Council [2002] 3 All ER 97   *19*
R (On the Application of Heather and Another) v Leonard Cheshire Foundation [2002] 2 All ER 936   *14*
R (On the Application of Hirst) v Secretary of State for the Home Department (2002) The Times 10 April   *10, 12*
R (On the Application of Howard) v Secretary of State for Health [2002] EWHC Admin 396   *8*
R (On the Application of International Transport Roth GmbH) v Secretary of State for the Home Department (2002) The Times 26 February   *120*
R (On the Application of McLellan) v Bracknell Forest Borough Council [2002] 1 All ER 899   *10*
R (On the Application of Persey) v Secretary of State for the Environment, Food and Rural Affairs (2002) The Times 28 March   *6*
R (On the Application of Potthoff) v Sheffield Croown Court Judgment of 18 July 2002 (nyr)   *38, 39*
R (On the Application of ProLife Alliance) v BBC [2002] 2 All ER 756   *107*
R (On the Application of Smeaton) v Secretary of State for Health (2002) The Times 3 May   *178*
R (On the Application of the Oxford Study Centre) v The British Council [2001] EWHC Admin 207   *18*
R (On the Application of Wagstaff) v Secretary of State for Health [2001] 1 WLR 292   *6, 7, 8*
Radwan v Radwan (No 2) [1973] Fam Law 35   *324*
Raja v Lloyds TSB Bank plc (2001) 82 P & CR 16   *175*
Rees v Darlington Memorial Hospital NHS Trust [2002] 2 All ER 177   *396*
Regal (Hastings) Ltd v Gulliver [1942] 1 All ER 378   *272*
Rhesa Shipping Co SA v Edmunds, The Popi M [1985] 1 WLR 918   *379*
Rhine Navigation Case Opinion 1/76 [1977] ECR 741   *284, 287*
Roerig v Valiant Trawlers Ltd [2002] 1 All ER 961   *100*

Roquette Frères v Commission Case 20/88 [1989] ECR 1553   *293*

Rose v Rose [2002] 1 FLR 978   *324, 325*

Royal Bank of Scotland v Etridge (No 2) [2001] 4 All ER 449   *331*

Royal Brompton Hospital NHS Trust v Hammond [2002] 2 All ER 801   *394*

Royal Brunei Airlines Sdn Bhd v Tan (Philip Kok Ming) [1995] 3 All ER 97   *273*

Royal National Orthopaedic Hospital Trust v Howard Judgment of 26 July 2002 (nyr) *230*

Rushbridger v Attorney-General [2001] EWHC Admin 529   *116*

Russell-Cooke Trust Company, The v Prentis [2002] EWHC 2227; [2002] NLJ 1719   *279*

Rutherford v Town Circle Ltd (T/A Harvest) and Secretary of State for Trade and Industry; Bentley v Secretary of State for Trade and Industry [2002] IRLR 768   *223*

Rutten v Cross Medical Ltd Case C–383/95 [1997] ICR 715   *95*

Rylands v Fletcher (1868) LR 3 HL 330   *401*

S, Re; W, Re (Children: Care Plan) [2002] 2 WLR 720   *341, 342*

S (Contact: Children's Views), Re [2002] 1 FLR 1156   *335*

S v S (Ancillary Relief: Consent Order) [2002] Fam Law 422   *327*

Saeed v Plustrade Ltd [2001] EWCA Civ 2011 *362*

Sahin v Germany [2002] 3 FCR 321   *335*

Sala (Maria Martinez) v Freistat Bayern Case C–85/96 [1998] ECR I–2691   *297*

Sanders Adour SNC and Guyomarc'h Orthez Nutrition Animale SA v Directeur des Services Fiscaux Des Pyrenées-Atlantiques Joined Cases C–149 and 150/91 [1991] ECR I–4337   *300*

Scarfe v Adams [1981] 1 All ER 843   *163*

Sealey v Trinidad and Tobago; Headley v Trinidad and Tobago (2002) The Times 5 November   *315*

Secretary of State for the Home Department v Wainwright and Another (2002) The Times 4 January   *130*

Secretary of State for Trade and Industry v Creegan [2002] 1 BCLC 99   *81*

Secretary of State for Trade and Industry v Deverall [2001] Ch 340   *83*

Sedleigh-Denfield v O'Callaghan [1940] AC 880 *401*

Sharif Garrett & Co [2002] 3 All ER 195   *400*

Shaw (Norman) v R [2002] Crim LR 140   *191*

Shell UK Ltd v Enterprise Oil plc [1999] 2 Loyd's Rep 456   *373*

Siebe Gorman v Barclays Bank Ltd [1979] 2 Lloyd's Rep 142   *79*

Six Constructions Ltd v Humbert Case 32/88 [1989] ECR 341   *95*

Sledmore v Dalby (1996) 72 P & CR 196   *277*

Smith v Royce Properties Ltd [2002] 2 P & CR 5 *162*

Smith v South Gloucestershire Council [2002] 38 EGLR 206   *167*

Sociaal Fonds v Brachfeld and Chougol Diamond Co Cases 2 and 3/69 [1969] ECR 211   *301*

Société National Industrielle Aerospatiale v Lee Kui Jak [1987] AC 871   *97*

Solle v Butcher [1950] 1 KB 671   *54, 55, 142*

Spiers v English [1907] P 122   *387*

Stafford v Director of Public Prosecutions [1974] AC 878   *263, 264*

Stelle v M'Kinlay (1880) 5 App Cas 754   *57*

Stuart v Bell [1891] 2 QB 341   *404*

Sulaiman v Juffali [2002] 2 FCR 427; [2002] Fam Law 97   *324*

Sunday Times v United Kingdom (1972) 2 EHRR 245   *118*

Sutherland v Hatton [2002] IRLR 263   *237*

Taylor v Chief Constable of Chester (1986) 84 Cr App R 191   *317*

Theakston v MGN Ltd [2002] EMLR 22   *137*

Thoburn v Sunderland City Council; Hunt v Hackney London Borough Council; Harman and Another v Cornwall County Council; Collins v Sutton London Borough Council (2002) The Times 22 February   *103*

Thomas v Hillingdon London Borough Council (200) The Times 4 October   *225*

Thompson (Robert) and John Venables, Re [2001] 1 Cr App R 401   *44*

Tinnelly and Sons Ltd and Others v United Kingdom; McElduff and Others v United Kingdom (1998) 4 BHRC 393   *115*

Toledo, The [1995] 1 Lloyd's Rep 40   *378*

Transpacific Eternity SA v Kanematsu Corporation and Another, The Anatares III [2002] 1 Lloyd's Rep 233   *375*

Trotter v Franklin [1991] 2 NZLR 92   *69*

TSN Kunststoffrecycling GmbH v Jurgens [2002] 1 WLR 2459   *100*

Turner v Grovit and Others [2002] 1 All ER 960 *97*

Twinsectra v Yardley [2002] 2 WLR 802; [2002] 2 All ER 377   *168, 267, 272*

UCB Corporate Services Ltd v Williams [2002] 3 FCR 448   *330*
UCB Group Ltd v Hedworth [2002] 46 EG 200   *159*
Unifrex v Council and Commission Case 281/82 [1984] ECR 1969   *293*
Unión de Pequeños Agricultores v Council of the European Union Case T–173/98 [1999] ECR II–3357   *289*
Unión de Pequeños Agricultores v Council of the European Union Case C–50/00P [2002] 3 CMLR 1   *289*

Van Gend en Loos [1963] ECR 1   *106*
Vaughan v Barlow Clowes International Ltd [1992] 4 All ER 22   *279*
Veba Oil Supply and Trading GmbH v Petrotrade Inc [2002] 1 Lloyd's Rep 295   *372*
VVG International and Metalsivas v Commission Case T–155/02 Order of 8 August 2002 (nyr)   *294*

W, Re [2001] 4 All ER 88   *168*
W (Children) (Education: Choice of School), Re [2002] 3 FCR 473   *334*
Waite and Kennedy v Germany (2000) 30 EHRR 261   *384*
Walker v Stones [2001] QB 902   *273*
Wallis Fashion Group Ltd v CGU Life Assurance Ltd (2001) 81 P & CR 393   *173*

Walsh v Lonsdale (1882) 21 Ch D 9   *177*
Webb v United Kingdom (1997) 24 EHRR CD 73   *380*
Weber v Universal Ogden Services Ltd [2002] 3 WLR 931   *94*
Wells v MHLG [1967] 2 All ER 1041   *13*
Western Fish Products Ltd v Penwith District Council [1981] 2 All ER 204   *14*
Wheeldon v Burrows (1879) 12 Ch D 31   *171*
White v White [2002] 2 FLR 981   *325, 326, 327*
Williams v Kiley T/A CK Supermarkets Ltd [2002] NPC 149   *172*
Willis (J) & Sons v Willis [1979] Ch 261   *277*
Wilsher v Essex Area Health Authority [1986] 3 All ER 801   *400*
Wilson and Others v United Kingdom (2002) The Times 5 July   *240*
Withers v Perry Chain Co Ltd [1961] 1 WLR 1314   *236, 397*
Woolnough, Re [2002] WTLR 595   *168*
WTO Case Opinion 1/94 [1994] ECR I–5267   *287, 288*

X v Bedfordshire County Council [1995] AC 633   *340*
X v X (Y and Z Intervening [2002] 1 FLR 508   *331*

Yaxley v Gotts & Gotts [1999] 3 WLR 1217   *162*

Z v United Kingdom (2001) 10 BHRC 384   *22*
Z v United Kingdom [2002] 2 FCR 245   *340*

Table of Statutes and Other Materials

Abortion Act 1967   *179*
Access to Justice Act 1999   *31, 32*
Adoption Act 1976
    s15(3)(b)   *337*
Adoption and Children Act 2002   *338*
    s111   *332*
    s112   *332*
    Sch 2   *338*
Anti-terrorism, Crime and Security Act 2001
   115–116, 192–193
    ss21–23   *116*
    s21   *115*
    s21(2)   *115*
    s26   *115*
    s28   *116*
    s30   *116*
    s39(4)   *192*
    s113   *192*
    s113(3)   *193*
    Pt 1   *115*
    Pt 2   *115*
    Pt 3   *115*
    Pt 4   *115*
    Pt 10   *116*
    Prt 11   *116*
    Pt 13   *116*
Arbitration Act 1996
    s69   *380*
Agricultural Holdings Act 1986   *173*

Banking Act 1987   *76*
Bermuda I Agreement   *280, 281, 282*
Bermuda II Agreement   *280, 281, 282, 283, 284*
    art 3(6)   *280*
    art 5   *280, 283*
Bill of Rights 1689   *105*
Broadcasting Act 1990   *107*
Brussels Convention on Jurisdiction and the
   Enforcement of Judgments in Civil and
   Commercial Matters 1968   *94, 95, 97, 102*
    art 5(1)   *94, 95*
    art 5(3)   *95*
    art 27   *102*
    art 27(1)   *102*
    art 27(2)   *101, 102*
Brussels Convention on Jurisdiction and the
   Recognition and Enforcement of Judgments
   in Matrimonial Matters and in the Matters of
   Parental Responsibility for the Children of
   Both Spouses 2001 (Brussels II)   *323*

Brussels Convention on Jurisdiction and the
   Recognition and Enforcement of Judgments
   in Matrimonial Matters and in the Matters of
   Parental Responsibility for the Children of
   Both Spouses 2001 (Brussels II) (*contd.*)
    art 2   *323*
    art 3   *323*
    art 11   *323*
Building Societies Act 1986   *76*

Carriage of Goods by Sea Act 1971
    s1(4)   *374*
Charter of Fundamental Rights of the European
   Union
    art 47   *291*
Child Support Act 1991
    s4(10)   *327*
Children Act 1989   *341, 342*
    s1   *333*
    s1(2)(c)   *334*
    s1(3)   *338*
    s4   *332*
    s4A   *332*
    s34   *343*
    s38(6)   *343*
    s39   *343*
Children and Young Persons Act 1963
    s29   *48*
Children and Young Persons Act 1969   *209, 211*
    s72(3)   *48*
    Sch 5   *48*
Civil Jurisdiction and Judgments Act 1982   *97*
    s2   *102*
    Sch 1 *see* Brussels Convention on
    Jurisdiction and the Enforcement of
    Judgments in Civil and Commercial
    Matters 1968
Civil Liability (Contribution) Act 1978   *68, 70, 274, 394*
    s1   *274*
    s1(1)   *68, 274, 394, 395*
    s1(4)   *274*
Civil Partnerships Bill 2002   *269, 329*
    s9   *269*
    s36(1)   *269*
Civil Procedure Rules 1998   *19, 25, 26, 27, 32, 260*
    Pt 1
      r1.3   *26*

Civil Procedure Rules 1998, Pt 1 (*contd.*)
    r1.4(2)(e) *26*
  Pt 17 *28*
    r17.4(2) *28*
  Pt 24 *30*
    r24 *30*
  Pt 31 *29*
    r31.20 *29*
  Pt 30 *16*
  Pt 36 *260, 261*
  Pt 44
    r44.3 *261, 386, 387*
  Pt 54 *15, 16*
    r54.1 *15*
    r54.2 *15*
    r54.20 *16*
Coal Industry Act 1994 *154*
Commonhold and Leasehold Reform Act 2002
  148
Commons Registration Act 1965 *152, 154*
Companies Act 1985 *70, 73, 77*
  s36A *140*
  s36C *72, 140*
  s36C(1) *71, 72, 139, 140*
  s263 *77*
  s270 *77*
  s330 *84*
  s341 *84*
  s350 *140*
  s395 *80*
  s404 *80*
  s459 *89*
Company Directors Disqualification Act 1986
  82
  s2 *81, 82*
  s6 *81, 82*
  s8 *82*
  s22(5) *83*
Consumer Credit Act 1974 *365*
  s138 *363, 364*
  s139 *364*
Contempt of Court Act 1981
  s10 *132, 133, 134, 135*
Contracts (Applicable Law) Act 1990 *98*
  Sch 1 *see* Rome Convention on the Law
    Applicable to Contractual Obligations
    1980
Convention against Torture and Other Cruel
  Inhuman or Degrading Treatment or
  Punishment 1984 *383, 385*
Courts and Legal Services Act 1990
  s8 *405, 406*
  s58 *142, 143*

Crime and Disorder Act 1998 *207, 216*
  s29 *192*
  s30 *192*
  s31 *192*
  s32 *192*
  Pt 2 *192*
Crime (Sentences) Act 1997
  s29 *46*
Criminal Appeal Act 1968
  s2(1) *50, 264*
  s11(1A) *49*
  s23 *263*
Criminal Evidence Act 1948
  s39 *314*
Criminal Justice Act 1967
  s9 *44*
Criminal Justice Act 1988 *383*
Criminal Justice Act 1991 *209*
  Sch 8 *48*
Criminal Justice and Court Services Act 2000
  s12(5)(b) *343*
Criminal Justice Bill 2002 *34*
Criminal Procedure and Investigations Act 1996
  186
  s29 *127*
Crown Proceedings Act 1947 *22*
  s10 *21, 2, 23, 393*
  s10(1) *22*
  s10(2) *22*
  s10(3) *22*
Crown Proceedings (Armed Forces) Act 1987
  393

Data Protection Act 1998 *132*
  s13 *131*
Disability Discrimination Act 1995 *231, 232,*
  233
  s1 *232*
  s6 *231*
Divorce (Religious Marriages) Act 2002 *322*
Domicile and Matrimonial Proceedings Act 1973
  s5(2) *323*

EC Council Directives
  68/151/EEC
    art 7 *71*
  80/181/EEC *103*
EC Council Regulations
  2299/89 *285, 288*
  2407/92/EEC *281, 285, 288*
  2408/92 *285, 288*
  2409/92 *285, 288*
  95/93 *285, 289*

EC Directives
   89/104/EEC
      art 7   *306*
      art 7(1)   *306*
      art 7(2)   *303, 304, 305, 306*
   90/364/EEC   *294, 295, 298*
EC Regulations
   1612/68
      art 10   *294*
      art 12   *294, 295, 296, 297*
   1638/89   *289, 290, 291*
EC Treaty 1957   *282, 284, 285, 286, 287, 292,*
  293, 297, 299, 300, 301, 302, 303, 349
   art 10   *282, 284, 292*
   art 18(1)   *296, 297, 298*
   art 25   *298, 299, 300, 301, 302, 303*
   art 30   *305*
   art 43   *280, 281, 282, 283, 284, 289*
   art 80(1)   *285*
   art 80(2)   *285*
   art 87   *298, 300, 302, 303*
   art 88   *298, 300, 302, 303*
   art 88(3)   *299, 302*
   art 90   *298, 299, 300, 301, 302, 303*
   art 133   *286*
   art 141   *229*
   art 141(1)   *229*
   art 226   *280, 281, 282, 284*
   art 230   *289, 290, 292, 294*
   art 230(4)   *290, 291, 294*
   art 234   *292, 294*
   art 235   *293*
   art 241   *292*
   art 288   *293*
   art 288(2)   *293*
   art 307   *280, 281, 282*
   art 307(1)   *282*
   art 307(2)   *282*
   art 308   *286*
Education Act 1996
   s548   *333*
Electronic Communications Act 2000   *148*
Employment Act 2002   *233*
   ss1–21   *234*
   ss22–28   *240*
   ss29–41   *226*
   s42   *233*
   s47   *234*
   Pt 1   *234*
   Pt 2   *240*
   Pt 3   *226*
Employment Rights Act 1996
   s94   *222*

Employment Rights Act 1996 (*contd.*)
   s94(1)   *222*
   s109   *223*
   s109(1)(b)   *222*
   s135   *223*
   s156   *223*
   s197   *219*
   s212(3)(c)   *226*
Employment Tribunals Extension of Jurisdiction
  (England and Wales) Order 1994
   art 3   *220*
   art 3(c)   *220*
Enduring Powers of Attorney Act 1985
   s6(6)   *168*
Enterprise Act 2002   *90, 91*
Equal Pay Act 1970   *229*
European Communities Act 1972   *103, 104,*
  105, 106, 107, 349
   s2   *103*
   s2(2)   *104*
   s2(4)   *104*
   s9(2)   *71, 72*
European Communities (Amendment) Act 2002
  264
European Convention for the Protection of
  Human Rights and Fundamental Freedoms
  1950   *10, 11, 15, 23, 45, 46, 114, 118, 119,*
  120, 121, 122, 123, 124, 126, 127, 186, 187,
  190, 311, 383, 384
   art 3   *46, 47, 340, 384, 385*
   art 5   *46, 47*
   art 5(1)   *116*
   art 6   *9, 21, 22, 23, 28, 30, 40, 46, 91,*
  114, 120, 121, 124, 125, 126, 178, 179,
  186, 190, 291, 339, 342, 380
   art 6(1)   *8, 22, 45, 120, 124, 125, 383,*
  384, 385, 393
   art 6(2)   *120, 123, 124, 125, 311, 312*
   art 6(3)   *120, 125*
   art 7   *49*
   art 8   *14, 17, 132, 321, 335, 336, 337,*
  339, 340, 342, 401
   art 8(1)   *335*
   art 8(2)   *335*
   art 9   *123, 124, 333*
   art 10   *6, 7, 8, 10, 11, 107, 108, 109,*
  116, 117, 123, 124, 126, 127, 128, 129,
  133, 135
   art 10(2)   *128, 131*
   art 11   *123, 124, 240*
   art 12   *321, 322, 340*
   art 13   *291, 340*
   art 14   *186, 335, 336*

European Convention for the Protection of
   Human Rights and Fundamental Freedoms
   1950 (*contd.*)
      Protocol 1
         art 1   *11, 120, 121, 393, 401*
Evidence Act 1851   *314*
   s7   *314*

Fair Employment (Northern Ireland) Act 1976
   s42   *114*
Family Law Act 1986
   s44(1)   *324*
   s46   *324*
   s55A   *343*
Family Law Reform Act 1969
   s21   *344*
Fatal Accidents Act 1976   *408*
Finance Act 1976
   s63(2)   *243*
Financial Services Act 1986   *76*
Financial Services and Markets Act 2000   *75,
   76*
      Pt 1   *76*
      Pt 2   *76*
      Pt 3   *76*
      Pt 6   *76*
Fires Prevention (Metropolis) Act 1774   *402*
   s86   *402*
First Council Directive on Harmonisation of
   Company Law *see* EC Council Directive
   68/151/EEC
Fixed-term Employees (Prevention of Less
   Favourable Treatment) Regulations 2002
   219
      reg 1   *219*
      reg 2   *219*
      reg 3   *219, 220*
      reg 4   *219*
      reg 5   *219*
      reg 6   *219*
      reg 7   *220*
      reg 8   *220*
Flexible Working (Eligibility, Complaints and
   Remedies) Regulations 2003 (draft)   *235*
Flexible Working (Procedural Requirements)
   Regulations 2003 (draft)   *235*
Friendly Societies Act 1992   *76*
Food and Drugs Act 1955
   s8(1)   *358*

Geneva Convention I 1949   *381*
Geneva Convention II 1949   *381*
Geneva Convention III 1949   *381*

Geneva Convention IV 1949   *381*
Geneva Protocol I Additional to the Geneva
   Conventions of 1949   *381*
Geneva Protocol II Additional to the Geneva
   Conventions of 1949   *381*
Government of Wales Act 1998   *105*

Hague Rules   *374*
   Arts I–VIII   *374*
Hague-Visby Rules   *373, 374, 377*
   Art I(b)   *374*
   Art III
      r1   *377, 378*
      r2   *377, 378*
   Art IV
      r5   *374*
      r5(a)   *374*
Highway Act 1835   *358*
   s78   *358*
Homes Bill 1999   *148*
Housing Act 1985   *149, 152*
Human Fertilisation and Embryology Act 1990
   s30   *344*
Human Rights Act 1998   *14, 15, 16, 40, 46, 49,
   105, 116, 117, 118, 119, 121, 122, 123, 124,
   125, 130, 136, 342, 401*
   s3   *28, 117, 122, 342*
   s4   *46*
   s6   *14, 117, 401*
   6(1)   *16, 117, 118*
   s6(2)(b)   *117, 118*
   s6(3)   *16*
   s6(3)(b)   *16, 17*
   s6(5)   *16*
   s7   *118, 119, 342*
   s7(1)   *119*
   s8   *342*
   s22   *130*
   Sch 1   *40, 117, 380*

Immigration and Asylum Act 1999   *125*
   Pt II   *120*
Indictments Act 1915
   s5   *41*
Inheritance (Provision for Family and
   Dependants) Act 1975   *328, 387, 388, 389*
   s3(1)(g)   *388*
   s25(4)   *328, 387, 388*
Inheritance Tax Act 1984   *390*
   s5(1)   *390*
   s49(1)   *392*
   s272   *390*

Insolvency Act 1986   *79, 91*
    s212   *85*
    s235   *92*
    s236   *92*
    s291(1)(a)   *91*
    s291(1)(b)   *91*
Insolvency Act 2000   *90*
Insurance Companies Act 1982   *76*
Interception of Communications Act 1985   *127*
Interpretation Act 1978   *186*

Land Charges Act 1972   *156*
Land Registration Act 1925   *149*
    s20   *160*
    s69   *160*
    s70(1)(g)   *159, 362, 363*
    s83   *161*
    s83(6)   *161*
Land Registration Act 2002   *148, 149–158*
    s3   *149*
    s4   *149*
    s5   *149*
    s6   *149*
    s7   *150*
    s8   *150*
    s9   *150*
    s10   *150*
    s11   *151*
    s12   *151*
    s15   *150*
    s23   *152*
    s24   *152*
    s26   *152*
    s27   *152, 154*
    s28   *153*
    s29   *153, 154*
    s30   *153, 154*
    s32   *154*
    s33   *154*
    s34   *154*
    s35   *154*
    s36   *154*
    s37   *154*
    s38   *154*
    s40   *155*
    s41   *155*
    s42   *155*
    s43   *155*
    s44   *155*
    s45   *155*
    s47   *155*
    s48   *155*
    s49   *155*

Land Registration Act 2002 (*contd.*)
    s51   *155*
    s52   *155*
    s54   *156*
    s55   *156*
    s56   *156*
    s57   *156*
    s58   *156*
    s60   *156*
    s62   *151, 158*
    s63   *151*
    s66   *156*
    s67   *156*
    s68   *156*
    s69   *156*
    s70   *156*
    s72   *156*
    s73   *156*
    s74   *156*
    s86   *156*
    ss91–95   *157*
    s96   *157*
    s115   *157*
    s116   *157*
    Pt 8   *157*
    Sch 1   *151, 153, 154*
    Sch 3   *153*
    Sch 4   *158*
    Sch 6   *157*
    Sch 8   *158*
Landlord and Tenant Act 1954   *173*
Landlord and Tenant Act 1985
    s11   *242*
Landlord and Tenant (Covenants) Act 1995
    173, 174
    s8   *173*
    s16   *174*
Late Payment of Commercial Debts (Interest)
    Act 1998
        s1(1)   *139*
        s5A   *139*
Late Payment of Commercial Debts Regulations
    2002   *139*
Law of Property Act 1925
    s1(2)(a)   *152*
    s1(2)(b)   *152*
    s1(2)(e)   *152*
    s53(1)(c)   *161*
    s62   *361, 363*
    s105   *156*
Law of Property (Miscellaneous Provisions) Act
    1989
        s2   *139, 140, 161, 162, 165*

Limitation Act 1980   *68, 70, 85, 151, 175*
    s5   *366*
    s10   *68, 70*
    s15(1)   *370, 371*
    s21(1)(b)   *85*
    s20   *366, 367*
    s32   *409*
    s32(2)   *409*
    s35(5)(a)   *28*
    Sch 1   *370*
Local Land Charges Act 1975   *167*
    s10   *167*

Magistrates' Courts Rules 1968
    r14(2)   *358*
Marriage Act 1949   *388*
Matrimonial Causes Act 1973   *322*
    s10A   *322*
    s11   *388*
    s25   *325, 332*
    s25(1)   *326, 327*
    s25(2)   *326*
    s25(2)(a)   *326*
    s25(2)(f)   *326, 332*
    s25(2)(g)   *326, 327*
Mental Health Act 1983
    s3   *19*
Metrication Directive *see* EC Council Directive
    80/181/EEC
Misuse of Drugs Act 1971   *180*
Misrepresentation Act 1967   *58*
Murder (Abolition of Death Penalty) Act 1965
46
    s1(1)   *46, 47*

National Assistance Act 1948   *14, 16, 17*
    s26   *17*

Offences Against the Person Act 1861
    s23   *181*
    s58   *179*
    s59   *179*
Official Secrets Act 1989   *127, 128, 129*
    s1   *127, 128*
    s1(1)   *127*
    s1(1)(a)   *128*
    s4(1)   *127, 128*
    s4(3)(a)   *128*
    s7   *127*

Partnership Act 1890
    s10   *274, 275, 395*
    s11   *275*
    s13   *275*

Police Act 1996
    s89(1)   *113*
Police and Criminal Evidence Act 1984   *37, 318*
    s17(1)(c)   *113*
    s24   *36, 113*
    s25   *113*
    s37   *36*
    s54   *116*
    s62(9)   *113*
    s64   *116*
    s78   *91*
    Sch 1A   *113*
Police Reform Act 2002   *112, 113, 214, 215*
    s10   *112*
    s10(8)   *112*
    s12   *112*
    s12(7)   *112*
    s19   *113*
    s48   *113*
    s50   *113*
    s54   *113*
    Pt 1   *112*
    Pt 2   *112*
    Pt 4   *113*
    Sch 6   *113*
Powers of Criminal Courts (Sentencing) Act 2000
    ss90–92   *196*
    s96   *46*
Private International Law (Miscellaneous
    Provisions) Act 1995   *100*
    s11   *100*
    s12   *100*
Prosecution of Offences Act 1985
    s22   *39*
    s22(3)(a)(iii)   *38*
Prosecutions of Offences (Custody Time Limits)
    Regulations 1987   *39*
Protection from Harassment Act 1997
    s2   *186*
    s4   *186*
Public Order Act 1986   *126*
    s1(1)   *49*
    s5   *126*
    s5(3)   *126*

Railway Clauses Consolidation Act 1845   *25*
Registered Homes Act 1984   *19*
Relationships (Civil Registration) Bill 2001   *329*
Road Traffic Act 1972
    s8(1)   *358*
Road Traffic Act 1988
    s3A   *311*
    s15   *311*

Road Traffic Act 1988 (*contd.*)
    s103(1)(b)   *113*
    s163   *113*
Rome Convention on the Law Applicable to
    Contractual Obligations 1980   *98–99*
    art 3   *98*
    art 4   *99*
    art 4(2)   *99*
Rules of the Supreme Court
    O.53   *15, 16*
    r1   *15*
    r4(1)   *21*

Sale and Supply of Goods Act 1994   *61*
Sale of Goods Act 1979   *58, 61, 62*
    s13   *59*
    s14(2)   *61, 146*
    s14(2A)   *61, 146*
    s14(2B)   *146*
    s19   *376*
    s49(1)   *64, 65*
    s49(2)   *65*
Scotland Act 1998   *105*
Settled Land Act 1925   *151, 153*
Sexual Offences Act 1956
    s6(1)   *186, 187*
    s6(3)   *186, 187*
Statute of Frauds 1677   *55, 56, 57, 58*
    s4   *55, 57, 58, 138*
State Immunity Act 1978   *383, 385*
Supreme Court 1981
    s30   *16*
    s31   *16*
    s37(1)   *96, 97*
Suicide Act 1961   *181*

Terrorism Act 2000   *116*
Theft Act 1968
    s2(1)(a)   *189*
    s5(1)   *188*
    s5(2)   *189*

Theft Act 1978
    s3   *113*
Town and Country Planning Act 1990
    s64   *12, 13*
Transfer of Undertakingsa (Protection of
    Employment) Regulations 1981
    reg 7   *228*
Treason Felony Act 1848   *117, 118, 119*
    s3   *116, 117, 118, 119*
Treaty of Amsterdam *see* Treaty on European
    Union 1997
Treaty of Nice   *264*
Treaty on European Union 1992
    art 48   *294*
    Title VI   *116*
Treaty on European Union 1997   *264*

UN Charter 1945
    art 2(1)   *381*
Unfair Contract Terms Act 1977   *63*
    s3(2)(b)   *364*
Unfair Terms in Consumer Contract Regulations
    1999   *63*
Units of Measurement Regulations 1994   *103*
Vienna Convention on Diplomatic Relations 1961
    art 41(2)   *381*
Vienna Convention on the Law of Treaties 1969
    art 30(4)   *282*
    art 31(3)   *384*

Water Act 1989   *166*
Weights and Measures Act 1963   *103*
    s8(2)   *103*
Weights and Measures Act 1985   *103, 104, 105*
    s1   *104*
Weights and Measures Act 1985 (Metrication)
    (Amendment) Order 1994   *103*
Working Time Regulations 1998   *238*
    reg 13   *239*

1

Administrative Law

Tribunals and Inquiries

The Leggatt report on the tribunals system

In March 2001 the report of the review of tribunals chaired by Sir Andrew Leggatt was published under the title *Tribunals for Users: One System One Service*.

Its main recommendations were as follows:

The tribunals system should be more independent of central government

This aim would be achieved by:

1. Ensuring separation between the ministers and other authorities whose policies and decisions are tested by tribunals, and the minister who appoints and supports tribunal members.
2. Making the administration of tribunals the responsibility of the Lord Chancellor.
3. Making the Lord Chancellor responsible for all appointments to tribunals (in consultation, as necessary) and that all appointments should be for a period of five or seven years. Subject to age, renewal for further such periods should be automatic, except for cause. Grounds for removal should be prescribed by the Lord Chancellor, with the concurrence of the appropriate minister in the devolved administrations, and the relevant head of the judiciary. A Judicial Appointments Commissioner should be responsible for supervising tribunal appointments, and in particular for the appointment of lawyers. Another Commissioner should be responsible for the appointment of non-lawyers. The Commission should establish a separate committee to oversee its work on tribunals.

The tribunals system should be made more coherent

This aim would be achieved by:

1. Presenting the citizen with a single, overarching structure, giving access to all tribunals.
2. Including local government tribunals, citizen and state tribunals and party and party tribunals in the tribunals system.
3. Giving tribunals the separate rules and procedures they need, with the Lord Chancellor's Department being required to adapt the civil justice reforms to the

different circumstances of litigation before tribunals as quickly as possible, to ensure that procedures are as speedy, proportionate and cheap as the nature of each case allows.

4. Establishing a Tribunals Service (as an executive agency of the Lord Chancellor's Department, separate from the Court Service) committed to producing a service and approach of the highest quality and responsive to the user. In addition to measures to test the efficiency and effectiveness of the tribunals system, the Tribunals Service should set out for users the standards of service which they can expect, and what to do if they do not think those standards have been met.

5. Establishing a tribunals system divided by subject-matter into divisions in a structure which is at once apparent to the user (the divisions composed by creating sensibly coherent areas of work), and by bringing together as far as possible the tribunals for which each government department currently has overall responsibility. First-tier tribunals should be grouped into eight divisions to deal with disputes between the citizen and the state, and one to deal with disputes between parties.

6. Establishing a single route of appeal for all tribunals to a single appellate division. This would involve creating appellate tribunal jurisdictions covering the areas of education, health and regulatory matters. Generally, there should be a right of appeal on a point of law, by permission, on the generic ground that the decision of the tribunal was unlawful, from first-tier tribunals to second-tier tribunals, and from second-tier tribunals to the Court of Appeal. The appellate body should have power in its discretion, if it upholds an appeal, to quash the decision, to remit it for reconsideration, to grant declaratory relief, or (if there was no substantial prejudice) to give no relief.

7. Introducing a common time-limit for appealing a tribunal's decision of six weeks from the date of issue of the tribunal's reasoned decision, or for particular tribunals such other period as may exceptionally be prescribed by statutory instrument.

8. Clarifying the rules on precedent so that first-tier tribunals should continue to consider each case on its merits and decide it as the public interest may require – their decisions should not set binding precedents. The system of designating binding cases (or limiting the cases which are permitted to be cited in argument) as used by the Social Security Commissioners and the Immigration Appeal Tribunal should be adopted throughout the appellate division. Decisions about binding precedents should be taken by the president of each appellate tribunal, with the approval of the Tribunals Board.

9. Enacting a statutory provision to exclude the decisions of second-tier tribunals from the supervisory jurisdiction of the High Court, and enacting a statutory provision excluding judicial review of the decisions of first-tier tribunals if rights of appeal have not been exhausted.

10. Appointing a High Court judge as the Senior President to head the tribunals system, and a Tribunals Board to direct the tribunals system, consisting of the

Senior President, the presidents of the appellate tribunals who are judges of the High Court, and the presidents of first-tier divisions, together with the Chairman of the Council on Tribunals, the Chairman of the Tribunals Committee of the Judicial Studies Board and the Chief Executive of the Tribunals Service. The Board's functions should include advising the Lord Chancellor's Department on qualifications for chairmen and members, overseeing the appointment of members, co-ordinating their training, investigating complaints against them, and recommending changes to the rules of procedure governing all divisions.

11. Basing tribunal practice on the Council on Tribunal's Model Rules, with procedures revised over time to achieve the greatest possible coherence across the system, whilst recognising the needs of different divisions (and perhaps classes of case within divisions) at least for different time-limits.

The tribunals system should be made more user-friendly

This aim would be achieved by:

1. Providing users with information about how to start a case, prepare it for submission to the tribunal and present it at a hearing – the aim being that tribunal users should be able to prepare and present their cases.
2. Developing a consistent approach and common standards on which the Council on Tribunals should be consulted.
3. Exploring the feasibility of specifying in regulations, rules of procedure or codes of practice the documents and information that decision-makers in both central and local government should be under a duty to supply to appellants.
4. Making provision for customer service points at all tribunal offices.
5. Providing appellants with timely advice and ensuring procedures are in place for examining financial eligibility for public funding, with the Community Legal Service contract scheme being extended to key advice organisations and used to assure the quality of advice and assistance users receive. State assistance should be directed to helping users to understand their case and its merits; to take a view about whether to proceed with an appeal; and, if so, to find out how to prepare for a hearing.
6. Exploiting IT to provide: common administrative systems across the tribunals system; case administration systems and electronic filing systems integrated as one system; document production systems that ensure the standard production of letters, directions, rulings, forms, decisions and publications; online publication of tribunal decisions; web-based interactive systems to help parties prepare their cases and web-based tracking to help them follow the progress of their actions; and a website to help citizens and organisations to identify the most appropriate forums for the resolution of their disputes.

The management and supervision of tribunals should be improved

This aim would be achieved by:

1. Emphasising in the advertisements for tribunal members the distinctive nature of tribunal proceedings and the need for interpersonal skills, as well as other professional skills and knowledge.
2. Requiring the presidents to: promote by leadership and co-ordination both consistency of decision-making and uniformity of practice and procedure; hear personally those cases which raise the most difficult, novel and complex issues, and those which raise general issues of practice and procedure for the system or its divisions; and be responsible for training and the co-ordination of the programmes developed by the Judicial Studies Board and the implementation of training in their respective divisions.
3. Ensuring that non-lawyers appointed as tribunal members are appointed on the basis of the specific contribution which each has to make to the tribunal's work, the relevant criteria for appointment being stipulated by Parliament. And that non-lawyers receive careful training and, where appropriate, guidance from the chairman in the process of finding facts and in the weighing of evidence.
4. Providing improved training for chairmen and members in the interpersonal skills peculiar to the distinctive approach of tribunals – the skills required for the efficient conduct of a tribunal being imparted by means of introductory training in core competencies, sustained by continuation training. Instruction should be provided in the additional competencies needed by chairmen, especially those needed to help them overcome the communication, language and literacy difficulties experienced by some users.
5. Giving the Judicial Studies Board responsibility for: the organisation and delivery of training for tribunal chairmen and members; recommending training policy; establishing national training standards; and monitoring the structure and content of training across all tribunals in England and Wales.
6. Encouraging the Council on Tribunals, through its programme of visits, to identify training needs, with the Judicial Studies Board consulting the Council on training requirements.
7. Extending the role of the Council on Tribunals to: encompass the monitoring of the development of the new tribunals system during the first few years of its existence, and check that the practices and procedures of government departments are compliant with the European Convention on Human Rights; champion users' causes; take evidence from user groups, from the Tribunals Service, from departments and from the Judicial Studies Board about how well the system is working; monitor the training of chairmen and members, proposals for procedural change, the development of IT, the usefulness of the information provided for users by the Tribunals Service and the adequacy of independent sources of assistance and advice for users; continue its own programme of visits, albeit scaled down, and after each visit report its findings at once to the Senior

President and to the president of the division concerned; ensure that the various mechanisms for redressing the grievances of users work together coherently and efficiently; commission research into the operation of administrative justice both in the UK and abroad; and promote conferences, more detailed tribunal information, more special reports and more guidance on standards and best practice. In the longer term, the Council should be made responsible for upholding the system of administrative justice and keeping it under review, for monitoring developments in administrative law, and for making recommendations to the Lord Chancellor about improvements that might be made to that system.

Tribunals should move towards a system of active case management

This aim would be achieved by:

1. Improving arrangements for scheduling hearings, inter alia, by: measuring the time taken for an appeal from the date of the initial decision; setting down time-limits to show when cases are expected to be heard; giving tribunals sanctions needed to ensure adequate case progression; and making effective use of IT to monitor work flow.
2. Making chairmen responsible for ensuring that cases adhere to time-limits, for supervising the listing and allocation of cases, for conducting hearings and for promulgating clear decisions promptly.
3. Ensuring difficulties are identified in advance by: making more use of pre-hearing procedures and review; giving directions about how to prepare for the hearing; appointing a legally qualified registrar to each division empowered to order the production and exchange of documents, to order parties and witnesses to attend oral hearings, to issue directions and to refer parties who abuse tribunal procedures to court for contempt action; empowering Registrars to carry out pre-hearing work for each tribunal, under its direction, and give legal or procedural advice to tribunal members and administrators, if required; and encouraging Registrars to consider the suitability of alternative dispute resolution during pre-hearing procedures.
4. Publishing rules and practice directions outlining the arrangements for case management, using that term in its widest sense to denote minding cases during their progress through the tribunal.
5. Ensuring that case management procedures approximate to modern court procedure.

OBP Textbook page 93, section 4.2.

Inquiry procedures

R (On the Application of Persey) v Secretary of State for the Environment, Food and Rural Affairs (2002) The Times 28 March Queen's Bench Divisional Court (Simon Brown LJ and Scott Baker J)

Inquiry – whether decision to hold inquiry in private irrational – whether any breach of art 10 European Convention on Human Rights involved

Facts
In the wake of the foot and mouth epidemic the Secretary of State for Environment, Food and Rural Affairs held an inquiry to investigate the causes of the outbreak and the way in which it had been dealt with (the 'Lessons Learned' inquiry). Some of those who had been adversely affected by the foot and mouth outbreak applied for judicial review of the decision to hold the inquiry in private.

Held
The application was dismissed. There was no legal presumption that an inquiry would be held in public. The Secretary of State for the Environment, Food and Rural Affairs had been vested with a discretion as to whether the inquiry should be held in public or not and the Minister had not acted illegally in determining that it should be held in private.

Contrasting the present case with the earlier case of *R (On the Application of Wagstaff)* v *Secretary of State for Health* [2001] 1 WLR 292 (where it had been held that it was unlawful for the Secretary of State to order the 'Harold Shipman' inquiry to proceed in private), Simon Brown LJ observed:

'The principal differences are surely these. The terms of reference of the [present] ... Inquiry are ... "markedly narrower" ... than those under consideration in *Wagstaff* ... Secondly, no-one suggests that an open public inquiry into FMD would take no longer than Dr Anderson's proposed six month inquiry (scheduled to report in June 2002). On the contrary, however inquisitorial the procedure and however firm the chairmanship, all experience dictates that an open inquiry would take very appreciably longer, even putting aside the need to set it up entirely afresh. One does not need to reflect on the Saville Inquiry to recognise the risk of timetables slipping. Thirdly, the case on candour which the defendant advances here seems to me both stronger than, and in an important respect different from, that advanced in *Wagstaff*. The Court there ... quoted a statement made by Sir Louis Blom-Cooper QC in support of public inquiries being conducted openly, remarking that "there was no evidence put before us to the opposite effect" (albeit reference was made to Sir Cecil Clothier's report on the Allitt Inquiry providing some support for the contrary view). In the present case not only is there a statement from a witness, Mr Richard Lingham, with great personal experience of health service inquiries, who expresses himself as "... firmly in favour of ... an inquiry that hears evidence in private" ... but Sir Louis himself takes a perhaps more ambivalent view than *Wagstaff* suggested. In his statement before us, he says this:

"It is frequently asserted that witnesses before an inquiry held in private are thereby more inclined to be candid about their testimony. My experience on the whole accords with that view, but there is a distinct downside to that benefit."

Having then explained that downside, essentially that witnesses in private tend to be careless about accusations against others, Sir Louis concludes:

"On balance I prefer the even-handed approach which gives equal weighting to the evidence".

A view arrived "on balance" hardly suggests that the evidence is all one way. In *Wagstaff*, moreover, the Court did not have the benefit of [the] ... evidence that, because the BSE Inquiry was held in public, "those with experience and knowledge [did not] make constructive suggestions about the management of the disease and its handling which could have contributed to the Inquiry's thinking". In other words, in an inquiry into a broadly comparable area of concern, witnesses tended to be defensive rather than constructive in their evidence.'

Simon Brown LJ concluded that the decision to proceed with the inquiry in private was one that was 'pre-eminently a judgment for government'.

The applicants had also contended that the decision to hold the inquiry in private violated the right to freedom of expression under art 10 of the European Convention on Human Rights (ECHR). The court rejected this on the basis that art 10 did not carry with it a right of access to information. As a result the Secretary of State was not under a legal duty to hold an inquiry in public by virtue of art 10. As Simon Brown LJ explained:

'... we have had the advantage of substantially fuller argument on the point than the Court enjoyed in *Wagstaff* and have been referred to a number of additional cases. In the result I for my part have come to the clear conclusion that art 10 is simply not engaged by a decision, as here, to hold a closed public inquiry. Let me as briefly as possible explain why ... the Court in *Wagstaff* cited part only of para 74 of *Leander* v *Sweden* (1987) 9 EHRR 433, the first of the three Strasbourg cases referred to, and observed that it could not assist the government's case. It seems to me, however, necessary to cite the paragraph rather more fully:

"... the right to freedom to receive information basically prohibits a government from restricting a person from receiving information that others wish or may be willing to impart to him. Article 10 does not in circumstances such as those of the present case, confer on the individual a right of access to a register containing information on his personal position, nor does it embody an obligation on the government to impart such information to the individual."

... The crucial point made by *Leander* is that freedom of expression – whether the right to receive, or the right to impart, information – is one thing, access to information quite another, and that art 10, whilst naturally conferring the former, does not accord the latter. That distinction appears to me central to this case. The true analysis of the complaint made here is that the form of inquiry decided upon by government and now being undertaken by Dr Anderson denies public access to the information being imparted at the closed sessions. That, to my mind, is not a legitimate complaint. The fact that a particular participant may be willing, even anxious, to have his contribution broadcast is nothing to the point. He is, of course, entirely at liberty to say what he likes to whomsoever he wishes. The conduct of the inquiry is not, however, in his hands and it is the willingness or unwillingness of whoever controls the inquiry's proceedings which must determine whether the public shall have direct access to the information being imparted. Someone attending a closed session of the Lessons Learned Inquiry is no more entitled to be accompanied by the press and television cameras than if he were invited to participate in a departmental meeting or, indeed, advise the Minister in his private office. In truth, under the guise of seeking merely to remove supposedly impermissible restrictions on the ability of willing participants to communicate their contributions more widely and more accurately than is possible without media intervention, the claimants and interveners are in reality seeking to enforce the setting up of a quite different form of inquiry, namely an open public inquiry such as Lord Phillips held into BSE. Article 10 contains no warrant for such an exercise. It is not a corollary of the right to freedom of expression that public authorities can be required to put in place additional opportunities for its exercise. Article 10 imposes no positive obligation on government to provide, in addition to existing means of communication, an open forum to achieve the yet wider dissemination of views. Article 10 prohibits interference with freedom of expression: it does not require its facilitation. In reality, as it seems to me, the claimants' argument here seeks to pull itself up by its own bootstraps. Had no inquiry been set up, art 10 would manifestly not be engaged. A closed form of inquiry having been determined upon, art 10 cannot then be invoked to transform it into some quite different process ... There seems to me to be some force too in the Attorney-General's argument that were art 10 to have the effect here contended for, it would not be necessary for art 6(1) to specify the entitlement of litigants to a "public hearing" of their disputes. The very fact that art 6 makes express provision for this suggests that no such right exists in relation to other forms of state inquiry.'

Comment

The decision suggests that the ruling in *R (On the Application of Wagstaff)* v *Secretary of State for Health* [2001] 1 WLR 292 should be seen as the exception rather than the rule. It should be borne in mind that in *Wagstaff* the terms of reference for the inquiry were very wide, and many people had received the clear impression that the inquiry would sit in public.

The court in *R (On the Application of Howard)* v *Secretary of State for Health* [2002] EWHC Admin 396 applied the ruling in *Persey* to conclude that the Secretary of State for Health had not acted unlawfully in refusing to hold an inquiry into professional misconduct by a doctor in public.

OBP Textbook page 115, section 4.9.

What Are the Requirements for a Fair Hearing?

Planning decision: compliance with Convention rights

R (On the Application of Adlard) v *Secretary of State for the Environment* [2002] EWCA Civ 735 Court of Appeal (Civil Division) (Simon Brown, Mummery and Dyson LJJ)

Planning decision – whether art 6 rights engaged – whether breach of natural justice could be cured by judicial review

Facts
A local planning authority received an application for planning permission for a 30,000 all-seater football stadium. An environmental impact study was carried out and the authority met to consider the application at a meeting attended by some 600 members of the public. Oral representations were not permitted. The application for planning permission was granted. By way of an application for judicial review the applicants sought to compel the Secretary of State to call in the application, thereby triggering the holding of a public inquiry. The applicants for review argued that the failure to provide a public inquiry violated their rights under art 6 of the European Convention on Human Rights (ECHR) to a hearing in respect of the determination of their civil rights. At first instance the application was dismissed and the applicants appealed.

Held
The appeal was dismissed. Article 6 ECHR rights were engaged but the availability of judicial review enabled the court to correct any perceived injustice that might arise.

As Simon Brown LJ explained:

'The question whether or not art 6 is satisfied, however, falls to be considered by reference not merely to the initial decision-making process but also in the light of the High Court's review jurisdiction ... For my part, I can find no warrant, whether in domestic or in Strasbourg jurisprudence, for concluding that where ... the administrative decisions taken at first instance are generally likely to turn on questions of judgment and discretion rather than on findings of fact, the statutory scheme must provide for an oral hearing at that initial stage. On the contrary, I have reached the clearest conclusion that the statutory scheme as a whole is plainly compliant with art 6 and that there is no need to resort to the Secretary of State's call-in power to make it so ... The remedy of judicial review in my judgment amply enables the court to correct any injustice it perceives in an individual case. If, in short, the court were satisfied that exceptionally, on the facts of a particular case, the local planning authority had acted unfairly or unreasonably in denying an objector any or any sufficient oral hearing, the court would quash the decision and require such a hearing to be given ... I should make it plain, however, that I am by no means persuaded that any oral hearing was required on the facts of the present case. Quintessentially the decision whether or not to permit this development (and the departure from the development plan which it represents) involves questions of discretion and planning judgment rather than the resolution of primary fact.'

Comment

See further on the extent to which administrative procedures can be cured by the availability of judicial review: *Adan* v *Newham London Borough Council* [2001] 1 All ER 930 and *R (On the Application of McLellan)* v *Bracknell Forest Borough Council* [2002] 1 All ER 899. In *R (On the Application of Beeson)* v *Dorset County Council* (2002) The Times 21 December the Divisional Court held that a local authority review panel, making decisions as to whether or not an applicant was required to contribute to the cost of residential care, was not sufficiently independent of the council as a majority of its members were council members. This unfairness could not be remedied by judicial review as the review panel was required to determine findings of fact – such as the assessing the credibility of claimants. It was impossible for a court on judicial review to determine whether or not the review panel's findings would have been affected by its connection with one of the parties. A reviewing court could not become an appeal body in relation to the panel's decisions.

OBP Textbook page 139, section 6.1.

Fettering Discretion

Adoption of a policy

R (On the Application of Hirst) v *Secretary of State for the Home Department* (2002) The Times 10 April Queen's Bench Divisional Court (Elias J)

Legality of policy – interference with the European Convention on Human Rights – whether proportionate

Facts

Under para 6.10 of Prison Service Order 4400, permission to call the media would be granted to prisoners only in exceptional circumstances. A policy was adopted whereby prisoners were denied the right to contact the media by telephone to comment on matters of legitimate public interest relating to prisons and prisoners.

The applicant applied for judicial review of the policy on the basis that it operated so as to deny him his right to freedom of expression as provided for by art 10 of the European Convention on Human Rights (ECHR).

Held

The application was allowed. The policy was being applied inflexibly and it appeared that in practice exceptions would only be made where a prisoner was illiterate and could not communicate with the media in writing, or where a prisoner was seeking to establish a miscarriage of justice. The respondent had not been able to justify what amounted to a blanket ban on contact with the media beyond pointing to the logistical difficulties of ensuring that any such communications where monitored to prevent unlawful activity. The court did not accept that this was sufficient reason for the interference with the claimant's art 10 rights.

Comment

This is another example of a public body adopting a policy that interferes with Convention rights. The aim of the interference was legitimate in this case but the extent of the interference was disproportionate. See further *Lindsay* v *Commissioners of Customs and Excise* (2002) The Times 27 February.

Lindsay v *Commissioners of Customs and Excise* (2002) The Times 27 February Court of Appeal (Civil Division) (Lord Phillips MR, Judge and Carnwath LJJ)

Policy – lack of flexibility – disproportionate interference with rights protected by the European Convention on Human Rights

Facts

L was returning to the United Kingdom from France. He was stopped at the controlled zone in Calais by British customs officers and a large quantity of tobacco was found in his vehicle. L claimed the tobacco was for personal use by himself and his friends and family. The customs officers did not accept this explanations. L was informed that, under the regulations in force and in accordance with the policy adopted by the Customs and Excise, the tobacco and the vehicle used to transport it would be forfeited. In November 2001 the VAT and Duties Tribunal held that officers' decision in accordance with the policy not to restore L's car was disproportionate and would cause him undue hardship. The Commissioners appealed.

Held

The appeal was dismissed. The power to issue circulars indicating the policy to be adopted by Customs and Excise officers regarding the forfeiture of smuggled goods and vehicles used for smuggling was not in question. The effect of the policy, however, was to interfere with L's right to the peaceful enjoyment of his possessions as enshrined in art 1 of Protocol 1 to the European Convention on Human Rights. The prevention of smuggling was a legitimate aim that could be pursued by interfering with that right, but any such interference had to be proportionate. In the present case the policy had been applied without sufficient flexibility. In particular, a policy of automatic forfeiture of vehicles ignored the relationship that the value of the car bore to the duty that should have been paid. Customs officers were required to consider each case on an individual basis. A general policy of forfeiture might have been appropriate in respect of 'professional' smugglers, but was unlawful when applied indiscriminately. In effect the policy was unlawful in its operation because it led officers to ignore relevant considerations such as the scale of the duty evasion.

Comment

The decision is a useful summary of how a variety of factors can operate together to render a policy unlawful, namely inflexibility of application, ignoring relevant considerations and disproportionate interference with Convention rights. See further *R (On the Application of Hirst)* v *Secretary of State for the Home Department* (2002) The Times 10 April.

OBP Textbook page 220, section 9.3.

Estoppel

R v *East Sussex County Council, ex parte Reprotech Ltd* [2002] 4 All ER 58 House of Lords (Lords Nicholls of Birkenhead, Mackay of Clashfern, Hoffmann, Hope of Craighead and Scott of Foscote)

Estoppel – operation in public law – whether public body bound

Facts

East Sussex County Council built a waste treatment plant operated by ESEL, a company owned by East Sussex County Council. In 1990 East Sussex County Council decided to sell the plant and advertised for tenders. A potential purchaser was interested in using the plant for the generation of electricity from waste treatment. No application for a material change of use under s64 of the Town and Country Planning Act 1990 was submitted. Instead the prospective purchasers sought an amendment to the conditions attaching to the grant of planning permission originally made to ESEL. ESEL agreed to make an application to East Sussex County Council for a variation of 'condition 10' so as to permit the operation of the plant for the generation of electricity 24 hours a day.

On 27 February 1991 the development control sub-committee of East Sussex County Council, as the planning authority, considered ESEL's application to vary 'condition 10'. The county planning officer reported to the committee that electricity generation would not involve a material change of use. In his view the only condition that needed to be varied was in relation to noise levels. The committee minuted its agreement with the planning officer's report but ESEL did not pursue the matter any further, leaving it to any future prospective purchaser to submit a noise attenuation scheme.

On 24 May 1991 Reprotech purchased ESEL. On the 18 March 1994 the secretary to East Sussex County Council wrote to Reprotech setting out the position as regards the plant. The letter made it clear that there had been no grant of planning permission resulting from the committee meeting of 27 February 1991, and the ESEL's application had been withdrawn from the register. The letter went on to confirm, however, that if a suitable noise attenuation scheme was submitted there was no reason why the resolution of the committee could not be implemented and permission granted. East Sussex County Council did not regard itself as bound by the planning officer's view that electricity generation would not involve a material change of use.

Reprotech's subsequent application for planning permission for a change of use in respect of the plant led to considerable local opposition. Reprotech then decided, as an alternative, to stand on its rights. Reprotech issued an originating summons asking for declarations, inter alia, that (1) the views expressed by the county planning officer in 1991 constituted a determination under s64 that no planning permission was required for the generation of electricity, or (2) the resolution of the development control sub-committee constituted such a determination. It also issued proceedings for judicial review, claiming a declaration that the County Council was not entitled to treat ESEL's application as withdrawn, and a mandamus requiring East Sussex County Council, subject to the submission of a satisfactory noise attenuation scheme, to issue a permission in accordance with the resolution of 27 February 1991. At first instance Tucker J granted declarations to the effect that the committee resolution was a s64 determination, and that the generation of electricity from recycled products did not require additional planning permission, and a mandatory order requiring the council to implement the resolution, subject to the submission of a satisfactory noise attenuation scheme, by the issue of planning permission. The Court of Appeal, by a majority, affirmed the judge's second and third declarations, and East Sussex County Council appealed to the House of Lords.

Held

The appeal was allowed. It was wrong to transplant private law concepts of estoppel into public law without amendment. Wider public interests had to be taken into account.

Lord Hoffmann:

'... I think that it is unhelpful to introduce private law concepts of estoppel into planning law. As Lord Scarman pointed out in *Newbury District Council* v *Secretary of State for the Environment, Newbury District Council* v *International Synthetic Rubber Co Ltd* [1981] AC 578 at 616, estoppels bind individuals on the ground that it would be unconscionable for them to deny what they have represented or agreed. But these concepts of private law should not be extended into "the public law of planning control, which binds everyone" ... There is of course an analogy between a private law estoppel and the public law concept of a legitimate expectation created by a public authority, the denial of which may amount to an abuse of power (see *R* v *North and East Devon Health Authority, ex parte Coughlan (Secretary of State for Health intervening)* [2001] QB 213). But it is no more than an analogy because remedies against public authorities also have to take into account the interests of the general public which the authority exists to promote. Public law can also take into account the hierarchy of individual rights which exist under the Human Rights Act 1998, so that, for example, the individual's right to a home is accorded a high degree of protection ... while ordinary property rights are in general far more limited by considerations of public interest ... It is true that in early cases such as *Wells'* case [*Wells* v *MHLG* [1967] 2 All ER 1041] and *Lever (Finance) Ltd* v *Westminster Corp* [1971] 1 QB 222, Lord Denning MR used the language of estoppel in relation to planning law. At that time the public law concepts of abuse of power and legitimate expectation were very undeveloped and no doubt the analogy of estoppel seemed useful. In the *Western Fish* case the Court of Appeal tried its best to reconcile these invocations of estoppel with the general principle that a public authority cannot be estopped from exercising a statutory discretion or performing a public duty. But the results did not give universal satisfaction ... It seems to me that in this area, public law has already absorbed whatever is useful from the moral values which underlie the private law concept of estoppel and the time has come for it to stand upon its own two feet.'

Comment

The decision suggests a significant move away from the approach in *Western Fish Products Ltd* v *Penwith District Council* [1981] 2 All ER 204. Lord Hoffmann's comments suggest that the public interest, for example in planning procedures being followed, should be paramount.

OBP Textbook page 227, section 9.5.

Introduction to Judicial Review

Identifying a public law body

R (On the Application of Heather and Another) v *Leonard Cheshire Foundation* [2002] 2 All ER 936 Court of Appeal (Civil Division) (Lord Woolf CJ, Laws and Dyson LJJ)

Charitable body – whether amenable to judicial review – whether discharging a public function – scope of the Human Rights Act 1998

Facts

The claimants were accommodated in care homes run by the Leonard Cheshire Foundation (LCF) pursuant to an agreement between the LCF and the local authority. The local authority owed a duty to the claimants, under the National Assistance Act 1948, to provide the claimants with accommodation. The LCF decided to close the care home occupied by the claimants, the local authority making arrangements for their relocation. The claimants applied for judicial review of the LCF, contending that it was a public body bound by the Human Rights Act (HRA) 1998 and as such the decision to close the care home would amount to a violation of the claimants' art 8 rights. At first instance the application was dismissed on the basis that the LCF was not a public body within s6 HRA 1998. The claimants appealed.

Held

The appeal was dismissed. The Court of Appeal addressed two points in the course of its decision. First, was an application for judicial review the appropriate procedure in this case? As Lord Woolf CJ explained the concept of 'public body' for the purposes of a HRA 1998 claim was not necessarily co-terminus with the concept as developed for the purposes of judicial review in domestic law.

Lord Woolf CJ:

'As is appropriately set out in Grosz, Beatson, Duffy *Human Rights: The 1998 Act and the European Convention* (2000) p61, as to the relationship between the scope of the 1998 Act and the scope of judicial review:

"4–04 The law on the scope of judicial review cannot, however, be determinative. First, it will be necessary for the English courts to take into account the Strasbourg jurisprudence which identifies the bodies whose actions engage the responsibility of the state for the purpose of the Convention, which, as we shall see, differs from the judicial review criteria in material respects. That jurisprudence also makes clear that the Convention's reach is determined by reference to 'autonomous' concepts of Convention law and not by the manner in which national law classifies bodies or their acts. Secondly, notwithstanding the Home Secretary's statement that 'the concepts are reasonably clear', the way English courts have drawn the distinction between 'public' and 'private' for the purpose of judicial review produced a complicated and not altogether consistent body of cases, using a variety of tests. Thirdly, as will be seen, not all the acts of 'obvious' public authorities are treated as 'public' for the purposes of judicial review. In contrast, the [Human Rights Act 1998] will apply to all their acts. Nevertheless, the case law on the judicial review jurisdiction is instructive." '

Lord Woolf CJ then went on to address the change of emphasis as regards the public/private procedural dichotomy:

'To the points made in *Human Rights*, there is to be added the distinction between the approach of RSC O.53 and CPR Pt 54. RSC O.53, r1, in identifying cases ... appropriate for an application for judicial review ... focused on the nature of the application. Was it an application for an order of mandamus, prohibition or certiorari or an application for a declaration or an injunction which could be granted on an application for judicial review, if having regard to the nature and matters in respect of which relief may be granted by way of one of the prerogative remedies, it would be just and convenient for the declaration or injunction to be granted on an application for judicial review? CPR 54.1 has changed the focus of the test so that it is also partly functions based. Now the relevant provisions of CPR Pt 54 provide:

"54.1 Scope and Interpretation
(1) This Part contains rules about judicial review.
(2) In this Part –
(a) a 'claim for judicial review' means a claim to review the lawfulness of –
(i) an enactment; or
(ii) a decision, action or failure to act in relation to the exercise of a public function ...

54.2 When This Part Must Be Used
The judicial review procedure must be used in a claim for judicial review where the claimant is seeking –
(a) a mandatory order;
(b) a prohibiting order;
(c) a quashing order; or

(d) an injunction under s30 of the Supreme Court Act 1981 (restraining a person from acting in any office in which he is not entitled to act) ...

54.20 Transfer
The court may
(a) order a claim to continue as if it had not been started under this Part; and
(b) where it does so, give directions about the future management of the claim.

(Part 30 (transfer) applies to transfers to and from the Administrative Court)."

These changes have not been reflected in any complementary change to s31 of the Supreme Court Act 1981, which still is in virtually the same language as RSC O.53. None the less, there was ... reflected in the decision of the court below ... with its reference to "A gap in judicial review", an idea that if LCF was not performing a public function, proceedings by way of judicial review were wrong. This is an echo of the old demarcation disputes as to when judicial review was or was not appropriate under RSC O.53. CPR Pt 54 is intended to avoid any such disputes which are wholly unproductive. In a case such as the present where a bona fide contention is being advanced (although incorrect) that LCF was performing a public function, that is an appropriate issue to be brought to the court by way of judicial review. Because LCF is a charity further procedural requirements may be involved ... We wish to make clear that the CPR provide a framework which is sufficiently flexible to enable all the issues between the parties to be determined. Issues, if any, as to the private law rights of the claimants have not been determined. A decision had to be reached as to what happened to these proceedings. In view of the decisions of Stanley Burnton J [at first instance] and this court the claimants have no public law rights. Stanley Burnton J dismissed the proceedings having given judgment. In view of a possibility of a misunderstanding as to the scope of judicial review we draw attention to this and the powers of transfer under CPR Pt 54.'

The second issue considered by the Court of Appeal was whether or not the provision of accommodation under the 1948 Act on behalf of the local authority was a public law function. Lord Woolf CJ stated:

'If the [local] authority itself provides accommodation, it is performing a public function. It is also performing a public function if it makes arrangements for the accommodation to be provided by LCF. However, if a body which is a charity, like LCF, provides accommodation to those to whom the authority owes a duty under [the legislative scheme] ... it does not follow that the charity is performing a public function. Before the [HRA] 1998 Act came into force, we doubt whether it would have even been contemplated that LCF in providing care homes for people in the position of the appellants would be performing a public function. Whether under the 1998 Act, LCF are performing a public function, is critical to this appeal because s6(1) of the 1998 Act makes it unlawful for a public authority to act in a way which is incompatible with a Convention right and s6(3) of the 1998 Act defines who is a public authority for the purpose of s6 in these terms: "In this section 'public authority' includes ... (b) any person certain of whose functions are functions of a public nature ..."

It is to be noted that s6(3) is not exhaustive as to who is a public authority, but LCF could only be a public authority under s6(3). A public authority can be a hybrid body. That is, a public authority in relation to some of its functions and a private body in relation to others. This is the combined consequence of s6(3) and (5). Section 6(5) states:

"In relation to a particular act, a person is not a public authority by virtue only of subs(3)(b) if the nature of the act is private."

The issue here can therefore be refined by asking, is LCF, in providing accommodation for the claimants, performing a public function?'

Lord Woolf CJ then referred to *Poplar Housing and Regeneration Community Association Ltd* v *Donoghue* [2001] 4 All ER 604, and in particular the factors that led the court in that case to conclude that the housing association in that case was performing a public function. These included the nature of the statutory powers under which a function was discharged, and the degree of control retained by the local authority. He concluded:

'If this were a situation where a local authority could divest itself of its art 8 obligations by contracting out to a voluntary sector provider its obligations under ... the 1948 Act, then there would be a responsibility on the court to approach the interpretation of s6(3)(b) [of the HRA 1998] in a way which ensures, so far as this is possible, that the rights under art 8 of persons in the position of the appellants are protected. This is not, however, the situation. The local authority remains under an obligation under ... the 1948 Act and retains an obligation under art 8 to the appellants even though it has used its powers under [the 1948 Act] to use LCF as a provider. In addition the appellants have their contractual rights against LCF in any event. There is also the possible protection which can be provided by the Attorney General's role but this is not a significant factor.

... In our judgment the role that LCF was performing manifestly did not involve the performance of public functions. The fact that LCF is a large and flourishing organisation does not change the nature of its activities from private to public. (i) It is not in issue that it is possible for LCF to perform some public functions and some private functions. In this case it is contended that this was what has been happening in regard to those residents who are privately funded and those residents who are publicly funded. But in this case ... there is no material distinction between the nature of the services LCF has provided for residents funded by a local authority and those provided to residents funded privately. While the degree of public funding of the activities of an otherwise private body is certainly relevant as to the nature of the functions performed, by itself it is not determinative of whether the functions are public or private ... (ii) There is no other evidence of there being a public flavour to the functions of LCF or LCF itself. LCF is not standing in the shoes of the local authorities. Section 26 of the 1948 Act provides statutory authority for the actions of the local authorities but it provides LCF with no powers. LCF is not exercising statutory powers in performing functions for the appellants. (iii) In truth, all that [counsel for the claimants] can rely upon is the fact that if LCF is not performing a public function the appellants would not be able to rely upon art 8 as against LCF. However, this is a circular argument. If LCF was performing a public function, that would mean that the appellants could rely in relation to that function on art 8, but, if the situation is otherwise, art 8 cannot change the appropriate classification of the function. On the approach adopted in [*Donoghue*] it can be said that LCF is clearly not performing any public function.'

Comment

The decision shows that a litigant should no longer agonise over whether a respondent is or is not a public body. The application for judicial review should be used in the knowledge that the proceedings can be transferred to be dealt with as a private law action if this is more appropriate. The issue of whether or not a function falls within the sphere of public law may still be vexed. The source of funding is not decisive, but the absence of statutory powers may be. See further *R (On the Application of A) v Partnerships in Care Ltd* (2002) The Times 11 April.

R (On the Application of the Oxford Study Centre) v The British Council [2001] EWHC Admin 207 Queen's Bench Divisional Court (Collins J)

Body involved in voluntary regulation – whether amenable to judicial review

Facts
The applicants operated a language school and agreed to participate in an accreditation scheme operated by the respondent organisation. Following an inspection visit undertaken by representatives of the respondents the applicants' accreditation was withdrawn. The applicants appealed against this decision on the basis that one of the inspectors had not been properly qualified to participate in the inspection. The respondents convened an appeal committee to consider the applicants' appeal against the decision. The secretary to the appeal committee was also the manager of the accreditation unit. She remained with the appeal committee whilst it deliberated. The appeal committee upheld the decision to withdraw accreditation and the applicants applied for judicial review on the basis that there had been a breach of natural justice on the basis that the secretary ought not to have remained with the appeal committee whilst it decided the outcome of the appeal. The committee contended that it was not a body amenable to judicial review.

Held
1. On the procedural issue. The respondent body was not a public law body, notwithstanding that it discharged a regulatory function. The key test was whether the respondents discharged a function that had been integrated into a system of governmental control. As the accreditation scheme was a purely voluntary arrangement it did not satisfy that key test. The court therefore determined to treat the application as an action for breach of contract.
2. On the natural justice issue. The secretary ought not to have remained with the appeal committee whilst it decided the outcome of the appeal as this raised the prospect of the committee considering irrelevant considerations or issues that the applicants would not have the opportunity to address. The applicants were therefore entitled to a declaration that the appeal committee had breached an implied term to act fairly.

Comment
Note that the court might have been willing to regard the respondents as a public body if there had been no basis for providing a contractual remedy. Compare this decision with that in *R (On the Application of A) v Partnerships in Care Ltd* (2002) The Times 11 April, where the court held that a private hospital, making changes as

to the provision of psychiatric care, was amenable to judicial review because the hospital was subject to specific statutory duties under the Registered Homes Act 1984. It was also considered significant that the hospital's patients were admitted under compulsion by virtue of s3 of the Mental Health Act 1983. The treatment of patients was, therefore, a matter of public concern and decisions as to their care were public law decisions.

OBP Textbook page 236, section 10.4.

Application for judicial review

Cowl v *Plymouth City Council* (2002) The Times 8 January Court of Appeal (Civil Division) (Lord Woolf CJ, Mummery and Buxton LJJ)

Judicial review – need to exhaust alternative remedies prior to applying for review

Facts
The applicants applied for judicial review to challenge a decision by the respondent local authority to close a residential home prior to carrying out detailed assessments of the residents' care needs and preparing individual care plans. The application was dismissed and the applicants appealed.

Held
The appeal was dismissed. The local authority had not acted unlawfully in shutting the residential home prior to carrying out the assessments, although it ought to have informed the residents of its strategy. The court stressed that this was a case where the applicants had resorted to litigation much too soon and had wrongly concluded that the respondent authority's complaints procedure did not constitute an alternative remedy. Lord Woolf CJ observed that the Civil Procedure Rules could be invoked to require the parties to attend a hearing to determine whether or not it was necessary to resort to litigation.

Comment
The decision underlines the point that judicial review should be seen as the last resort in contesting the actions of a public body. It also illustrates the willingness of the courts to adopt a more proactive approach under the Civil Procedure Rules to deter unnecessary litigation.

R (On the Application of Burkett) v *Hammersmith and Fulham London Borough Council* [2002] 3 All ER 97 House of Lords (Lord Phillips MR, Lords Slynn of Hadley, Steyn, Hope of Craighead and Millett)

Application for judicial review – time limits – when does time run – appellate jurisdiction of the House of Lords

Facts

In November 1999 Hammersmith and Fulham London Borough Council passed a resolution that a planning officer could grant planning permission provided two conditions precedent were met. In May 2000 the claimants submitted an application for judicial review of that resolution. On 12 May 2000 the developer met the conditions precedent and outline planning permission was granted. On 18 May 2000 the claimants' application for judicial review was refused both on its merits and due to the delay in bringing the challenge to the November 1999 resolution. Having appealed unsuccessfully to the Court of Appeal the claimants appealed further to the House of Lords.

Held

The appeal was allowed. The time-limit for applying for judicial review ran from the date of the grant of planning permission, not the date of the resolution. The application for review could be amended so as to be directed at the grant of planning permission. As regards the issue of whether time should run from the date of the resolution, Lord Steyn observed:

'In law the resolution is not a juristic act giving rise to rights and obligations. It is not inevitable that it will ripen into an actual grant of planning permission. In these circumstances it would be curious if, when the actual grant of planning permission is challenged, a court could insist by retrospective judgment that the applicant ought to have moved earlier for judicial review against a preliminary decision "which is the real basis of his complaint" … Moreover, an application to declare a resolution unlawful might arguably be premature and be objected to on this ground. And in strict law it could be dismissed … For my part the substantive position is straightforward. The court has jurisdiction to entertain an application by a citizen for judicial review in respect of a resolution before or after its adoption. But it is a jump in legal logic to say that he must apply for such relief in respect of the resolution on pain of losing his right to judicial review of the actual grant of planning permission which does affect his rights. Such a view would also be in tension with the established principle that judicial review is a remedy of last resort.

At this stage it is necessary to return to the point that the rule of court applies across the board to judicial review applications. If a decision-maker indicates that, subject to hearing further representations, he is provisionally minded to make a decision adverse to a citizen, is it to be said that time runs against the citizen from the moment of the provisional expression of view? That would plainly not be sensible and would involve waste of time and money. Let me give a more concrete example. A licensing authority expresses a provisional view that a licence should be cancelled but indicates a willingness to hear further argument. The citizen contends that the proposed decision would be unlawful. Surely, a court might as a matter of discretion take the view that it would be premature to apply for judicial review as soon as the provisional decision is announced. And it would certainly be contrary to principle to require the citizen to take such premature legal action. In my view the time limit under the rules of court would not run from the date of such preliminary decisions in respect of a challenge of the actual decision. If that is so, one is entitled to ask: what is the qualitative difference in town planning? … Undoubtedly, there is a need for public bodies to have certainty as to the legal validity of their actions. That is the rationale of O.53, r4(1). On the other hand, it is far from clear that the selection of the actual grant of planning permission as the critical date would disadvantage developers and local authorities.

For my part the arguments in favour of time running from the date of resolution in the present case have been given undue weight by the Court of Appeal. In any event, there are a number of countervailing policy considerations to be considered ... legal policy favours simplicity and certainty rather than complexity and uncertainty. In the interpretation of legislation this factor is a commonplace consideration. In choosing between competing constructions a court may presume, in the absence of contrary indications, that the legislature intended to legislate for a certain and predictable regime. Much will depend on the context. In procedural legislation, primary or subordinate, it must be a primary factor in the interpretative process, notably where the application of the procedural regime may result in the loss of fundamental rights to challenge an unlawful exercise of power. The citizen must know where he stands. And so must the local authority and the developer. For my part this approach is so firmly anchored in domestic law that it is unnecessary, in this case, to seek to reinforce it by reference to the European principle of legal certainty ... I am satisfied that the words "from the date when the grounds for the application first arose" refer to the date when the planning permission was granted.'

Comment

Note that the House of Lords also rejected the assertion that it had no jurisdiction to hear appeals from the Court of Appeal against a decision to refuse to give permission to apply for judicial review.

OBP Textbook page 266, section 10.6.

Liability of the Crown and Public Bodies in Contract and Tort

Crown immunity

Matthews v *Ministry of Defence* [2002] 3 All ER 513 Court of Appeal (Civil Division) (Lord Phillips MR, Mummery and Hale LJJ)

Crown immunity – s10 Crown Proceedings Act 1947 – whether compatible with the European Convention on Human Rights

Facts

The claimant served in the Royal Navy between 1955 and 1968. In September 1999 he was diagnosed as having an illness related to his exposure to asbestos dust whilst serving in the Royal Navy. The claimant alleged that his condition resulted from the negligence of fellow Royal Navy servicemen and/or breach of statutory duty by the Royal Navy and the Ministry of Defence. A preliminary hearing was held at which Keith J declared that s10 of the Crown Proceedings Act 1947 was incompatible with art 6 of the European Convention on Human Rights (ECHR) on the basis that s10 interfered with the claimant's right of access to the court as provided for by art 6 ECHR. The Ministry of Defence appealed.

Held

The appeal was allowed. Section 10 of the Crown Proceedings Act 1947 was substantive, as opposed to procedural, in its effect. If the terms of s10 were met a claimant had no cause of action in negligence. The issuing of a certificate under s10 that prevented any cause of action arising gave rise to a defence that existed as a matter of substantive law. There had, therefore, been no violation of art 6.

Lord Phillips MR:

'Article 6(1) is essentially concerned with judicial process. Its effects include an entitlement to a fair, public and reasonably prompt hearing in respect of any assertion of an infringement of a civil right. A claim that a civil right has been infringed may involve a seminal question of law of whether the civil right, which the claimant asserts has been infringed, exists at all. English civil procedure is accustomed to resolving such seminal issues as preliminary points of law, before the facts that are alleged to give rise to the infringement of the right are investigated by the court. Whether a civil right exists is a matter of the substantive law of the contracting states. If a preliminary issue as to the existence of a civil right is decided against a claimant, there will be a procedural bar to his exploring the facts before the court. The nature of this procedure does not appear to have been fully appreciated by the Strasbourg court in *Osman* v *United Kingdom* (1998) 5 BHRC 293. The court has, however, since recognised that this procedure does not infringe art 6 (see *Z* v *United Kingdom* (2001) 10 BHRC 384) … With the exception of *Osman* v *United Kingdom* … we have not been referred to any decision where the Strasbourg court has held that a rule of substantive law conferring immunity from liability on a category of persons infringes art 6(1). In so saying we distinguish between immunity from liability, which is substantive, and immunity from suit, which is procedural, although sometimes it is not easy to distinguish between the two … The Bill, which became the 1947 Act, was introduced into the House of Lords by the Lord Chancellor. The debate there shows that the Bill was always subject to the s10 exception, which was not initially qualified by the requirement for a certificate. Provision was made for the "conclusive" certificates under s10(3) and there was considerable discussion about these. The requirement for the s10(1) and (2) certificate was introduced in the committee stage by the Attorney General. In moving these amendments the Lord Chancellor explained (151 HL Official Report (5th series) col 849, 31 July 1947):

"It is thus apparent that it was never intended that the question of whether or not a serviceman should enjoy a right of action against a fellow serviceman or the Crown for personal injuries sustained in service should be at the option of the Secretary of State. The requirement for a certificate was introduced as a prerequisite to the loss of the cause of action in order to establish conclusively that the circumstances which had deprived the serviceman of a cause of action had entitled him, provided other relevant criteria were satisfied, to a pension. While reference to Hansard makes this quite clear, it is the conclusion to which we would have come without that assistance." '

Comment

Note that as the ECHR was not engaged in this case, arguments as to whether s10 amounted to a proportionate interference with art 6 ECHR rights did not arise.

OBP Textbook page 340, section 14.4.

2

Civil and Criminal Procedure

PART I – CIVIL PROCEDURE

The Choice of Court

Introduction

As the fourth anniversary of the implementation of Woolf approaches, the practical effects of the reforms continue to provoke interest amongst politicians as well as members of the judiciary and legal practitioners. The Judicial Statistics (July 2002), published on behalf of the Lord Chancellor's Department, confirm the trend of each year since the implementation of the Woolf reforms of a significant drop in the number of new cases reaching the courts. Claims in the Queen's Bench Division were down by 20 per cent to 22,000, compared to 180,000 ten years ago. The number of claims lodged in the county court were down by 7 per cent on the previous year. In the High Court, the time taken between issue and trial has gone up to 173 weeks, whilst in the county court the period is 73 weeks.

In announcing the conclusions of a longer term study of the effects of the Woolf reforms, Baroness Scotland, parliamentary secretary at the Lord Chancellor's Department, said that overall there had been a drop in the number of claims issued where the new Civil Procedure Rules 1998 had been introduced. The use of pre-action protocols and claimant offers to settle have diverted cases from being litigated in the courts, with the result that only 8 per cent of cases listed for trial settle at the trial at the court, while 70 per cent settle much earlier. The report also shows that the average time from issue to trial in the county court has fallen from 640 days in 1997 to 500 in 2000–2001.

In May 2002, the Court Service published a progress report outlining a plan to establish a network of primary hearing centres and part-time local centres for some small claims, family and possession work. The main effect of the plans, if implemented, would be to increase the number of courts from the present 220 to 275. Pilot schemes have also been commenced in relation to the electronic issue of proceedings and the payment of court fees.

In their research paper *More Civil Justice? The Impact of the Woolf Reforms on Pre-action Behaviour* (May 2002), the Law Society and the Civil Justice Council assessed the success of the pre-action procedures introduced by Woolf. Most of the respondents were positive about the 'new' pre-action procedures, even in those areas where there are no pre-action protocols. Personal injury practitioners and insurers appear to have welcomed the additional information that the protocol requires to be disclosed during the early stages of the action, as it facilitates early settlement and restricts the unnecessary incursion of legal costs.

Finally, the Working Party on Expert Evidence, which was established by the Head of Civil Justice, has produced a Code of Guidance on Expert Evidence. The purpose of the Code is to provide appropriate guidelines to experts and those instructing them in civil cases for all cases where the Civil Procedure Rules 1998 apply, and to facilitate better communication and dealings between the expert and the instructing parties and between the parties.

HLT Textbook page 3, section 1.1.

Court proceedings or alternative dispute settlement?

Dunnett v *Railtrack plc* [2002] 2 All ER 850 Court of Appeal (Civil Division) (Brooke, Sedley and Robert Walker LJJ)

Costs sanctions – alternative dispute settlement

Facts
Ms Dunnett (D) kept horses in a field adjoining a railway line owned by Railtrack. A gate in the field was used by Railtrack to gain access to the field to carry out repairs to the line. Railtrack had replaced the 'old' gate with a new one that was not self-closing. In D's absence, the gate was left open and her horses were killed by a train when they strayed onto the line. The gate was later replaced by a fixed fence. D brought proceedings against Railtrack in negligence for failing to take notice of her request that the gate should be locked, which she lost at first instance. D applied for leave to appeal against the first instance decision on the ground that she now sought to rely on breach of statutory duty by Railtrack under the duties imposed by the Railway Clauses Consolidation Act 1845. In granting D's right to appeal, the Court strongly suggested that the parties should resolve the matter by either mediation or arbitration. In spite of the Court's strong direction on the point, Railtrack refused to contemplate any form of alternative dispute resolution with D.

Held
In making no order as to costs, the Court stated that, if a party rejected alternative dispute resolution out of hand, when it had been suggested by the Court, they would suffer the consequences when costs came to be decided. Even though D's appeal was dismissed, the Court of Appeal refused to order that she pay Railtrack's costs, because the Court considered that the appeal hearing could have been avoided if Railtrack had resolved to settle the dispute by alternative dispute resolution.

Hurst v *Leeming* [2002] CP Rep 59 High Court (Chancery Division) (Lightman J)

Availability of mediation – costs

Facts

H, a solicitor, brought proceedings against his former partners in which Mr Leeming QC (L) was instructed to act on his behalf. The proceedings were unsuccessful and H subsequently brought an action against L in professional negligence. Both parties applied for summary judgement and at the hearing of the application, H conceded that his claim was without merit but argued that L should not be entitled to his costs because he had refused H's offer to have the matter settled by arbitration.

Held

The application was refused on the grounds that, in the exceptional circumstances of the case, it was inappropriate to penalise L in costs following his refusal of a pre-trial offer of mediation in view of H's attitude, character and status as an undischarged bankrupt. Further, L had been justified in refusing mediation, as H's claim clearly had no realistic prospect of success.

Comment

An integral part of the Woolf proposals (see the Interim Report's chapter on 'Alternative Approaches to Dispensing Justice') was making greater use of alternative dispute resolution (ADR) procedures. ADR procedures, including ombudsman schemes and mediation, are considered to be more cost effective and quicker than mainstream civil proceedings. The availability of ADR is contained in the Civil Procedure Rules (CPR) 1998 as part of the court's case management powers by imposing an obligation to encourage the use of ADR in pursuance of the overriding objectives under r1.4(2)(e) CPR 1998. This obligation also extends to the parties to assist the court under r1.3 CPR 1998: they should take an active part to assist the court by resolving the dispute by ADR where appropriate. Whilst the use of ADR clearly falls within the philosophy and practice of the Rules, until the decision in *Dunnett* v *Railtrack plc* there appears to have been no reported decision where a party had been punished by refusing to consider the use of ADR. It remains to be seen whether the decision is the beginning of a more punitive approach by the courts by imposing sanctions against those parties, which, for no compelling reason, refuse to contemplate mediation or arbitration.

Clearly, in *Hurst* v *Leeming* the court was satisfied that the party did have a compelling reason to refuse to go to arbitration – although before coming to this conclusion the court rejected four out of the five reasons put forward by L. In refusing the offer of arbitration, L had unsuccessfully put forward the following reasons: that he had already incurred heavy costs in meeting the allegations; that the allegation of professional misconduct that had been made against him was serious; that he believed there was no substance in H's case; and finally, that he had already supplied a full refutation of H's case. Whilst none of these reasons were accepted by the court as justifying the refusal to arbitrate, the final reason was accepted that, when objectively viewed, H had shown himself to be incapable of making a balanced evaluation of the facts, and that his sole intention in seeking arbitration was to obtain a substantial sum from L when there was clearly no merit to his claim.

HLT Textbook pages 4 and 158, sections 1.3 and 17.5.

The Issue of Proceedings

Phoenix Finance Ltd v *Federation International de l'Automobile* (2002)
The Times 27 June High Court (Chancery Division) (Sir Andrew Morrit V-C)

Letter before action under the Civil Procedure Rules 1998

Facts
The issue before the court was whether the second and third defendants' costs should be assessed on an indemnity basis because of the conduct of the claimant in failing to send a letter before action or any comparable warning.

Held
In ordering the payment of the second and third defendants' costs on an indemnity basis, his Lordship stated that a letter before action was required under the Civil Procedure Rules (CPR) 1998 as much as under the 'old' rules. If a claimant failed to give any warning of proceedings which he later lost, he could not complain if he was required to pay indemnity costs.

Comment
The position before the CPR 1998 was that a letter before action was required in all but the most exceptional cases. Under the new rules, even where there was no pre-action protocol that was directly applicable to the instant case, the whole thrust of the CPR 1998, and particularly the overriding objective, made it plain that a letter before action was necessary under the new rules.

HLT Textbook pages 13 and 158, sections 3.1 and 17.5.

Amendment and Striking Out of Pleadings

Amendment of the pleadings

Goode v *Martin* [2002] 1 WLR 620 Court of Appeal (Civil Division) (Brook, Kay and Latham LJJ)

Amendments – causes of action – limitations – statements of case

Facts

G had been injured in an accident on board a yacht owned by M. As a result of the head injuries she sustained in the accident, she was unable to remember events in the ten minutes before the accident and had to rely on others to tell her what had happened. In an action in negligence against M, she sought to amend her statement of case in the light of events contained in M's amended defence. G unsuccessfully applied to amend her statement of case (reported at [2001] 3 All ER 562) and appealed against the decision to the Court of Appeal. At the hearing of the appeal, G contended that if her amendment was disallowed on a conventional interpretation of Pt 17, r17.4(2) Civil Procedure Rules (CPR) 1998 then pursuant to the interpretive obligation imposed by s3 Human Rights Act 1998, a more unconventional approach should be taken to avoid an infringement of her right to a fair trial under art 6 European Convention on Human Rights 1950.

Held

In allowing the appeal, the Court ruled that the interpretive obligation under s3 of the 1998 Act made it possible for r17.4(2) CPR 1998 to be interpreted as though it contained the additional words 'already in issue on' after 'the same facts as' as per *R v A (Complainant's Sexual History)* [2001] 3 All ER 1. This meant that a statement of case could be amended after the expiry of the relevant limitation period to add a new claim which was founded on the defendant's version of the facts rather than those in the claimant's existing claim. In the instant case, no new facts were being introduced, as all G was seeking to do was to say that negligence was established, no matter whether G's or M's version of events were correct.

Comment

Whilst the obligation imposed on the courts by s3 Human Rights Act 1998 to interpret domestic legislation, so far as is possible, in a way that ensures compliance with Convention rights has already had a significant influence on the development of the rules of criminal practice, the pervasive influence of s3 in civil proceedings is well-illustrated by the decision in *Goode* above. Rule 17.4(2) CPR 1998 permits a party to amend or substitute a new claim after the limitation period has expired provided the new claim arises out of the same or substantially the same facts as the original claim. This power is also reflected in s35(5)(a) Limitation Act 1980, which permits the rules of the court to allow a claimant to add, after the expiry of the limitation period, a new claim which arises out of the original claim. In deciding to allow the amendment in *Goode*, in order to comply with the requirements of the party's right to a fair trial in the determination of his civil rights under art 6, the Court of Appeal extended the meaning of the provision to allow a new claim which arises out of the same facts as are already in issue in the original claim. In interpreting the domestic law in a Convention-compliant way, the approach adopted by the House of Lords in *R v A (Complainant's Sexual History)* [2001] 3 All ER 1 was applied.

HLT Textbook page 75, section 10.3.

Disclosure of Documents

Use of disclosed documents

Al Fayed and Others v *Commissioner of Police of the Metropolis and Others* (2002) The Times 17 June Court of Appeal (Civil Division) (Lord Phillips MR, Clarke and Walker LJJ)

Disclosure and inspection – mistake – legal professional privilege – public interest immunity

Facts

A appealed against an order (reported at [2002] EWHC 562) requiring him to deliver up to the solicitors representing the Commissioner of Police two opinions of counsel which had been disclosed by mistake, and restraining him from making use of those opinions save for the purposes of an appeal. A had been arrested on suspicion of theft or criminal damage but a decision had been made not to charge him. A brought proceedings against the Commissioner of Police alleging wrongful arrest and false imprisonment. Counsel's opinions, which had influenced the decision not to charge A, were inadvertently sent to A's solicitors when documents were inspected under Pt 31 Civil Procedure Rules (CPR) 1998. The Commissioner of Police argued that the opinions were subject to legal professional privilege and public interest immunity, and therefore should not be used by A's solicitors.

Held

The appeal was allowed. In cases where a party had inspected documents subject to legal professional privilege, the Court of Appeal reaffirmed the well-established position that, where privileged documents were mistakenly disclosed for inspection by one party to litigation, in circumstances in which it would not have been obvious to a reasonable solicitor that a mistake had been made, the disclosing party was not entitled to an injunction ordering the receiving party to return the documents. Where the documents were received in this way, the receiving party should be permitted to make proper use of the documents on the basis that they were no longer subject to legal professional privilege or public interest immunity, subject to the court's case management powers. On the facts of the present case, it could not be said that it should have been obvious to A's solicitors that the opinions had been made available by mistake. Two experienced solicitors acting for A had genuinely believed that the opinions had been disclosed deliberately. Furthermore, there appeared to have been a careful approach to disclosure and it had not been obvious that legal professional privilege or public interest immunity would be relied on. It was therefore appropriate to discharge the order.

Comment

The position where documents protected by legal professional privilege are mistakenly disclosed to the another party in the case is governed by r31.20 CPR

1998, which states: 'Where a party allows a privileged document to be inspected, the party who has inspected the documents may use it or its contents only with the permission of the court'. The leading case on the issue following the implementation of the CPR 1998 is *Breeze* v *John Stacey* (1999) The Times 8 July, in which the Court of Appeal stated that if the mistake was obvious and it was clear that the documents had been inadvertently disclosed, the privileged material should be returned. If the mistake was not apparent, then, as in *Al Fayed and Others* v *Commissioner of Police for the Metropolis and Others* above, it must be decided if a reasonable, hypothetical solicitor would have concluded that disclosure must have occurred as the result of a mistake.

HLT Textbook page 91, section 11.11.

Payment into Court

Procedure

Anglo-Eastern Trust Ltd v *Kermanshahchi* [2002] EWCA Civ 198 Court of Appeal (Civil Division) (Brooke and Mance LJJ, Park J)

Payment into court – right to a fair trial – summary judgments

Facts

The claimant company had sought summary judgement against Kermanshahchi, a debtor. The application for summary judgement had been refused at first instance as it had been held that, although it was improbable that Kermanshahchi's defence would succeed, the prospect of success could not be ruled out. A conditional order had been made under Pt 24, r24 Civil Procedure Rules (CPR) 1998, requiring Kermanshahchi to pay £1 million into court. No evidence of Kermanshahchi's means had been adduced. Kermanshahchi appealed against the order requiring him to make the payment into court on the basis that he could not afford to pay £1 million, and was therefore prevented from defending the action.

Held

Allowing the appeal in part, Kermanshahchi was permitted to adduce fresh evidence of his means, as the absence of evidence in the first instance was not his fault. On the evidence, Kermanshahchi did not have the sum ordered, with the result that the payment into court would have prevented him from defending the action. That was in breach of art 6 European Convention on Human Rights 1950. The payment was therefore reduced to £75,000.

Comment

In giving its judgement, the Court of Appeal cited with approval *Ladd* v *Marshall* [1954] 3 All ER 745 concerning the reception of new evidence on appeal. The case was, however, decided under the 'old' rules and in *Hertfordshire Investments Ltd* v

Bubb [2000] 1 WLR 2318, the Court stated that that the principles set out in *Ladd* should be regarded as establishing the relevant factors to be considered, rather than laying strict guidelines.

HLT Textbook page 136, section 15.2.

Costs

Callery v *Gray (Nos 1 & 2)* [2002] 1 WLR 2000 House of Lords (Lords Bingham of Cornhill, Nicholls of Birkenhead, Hoffmann, Hope of Craighead and Scott of Foscote)

Conditional fees – costs – insurance premiums

Facts
The claimant, who had suffered minor injuries in a road traffic accident, entered into a conditional fee agreement, on first instructing solicitors, and agreed a 60 per cent success fee. Before the defendant's response to the claim was known, the claimant also paid the premium for the after the event insurance cover against the risk of his incurring liability as to costs. The claim settled quickly without recourse to proceedings. In costs-only proceedings, the judge, upholding the district judge, had reduced the success fee to 40 per cent and held the after the event premium recoverable. The Court of Appeal held in *Callery* v *Gray (No 1)* [2001] 1 WLR 2112 that first, 20 per cent is the maximum uplift that could reasonably be agreed, and second (*Callery* v *Gray (No 2)* [2001] 1 WLR 2142) that, in principle, an after the event insurance premium is recoverable, and the premium in the instant case was not manifestly disproportionate to the risk. The defendant was granted leave to appeal to the House of Lords on a point of law of public importance.

Held
Their Lordships (with Lord Scott dissenting in part) held, in dismissing points of appeal, that: (1) they would uphold the order made by the Court of Appeal that, in principle, the after the event insurance premium was recoverable so long as they were each in a reasonable amount and that the maximum allowable success fee was 20 per cent in such a modest and straightforward case as the present one; and (2) they would uphold the order made by the Court of Appeal that on receipt of further evidence, the amount of the after the event insurance premium of £350 was not manifestly disproportionate to the risk and was therefore recoverable. Their Lordships also went on to state that responsibility for supervising the developing practice by which the new funding regime under the Access to Justice Act 1999, particularly with regard to personal injury litigation, lay with the Court of Appeal and not the House of Lords, which should ordinarily be slow to intervene.

Comment

The long-running saga of this case was first considered in *Law Update 2002*. It is to be welcomed that the House of Lords has finally clarified the uncertainties that inevitably arose out of the earlier decisions in the case. In his speech in *Callery* v *Gray (Nos 1 & 2)*, Lord Bingham referred to the defects in the previous system of public funding and to the new funding regime, in particular with regard to personal injury litigation introduced by the Access to Justice Act 1999, which (along with its accompanying regulations) had, for the present purposes, three aims. First, to contain the rising cost of legal aid to public funds and enable existing expenditure to be refocused on causes with the greatest public need to be funded at public expense. Second, to improve access to the courts for members of the public with meritorious claims; it was appreciated that the risk of incurring substantial liabilities in costs was a powerful disincentive to all but the very rich from becoming involved in litigation, and it was therefore hoped that the new arrangements would enable claimants to protect themselves against liability for paying costs either to those acting for them or, if they chose, to those on the other side. Third, to discourage weak claims and enable successful defendants to recover their costs in actions brought against them by indigent claimants. To achieve these objectives, publicly funded assistance was withdrawn from run-of-the-mill personal injury claimants requiring the parties to enter into conditional fee agreements with their lawyers. Under this new regime, litigants transferred the entire cost of funding litigation to the liability insurers of the unsuccessful party. The frontline responsibility for making the new funding regime work fairly and in accordance with the overriding objectives of the CPR 1998 lay with lawyers agreeing to act under conditional fee agreements and insurers offering after the event insurance. The responsibility for curbing excesses in the new funding regime lay with the judiciary and finally with the Court of Appeal.

HLT Textbook page 160, section 17.7.

PART II – CRIMINAL PROCEDURE

Introduction

As any criminal litigator will be aware, in recent years the criminal justice system has been at the forefront of discussion, debate and legislative reform. The reforming process has continued during the spring and summer of 2002 with the introduction of the revised Code D of the Codes of Practice governing the conduct of identification procedures used by the police. These changes are considered in detail below. This period of legislative change is set to continue after the publication in July 2002 of the government's White Paper, *Justice for All*. The recommendations in the long-awaited White Paper are based on the proposals contained in Auld LJ's

Report into the criminal justice system (January 2002) and the Halliday Report on sentencing (May 2001), which were both considered in *Law Update 2002*.

The stated aims of *Justice for All* seek to introduce reforms at all stages of the criminal justice process, from the investigation of crime, to trial procedures and the court's powers of sentencing. Not only are the proposals important for the rules of criminal procedure, but they are also significant for the procedural context in which the rules of evidence operate in criminal cases and attempt to simplify and modernise the approach to evidence.

Detection of crime

Justice for All made the following recommendations:

1. to increase police numbers to 130,000;
2. to increase expenditure on operational policing;
3. to have greater specialisation in detective skills;
4. to have more effective use of science and technology in the detection of crime.

Pre-trial procedures

Further recommendations were:

1. to continue the extension of locating police and Crown Prosecution Service staff in joint Criminal Justice Units in police stations;
2. Crown Prosecution Service staff to assume greater responsibility for deciding the appropriate charge for the defendant;
3. Crown Prosecution Service staff to give an early indication of possible sentence to the defendant to encourage an early guilty plea;
4. to extend magistrates' custodial sentencing powers to 12 months;
5. to extend police powers to impose bail conditions on a suspect before charge;
6. to extend the prosecution's right to appeal against bail for all imprisonable offences;
7. to improve the procedures for the pre-trial disclosure of prosecution and defence evidence;
8. to extend the availability of preparatory hearings to include 'serious' offences as well as those that are regarded as 'complex'.

At trial

There are also proposals:

1. to allow for trial with a judge sitting alone in complex and lengthy trials and/or where there is a risk of jury intimidation;

2. to allow the court to be informed of the defendant's previous convictions where it is 'relevant';
3. to give witnesses greater access to their original statements when giving evidence;
4. to extend the use of hearsay evidence where there is a 'good' reason for the witness not attending trial;
5. to remove the double jeopardy rule for serious offences where fresh evidence comes to light;
6. to give the prosecution the right of appeal against rulings by the judge which terminate the prosecution case before the jury decides;
7. to increase the proportion of the public who are eligible for jury service.

After conviction

It will also be necessary to ensure uniformity in sentencing through the creation of a Sentencing Guidelines Council.

Criminal Justice Bill 2002

Based on the proposals contained in *Justice for All* and as part of its legislative proposals for the then forthcoming parliamentary session in November 2002, the government published its Criminal Justice Bill 2002. The Bill includes the following proposals:

1. introducing powers to impose conditions on police bail before charge;
2. improving procedures for prosecution and defence pre-trial disclosure of evidence;
3. reducing exemption from jury service;
4. providing for judge-only trials in complex fraud cases and in cases of witness intimidation;
5. providing clearer and more severe community punishments;
6. extending the magistrates' custodial sentencing powers from six to 12 months.

The latest Criminal Justice Bill 2002 is yet another attempt by successive governments to make the criminal justice system more efficient in its working practices and more responsive to the victims of crime by bringing more offenders to justice. At the present time it is estimated that only 20 per cent of crimes reported to the police result in a conviction. This is probably the most radical solution to date, with an overhaul of many of the key stages of a criminal case by increasing the powers of the police on the streets, the speed with which offenders are dealt with in court and creating a more consistent and rigorous approach to custodial sentences and community punishments. It remains to be seen whether this initiative, like many of its predecessors, fails to deliver its promises.

HLT Textbook pages 211, 216, 275 and 306, sections 22.1, 23.5, 28.3 and 30.6.

Practice Direction (Criminal Proceedings: Consolidation) [2002] 1 WLR 2870 Lord Chief Justice's Court (Lord Woolf CJ)

Lord Woolf, the Lord Chief Justice, issued this *Practice Direction*, which is primarily a consolidation of existing practice with some amendments as they affect proceedings in the Court of Appeal (Criminal Division), the Crown Court and the magistrates' court, with the exception of the *Practice Directions* which relate to costs. Part I deals with directions of general application, including appropriate mode of court dress, restrictions on reporting proceedings, spent convictions and the words to be used when passing sentence. Part II provides further directions for parties when applying to the Criminal Division of the Court of Appeal, including when drafting a notice of appeal and making an application for leave to appeal, and guidance on citing judgements in court and extracts from Hansard. Part III has general application for procedures in the Crown Court and the magistrates' court, including guidance on the classification of Crown Court business and allocation to Crown Court centres, the facts to be stated on a guilty plea, guidance on the granting of bail during the trial, disclosure of the accused's antecedents and the personal statements of victims. Part IV provides further directions applying in the Crown Court to include modes of address and titles of judges, the allocation of business within the Crown Court, the procedure to be followed when preferring voluntary bills of indictment and guidance about citing from Hansard. Part V provides further directions applying in magistrates' courts relating to the procedure to be adopted at mode of trial hearings, committals for sentence and the procedure to be followed when the clerk retires with the magistrates.

HLT Textbook pages 211, 224 and 246, sections 22.1, 24.1 and 25.15.

Arrest and Prosecution

Grounds for a lawful arrest without warrant

Al-Fayed and Others v *Commissioner of Police of the Metropolis*
Judgment of 13 August 2002 (not yet reported) Queen's Bench Divisional Court (Cresswell J)

False imprisonment – 'reasonable suspicion'

Facts
This involved an action by the claimants for damages for alleged false imprisonment following their arrest by the second to fourth defendants, who were officers in the Metropolitan Police's Organised Crime Group (OCG), in connection with the opening of the late Tiny Rowland's safe deposit box at Harrods. The first claimant was the chairman of the Harrods group of companies which operated a safe depository located at the Harrods store in Knightsbridge. The other claimants were

employees of Harrods. On various dates in March 1998 the claimants were arrested on suspicion of theft and criminal damage in connection with the alleged theft and damage to the contents of the deposit box. The claimants were subsequently released without charge. The OCG investigation was brought to an end in July 1998 without any charge being brought against the claimants. The claimants' case was that the arrests were wrongful and that the defendants were liable for false imprisonment on the grounds that: (1) they did not suspect the claimants of having committed the offences in question; (2) even if they did, they had no reasonable grounds for that suspicion; and (3) the decision to arrest the claimants and/or their continued detention after arrest was, under s37 Police and Criminal Evidence Act (PACE) 1984, unlawful, irrational and perverse.

Held

In relation to (1), the court was satisfied that on the evidence before it, each arresting officer not only reasonably suspected that the offences in question had been committed by someone, but also suspected, in the case of each claimant arrested, that the person was guilty of those offences on the basis of joint enterprise. In relation to (2), the materials available to the arresting officers were such that a reasonable man would have been of the opinion that there were reasonable grounds for suspecting each claimant to be guilty of the offences in question. In relation to (3), the decision to arrest was exercised lawfully in the case of each claimant. No irrelevant consideration was taken into account and no relevant consideration was ignored. The decision to arrest the claimants was not perverse, as considered in *Associated Provincial Picture Houses Ltd* v *Wednesbury Corporation* [1948] 1 KB 223.

Comment

In giving his judgement in the case, Cresswell J confirmed that when arresting a suspect under s24 PACE 1984, the ground of 'reasonable suspicion' would be satisfied where the information available to the arresting officers was such that a reasonable man would have been of the opinion that there were reasonable grounds for suspecting that each of the claimants in the civil action was guilty of the offences in question. The modern authority to determine the existence of reasonable suspicion is the House of Lords' decision in *O'Hara* v *Chief Constable of the Royal Ulster Constabulary* [1997] 2 WLR 1, where a two-stage test was identified. First, there must be actual suspicion on the part of the arresting officer (the subjective test) and second, there must be reasonable grounds for that suspicion (the objective test). This approach was later upheld by the European Court of Human Rights in *O'Hara* v *United Kingdom* (2002) 34 EHHR 32. The *Al-Fayed* case can be found on Lawtel at transcript no C0103766.

HLT Textbook page 214, section 23.3.

Detention and police bail

Identification procedures used by the police

During the police investigation of a criminal offence, in order to test the ability of a witness to identify a suspect and to safeguard against mistaken identity, the police employ a number of identification procedures, which are governed by the Police and Criminal Evidence Act 1984 Codes of Practice, those being Code D and its annexes A–E. A revised Code D and the annexes to Code D were introduced in April 2002.

Paragraph 2.14 of the revised Code D requires that whenever a suspect disputes an identification made by a witness, an identification procedure shall be held if practicable or if the officer in charge of the police investigation considers that it would be useful. The identification procedure should be instigated as soon as possible. The presumption in favour of convening an identification procedure is rebutted where para 2.15 of Code D applies, stating that an identification procedure will not be necessary where, in all the circumstances, it would serve no useful purpose in proving or disproving whether the suspect was involved in the offence, including, for example, where the suspect is well known to the witness making the identification.

Paragraphs 2.14 and 2.15 appear to fully embrace the House of Lords' decision in *R* v *Forbes* [2001] AC 473, except that the police now have a choice to use either a video identification or an identification parade. The test of 'no useful purpose' in para 2.15, which as *Forbes* confirms is interpreted restrictively, would appear to be satisfied where the suspect is well known to the police or where there is no possibility that the witness would identify the suspect.

Code D requires that where the witness has previously identified a person, the police should make a record of the witness's description before the witness takes part in any further identification procedures. A record of the witness's description should be given to the suspect or to his lawyer.

The revised Code D introduces a hierarchy of identification procedures by giving the police officer in charge of the criminal investigation a free choice to decide between a video identification or an identification parade, and the identification officer considers whether it is practicable to arrange one of these forms of identification. Therefore, as a result of the revision, video identification has been elevated to the same status as an identification parade and is likely to result in the much wider use of video identification procedures, as they can be often undertaken sooner than an identification parade and they are much less intimidating for the witness.

If none of these procedures are practicable, the identification officer has the discretion to arrange a covert video identification or covert group identification, or in the last resort, a confrontation.

Code D prescribes the appropriate procedures to be followed, depending on whether the suspect is known and is available to take part in the procedures, or whether the suspect is known but is not available, or whether the suspect is not known. For example, in cases of disputed identity where the suspect is known and is available, the police are required to use either a video identification or an identification parade or a confrontation, subject to the requirements of Code D and its annexes.

Where the suspect's identity is known but he is not available to participate in the identification procedures, the identification officer has the discretion to make arrangements for a video identification to be used. If the suspect's identity is not known, a witness may be taken to a particular neighbourhood or place to see whether the witness can identify the person he had seen on a previous occasion. The revised annexes to Code D deal with the following procedures:

1. annex A: video identification;
2. annex B: identification parades;
3. annex C: group identification;
4. annex D: confrontation by a witness;
5. annex E: showing photographs.

HLT Textbook page 216, section 23.5.

Custody time limits

R (On the application of Potthoff) v *Sheffield Crown Court* Judgment of 18 July 2002 (not yet reported) Queen's Bench Divisional Court (Buxton J)

Judicial review – extension of custody time limits

Facts
The hearing was an application for judicial review of the decision of Baker J to extend a custody time limit that was due to expire on 7 June 2002. P, the applicant, was one of nine defendants against whom criminal proceedings were pending. At a directions hearing on 11 March 2002, the case was fixed for trial on 1 July 2002. However, it was only at a further directions hearing on 27 March 2002 that it was appreciated that an issue relating to the custody time limit arose. The trial date was then fixed 29 July 2002 and the judge on that occasion concluded that the custody time limit should be considered by the judge who would preside at the trial: the custody time limit was not considered until 30 May 2002. Before Baker J, it was accepted that the prosecution had acted with all due diligence and expedition and the issue on custody time limits turned on whether delays due to the availability of the judge and an appropriate size court constituted a 'good and sufficient cause' for an extension of custody time limits under s22(3)(a)(iii) Prosecution of Offences Act 1985. In his submission before the Court of Appeal, P argued that: (1) the exercise of the judge's discretion was inappropriate, as a factual finding was required; (2) the unavailability of a court or judge could be a good and sufficient cause provided that there was rigorous scrutiny; and (3) in the absence of a clear investigation into

whether an alternative venue was available, the judge was not entitled to have come to the conclusion he did.

Held

In dismissing P's application, Buxton J held that: (1) the wording the judge had used did not stand in the way of upholding his judgement. In relation to (2), it was plain from the authorities that a court extending the custody time limit could do so only after exercising caution. The judge had given very careful consideration to all the facts, the chronology, the nature of the case and the matters brought to his attention. Notwithstanding the absence of express evidence that the trial could have been elsewhere, it was not perverse to have reached the conclusion reached.

Comment

Section 22 Prosecution of Offences Act 1985 and the Prosecution of Offences (Custody Time Limits) Regulations 1987 prescribe the maximum period for which the defendant can be kept in detention before the completion of a particular stage of the proceedings. Once the time limit has expired, the defendant has an absolute right to bail unless the court is satisfied that 'there is good and sufficient cause' to extend the suspect's custody time limit. On the facts of *Potthoff*, the 'good and sufficient cause' test was satisfied where difficulties were encountered with the availability of both a judge and a court that was large enough to accommodate the trial. In reaching this decision, Buxton J was satisfied that the prosecution had acted with the necessary due diligence in preparing the case for trial. The House of Lords' decision in *R* v *Leeds Crown Court, ex parte Wardle* [2001] 2 WLR 865, which was considered in *Law Update 2002*, was cited with approval. *R (On the application of Potthoff)* v *Sheffield Crown Court* can be found on Lawtel at transcript no C9500869.

HLT Textbook page 222, section 23.12.

Committal Proceedings

Summary trial

Moran v *Director of Public Prosecutions* (2002) The Times 6 February Queen's Bench Divisional Court (Maurice Kay J)

Summary trial – duty to give reasons – right to a fair trial

Facts

M appealed against a decision of the magistrates to reject a submission of no case to answer. Three informations had been preferred against M in relation to his alleged role in a fracas in a take-away food shop. Submissions of no case to answer were rejected in respect of each of the informations and M was subsequently convicted. He maintained the justices' failure to give reasons for rejecting the submission of no case to answer had breached his right to a fair trial under art 6 European Convention on Human Rights 1950.

Held
The appeal was dismissed: although now it was usual for magistrates to give reasons following a finding of guilt there was still no legal obligation upon the justices to give reasons for rejecting a submission of no case to answer. Given the highly specific nature of summary proceedings, the interests of justice would not be served by the imposition of a requirement that that magistrates give detailed reasons for their assessment of the evidence and witnesses at the end of the prosecution case. The defendant's right to a fair trial contained in art 6 of the Convention and in Sch 1 to the Human Rights Act 1998 had not been breached by the magistrates' refusal to give reasons.

Comment
It is well established that a significant development following the implementation of the Human Rights Act 1998 has been the requirement for courts to give reasons for their decisions. Whilst this provision is seen as a fundamental aspect of the defendant's right to a fair trial under art 6 European Convention on Human Rights 1950, it is not an absolute right, and in the *Moran* case it was held that the duty to give reasons for a court's decision does not extend to summary proceedings where a defence submission of no case to answer is not upheld by the justices. In reaching this verdict the decision in *Harrison* v *Department of Social Security* [1997] COD 220 was followed. The court was satisfied that any injustice suffered by M could have been remedied by an appeal by way of rehearing or appeal by way of case stated, or by an application for judicial review, depending on the nature of the alleged breach of M's right to a fair trial.

HLT Textbook page 239, section 25.3.

The Bill of Indictment

Joinder of accused in the same court

R v *Palmer* (2002) The Times 18 April Court of Appeal (Criminal Division) (Rose LJ VP, McKinnon and Poole JJ)

Indictment – joinder of defendants

Facts
During the course of the proceedings a co-defendant was added to the indictment, which alleged conspiracy to defraud. Subsequently, the prosecution offered no evidence against the co-defendant. The original indictment had been signed, but the defence submitted that adding the co-defendant created a new indictment, which had not been signed. The issue before the Court of Appeal was whether the trial

had become a nullity because the indictment upon which P had been convicted had not been signed.

Held

In refusing P's application to appeal against his conviction of conspiracy to defraud, the Court of Appeal held that the judge had ordered the amendment of the indictment, and the fact that the court clerk had mistakenly written 'joinder indictment' on the document did not make the indictment a nullity. The adding of the co-defendant to the indictment was a proper exercise of judicial discretion under s5 Indictments Act 1915, and no injustice had been suffered by the defendant, as, on the facts, there was nothing ineffective, misleading or inappropriate in what the judge had ordered.

Comment

The issue on appeal was whether the trial had been rendered a nullity because the indictment on which the appellant had been convicted had never been signed. In support of this point the appellant submitted that first, there could not have properly been an amendment to the original indictment: such an indictment that had resulted from the purported amendment was a new indictment which had never been signed; second, the deletion of the co-accused was not a defect of the indictment capable of being remedied by s5 Indictments Act 1915; and, third, the judge had not properly approved the amendments. In rejecting these arguments the Court was satisfied that nothing done or failed to be done by the court clerk could subsequently alter the effect of, or render nugatory, that which the judge had done. In reaching this conclusion on the facts of the case, *R* v *Jackson* [1997] 2 Cr App R 297 and *R* v *Ismail* (1991) 92 Cr App R 92 were cited with approval.

HLT Textbook page 255, section 26.7.

Arraignment and Plea

Presence of the accused

An important case dealing with the defendant's right to be present at his trial has been heard by both the Court of Appeal and the House of Lords. Whilst the case specifically concerned trial in the Crown Court, the principle applies equally to summary proceedings.

R v *Jones (Anthony William) and Others* [2002] 2 All ER 113 House of Lords (Lords Bingham of Cornhill, Hoffmann, Hutton, Nolan and Rodger of Earlsferry)

Absconding – absence of the defendant – right to a fair trial

Facts

In August 1987 a robbery had taken place in Liverpool and some £87,000 had been stolen. The appellant had been arrested and charged. On 3 December 1997, he and a co-defendant had been committed on bail for trial. In January 1998 they had been arraigned and pleaded not guilty. A trial date had been fixed for 9 March 1998, but had subsequently been vacated and replaced with 1 June 1998. On that date neither defendant had surrendered and warrants had been issued for their arrest. The trial had been re-listed to commence on 5 October 1998. Neither had been arrested or had surrendered by that date.

The case had been adjourned until the next day, when they had still not been arrested or surrendered. Both the defendant's legal representatives had withdrawn from the court from their failure to appear at trial.

The judge had been reluctant to embark on the trial but it had been urged upon him that further delay would be unfair to the witnesses, some of whom had undergone a traumatic experience. Taking the view that the defendants had deliberately frustrated the prosecution's attempt to have the case finally concluded, the judge had ruled that the trial should begin. He warned the jury not to hold the defendant's absence against them. On 9 October 1998 both defendants had been convicted by a unanimous verdict and sentenced to 13 years imprisonment. At the end of December 1999 the appellant had been arrested and appealed to the Court of Appeal against his conviction. In the Court of Appeal, the appellant had conceded that his failure to attend trial was deliberate, as he thought that the court could not proceed in his absence.

In refusing the appeal, the Court of Appeal stated that a defendant had a general right to be present at his trial and to be legally represented, but that those rights could be waived, wholly or in part, by the defendant. The trial judge had discretion whether a trial should take place or to continue in the absence of the defendant and/or his legal representatives, but that discretion had to be exercised with great care and had to take into account fairness to the prosecution as well as the defendant.

In giving the reserved judgment of the Court, Rose LJ reviewed both English and European authorities and provided the following guidance to the courts in relation to trying a defendant in his absence.

1. A defendant had, in general, a right to be present at his trial and a right to be legally represented.
2. Those rights could be waived, separately or together, wholly or in part, by the defendant himself. They might be waived when, knowing where his trial was to take place, he deliberately and voluntarily absented himself and/or withdrew his instructions from his legal representative. The defendant could waive his rights in part, where he behaved in such a way that he obstructed the proper course of justice and/or withdrew his instructions from his legal representative.

3. The trial judge had a discretion as to whether a trial should take place or continue in the absence of a defendant and/or his legal representative.
4. That discretion had to be exercised with great care, and only in a rare case in favour of the trial taking place or continuing, particularly if the defendant was unrepresented.
5. In exercising the discretion, fairness to the defence was of prime importance but fairness to the prosecution also had to be taken into account. The judge had to have regard to all the circumstances of the case.

Leave was granted to appeal to the House of Lords, which also dismissed his appeal. In coming to this decision, the House of Lords held that a trial judge had a discretion to commence a trial for robbery in the absence of the defendant, and that the fair trial provisions of the European Convention on Human Rights 1950 had not been breached.

Held
In giving the leading opinion in the House of Lords, Lord Bingham stated that whilst the Court of Appeal's check-list was of useful guidance, it was not exhaustive. His Lordship made two general observations. First, the judge's overriding concern would be to ensure that the trial would be as fair as the circumstances permitted and lead to a just outcome. Those objects were equally important whether the offence was serious or relatively minor. Second, it was generally desirable that a defendant be represented even where he had voluntarily absconded. That provided a valuable safeguard against the possibility of error and oversight. For that reason, judges routinely ask counsel to continue to represent a defendant who had absconded during the trial. The court's priority was to ensure that a trial was as fair as possible as the circumstances permitted and that it achieved justice, regardless of the seriousness of the offence. Whilst it is desirable that a defendant was represented at trial, on the facts of the present case, the fact that the defendant was not represented at his trial did not constitute a ground for complaint.

HLT Textbook page 272, section 27.12.

Sentencing of Adult Offenders

Victim personal statements

Practice Direction (Crime: Victim Personal Statements) [2001] 4 All ER 640 Lord Chief Justice's Court (Lord Woolf CJ)

From 1 October 2001 the victims of crime have had a more formal opportunity to say how a crime has affected them. Where there is a victim personal statement, that statement and any evidence in support should be taken into account by the court prior to passing sentence. Evidence of the effects of the offence should be contained in a s9 Criminal Justice Act 1967 statement and must be served on the defence prior to sentence. The opinions of the victim and of the victim's close relatives as to what sentence should be imposed are not relevant.

The sentencing framework

In *R* v *R (Informer: Reduction in Sentence)* (2002) The Times 18 February, the Court of Appeal held that a sentenced defendant is entitled to receive a discount where he provides information within a reasonable time after he has been sentenced. In this case, the defendant's sentence of seven and a half years imprisonment for possession of a class A drug with intent to supply should be reduced to five years, as the defendant had pleaded guilty and had given further information to the police before sentence and further significant information after sentence.

HLT Textbook page 304, section 30.2.

Life sentences

Practice Statement (Crime: Life Sentences) [2002] 1 WLR 1789 Lord Chief Justice's Court (Lord Woolf CJ)

The Lord Chief Justice has issued a *Practice Statement* applicable to all murder cases where sentence is passed after 31 May 2002. The *Practice Statement* applies where an adult defendant has been sentenced to a term of life imprisonment under either a discretionary or a mandatory power, and in relation to 'serious' sentences for young offenders. The guidelines are laid down in the *Practice Statement (Crime: Life Sentences)* [2002] 1 WLR 1789. The guidelines, which are advisory only and from which the judge can depart where it is appropriate to do so, are based on the recommendations of the Sentencing Advisory Panel. Under the *Practice Statement*, the term 'tariff' when indicating the recommended length of sentence to be served should no longer be used. It is more appropriate to use the term 'minimum sentence' at the end of which the defendant may be eligible to be released on licence. In most cases an offender is unlikely to be released at the expiration of the minimum term, and for the purpose of calculating the earliest date for normal release on licence the minimum term was approximately equivalent of a determinate sentence twice its length. So, a minimum term of 14 years was equivalent to a determinate term of 28 years, as in *Re Robert Thompson and John Venables* [2001] 1 Cr App R 401.

When the judge indicates the minimum term the defendant is required to serve, he should make it clear how that term was arrived at. In relation to adult offenders convicted of murder, the trial judge and the Lord Chief Justice would make their recommendations to the Home Secretary as to the minimum sentence the offender should serve. The Home Secretary would then make the final decision as to the minimum term. The Parole Board would then have to be satisfied that before the offender was released he was no longer a threat to the public before he would be released on licence.

The normal starting point for the minimum term for the murder of an adult victim would be 12 years. A case falling into this category would arise, for example, from a quarrel between two people known to each other, subject to any mitigating or aggravating factors. Mitigating factors would include:

1. where the case was borderline between murder and manslaughter;
2. where the case involved an over-reaction to self defence or provocation;
3. where the offence was a mercy killing.

The starting point for a minimum sentence in more serious cases is 15/16 years. This is where the defendant has high culpability or where the victim was particularly vulnerable. Such cases would be characterised as serious where the killing was for a political motive, or was a contract killing, or the victim was a child, or the killing was racially aggravated. With respect to both categories of cases, the judge should move the starting point up or down, depending on any aggravating or mitigating factors. Important aggravating factors include:

1. where the killing was planned;
2. where a firearm was used;
3. where there was the concealment of the body;
4. in cases of domestic violence, where the killing was the culmination of cruel or violent behaviour by the accused over a period of time.

Finally, in very serious cases involving adult offenders, where for example the offender has committed multiple murders, the minimum term might be 30 years. Where the victim was a prison officer, or the victim of a sadistic murder, or a young child, the minimum term was likely to be 20 years and upwards, as appropriate.

R (On the application of Anderson) v *Secretary of State for the Home Department* [2002] 4 All ER 1089 House of Lords (Lords Bingham of Cornhill, Nicholls of Birkenhead, Steyn, Hutton, Hobhouse of Woodborough, Scott of Foscote and Rodger of Earlsferry)

Executive power to fix the tariff in a life sentence – compatibility with the European Convention on Human Rights 1950

Facts
The appellant appealed to the House of Lords from the decision of the Court of Appeal (Criminal Division) (reported at [2002] 1 WLR 1143) against the refusal of his application for the judicial review of the Home Secretary's decision to fix the tariff term at a longer period than that recommended by the Home Secretary.

Held
The Home Secretary had acted incompatibly with art 6(1) European Convention on

Human Rights 1950 in fixing the tariff term to be served for punitive purposes by a defendant who, on conviction of murder, received a mandatory sentence of life imprisonment under s1(1) Murder (Abolition of Death Penalty) Act 1965. The House of Lords so held in:

1. allowing the appeal in part against the decision of the Court of Appeal's refusal to allow the judicial review of the Home Secretary's decision to fix the tariff term at a longer period than that recommended by the Home Secretary;
2. making a declaration under s4 Human Rights Act 1998 that s29 Crime (Sentences) Act 1997, which conferred on the Home Secretary control of the release of mandatory life sentence prisoners, was incompatible with the right under art 6 to have a sentence imposed by an independent impartial tribunal.

Comment

The above case is one of the most significant developments since the implementation of the Human Rights Act 1998, and it can be no coincidence that in considering the persuasive force of the case, seven of their Lordships sat in judgement rather than the normal five Law Lords. The decision puts the judiciary in direct conflict with senior government officers, including the Home Secretary, in confirming that to comply with the provisions of art 6 of the Convention, the decision about the tariff a life prisoner should serve should be taken by a member of the judiciary who is regarded as being an independent and impartial tribunal. The Home Secretary was not regarded as being an independent tribunal, as the word 'independent' required the decision-maker to be independent of the parties and the executive.

It is thought that the decision opens the way for the sentence review of 2,000 murderers. Of the 2,000, it may be that up to 215 could have their sentence reviewed by a judge, of which between 60 and 70 could be the subject of early release on parole. The government's early response to the House of Lords' decision appears to suggest that primary legislation is being considered to reverse the ruling.

R v *Lichniak; R Pyrah* [2002] 4 All ER 1122 House of Lords (Lords Bingham of Cornhill, Nicholls of Birkenhead, Steyn, Hutton, Hobhouse of Woodborough, Scott of Foscote and Rodger of Earlsferry)

Compatibility of mandatory life sentences under the European Convention on Human Rights 1950

Facts

The appellants appealed against the decision of the Court of Appeal (Criminal Division) (reported at [2002] QB 296) against their mandatory life sentences for murder imposed under the Murder (Abolition of Death Penalty) Act 1965 on the ground that such sentences were arbitrary and disproportionate and contrary to arts 3 and 5 European Convention on Human Rights 1950.

Held

The mandatory sentence of life imprisonment imposed under s1(1) Murder (Abolition of Death Penalty) Act 1965 on adults in England and Wales on their conviction was not incompatible with arts 3 and 5 European Convention on Human Rights 1950.

Comment

The appellants' counsel submitted to their Lordships that neither appellant was to present any future danger to the public, and had the trial judges enjoyed any discretion in sentencing, it is unlikely that the appellants would have received terms of life imprisonment. Under the Convention law, the statutory requirement to impose a term of life imprisonment was arbitrary, excessive and disproportionate in cases where the accused, like the appellants, was considered to be no danger to the public. In rejecting these points, Lord Bingham stated that the appellants' complaints were not sufficiently grave to invoke arts 3 or 5 of the Convention. In addition, those convicted of murder were not sentenced to an arbitrary, rule-of-thumb term. Those responsible did their best to match the respective terms served to the particular circumstances of the case. Finally, as with the case of *R (On the application of Anderson)* v *Secretary of State for the Home Department* (above), this decision was based on a panel of seven Law Lords.

HLT Textbook page 314, section 30.19.

Trial and Sentence of Juveniles

Mode of trial

R v *Southampton Youth Court, ex parte W; R* v *Wirral Borough Magistrates' Court, ex parte K* Judgment of 23 July 2002 (not yet reported) Queen's Bench Divisional Court (Lord Woolf CJ and Kay LJ)

Place of trial – juveniles – youth court – court's sentencing powers

Facts

The first claimant, W, was 14 years old and had been charged with robbing a 13-year-old boy of his bike, during the course of which it was alleged that W had threatened the victim with a broken bottle. The district judge had decided that the case should be tried in the Crown Court as she considered that it was unlikely that the Court would find that a two-year detention limit would be sufficient. In the second case, K, the claimant, who was 13 years old, had been charged with two offences of indecently assaulting a six-year-old boy. His case had also been transferred to the Crown Court for trial.

Held

The Divisional Court, which included Lord Woolf CJ, held that, first, in deciding the appropriate place of trial for a juvenile, while the need to impose the appropriate sentence was important, so was the need to ensure that wherever possible an appropriate a trial should take place in appropriate surroundings, which would be much more satisfactorily achieved in the youth court rather than the Crown Court. Second, magistrates should start off with a strong presumption against sending a case to the Crown Court unless they were satisfied that it was clearly required that the juvenile should be tried on indictment. Third, the justices should also have in mind that if they send the case to the Crown Court for trial, it is because the youth court had no power to make a Detention and Training Order (DTO), or if a case required the imposition of a DTO of more than two years. On the facts of the present cases, W's offence was serious and the district judge had not misdirected herself in any way. It could not be said that the decision to transfer the case to the Crown Court was wrong. K's case did not come anywhere near the threshold and the case should have remained in the youth court. This case can be found on Lawtel at transcript no C9500874.

HLT Textbook page 318, section 31.2.

Sentencing in the youth court

Aldis v *Director of Public Prosecutions* (2002) The Times 6 March Queen's Bench Divisional Court (Keene LJ and Goldring J)

Sentencing at age of the offence

Facts

A appealed by way of case stated by Brighton and Hove youth justices on 12 November 2001 against their decision not to substitute four concurrent detention and training orders totalling 18 months, which they had imposed on A on 29 October 2001 for two offences of wounding with intent to do grievous bodily harm and two offences of common assault, with an order of detention in a young offenders' institution which would have been subject to a maximum of 12 months.

Held

In dismissing the appeal, a court was entitled to impose a detention and training order on a youth who had attained the age of 18 prior to his conviction and sentence for the relevant offence by virtue of s29 Children and Young Persons Act 1963, as amended by s72(3) and para 49 of Sch 5 Children and Young Persons Act 1969 and para 3 of Sch 8 Criminal Justice Act 1991.

R v *Ghafoor (Imran)* (2002) 166 JP 601 Court of Appeal (Criminal Division) (Dyson LJ, Silber and Goddard JJ)

Sentencing – Human Rights Act 1998 – age of offender at the date of the commission of the offence – s11(1A) Criminal Appeal Act 1968

Facts

The appellant, G, had pleaded guilty to riot contrary to s1(1) Public Order Act 1986, which had been committed when he was 17 years old. When G was 18 years old, he was sentenced to four-and-a-half years' detention in a young offenders' institution pursuant to s96 Powers of Criminal Courts (Sentencing) Act 2000. The maximum sentence that could have been imposed for a 17-year-old for the same offence was one of a two-year detention and training order. It appeared that the longer sentence that had been imposed on G was incompatible with art 7 European Convention on Human Rights 1950, which prohibited the imposition of a heavier penalty than the one applicable at the time the criminal offence was committed. G applied to the sentencing judge to vary his sentence on the ground that he had erred in principle in passing a sentence that was heavier than he would have had the power to impose at the date when the offence was committed. The judge considered that the matter could only be resolved by a declaration of incompatibility under the Human Rights Act 1998 and accordingly issued a certificate under s11(1A) Criminal Appeal Act 1968 that the case was fit for appeal.

Held

1. The sentence passed had been wrong in principle and should not have been in excess of 18 months detention. Article 7 of the Convention did not need to be considered as per *R* v *Fowler* [2002] Crim LR 521.
2. Where a defendant crossed a relevant age threshold between the date of the commission of the offence and the date of conviction, the starting point was the sentence the defendant was likely to have received if he had been sentenced at the date of the commission of the offence. Sentences higher than the maximum would rarely be imposed.
3. Had G been sentenced at the commission of the offence, taking into consideration his guilty plea, he should have received a sentence of an 18 months' detention and training order, the equivalent for an 18-year-old being 18 months' detention in a young offenders' institution. That was the starting point that the sentencing judge should have used, and due to the short period between the commission of the offence and the date of the sentence there were no good reasons for departing from the starting point. The appeal was allowed and a sentence of 18 months substituted.

HLT Textbook page 321, section 31.10.

Appeals

Fresh evidence

R v *Hanratty (James) (Deceased)* (2002) The Times 16 May Court of
Appeal (Criminal Division) (Lord Woolf CJ, Mantell LJ and Leveson J)

Appeals against conviction

Facts

An appeal was made on behalf of the deceased appellant against his conviction for
murder on 17 February 1962. The appellant was executed on 4 April 1962.

Held

In dismissing the appeal, the Lord Chief Justice stated that on an appeal against
conviction the Crown could introduce fresh evidence even if it did not directly
address the grounds of appeal and was intended to weaken the appeal. The
overriding purpose of admitting the fresh evidence was to assist the court in
furthering the interests of justice. On the facts of the case, the deceased appellant's
trial had met the basic standards of fairness and accordingly he had suffered no
prejudice.

R v *Pendleton* [2002] 1 All ER 524 House of Lords (Lords Bingham of
Cornhill, Hobhouse of Woodborough, Hope of Craighead, Mackay of
Clashfern and Steyn)

Correct test for assessment of fresh evidence

Facts

P, who had been convicted in 1986 of murder, appealed against the decision of the
Court of Appeal upholding his conviction. Some 14 years after commission, P had
been re-arrested and, after three days of interviews with the police, had admitted
that he had been in the vicinity of the crime, but strenuously denied being a party
to violence. P informed his lawyers that the admissions were untrue, claiming that
they had been made under pressure. However, counsel was concerned that a jury
would be unlikely to accept P's retraction and with P's consent, it was decided that
he would not give evidence. Upon reference by the Criminal Cases Review
Commission, P applied to the appellate court to receive fresh psychological evidence
and documents dating from the time of the commission of the offence but not
adduced at trial.

Held

In allowing the appeal, the House of Lords held that s2(1) Criminal Appeal Act
1968 imposed a duty of judgment on the appellate court to assess the safety of the
conviction, as the primacy of the jury decision precluded judicial intrusion upon the

issue of the appellant's guilt. The proper approach for the appellate court to take was whether, in assessing the new evidence, the court might reasonably have affected the jury's decision to convict. In the light of the fresh evidence, it was impossible to be sure that P's conviction was safe, as the jury never had the chance to hear P's true defence, nor were they allowed to assess the reliability of his admissions. In finding otherwise, the Court of Appeal had strayed beyond its true function of review and had come perilously close to making its own determination on the issue of P's guilt. P's appeal was allowed.

Comment

Pendleton confirms that, in deciding an appeal on the basis of receiving fresh evidence, the Court of Appeal was required to consider the safety of the defendant's conviction and not the guilt of the accused, which was an issue that should lie exclusively with the jury. In criticising the Court of Appeal's decision in *Pendleton*, the House of Lords suggested that the Court had strayed beyond its true function of review and had come perilously close to making its own determination on the issue of P's guilt. The proper approach that should have been taken by the Court was contained in the decision of *R* v *Parks (Sydney Alfred)* [1961] 1 WLR 1484.

HLT Textbook page 339, section 33.14.

3

Commercial Law

SALE OF GOODS

Formation of the Contract and Formalities

Mistake

Great Peace Shipping Ltd v *Tsavliris Salvage (International) Ltd, The Great Peace* [2002] 4 All ER 689 Court of Appeal (Lord Phillips MR, May and Laws LJJ)

Contract and mutual mistake

Facts

The appeal concerned two vessels, the Cape Providence (the appellants) and the Great Peace (the respondents). The Cape Providence was carrying a cargo of iron ore from Brazil to China in September 1999 and during the voyage the vessel incurred serious structural damage in the middle of the South Indian Ocean. The respondents (Great Peace) offered their salvage services which were accepted. The respondents were to obtain a tug and rendezvous with the Cape Providence. The purpose of the rendezvous was to escort her into safety and, if necessary, assist with the evacuation of her crew if she was in danger of sinking. The respondents contacted a firm of brokers, explained the situation and stressed the urgency in getting a tug to the Cape Providence. The brokers, a Mr Little and Mr Holder, informed the respondents that a vessel was available but would take an estimated five or six days to reach the Cape Providence. This information was received with consternation as the vessel might have sunk resulting in the loss of lives. Captain Lambrides, the appellants' representative, instructed Mr Little to find an alternative tug. Mr Little contacted Ocean Routes, an organisation which provides reports about vessels at sea and weather forecasts. Mr Little received the names of four vessels within the vicinity of the Cape Providence. One of these vessels was the Great Peace and Mr Little was informed this vessel was the nearest to the Cape Providence, with an estimated rendezvous time of 12 hours. However, the estimated position of the Cape Providence and rendezvous time was incorrect. Mr Little contacted Great Peace's managers and spoke to a Mr Lee. The circumstances were explained to Mr Lee but at no time was the location of the vessels discussed. Mr Little further informed Mr Lee that he believed, from the information supplied by Ocean Routes, that the Great Peace was the closest vessel to the Cape Providence. Mr Lee informed Mr Little the Great Peace was currently under charter, transporting soya beans from New Orleans to China, but he would first need to consult the charterers. Mr Lee requested the information by fax with the intention of informing Mr Little. Mr Little sent Mr Lee the following fax:

'Further to our telcon at 22.22 hours BST 24 September, we are working on behalf of the owners of a cape size bulk carrier which has suffered serious structural damage in the southern Indian Ocean. Her position at 10.27 hours BST today was 29 40S/80 20 E. She is proceeding at 5 knots on course 050 degrees direction Sunda Strait. Owners have mobilised a tug from Singapore which should reach the casualty in the next 5/6 days. We understand from Ocean Routes that your vessel "Great Peace" is in close proximity to the casualty and have been asked by hirers to check whether it would be possible to charter the "Great Peace" on a daily hire basis to escort the casualty until arrival of the tug.

We would appreciate if you can check soonest with the charterers whether they can agree to the request, bearing in mind that the casualty is in serious danger.'

At approximately midnight, Mr Lee telephoned Mr Holder and offered the Great Peace for charter. The terms of the charter were discussed, these included a minimum hire of five days and the purpose of the hire which was to escort and stand-by the Cape Providence in case she sank. Mr Holder asked Mr Lee to confirm the position of the Great Peace and her speed. Mr Lee would obtain this information when he had discussed the matter further with the master when he was certain the appellants were interested in the terms of the offer.

At 06.40 Captain Lambrides instructed Mr Holder to fix the vessel at a gross rate of US$16,500 per day. Mr Holder contacted Mr Lee and they confirmed the terms of the contract. Mr Holder then sent a fax to Mr Lee thanking him for his assistance and gave details of the Cape Providence's latest position, course and speed to ensure the vessels were able to meet as soon as possible. He ended his correspondence with the following sentence:

'Please instruct your master to contact the master of Cape Providence and alter course to rendezvous with the vessel as soon as possible.'

Mr Lee followed out these instructions and requested the Great Peace alter course and head for the Cape Providence. He sent a copy of his request to Mr Holder, which Mr Holder then passed to Captain Lambrides. Captain Lambrides then discovered, and informed Mr Holder, the vessels were 410 miles apart from each other. These details were unknown to either Mr Holder or Mr Lee. Captain Lambrides then informed Mr Holder he intended to cancel the Great Peace but would first wait and see whether an alternative vessel would be available first. By luck, a vessel called the Nordfarer was passing the Cape Providence and was able to give assistance to the Cape Providence.

The appellants informed Mr Holder they had contracted with the Nordfarer and instructed Mr Holder to cancel the agreement with the Great Peace. Mr Holder carried out these instructions by contacting Mr Lee and informing him the Great Peace was no longer needed and discussed the cancellation fee. Mr Lee sent a fax to

Mr Holder informing him he would attempt to negotiate a cancellation fee of two days hire with the Great Peace instead of the minimum five days due under the contract. Mr Holder discussed the contents of the fax with the appellants and was instructed to inform Mr Lee they were not prepared to pay any cancellation fee. Mr Lee was informed of the appellants refusal to pay a cancellation fee and informed the respondents who issued proceedings.

The claimants/respondents claimed a sum of $82,500 under the terms of the contract, or, alternatively the same amount would be payable as damages for wrongful repudiation of the contract. The defendants/appellants defended the action by claiming the contract had been concluded while both parties laboured under a fundamental mistake of fact. They claimed the contract was either void under common law or voidable in equity due to the mutual mistake that both parties believed the Great Peace was in close proximity to the Cape Providence when the contract was concluded, which was not in fact true. However, at first instance Toulson J rejected the defendants' defence and awarded the sum claimed by the claimants. However, the defendants appealed against this decision and reasserted their original defence based upon the vitiating factor of mistake.

Held

It is a common factor, in contract law, that the parties to the contract must have a consensus ad idem, a meeting of the minds, in order for an agreement to be formed. If this is not evident from the facts in question the parties who formed the agreement will not be of the same mind and by operation of law thus will render the contract either void or voidable. To find out whether or not a contract has been concluded the Court of Appeal had to carry out an objective appraisal of the circumstances to reveal whether an agreement had been formed.

Lord Phillips MR carried out an exposition of the cases of *Bell* v *Lever Brothers* [1932] AC 161 and *Solle* v *Butcher* [1950] 1 KB 671 to review the existing legal principles that apply to common mistake. Through the use of these cases and others he was able to examine the common law rules that apply to mistake. In particular, the legal principles that apply to mistake may be seen to be harsh but to some extent the courts have supplemented the harshness of the common law with its equitable jurisdiction. For example, a contract may be void at common law but would be voidable in equity. This was the crux of this appeal: to review the difficulties between the common law and equitable application of the legal rules developed by the courts.

The operative mistake claimed was that the parties were at cross purposes to the location of the vessels and that the Great Peace would take approximately 39 hours to reach the Cape Providence. The appellants were contending that this was a fundamental mistake and that no agreement was ever reached. Lord Phillips MR examined the application of *Bell* v *Lever Brothers* to this case in order to decide whether the fulfilling of the contract would have produced an outcome that neither party contemplated. If this was in fact the case the mistake would deprive the parties from achieving the purpose of the contract and the effect would be to render the contract void. However, should the court consider the common jurisdiction not apply they may, in prescribed circumstances, apply the equitable principles of mistake, as held by Lord Denning in the case of *Solle* v *Butcher*. However, the Court of Appeal's interpretation of *Solle* v *Butcher* was that a party who had entered a contract to discover the bargain to be bad should be allowed to avoid the contract. The Court of Appeal were not prepared to follow this decision and found *Solle* v *Butcher* was not good law.

The Court of Appeal then referred back to the facts in question: was the distance between the two vessels likely to render the purpose of the contract impossible to perform? It was found, at first instance, the vessels would have rendezvoused within 22 hours. The defendants did not immediately cancel the agreement and this suggested the purpose of the contract could be achieved, otherwise they would have cancelled immediately. Thus, it was the conclusion of the Court of Appeal that the contractual adventure entered into by the parties could be achieved and was not impossible to perform. They found the parties had entered into a legally binding agreement for the hire of the Great Peace and the appellants were entitled to cancel the agreement subject to the cancellation fee of five days hire. When the appellants engaged the services of the Nordfarer this cancelled the agreement with the Great Peace and the appellants became liable for the cancellation fee.

Comment
This appeal tested the common law and equitable doctrine of mutual/common mistake. Lord Phillips used the cases of *Bell* v *Lever Brothers* and *Solle* v *Butcher* to draw a comparison between the common law and equitable rules. He demonstrated the principles in these cases and considered the decision in *Solle* v *Butcher* to be wrong. The decision has reviewed the area of common mistake and illustrated the problems produced through case law.

OBP Textbook page 20, section 2.2.

Formal requirements

Actionstrength Ltd v *International Glass Engineering IN GL EN SpA and Another* [2002] 1 WLR 566 Court of Appeal (Simon Brown, Peter Gibson and Tuckey LJJ)

Guarantee and enforceability under the Statute of Frauds 1677

Facts
This was an appeal by the second defendant, Saint-Gobain Glass UK Ltd (SG), who believed the claimant, Actionstrength Ltd (trading as Vital Resources) (AS), did not have a genuine arguable defence and had applied for summary judgment which had been refused. SG based the appeal on a point of law under s4 of the Statute of Frauds 1677.

The first defendant, International Glass Engineering IN GL EN SpA (IGE), contracted with the second defendant (SG) to build a float glass factory at Eggborough in Yorkshire. IGE entered into an agreement with the claimant (AS) to provide the labour to build the float glass factory. IGE was persistently late in making payment to the claimant, which resulted in a substantial sum outstanding.

The claimant (AS) complained to the second defendant (SG) and threatened to withdraw his labour unless the first defendant paid him the arrears. AS alleged that SG made a verbal agreement with AS stating that if AS did not withdraw his labour from the building site he (SG) would speak to the first defendant regarding the money owed to the claimant. Also, if the first defendant did not meet his obligations with the claimant, SG promised he would withhold his payment to IGE and use this payment to pay the claimant the amount outstanding.

The claimant, in reliance on the second defendant's promise, agreed not to withdraw his labour and to proceed toward completion of the factory. However, by March 2000 the first defendant owed the claimant £1.3 million. It became apparent that IGE was unable to meet his obligation to the claimant and SG would have to make payment to the claimant. SG refused to make payment and the claimant withdrew his labour from the building site.

The claimant commenced proceedings against IGE and obtained default judgment on the 12 June 2000. However, the judgment proved worthless as the first defendant had been put into liquidation in Italy. Therefore, the claimant pursued his claim against the second defendant (SG) and pleaded, at para 5, that the second defendant:

> 'Agreed that in consideration of the claimant not withdrawing its labour from the site as aforesaid – ie as it had told the second defendant it proposed to do – the second defendant would ensure that the claimant received any amount due to it from the first defendant under the supply contract if necessary by redirecting to the claimant payments due by the second defendant to the first defendant.' (p569)

SG had resisted the claim by denying any such agreement was ever entered into with the claimant and, also, if any such agreement had been entered into it would constitute a guarantee, which in the absence of being evidenced in writing is unenforceable by virtue of s4 of the Statue of Frauds 1677, which states:

> 'No action shall be brought ... whereby to charge the defendant upon any special promise to answer for the debt, default or miscarriages of another person ... unless the agreement upon which such action shall be brought, or some memorandum or note thereof, shall be in writing, and signed by the party to be charged therewith, or some other person thereunto by him lawfully authorised.'

The claimant contended that the Statute of Frauds 1677 had no application to the agreement and the second defendant was estopped from relying upon the Statute.

Held
At first instance, Mitting J, concluded that the second defendant undertook a

primary obligation to pay the claimant and the facts should be examined at trial and refused summary judgment. Mr Soole, who acted for the second defendant, on appeal challenged the decision of the court of first instance and this was discussed by Simon Brown LJ:

'... the question whether or not a guarantee is within the Statute of Frauds 1677 must be approached as a matter of substance rather than form. It is the essence of the second defendant's case that, however, precisely one construes the terms of this agreement, in substance it imposed only a secondary liability upon the second defendant, a liability contingent upon the first defendant defaulting on its primary obligation under the subcontract with the claimant. Such liability, submits Mr Soole, falls foul of s4.' (p570)

Simon Brown LJ (at p571) referred to the case of *Motemtronic Ltd* v *Autocar Equipment Ltd* (unreported) 20 June 1996 (CA (Civil Division)) and made reference to the following statement:

'Mrs Ford. Where would money come from if M [the principal debtor] had to repay £1m? Colin Searle [the second defendant, M's chairman]. From wherever in the group the money was at the relevant time. I'll make sure it is there, I'm good for £1m.'

The Court of Appeal, in that case, found the wording merely constituted a statement of comfort and such a promise would fall within s4. Simon Brown LJ (at p572) discussed the dictum of Lord Diplock in the case of *Moschi* v *Lep Air Services Ltd* [1973] AC 331 (at 347H):

'The reason for the need for such formality was set out by Lord Blackburn in *Stelle* v *M'Kinlay* (1880) 5 App Cas 754, 768: "It was thought by the English Legislature that there was a danger of contracts of particular kind being established by false evidence, or by evidence of loose talk, when it never was really meant to make such a contract; and there it was provided ... " and s4 is set out. The policy behind the Statute is to seek to introduce certainty in any case where a party accepts secondary liability for another's failure to meet his promise ... I have made it clear that in my judgment the mischief aimed at by s4 of the Statue of Frauds 1677 remains as valid as ever it did. If follows from this that in examining whether an oral contract is within or without the Statute, it is necessary to look at the substance rather than the form ... The first basis requirement of a contract of guarantee within s4 is that there must be someone other than the surety who is primarily liable ...'

Simon Brown LJ was of the opinion that the second defendant, as in the case of *Motemtronic Ltd* v *Autocar Equipment Ltd*, took on a secondary liability and was answerable for the debt of the defaulter (in the aforementioned case it was Autocar), in this instance it is the first defendant (IGE).

However, Mr McGhee, the claimant's representative, argued the contrary and used the case of *Andrews* v *Smith* (1835) 2 CM & R 627 using the dictum recorded at pp629–630:

'This is not a promise to answer for the debtor default of another, within the meaning of the Statute of Frauds. It is not a promise to be answerable out of the defendant's own funds, but to pay out of the funds of another, on receiving his direction for that purposes

'... such a contract is direct, and not collateral, and therefore binding without being in writing.'

Simon Brown LJ, having heard the arguments rejected the claimant's submission and found the in favour of the second defendant. The promise made by the second defendant was unenforceable by virtue of s4 of the Statute of Frauds 1677. The appeal was allowed and the claim against the second defendant was struck out.

Comment
This case clearly demonstrates the Statute of Frauds 1677 is still alive and enforceable when it comes to formation of contract. The facts of this case should send a clear message to those involved with secondary debtors: guarantees must be evidenced in writing.

OBP Textbook page 22, section 2.4.

Types of Obligations Created

Representations

Richard Drake v *Agnew & Sons Limited* [2002] EWHC 294 Queen's Bench Division (Buckley J)

Representation or term of the contract – Misrepresentation Act 1967 and Sale of Goods Act 1979

Facts
The claimant, Mr Drake, employed an agent, Mr Callan, to find and purchase a painting by one of the Old Masters such as van Dyck. It was agreed that Mr Callan would receive 5–10 per cent commission and reimbursement costs for transportation. Mr Callan visited Agnew, the defendant, and spoke to Miss Gabriel Naughton, a director of the company. He explained he was a dealer looking for a painting by one of the Old Masters, but did not disclose the name of his principal. Miss Naughton showed Mr Callan a picture and said it was by Sir Anthony van Dyck and the price was £2,000,000. Mr Callan said he would be in touch. Agnew had purchased the picture from Sothebys and had paid £30,000. The catalogue sale at the auction had described the painting as: 'After Sir Anthony van Dyck (1599–1641)'. This suggested the portrait was not by van Dyck and Mr Agnew carried out further research on the painting. He sought the advice of Sir Oliver Millar, a leading expert on van Dyck portraits. Sir Millar did accept the painting as a van Dyck.

Mr Callan sent a copy of a sales brochure to Mr Drake and it was found that the last two words had been covered with tipp-ex: the brochure had been doctored. The original should have read:

'Sir Anthony van Dyck (1599–1641) James Stuart 4th Duke of Lennox and 1st Duke of

Richmond as Paris. Oil on canvas 40 x 29½ inches (101.5 x 75 cms). Collection: in the collection of the family of the Marquess of Bristol from before 1819 (probably acquired by Frederick Hervey, 1st Marquess) until 1996.'

The deletion of the last two words gave the impression that the painting had been in the possession of the Marquess of Bristol's collection until the sale to Mr Drake, whereas it left the collection in 1996. Mr Callan had been dishonest and his motive, it was suggested by the court, was to complete the sale and claim his commission.

Mr Drake alleged the statement was an express term of the contract. If this was to be accepted by the court the breach would be contrary to s13 of the Sale of Goods Act 1979, an implied term that the painting should correspond with the description. The defendant denied this allegation and argued that he intended any such statement to be merely an opinion and not a term of the contract. Mr Drake further contested that if the statement was not accepted as a term of the contract it constituted a misrepresentation, ie an untrue statement of fact which induced Mr Drake to enter the contract.

Held

Buckley J considered the arguments by both counsel and in particular the authority of *Harlingdon and Leinster Enterprises Ltd* v *Christopher Hull Fine Art Ltd* [1991] 1 QB 564 which also dealt with a picture that later turned out to be fake. The Court of Appeal, in *Harlingdon*, made reference to the intentions of the parties and whether the description was influential and became a term of the contract. The Court of Appeal found the statement not to be a term of the contract. They believed the attribution of artistic work is not an exact science and anyone dealing within the art world is taking a calculated risk. Buckley J focused on the intention of the parties when they entered the contract and made an objective assessment of all the circumstances. Buckley J considered Mr Callan's role and why he did not ask additional questions and pursue his own research to ascertain whether the picture was indeed a van Dyck. Mr Callan was more concerned with obtaining his commission and decided to proceed with the sale. Buckley J concluded there was no term in the contract which stated the painting was by van Dyck and thus no breach of an implied term under s13 of the Sale of Goods Act 1979. He based his decision on the premise that no responsible buyer would hold Agnew's statement out without carrying out further investigation in such circumstances. Mr Callan had obtained information and had not relied on Agnew's statement.

Buckley J was not satisfied that the statement constituted a misrepresentation. Again, this was due to Mr Callan's actions. As agent for Mr Drake, Mr Callan's motive and state of mind were considered. It was found that Agnew's opinion had not influenced the purchase of the painting. Buckley J believed that Mr Callan knew that Agnew had purchased the painting for £30,000 in 1996 and Mr Callan had attempted to keep this information from his principal, Mr Drake, by doctoring the brochure which demonstrated the 1996 sale. Mr Callan was determined the sale should proceed so that he would earn the substantial commission from the sale, and he hoped that Mr Drake would not investigate the facts after the event. Buckley J found that Agnew could not be liable for Mr Drake's agent's deception. Mr Callan and not Agnew engineered the whole fiasco. Thus, there was no term in the contract stating the picture was a van Dyck and there was no misrepresentation; the claimant's action failed.

Comment

This was a judgment that initially portrayed either a breach of contract or misrepresentation. However, the crux of the matter was the agent's fiduciary duty towards his principal. Given the facts, judgment could have been given in favour of the claimant had the agent performed his duties accordingly. However, the ruling adhered to the principal enunciated in *Harlingdon & Leinster Ltd* v *Christopher Hull Fine Art Ltd* which examined the intention of the parties and the influence of any such statement made. This approach reinforces the predicament of the court when attempting to view all the facts objectively, whilst hearing the facts from parties that cannot be wholly objective because of their prior involvement.

OBP Textbook pages 23 and 66, sections 3.2 and 5.2.

Duties of the Seller II: Quality

Implied terms

Jewson Ltd v *Kelly* (2002) The Times 3 October Queen's Bench Division (Mr David Foskett QC)

Implied terms – satisfactory quality and misrepresentation

Facts

The claimant, Jewson, a building merchant, sold and delivered 12 Amptect electric boilers to the defendant, Kelly, to be installed within self-contained flats that were being converted from a former convent school building by Kelly. Jewson claimed the sum of £53,322.43; the defendant counterclaimed for breach of contract and consequential losses and sought to set off his claim against the outstanding sum owed to Jewson.

The defendant decided to install electric boilers which had been manufactured by a company known as Amptec Heating Technology Ltd (Amptec). The defendant purchased the boilers from Jewson and the total expenditure was in the region of £6,000. The claimant's contention was the suitability of these boilers and the defendant's liability for the losses. The claimant's standard terms and conditions applied to the sale and had been relied upon to resist the defendant's counter-claim. Clause 8.7 was as follows:

> 'The Customer is deemed to be fully conversant with the nature and performance of the goods including any harmful or hazardous effects resulting from their usage and shall not

be reliant in any way upon the advice, skill or judgment of the Company. The Company's employees or agents are not authorised to make any representations concerning the goods other than those confirmed by the Company in writing.'

Whilst clause 8.10 stated:

'The Company shall not be liable for any consequential loss or indirect loss suffered by the Customer or any third party in relation to this contract (except personal injury directly attributable to the negligence of the Company) and the Customer shall hold the company fully and effectively indemnified against such losses whether from breach of a duty in contract or loss in any way including losses arising from the Company's negligence.'

The court accepted that these clauses were deemed reasonable given the relationship between the parties and nature of the circumstances.

Jewson were aware of the particular purpose for which the boilers were intended and had informed Kelly during their negotiations that the boilers were suitable for his requirements. Kelly alleged the boilers had an unsatisfactory Standard Assessment Procedure (SAP) rating for the individual properties in question. The SAP refers specifically to energy efficiency of the heating system for an individual residential property. The building regulations in force at the time for a 'new build' dwelling specified an energy efficiency in the region of 80–85, which varied depending on the floor size. There was no statutory minimum when dealing with a conversion and thus there was no refusal under the building regulations based upon an unsatisfactory SAP. However, the SAP calculations will be considered by a potential lender and their surveyor when carrying out a valuation on the property. Kelly claimed that the unsatisfactory low SAP readings led to the loss of potential purchasers and further claimed Jewson were in breach of contract under the Sale of Goods Act 1979 (as amended by the Sale and Supply of Goods Act 1994), s14(2) and (2A) of which state as follows:

'(2) Where the seller sells goods in the course of a business, there is an implied term that the goods supplied under the contract are of satisfactory quality.
(2A) For the purposes of this Act, goods are of satisfactory quality if they meet the standard that a reasonable person would regard as satisfactory, taking into account any description of the goods, the price (if relevant) and all other relevant circumstances.'

The SAP rating, for these flats, should have been in the region of between 55 and 100. However, expert opinion was given that these boilers scored a rating of between 44, 30, ten and below. The literature supplied by the manufacture (Amptec) that accompanied the boilers made various claims, for example:

'The Amptec boiler processes very low volumes of water at very high speeds making it 99.6 per cent heat efficient and impressively cheap to run.
    Because it's so compact, the Amptec boiler is particularly suitable for house, flats, small shops and mobile homes. Because it's electric, it's ideal when there's no gas main; for new housing, properties in rural areas and renovations.'

Similar claims were made throughout the literature which emphasised the unobtrusive nature of the boiler, its safety, efficiency, ease of installation and economy. These claims were not in dispute: the SAP ratings were. Several of the 13 flats had been purchased for the prices expected and in certain cases the price had been exceeded. There was no direct evidence that the Amptec boilers were not working satisfactorily. However, the defendant alleged the boilers were not of satisfactory quality under the implied terms of the Sale of Goods Act 1979 as potential purchasers, which he claimed there was a number, were deterred from proceeding with their purchase due to the SAP ratings. The defendant claimed their mortgagee's surveyor put them off, as they would not be able to obtain a mortgage on the flats in question because of the low SAP ratings.

Held

Foskett J found in favour of the defendant. He was of the opinion that the claimant was aware that the boilers were to be installed in the flats which were being converted for profit. The low SAP ratings caused a delay in sale and were therefore not fit for their purpose and not of satisfactory quality. The claimant was responsible for supplying goods that were not of a correct quality and was in breach of contract. The use of the Amptec boilers substantially increased the risk that any sale proposal would either be delayed or abandoned. It was found that the defendant had relied upon the claimant's skill and judgment and assumed responsibility for the fitness for purpose of the boilers and this responsibility was within the performance of their contractual duties. Regarding Clause 8.10 of the claimant's standard conditions of sale which referred to the exclusion of and 'consequential ... or indirect' losses, in this instance it was found that the breach of contract had resulted in losses 'directly and naturally' arising from the breach. Thus the losses fell within the first rule laid down within *Hadley* v *Baxendale* (1854) 9 Ex 341 and could not be excluded.

Comment

This case demonstrates that the courts are still attempting to interpret and apply the Sale of Goods Act 1979 (as amended) when dealing with satisfactory quality and fitness for purpose. However, progress is being made and as this case illustrates a number of difficult issues were discussed and clarified.

OBP Textbook page 86, section 5.4.

Exclusion of Liability

Unfair terms in contracts

A Joint Consultation Paper

The Law Commission Consultation Paper No 166 (August 2002); Scottish Law Commission Discussion Paper No 119

Exclusion clauses or limitation clauses are currently regulated through common law, domestic legislation and EU directives. This has led to a system which offers protection to traders and consumers through either the Unfair Contract Terms Act (UCTA) 1977 or, in the case of consumers, the Unfair Terms in Consumer Contracts Regulations (UTCCR) 1999. However, before dealing with an alleged unfair term it must first be established, using case law as reference, whether or not the term has been incorporated within the contract. Incorporation, under the common law, may take place through signature, notice or previous course of dealings. If the term has been incorporated it is then necessary to examine the construction of the exclusion/limitation clause in question, in the light of the nature and circumstances prevailing, to see whether it covers the exclusion/limitation. If the term covers the exclusion/limitation it is then necessary to refer to either the UCTA 1977 or the UTCCR 1999 to see whether the term is void or reasonable. The former piece of legislation covers both business and consumer contracts, whereas the latter covers only consumers. There are a number of differences between the two pieces of legislation and to some extent they overlap but also have a different scope and application. This has resulted in a complex system and arguably may lead to inconsistencies when attempting to apply the law. Thus, the Law Commission are looking at reforms.

The Law Commission is looking at reforms to combat unfair terms and exclusion clauses which exclude or limit liability in contracts. They are scrutinising the UCTA 1977 and the UTCCR 1999. They are considering the feasibility of a single piece of legislation that will replace the current legislation. The new legislation will cover both consumer and non-consumer contracts and will extend the protection currently given to consumers and also to business-to-business contracts when dealing with unfair terms. This protection is not provided within the UCTA 1977 but has been extended to consumers through the UTCCR 1999. It is intended that the draft legislation will be easier to read than the current legislation and in a simpler style which will ensure understanding and avoid confusion. The new legislation is intended to implement the directives on unfair terms and sale of consumer goods and associated guarantees.

Comment

The Law Commission's proposals are pragmatic and would cure many of the defects that currently exist. The recommendations outlined in their consultation paper would not only amalgamate existing legislation but would also simplify and clarify the application of domestic legislation and the language of the EU directives.

OBP Textbook page 137, section 7.11.

Personal Remedies of the Seller

The action for the price of the goods sold

Otis Vehicle Rentals ALS Ltd (Formerly Brandrick Hire (Birmingham) Ltd) v Ciceley Commercials Ltd [2002] EWCA Civ 1064 (Peter Gibson and Potter LJJ, Sir Murray Stuart-Smith)

Section 49(1) Sale of Goods Act 1979 – action in debt for the price due or contractual damages

Facts

The appeal by the defendants/appellants, Ciceley Commercials Limited, was based upon the interpretation of s49(1) of the Sale of Goods Act (SGA) 1979. The defendants sold commercial vehicles and the claimants/respondents (Otis) were engaged in the business of selling and letting such vehicles. Under the terms of the agreement the claimants purchased 14 Mercedes Benz tractor units (the vehicles) from the defendants with the use of credit from Mercedes Benz Finance Limited (MBFL). Thus, in effect the vehicles were sold to MBFL and hired to Otis until the final payment would transfer ownership to Otis. Payments were to be made monthly to MBFL and the final payment, for each vehicle, was to be an increased payment, known in the trade as a 'balloon' payment. This was a common clause to be included, particularly when the property in question was subject to a buy-back agreement which would usually operate as the source of income to cover this inflated final payment under the finance agreement.

Otis claimed the initial agreement with the defendants included the following clause:

'... that if the Plaintiffs entered into a hire purchase agreement with a finance company in respect of the said Tractor Units (for the purpose of which the Defendants would sell the Tractor Units to the finance company) the Defendants would repurchase the said vehicles from the Plaintiffs at the Plaintiffs' option after with two or three years; [and] ... the repurchase price would be either 60 per cent or 45 per cent of the purchase price of each vehicle depending on whether it was after two or three years ...'

Three years later Otis notified the defendants in writing they wished to exercise the buy-back agreement and the re-purchase of each Tractor Unit would be £19,153.53p. However, the defendants responded by denying the vehicles had ever been the subject of a buy-back agreement and refused to re-purchase them at the said price. This resulted in Otis successfully requesting an extended 12 months to pay off the outstanding debt to MBFL by re-financing the balloon payments payable on each vehicle. Thus, Otis continued to lease out the vehicles and eventually sold off all 14 vehicles between June 1999 and April 2000 to meet their obligations to MBFL.

Otis commenced an action against the defendants under s49(1) SGA 1979, which provides:

> 'Where, under a contract of sale, the property in the goods has passed to the buyer and he wrongfully neglects or refuses to pay for the goods according to the terms of the contract, the seller may maintain an action against him for the price of the goods.'

Otis claimed they were ready, willing and able to deliver the vehicles to the defendants and the defendants were indebted to them for the price of the vehicles, plus interest amounting to £315,075.57p. They supported this argument under s49(2) SGA 1979, which provides:

> 'Where, under a contract of sale, the price is payable on a day certain irrespective of delivery and the buyer wrongfully neglects or refuses to pay such a price, the seller may maintain an action for the price, although the property in the goods has not passed and the goods have not been appropriated to the contract.'

The defendants/appellants believed the claim should have been for breach of contract and an award of damages in the sum of £150,003.91p should be made.

Held

Potter LJ examined the effect of s49(1) in light of the circumstance and was of the opinion that by allowing recovery of the price (debt) the court would in effect be granting specific performance in circumstances where damages would be an adequate remedy. He believed the appellants' ground for appeal was justified and that it was wrong to have given judgment for the price under the buy-back agreement instead of awarding damages.

Potter LJ was mindful of the balloon payment, which was to be met through the buy-back agreement, as such an arrangement would indemnify the claimants. However, such an arrangement would involve the defendants paying either MBFL or the claimants to ensure the hire-purchase agreements were met and title was allowed to pass to the claimants and then back to the defendants. Such an agreement, a buy-back agreement, which was to take place three years from the original contract did not comply with s49(2): it could not be ascertained that the price was to be payable on a day certain irrespective of delivery. Also, Potter LJ made it clear that even if s49(2) had been complied with the seller's right to sue for the price would also depend upon his continuing willingness to deliver the goods and in this instance the goods had been sold, leaving a claim for damages. Thus, the appeal was allowed and damages substituted the original award.

Comment

This case clearly showed the difference between suing for the price of the goods or for damages. The facts illustrated the crucial distinction between suing for an outstanding debt or for damages. Under the former the price is due and there is no need to mitigate any losses; whereas, in the latter, the claimant must not only mitigate their losses but also demonstrate their damages are not too remote. It was easy to see why Otis elected to sue for the price instead of damages, as the latter offers a secure and favourable position in comparison to damages.

OBP Textbook page 229, section 12.2.

CONSUMER CREDIT

Default by the Debtor

Security for credit

AIB Group (UK) plc v *Martin and Another* [2002] 1 WLR 94 House of Lords (Lord Irvine of Lairg LC, Lords Hutton, Millett, Scott of Foscote and Rodger of Earlsferry)

Joint and several liability – guarantees – primary and secondary debtors

Facts

The House of Lords was asked to consider the construction and interpretation of various clauses contained within a mortgage agreement. The appeal was brought by the second defendant, Alan Clive Gold, who was found to be liable by the Court of Appeal (upholding the decision of the court of first instance) to the claimant bank AIB Group (UK) plc (formerly known as Allied Irish Bank plc and AIB Finance Ltd).

There were two mortgagors, Mr Gold and Mr Martin. Mr Gold was a dentist by trade but formed a business partnership with Mr Martin, a property dealer. Together they acquired a number of properties together and financed these purchases by borrowing from AIB Group plc (the bank). Mr Martin also acquired additional properties by himself, funded through various loans from the bank. In 1993 the bank restructured the joint borrowing and wrote to Mr Gold and Mr Martin offering them a joint facility of £1,710,000 to be secured on 46 specified properties. Mr Martin owned 28 of the properties, Mr Gold owned two and the remainder were held jointly. The acceptance by the borrowers (mortgagors) of this facility was in a standard form and the outcome was that the mortgagors undertook joint and several liability for all outstanding debts. This obligation meant that they were liable for their joint debts, individual debts and had guaranteed to pay the debts of the other if there was a shortfall. It was the latter covenant that led to this appeal. For reasons that were not material to the case the bank called in their loans and at first instance and in the Court of Appeal it was found that Mr Martin and

Mr Gold had agreed to be joint and severally liable for all outstanding loans. There was a short fall to repay all of Mr Martin's debt and Mr Gold was asked to make up this deficit. Mr Gold now appealed to the House of Lords.

Held

Their Lordships examined the construction and interpretation of the clauses contained within the standard form agreement. The relevant operative clause was 2(1) which stated:

> 'The mortgagor hereby covenants with ... the bank ... that it will on demand pay or discharge to the bank ... all sums of money ... advanced to the mortgagor by the bank ...'

In this instance the mortgagor is Mr Martin and Mr Gold. Clause 1 of the mortgage is an interpretation clause and in this instance it defined 'mortgagor' as the person(s) named in the agreement, ie Mr Gold and Mr Martin. The last sentence of clause 1 then states:

> 'If the expression "the mortgagor" includes more than one person it shall be construed as referring to all and/or any one of those persons and the obligations of such persons shall be joint and several.'

Lord Scott of Foscote discussed these clauses (p100–101) and whether such covenants made Mr Gold liable to the bank for Mr Martin's indebtedness, which included advances made solely to Mr Martin. This was the crux of Mr Gold's appeal. At first instance Jacob J, and then the Court of Appeal, found in favour of the bank and Mr Gold liable. Lord Scott (at p103) referred to the leading judgment in the Court of Appeal by Morritt LJ:

> 'Once it is recognised that each reference to mortgagor includes Mr Martin and Mr Gold jointly, and Mr Martin and Mr Gold severally and in isolation from the other, then both the obligation to pay and the liability which that obligation extends to, is a several obligation of Mr Gold in relation to a several liability of Mr Martin, as well as the other way round ...'

Lord Scott heard argument from Mr Davidson, counsel for Mr Gold, but was not persuaded by his submissions. Instead Lord Scott formed the opinion that:

> 'The clause starts with a joint covenant by Mr Gold and Mr Martin. It is not three separate covenants, one by them jointly and one by each of them individually. It is a single joint covenant. Their liability under this joint covenant is declared to be joint and several.' (p103)

This may have given the answer to the question of joint and several liability, but what are they joint and severally liable for? Lord Scott then referred to clause 2(1) which makes reference to 'all sums of money ... advanced to the mortgagor by the bank'. Thus, they were joint and severally liable for all funds advanced and Lord Scott agreed with the decision of the Court of Appeal and dismissed the appellant's appeal.

Comment
The House of Lords answered many questions and clarified the law on joint and several liability. The decision will place advisors on mortgage offers on their guard and ensure clauses that give rise to joint and several liability are fully explained. This case also gives rise to the format of mortgage offers and supports the call for standardisation. If mortgage offers were to be standardised there would be less confusion over the construction and interpretation when they are employed for the correct circumstances.

Security for credit and guarantees

Hampton v *Minns* [2002] 1 WLR 1 Chancery Division (Kevin Garnett QC sitting as a deputy High Court judge)

Guarantee – debt – surety's liability and the Limitation Act 1980

Facts
The case involved the claimant, a Mr Bernard Roy Hampton, and the defendant, a Mr Dennis Rodney Minns, who set up a property development company called Banobury Homes (the company). The venture involved the purchase of land and construction and the sale of houses. Mr Minns had previously been involved with purchasing land on behalf of Bovis Homes and therefore had previous knowledge and experience in dealing with the acquisition of land, which also involved obtaining planning permission to develop land for residential purposes. Mr Hampton was to put up the capital as Mr Minns was not in a financial position to inject any capital into the company, and deal generally with the financial arrangements.

The claimant and defendant were directors of the company and Mr Minns was to be employed by the company, receiving a salary of £27,500, a company car, plus pension contributions, whilst Mr Hampton would not receive any director's fee or salary. The shareholding of the company was 80:20 between Mr Hampton and Mr Minns, accordingly. However, the company needed additional funds and took out various secured loans but the bank (Barclays Bank) requested additional security in the form of a personal guarantee. On 9 June 1988 both the claimant and defendant signed a joint and several guarantee for the company's liabilities.

The company did not prosper and was wound up leaving a vast amount outstanding to the bank. The bank recovered a large amount of the loan and also enforced the guarantee against the claimant, Mr Hampton, to an agreed shortfall of £478,400.36. The claimant responded by claiming a contribution of half the amount, £239,200.18, from the defendant.

The defendant resisted the claim by referring to s1(1) of the Civil Liability (Contribution) Act 1978, and argued that any contribution to be paid was statute barred under s10 of the Limitation Act 1980, which applies a two-year limitation period for claims brought under the 1978 Act.

Held

Kevin Garnett QC explained that, in equity, where one person meets the whole debt of a joint guarantee the guarantor is entitled to a contribution from his co-guarantor and in equity each guarantor should bear equal responsibility for the debt. However, Murray Shanks, who acted for the defendant, argued that the normal rule of equality of the burden should not apply in this instance as Mr Hampton owned 80 per cent of the shares in the company, whilst Mr Minns owned only 20 per cent. He further argued that from the outset of the venture it was implicit that Mr Minns was not to be equally liable for the debts incurred and attempted to persuade Kevin Garnett QC with the dictum of Tipping J taken from the High Court of New Zealand in *Trotter* v *Franklin* [1991] 2 NZLR 92, at p98:

'As the right to contribution is founded in equity the ultimate question is what is a just apportionment between the co-sureties. Ordinarily the justice of the matter will require equality of sharing. Obviously if the parties have expressly provided to the contrary then justice will require such contrary arrangement to be enforced. It seems to be however that equity may well require unequal sharing if the court can discern by clear implication either that this is what the parties must have intended or that such unequal sharing is necessary to do justice in the particular case.'

Mr Shanks suggested that his client, Mr Minns, regarded Mr Hampton as being liable for all financial transactions carried out in the company's name and that his client had no recollection of signing any guarantees.

Kevin Garnett QC considered Mr Shank's argument but was also mindful to the fact that Mr Hampton had provided all the additional funding for the company. He also noted that Mr Hampton did not draw a salary for the work he carried out whilst Mr Minns received a salary and 20 per cent of the shareholding in the company, without putting in any capital. The balance of power may have been uneven but the benefits being received in return for any burden was also unbalanced. Thus, he rejected Mr Shank's argument to vary the equal sharing of the debt in equity and did not believe the dictum of Tipping J was 'a correct statement of English law in the absence, for example, of something in the nature of an estoppel.'

He further examined the limitation period between co-sureties by referring to *Halsbury's Laws of England* (4th ed reissue, vol 20 (1993), para 278) which deals with the applicable limitation period, which states:

'... the guarantor's primary cause of action against a co-guarantor for contribution is for money paid to the debtor's use at his request. Such a claim is treated as one of six years from the date on which the cause of action accrued ... It is not clear whether the Civil Liability (Contribution) Act 1978 applies to claims between co-guarantors.'

He also referred to vol 28, para 875:

'As between co-guarantors, co-contractors, or co-debtors, the statue of limitation runs against the right of contribution of one who has paid more than his share from the time of such payment.'

Kevin Garnett QC was not persuaded by Mr Shanks argument and gave his reasoning (at p28):

> 'In my judgment, what Mr Hampton and Mr Minns agreed to do, when a demand to do so was made on them, was to pay to the bank whatever it was that the company owed to the bank. This obligation created a debt ... I would expect if such a person were called upon to pay damages under the guarantee he or she would respond: "I only agreed to pay whatever it was that the company owed, not to pay you damages."'

Therefore, he found that the 1978 Act was applicable for a claim in damages but not for a debt. The construction of this agreement had resulted in a debt owed to the bank and the obligations placed upon the parties were to meet this debt. The claim against the defendant was a debt and not damages, which excluded the two-year limitation period in s10 of the 1980 Act. The time limit in this case was six years and the case had been brought within the period of time and was not statute barred. Thus, judgment was given for the claimant for £239,200.18p, plus interest and costs.

Comment

This was an interesting case which gave an excellent interpretation of the Civil Liability (Contribution) Act 1978 and the application of the Limitation Act 1980. The legal arguments, supported with relevant case law, demonstrated the persuasive skills and tactical manoeuvres of counsel when attempting to distinguish between damages and a debt. The case answered many questions when dealing with the liabilities of co-sureties and their legal rights against each other when seeking a contribution from a co-surety.

OBP Textbook page 365, section 20.6.

AGENCY

The Creation of Authority

Authority and pre-incorporation contracts

Braymist Ltd and Others v *Wise Finance Co Ltd* [2002] 2 WLR 322 Court of Appeal (Judge, Latham and Arden LJJ)

Agency – authority – pre-incorporation contracts and the Companies Act 1985

Facts

The appeal involved the defendant/appellants, Wise Finance Company Ltd (WFC), and the fourth claimant/respondents, William Sturges & Co (a firm) (WS). WFC agreed to purchase a piece of land from the first claimant, Braymist Ltd, (the vendor), which was owned by the second claimant, Plumtree Ltd. The third claimant was Colin Anthony Pool who owned 75 per cent of the shareholding in Pique Holding plc, which also owned the second claimant, Plumtree Ltd

The fourth claimant, WS, signed the agreement for the sale of the piece of land as solicitors and agents for the first claimant, Braymist Ltd, who had not, at the time, been incorporated. This was primarily a pre-incorporation contract and s36C(1) of the Companies Act (CA) 1985 applied. This states:

'A contract which purports to be made by or on behalf of a company at a time when the company has not been formed has effect, subject to any agreement to the contrary, as one made with the person purporting to act for the company or as agent for it, and he is personally liable on the contract accordingly.'

When the appellants found out Braymist Ltd had not been incorporated they refused to complete. However, if the respondents were to be personally liable they also believed they should be able to enforce the contract against The Wise Finance Company Ltd (WFC). Therefore, based upon the appellants' actions the respondents issued a notice to complete the purchase, pursuant to Condition 22 of the National Conditions of Sale (20th ed) which had been incorporated into the contract. When the notice expired and WFC failed to complete WS informed WFC's solicitor that Braymist Ltd had rescinded the agreement, forfeited the deposit and brought an action for breach of contract against the appellants. At first instance the court found in favour of the fourth claimant and ordered the £5,000 deposit paid by the appellants be forfeited to the fourth claimant and also to pay them £67,700.58p, representing damages for breach of contract and interest.

WFC appealed and the crux of the appeal was based upon the interpretation of s36C(1) CA 1985 and whether the section merely granted rights of action against the agent in favour of the purporting contracting party (WFC) or also conferred a benefit (the right to enforce the contract) upon the agent of the non-existent purported principal.

Held

The Court of Appeal examined the judgment of Etherton J, at first instance, which dealt with the WS's right to enforce the agreement under s36C(1). Etherton J considered the enactment of this piece of legislation and that it emanated from s9(2) of the European Communities Act 1972, which has attempted to give force to art 7 of the First Council Directive on Harmonisation of Company Law (68/151/EEC). The Court of Appeal also noted (at p325), that Etherton J made reference to the text of art 7, which states:

'If, before a company being formed has acquired legal personality, action has been carried out in its name and the company does not assume the obligation arising from such action, the persons who acted shall, without limit, be jointly and severally liable therefore, unless otherwise agreed.'

Based upon this Etherton J, at first instance, held that s36C(1) would give the agent of an unformed company the right to enforce the contract and supported this finding using the case of *Phonogram Ltd* v *Lane* [1982] QB 938, which was the first case to come before the court of appeal to deal with the construction of s9(2) of the 1972 Act.

On appeal Mark Blackett-Ord, who acted for WFC, believed it would be a bizarre result to allow an agent to be able to enforce a contract in such circumstances. He argued that:

> '... no agent has succeeded on this basis and that there is no reported case in which the point has been taken. If the judge is right, agents for non-existent companies will get an advantage. They can take advantage of their own carelessness in making the contracts on behalf of unformed companies ... A further bizarre result is that the third party becomes liable to a party with whom he did not intend to contract ... The effect may be to impose a contract on a party who particularly wished to contract with the company which was in course of incorporation ... There is no reason why Parliament should want to confer the benefit on agents.' (pp328–329)

However, Arden J pointed out (at p329): 'In this case the identity of the vendor was of no particular concern to Wise.' Also, Arden J notes the argument put forward by Barbara Rich, who acted for the fourth claimant (at pp330–331), that 's36C states that the contract takes effect as a contract to which the agent is a party. The court must give effect to this wording. ... where identity is relevant, the counterparty can rescind the contract, but that is not the case here.'

Arden J examined the evidence and various authorities and concluded that:

> '... the general law is not that an agent can in all circumstances come in and claim to be principal on a contract which he made as agent ... In my judgment, it should not be assumed that Parliament intended in that situation that the agent should be able to enforce the contract to the same extent as if he had been the company itself. As to what the rules should be in a situation which I have postulated, that matter will have to await another case. It is clear in that in this particular instance it is of no moment to the defendant whether the party selling the property is Braymist or sturges ... I conclude that sturges are entitled to enforce the agreement.' (p338)

Comment

This case demonstrates that in certain circumstances, for example, when the identity of the principal is not important, the court is prepared to allow an agent who has the burden imposed by s36C(1) to also take the benefit under the contract. However, this was an exception to the rule and the dictum of Judge, Latham and Arden LJJ suggest it will remain at the discretion of the court unless Parliament intervenes and amends s36C(1).

OBP Textbook pages 432 and 452, sections 25.4 and 27.2.

4

Company Law

Introduction and Corporate Personality

The scope of the law

Reform

The White Paper *Modernising Company Law* was presented to Parliament by Patricia Hewitt, the Secretary of State for Trade and Industry, in July 2002 (Cmnd 5553–I).

A thorough overhaul of company law was needed to make the law clearer and more accessible, so the government established the independent Company Law Review to develop proposals for reform. This was led by a Steering Group of company law experts, academics and business people, and was supported by a widely-based Consultative Committee and a range of working groups and working parties. The Steering Group produced nine consultation documents during the Review and the final report to government was published on 26 July 2001: the White Paper is the first part of the government's response. Other information which will feed into the Bill includes an independent review of the role and effectiveness of non-executive directors, and the work undertaken in the wake of the collapse of Enron.

The government believes that the starting point for company law should be small companies, with additional provisions being added for larger companies where necessary. This means that there will be a reversal in the way in which the new Companies Act will be written. The Companies Act 1985 operates on a 'top down' principle, with the legislation being drafted from the perspective of large public companies. For years this approach has caused operational difficulties for small private companies, who have found themselves stifled by the red tape imposed by the legislation, despite numerous attempts to lessen this burden on them.

There is also an indication that a more stakeholder approach to company law may be adopted in the new legislation, as the White Paper talks about the need to balance various interests, for example those of shareholders, directors, employees, creditors and customers.

The White Paper proposes modernisation and simplification to the ways in which companies take decisions. The requirement for private companies to hold an annual general meeting (AGM) will be removed unless the members want to hold such meetings. This means that instead of opting out of the procedure, private companies will have to opt in, and such a decision will be taken by way of an ordinary resolution. Where the decision has been taken to hold AGMs, then the timing of the meeting will now be linked to the company's annual reporting cycle. In future the proposal is that the AGM should be held within ten months of the end of the financial year. This time limit is reduced to six months for public companies.

With regard to resolutions, it is proposed to abolish the category of extraordinary resolution and to use the special resolution procedure in its place. A written resolution will require a majority of 75 per cent of the eligible votes, rather than the 100 per cent presently required, as it is considered that such an alteration will make it easier for private companies to take decisions.

The government agrees that neither the 'objects clauses' nor the split between the memorandum and the articles continues to serve a useful purpose, so it is now proposed that a company's constitution should be contained in a single document. The constitution would be permitted to contain an objects clause: however, that clause would be effective only as between the directors and the members. Effectively this also means that any third party doing business with a company in good faith will not need to worry about the details of that company's constitution. It also means that there will need to be a review of the standard form of articles of association. The proposals further enable shareholders to require the scrutiny of a poll and give proxies extended rights.

With regard to directors, the government agrees that the primary role of directors should be to promote the success of the company for the benefit of its shareholders as a whole, and that directors' general duties to the company should be codified. There will also be clear guidance given to new directors on what their duties entail. The draft duties make it clear that a director must exercise the care, skill and diligence of a reasonably diligent person with both the knowledge, skill and experience which may reasonably be expected of a director in his or her position, and any additional knowledge, skill and experience which the particular director has.

A further report into the role of non-executive directors, *The Review of the Role and Effectiveness of Non-executive Directors*, was published on 20 January 2003. This report, by Derek Higgs (a former international banker) recommends, instead of legislation, a voluntary set of guidelines for companies to follow in their appointment of non-executive directors. The voluntary guidelines would come under the UK's Combined Code, with the effect that companies may choose to ignore the guidelines, provided they give reasons for their refusal to adopt them. It is hoped that these guidelines will lead to a fairer and more open recruitment process among non-executive directors (the report discovered that nearly half of non-executive directors were recruited through personal contacts and friendships), and they have been welcomed by City fund managers.

The report also proposes to give non-executive directors more power by ensuring that they are in a majority on the board. This proposal has been criticised in that it will encourage disparate interests on the board and could make the decision-making process even more difficult. A further proposal is that non-executive directors should hold one directorship only. The Higgs report was commissioned in response to the Enron crisis and the results are being questioned as 'a possible political over-reaction to a corporate crisis that is peculiarly American': *Sunday Times* 26 January 2003, p7. Overall what is important is that any board of directors works together as a cohesive unit: it is also necessary to realise that non-executive directors are no better than the information they are given.

Corporate directors will in future be prohibited

In terms of auditing and reporting, the proposals are to replace the directors' report, and for small companies replace it with a short supplementary statement. Companies will therefore need to produce financial statements and a supplementary statement: the very largest companies only will have to produce an operating and financial review, which is a narrative report on a company's business, its performance and future plans; for quoted companies only, a directors' remuneration report and an optional summary statement will be needed.

The government realises that it is important to keep the law up to date and ensure it continues to meet all users' needs, and so proposes to put elements that are likely to need regular updating into secondary legislation.

The White Paper also proposes to abolish the requirement for private companies to have an authorised share capital, to remove the prohibition on the giving of financial assistance by private companies for the purchase of their own shares, and to change the procedure by which private companies redeem or purchase their own shares out of capital. It is also proposed that private companies will no longer be required to have a company secretary, as that specific role is not considered essential to good corporate governance, which is the responsibility of the directors.

The White Paper is available from the *Modernising Company Law* pages on the DTI's website (http://www.dti.gov.uk/companiesbill) and it contains about one third of the draft clauses of the forthcoming Companies Bill (that being about 200 draft clauses). Further draft clauses will be published over the coming months for consultation. The government hopes, although it cannot be guaranteed, that the Bill will be introduced before the end of this Parliament (ie before the next election).

OBP Textbook pages 2–3, section 1.1.

Company Formation

Flotation

The Financial Services and Markets Act 2000

This Act was given the Royal Assent on 14 June 2000, with the main provisions coming into force in 2001. The Act provides the legal framework for the Financial Services Authority (FSA), which takes over as the single regulator of the financial services industry, and it gives the FSA a range of statutory powers. The FSA will take over responsibility for various self-regulating organisations, such as the Personal Investment Authority, the Investment Management Regulatory Organisation, the Building Societies Commission, the Insurance Directorate of the Treasury, the Friendly Societies Commission and the Registry of Friendly Societies.

The Act is also intended to co-ordinate and modernise financial regulation that has previously been covered by several different Acts, such as the Insurance Companies Act 1982, the Financial Services Act 1986, the Building Societies Act 1986, the Banking Act 1987 and the Friendly Societies Act 1992.

Part 1 of the Act covers the Regulator and sets out the general duties and statutory objectives of the FSA. Its overall objectives are: market confidence; public awareness; consumer protection; and the reduction of financial crime. It must follow the principles of good governance and have effective consultation arrangements.

Part 2, which deals with regulated or prohibited activities, prohibits people who are not authorised to carry on a regulated activity in the UK, or exempt from the need to obtain authorisation, from carrying on a regulated activity in the UK and from holding themselves out to be authorised or exempt. It also sets out arrangements for the regulation of financial promotion, similar to the regulation of advertisements and cold calling under the Financial Services Act 1986, and provides for criminal offences relating to these areas. The way to become an authorised person is set out in Pt 3. There is a single route to authorisation which will operate in the financial services industry that is granted by the FSA. The FSA will also have the power to ensure that people who work for authorised persons are fit and proper, and it has the power to issue prohibition orders against anyone considered not to be fit and proper.

Part 6 covers the listing rules. The FSA becomes the competent authority to maintain the official list of securities instead of the London Stock Exchange, and it also has control over the listing particulars. Part 6 also contains the legal duties of those people who are responsible for listing particulars and prospectuses, and includes the penalties and rights of civil action for giving misleading particulars.

These are the main aspects of this Act that cover the area of company law. To some extent the enormous growth and complexity of regulatory control of the financial services industry, which relates to company securities in particular, means that this area could be regarded as a separate, but related, area of law. The extent to which this piece of legislation needs to be considered in a company law module on an undergraduate law degree will depend on the definition of the syllabus in each institution.

OBP Textbook pages 90–99, section 5.2.

Capital

Dividends

Liability in respect of unlawful dividends

Bairstow v Queens Moat Houses plc [2001] 2 BCLC 531 Court of Appeal (Civil Division) (Sir Andrew Morritt V-C, Robert Walker and Sedley LJJ)

Illegal distributions must be repaid whether or not the company was solvent or insolvent at the time of the distribution

Facts

Three joint managing directors and a finance director of the defendant company authorised the payment of interim and final dividends for 1990 and 1991 and an interim dividend for 1992. The defendant company then suffered a major financial crisis and by 1993 shares in the company were suspended. Subsequently, the four directors were dismissed. They were found guilty of gross misconduct and willful neglect because they had given an untrue picture of the company's profitability in the annual accounts. The judge at first instance held that payment of the dividends had been unlawful and contrary to s263 Companies Act 1985 (a company can make distributions only out of the profits available for that purpose) and s270 Companies Act 1985 (any distribution has to be justified by reference to a company's accounts). The directors appealed.

Held

If a company has made an illegal distribution, the directors who authorised it are liable to repay the money to the company. This applies whether the company is solvent or insolvent when it claims repayment. The provisions of s270 are strict and are there to ensure that the power to make a dividend payment is linked to the requirements laid down in the Companies Act 1985 covering company accounts.

Comment

The onerous nature of the directors' duties is reflected in the remedies available for breach of those duties, and the object of the remedy is restitution, as in *Allied Carpets Group plc v Nethercott* [2001] BCC 81.

OBP Textbook pages 135–140, section 6.5.

Debentures

Charges on company property

Agnew v *Inland Revenue Commissioner* [2001] 2 AC 710 Privy Council
(Lords Bingham of Cornhill, Nicholls of Birkenhead, Hoffmann, Hobhouse
of Woodborough and Millett)

Are book debts fixed or floating charges?

Facts
A company granted a charge over uncollected book debts so that it could continue to
use the proceeds in the ordinary course of business, but it was not able to assign the
debts. The charge was expressed to be a fixed charge. The company then went into
liquidation and the only assets available for distribution were the book debts. The
question which fell to be determined was the nature of the charge that had been
created: was it fixed or floating? The judge at first instance held that it was a fixed
charge. The New Zealand Court of Appeal reversed this decision.

Held
In a judgment delivered by Lord Millett, the court adopted a two-stage process to
answer this question. The first thing to establish was the intention of the parties and
how the instrument creating the charge should be construed. The second stage was
then the categorisation of the charge, which was a matter of law. A provision in the
charge contract that the charge is fixed, but that all charged assets are released from
the charge and instead subject to a floating charge until the chargee declares
otherwise means that a charge is a floating charge from the outset, otherwise any
floating charge could be declared to be a fixed charge.

Comment
The instrument by which the charge was created was closely modelled on the
instrument which was the subject of the decision in *Re New Bullas Trading Ltd*
[1994] 1 BCLC 449, and which has now been overruled by this case. The present
case also contains a very useful review of the cases dealing with this area of the law.

Arthur D Little Ltd (In Administration) v *Ableco Finance LLC* [2002] 3
WLR 1387 Chancery Division (Mr Roger Kaye QC)

Distinction between fixed and floating charges

Facts
Arthur D Little Ltd was registered in Scotland and had a subsidiary company called
CCL. Arthur Little purported to create, in favour of the defendant company, a first
fixed charge over the shares of CCL: however, this charge was not registered in
Scotland. The company went into administration and the administrators alleged that
they should be free to deal with the shares in CCL as they thought fit, as they

contended that what had been created was a floating charge, and that, as it had not been registered, it was therefore void as against the administrators. Arthur Little was not in the business of trading in shares.

Held
The charge was a valid fixed charge because it was taken over an asset which did not, in the ordinary course of business, change from time to time. It does not matter that the company can deal with the assets without the chargee's permission. As the charge was a fixed charge, it did not need to be registered, and so the administrator would need leave of the court to sell the shares under the terms of the Insolvency Act 1986.

Comment
It is already established law that a licence to deal with charged property does not necessarily mean that the charge is a floating charge. It depends on the extent of the licence and also on the nature of the assets charged.

Re CIL Realisations Ltd [2000] 2 BCLC 361 Chancery Division (Hart J)

Is a charge over book debts a fixed or floating charge?

Facts
In 1994 the company borrowed money from the NDB Bank secured against debentures, which provided that all the company's book and other debts were the subject of a fixed charge in favour of the NDB Bank. The debenture further provided that the company was not entitled to deal or dispose of its assets without the debenture holder's written consent, and that all of the property not covered by a fixed charge would be covered by a floating charge. The company agreed to collect all the book debts owed to it and pay them into its account with the NDB Bank. At that time the company did not have a current account with the NDB Bank, so the NDB Bank instructed it to pay the moneys into its current account with the M bank until further notice. In 1995 the NDB Bank appointed a receiver, and in 1997 the company went into liquidation. The question arose as to whether the money in the M Bank was held subject to a fixed or a floating charge.

Held
Even where payments must be made into a designated bank account, if the company is then free to use the money without reference to the chargee, the charge will be floating and not fixed. Had the money been paid into the account with the NDB Bank it would have been the subject of a fixed charge.

Comment
This case considered the judgment in *Siebe Gorman* v *Barclays Bank Ltd* [1979] 2 Lloyd's Rep 142, distinguished the decision in *Re New Bullas Trading Ltd* [1994] 1 BCLC 449, and applied the decision in *Re Brightlife Ltd* [1986] BCLC 418.

OBP Textbook pages 163–169, section 7.2.

Registration and priority of charges

Barclays Bank plc v *Stuart London Ltd* [2001] 2 BCLC 316 Court of Appeal (Civil Division) (Chadwick and Peter Gibson LJJ)

Late registration of a charge and the protection of the parties involved

Facts

A company executed two charges in respect of the purchase of a property and a business. One charge was to the bank, and the second was to the vendor. The charge to the vendor provided that it would rank in priority after the charge to the bank. The charge to the vendor was registered within the 21-day time limit set by s395 Companies Act 1985: however, registration of the bank's charge was overlooked. Subsequently, when it became virtually certain that the company was going to wind up, the bank applied under s404 Companies Act 1985 to have the charge registered out of time. A district judge made an ex parte decision to allow the late registration, but made the order without prejudice to the rights acquired by the parties prior to the actual date of registration. The vendor then applied to vary the order, and the district judge commented that the order would be of very little benefit to the bank, as the liquidator would be sure to set it aside. The bank appealed.

Held

If other chargees have already agreed that their charges are to rank after a charge which was accidentally or inadvertently not registered, the court will preserve the contractually agreed priorities. In this case, the order of the district judge had given protection to unsecured creditors and had also protected the bank's interests. The appeal was allowed.

Comment

If a person acquired property, or a charge on it, on the express terms that the charge (not in fact registered) is to take priority over his interest, it preserves that priority in spite of the failure to register. There is a good article dealing with the late registration of charges entitled 'Late Registration of a Charge' in *Accountancy* December 2001, vol 1300, p82.

OBP Textbook pages 169–176, section 7.3.

Directors

Management of the company

Disqualification for unfitness

Secretary of State for Trade and Industry v *Creegan* [2002] 1 BCLC 99
Court of Appeal (Civil Division) (Potter and Ward LJJ, Sir Martin Nourse)

The test for unfitness is twofold

Facts
The respondent was employed as a warehouse manager by a company which went into liquidation in 1997, owing over £1 million. The shareholders and owners of the company bought an off-the-shelf company to carry on the business of the liquidated company, and the respondent was appointed as a director of the new company. Later in 1997, the respondent was removed as a director of the new company, which subsequently went into liquidation in 1998. An action was brought to disqualify the respondent under s6 Company Directors Disqualification Act 1986 on the grounds of his incompetent behaviour, causing the company to trade whilst it was insolvent. He was disqualified for two years.

Held
Unfitness (of directors) is not demonstrated merely by allowing a company to trade while knowing it to be insolvent: it must also be shown that the director knew, or ought to have known, that there was no reasonable prospect of meeting creditors' claims.

Comment
It is important to note that both elements of the test must be satisfied to show that a director is unfit to hold office.

Disqualification of directors

Re Cedarwood Productions Ltd (2001) The Times 12 July Court of Appeal (Civil Division) (Chadwick LJ and Rougier J)

Disqualification in relation to a criminal offence does not bar an action for disqualification for a civil matter

Facts
Two company directors, who had been disqualified for two years from acting as company directors as a result of criminal proceedings taken against them, applied to appeal against a decision of the Secretary of State to instigate further disqualification proceedings against them in the Companies Court. The disqualification in the criminal court was under s2 Company Directors Disqualification Act 1986. The Secretary of State was initiating proceedings under s6 Company Directors

Disqualification Act 1986 on the grounds that the directors were unfit to be directors.

Held

If a criminal court disqualifies as person under s2 Company Directors Disqualification Act 1986 after conviction for an offence in relation to a company, it is not necessarily an abuse of power to apply for a further disqualification order to be made against the same person under ss6 or 8 of the same Act based on their conduct while a director of the same company. The application was refused.

Comment

It is perhaps worth noting here that a disqualification order made as a result of a criminal action is penal in nature. An order made in civil proceedings under ss6 or 8 Company Directors Disqualification Act 1986 is made with the intention of protecting the public.

Re Hopes (Heathrow) Ltd [2001] 1 BCLC 575 Chancery Division (Companies Court) (Neuberger J)

Delaying payment to creditors – may amount to unfitness to hold office – may still be the case even if the company is solvent at the time

Facts

In July 1993 the appellant was appointed as the financial director and company secretary of Hopes (Heathrow) Ltd, a haulage company that had been trading for about six months. The managing director of the firm had committed several Road Traffic Act 1988 offences, and it was felt that he was no longer suitable to be a director of the company. He tendered his resignation in 1993, but rejoined the board in 1994. The company also owed the Inland Revenue large amounts of money. The appellant reached an agreement with the Inland Revenue that the sum could be paid off by instalments: however, the repayments were never made. In 1994 the company went into voluntary liquidation. The Secretary of State applied for a disqualification order under the Company Directors Disqualification Act 1986 against the appellant, on the grounds of non-repayment of money owed to the Inland Revenue, and the fact that he had stated that the managing director had resigned when he clearly had not. The Registrar disqualified the appellant for five years on the grounds of his improper conduct, even though the appellant was not cross-examined on certain relevant facts and issues.

Held

The findings of improper conduct were unjust, but that the appellant had still been careless and had behaved in an irresponsible manner. As a result, the period of disqualification was reduced to four years.

Comment

It would appear that, where a company adopts a policy of not paying creditors who do not press for payment, even though the company is solvent, this may still demonstrate that directors are unfit to hold office.

OBP Textbook pages 214–222, section 9.1.

Shadow directors

Secretary of State for Trade and Industry v Deverall [2001] Ch 340 Court of Appeal (Civil Division) (Morritt and Potter LJJ, Morison J)

Construction of s22(5) Company Directors Disqualification Act 1986 – definition of a shadow director

Facts

The judge at first instance did not make disqualification orders against two shadow directors of a company. On his construction of s22(5) Company Directors Disqualification Act 1986, the term 'advice' was not covered by the terms 'directions' and 'instructions' contained in that section. The Secretary of State for Trade and Industry appealed.

Held

The appeal was allowed as the judge at first instance had construed the legislation too strictly. In order to establish that a person is a shadow director of a company:

1. it is not necessary to show that the person gives directions or instructions on every matter on which the directors act, but it must be shown that the person has a real influence in the company's corporate affairs;
2. whether any particular communication should be classed as a direction or instruction is for the court to determine objectively;
3. advice (provided it is not professional advice) may be a direction or instruction;
4. it is not necessary to show that the directors adopted a subservient role or surrendered their discretion;
5. despite the use of the term 'shadow director', it is not necessary to characterise the person as 'lurking in the shadows': it is possible for a person to be a shadow director quite openly.

Comment

This case provides a very useful summary of the requirements for a shadow director.

OBP Textbook page 215, section 9.1.

Loans to directors

Ciro Citterio Menswear plc v Thakrar [2002] 1 WLR 2217 Chancery Division (Companies Court) (Anthony Mann QC)

Loan to a company director – not necessarily a misapplication of company funds giving rise to a constructive trust

Facts

N and K were shareholders and directors of the company. In 1999, N purchased a house for £562,000. Of this, £250,000 was borrowed from a building society and the balance came from funds paid by the company. This was reflected as debit entries for N's director's account with the company. The company went into administration and the liquidator claimed an interest in the house, on the grounds that N was a constructive trustee of the balance paid by the company.

Held

Under s341 Companies Act 1985, a loan by a company to a director in contravention of s330 Companies Act 1985 was voidable only, and therefore stood until it was avoided. It was not necessarily a misapplication of company funds, and so it did not give rise to a constructive trust.

Comment

There are some useful articles on the subject of constructive trusts and loans to directors to be found: see 'Expensive Holidays' in *Accountancy* October 2002, vol 1310, p108 and 'Illegal Loan to a Director: No Tracing to Property' in *Accountancy* October 2002, vol 1310, p84.

Currencies Direct Ltd v Ellis [2002] 1 BCLC 193 Queen's Bench Divisional Court (Gage J)

Directors' liabilities and the ability to recover illegal loans from directors

Facts

The defendant was a shareholder and former director of the claimant company, which dealt with foreign exchange. Between May 1997 and April 2000 he was forced out of the company. It was company policy to pay some personal expenses, such as credit card bills and school fees. However, to avoid the company becoming insolvent, the majority of these payments were shown as loans to the directors. When the defendant left, the company claimed repayment of the 'loan'. The defendant claimed that the monies had been paid by way of remuneration, and that if they had been a loan, the payment would have been illegal under s330 Companies Act 1985, and therefore unenforceable.

Held

Most of the sums had been paid by way of remuneration: however, where they did amount to a loan, that loan had been genuine and was to have been repaid out of future salaries.

Comment

There is a useful article on this subject: see 'Loans to a Company Director' in *Accountancy* June 2002, vol 1306, p89. What used to be called misfeasance reappears in s212 Insolvency Act 1986, giving a summary remedy against delinquent directors. For an example of this remedy, see *Re D'Jan of London Ltd* [1993] BCC 646.

OBP Textbook pages 227–228 and 345, sections 9.1 and 13.6.

Duties of directors

Director's fiduciary duty

Miller v Bain (Director's Breach of Duty) [2002] 1 BCLC 266 Chancery Division (Companies Court) (Richard Field QC sitting as Deputy Judge of the High Court)

Whether the claim by a liquidator against a director is time barred under the Limitation Act 1980

Facts

This was an action by the liquidator of Panetone 485 Ltd against a Mr Bain. Mr Bain was the owner and director of three companies and he caused one of the companies that he owned to incur a debt for the benefit of one of the other companies that he owned. The question arose as to whether the action by the liquidator against Mr Bain would be time barred under the Limitation Act 1980.

Held

Where an allegation is made that a director has acted in breach of his fiduciary duty, as happened in this case, the action will not be time barred under the Limitation Act 1980. A director in this situation is a trustee and therefore the claim by the liquidator falls within s21(1)(b) Limitation Act 1980. This principle applies where the director is a director of a group of companies where fiduciary duties are owed to each company in the group.

Comment

Directors owe fiduciary duties to their companies. If the company is solvent, then the directors must act in what they honestly believe to be the best interests of the present and future shareholders as a whole. They do no owe fiduciary duties to any particular section of members. When a company becomes insolvent, the directs owe fiduciary duties to the company's creditors and not to the shareholders. A person who is a director of a number of companies owes fiduciary duties to each company, as each one is a separate legal entity, and a director of one company is not entitled to sacrifice the interests of that company in favour of another company in a group of which he or she is also a director.

Peskin v *Anderson* [2001] 1 BCLC 372 Court of Appeal (Civil Division) (Mummery, Simon Brown and Latham LJJ)

No existence of special circumstances to justify the imposition of a duty for the directors to disclose information to previous shareholders of a company

Facts

RACL owned the RAC and a motoring services business called RACMS. Members of the RAC were also shareholders in RACL. In 1998, RACMS was sold and the existing RAC members received about £34,000 each. This caused difficulties with people who had recently ceased to be members of the RAC. Under the rules of the RAC, a member who resigned and was not expelled from the club might re-apply for membership within three years of their resignation, and could be re-elected without the need to be proposed and seconded. Ex-members of the club who fell within this three-year rule alleged that when the committee began to consider the sale of RACMS, they should have informed the former members, everyone of whom had received letters since their resignation reminding them that they could re-apply if they so wished. The judge at first instance dismissed the claim on the grounds that the directors of RACL did not owe any fiduciary duties to members who had resigned.

Held

In a judgment delivered by Mummery LJ, the directors did not owe a fiduciary duty to the shareholders or the claimants. It was not ultra vires for the directors to authorise the expenditure of company money to look at the proposals to sell off RACMS, nor were there any special circumstances that would justify the imposition of a duty of disclosure. The directors' actions were not linked to the claimants' decisions to resign.

Comment

It is difficult to see how any duty could have been owed to the shareholders by the directors, as the general rule is that a fiduciary duty is owed to the company. Although this is traditionally taken to mean the shareholders as a collective body, it refers only to present and future shareholders.

OBP Textbook pages 233–234 and 238, section 9.2.

Minority Protection

Rule in *Foss* v *Harbottle*

Voidable transactions and compensation

Day v *Cook* [2002] 1 BCLC 1 Court of Appeal (Civil Division) (Arden, Tuckley and Ward LJJ)

Is the loss recoverable by the shareholder or the company?

Facts

The claimant, Mr Day, was a businessman who, in 1987, owned 82 per cent of the shares in a company which had recently sold a nursing home business for £1.8 million. Mr Cook, the defendant, acted as Mr Day's solicitor. On Mr Cook's advice, Mr Day then made investments in certain new businesses, including a solicitor and estate agency business that Mr Cook was interested in. The investments went wrong and Mr Day sued Mr Cook for negligence. The judge at first instance held that Mr Cook had been negligent, but that as it was the company that had suffered the loss, the company was the proper plaintiff to the action and Mr Day could therefore recover only personal losses. The issue on appeal concerned where Mr Cook's duty lay.

Held

Where there was a breach of duty to the shareholder and the company, and the loss suffered by the shareholder was a reflection of the loss suffered by the company, the shareholder would not be able to recover. *Johnson* v *Gore Wood & Co (No 1)* [2002] 2 AC 1 had established that the company's claim would take precedence over the shareholder's claim unless the shareholder had incurred some additional loss.

Giles v *Rhind* [2001] 2 BCLC 582 Chancery Division (Blackburne J)

Damages reflective of a company's loss cannot be recovered by an individual shareholder

Facts

Mr Giles (G) and Mr Rhind (R) were directors and shareholders of Surrey Hills Food (SHF), a company that was formed in 1987. They each held just under 50 per cent of the issued shares. In 1990, the company restructured and G and R were left with about 20 per cent of the shareholding. G was the managing director of the company and R was its commercial director. In 1993, G and R fell out to the extent that R left the company and set up on his own. Several other members of staff joined R, and an important contract was also diverted to R's new company. SHF commenced proceedings against R but, before the matter was determined, SHF went into liquidation: the proceedings against R were accordingly discontinued because of a lack of funds. The administrator had also given an undertaking that SHF would not recommence the claim. In 1996, G recommenced proceedings against R, and the deputy judge held that R had used confidential information to take the important contract away from SHF and was therefore in breach of his duty of confidentiality.

Held
The damages claimed by Mr Giles were only reflective of the company's losses, so he could not sue for them personally.

Comment
This case demonstrates the logical extension of the rule in *Foss* v *Harbottle* (1843) 2 Hare 461 that where a wrong is done to a company, the company is the proper plaintiff.

Johnson v *Gore Wood & Co (No 1)* [2002] 2 AC 1 House of Lords (Lords Bingham of Cornhill, Cooke of Thorndon, Goff of Chieveley, Hutton and Millett)

Recoverable loss by shareholder – question of whether losses were due to the shareholder or the company

Facts
The plaintiff was a member of several companies which he used to run his businesses. He held all but two shares in W Ltd, a company that wanted to buy some land for the purposes of development. He instructed a firm of solicitors, the defendants, to act for W Ltd in the proposed purchase. The purchase was very long and drawn out and eventually resulted in an order for specific performance being made against the vendor of the land. By then, W Ltd had suffered substantial losses as a result of the court hearings leading to the grant of the order for specific performance and the collapse of the property market. In 1991, W Ltd commenced proceedings against the defendant solicitors for professional negligence. The plaintiff also had a personal claim against the solicitors arising from the same matter, but he intended to pursue that at a later date. W Ltd's claim was eventually settled during the trial. In 1993, the plaintiff issued proceedings against the defendants for his personal claim. In 1997, the defendants applied for the action to be struck out as an abuse of process, and they questioned whether they owed the plaintiff any duty of care.

Held
The action by the plaintiff did not constitute an abuse of process. When deciding whether a claim should have been brought in earlier proceedings, the court should adopt a broad merits-based approach. On an application to strike out damages claimed by a shareholder, the court should scrutinise pleadings carefully to see if the losses were due to the shareholder or the company. In this case, the majority of the losses claimed by the plaintiff were recoverable, as they did not merely reflect the loss that had been suffered by W Ltd.

Comment

Although this is a case that is concerned mainly with civil procedure, it has been included because of the comparison with *Giles* v *Rhind* [2001] 2 BCLC 582 on the matter of recoverable losses. It also contains an interesting discussion about estoppel. Lord Bingham was of the opinion that the test required to establish estoppel was that given by Lord Denning in *Amalgamated Investment & Property Co Ltd (In Liquidation)* v *Texas Commerce International Bank Ltd* [1982] QB 84. Lord Goff was of the opinion that it is not possible to adopt common criteria for the various forms of estoppel.

OBP Textbook pages 263–264, section 11.1.

Statutory rights of a minority

Statutory protection of minorities

Re Guidezone Ltd [2000] 2 BCLC 321 Chancery Division (Companies Court) (Jonathan Parker J)

Section 459 Companies Act 1985 – the definition of unfairness

Facts

A family company which owned and ran a hotel had four directors: the father of the family and his three sons. Each director held 25 per cent of the shares. One of the sons was the managing director of the hotel and he fell seriously ill. On his recovery, he wanted to sell the hotel and distribute the proceeds among the shareholders. The rest of the family did not agree and wanted to keep the hotel. The son issued a petition under s459 Companies Act 1985, because he understood that the hotel was acquired on the basis that he would have the final say in what happened to it.

Held

Unfairness for the purposes of s459 Companies Act 1985 was not to be judged by reference to subjective notions of fairness, but rather by testing whether, applying established equitable principles, the majority had acted in a manner which equity would regard as contrary to good faith. This was a case of a quasi-partnership company in which exclusion of a minority from participation in the management of the company provided clear evidence of conduct which would be regarded as contrary to good faith. Unfairness for the purposes of s459 might also occur when an event occurred which put an end to the basis on which the parties had entered into an agreement with each other, making it unfair that one shareholder should insist on continuing the arrangement. Taking into consideration all the facts, there was no unfairness in this case.

Comment

The case of *Ebrahimi* v *Westbourne Galleries Ltd* [1973] AC 360 comes up for consideration again. *Guidezone* deals with exclusion from management and the issues of quasi-partnership companies. See also *O'Neill* v *Phillips* [1999] BCC 600, an important case which considers shareholders' agreements and s459 Companies Act 1985.

OBP Textbook pages 271–282, section 11.2.

Insolvency

Introduction

The fee structure of the insolvency regime is being modernised, with the intention of ensuring increased transparency and simplicity. Implementation of the measures contained in the Enterprise Act 2002 is subject to commencement orders. The secondary legislation on insolvency is expected to be started early in the 2003 financial year, and the changes to the Insolvency Service's financial regime are expected to come into force early in the 2004 financial year. This will provide time for the necessary changes to the infrastructure to be made, and any relevant staff training to be carried out.

OBP Textbook page 308, section 13.1.

Company voluntary arrangements

Inland Revenue Commissioners v Adam & Partners Ltd [2001] 1 BCLC 222 Court of Appeal (Civil Division) (Mummery, Gibson and Latham LJJ)

Valid imposition of a voluntary arrangement

Facts
The majority of the creditors of A Ltd approved a voluntary arrangement with the company. The Inland Revenue, which was a preferential unsecured creditor of A Ltd, challenged this approval.

Held
As a majority of the creditors had approved the arrangement, it had been validly approved. In effect the scheme imposed a moratorium, but the creditors were not prevented from pursuing their contractual rights when the moratorium came to an end.

Comment
The Insolvency Act 2000 introduces a moratorium in company voluntary arrangements that are proposed by the company's directors (but not administrators or liquidators). This procedure is limited to small companies according to the accountancy definition.

Enterprise Act 2002

The Enterprise Act 2002, which contains provisions to modernise insolvency law in the areas of both company insolvency and individual bankruptcy, received Royal Assent on 7 November 2002. The 2002 Act makes provision for improving the rescue procedure of viable companies, and where this is not possible, the achievement of a better result for the company's creditors as a whole than was previously the case under the insolvency legislation. The 2002 Act streamlines the administration procedure by removing the need for a court hearing for floating charge holders and companies making an application for an administration order. The aim of this is to make an application for an administration order more widely accessible and successful.

To aid the opening up of the administration procedure, the use of administrative receivership is to be restricted. Precipitate and excessive use of the administrative receivership procedure is seen as being a major cause of the failure of the rescue provisions in the Insolvency Act 1986. The administrative receiver represents only the interests of the appointing floating charge holder, and not the interests of the creditors generally. The administration procedure is a collective procedure which takes account of the interests of all the creditors.

OBP Textbook pages 311–313, section 13.1.

Compulsory liquidation

Attorney-General's Reference (No 7 of 2000) [2001] 1 WLR 1879 Court of Appeal (Criminal Division) (Rose LJ, Rosier and McCombe JJ)

Use in a second trial of evidence given to the official receiver under compulsion

Facts
A defendant was declared bankrupt, owing money to his former employer. He was under a duty under s291(1)(a) and (b) Insolvency Act 1986 to deliver up to the official receiver possession of his estate and all books and papers relating to it. Because of the answers he gave under compulsion to the official receiver he was subsequently charged with another offence.

The question for reference was whether the use by the prosecution of the documents delivered up to the official receiver, under compulsion, violated his rights under art 6 European Convention on Human Rights 1950.

Held
No, it did not. The privilege against self-incrimination was not absolute. Documents obtained under compulsion are admissible as a matter of English law, subject to the trial judge's discretion to exclude them on the grounds of fairness under s78 Police and Criminal Evidence Act 1984.

Re Bellmex International Ltd (In Liquidation) [2001] 1 BCLC 91
Chancery Division (Evans-Lombe J)

Directors – not entitled to rely on the privilege against self-incrimination

Facts
The company, a wholesaler and distributor of cigarettes, entered into a contract with a tobacco company for the supply of cigarettes. The tobacco company supplied some cigarettes from Zimbabwe and some from South Africa. Because of an international convention on tariffs, the cigarettes imported from Zimbabwe received more favourable financial treatment than those from South Africa. The company went into liquidation, leaving unsecured creditors out of pocket to the sum of £4.5 million, and the liquidator applied for an order under s236 Insolvency Act 1986 requiring the regional manager for Africa of British American Tobacco to attend a private examination, as he was responsible for a transaction which produced a debt.

Held
It was for the creditor to justify his claim. In this case it seemed clear that the unsecured creditors would receive nothing, as the assets of the company were worth no more than £500: it was not apparent what an order under s236 would achieve.

Comment
A director of a company is not entitled to rely on the privilege against self-incrimination to refuse to answer questions put to him by the provisional liquidators under ss235–236 Insolvency Act 1986, but such privilege is available to a fiduciary from whom the principal is seeking information about dealings with trust money under the general law.

OBP Textbook page 323, section 13.3.

Assets and liabilities in liquidation

The Crown's preferential rights to recover unpaid taxes ahead of other creditors is abolished in the new legislation, with the intention of giving a real benefit to unsecured creditors, many of whom will be small firms.

OBP Textbook pages 335–336, section 13.5.

5

Conflict of Laws

Preliminary Topics

Public international law and the conflict of laws

Kuwait Airways Corp v *Iraqi Airways Co (No 3)* [2002] 3 All ER 209
House of Lords (Lords Nicholls of Birkenhead, Steyn, Hoffmann, Hope of
Craighead and Scott of Foscote)

Conflict of laws – foreign law in breach of international law – whether English court
should recognise or refuse recognition in view of breach of international law

Facts
The facts of this case are the same as *Kuwait Airways Corp* v *Iraqi Airways Co (No
2)* (1998) The Times 12 May and *Kuwait Airways Corp Co* v *Iraqi Airways Co (No
1)* [1995] 3 All ER 694. Briefly, it related to the seizure of aircraft belonging to the
plaintiffs by the Iraqi government, which subsequently allowed the defendants to
incorporate the aircraft by way of a legislative decree. In the first case, the House of
Lords agreed that the seizure of the aircraft was in the exercise of sovereign
authority. In the second case, it was held that the defendants could rely on the
defence of state immunity. The second case also illustrated the relationship between
state immunity and the principle of non-justicability. In the present case the trial
concerned issues relating to quantum of damages. The judge at first instance held
that the claimant would have suffered the losses claimed even if the defendant had
not wrongfully interfered with the aircraft and accordingly the action was dismissed.
On appeal, the Court of Appeal reversed that decision and held that the claimant
was entitled to recover for all losses except under one head. The defendant appealed
to the House of Lords.

Held (Lord Scott of Foscote dissenting)
Appeal dismissed. The main issue was whether an English court was entitled to
refuse recognition of foreign law on the grounds of breach of international law, as
well as whether the non-recognition extended to both limbs of the rule of double
actionability in tort. Their Lordships noted that whilst the seizure of the aircraft
could be described as an act of state, thereby attracting the defence of state
immunity, the subsequent passing of a legislative decree to enable the Iraqi Airways
Corporation to incorporate the seized aircraft could not be seen nor accepted as an
exercise of sovereign authority and consequently did not attract the state immunity

defence. This, the Court held, amounted to a breach of an established principle of international law. As a result, in the interest of public policy, the English court would decline to recognise the decree or resolution as being effective so as to divest Kuwaiti Airways of its title to the seized aircraft. As the resolution itself is disregarded, there was no necessity to ensure compliance with the double actionability rule.

OBP Textbook page 43, section 2.5.

Jurisdiction in Personam

Actions in personam where the defendant is 'domiciled' in the EC

Weber v *Universal Ogden Services Ltd* [2002] 3 WLR 931 European Court of Justice

Conflict of laws – contract – determination of appropriate forum – jurisdiction under the Brussels Convention

Facts
The claimant, a cook of German nationality, was employed by the defendant, a Scottish company. Throughout the claimant's employment, which spanned a period of six years, the claimant had worked in various places, as required by the defendants. These places included on board ships or drilling rigs operating on or over the Netherlands continental shelf, as well as on board a floating crane in Danish territorial waters. As a result of a dispute in connection with the employment contract, the claimant initiated an action in the Netherlands. The Dutch lower courts accepted jurisdiction in the first instance, but on appeal to the Dutch Court of Appeal it was held that a decision could not be reached without first obtaining a preliminary ruling from the European Court of Justice (ECJ) in relation to two issues. First, whether the work carried out on or above the Netherlands continental shelf was to be regarded as work carried out in the Netherlands and, second, how in the circumstances the place whose courts had jurisdiction under art 5(1) of the Brussels Convention on Jurisdiction and the Enforcement of Judgments in Civil and Commercial Matters 1968 was to be determined.

Held
The ECJ in ruling on the reference held that: first, the work carried out on or above the part of the continental shelf was to be treated as work carried out in the territory of that state; and, second, for the purpose of art 5(1) of the Convention the place of performance of the contract, either wholly or substantially, would determine the issue of jurisdiction.

Comment
In arriving at its decision the ECJ appears to have consulted the following cases

(which also raised the question of the determination of the place of performance of the employment contract in situations where the employee carries out work in different jurisdictions): *Six Constructions Ltd* v *Humbert* Case 32/88 [1989] ECR 341, *Mulox IBC Ltd* v *Geels* Case C–125/92 [1993] ECR I–4075 and *Rutten* v *Cross Medical Ltd* Case C–383/95 [1997] ICR 715. In all three cases it follows that art 5(1) must be interpreted as meaning that, as regards contracts of employment, the place of performance of the relevant obligation, for the purposes of that provision, is the place where the employee actually performs the work covered by the contract with his employer. The consistency of these cases was recently affirmed by the ECJ in *GIE Groupe Concorde* v *Master of the Vessel Suhadiwarno Panjan* [1999] ECR I–6307. The ECJ in the instant case (*Weber*) stressed the importance of avoiding any multiplication of courts having jurisdiction in order to preclude the risk of irreconcilable decisions. Accordingly, they found that art 5(1) cannot be interpreted as conferring concurrent jurisdictions on the courts of each contracting state in whose territory the employee performs part of his work.

OBP Textbook page 92, section 4.3.

Henderson v *Jaouen and Another* [2002] 1 WLR 2971 Court of Appeal (Peter Gibson and Mantell LJJ, Wall J)

Conflict of laws – tort – place of harmful event – jurisdiction under the Brussels Convention – whether English court has locus

Facts
The claimant was a victim of a road accident caused by the first defendant, in France. The accident occurred in 1978 at which time the claimant was residing in France. He successfully sued the defendant and his insurers, the second defendants, in France, and obtained compensation. The French court also granted the claimant a right to seek a further award in the event of a subsequent deterioration in his condition which would give rise to a French law cause of action known as 'cas d'aggravation'. Since obtaining compensation in 1983 the claimant had lived in England. In 1995 the claimant, through French lawyers, issued fresh proceedings in France on the basis of 'cas d'aggravation' and in 1996 a provisional payment was made. The claimant, however, did not pursue the matter before the French tribunal but decided to issue, in May 2000, a claim in the Queen's Bench Division, arguing that the English court had jurisdiction because his condition had deteriorated whilst he was residing in England and therefore England was the place where the requisite 'harmful event' took place. At first instance the Master held that the English courts did possess sufficient jurisdiction. The defendants appealed.

Held
Appeal allowed. The 'harmful event' in art 5(3) of the Brussels Convention on Jurisdiction and the Enforcement of Judgments in Civil and Commercial Matters 1968 was the original event that took place in France in 1978 and, as such, the

aggravation was not a fresh wrong but a worsening of his condition deriving directly from the original wrong.

Comment

First, it is noteworthy that the Court of Appeal, in allowing the defendants' appeal, refused permission for a further appeal to the House of Lords by the respondents in this case.

The Master (in the first instance) was clearly influenced by the decision of the ECJ in *Handelswekerij G J Bier BV* v *Mines de Potasse* Case 21/76 [1978] QB 708, on the basis that France was the place which gave rise to the origin of the case or the damage, whilst England was the place where the subsequent damage occurred.

The Court of Appeal, however, sought to distinguish the *Bier* case ad held that the *Bier* case should apply to situations where the 'harmful event' in question is unclear, for example, to cases which involve water or atmospheric pollution beyond the frontiers of a state.

For the present purpose, it is very clear that the accident was the main cause of the plaintiff's suffering, and the accident took place in France. The worsening of his condition is, therefore, not a new cause, but a related and consequential cause of action which must therefore be followed up in France where the initial case was decided.

OBP Textbook page 100, section 4.3.

Forum conveniens

Donoghue v *Armco Inc and Others* [2002] 1 All ER 748 House of Lords (Lords Bingham of Cornhill, Mackay of Clashfern, Nicholls of Birkenhead, Hobhouse of Woodborough and Scott of Foscote)

Conflict of laws – restraint of foreign proceedings – circumstances in which the court will award restraint – the 'proper' forum

Facts

The claimant worked for the defendants, a conglomerate based in the United States. The claimant was based in New York where he was named as one of the defendants in an action for contractual fraud initiated by Armco Incorporated, the respondents in this case. The fraud case was filed in New York. The case concerned three key contracts which contained exclusive jurisdiction clauses which provided that the parties irrevocably submit themselves to the jurisdiction of the English courts in settling any dispute which may arise out of, or in connection with, the contracts. Accordingly, the claimant applied for an anti-suit injunction under s37(1) of the Supreme Court Act 1981. The issue was whether the English court should grant the anti-suit injunction in respect of the New York proceedings. The judge at first instance refused the injunction. On appeal the Court of Appeal exercised its discretion in favour of the injunction. The defendant appealed to the House of Lords.

Held

Appeal allowed. In allowing the appeal their Lordships held that notwithstanding the exclusive jurisdiction clause (which ordinarily would have a binding effect), the court could deny an injunction or a stay of proceedings. This is purely to prevent parallel proceedings which would lead to the possibility of inconsistent decisions. This is so, particularly where the interests of the parties (other than the parties who are bound by the exclusive jurisdiction clause) are not directly related to the subject matter of the clause in issue.

Comment

The student is invited to revisit the Privy Council's decision in *Société National Industrielle Aerospatiale* v *Lee Kui Jak* [1987] AC 871, wherein the Privy Council laid down several propositions about the way in which the issue of 'controversial' jurisdictions should be decided.

Turner v *Grovit and Others* [2002] 1 All ER 960 House of Lords (Lords Nicholls of Birkenhead, Hoffmann, Hobhouse of Woodborough, Millett and Scott of Foscote)

Conflict of laws – jurisdiction – challenge to jurisdiction – whether English court has jurisdiction to grant anti-suit injunction in respect of proceedings in a foreign state

Facts

The claimant was working as a solicitor for a group of companies but had a contract of employment with an Irish member of the group based in London. When asked to relocate to Madrid from London, the claimant resigned and claimed constructive dismissal in England. At the same time, the Spanish member of the group sued the claimant in Spain for a breach of contract. The claimant therefore applied under s37(1) of the Supreme Court Act 1981 for an anti-suit injunction in respect of the proceedings in Spain. At first instance, the application was refused. The claimant then successfully appealed to the Court of Appeal. The defendants appealed to the House of Lords.

Held

The House of Lords have referred the matter to the European Court of Justice (ECJ) for a preliminary ruling as to whether the grant of an anti-suit injunction would be consistent with the Brussels Convention on Jurisdiction and the Enforcement of Judgments in Civil and Commercial Matters 1968 as set out in Sch 1 to the Civil Jurisdiction and Judgments Act 1982.

Comment

Whilst their Lordships undoubtedly have the wisdom and experience of deciding as to whether or not to grant an anti-suit injunction in respect of foreign proceedings (as they have shown on past occasions), the fact that they have, however, referred the case to the ECJ for a preliminary ruling on this point indicates two things. One is the maintenance of consistency in the making of decisions, both on a national as well as a Community level, and the other is to avoid the absurdity that would result if multiple courts possessing similar powers or competent jurisdiction are recognised in relation to a case or a series of connected cases. It is evident that their Lordships are eminently attempting to preclude the risk of irreconcilable decisions.

It would be interesting to read the findings of the ECJ.

OBP Textbook page 132, section 4.4.

Choice of Law in Contract

Choice of law

Ennstone Building Products Ltd v *Stanger Ltd* [2002] 1 WLR 3059 Court of Appeal (Potter and Keene LJJ)

Choice of law – contract – proper law – whether contract is governed by English or Scottish law

Facts ·
The claimant supplied stone for use in building work and the defendant provided testing and consultancy services. The claimant had contracted with the defendant to investigate the staining of a stone that it had supplied for a building. Both companies operated in England as well as Scotland and there was no choice of law clause in the contract, although both parties anticipated that the contract would be performed in Scotland. The defendant carried out the required testing and investigation and made some recommendations to the claimant. When the claimant followed the recommendations of the defendant, the problem was exacerbated. The claimant alleged that the defendant was both negligent and in breach of contract in failing to exercise due care and skill. The Technology and Construction Court in Birmingham, where the action was initially heard, held that the contract was governed by Scottish law. The claimant appealed to the Court of Appeal.

Held
Appeal allowed. The proper law of the contract was that of English law.

Comment
The principle issue in this case was whether English law could be said to be the proper law governing the contract between the parties. As the contract did not include an express choice of law or a choice that could be inferred, the Contracts (Applicable Law) Act 1990 deserves to be examined, especially Sch 1 art 3.

Although the Rome Convention on the Law Applicable to Contractual

Obligations 1980 has been subject to criticism in recent times as being unclear, the learned judges nevertheless referred to art 4 of the Rome Convention which basically stipulates that the applicable law is to be the law of the country with which the contract is most closely connected. The presumption raised by art 4(2) could not be rebutted owing to the insufficient linkage with Scotland and, accordingly, the proper law of the contract was that of England.

OBP Textbook page 155, section 5.2.

Choice of Law in Tort

Choice of law

Ennstone Building Products Ltd v *Stanger Ltd* [2002] 1 WLR 3059 Court of Appeal (Potter and Keene LJJ)

Choice of law – tort – issue of place where tort was committed – whether claim in tort is governed by English law

Facts
As per the contract case (above).

Held
Appeal allowed. The act or omission complained of constituted an English tort so English law would therefore apply.

The Court (rightly so) held that although the investigating and testing was done in Scotland, the fundamental feature of what the defendant was to do was advising on the problem of staining, and since that advice was received in England the alleged tort was English. It was only on receipt of the advice that the proposed recommendations were put into practice. Hence, the material issue is the advice.

Comment
This decision is consistent with the decision in *Metall und Rohstoff AG* v *Donaldson Lufkin and Jenrette Inc* [1990] 1 QB 391. Similarly, the court held in *Diamond* v *Bank of London and Montreal* [1979] QB 333 that where the tort consists in essence of the giving of negligent advice, that tort is committed where the advice is received. The overriding consideration in matters involving choice of law with respect to tort is, as always, provided by the case of *Boys* v *Chaplin* [1971] AC 356.

OBP Textbook page 183, section 6.4.

Private International Law (Miscellaneous Provisions) Act 1995

Roerig v *Valiant Trawlers Ltd* [2002] 1 All ER 961 Court of Appeal (Simon Brown, Waller and Sedley LJJ)

Conflict of laws – assessment of damages in tort – whether Dutch law or English law more appropriate

Facts

The claimant was a Dutch national who brought the action as a dependant of her husband, a Dutchman who was tragically killed whilst working on an English registered trawler which was owned by the defendants, an English company. There was no dispute in relation to liability. The only issue which the defendants contended were that damages should be assessed according to Dutch law and not English law. The court at first instance held that English law was the proper law to be used for the purpose of assessment of damages. The defendants appealed to the Court of Appeal.

Held

Appeal dismissed. The proper law of the tort was English law.

In deciding the issue, Waller LJ consulted the Private International Law (Miscellaneous Provisions) Act 1995, of which s11 provided that:

> 'The general rule is that the applicable law is the law of the country in which the events constituting the tort or delict in question occur.'

Since the accident occurred on the English-registered trawler, the governing law should clearly be English law. The defendants' attempt to rely on s12 of the 1995 Act, which has the effect of displacing the general rule in s11, was firmly rejected by Waller LJ. The law of lex loci was therefore strictly enforced in the absence of the defendants establishing a significant connection between it and the tort.

OBP Textbook page 187, section 6.7.

Recognition and Enforcement of Foreign Judgments

Judgments rendered within the EC

TSN Kunststoffrecycling GmbH v *Jurgens* [2002] 1 WLR 2459 Court of Appeal (Robert Walker, Rix and Dyson LJJ)

Conflict of laws – recognition of foreign judgment – whether foreign judgment registered in English court can be set aside

Facts

In 1998 the claimant, a German company, initiated proceedings in a German court against the defendant who was a Dutch national and who was residing in England. The defendant was served with notice of the proceedings at his home in England and failed to enter a notice of appearance or intention to defend. Accordingly, judgment in default was entered against the defendant by the German court after the 14-day period to file the response had expired. The claimant then applied to register the judgment in England for enforcement purposes. The defendant applied to set aside registration of the judgment but the court refused it. The defendant then appealed that he was not given sufficient time to file his response, and that the exception provided by art 27(2) of the Brussels Convention on Jurisdiction and the Enforcement of Judgments in Civil and Commercial Matters 1968 was satisfied.

Held
Appeal dismissed. Decision of the court of first instance affirmed.

The Court was of the opinion that the 14-day period to file a response was indeed more than sufficient because all the defendant needs to do is to merely enter an appearance which would in fact prevent the issue of judgment by default. Once that is done, the defendant is entitled to apply to the court for extension of time provided the application for extension is appropriately substantiated with strong grounds. The court may exercise its discretion to grant the extension if it is fair and justified under the circumstances. In this instance, however, the defendant did absolutely nothing.

The Court held that in order to do justice both to the need to protect the defendant's right to a fair hearing and to the underlying purpose of the Brussels Convention to ensure the free movement of judgments between contracting states, the exception provided by art 27(2) should not be expanded further than is reasonably necessary.

OBP Textbook page 237, section 8.3.

Maronier v *Larmer* [2002] 3 WLR 1060 Court of Appeal (Lord Phillips MR, Robert Walker and Clarke LJJ)

Conflict of laws – foreign judgments on action brought in Netherlands stayed by claimant – reactivated after 12 years – new judgment obtained and registered in England – whether judgment should be recognised – whether it should be set aside

Facts
The claimant, who was a Dutch national, brought an action in 1984 against the defendant, a dental surgeon, for negligent treatment in 1983. The defendant filed a defence but the claimant applied for a stay of proceedings in 1986. The defendant moved to the UK in 1991 but left his address in England with the Dutch authorities. The claimant, after 12 years, decided to revive the action and pursued the claim in 1998. The defendant's solicitors withdrew as they had lost contact with him. The defendant was never contacted by the claimant nor the Dutch court. The Dutch court gave judgment to the claimant in December 1999. The judgment was

registered in the High Court in London in July 2000. The defendant had by this time lost his right to appeal. The defendant, nonetheless, appealed against the registration of the judgment in the English court by the claimant and the appeal was allowed by the Deputy Master. The claimant appealed to a High Court judge, who affirmed the decision of the Queen's Bench Division. The claimant then appealed to the Court of Appeal.

Held

Appeal dismissed. The Court evidently gave due regard to the Brussels Convention on Jurisdiction and the Enforcement of Judgments in Civil and Commercial Matters 1968 which has the force of law in the UK by virtue of the provisions of s2 of the Civil Jurisdiction and Judgments Act 1982. Article 27 of the Convention states that:

> 'A judgment shall not be recognised:
> 1. if such recognition is contrary to public policy in the state in which recognition is sought;
> 2. where it was given in default of appearance, if the defendant was not duly served with the document which instituted the proceedings or with an equivalent document in sufficient time to enable him to arrange for his defence ...'

Clearly the irregularities of the case fall within the above and, in the circumstances, the Court was correct to conclude as it did.

OBP Textbook page 240, section 8.3.

6

Constitutional Law

The Sovereignty of Parliament

Constitutional statute: implied repeal

Thoburn v *Sunderland City Council; Hunt* v *Hackney London Borough Council; Harman and Another* v *Cornwall County Council; Collins* v *Sutton London Borough Council* (2002) The Times 22 February Queen's Bench Divisional Court (Laws LJ and Crane J)

European Communities Act 1972 – constitutional statute – no implied repealed – effect of Weights and Measures Act 1985

Facts

The Weights and Measures Act 1963 had permitted the sale of goods in imperial units. A provision known as a 'Henry VIII' clause was contained in s8(2) of the 1963 Act conferring a power on the relevant minister to amend the statute itself. Section 2 of the European Communities Act 1972 also created a Henry VIII power enabling any designated minister, by way of regulations, to make provision for the purpose of implementing any Community obligation of the United Kingdom – ie this extended to the power to amend primary legislation. The Metrication Directive (Council Directive 80/181/EEC (as amended)) permitted the use of imperial units for the sale of loose goods from bulk until 31 December 1999. Thereafter metric units would have to be used if criminal liability was to be avoided.

The Weights and Measures Act 1985 was enacted as a consolidating statute which preserved the Henry VIII power provided for in the 1963 Act. Various statutory instruments were introduced to give effect to the Metrication Directive: see the Weights and Measures Act 1985 (Metrication) (Amendment) Order 1994 and the Units of Measurement Regulations 1994. The position was, therefore, that although the 1985 Act consolidated the legality of using imperial units, the delegated legislation introduced to give effect to EC law amended the 1985 Act so as to make the use of imperial units unlawful after a specified period.

All but one of the appellants were market traders convicted of offences contrary to the Weights and Measures Act 1985 and Orders made thereunder. The offences arose out of the appellants' continued practice of selling loose fruit and vegetables in imperial units. Collins appealed by way of cases stated against the dismissal by Sutton Justices of his appeal against conditions imposed upon the renewal of his street trading licence.

The appellants contended that the 1985 Act had impliedly repealed the European Communities Act (ECA) 1972 to the extent that the latter empowered the making of any provision by way of subordinate legislation, whether so as to amend primary legislation or otherwise, which would be inconsistent with s1 of the Weights and Measures Act 1985.

Their argument was that s1 of the 1985 Act must be taken to have forbidden any amendment by means of s2(2) of the 1972 Act which would prohibit the continued use of imperial and metric measures: they were inconsistent with and repugnant to the terms of s1 as enacted and were therefore unlawful. They were not authorised by s2(2) ECA 1972 as impliedly amended.

In particular it was contended that the Henry VIII power could only be used to amend existing legislation (ie that enacted prior to the 1972 Act coming into effect) and not later Acts.

Held

The appeals were dismissed. There was in fact no inconsistency between the terms of the 1985 Act and the 1972 Act, hence no implied appeal argument arose in this case. A Henry VIII power could extend to future legislation, thus limiting the scope for the application of the doctrine of implied repeal. The ECA 1972 belonged to a category of 'constitutional' statutes and as could not be impliedly repealed.

Laws LJ:

'The common law has in recent years allowed, or rather created, exceptions to the doctrine of implied repeal: a doctrine which was always the common law's own creature. There are now classes or types of legislative provision which cannot be repealed by mere implication. These instances are given, and can only be given, by our own courts, to which the scope and nature of Parliamentary sovereignty are ultimately confided. The courts may say – have said – that there are certain circumstances in which the legislature may only enact what it desires to enact if it does so by express, or at any rate specific, provision. The courts have in effect so held in the field of European law itself, in the *Factortame* case, and this is critical for the present discussion. By this means, as I shall seek to explain, the courts have found their way through the impasse seemingly created by two supremacies, the supremacy of European law and the supremacy of Parliament.

The present state of our domestic law is such that substantive Community rights prevail over the express terms of any domestic law, including primary legislation, made or passed after the coming into force of the ECA [European Communities Act], even in the face of plain inconsistency between the two. This is the effect of *Factortame (No 1)* [1990] 2 AC 85. ...

... It seems to me that there is no doubt but that in *Factortame (No 1)* the House of Lords effectively accepted that s2(4) could not be impliedly repealed, albeit the point was not argued ... Where does this leave the constitutional position which I have stated? ... In the present state of its maturity the common law has come to recognise that there exist rights which should properly be classified as constitutional or fundamental. ... And from this a further insight follows. We should recognise a hierarchy of Acts of Parliament: as it were "ordinary" statutes and "constitutional" statutes. The two categories must be distinguished on a principled basis. In my opinion a constitutional statute is one which (a) conditions the legal relationship between citizen and State in some general, overarching manner, or (b) enlarges or diminishes the scope of what we would now regard as fundamental constitutional rights. (a) and (b) are of necessity closely related: it is difficult to think of an instance of (a) that is not also an instance of (b). The special status of constitutional statutes follows the special status of constitutional rights. Examples are the Magna Carta, the Bill of Rights 1689, the Act of Union, the Reform Acts which distributed and enlarged the franchise, the HRA, the Scotland Act 1998 and the Government of Wales Act 1998. The ECA clearly belongs in this family. It incorporated the whole corpus of substantive Community rights and obligations, and gave overriding domestic effect to the judicial and administrative machinery of Community law. It may be there has never been a statute having such profound effects on so many dimensions of our daily lives. The ECA is, by force of the common law, a constitutional statute.

Ordinary statutes may be impliedly repealed. Constitutional statutes may not. For the repeal of a constitutional Act or the abrogation of a fundamental right to be effected by statute, the court would apply this test: is it shown that the legislature's actual – not imputed, constructive or presumed – intention was to effect the repeal or abrogation? I think the test could only be met by express words in the later statute, or by words so specific that the inference of an actual determination to effect the result contended for was irresistible. The ordinary rule of implied repeal does not satisfy this test. Accordingly, it has no application to constitutional statutes. I should add that in my judgment general words could not be supplemented, so as to effect a repeal or significant amendment to a constitutional statute, by reference to what was said in Parliament by the minister promoting the Bill pursuant to *Pepper* v *Hart* [1993] AC 593. A constitutional statute can only be repealed, or amended in a way which significantly affects its provisions touching fundamental rights or otherwise the relation between citizen and State, by unambiguous words on the face of the later statute.

This development of the common law regarding constitutional rights, and as I would say constitutional statutes, is highly beneficial. It gives us most of the benefits of a written constitution, in which fundamental rights are accorded special respect. But it preserves the sovereignty of the legislature and the flexibility of our uncodified constitution. It accepts the relation between legislative supremacy and fundamental rights is not fixed or brittle: rather the courts (in interpreting statutes, and now, applying the HRA) will pay more or less deference to the legislature, or other public decision-maker, according to the subject in hand. Nothing is plainer than that this benign development involves, as I have said, the recognition of the ECA as a constitutional statute. ...

In my judgment (as will by now be clear) the correct analysis of that relationship involves and requires these following four propositions. (1) All the specific rights and obligations which EU law creates are by the ECA incorporated into our domestic law and rank supreme: that is, anything in our substantive law inconsistent with any of these rights and obligations is abrogated or must be modified to avoid the inconsistency. This is true even where the inconsistent municipal provision is contained in primary legislation. (2) The ECA is a constitutional statute: that is, it cannot be impliedly repealed. (3) The truth of (2) is derived, not from EU law, but purely from the law of England: the common law recognises a category of constitutional statutes. (4) The fundamental legal basis of the United Kingdom's relationship with the EU rests with the domestic, not the European, legal powers. In the event, which no doubt would never happen in the real world, that a European measure was seen to be repugnant to a fundamental or constitutional right guaranteed by the law of England, a question would arise whether the general words of the ECA were sufficient to incorporate the measure and give it overriding effect in domestic law. But that is very far from this case.

I consider that the balance struck by these four propositions gives full weight both to the proper supremacy of Community law and to the proper supremacy of the United Kingdom Parliament. By the former, I mean the supremacy of substantive Community law. By the latter, I mean the supremacy of the legal foundation within which those substantive provisions enjoy their primacy. The former is guaranteed by propositions (1) and (2). The latter is guaranteed by propositions (3) and (4). If this balance is understood, it will be seen that these two supremacies are in harmony, and not in conflict. [The argument put forward by Counsel for the appellant Collins] is wrong because it would undermine the first supremacy; [the argument put forward by counsel for Sunderland is wrong] because it would undermine the second.'

As to the effect of EC membership on parliamentary sovereignty Laws LJ observed:

'[The argument put forward by counsel for Sunderland] ... appears to me to entail the proposition that the legislative and judicial institutions of the EU may set limits to the power of Parliament to make laws which regulate the legal relationship between the EU and the United Kingdom ... [this submission forgets] ... the constitutional place in our law of the rule that Parliament cannot bind its successors, which is the engine of the doctrine of implied repeal. Here is her argument's bare logic. (1) The ECA incorporated the law of the EU into the law of England. (2) The law of the EU includes the entrenchment of its own supremacy as an autonomous legal order, and the prohibition of its abrogation by the Member States: *Van Gend en Loos* [1963] ECR 1 and *Costa v ENEL* [1964] ECR 585. Therefore (3) that entrenchment, and that prohibition, are thereby constituted part of the law of England. The flaw is in step (3). It proceeds on the assumption that the incorporation of EU law effected by the ECA (step (1)) must have included not only the whole corpus of European law upon substantive matters such as (by way of example) the free movement of goods and services, but also any jurisprudence of the Court of Justice, or other rule of Community law, which purports to touch the constitutional preconditions upon which the sovereign legislative power belonging to a member State may be exercised.

Whatever may be the position elsewhere, the law of England disallows any such assumption. Parliament cannot bind its successors by stipulating against repeal, wholly or partly, of the ECA. It cannot stipulate as to the manner and form of any subsequent legislation. It cannot stipulate against implied repeal any more than it can stipulate against express repeal. Thus there is nothing in the ECA which allows the Court of Justice, or any other institutions of the EU, to touch or qualify the conditions of Parliament's legislative supremacy in the United Kingdom. Not because the legislature chose not to allow it; because by our law it could not allow it. That being so, the legislative and judicial institutions of the EU cannot intrude upon those conditions. The British Parliament has not the authority to authorise any such thing. Being sovereign, it cannot abandon its sovereignty. Accordingly there are no circumstances in which the jurisprudence of the Court of Justice can elevate Community law to a status within the corpus of English domestic law to which it could not aspire by any route of English law itself. This is, of course, the traditional doctrine of sovereignty. If is to be modified, it certainly cannot be done by the incorporation of external texts. The conditions of Parliament's legislative supremacy in the United Kingdom necessarily remain in the

United Kingdom's hands. But the traditional doctrine has in my judgment been modified. It has been done by the common law, wholly consistently with constitutional principle.'

Comment

The decision is significant for two reasons. First, it provides further evidence of the evolution of the implied repeal rule as regards 'constitutional' statutes. Essentially if a statute is held to fall within this category the rules on implied repeal are suspended. This is a 'soft' form of entrenchment. Second, because it provides a clear analysis of the constitutional impact of the enactment of the European Communities Act 1972.

OPB Textbook pages 92 and 103, section 4.4 and 4.7.

The Electoral System

Party political broadcasts: freedom of expression

R (On the Application of ProLife Alliance) v *BBC* [2002] 2 All ER 756 Court of Appeal (Civil Division) (Simon Brown, Laws and Jonathan Parker LJJ)

Freedom of expression – refusal of broadcasters to permit party political broadcast – whether a violation of art 10 of the European Convention on Human Rights

Facts

The ProLife Alliance fielded sufficient candidates in Wales to qualify for the broadcasting of its party election broadcasts (PEBs) in that country. It sought permission from the relevant broadcasters to show the film containing images of abortions being carried out. Broadcasters refused to show the video, relying on their various legal duties not to broadcast material that would offend against good taste and decency as laid out in the Broadcasting Act 1990 and in the BBC's agreement with the Secretary of State for National Heritage.

The ProLife Alliance applied for judicial review of the broadcasters' decisions. Permission was refused at first instance but granted on appeal. The Court of Appeal, treating the first instance decision on permission as a disposal of the application for the purposes of judicial review, proceeded to treat the hearing before it as the substantive appeal.

The ProLife Alliance contended that the refusal to broadcast the video was a contravention of its art 10 rights. The broadcasters argued that due deference had to be shown to their discretion to determine what was likely to offend good taste and decency.

Held

The appeal was allowed and a declaration granted that the broadcasters had acted unlawfully in refusing permission to broadcast the video.

Laws LJ (outlining what he saw as the real issue):

'In my view the court has to decide whether those considerations of taste and offensiveness, which moved the broadcasters, constituted a legal justification for the act of censorship involved in banning the appellant's proposed PEB (primarily as it was contained in the first video which was submitted). It will at once be clear that this formulation does not treat the reasonableness or rationality of the broadcasters' decision as conclusive of the issue falling for decision. That would have been the approach upon the conventional jurisprudence dealing with judicial review of a public body's exercise of discretionary power: *Associated Provincial Picture Houses Ltd* v *Wednesbury Corp* [1948] KB 223 ... and *Council of Civil Service Unions* v *Minister for the Civil Service* [1985] AC 374 ... [this is] ... in my view a profoundly mistaken approach. At least it falls to be so regarded today.'

Laws LJ went on to explain that the real issue was one of proportionality. Article 10 envisaged some restrictions being placed on freedom of expression, but the court had to determine whether the decision-maker had exercised proper judgment in deciding that restrictions should be imposed. He rejected the view that the courts ought to give way to the views of broadcasters on the basis that the latter enjoyed a 'margin of appreciation'. He observed:

'We are not, therefore, bidden to accord a "margin of appreciation" properly so called to the broadcasters, and we should fall into confusion and error if we did so. That is not to say that some margin of discretion or deference is not to be paid by this court to the statutory decision-maker. ... There is, I think, some relationship between the margin of appreciation doctrine and the judgment of a domestic court upon the margin of discretion to be accorded to the domestic decision-maker ... [the decisions of the court at Strasbourg tend] ... in my judgment to show that in the Strasbourg court's view the state in principle should possess little discretion to interfere with free political speech: especially at the time of an election. ... That view is not a function of the margin of appreciation. On the contrary it expresses a standard which the signatory states must fulfil for compliance with art 10. The reference to a "wider margin of appreciation" in the context of speech liable to offend personal moral or religious convictions indicates that in such matters the signatory states, consistently with their obligations under the ECHR, are at greater liberty to choose between more or less liberal or conservative regimes. The insight which this provides is that the scope or width of the margin of appreciation which in any given case the European Court of Human Rights will accord to the national authorities depends at least in part upon the court's judgment of the extent to which, giving full weight to municipal culture and practice, there may in principle be a range of different views and approaches relating to the matter in hand.'

Turning to consider the role of the courts in upholding the right to freedom of expression, Laws LJ expressed the view that:

'... as a matter of domestic law the courts owe a special responsibility to the public as the constitutional guardian of the freedom of political debate. This responsibility is most acute at the time and in the context of a public election, especially a general election. It has its origin in a deeper truth, which is that the courts are ultimately the trustees of our democracy's framework. ... Freedom of expression is plainly ... a constitutional right, and its enjoyment by an accredited political party in an election contest must call, if anything, for especially heightened protection. We are in any case long past the point when interference with fundamental rights by public authorities can be justified by a bare demonstration of rationality or reasonableness: see *R* v *Secretary of State for the Home Dept, ex p Daly* [2001] 2 AC 532 ...'

Explaining his use of the word 'censorship' to describe the refusal of the broadcasters to show the films in question, Laws LJ added:

'... this court must, and I hope the broadcasters will, recognise unblinking that censorship is exactly what this case is about. I should say that I do not mean it as a term of abuse; there are of course contexts in which Parliament and the common law have accepted that some forms of censorship are well justified. But we should know the beast we are dealing with. In the context of political speech, it needs to be kept in its cage.'

Comment

Strictly speaking this is not an application of art 10 as such but the development of the common law principles of judicial review to give effect to a constitutional right to freedom of expression. As regards the issue of whether the courts would uphold any prohibition on material intended for broadcast in a PEB, Laws LJ commented that:

'There may be instances, even in the context of a general election, in which political speech may justifiably be censored on grounds of taste or offensiveness. But in my judgment it would take a very extreme case, most likely involving factors ... such as gratuitous sensationalism and dishonesty.'

The applicants were only granted declaratory relief as the judgment was not delivered until well after the completion of the election campaign in question, but broadcasters will be bound by in respect of forthcoming elections.

OPB Textbook pages 119 and 417, sections 5.6 and 15.1.

The House of Lords

Reform

Joint Committee on House of Lords Reform – first report

In December 2002 the Joint Committee on House of Lords Reform published its first report. The proposals for reform envisage 'a continuation of the present role of the House of Lords, and of the existing conventions governing its relations with the House of Commons.'

The Committee identified what it saw as 'five qualities desirable in the makeup of a reformed second chamber.' These were: legitimacy; representativeness; no domination by any one party; independence; and expertise.

On the basis of a reformed second chamber of about 600 members (tenure being for 12 years), with most appointed by a new Appointments Commission (the Prime Minister of the day to retaining a power of nomination, such nominations being subject to scrutiny by the Appointments Commission), the Committee agreed that seven options regarding composition should be considered by Parliament.

The first option is that of a fully appointed second chamber. The report states (paras 63–65):

'A fully appointed House would most closely resemble the existing House of Lords, with the remaining hereditary element removed. Although the legitimacy of such a House would be challenged, this could be mitigated if a new independent and respected Appointments Commission was set up by statute. We have said that we consider that there is a place for political appointments to the House but, to ensure the integrity of the process, all such appointments should be scrutinised by the Appointments Commission. ... It would be the responsibility of the ... Appointments Commission, to ensure that ... representativeness was achieved. ... A fully appointed House could also provide a method for the inclusion of independent members and experts. It could continue to provide part-time members who could bring contemporary professional experience to bear on the duties of scrutiny and the passing of legislation.'

The second option is that of a fully elected second chamber. The report states (paras 67–69):

'The principal argument in favour of a fully elected House is that it would have greater legitimacy and accountability. That view rests upon the premise that legitimacy and accountability are conferred by election. On the other hand the existing House, in exercising independence and in applying expertise, has contributed significantly to the process of parliamentary scrutiny. That may also be considered a basis of legitimacy, important but different from legitimacy conferred by election. Legitimacy based entirely on election may well result in a House which is more assertive. While a reformed second chamber could not unilaterally increase its formal powers, it is a matter for consideration just how far it might feel disposed, by more vigorous use of its existing powers, to challenge the House of Commons and the Government. Such developments could represent a significant constitutional change. ... An elected House is also likely to have few if any independent members ... the domination of the House by elected party politicians would irrevocably change the nature of the House and the attitude and relationship of the House to the Commons and to the Government. In a fully elected House there could be no question of continuing membership for the law lords or Church of England bishops ... the cost is likely to be greater because elected members will expect to be salaried and will expect facilities on a par with those in the House of Commons.'

The third option is to have an 80 per cent appointed/20 per cent elected second chamber. Of this the report observes (para 70):

'We do not share the view that a House of mixed composition is necessarily undesirable. Indeed, in certain senses the House of Lords has always been a mixed House (comprising hereditary peers by succession, hereditary peers of first creation, ex officio members, and in recent times life peers). However, although this model would ensure the entry to the House of a sufficient number of independents, we can foresee difficulties in holding a direct election for only twenty per cent of the second House. Turnout in all elections has fallen to a worryingly low level. We cannot see an election for a small proportion of the new House raising any enthusiasm or contributing to a sense of the importance of the reformed House in the eyes of the electorate.'

The remaining options for reformed compositions are variations on the third, namely: an 80 per cent elected/20 per cent appointed second chamber; a 60 per cent appointed/40 per cent elected second chamber; a 60 per cent elected/40 per cent appointed second chamber; a 50 per cent appointed/50 per cent elected second chamber. Of these variations the report states (paras 71–74):

'... if the appointed element is pitched as low as 20 per cent, difficulties will arise. The current working House consists of 300 or so members but it is a frequently changing 300, depending on the business being considered. The independent element and the element of expertise need to have a sufficiently wide base to provide opinion on a vast range of subjects as they arise in the course of the House's business. With a smaller appointed element in an elected House of reduced size, that provision is unlikely to be sufficient or satisfactory. The law lords and the bishops (or other religious representatives) could not easily be retained. Moreover, a House of largely elected members is bound to change the culture of the second House, making it less attractive for those who wish to remain unaffiliated to party. ... [a 60 per cent appointed/40 per cent elected mix] ... would provide a more reasonable basis of independent members and experts who do not wish to stand for election. It would, on the other hand, provide a significant elected element, to go some way to meet the demands of legitimacy. ... [a 60 per cent elected/40 per cent appointed split] ... retains the advantages of a mixed House. Nevertheless, it is a matter of judgment as to whether a 40 per cent appointed House is sufficient to provide the necessary diversity of expertise. ... The above arguments broadly apply to [the 50 per cent elected/50 per cent appointed option]. ... However, the exact half-way House may have some appeal on grounds of mathematical neatness. It would provide an apparently sufficient balance of electoral legitimacy on the one hand and of independence and expertise from appointment on the other.'

Regarding the method used to elect any members to the second chamber, the report observes (para 53):

'Most opinion concludes that, if the second chamber is to be different from the first ... the method of election needs to be different, and elections should be held on different dates from general elections. The context should not be the election of a government, and, in any case, without fixed-term Parliaments there would be practical difficulties ... the electoral systems recommended by the Commons Public Administration Committee (open regional lists or Single Transferable Vote) both have the advantages that they provide for much larger constituencies than for MPs, minimising the risk of overlap. "First-past-the-post", especially if applied to a smaller percentage of a smaller sized House, would both rule out minor parties and independents, and give an undue preponderance to the largest party.'

It is envisaged that the options will be voted on once both Houses have had the opportunity to consider the report in detail.

Once Parliament has made a decision regarding the composition of the second chamber, the Committee will examine the conventions that regulate relations between the two chambers, and whether any additional powers should be given to the second chamber.

OPB Textbook page 198, section 7.4.

Organisation and Accountability of the Police

Reform

Police Reform Act 2002 (c 30)

The Police Reform Act 2002 is based largely upon the proposals canvassed in the White Paper *Policing a New Century: A Blueprint for Reform* (Cm 5326). It reflects the government's aim of reforming the police service so as to ensure that its crime reduction policies could be carried out more effectively.

Part 1 of the Act provides the Secretary of State with additional supervisory powers as regards police forces. In particular, he is empowered to issue codes of practice to chief officers and police authorities, issue directions to police authorities, and is given extended powers to make regulations regarding the governance of police forces. The Act also places the Secretary of State under a duty to produce an annual National Policing Plan that has to be presented to Parliament.

Part 2 of the Act deals with reforms to the system for dealing with complaints against the police. The Police Complaints Authority is replaced by a new body to be known as the Independent Police Complaints Commission (IPCC). The aim of these reforms is to increase public confidence in the police complaints machinery by providing a more independent and transparent process.

The key roles assigned to the IPCC are those set out in is set out in s10 of the 2002 Act, which provides that the IPCC functions are (inter alia): to secure public confidence in the complaints procedures; to handle complaints made about the conduct of persons serving with the police; and to record matters from which it appears that there may have been conduct by such persons which constitutes or involves the commission of a criminal offence or behaviour justifying disciplinary proceedings. Section 10(8) expressly excludes the IPCC from dealing with complaints where the subject matter relates to the direction and control of a police force by the chief officer of police of that force or a person for the time being carrying out the functions of the chief constable.

What constitutes a complaint is set out in s12, which provides that it can encompass any 'complaint about the conduct of a person serving with the police which is made': (a) by a member of the public who claims to be the person in relation to whom the conduct took place; (b) a member of the public not falling within (a) who claims to have been adversely affected by the conduct; (c) a member of the public who claims to have witnessed the conduct; and (d) a person acting on behalf of a person falling within (a), (b) or (c). Section 12(7) extends the range of those against whom complaints can be made to include employees of police authorities acting under the direction and control of a chief officer and special constables. Hence, the right to make a complaint will no longer be limited to the victim of the police action and complaints can be pursued by independent organisations.

All serious cases will be referred to the IPCC regardless of whether or not a complaint has been made. It will also have its own powers of investigation exercised by a body of independent investigators. Where it carries out an investigation a chief officer of police will be required to co-operate with the IPCC, and will be under a legal obligation to provide investigators with access to documentation or other material. As appropriate it will also have the power to manage or to supervise police investigations of complaints. If necessary the IPCC will be able to call in any case being investigated by the police. Section 19 provides that, if necessary, the Secretary of State may authorise the use of directed and intrusive surveillance, and the conduct and use of covert human intelligence sources, for the purposes of carrying out of the Commission's functions.

Amendments to police powers of arrest under s24 of the Police and Criminal Evidence Act 1984 (PACE) are effected by s48 of Pt 4 of the 2002 Act. The list of arrestable offences in s24 PACE is replaced by a new Sch 1A to PACE: see Sch 6 of the 2002 Act. Three offences are added to this list, namely: making off without payment contrary to s3 of the Theft Act 1978; driving while disqualified contrary to s103(1)(b) of the Road Traffic Act 1988; and assaulting a police officer in the execution of his duty or a person assisting such an officer contrary to s89(1) of the Police Act 1996 Act.

Section 24 is further amended to make it clear that attempting to commit an offence only constitutes an arrestable offence where the offence being attempted is triable on indictment or triable either-way.

Section 17(1)(c) PACE is amended by the addition of a new sub-paragraph (iiia) which creates a power to enter and search premises to arrest a suspect for an offence contrary to s163 of the Road Traffic Act 1988 (failing to stop when requested to do so by a constable in uniform). Section 54 of the 2002 Act amends s62(9) PACE to permit registered health care professionals to take intimate body samples.

A person acting in an anti-social manner can be required to give his or her name an address by virtue of s50 of the 2002 Act. Failure to do so is made a summary offence. Presumably this would also open up the possibility of the use of the power of arrest for non-arrestable offences under s25 PACE.

The Act received Royal Assent on 24 July 2002

OPB Textbook pages 251, 381 and 387, sections 9.6, 14.7 and 14.11.

The European Convention on Human Rights

Article 6: right to a fair trial

Devenney v *United Kingdom* (2002) The Times 11 April European Court of Human Rights

Denial of access to the courts – whether interference with art 6 rights disproportionate

Facts

The applicant, a Roman Catholic, had been employed as a waiter at an hotel in Belfast. The hotel guests included members of the security forces. The applicant was informed that his employment was to be terminated. No reasons were given. The claimant contended that the decision to terminate his employment had been based on the fact that he was a Catholic and as such was discriminatory. The Secretary of State for Northern Ireland issued a certificate under s42 of the Fair Employment (Northern Ireland) Act 1976 certifying that the applicant's contract of employment had been terminated in order to protect public safety and public order. The result was that the applicant was unable to have the legality of his dismissal determined by a Fair Employment Tribunal. The applicant contended that the issuing of the certificate resulted in a violation of his rights under article 6 of the European Convention on Human Rights (ECHR) as regards right of access to the courts.

Held

The application was allowed. There had been a violation of art 6 rights. The right of access to the courts was not absolute. It could be subject to limitations in respect of which contracting states enjoyed a certain margin of appreciation. The Court had to be satisfied that: (i) any limitations imposed did not restrict or reduce the access to the courts so as to undermine the very essence of the right in question; (ii) any limitation was imposed in pursuit of a legitimate aim as determined by the wording of art 6 ECHR; and (iii) there was a reasonable relationship of proportionality between the means employed and the aim sought to be achieved.

Whilst the protection of national security was undoubtedly a legitimate aim that could be pursued by limiting access to a court, the United Kingdom had failed to show that there was a reasonable relationship of proportionality between the concerns for the protection of national security invoked by the authorities and the impact that these restrictions would have on the applicant's right of access to a tribunal. A s42 certificate denied the applicant any information as to the grounds for his dismissal, and he had no means of determining whether any such information was correct. Hence, the conclusion that the s42 certificate constituted a disproportionate restriction on the applicant's right of access to a court.

Comment

The ruling effectively follows that in *Tinnelly and Sons Ltd and Others* v *United Kingdom; McElduff and Others* v *United Kingdom* (1998) 4 BHRC 393. The Court felt that the United Kingdom had failed to identify any new elements that might lead it to depart from its conclusion in the *Tinnelly* case. What the Court is particularly concerned about in cases such as this is permitting the denial of access to the courts on the basis of executive ipse dixit, particularly where there are no effective legal safeguards such as independent judicial review.

OPB Textbook page 309, chapter 12.3.

The Anti-terrorism, Crime and Security Act 2001

The Anti-terrorism, Crime and Security Act 2001 was enacted as part of the government's response to the increased threat from international terrorism in the wake of the attacks in New York City on 11 September 2001.

The Act runs to almost 130 sections, spread across 14 Parts, and has eight Schedules. Parts 1 and 2 provide extended powers to confiscate terrorist property and to make freezing orders in respect of bank accounts and similar assets. Part 3 extends the basis upon which public authorities can disclose information where a criminal investigation is taking place.

Part 4 of the Act attracted perhaps most attention when the Bill was going through Parliament.

Under s21 the Secretary of State may issue a certificate in respect of a person where he reasonably believes that the person's presence in the United Kingdom is a risk to national security, and he suspects that the person is a terrorist. For these purposes 'terrorist' is defined as a person who '(a) is or has been concerned in the commission, preparation or instigation of acts of international terrorism, (b) is a member of or belongs to an international terrorist group, or (c) has links with an international terrorist group': see s21(2).

If a person is certified as a terrorist under s21 he or she can be detained indefinitely without charge. The rationale for these exceptional powers is that there may be cases where there is insufficient evidence to charge a suspected terrorist or the suspect may be subjected to the death penalty if deported to another country.

Legal challenge to certification can only be brought as provided for under the 2001 Act – in effect the normal jurisdiction of the courts has been ousted.

Appeal against certification lies to the Special Immigration Appeals Commission (SIAC). On an appeal the SIAC must cancel the certification if it considers that there are no reasonable grounds for a belief or suspicion of the kind referred to in s21 or it considers that for some other reason the certificate should not have been issued. If the SIAC determines not to cancel a certificate it must dismiss the appeal. In any event certification is subject to review under s26, the SIAC being placed under a duty to hold a first review of each certificate issued under s21 as soon as is reasonably practicable after the expiry of the period of six months beginning with the date on which the certificate is issued.

Section 28 of the Act places the Secretary of State under a duty to appoint a person to review the operation of ss21–23 within 14 months of the provisions coming into effect. The certification power, unless renewed, expires at the end of the period of 15 months beginning with the day on which the Act was passed.

The certification and detention powers are clearly at odds with the rights provided for under art 5(1) of the European Convention on Human Rights, hence the government has had to apply for a derogation, pleading the threat caused by international terrorism as the reason: see further s30 of the 2001 Act.

Part 10 of the Act amends the Terrorism Act 2000, and ss54 and 64 of the Police and Criminal Evidence Act 1984, to provide the police with extended powers to search, fingerprint and photograph suspects. Part 11 makes further provision for the retention and delivery of data by internet service providers where there is suspected terrorist activity. Part 13 of the Act empowers the relevant minister to make regulations for implementing the United Kingdom's obligations under Title VI of the Treaty on European Union (Pillar 3). Essentially, this would enable the implementation of certain anti-terrorist measures agreed by the Justice and Home Affairs Committee and the European Council in the wake of the September 11th attacks. The government has accepted that measures to introduce the proposed European arrest warrant will have to be enacted separately by means of primary legislation.

OBP Textbook pages 322 and 365, sections 12.3 and 13.7.

Pursuing a Human Rights Act claim before the domestic courts

Rushbridger v *Attorney-General* [2001] EWHC Admin 529 Queen's Bench Division (Administrative Court) (Rose LJ and Silber J)

Human Rights Act 1998 – whether domestic law relating to treason in breach of art 10 of the European Convention on Human Rights – whether a free-standing right to bring challenges under the 1998 Act

Facts
The applicants were the editor of *The Guardian* newspaper and a journalist. They intended to publish a series of articles supporting the abolition of the monarchy and the establishment of a republic in the United Kingdom. Under s3 of the Treason Felony Act 1848 it is an offence to

'Compass, imagine, invent devise, or intend to deprive or depose ... the Queen ... or to levy war against Her Majesty ... or in order to put any force or constraint upon ... either House of Parliament, or to move or to stir any foreigner or stranger with force to invade the United Kingdom.'

The applicants wrote to the Attorney-General seeking assurances that if the articles were published there would be no prosecution under the 1848 Act, on the basis that the Act had to be applied by the Attorney-General in a manner consistent with the Human Rights Act 1998. The applicant contended that if a prosecution did follow the publication of the articles the trial court would be required to 'read down' s3 of the 1848 Act, or grant a declaration of incompatibility on the basis that s3 was incompatible with the right to free expression guaranteed by art 10 of the European Convention on Human Rights (ECHR), as incorporated into domestic law by the Human Rights Act 1998. The Attorney-General declined to give the undertaking sought, contending that only Parliament could disapply current legislation.

The applicants thereupon sought two declarations to the effect that:

1. by virtue of the operation of s3 and Sch 1 of the Human Rights Act 1998, s3 of the Treason Felony Act 1848 did not apply to persons who evinced in print or in writing an intent to depose the monarch or deprive her of her imperial status or to establish a republican form of government unless their intent was to achieve this by acts of force, constraint or other unlawful means;
2. the decision of the Attorney-General was erroneous in law and in breach of s6 of the Human Rights Act 1988.

As an alternative a third declaration was sought that the Treason Felony Act 1848 was incompatible with art 10 ECHR.

Held
The applications were dismissed on the basis that as judicial review proceedings there was no 'decision' of the Attorney-General to be challenged (the letter simply stating his view of the law). Rose LJ accepted the submission of Mr Sales (appearing on behalf of the Attorney-General), which he summarised in these terms:

'As to the merits of the claim against the Attorney-General, Mr Sales submits that there are a number of insurmountable hurdles, particularly in relation to the second declaration sought. First of all, he submits that the Attorney-General made no decision amenable to challenge by way of the second declaration. ... He submits that the letters written by the Attorney-General merely explained the basis upon which decisions to prosecute are taken and the fact that the Human Rights Act preserves the sovereignty of Parliament.

Mr Sales submits that it would be curious if such an unobjectionable statement of the law were amenable to judicial review and there is no authority to suggest that it is. Similarly, he says, it would be a distortion of language to describe such an expression of view as to the law as an act falling within section 6(1) of the Human Rights Act. As a matter of language, the fact that the Attorney-General holds wholly unexceptionable views, as set out in his letters, constitutes his having a particular state of mind. It does not constitute an action or omission on his part.

Secondly, Mr Sales submits that these claimants are not victims of any relevant act of the Attorney-General and in this regard he draws attention to the linkage between section 6(1) and section 6(2)(b) [of the Human Rights Act 1998]. He submits that there is no unlawful act under s6(1) because, whatever the construction of section 3 of the 1848 Act, there is no unlawfulness by the Attorney-General. That is because either section 3 can properly be read down, in which case there is no incompatibility with the European Convention, or it cannot be read down. But, if the Attorney-General sought to enforce s3, s6(2)(b) would apply and his action would simply not be unlawful under s6(1).

There is, submits Mr Sales, no duty on the Attorney-General to give an answer, such as was sought in this correspondence, and the requirement for such an answer, if it were wellfounded, would ignore the supremacy of Parliament and the interaction between section 6(1) and (2)(b).

Mr Sales submits that the true nature of the present claim is to obtain an advisory opinion from the courts on the nature of the legislation, but that has nothing at all to do with the Attorney-General. The purpose of the present claim, submits Mr Sales, is to harness the court to law reform, whereas the Human Rights Act makes plain that Parliament remains supreme in this area.

So far as the alleged victim status of the claimants is concerned, Mr Sales submits that the Treason Felony Act has to be interpreted by reference to section 3 of the Human Rights Act. As to the true interpretation, Mr Sales makes no submission, but he points out that it appears from the terms of the first letter to the Attorney-General, and from the skeleton argument on behalf of the complainants, that case of the claimants is that section 3 would be read down so as to ensure compatibility between the 1848 Act and the Human Rights Convention. Furthermore, says Mr Sales, *The Guardian* published the article to which their second letter refers. That being so, submits Mr Sales, the claimants have not established that they can claim victim status even in relation to the 1848 Act. But much more fundamentally, he submits that there is no arguable case that they are victims of any unlawful act or failure to act on the part of the Attorney-General. They fail, in consequence, to satisfy the victim test of section 7 [Human Rights Act 1998], namely that they should be victims of an unlawful act and, in so far as they are victims of anything, it is the 1848 Act which is itself a piece of primary legislation, not the responsibility of the Attorney-General.

Mr Sales submits that domestic constitutional law presents an insuperable problem to the claimants. Whereas the court in Strasbourg looks at the state as a whole and it does not matter there which organ of the state is responsible for the unlawful act about which complaint is made, that approach is simply not available to the domestic courts of this country because the distinction between the different roles of Parliament and the prosecution authority is of vital importance in municipal law. It is not for the Attorney-General to disapply the law (see *Ex parte Blackburn* [1968] 2 QB 118), hence the second of the Attorney General's letters was entirely correct.

Mr Sales submits that judicial review of a decision to prosecute or not to prosecute is available only in exceptional cases as is apparent from the judgment of Woolf J in the case of *A-G v Able* [1984] QB 795.

Furthermore, Mr Sales submits, it is for the courts, not the Attorney-General, to rule on the effect of statutes. The present case, he submits, is even stronger in terms of being outwith the principle of challenge to decisions whether or not to prosecute illustrated by *Kebilene* [[1999] 3 WLR 175], because, in the present case, there has been no decision to prosecute. The claimants are seeking an advisory opinion from the Attorney-General and, that having failed in correspondence, they are seeking an advisory opinion from the court. Mr Sales also referred to *The Sunday Times* v *United Kingdom* (1972) 2 EHRR 245 where paragraph 49 of the judgment indicates that the law must be accessible, but need not be absolutely certain: from that accessibility arises the ability of individuals to obtain legal advice as to their conduct and to behave accordingly, as has happened in the present case.

... For these reasons, Mr Sales submits that the claim against the Attorney General is misconceived.

[The claims in relation to] ... declarations (1) and (3) ... Mr Sales submits, necessarily [fail] because, by virtue of section 7(1), under which those claims are brought, there is no unlawful act such as that section requires.

So far as declarations in relation to the criminality or otherwise of conduct are concerned, Mr Sales relies on the judgment of Woolf J in *A-G* v *Able* as stressing that it is only in exceptional circumstances that such declarations should be made and the present, he submits, is not an exceptional case. None of these principles, he submits, has been changed by the Human Rights Act and, as I have indicated, he relies on the approach of the majority of the House of Lords in *Kebilene*. He submits that an advisory declaration simply cannot be sought or made under section 7.

... although a European Community law is capable of, as he put it, trumping English domestic law, that is not the position under the Human Rights Act, whereby Parliament's sovereignty is preserved, and there is no scope for a declaration under that Act that domestic law should be set aside. For my part, I accept Mr Sales' submissions.

Furthermore, the claimants are not the victims of any unlawful act of the Attorney-General, even if, which seems to me to be doubtful, they are victims of section 3 of the 1848 Act.

The first and third declarations are, in my judgment, not obtainable under section 7 because there is no unlawful conduct by the Attorney-General. In any event, in the light particularly of *Kebilene*, it is not, in my judgment, appropriate for declarations as to the criminality or otherwise of conduct to be made, save in exceptional circumstances, and certainly not, generally speaking, before the conduct has itself occurred.'

Comment

Although not widely reported the decision is a useful reminder of how the Human Rights Act 1998 operates. Contrary to what some casual observers may have thought the 1998 Act does not create any freestanding right to challenge domestic legislation simply because it is thought to be incompatible with Convention rights. There must be an issue at stake between two parties, ie the applicant must be the victim of action taken by a public body pursuant to a domestic provision that he alleges contravene his Convention rights. The applicants in the present case attempted to create such an issue in writing to the Attorney-General seeking assurances of non-prosecution. As the court rightly held, however, the refusal of the Attorney-General to provide any such assurance could not be viewed as an 'action' by a public body. Hence, the applicants were unable to acquire their sought-after 'victim' status. Had the Attorney-General advised that there would be a prosecution, having seen drafts of the article, the applicants would have had a much stronger case, either by way of judicial review or by way of defence to criminal proceedings. The refusal of the courts to provide what would in effect have been advisory opinions on the status of the 1848 Act is understandable and consistent with previous rulings regarding the availability of declaratory relief.

OPB Textbook page 323, section 12.4.

Violation of Convention rights

R (On the Application of International Transport Roth GmbH) v
Secretary of State for the Home Department (2002) The Times 26
February Court of Appeal (Civil Division) (Simon Brown, Laws and
Jonathan Parker LJJ)

Fines regime for bringing illegal immigrants in the UK – whether proportionate – incompatibility with European Convention on Human Rights

Facts

A scheme imposing fixed penalties on carriers for bringing clandestine entrants into the United Kingdom was established pursuant to Pt II of the Immigration and Asylum Act 1999. If any clandestine entrants were discovered on carriers' vehicles the scheme provided that hirers, drivers or operators could be subject to a fixed penalty of £2,000 in respect of each clandestine entrant. Fault was established if it could be shown that a carrier had been negligent in permitting his vehicle to be used for the clandestine entry. If this was the case, the burden was then on the carrier to show that he had been acting under duress, or that he had had neither actual nor constructive knowledge of the presence of the clandestine entrant, that an effective system for preventing the carriage of clandestine entrants had been in place and that that system had been operating properly at the relevant time. Under the scheme a senior immigration officer was empowered to detain a vehicle used by a clandestine entrant if he considered that there was a serious risk that the penalty would not be paid and satisfactory alternative security had not been given. A number of lorry drivers applied for judicial review of the scheme on the basis that it contravened both the European Convention on Human Rights and Community law. At first instance it was held that (in addition to the scheme being in contravention of Community law) the scheme contravened art 6 of the European Convention on Human Rights (ECHR) because it involved the determination of a 'criminal charge' and therefore failed to meet the procedural requirements of art 6(1), (2) and (3). Furthermore it was held that the scheme contravened art 1 of Protocol 1 of the ECHR, because the provisions for the detention of vehicles constituted an unjustifiable infringement of the right to property. The Secretary of State appealed.

Held

The appeal was allowed in part. The scheme did violate Convention rights (Laws LJ dissenting on this point) but was not incompatible with Community law. Regarding compatibility with Convention rights Simon Brown LJ, having determined that the proceedings under the scheme were 'criminal' in nature (thus engaging the provisions of art 6), observed:

'The mere fact, therefore, that the burden of disproving dishonesty and negligence is placed by the scheme upon the carrier does not of itself seem to me to violate of Article 6. The reverse onus, however, cannot be ignored. Rather, in combination with the vehicle detention provisions and the inflexibility of the substantial financial penalties, it places an immense burden on carriers. It is, for example, one thing to put the burden of disproving culpability upon the carrier; quite another to allow his vehicle to be detained until he has discharged that burden. I know of no other such provision in our law. ... Insofar as the liability is suggested to be civil and not to involve moral culpability on the driver's part, the penalty far exceeds what any individual ought reasonably to be required to sacrifice in the interests of achieving improved immigration control. ... But even assuming, as I do, that the scheme is directed towards punishing carriers for some fault, it cannot to my mind be right to impose so high a fixed penalty without possibility of mitigation. The hallowed principle that the punishment must fit the crime is irreconcilable with the notion of a substantial fixed penalty. It is essentially, therefore, on this account rather than because of the reversed burden of proof that I would regard the scheme as incompatible with Article 6. What in particular it offends is the carrier's right to have his penalty determined by an independent tribunal. To my mind there surely is such a right ... I cannot think, however, that other substantial fixed penalties can properly be put beyond the court's purview. Sentencing is, like all aspects of the criminal trial, a function that must be conducted by an independent tribunal. If, as I would hold, the determination of liability under the scheme is properly to be characterised as criminal, then this fixed penalty cannot stand unless it can be adjudged proportionate in all cases having regard to culpability involved.'

Regarding the violation of art 1 of Protocol 1 Simon Brown LJ noted that, in order to be permissible under the ECHR, an interference with property not only had to be in the public or general interest, but also had to satisfy the requirement of proportionality, ie the impairment of the individual's property rights had to be no more than was necessary for the attainment of the public policy objective sought, and should not impose an excessive burden on the individual concerned. He continued:

'The requisite balance will not be found if the person concerned has had to bear an "individual and excessive burden". That principle seems to me of the first importance here. If, therefore, contrary to my belief, the scale and inflexibility of the penalty, taken in conjunction with the other features of this scheme, are not such as to deprive the carriers of a fair trial under Article 6, then I would hold them instead to impose an excessive burden on the carriers such as to violate Article 1. Even acknowledging, as I do, the great importance of the social goal which the scheme seeks to promote, there are nevertheless limits to how far the state is entitled to go in imposing obligations of vigilance on drivers (and vicarious liability on employers and hirers) to achieve it and in penalising any breach. Obviously, were the penalty heavier still and the discouragement of carelessness correspondingly greater, the scheme would be yet more effective and the policy objective fulfilled to an even higher degree. There comes a point, however, when what is achieved is achieved only at the cost of basic fairness. The price in Convention terms becomes just too high. That in my judgment is the position here.'

Finally he concluded with some observations on the impact of the Human Rights Act (HRA) 1998 on the relationship between the courts and the legislature:

'... this ... case ... raises questions as to the degree of deference owed by the courts to the legislature and executive in the means used to achieve social goals ... judges nowadays have no alternative but to apply the Human Rights Act. Constitutional dangers exist no less in too little judicial activism as in too much. There are limits to the legitimacy of executive or legislative decision making, just as there are to decision making by the courts. Difficult and worrying though I have found this case to be, in the last analysis, affording all such deference as I believe I properly can to those responsible for immigration control and for devising and enacting the legislation necessary to achieve it, I have come to regard this scheme as, quite simply, unfair to carriers. Nothing in the Convention itself, nor in the extensive jurisprudence upon it, dictates, or ever could dictate, precisely when a measure such as this is unfair – when, that is, the limits of permissible individual sacrifice have been exceeded. All that the Convention really provides are the central principles and touchstones by which such a judgment can be made.'

Simon Brown LJ rejected the invitation from the appellants to construe the legislation so as to eliminate any injustice or unfairness (ie to use the powers of interpretation provided for by s3 HRA 1998). He confirmed that, in his view, the court's task was to 'distinguish between legislation and interpretation, and confine itself to the latter.'

Laws LJ, whilst dissenting on the issue of the scheme's incompatibility with the ECHR, dealt with a number of useful and wide-ranging observations on the nature of the British constitution in the wake of the enactment of the HRA 1998. First, he explained the impact that the enactment of the 1998 Act had had on the nature of parliamentary sovereignty, in particular the move towards what he described as an intermediate position somewhere between pure parliamentary sovereignty on the one hand and constitutional sovereignty on the other.

'Not very long ago, the British system was one of parliamentary supremacy pure and simple. Then, the very assertion of constitutional rights as such would have been something of a misnomer, for there was in general no hierarchy of rights, no distinction between "constitutional" and other rights. Every Act of Parliament had the same standing in law as every other, and so far as rights were given by judge-made law, they could offer no competition to the status of statutes. The courts evolved rules of interpretation which favoured the protection of certain basic freedoms, but in essence Parliament legislated uninhibited by claims of fundamental rights.

In its present state of evolution, the British system may be said to stand at an intermediate stage between parliamentary supremacy and constitutional supremacy ... Parliament remains the sovereign legislature; there is no superior text to which it must defer (I leave aside the refinements flowing from our membership of the European Union); there is no statute which by law it cannot make. But at the same time, the common law has come to recognise and endorse the notion of constitutional, or fundamental rights. These are broadly the rights given expression in the European Convention on Human Rights and Fundamental Freedoms ("ECHR"), but their recognition in the common law is autonomous. ... The Human Rights Act 1998 ("HRA") now provides a democratic underpinning to the common law's acceptance of constitutional rights, and important new procedural measures for their protection. Its structure, as has more than once been observed, reveals an elegant balance between respect for Parliament's legislative supremacy and the legal security of the Convention rights.

This being our constitution's present nature, there exists a tension between the maintenance of legislative sovereignty and the vindication of fundamental, constitutional rights. How are their respective claims to be reconciled? Where is the point of escape if the legislature tramples on the territory of rights? This tension is hardly to be found in a system of pure parliamentary supremacy, and is less acute in a system of constitutional supremacy. In the former, fundamental rights are not recognised as such. The majoritarian principle, expressed and made good by a sovereign Parliament, comes first. In the latter, the majoritarian principle gives way to fundamental rights. In practice, the constitutions and jurisprudence of sovereign States in the civilised world show that this distinction is by no means always clear-cut; and to the extent in any concrete instance that it is not clear-cut, the tension to which I refer will arise. Moreover, although it may create difficulties, and its resolution case by case requires firmness of purpose and good judgment, this tension is a welcome inhabitant of a democratic State. ...

... In the British State, there are at least two means by which the courts seek to resolve this tension. The first, not directly relevant in the present case, arises where it is suggested that a statute has effected or authorised what would undoubtedly amount to a violation of a fundamental or constitutional right. Here the courts protect the right in question, while acknowledging the legislative supremacy of Parliament, by means of a rule of construction. The rule is that while the legislature possesses the power to override fundamental rights, general words will not suffice. It can only be done by express, or at any rate specific, provision. ...

... The second means by which constitutional rights are recognised consistently with the sovereignty of Parliament is engaged where a statute admittedly travels in the field of a constitutional right, and the issue is whether the right is violated, or if it is whether the extent of the statute's intrusion is acceptable or justified. Such questions characteristically arise where the right is one guaranteed by the ECHR, and the court acts pursuant to its duty under the HRA. Where one of the political rights is under consideration (that is, any of those guaranteed by ECHR Articles 9 to 11), the issue most often falling for decision is whether there is shown sufficient justification, under paragraph 2 of the Article in question, for the right's infringement. But the question may be, whether there has been a violation at all; and that question may of course arise in the context of Convention rights as regards which the ECHR provides no express exceptions or qualifications. ...

In this second area the court's task is quite unlike its duty in deciding whether on its true construction a statute allows or perpetrates an undoubted violation of a constitutional right. The rule of construction, that only express or at least specific words will suffice to effect such a result, is a brightline rule whose edge is sharp. In this present context, there is no brightline rule. It is because here, the court has to strike a balance between the claims of the democratic legislature and the claims of the constitutional right. Sometimes, of course, it will be plain and obvious which way the scales fall. In the field of ECHR Article 10, the justification of certain specified restrictions upon the right of free expression may be clear beyond argument in time of war or other national emergency. On the other hand, an attempt to curtail free speech merely to avoid embarrassment to the Government would, no less obviously, lack any colour of justification. In the far more frequent case where the answer is by no means so plain, and a balance has to be struck between contradictory interests each possessing some substance of legitimacy, a critical factor in the court's appreciation of the balance will be the degree or margin of deference it pays to the democratic decision-maker. This deference – and its limits – have to be fashioned in a principled but flexible manner, sensitive to the particular case and its context. In some contexts the deference is nearly absolute. In others it barely exists at all. The development of principle in this field is one of the most important challenges which the common law must meet, in face of the provisions of the HRA and our own domestic acceptance of the idea of constitutional rights. The reach of the deference which the judges will pay to the democratic decision-maker, the giving and withholding of it, is the second means by which the courts resolve the tension between parliamentary sovereignty and fundamental rights in our intermediate constitution.'

The second issue addressed by Laws LJ was the extent to which the courts, in assessing whether or not executive action should be invalidated on grounds of non-compliance with the ECHR, should or should not show deference to the executive decision-maker.

Where difficult choices may have to be made by the executive or the legislature between the rights of the individual and the needs of society he recognised that it would be appropriate for the courts to recognise an area of judgment within which the judiciary would, on democratic grounds, defer to the considered opinion of the elected body or person. This he described as the 'discretionary area of judgment'. It should not be assumed that the domestic courts will slavishly apply the Strasbourg doctrine of the margin of appreciation. Laws LJ was keen to ensure that domestic courts showed the deference owed to democratic powers, reflecting the culture and conditions of the British state leading to the development of an autonomous, as opposed to merely an adjectival, human rights jurisprudence. Laws LJ went on to formulate what he saw as four principles that would help guide a court as to the deference to be shown to a decision-maker alleged to have violated Convention rights.

The first was that greater deference would be paid to an Act of Parliament than to a decision of the executive or a subordinate measure. He explained:

'Where the decision-maker is not Parliament, but a minister or other public or governmental authority exercising power conferred by Parliament, a degree of deference will be due on democratic grounds – the decision-maker is Parliament's delegate – within the principles accorded by the cases. But where the decision-maker is Parliament itself, speaking through main legislation, the tension of which I have spoken is at its most acute. In our intermediate constitution the legislature is not subordinate to a sovereign text, as are the legislatures in "constitutional" systems. Parliament remains the sovereign legislator. It, and not a written constitution, bears the ultimate mantle of democracy in the State.'

The second principle was that there was more scope for deference where Convention rights were expressed in terms of the executive having to strike a balance between competing interests, rather than where a Convention right was expressed in unqualified terms. Explaining this in the context of the case before the court, he observed:

'In the present case we are principally concerned with Article 6, which does not on its face require any balance to be struck: it contains no analogue of paragraph 2 in Articles 9–11, dealing with political rights. It is thus a context which militates against deference. But even here, there is no sharp edge. The right to a fair trial under ECHR Article 6(1) is certainly unqualified and cannot be abrogated. So also is the presumption of innocence (in a criminal case) arising under Article 6(2). But what is required for fairness, what is required to satisfy the presumption of innocence, may vary according to context ... I think it misleading to describe Article 6 rights as "absolute", an adjective which tends to suggest that the nature of such rights is uniform, the same for every class of case (bar the distinction between civil and criminal). That is not right. The requirements of independence and impartiality are perhaps as close as one can get to uniform requirements. But even there, there may be scope for reasonable differences of view as to the conditions which have to be met.'

The third principle was that greater deference would be awarded to democratic powers where the subject matter was something peculiarly within the decision-maker's constitutional responsibility. Less deference would be afforded where the issue was something more appropriately within the constitutional responsibility of the courts. Laws LJ gave the following example:

'The first duty of government is the defence of the realm. It is well settled that executive decisions dealing directly with matters of defence, while not immune from judicial review (that would be repugnant to the rule of law), cannot sensibly be scrutinised by the courts on grounds relating to their factual merits. ... The first duty of the courts is the maintenance of the rule of law. That is exemplified in many ways, not least by the extremely restrictive construction always placed on no certiorari clauses.

Now this is not a case, of course, in which the courts are intruding in defence policy, or the democratic powers in the rule of law. There are no tanks on the wrong lawns. But ... the constitutional responsibility of the democratic powers particularly includes the security of the State's borders, thus including immigration control, and that of the courts particularly includes the doing of criminal justice. If the scheme of the 1999 Act is essentially to be treated as an administrative scheme for the betterment of immigration control in a context – clandestine entrants in vehicles – acknowledged to be especially acute, the courts will accord a much greater deference to Parliament in deciding whether there is any violation of Convention rights than if it is to be regarded as a criminal statute. In the latter case, the courts are of course obliged to apply Article 6(2) and (3) as well as (1). They would do so rigorously, with much less deference to the legislature, not only in fulfilment of their duty under the HRA but also because their own constitutional responsibility makes the task a necessarily congenial one.'

The fourth principle identified by Laws LJ was that greater or lesser deference would be permitted depending upon the extent to which the subject matter fell within the actual or potential expertise of the democratic powers or the courts. By way of example he indicated that, in his view, decisions in the area of macro-economic policy would be remote from judicial control. He added:

'I have no doubt that the social consequences which flow from the entry into the United Kingdom of clandestine illegal immigrants in significant numbers are far-reaching and in some respects complex. While the evidence before us gives more than a flavour of the problems, the assessment of these matters (and therefore of the pressing nature of the need for effective controls) is in my judgment obviously far more within the competence of government than the courts.'

Comment

Note that permission to appeal and to cross-appeal to the House of Lords was granted. Although it is normally said that the ECHR cannot be used to challenge the validity of substantive criminal law, this is a case where the courts come close to doing so. Unfairness per se is not a ground of challenge under art 6, but the majority in this case was persuaded that the cumulative effect of the impugned provisions was to place an unfair burden on individual carriers. The views expressed by Laws LJ, whilst obiter, are further evidence of the redefining of the concept of parliamentary sovereignty in the post-incorporation era.

OPB Textbook pages 92 and 327, sections 4.4 and 12.4.

Freedom of Assembly and Association

Offences under the Public Order Act 1986

Percy v *Director of Public Prosecutions* (2002) The Times 21 January
Queen's Bench Divisional Court (Kennedy LJ and Hallet J)

Desecration of the United States flag – whether an offence under s5 of the Public Order Act 1986 – whether prosecution a violation of the right to freedom of expression under art 10 of the European Convention on Human Rights

Facts
P was involved in a flag desecration protest outside a United States airbase. She was convicted of an offence contrary to s5 of the Public Order Act (POA) 1986 (using threatening, abusive or insulting words or behaviour, or disorderly behaviour, or displays any writing, sign or other visible representation which is threatening, abusive or insulting, within the hearing or sight of a person likely to be caused harassment, alarm or distress thereby). P appealed against conviction on the basis that the prosecution was an unlawful interference with her right to freedom of expression under art 10 of the European Convention on Human Rights (ECHR).

Held
The appeal was allowed. The district judge had erred in placing too much weight on the fact that others might have been insulted by P's behaviour. There was a presumption in favour of freedom of expression that the judge had failed to give due weight to. He had also failed to consider the issue of proportionality sufficiently.

Comment
This is not a decision to the effect that s5 POA 1986 is incompatible with art 10 ECHR. The restrictions imposed by s5 passed the 'prescribed by law' test despite the vagueness of the terms deployed. If P's expression was reasonable within the terms of s5(3) of the 1986 Act the burden fell upon the prosecution to show that the interference with Convention rights caused by the use of s5 was both legitimate and proportionate.

OPB Textbook page 359, section 13.4.

Freedom of Expression

Official Secrets Act 1989

R v *Shayler* [2002] 2 All ER 477 House of Lords (Lords Bingham of Cornhill, Hope of Craighead, Hutton, Hobhouse of Woodborough and Scott of Foscote)

Official Secrets Act 1989 – defendant claiming public interest justification for disclosures – whether 1989 Act compliant with the European Convention on Human Rights

Facts

The defendant was a former member of the security services. After leaving the employment of the security services he supplied a national newspaper with information which was published in an article. He claimed his motivation in disclosing the information had been to show that the British people were being put at risk of harm as a result of the inadequacies of the security services. The information disclosed was such that he could only have obtained it as a result of his employment with the security services. The defendant was charged on two counts of disclosing documents relating to security or intelligence without lawful authority, contrary to s1(1) of the Official Secrets Act 1989, and one count of disclosing information obtained under warrants issued under the Interception of Communications Act 1985, contrary to s4(1) of the 1989 Act. At a preparatory hearing under s29 of the Criminal Procedure and Investigations Act 1996, prior to the commencement of his trial, the defendant had raised issues regarding the extent to which he might be allowed to rely upon the defence of necessity in relation to the disclosures, and the extent to which the prohibitions laid down in the 1989 Act amounted to a breach of his rights under art 10 of the European Convention on Human Rights (ECHR). Having had rulings against him made on both points the defendant appealed unsuccessfully to the Court of Appeal from whence he appealed further to the House of Lords.

Held

The appeal was dismissed. Neither serving nor former members of the security services were permitted any public interest defence in respect of disclosures that contravened the Official Secrets Act 1989. Further, s1 of the 1989 Act was compatible with art 10 ECHR, therefore the defendant should stand trial on the charges that had been brought against him. There was scope, on the facts, for the application of any defence based on necessity.

Lord Bingham of Cornhill explained that under the 1989 Act a member of the intelligence and security services would commit an offence if, without lawful authority, he disclosed any information relating to security or intelligence which he acquired by virtue of his position as a member of any of those services. Under s7 lawful authority permits disclosures to a Crown servant for the purposes of his functions as such or in accordance with an official authorisation (ie authorisation given by an appropriate Crown servant). Effectively this meant that any member of the security services who had misgivings about security arrangements had the right to take the matter up with a senior civil servant, rather than passing details onto the press.

Regarding the existence of any public interest defence for disclosures he observed:

'It is in my opinion plain, giving sections 1(1)(a) and 4(1) and (3)(a) their natural and ordinary meaning and reading them in the context of the OSA 1989 as a whole, that a defendant prosecuted under these sections is not entitled to be acquitted if he shows that it was or that he believed that it was in the public or national interest to make the disclosure in question or if the jury conclude that it may have been or that the defendant may have believed it to be in the public or national interest to make the disclosure in question. The sections impose no obligation on the prosecution to prove that the disclosure was not in the public interest and give the defendant no opportunity to show that the disclosure was in the public interest or that he thought it was. The sections leave no room for doubt.'

Regarding the extent to which s1 of the 1989 Act was compatible with art 10 ECHR, Lord Bingham of Cornhill set out the tests as being: (i) whether or not the restriction was prescribed by law; if so, (ii) whether the restriction sought to achieve one or more of the objectives permitted by art 10(2); if so, (iii) whether or not the restriction was necessary in a democratic society – in relation to which he observed that:

' "Necessary" has been strongly interpreted: it is not synonymous with "indispensable", neither has it the flexibility of such expressions as "admissible", "ordinary", "useful", "reasonable" or "desirable". ... One must consider whether the interference complained of corresponded to a pressing social need, whether it was proportionate to the legitimate aim pursued and whether the reasons given by the national authority to justify it are relevant and sufficient under art 10(2).'

Concluding that there was a pressing social need for the restrictions imposed under the 1989 Act Lord Bingham of Cornhill observed:

'There is much domestic authority pointing to the need for a security or intelligence service to be secure. The commodity in which such a service deals is secret and confidential information. If the service is not secure those working against the interests of the state, whether terrorists, other criminals or foreign agents, will be alerted, and able to take evasive action; its own agents may be unmasked; members of the service will feel unable to rely on each other; those upon whom the service relies as sources of information will feel unable to rely on their identity remaining secret; and foreign countries will decline to entrust their own secrets to an insecure recipient.'

As to whether the scheme provided for under s1 of the 1989 Act whereby a member of the security services could take up his concerns about security with a senior civil servant, Lord Bingham of Cornhill commented:

> 'One would, again, hope that requests for authorisation to disclose would be granted where no adequate justification existed for denying it and that authorisation would be refused only where such justification existed. But the possibility would of course exist that authority might be refused where no adequate justification existed for refusal ... In this situation the former member is entitled to seek judicial review of the decision to refuse, a course which the OSA 1989 does not seek to inhibit. ... For the appellant it was argued that judicial review offered a person in his position no effective protection, since courts were reluctant to intervene in matters concerning national security and the threshold of showing a decision to be irrational was so high as to give the applicant little chance of crossing it. ... There are in my opinion two answers to this submission. First the court's willingness to intervene will very much depend on the nature of the material which it is sought to disclose. If the issue concerns the disclosure of documents bearing a high security classification and there is apparently credible unchallenged evidence that disclosure is liable to lead to the identification of agents or the compromise of informers, the court may very well be unwilling to intervene. If, at the other end of the spectrum, it appears that while disclosure of the material may cause embarrassment or arouse criticism, it will not damage any security or intelligence interest, the court's reaction is likely to be very different. Usually, a proposed disclosure will fall between these two extremes and the court must exercise its judgment, informed by article 10 considerations. The second answer is that in any application for judicial review alleging an alleged violation of a Convention right the court will now conduct a much more rigorous and intrusive review than was once thought to be permissible.'

Comment

Given the avenues open to a member of the security services to raise his or her concerns the decision was perhaps inevitable. As Wadham explains ([2002] NLJ 556), these avenues include: discussing concerns with a staff counsellor; raising issues about breaches of the criminal law with the Attorney-General, Director of Public Prosecutions or Head of the Metropolitan Police; and raising issues about maladministration with the Home Secretary, other relevant minister or Secretariat of the Parliamentary Intelligence and Security Committee. In a sense, however, the decision is a significant advance for freedom of expression as the House of Lords has made clear that any inadequacies in the administrative framework for regulating freedom of expression will be subject to a more robust form of judicial review given that Convention rights are in play

The decision is also noteworthy for Lord Bingham's obiter comments on why, in his view, freedom of expression is a constitutionally important matter. He stated:

> 'Modern democratic government means government of the people by the people for the people. But there can be no government by the people if they are ignorant of the issues to be resolved, the arguments for and against different solutions and the facts underlying those arguments. The business of government is not an activity about which only those professionally engaged are entitled to receive information and express opinions. It is, or should be, a participatory process. But there can be no assurance that government is carried out for the people unless the facts are made known, the issues publicly ventilated.

Sometimes, inevitably, those involved in the conduct of government, as in any other walk of life, are guilty of error, incompetence, misbehaviour, dereliction of duty, even dishonesty and malpractice. Those concerned may very strongly wish that the facts relating to such matters are not made public. Publicity may reflect discredit on them or their predecessors. It may embarrass the authorities. It may impede the process of administration. Experience however shows, in this country and elsewhere, that publicity is a powerful disinfectant. Where abuses are exposed, they can be remedied. Even where abuses have already been remedied, the public may be entitled to know that they occurred. The role of the press in exposing abuses and miscarriages of justice has been a potent and honourable one. But the press cannot expose that of which it is denied knowledge.'

OPB Textbook page 427, section 15.2.

Privacy

Secretary of State for the Home Department v *Wainwright and Another* (2002) The Times 4 January Court of Appeal (Civil Division) (Lord Woolf CJ, Mummery and Buxton LJJ)

Privacy – whether any residual common law right

Facts
The claimants visited a relative in prison in January 1997. As a condition of being allowed entry the claimants consented to being strip-searched. The claimants subsequently sued for trespass to the person in respect of the searches, claiming that the searches had involved a breach of their privacy rights. At first instance McGonigal J at Leeds County Court granted the claimants basic and aggravated damages for the manner in which they were strip-searched by prison officers. The Secretary of State appealed.

Held
The appeal was allowed. The events complained of took place prior to the Human Rights Act 1998 coming into force. That Act could operate retrospectively but only where Parliament had so indicated: see s22 of the 1998 Act. The present case was not one where those retrospectivity provisions applied, hence the Convention could not be relied upon. The Court went on to confirm that, in the absence of a Convention right to privacy there was no residual common law right to privacy that could be relied upon to justify the award of aggravated damages.

Comment
The Court accepted that the manner in which the searches were conducted could be relied upon to support a claim for damages in respect of the battery inflicted upon each claimant. The decision regarding privacy seems rational as regards events occurring pre-October 2000, but begs the question as to whether or not, in respect of events occurring post-October 2000, the courts would be willing to develop

common law concepts such as trespass to the person so as to ensure the protection of privacy in dealings between private parties, eg a search of a suspected shoplifter by a store detective.

OPB Textbook page 448, section 15.6.

Campbell v *MGN Ltd* (2002) The Times 29 March Queen's Bench Divisional Court (Morland J)

Disclosure of personal information – whether breach of privacy – remedies available

Facts
The claimant was a famous fashion model. The defendant newspaper published articles detailing the claimant's drug addiction problems and details of her attendance at meetings of Narcotics Anonymous. The claimant accepted that the defendant newspaper could publish facts about her being a drug addict, but argued that details of her therapy and her attendance at therapy sessions were private and confidential matters publication of which could not be justified by reference to any overriding public interest in disclosure.

The defendant newspaper contended that publication was justified because the claimant was a figure in the public eye, had courted publicity and had publicly denied receiving treatment for drug abuse, thereby misleading the public.

Held
The claimant was awarded damages for breach of confidentiality and was awarded compensation under s13 of the Data Protection Act 1998. Morland J explained that three factors had to be established to support a successful claim for breach of confidence:

1. the material divulged had to have the 'necessary quality of confidence' about it;
2. the details must have been imparted in confidence; and
3. the publication of the details must have been to the claimant's detriment.

As regards (1) he was satisfied that details of the claimant's attendance at Narcotics Anonymous did have the necessary quality of confidence. It was easily identifiable as private, and disclosure of such information would be highly offensive to a reasonable person of ordinary sensibilities. As to (2) the duty of confidence arose from the circumstances in which the information was imparted. The test to be applied was that of the court viewing the circumstances objectively to determine whether the defendant was clothed in conscience with the duty of confidentiality. The test in (3) was also satisfied on the facts, as disclosure was likely to effect adversely the claimant's attendance and participation in therapy meetings.

Even those in public life who openly courted publicity were entitled to respect for their private lives provided this restriction could be justified within the terms of art 10(2) of the European Convention on Human Rights (ECHR). On the facts the defendant newspaper was justified in publishing information that showed the claimant to have misled the public as to her having had problems with drug abuse. It had overstepped the mark, however, in publishing details of the claimant's treatment. The court was bound to give effect to art 8 ECHR by extending the protection of confidentiality to such material.

Comment

The result is something of a token victory for the claimant, as she would obviously have preferred to obtain some form of injunctive relief to prevent publication in the first place. Note that the defendant newspaper was also found to have been in breach of the Data Protection Act 1998 as regards its processing of data concerning the claimant's physical or mental health. The claimant was awarded £2,500 in respect of this breach.

OPB Textbook page 455, section 15.6.

Protection of journalistic sources

Interbrew SA v *Financial Times Ltd and Others* [2002] EWCA Civ 274
Court of Appeal (Civil Division) (Ward, Sedley and Longmore LJJ)

Innocent party in receipt of unlawfully obtained material – whether legally required to deliver up material – protection of sources – freedom of expression

Facts

Interbrew commissioned an analyst's report on a company it considered purchasing – South African Breweries (SAB). A third party (the source) obtained a copy of the report and, with a view to creating a false market in the shares of SAB, made fraudulent alterations to the report and passed it on to the defendant newspapers. The altered report was used by the defendant newspapers as the basis for articles that were subsequently published. The publications had a significant impact on the share values of both Interbrew and SAB. Interbrew applied to the court for an order compelling the defendants to deliver up the copies of the report supplied by the source with a view to identifying the source. Reliance was placed on the court's jurisdiction, in the wake of the decision in *Norwich Pharmacal Co* v *Commissioners of Custom and Excise* [1974] AC 133, to order the disclosure of evidence of wrongdoing in the possession of a party not directly involved in the commission of the wrongdoing. At first instance disclosure was ordered. The defendant newspapers appealed.

Held

The appeal was dismissed. Given that Interbrew had established that it had suffered a civil wrong, and that the defendants had, albeit innocently facilitated the commission of that wrongful act, the question arose as to whether or not s10 of the Contempt of Court Act 1981 could be relied upon to prevent the court from ordering disclosure on the basis that upholding freedom of expression involved allowing journalists to refuse to comply with requests that might reveal the source of information received. Section 10 provides:

> 'No court may require a person to disclose, nor is any person guilty of contempt of court for refusing to disclose, the source of information contained in a publication for which he is responsible, unless it be established to the satisfaction of the court that disclosure is necessary in the interests of justice or national security or for the prevention of disorder or crime.'

The court was required to balance the defendants' rights to freedom of expression against the need to prevent the commission of crime and the need to prevent breaches of confidentiality. On the facts the granting of the order at first instance had been justified because it was necessary in order to enable Interbrew to identify who had committed a breach of confidence, a basis for disclosure expressly adverted to in s10 of the 1981 Act.

Comment
Critical to this decision was the fact that the source could not have been claiming to act in any wider public interest. On the contrary, all the evidence suggested that the source had acted either with a view to personal gain, or at least out of malevolence towards the applicants. This was not, therefore, a case where it could be said that requiring journalists to disclose their sources would in any way inhibit the flow of information to journalists that it might be in the public interest to have disclosed. As Sedley LJ observed:

> '... is the public interest in the doing of justice sufficient in the particular circumstances of this case to make disclosure necessary? ... What in my judgment matters critically, at least in the present situation, is the source's evident purpose. It was on any view a maleficent one, calculated to do harm whether for profit or for spite, and whether to the investing public or Interbrew or both. ... The public interest in protecting the source of such a leak is in my judgment not sufficient to withstand the countervailing public interest in letting Interbrew seek justice in the courts against the source.'

Ashworth Hospital Authority v *MGN Ltd* [2002] 4 All ER 193 House of Lords (Lord Woolf CJ, Lords Slynn of Hadley, Browne-Wilkinson, Nolan and Hobhouse of Woodborough)

Contempt of Court Act 1981, s10 – duty to reveal journalistic sources – whether a breach of art 10 of the European Convention on Human Rights – confidentiality of journalistic sources – when in the public interest to order disclosure

Facts
A person employed at Ashworth Security hospital downloaded 17 pages of medical notes relating to the hunger strike of Ian Brady, a prisoner at the hospital. The material was passed to an intermediary who in turn sold the information to Mirror Group Newspapers (MGN) who published the information verbatim. Ashworth Hospital obtained an order compelling MGN to serve a witness notice upon the

hospital providing evidence as to the identity of the intermediary. MGN appealed unsuccessfully against this notice, citing the need to protect the confidentiality of journalistic sources. The Court of Appeal held that disclosure was necessary in the interests of justice under s10 of the Contempt of Court Act 1981, a conclusion arrived at by extending the scope of the decision in *Norwich Pharmacal Co* v *Commissioners of Customs and Excise* [1974] AC 133 to encompass a third party that became mixed up in wrongdoing that was not tortious but involved activity such as a breach of confidence. The newspaper appealed to the House of Lords.

Held

The appeal was dismissed. The *Norwich Pharmacal* jurisdiction to order the delivery up of material was not contingent upon establishing that the party in possession of the material was a wrongdoer. It was sufficient that the party in possession was involved in some way.

Lord Woolf CJ:

'Under this jurisdiction, there is no requirement that the person against whom the proceedings have been brought should be an actual wrongdoer who has committed a tort or breached a contract or committed some other civil or criminal wrongful act. In *Norwich Pharmacal* Co v *Comrs of Customs and Excise* ... itself, the Customs and Excise Commissioners were an entirely innocent party. The commissioners had, however, because of their statutory responsibilities become involved or mixed up in the illicit importation of the chemicals manufactured abroad which Norwich Pharmacal alleged infringed their patent. The *Norwich Pharmacal* case clearly establishes that where a person, albeit innocently, and without incurring any personal liability, becomes involved in a wrongful act of another, that person thereby comes under a duty to assist the person injured by those acts by giving him any information which he is able to give by way of discovery that discloses the identity of the wrongdoer. While therefore the exercise of the jurisdiction does require that there should be wrongdoing, the wrongdoing which is required is the wrongdoing of the person whose identity the claimant is seeking to establish and not that of the person against whom the proceedings are brought.'

The court, he felt, should exercise its discretion to determine where and how the line would be drawn to distinguish between parties involved in the wrongdoing and parties that were mere onlookers:

'It is sufficient that the source was a wrongdoer and MGN became involved in the wrongdoing which is incontestably the position. Whether the source's wrongdoing was tortious, or in breach of contract in my judgment matters not. If there was wrongdoing then there is no further requirement that [the] conduct should also be wrongful. It is sufficient ... that there was "involvement or participation". As MGN published the information which was wrongfully obtained, the answer as to whether there was involvement or participation must be an emphatic Yes.

... Although this requirement of involvement or participation on the part of the party from whom discovery is sought is not a stringent requirement, it is still a significant requirement. It distinguishes that party from a mere onlooker or witness. The need for involvement, the reference to participation can be dispensed with because it adds nothing to the requirement of involvement, is a significant requirement because it ensures that the mere onlooker cannot be subjected to the requirement to give disclosure. Such a requirement is an intrusion upon a third party to the wrongdoing and the need for involvement provides justification for this intrusion.'

Lord Woolf CJ went on to explain that an order for the disclosure of journalistic sources would only be granted in exceptional circumstances given the terms of s10 of the Contempt of Court Act 1981 and art 10 of the European Convention on Human Rights. Any such disclosure would have to be justified on the basis of pressing social need and would have to be proportionate. As to why those exceptional factors were made out in the present case, he made the following observations:

'The fact is that information which should be placed in the public domain is frequently made available to the press by individuals who would lack the courage to provide the information if they thought there was a risk of their identity being disclosed. The fact that journalists' sources can be reasonably confident that their identity will not be disclosed makes a significant contribution to the ability of the press to perform their role in society of making information available to the public. It is for this reason that it is well established now that the courts will normally protect journalists' sources from identification. ... The situation here is exceptional, as it was in *Financial Times Ltd* v *Interbrew SA* [2002] EMLR 446 and as it has to be, if disclosure of sources is to be justified. The care of patients at Ashworth is fraught with difficulty and danger. The disclosure of the patients' records increases that difficulty and danger and to deter the same or similar wrongdoing in the future it was essential that the source should be identified and punished. This was what made the orders to disclose necessary and proportionate and justified. The fact that Ian Brady had himself disclosed his medical history did not detract from the need to prevent staff from revealing medical records of patients. Ian Brady's conduct did not damage the integrity of Ashworth's patients' records. The source's disclosure was wholly inconsistent with the security of the records and the disclosure was made worse because it was purchased by a cash payment.'

Comment

This ruling leaves the law in an uncertain state for journalists as so much now rests on judicial discretion. It may be significant that the disclosures in this case served no obvious public interest beyond providing lurid and sensationalist tabloid coverage.

OPB Textbook page 471, section 15.7.

Confidentiality

A v *B (A Company) and Another* [2002] 2 All ER 545 Court of Appeal (Civil Division) (Lord Woolf CJ, Laws and Dyson LJJ)

Confidentiality – determining which relationships give rise to a duty of confidentiality

Facts

The claimant was a professional footballer, married with children. He had had extra-marital sexual relations with two women, C and D, for approximately three and 12 months respectively. The women subsequently sold their stories to B, a national newspaper. B intended to publish this information, prompting the claimant to seek an injunction. His claim was based on the assertion that the publication could prejudice his marriage and indirectly harm his children. At first instance the injunctive relief was granted, a decision from which the newspaper now appealed.

Held

The appeal was allowed. Lord Woolf CJ, having alluded to the impact of the Human Rights Act 1998 on the area of law concerned with claims for breach of confidence, proceeded to offer a set of guidelines that courts might follow when balancing the competing demands of, on the one hand, the public's interest in the private lives of celebrities and sports stars and, on the other, the right of individuals to have details of their personal lives kept confidential.

Any interference with the freedom of the press to publish had to be justified in the public interest. Whilst a court would have regard to whether or not publication was in the public interest, it did not follow that publication of any given material had to be desirable in order for publication to be in the public interest. If privacy was to be protected in dealings between private parties it was through the use of breach of confidence rather than the development of any new free-standing cause of action.

Central to any claim for breach of confidence would be the existence of an interest of a private nature. The less evidence there was of any private interest the greater the probability that it would be outweighed by the right to freedom of expression. Each case would depend to a large extent on its own facts.

Lord Woolf CJ:

> 'A duty of confidence will arise whenever the party subject to the duty is in a situation where he either knows or ought to know that the other person can reasonably expect his privacy to be protected. ... The range of situations in which protection can be provided is therefore extensive. Obviously, the necessary relationship can be expressly created. More often its existence will have to be inferred from the facts. Whether a duty of confidence does exist which courts can protect, if it is right to do so, will depend on all the circumstances of the relationship between the parties at the time of the threatened or actual breach of the alleged duty of confidence.'

It is thus more likely that a duty of confidence will arise in situations if an intrusion relates to a situation where a person can reasonably expect his privacy to be respected. The bugging of someone's home or the use of other surveillance techniques were cited as obvious examples of such intrusions, but his Lordship noted that the fact that information is obtained as a result of unlawful activities does not mean that its publication would necessarily be restrained by an injunction on the grounds of breach of confidence.

Where one party to a sexual relationship outside marriage wishes to divulge details of it there is a conflict between one party's right to privacy and the other party's right of freedom of expression. The more stable the relationship the greater will be the significance attached to it by the courts. Hence the courts will be willing to extend a duty of confidentiality to stable relationships outside marriage, but not fleeting or transient affairs (ie one-night stands).

Regarding the position of those in the public eye, Lord Woolf CJ observed:

'A public figure is entitled to a private life. The individual, however, should recognise that because of his public position he must expect and accept that his actions will be more closely scrutinised by the media. Even trivial facts relating to a public figure can be of great interest to readers and other observers of the media. Conduct which in the case of a private individual would not be the appropriate subject of comment can be the proper subject of comment in the case of a public figure. The public figure may hold a position where higher standards of conduct can be rightly expected by the public. The public figure may be a role model whose conduct could well be emulated by others. He may set the fashion. The higher the profile of the individual concerned the more likely that this will be the position. Whether you have courted publicity or not you may be a legitimate subject of public attention. If you have courted public attention then you have less ground to object to the intrusion which follows. In many of these situations it would be overstating the position to say that there is a public interest in the information being published. It would be more accurate to say that the public have an understandable and so a legitimate interest in being told the information. If this is the situation then it can be appropriately taken into account by a court when deciding on which side of the line a case falls. The courts must not ignore the fact that if newspapers do not publish information which the public are interested in, there will be fewer newspapers published, which will not be in the public interest. The same is true in relation to other parts of the media ... In drawing up a balance sheet between the respective interests of the parties courts should not act as censors or arbiters of taste. ... If there is not a sufficient case for restraining publication the fact that a more lurid approach will be adopted by the publication than the court would regard as acceptable is not relevant. If the contents of the publication are untrue the law of defamation provides prohibition.'

Comment

The appeal succeeded essentially because the judge at first instance had failed to distinguish between the varying degrees of confidentiality attaching to different relationships. Note also that the Court of Appeal was not convinced that it was in the interests of the claimant's wife to remain in ignorance regarding his extra-marital sexual activities. See further *Theakston* v *MGN Ltd* [2002] EMLR 22, where the court observed that a transitory engagement in a brothel was at the very limits of what could be protected by the law of confidence, as the relationship between a prostitute in a brothel and the customer was not confidential in nature. The mere fact that sexual activity had taken place did not, of itself, create a relationship of confidentiality. The court was willing, however, to grant an injunction to prevent the publication of photographs taken of the claimant at the brothel without his consent.

OPB Textbook page 473, section 15.7.

7

Contract Law

Certainty and Form of the Contract

Contracts of guarantee

Actionstrength Ltd v *International Glass Engineering IN GL EN SpA*
[2002] 4 All ER 468 Court of Appeal (Simon Brown, Peter Gibson and
Tuckey LJJ)

Guarantee – specific assets – s4 of the Statute of Frauds 1677

Facts
An employer contracted with the main contractor for the building of a factory, and
the claimant subcontractor agreed with the main contractor to provide the necessary
labour. Because of late payment by the main contractor, the subcontractor
threatened to cease work. According to the subcontractor, the employer agreed with
the subcontractor that if it remained at work, the employer would ensure that it
received any amount due to the subcontractor from the main contractor, if necessary
by redirecting moneys due to the main contractor. There was no written note or
memorandum of the alleged agreement, so when the subcontractor sued the
employer to enforce it the employer relied upon s4 of the Statute of Frauds 1677.

Held
The alleged agreement was unenforceable since, contrary to the subcontractor's
contention, s4 of the Statute was not confined to a liability imposed on the
promisor's assets generally as distinct from one imposed (as here, according to the
subcontractor) on a particular asset or source.

Comment
The Appeal Committee of the House of Lords gave permission to appeal against this
decision.

OBP Textbook page 88, section 5.5.

Contents of Contracts

Terms implied by statute

Consideration

By virtue of the Late Payment of Commercial Debts Regulations 2002, s5A is inserted in the Late Payment of Commercial Debts (Interest) Act 1998. This new section, which came into force on 7 August 2002, provides that once statutory interest begins to run in relation to a qualifying debt, the supplier is entitled to a fixed sum (in addition to the statutory interest on the debt). That sum is:

1. for a debt less than £1,000, the sum of £40;
2. for a debt of £1,000 or more, but less than £10,000, the sum of £70;
3. for a debt of £10,000 or more, the sum of £100.

The obligation to pay an additional fixed sum under this new section in respect of a qualifying debt is treated as part of the term implied by s1(1) of the 1998 Act in the contract creating the debt.

OBP Textbook page 117, section 6.10.

Incapacity

Corporations

Braymist Ltd v *Wise Finance Co Ltd* [2002] 2 All ER 333 Court of Appeal (Judge, Latham and Arden LJJ)

Contract – unformed company – agent's ability to sue

Facts
Braymist Ltd contracted to sell Wise Finance Co Ltd a parcel of land. At the time, Braymist was in the process of incorporation: its solicitors (Sturges) signed the agreement as agents and solicitors for it. Wise did not know that Braymist had yet to be incorporated. Sturges sought to enforce the contract against Wise by virtue of s36C(1) Companies Act 1985 and the judge found in their favour. He also concluded that the signing of the agreement by Sturges as agents satisfied the requirements of s2 Law of Property (Miscellaneous Provisions) Act 1989.

Held
The judge's decision on both points had been correct: Wise's appeal would be dismissed.

Judge LJ:
'The critical question for decision is whether s36C(1) of the Companies Act 1985 not only

provides a remedy for a person (A) who has purported to enter into a contract with a company when it was unformed (the narrow view) but also imposes obligations enforceable against A's wishes by the person purporting to act for or as agent of the unformed company (B). ... The insurmountable difficulty with the narrow view is that it requires s36C(1) to be read as if it created a complete option for someone in A's position, but never for someone in B's position, either to adopt or reject the contract, a choice to be made unilaterally by him, for good, bad, or no reason. The statutory language could, of course, have been drafted so to provide. Instead s36C(1) specifies that contract has "effect", language remote from the concept of an "option" or, as here, the wish of the party in A's position to be protected from the consequences of the deemed contract simply because the bargain is no longer as commercially attractive as it once was. Accordingly, dealing with the issue as a matter of construction, I prefer the broad rather than the narrow view of the meaning and effect of s36C(1).'

Arden LJ:

'Section 2 of the 1989 Act refers to signature "by or on behalf" of a party. In my judgment, having concluded that Sturges is a party to the agreement by virtue of s36C and that there is no common law bar to enforcement of the contract by Sturges, in my judgment Sturges is properly to be treated as having signed the agreement on its own behalf for the purposes of s2. I reach this construction in order to make both sections work properly together. Otherwise, Sturges having shown that it is entitled to enforce the contract under s36C would be unable to do so because of over-literal construction of s2 of the 1989 Act. I agree with the judge that this cannot be the policy of s2. My interpretation does no violence to the language: Sturges did sign the contract. Because it renders ss36C and 2 more efficacious, in my view the judge's consideration is to be preferred.'

OBP Textbook pages 78 and 167, sections 5.4 and 9.11.

OTV Birwelco Ltd v *Technical and General Guarantee Co Ltd* [2002] 4 All ER 668 Queen's Bench Division (Technology and Construction Court) (Judge Thornton QC)

Company – bond – use of trading name – enforceability

Facts
Following a management buy-out, the new company usually traded under the original company's name. The new company entered into a performance bond with the defendant surety, in respect of a contract with the claimant. The bond was made by deed in which, and on its seal on which, the new company used the original company's name. The new company ceased trading: could the claimant enforce the bond?

Held
It could, since (1) s36A Companies Act 1985 did not require a company to use its registered name rather than its trading name in the body of a deed, and (2) non-compliance by the new company with s350 of the 1985 Act did not render the bond

a nullity nor make the claimant's third party rights created by the bond unenforceable by the claimant against the defendant.

OBP Textbook page 167, section 9.11.

Mistake

Mistake at common law

Great Peace Shipping Ltd v *Tsavliris Salvage (International) Ltd, The Great Peace* [2002] 4 All ER 689 Court of Appeal (Lord Phillips MR, May and Laws LJJ)

Mistake – common law and equity – contract void?

Facts

While taking a cargo of iron ore from Brazil to China, the Cape Providence suffered serious structural damage in the South Indian Ocean. The appellants offered and had accepted their salvage services on standard terms. On finding that it would take five or six days for a tug to reach the Cape Providence, and since there was serious concern for the safety of the crew, through brokers the appellants sought a merchant vessel in the vicinity of the Cape Providence. The brokers were told, by a respected source, that the respondents' vessel, the Great Peace, was about 12 hours (35 miles) away and they agreed with the respondents that it would go to the rescue, again on standard terms. In fact, the Great Peace was 39 hours (410 miles) away from the Cape Providence and, by chance, another vessel, the Nordfarer, passed by and provided the necessary assistance. The appellants contracted directly with the Nordfarer's owners for these services and instructed the brokers to cancel the contract with the respondents. The respondents claimed damages for breach of contract, a claim which the appellants resisted on the ground of common mistake or, alternatively, that the facts had given rise to a right to rescind the contract in equity.

Held

The respondents would succeed since the mistake as to the distance between the two vessels had not rendered the services that the respondents' vessel was in a position to provide something essentially different from those which the parties had agreed.

Lord Phillips MR:

> '... what we are here concerned with is an allegation of a common mistaken assumption of fact which renders the service that will be provided if the contract is performed in accordance with its terms something different from the performance that the parties contemplated. This is the type of mistake which fell to be considered in *Bell* v *Lever Bros Ltd* [1932] AC 161. We shall describe it as "common mistake", although it is often alternatively described as "mutual mistake". ... We agree ... that, on the facts of the present case, the issue in relation to common mistake turns on the question of whether

the mistake as to the distance apart of the two vessels had the effect that the services that the Great Peace was in a position to provide were something essentially different from that to which the parties had agreed. ... The appellants would have wished the contract to be performed but for the adventitious arrival on the scene of a vessel prepared to perform the same services. The fact that the vessels were further apart than both parties had appreciated did not mean that it was impossible to perform the contractual adventure. The parties entered into a binding contract for the hire of the Great Peace. That contract gave the appellants an express right to cancel the contract subject to the obligation to pay the "cancellation fee" of five days hire. When they engaged the Nordfarer they cancelled the Great Peace. They became liable in consequence to pay the cancellation fee. There is no injustice in this result.'

Comment

At first instance Toulson J held that equity neither gave a party a right to rescind a contract on grounds of common mistake nor conferred on the court a discretion to set aside a contract on such grounds: *Solle* v *Butcher* [1950] 1 KB 671 had been wrongly decided. The Court of Appeal shared this view. The Master of the Rolls said:

'In this case we have heard full argument, which has provided what we believe has been the first opportunity in this Court for a full and mature consideration of the relation between *Bell* v *Lever Bros Ltd* and *Solle* v *Butcher*. In the light of that consideration we can see no way that *Solle* v *Butcher* can stand with *Bell* v *Lever Bross Ltd*.'

OBP Textbook page 194, section 10.4.

Illegality

Contracts contrary to public policy

Maintenance and champerty

Factortame Ltd v Secretary of State for the Environment, Transport and the Regions (No 2) [2002] 4 All ER 97 Court of Appeal (Lord Phillips MR, Robert Walker and Clarke LJJ)

Contingency fee agreement – accountants' fees percentage of final settlement – s58 Courts and Legal Services Act 1990

Facts

It having been decided that the claimant fishing companies were entitled to compensatory damages in respect of the United Kingdom Government's breach of Community law, the claimants agreed to pay a firm of accountants 8 per cent of the final settlement received as their fees for preparing and submitting the claimants' claims for damages. The claimants sought to recover these fees as costs, but the Secretary of State resisted this claim, contending that the agreement as to fees was champertous.

Held

This was not the case.

Lord Phillips MR:

> 'The costs judge concluded that the ... agreements [with the accountants] lacked the characteristics that might have rendered them contrary to public policy under the vestigial remnants of the law of champerty. As we considered the evidence and heard the argument unfold we became increasingly convinced that he was correct. Reflection after reserving our judgment has not shaken that conclusion. The claimants had been brought low by the initial wrong done to them and by the costs and stress of prolonged litigation in which no quarter was given. They were faced with an extraordinarily complicated task in proving the damage that they had suffered and there was a real risk that lack of funds might result in their losing the fruits of their litigation. The ... agreements ensured that they continued to enjoy access to justice. They did this without putting justice in jeopardy. The ... agreements were not champertous.'

Comment

His Lordship affirmed that s58 Courts and Legal Services Act 1990 does not apply to expert witnesses and the Court considered that it would be in a very rare case indeed that the court would be prepared to consent to an expert being instructed under a contingency fee agreement. Here, the accountants were not expert witnesses: they had engaged others to perform that role.

OBP Textbook page 254, section 13.3.

Enforcement of illegal contracts

Callery v *Gray (Nos 1 and 2)* [2002] 3 All ER 417 House of Lords (Lords Bingham of Cornhill, Nicholls of Birkenhead, Hoffmann, Hope of Craighead and Scott of Foscote)

Conditional fee agreement – success fee uplift – after-the-event insurance cover

Facts

Following a motoring accident in which he had suffered minor injuries, the claimant entered into a conditional fee agreement with his solicitors providing for a success fee of 60 per cent. A few days later he took out an after-the-event insurance policy (premium £350) to protect himself against the possibility of liability for the defendant's costs. On the same day, his solicitors sent the defendant a letter before action. The claim was settled before proceedings were issued and the defendant agreed to pay the claimant's reasonable costs and disbursements. Since the parties were unable to agree the amount of costs and disbursements, the claimant commenced costs-only proceedings. The district judge reduced the success fee to 40 per cent but allowed the premium; on appeal, the judge upheld the district judge's decision; on a further appeal the Court of Appeal upheld the judge as to the premium but reduced the success fee to 20 per cent.

Held

The appeal against the Court of Appeal's decision would be dismissed, although Lord Scott of Foscote would not have allowed recovery of the insurance premium.

Lord Bingham of Cornhill:

> 'There are none the less two reasons which lead me to the conclusion that the House should not intervene. The first is that the responsibility for monitoring and controlling the developing practice in a field such as this lies with the Court of Appeal and not the House, which should ordinarily be slow to intervene. The House cannot respond to changes in practice with the speed and sensitivity of the Court of Appeal, before which a number of cases are likely over time to come ... I would [also] decline to intervene because, as the Court of Appeal repeatedly stressed, the present issues arise at a very early stage in the practical development of the new funding regime, when reliable factual material is sparse, market experience is meagre and trends are hard to discern ... I feel sure that district and costs judges, circuit judges and in the last resort the Court of Appeal can be relied on to maintain a fair and publicly beneficial balance between competing interests.'

OBP Textbook page 265, section 13.5.

Remedies for Breach of Contract – Damages

Causation

Bank of Credit and Commerce International SA v Ali (No 2) [2002] 3 All ER 750 Court of Appeal (Pill, Robert Walker and Jonathan Parker LJJ)

Breach of implied term of trust and confidence – stigma – financial loss

Facts

When the respondent bank was wound up in 1991 it became clear that part of its business had been carried on in a corrupt and dishonest manner and some employees sought damages for the stigma (and handicap in obtaining other employment) of their association with the bank. In *Malik* v *Bank of Credit and Commerce International SA* [1997] 3 All ER 1, the House of Lords held that, in a contract of employment, there is an implied obligation on an employer not to carry on a dishonest or corrupt business. If there is a breach of that obligation as a result of which the employee's future employment prospects are handicapped, damages may be recoverable for financial losses sustained. When the appellant former employees made such claims, the trial judge said that the attitude of a prospective employer had to be proved in every particular case: there was no general prejudice against the bank's former employees and loss should not necessarily be assumed or inferred.

Held

The appeals against this decision would be dismissed.

Jonathan Parker LJ:

> 'I accept ... that had the appellants succeeded in establishing a general prejudice in the employment market against former employees of BCCI as a result of stigma, it would have been open to them to invite the Court to infer that but for that general prejudice a claimant would have succeeded in obtaining – albeit not a particular job – a job of a particular type or at a particular level of salary. In the event, however, the judge found as a fact (as in my judgment he was entitled to do) that no such general prejudice existed. Absent general prejudice, it was necessary for the appellants to prove that stigma was an effective cause of the failure of their job applications on what the judge described as a "job-specific" basis. In other words, it was necessary for them to show that stigma was an effective cause of the failure of a particular job application. That too they failed to do on the findings of the judge (findings which, once again, he was in my judgment entitled to make).'

OBP Textbook page 319, section 16.4.

Quasi-contract

Action for money had and received

National Westminster Bank plc v *Somer International (UK) Ltd* [2002] 1 All ER 198 Court of Appeal (Peter Gibson, Potter and Clarke LJJ)

Estoppel – money paid by mistake – recovery

Facts

The defendant company sometimes received payments from its customers in dollars directly into its dollar account with the claimant bank. Knowing that the defendants were expecting to receive from their customer Mentor a payment of between $US70,000 and $US80,000, having received a payment of $US76,708 from Moffett intended for another of the claimants' customers, the claimants notified the defendants that the moneys they were expecting had been received into their account. On hearing this, the defendants released to Mentor further goods to the value of £13,180. Some nine months later, having discovered their mistake, the claimants notified the defendants that the payment received had been credited to their account in error and requested repayment. By this time, Mentor had ceased to trade and had effectively disappeared. The claimants now sued to recover the payment of $US76,708.

Held

The claimants were entitled to recover the amount mistakenly credited to the defendants' account less the value of the goods subsequently sent by the defendants to Mentor.

Peter Gibson LJ:

'The test is whether it would be unconscionable and inequitable for the recipient of the moneys mistakenly paid to retain the moneys having regard to what the recipient did in reliance on the representation made to him. I fully accept that the Court, when assessing detriment, should not apply too demanding a standard of proof because of the practical difficulties faced by a defendant conducting a business who has been led to believe that the moneys paid by mistake are his ... But in view of the clear findings of fact made by the judge as to the extent of the detriment suffered by [the defendants] and in particular his outright rejection of the argument that [they were] induced to forgo the opportunity to pursue Mentor for payment, I am not able to accede to [counsel for the defendants'] submission that this is a case where it would be unjust not to give full effect to the estoppel. On the contrary, the circumstances here, as found by the judge, are such that the disparity between the $US76,708 mistakenly credited to [the defendants] and £13,180, being the value of the goods despatched by [the defendants] in reliance on the bank's representation, makes it unconscionable and inequitable for [the defendants] to retain the balance.'

OBP Textbook page 356, section 18.2.

Sale of Goods, Consumer Credit and Supply of Goods and Services

Implied terms

Jewson Ltd v *Kelly* (2002) The Times 3 October Queen's Bench Division (Mr David Foskett QC)

Boilers – satisfactory quality – test

Facts
The claimant sold 12 electric boilers to the defendant. When the claimant sued to recover the purchase price, the preliminary issue arose as to whether the claimant had been in breach of the term implied by s14(2) Sale of Goods Act 1979 that the goods supplied were of satisfactory quality.

Held
The boilers had not passed this test. Mr David Foskett QC explained that it was necessary to ask whether the reasonable person having considered the matters set out in s14(2A) and (2B) of the 1979 Act would have regarded the boilers as of satisfactory quality. The fact that the boilers intrinsically worked satisfactorily was not sufficient for them to be of satisfactory quality, since a reasonable person would have said that a new form of electric boiler, claiming to provide efficient low-cost heating in residential dwellings, ought to be capable of being shown to meet such a claim within the tests or procedures then prevailing. Furthermore, a reasonable person would say that without meeting such tests or procedures (or without an

explanation as to why they were not satisfied), he or she would understand a proposed purchaser of a dwelling delaying, or even pulling out of the purchase. A reasonable person would therefore on balance have said that the boilers were not of satisfactory quality.

OBP Textbook page 380, section 20.6.

8

Conveyancing

Introduction and Overview

The Land Registration Act 2002 (see below) will effect far-reaching changes to land law and conveyancing. It lays the foundations for a radical change in procedures by making provision for the introduction of a comprehensive system of e-conveyancing – electronic conveyancing. The Electronic Communications Act 2000 was the first piece of legislation which specifically addressed the problems of e-commerce, and following that, matters have continued to develop. In the conveyancing field, there is already the Land Registry Direct, allowing direct access by computer to the Land Registry, and the introduction of the National Land Information System. This latter is a means whereby searches can be done electronically, the idea being that a variety of information providers, of whom inquiry has to be made, will link into the system so that one inquiry effects several searches, with a consequent saving of time. The Council of Mortgage Lenders' Handbook, which deals with procedures to be followed when solicitors are acting for lenders, is now only available on-line. In February 2002 it became possible to lodge some applications at the Land Registry electronically. These were relatively minor – applications to change a name following marriage or a deed poll; change of address for service; change of property description; death of a joint proprietor; and entry of a restriction following the severance of a joint tenancy – but the precedent has been set and it is planned that electronic access will increase. A period of consultation by the Land Registry and the Lord Chancellor's Department over the means of implementing e-conveyancing closed at the end of summer 2002 and the findings are currently under consideration. Particular problems which will need to be resolved include the security of transactions and how documents can be signed when they are in electronic form. The Lord Chancellor has indicated a target date of 2006 for the introduction of a system of e-conveyancing.

The Commonhold and Leasehold Reform Act 2002 was passed in 2002: it establishes a new regime for the ownership of properties such as blocks of flats. In the Queen's speech at the end of 2002 it was announced that the proposals for the introduction of a seller's pack, initially envisaged in the Homes Bill of 1999, will reappear.

OBP Textbook Chapter 1.

Land Registration

Land Registration Act 2002

This Act is scheduled to come into force in October 2003, and will repeal the Land Registration Act 1925 in its entirety. The detail of many matters will be dealt with in Rules and Regulations to be made under the Act. This outline refers to the registered proprietor of a registered estate: with appropriate amendments the provisions apply to the proprietor of a registered charge, and also the proprietor of a rentcharge, franchise or profit à prendre in gross, which can now be the subject of substantive registration. The most significant alterations are:

1. leases of over seven years are now registrable;
2. the system of protecting third party rights is changed;
3. overriding interests as previously known cease to exist and there will be two categories of overriding rights, those which override first registration and those which override a registered disposition or charge; and
4. a new system of adverse possession applying to registered land.

References to sections are to the Land Registration Act 2002 unless otherwise stipulated.

First registration

Voluntary first registration remains available and any person who owns an estate in land can apply to be registered as proprietor unless the estate owned is a lease with less than seven years to run: s3.

Compulsory registration applies to a qualifying estate, defined as a fee simple or a lease with over seven years to run at the time of the event triggering first registration. Registration of title is compulsory on the occurrence of any of the following (s4):

1. the transfer of a qualifying estate for valuable or other consideration, by way of gift or in pursuance of a court order;
2. assents relating to a qualifying estate;
3. certain transfers and grants of leases under the Housing Act 1985;
4. the grant of a lease for over seven years for valuable or other consideration, by way of gift or in pursuance of a court order;
5. the grant of a lease to take effect in possession after three months;
6. the creation of a first legal mortgage of a qualifying estate.

The Lord Chancellor has a power to extend the situations when compulsory first registration applies: s5. Where compulsory registration is applicable, the estate owner, the transferee or the mortgagor has to apply for first registration within two months of completion: s6. If this is not done, the transaction is void as regards the legal estate. If the transaction is a transfer or assent, then the legal title reverts to the transferor who holds it on bare trust for the transferee. If the transaction is a lease or mortgage, the transaction takes effect as a contract for valuable consideration to create or convey the estate or interest: s7. If this occurs, the person in default is liable for the costs and also has to indemnify any other party in respect of liabilities incurred: s8.

Cautions against first registration

A person who claims to be the owner of a qualifying estate or entitled to an interest affecting a qualifying estate may apply to the registrar for the registration of a caution against first registration: s15. When an application for first registration is made, the registrar must then give the cautioner notice of the application and his right to object to it. The application cannot be completed before the end of such period as is prescribed for the cautioner to object, unless the cautioner has objected during that period or has indicated he will not object to the registration proceeding. A caution against first registration may be withdrawn at any time by the cautioner. The owner of the estate affected by the caution may also apply to the registrar for the caution to be cancelled. The registrar must then give notice of that application to the cautioner, and unless the cautioner objects to the cancellation within the prescribed period, the caution must be cancelled. The registrar has to keep a register of cautions against first registration.

Classes of title

Freeholds (s9)
1. Absolute title – if the registrar is of the opinion that the title is such as a willing buyer could properly be advised by a competent professional adviser to accept; any defects which will not cause the holding to be disturbed can be ignored.
2. Qualified title – if the title has been established only for a limited period or is subject to a qualification which cannot be ignored.
3. Possessory title – if the person is in actual possession and there is no other class of title with which he can be registered.

Leaseholds (s10)
1. Absolute leasehold title – as for freehold, and if the registrar approves the lessor's title to grant the lease.
2. Good leasehold title – if the registrar is of the opinion that the title is one which a willing buyer could properly be advised by a competent professional to accept. (In relation to these two titles ('absolute' and 'good'), a defect which will not cause any disturbance can be ignored.)
3. Qualified leasehold title and possessory leasehold title – as for freeholds above.

A freehold possessory or qualified title can be upgraded to absolute if the registrar is satisfied as to the title. A good leasehold title can be upgraded to absolute if the registrar is satisfied as to the superior title. If a leasehold is registered with possessory or qualified title, the registrar can upgrade it to good leasehold if satisfied as to the title, or absolute if satisfied as to the title and the superior title: ss62 and 63.

Effect of first registration

Freeholds (s11)
Registration of a person with absolute title vests the estate in him, together with all interests subsisting for the benefit of the estate, subject only to the following interests which affect the estate at the time of registration:

1. interests which are the subject of an entry in the register;
2. unregistered interests which fall within Sch 1;
3. interests acquired under the Limitation Act 1980 of which the proprietor has notice;
4. if the proprietor is not entitled to the estate for his own benefit, as between him and the persons beneficially entitled, subject to such of their interests of which he has notice.

Registration with qualified title has the same effect, except that it does not affect the enforcement of any matter which appears from the register to be excepted from the effect of registration. Registration with a possessory title has the same effect, except that it does not affect the enforcement of any matter affecting the proprietor's title which is subsisting at the time of registration.

Leaseholds (s12)
1. Absolute, qualified and possessory titles – registration with any of these titles has the same effect as above in relation to freeholds, but in all cases is also subject to the covenants, obligations and liabilities contained in the lease.
2. Good leasehold title – registration with this title has the same effect as registration with absolute leasehold, but it does not affect the enforcement of any matter affecting the title of the lessor to grant the lease.

Schedule 1: unregistered interests which override first registration
1. Leases of less than seven years.
2. The interest of a person in actual occupation so far as it relates to land of which he is in actual occupation, but excluding an interest under the Settled Land Act 1925.
3. A legal easement or profit.
4. A customary right.
5. A public right.
6. A local land charge.
7. An interest in coal or coal mines.
8. Rights to mines created before 1898 in the case of land registered before 1898.

9. Where the title was registered between 1898 and 1925, rights to mines and minerals created before the title was registered.
10. A franchise.
11. A manorial right.
12. A right to rent reserved to the Crown in respect of a freehold.
13. A non-statutory right in respect of an embankment or sea or river wall.
14. A right to payment in lieu of tithe.

(Those interests in 10–14 above cease to be protected at the end of ten years from the date the Land Registration Act 2002 comes into force.)

Dispositions of registered land

The registered proprietor may exercise owner's powers, defined as the power to make a disposition of any kind permitted by the general law and also to charge the estate at law with the payment of money. A registered proprietor does not have the power to create a mortgage by demise: ss23 and 24.

A person's right to exercise owner's powers is to be taken to be free of any limitation affecting the validity of a disposition unless that limitation is reflected by an entry in the register or is imposed under the Land Registration Act 2002: s26. (Note: this only operates to protect the title of a person to whom a disposition is made; it does not affect the lawfulness of the disposition.)

If a disposition has to be completed by registration, it does not operate at law until the relevant registration requirements are met. The dispositions requiring completion by registration are:

1. a transfer;
2. the grant of a term of years for more than seven years, or to take effect in possession after three months, or where the right to possession is discontinuous, or certain leases under the Housing Act 1985;
3. the express grant or reservation of an interest of a kind contained in s1(2)(a) Law of Property Act 1925 (easement) other than a right registrable under the Commons Registration Act 1965;
4. the express grant or reservation of an interest contained in s1(2)(b) Law of Property Act 1925 (rentcharge) or s1(2)(e) Law of Property Act 1925 (right of entry);
5. the grant of a legal charge.

This requirement of completion by registration also applies to a disposition by operation of law, except a transfer on the death or bankruptcy of an individual, a transfer on the dissolution of a corporate proprietor or the creation of a local land charge: s27.

Effect of dispositions on priority

The general rule (s28) is that a disposition has no effect on the priority of an interest affecting a registered estate except as provided by ss29 and 30. Section 29 states that if a registrable disposition of a registered estate is made for valuable consideration, completion of the disposition by registration has the effect of postponing to the interest under the disposition any interest affecting the estate which is not protected. The priority of an interest is protected for this purpose if:

1. it is a registered charge or is the subject of a notice in the register;
2. it falls within Sch 3, unless the interest has at any time been protected by a notice;
3. it appears from the register to be excepted from the effect of registration;
4. in the case of leasehold land, the burden of the interest is incident to the estate.

Where the grant of a lease out of registered land does not involve a registrable disposition, this section has effect as if the grant did involve such a disposition and the disposition were registered. Section 30 contains provisions in similar terms applying to registered charges.

Schedule 3: unregistered interests which override a registered disposition or charge

1. A lease granted for less than seven years, except a lease which has to be registered.
2. An interest belonging at the time of the disposition to a person in actual occupation so far as it relates to land of which he is in actual occupation, except:

   a) an interest under the Settled Land Act 1925;
   b) the interest of a person of whom inquiry was made and who failed to disclose the interest when he could reasonably have been expected to do so;
   c) an interest which belongs to a person whose occupation would not have been obvious on an inspection, and of which the person to whom the disposition is made does not have actual knowledge;
   d) a leasehold estate granted to take effect after the end of three months and which has not taken effect in possession.
3. A legal easement or profit, except an easement or profit which is not within the actual knowledge of the person to whom the disposition is made and which would not have been obvious on an inspection of the land. This exception does not, however, apply if the person claiming the easement or profit proves that it has been exercised within the period of one year ending with the date of disposition.
4. The same interests as those contained in points 4–14, Sch 1 Land Registration Act 2002 (see above). (Those interests in points 10–14, Sch 1 cease to be protected at the end of ten years from the date the Land Registration Act 2002 comes into force.)

Notices

A notice is an entry on the register in respect of the burden of an interest affecting a registered estate, and is made against the registered estate affected. The fact that an interest is the subject of a notice does not of itself mean that the interest is valid, but if the interest is valid then priority is protected for the purposes of ss29 and 30: s32. Certain matters cannot be protected by the registration of a notice. No notice can be entered to protect an interest under a trust of land or a strict settlement; a lease for less than three years which is not required to be registered; a restrictive covenant as between a lessor and lessee; an interest which can be registered under the Commons Registration Act 1965; and an interest in coal mines under the Coal Industry Act 1994: s33.

A person claiming to be entitled to the benefit of an interest may apply to the registrar for the entry of a notice. The application may be for an agreed notice or a unilateral notice. The registrar can only approve an application for an agreed notice if:

1. the applicant is the registered proprietor or a person entitled to be registered as such;
2. the registered proprietor, or a person entitled to be registered, consents;
3. the registrar is satisfied as to the validity of the applicant's claim: s34.

If an agreed notice cannot be entered, then a unilateral notice has to be entered. If a unilateral notice is entered, the registrar must serve notice of the entry on the proprietor and any other person specified. The unilateral notice must state that it is such and specify the beneficiary of the notice. The beneficiary of the notice may apply at any time for the notice to be removed: s35. The registered proprietor of the estate affected by a unilateral notice may apply for the cancellation of the notice. Where such an application is made, the registrar must give the beneficiary of the notice notice of the application. If the beneficiary does not object within the prescribed period to the cancellation, the registrar must cancel the unilateral notice: s36. If the registrar is of the opinion that a registered estate is subject to an unregistered interest specified in Sch 1 which is not excluded by s33, he may enter a notice of that interest on the register. Rules will state who is to be served with notice of such an entry: s37. Where an interest other than a transfer is registered under s27, the registrar must enter a notice of that interest against the estate affected: s38.

Restrictions

A restriction is an entry on the register regulating the circumstances in which a disposition can be registered. It may prohibit the making of an entry in respect of any disposition or a disposition of a specified kind, or prohibit the making of an entry indefinitely, for a specified period or until the occurrence of a specified event.

The specified events may include: the giving of notice; the obtaining of a consent; or the making of an order by the court or registrar: s40.

Where a restriction is entered, no entry may be made on the register except in accordance with the restriction: s41. The registrar may enter a restriction if it appears to him to be necessary or desirable to do so:

1. to prevent invalidity or unlawfulness in relation to dispositions;
2. to secure that overreachable interests are overreached;
3. to protect a right or a claim in relation to a registered estate.

However, no restriction may be entered under (3) above to protect an interest which is, or could be, the subject of a notice.

Notice of the entry of a restriction must be given to the registered proprietor: s42. A person may apply to have a restriction entered if he is the registered proprietor, the proprietor consents, or he otherwise has a sufficient interest in the making of the entry: s43. Notice of an application must be served on the proprietor and any other person prescribed, and the application may not be determined before the end of the period allowed for objections, unless the proprietor and any other relevant person has indicated no objection or has objected. Notice need not be given, however, if the application is made by or with the consent of the registered proprietor, or is made in pursuance of rules or an order of the court or registrar or an undertaking in lieu: s45.

If two or more persons are registered as proprietor, the registrar must enter such restrictions as Rules will provide, to ensure that overreachable interests are overreached: s44. The court can also order the registration of a restriction, except that it cannot order that an interest be protected by a restriction if it could be protected by the entry of a notice: s47.

Charges

Charges rank in the order shown in the register: s48. Further advances can be tacked and have priority over a subsequent charge if the chargee has not received notice of the subsequent charge. A further advance can also be tacked and have priority if the advance is made in pursuance of an obligation to make further advances, and that obligation is entered on the register. A further advance can also be tacked and have priority if the parties have agreed a maximum amount to be secured, and that agreement was entered on the register. In any other circumstance, tacking is only possible with the agreement of a subsequent chargee: s49.

Once registration is completed, a charge has effect as a charge by deed by way of legal mortgage: s51. The proprietor of the charge is to be taken to have the powers of the owner of a legal mortgage, subject to any entry on the register to the contrary: this, however, only prevents the title of a disponee being questioned and does not affect the lawfulness of a disposition: s52. Thus, as between the mortgagor and mortgagee, the issue of whether a power of sale is exercisable needs to be considered, although that does not affect a purchaser.

If a mortgagee sells, for the purposes of s105 Law of Property Act 1925 (application of the proceeds) he is deemed to have notice of any matter which is registered: s54. If a charge is a local land charge, it can only be realised if it is entered on the register: s55. Where a charge is registered in the name of two or more, a valid receipt can be given by the proprietors of the charge, the survivor or survivors, or the personal representatives of the last survivor: s56. Rules may be made concerning entry on the register of a right of consolidation: s57.

Registration – general

Once a person is entered on the register as proprietor, the legal estate is deemed to be vested in him even though otherwise it would not be: s58. The boundary of a registered estate as shown for the purposes of the register is a general boundary unless determined, and a general boundary does not determine the exact line of the boundary. Rules may, however, make provision for a procedure to be followed for the exact line of a boundary to be determined, and as to how that fact is to be recorded on the register: s60.

Any person may inspect the register and take copies of the register or of filed documents: s66. Official copies of the entries on the register of documents are admissible in evidence to the same extent as the original. A person who relies on an official copy in which there is a mistake is not liable for loss suffered by another by reason of that mistake: s67.

The registrar must keep an index to enable it to be ascertained whether land is registered, how it is to be identified, whether it is affected by a caution against first registration and any other matter prescribed: s68. The registrar may, on application, provide information about the history of a title: s69. Rules will provide for official searches of the register: s70.

Priority periods will be dealt with in Regulations. An application for an entry on the register will be protected if it is one to which a priority period relates and it is made within that period. Where an application is so protected, any entry made in the register during the priority period is postponed to it: s72.

The general rule is that anyone may object to any application to the Land Registry. There are exceptions, in that only the beneficiary of a caution against first registration, or the beneficiary of a restriction, may object to its cancellation: s73.

An entry made in the register in relation to an application for registration of an unregistered estate or a registrable disposition has effect from the time of the making of the application: s74.

A petition in bankruptcy and a bankruptcy order are not interests affecting an estate. As soon as possible after a bankruptcy petition is registered under the Land Charges Act 1972, the registrar must enter a notice in the register. As soon as a bankruptcy order is made, a restriction must be entered. A person who acquires land from a bankrupt for value in good faith when no notice or restriction is registered obtains a good title if he had no notice of the bankruptcy proceedings: s86.

A right of pre-emption, an equity by estoppel or a mere equity have effect as interests in land which are capable of binding successors (subject to the rules about the effect of dispositions on priorities): ss115 and 116.

Electronic conveyancing

Part 8 (ss91–95) contains provision for the introduction, extension and use of electronic conveyancing. The implementation will be effected by Regulations, but matters which will be dealt with include electronic documents and electronic signatures. Documents to which relevant requirements apply will be deemed to be in writing or be deeds. The Land Registration Act 2002 makes provision for the establishment of a Land Registry electronic communications network, and Rules may provide for registration requirements to be followed and also for the electronic settlement of financial matters.

Adverse possession

The Limitation Acts do not apply to registered land: s96. A separate set of Rules and procedures relating to adverse possession and registered land is set out in Sch 6 to the Land Registration Act 2002.

A person can apply to be registered with a title to land by adverse possession if he has been in adverse possession for ten years, or if he had ceased to be in occupation within six months because of eviction by the registered proprietor, and on the day before eviction he had been in adverse possession for ten years and the eviction was not in pursuance of a court order. A person cannot make such an application if he is a defendant in possession proceedings or judgment has been given against him in the previous two years. Notice of an application must be given to the registered proprietor, any registered chargee, if the property is leasehold any superior title owner and anyone else specified. Anyone to whom notice is given may request that the application be dealt with under para 5 of Sch 6. If no such request is made, the applicant can be registered as proprietor. Under para 5 the applicant can only be registered if:

1. it would be unconscionable because of an equity by estoppel for the registered proprietor to seek to dispossess the applicant, and the circumstances are such that the applicant ought to be registered;
2. the applicant is for some other reason entitled to be registered as proprietor;
3. the land to which the application relates is adjacent to land owned by the applicant, the exact boundary line has not been determined, for at least ten years the applicant reasonably believed the land belonged to him and the estate was registered more than 12 months previously.

When a person is registered as proprietor, the title which he had by adverse possession is extinguished and replaced by the new registered title. Registration does not affect the priority of an interest affecting the estate. Registration extinguishes any charge, unless the application was one determined under para 5.

Alteration of the register (Sch 4)

Rectification is defined as an alteration of the register which involves the correction of a mistake and prejudicially affects the title of registered proprietor. The court can order the alteration of the register to correct a mistake, bring the register up to date, or give effect to any estate, right or interest excepted from the effect of registration. If the alteration is a rectification, then no order can be made by the court without the registered proprietor's consent, unless he has by fraud or lack of proper care caused or substantially contributed to the mistake, or it would for some other reason be unjust for the alteration not to be made.

The registrar may alter the register to correct a mistake, bring the register up to date, give effect to any matter excepted from the effect of registration or to remove a superfluous entry. No alteration affecting the title of a registered proprietor may be made without the proprietor's consent, unless he has by fraud or lack of proper care caused or substantially contributed to the mistake, or it would for some other reason be unjust for the alteration not to be made. Where the register is rectified, the alteration may affect for the future the priority of any interest affecting the registered estate.

Indemnities (Sch 8)

A person is entitled to be indemnified if he suffers loss because of:

1. rectification of the register;
2. a mistake whose correction would involve rectification;
3. a mistake in an official search or an official copy;
4. a mistake in a document kept at the Registry;
5. the loss or destruction of a document kept at the Registry; and
6. a mistake in the cautions register.

A person who suffers loss by reason of a change of title under s62 (upgrading) is to be treated as having suffered loss for this purpose, and a proprietor claiming in good faith under a forged disposition is also deemed to have suffered loss. No indemnity is payable if the person claiming an indemnity has suffered loss wholly or partly because of his own fraud, or wholly as the result of his own lack of proper care. If a claimant suffers loss partly as the result of his own lack of care, any indemnity is to be reduced to such extent as is fair, having regard to his share in the responsibility for the loss.

OBP Textbook Chapter 2.

Third party rights

In *UCB Group Ltd* v *Hedworth* [2002] 46 EG 200 the Court of Appeal considered the nature of occupation for the purposes of s70(1)(g) Land Registration Act (LRA) 1925. In that case, the defendant's husband was the registered proprietor, and in 1990 he granted the claimant a first legal charge over the property. It was accepted by all parties that at the date of the charge the husband held the property upon a bare trust for the defendant's wife. The wife had been in receipt of weekly payments made to her by her husband under a tenancy which she had granted to him in her capacity as beneficial owner. In 1997 the wife registered a caution to protect her interest and the claimant applied to have the caution vacated. Under s70(1)(g) LRA 1925, the rights of a person in actual occupation, or in receipt of the rents and profits, are an overriding interest, and the issue here was whether the wife was in receipt of the rents and profits. The Court held that a beneficiary under a bare trust who was in receipt of payments made by the registered proprietor under a tenancy by estoppel was not in receipt of the rents and profits of the land for the purposes of s70(1)(g) LRA 1925, and therefore did not have an overriding interest: the caution should be vacated.

In *Lloyd* v *Dugdale* [2002] 2 P & CR 13 the Court of Appeal emphasised the need for occupation by the person with the benefit of the rights. In this case, D was the major shareholder and managing director of a company, J Ltd. In 1987, D entered into an oral agreement with I, the owner of property held under a long lease, that I would grant a sub-lease of a unit in a block, apparently to D personally. There seemed to be some uncertainty as to who would be the prospective tenant, as in correspondence solicitors referred to the proposed lease to J Ltd. I agreed that D and J Ltd could go into occupation before completion of the lease, and with I's knowledge J Ltd spent £15,000 on alterations. The terms of a lease to D personally were agreed but no lease was executed, and in 1989 I issued proceedings against D and J Ltd claiming possession. D counterclaimed, contending that I was bound to grant the lease. In 1992 I died, and in 1993 his executors purchased the freehold. Up to 1993, J Ltd had paid rent. In 1994 I's executors sold the freehold to the claimants, expressly subject to existing rights of use and occupation and the existing legal proceedings between I, D and J Ltd. In 1995 J Ltd went into liquidation, and in 1996 the claimant issued fresh possession proceedings against D and J Ltd. The Court held that I had orally represented that he would lease the premises to D. But for I's representation, D would have found alternative premises and it would have been unconscionable for I to resile from the agreement. D could therefore have sustained the claim against I and I's executors by virtue of proprietary estoppel. However, when the executors sold the property to the claimants, the situation changed. At the time of the sale to the claimants, D was not in actual occupation; on the facts, J Ltd was. A distinction had to be drawn between D and J Ltd. D attended the premises in his capacity as managing director of J Ltd and in no other capacity, and therefore J Ltd was in occupation, not D personally. There was not sufficient evidence to justify the finding of a constructive trust in favour of D. The fact that the claimants acquired with notice of D's claim was not sufficient; there had to be something more. D therefore did not have an equity binding on the claimants.

OBP Textbook page 13, section 2.5.

Rectification and indemnity

Rectification

In the case of *Malory Enterprises Ltd* v *Cheshire Homes (UK) Ltd* [2002] Ch 216 the Court of Appeal emphasised the fact that once a person is registered as proprietor he has the legal estate, and considered the issue of rectification. In this case, a company, X Ltd, dishonestly obtained a land certificate in its own name relating to land of which the claimant, Malory Enterprises Ltd, was the registered proprietor. X Ltd sold the land to the first defendant, which was registered as proprietor on 12 January 1999. The land was used for storage by a company under the same control as the claimant. At the time of the transfer to the first defendant, the claimant found that the locks on the fence had been changed. The claimant sought rectification of the register and damages for trespass. At first instance the court ordered rectification, effective from 12 January 1999. The Court of Appeal held that although X Ltd had no title to convey to the first defendant, once the first defendant was registered as proprietor under s69 Land Registration Act 1925, it had vested in it the fee simple. Section 69, however, only dealt with the legal estate, and did not vest in the first defendant the legal estate together with all rights, privileges and appurtenances. On first registration, the fee simple was vested in the proprietor together with all rights, privileges etc. That was not the case under s69. As s69 only dealt with the legal estate, the transfer to the first defendants was not a disposition for the purposes of s20 Land Registration Act 1925 as it was of no effect. The transfer to the first defendant was therefore subject to the rights of the claimant as beneficial owner. The Court indicated that a right to apply for rectification of the register could be an overriding interest. It declined to make the rectification retrospective, but did not consider it was in any event necessary as the claimant was always entitled to possession as against the first defendant, and could therefore claim in trespass. There was a divergence of opinion among the members of the Court as to whether rectification could be retrospective or could only take effect from the date of application.

OBP Textbook page 19, section 2.7.

Indemnity

In *Prestige Properties Ltd* v *Scottish Provident Institution* [2002] 3 WLR 1011 Lightman J had to consider the issue of an indemnity and how to apportion responsibility for loss. The claimant purchased land in 1997 and obtained a search certificate from the Land Registry confirming that part was not registered. The claimant did not apply for first registration but, relying on the certificate, sold the land to the first defendant on the basis that the first defendant could retain a sum of money if it could not procure registration within six months. When the first defendant applied to register the title, errors in the original search certificate were discovered. The piece of land was in fact three pieces and all were registered. The first defendant already owned one part, and the other two parts were parts of other registered titles. The first defendant refused to pay the retention and claimed an indemnity under s83 Land Registration Act (LRA) 1925. The court held that, in order to be able to claim an indemnity, a claimant had to establish that he had suffered loss because of an error in an official search. The error had to be a cause, but not necessarily the sole effective cause. The indemnity could, however, be reduced under s83(6) LRA 1925 to the extent that the claimant had contributed to the loss because of a lack of proper care. The court stated that, in order to assess the care to be expected of a claimant, the duty owed by a solicitor to his client provided a measure. The court emphasised that the whole purpose of the legislative scheme was that search certificates could be relied on, and a solicitor need not go behind what a search certificate said. Although the claimant was not under a statutory duty to register the title after it purchased, it should have done so in order to protect its interests. In this case there was an error in the certificate; the claimant was entitled to rely on the certificate, and in relying on the certificate had exercised proper care. However, had the claimant applied for first registration, the error would have come to light at that stage. The claimant was therefore partly responsible for its loss and the indemnity was reduced by 10 per cent to reflect the claimant's responsibility.

OBP Textbook page 20, section 2.7.

The Contract – Formalities

Formalities

The case *Clark* v *Chandler* [2002] EWCA Civ 1249 considered the relationship between s2 Law of Property (Miscellaneous Provisions) Act 1989 and s53(1)(c) Law of Property Act (LPA) 1925. In 1988 Mrs Chandler purchased a house in her sole name. In 1997 she and her husband agreed to divorce, and a document was prepared and signed by Mr Chandler which purported to transfer his beneficial interest to Mrs Chandler in return for a sum of money, although the precise terms were not finalised. Mr Chandler made a will appointing Mrs Clark his executrix and beneficiary. The divorce was concluded and then Mr Chandler died. It was first held that, as the agreement was not signed by both parties, it was void as a contract as it did not comply with s2 of the 1989 Act, nor did the document take effect as a disposition under s53(1)(c) LPA 1925. It was not an unconditional and immediate disposition. It was drafted to assist in processing the divorce, Mr Chandler had not intended to make an unconditional transfer of his beneficial interest, and it was not successful as a conditional disposition as the condition had not been fulfilled. Mrs and Mr Chandler had held the property as joint tenants, and she therefore had the entire beneficial interest.

OBP Textbook page 22, section 3.2.

Constructive trusts and estoppel

In *James* v *Evans* [2000] 3 EGLR 1 the Court of Appeal emphasised that it is not easy to establish an estoppel or constructive trust when the relevant contractual formalities are not observed. Here, H, the owner, was negotiating with E for a ten-year lease of a farm. E was let into possession to look after sheep which he was to acquire under the contract and matters were agreed. E sent his part of the contract signed to H's solicitors. H then became ill and, during a telephone conversation, H's solicitor asked that money be sent: accordingly a cheque was sent for the price of the sheep, half the valuation expenses and six months' rent. H died. All the negotiations had been headed subject to contract. H's personal representative commenced possession proceedings and E opposed, contending that he was entitled to remain either under a constructive trust or because of a proprietary estoppel based upon H's solicitor's request that he pay money. The Court held that E's claim failed. There was no estoppel arising out of the solicitor's request. A solicitor does not have ostensible or apparent authority to conclude a contract binding on his client, actual authority being needed, which also was not present. There was no contract as required by s2 Law of Property (Miscellaneous Provisions) Act 1989, and no estoppel or constructive trust. The Court distinguished *Yaxley* v *Gotts & Gotts* [1999] 3 WLR 1217, because in that case there was a joint enterprise which one party did not wish to pursue, whereas here there were simply negotiations for a lease which had not been concluded.

OBP Textbook page 28, section 3.3.

The Contract – Contents

The contract

In *Smith* v *Royce Properties Ltd* [2002] 2 P & CR 5 the Court of Appeal considered the interpretation of a contract when the description of the property is not clear. In 1977 the claimant trustees sold land to the defendant's predecessors which included two parcels, Ordnance Survey 0062 and 0052. The conveyance granted the trustees an option to repurchase if, within 20 years, planning permission was granted for 0062, but no mention was made of 0052. There were several plans on which the precise extent of the land involved was ambiguous. The registered plan included 0052 and 0062. In 1996 the trustees obtained planning permission for use of the land as allotments with access and parking. This was part of a larger scheme. The application included allotments on 0052 and 0062, and a car park was to be built on 0052. The trustees contended that this entitled them to exercise the option in respect of 0052 and part of 0062. At first instance it was held that they could not. Parcel 0052 was not in terms included in the option plan, and the words did not include it. The option was not triggered as no planning permission was needed to change the use from agriculture to allotments.

The Court of Appeal allowed the appeal. The judge at first instance had not placed sufficient weight on the registered plan, and having concluded that there was ambiguity between the plan and the wording of the option, more weight should have been attached to the commercial context. A common sense approach would indicate that the parties had intended the option to relate to both 0052 and 0062. It made no commercial sense to exclude 0052. There was no physical boundary between 0052 and 0062, the only boundary being the grid line on the Ordnance Survey map. The filed plan controlled the verbal description and produced a sensible commercial result. The option was exercisable. Whether a triggering event occurred was simply a matter of construction. The option referred to the grant of planning permission in respect of any part of the land, and that was satisfied. In *Clarke* v *O'Keefe* (2000) 80 P & CR 127 the Court of Appeal accepted that where there had been a plan on the contract at the scale of 1:2500, with a larger scale plan attached to the transfer, and there had been an acceptance that the precise boundary was not clear and there had been meetings on site in order to try define precisely the boundary line, extrinsic evidence could be admitted to define the precise line of the boundary, as the small scale plan was not precise enough to do so, the width of the area in dispute being only about 12 feet. The Court applied *Scarfe* v *Adams* [1981] 1 All ER 843 and said that a small scale plan is useless in defining precise boundaries.

The position of a stakeholder was considered by the Court of Appeal in *Gribbon* v *Lutton* [2002] QB 902. G was negotiating to sell land to W and it was agreed that a non-refundable deposit would be paid by W to be held by L, G's solicitor, as stakeholder. If a contract was concluded within a specified time, the deposit would be a part payment; if no contract was concluded, then it would be forfeited to G unless the failure to conclude the contract arose because of G's default. The deposit was paid to L but no contract was concluded. L issued interpleader proceedings before a recorder to determine entitlement as between G and W, and the recorder held that the deposit was repayable to W. That decision was not appealed. G then sued L, alleging that L had been negligent in not ensuring that the deposit was not refundable, or alternatively alleging that the recorder's decision was wrong. The Court of Appeal set out some basic principles.

In a normal case where a deposit is held by a stakeholder under a contract, there are actually two contracts: a bilateral contract between the seller and purchaser, and a separate contract between the seller, purchaser and stakeholder. Where there is a pre-contract deposit, the usual rule is that it has to be returned to the purchaser unless a contract is concluded. The Court emphasised that the position of a stakeholder is governed by contract, and the stakeholder is not a fiduciary or a trustee. Entitlement to a deposit could not be determined by a tripartite contract between seller, purchaser and stakeholder in the absence of a bilateral contract between seller and purchaser. It was found as a fact that G provided no consideration, and there was therefore no contract between G and W. The Court emphasised that the entitlement to the deposit is determined by the bilateral contract and not the tripartite contract. In *Chillingworth* v *Esch* [1924] 1 Ch 97, where a purchaser had paid a sum before contract as a deposit and part payment to the vendor, when no contract was concluded the Court of Appeal held that the deposit was to be returned, and dealt with the matter purely as contractual. In the instant case, in the absence of an express lock out clause, the seller G had provided no consideration and the deposit should be refunded to W. Had there been a lock out clause, then the seller would have provided consideration and the outcome would have been different. The Court stated that in interpleader proceedings between a seller and purchaser as to entitlement, the stakeholder was not entitled to take part, as his duty was simply to deal with the deposit in accordance with the bilateral contract. The Court also indicated that L should not have been allowed to reopen the matter of entitlement to the deposit in the way in which he did, although there was some disagreement as to the precise reason: either because of issue estoppel or alternatively because of abuse of process, as the matter was res judicata.

OBP Textbook page 34, section 4.2.

Special conditions

There have been several recent cases involving the interpretation of options and rights of pre-emption. In *Bircham & Co Nominees (No 2) Ltd* v *Worrell Holdings Ltd* [2001] 3 EGLR 83 the Court of Appeal considered the effect of pre-emption rights. In this case, the tenant had a lease and the lease contained a clause to the effect that if the tenant wished to assign the lease, the tenant should first offer the lease to the landlord, stating the price at which it was to sell. If the landlord did not respond within 21 days, the tenant could proceed to dispose of the lease at a price not less than that at which the lease had been offered to the landlord. On 28 October 1997 after receiving an offer for the lease of £1.7 million, the tenant offered the lease to the landlord for the same sum. On 18 November 1997 the landlord replied that it wished to exercise the option and would offer £1.7 million to include furnishings. By January 1998 the tenant was contending that there was no binding contract. The landlord contended that the letter of 28 October 1997, coupled with the lease, created a binding contract and that the effect of that letter and the lease was to confer an equitable interest on the landlord. The Court of Appeal found for the tenant and held that the effect of a pre-emption clause depended on its own terms. The clause did not impose an obligation on the tenant to offer the lease to the landlord at any time earlier than before entering into a contract to assign the lease. There was no obligation to keep the offer open for any particular period. The only time limit was that within which the landlord had to respond.

A pre-emption clause did not create an equitable interest in property where, as here, the offer could could be withdrawn at any time. If under a right of pre-emption the offer cannot be withdrawn for a specified period, an equitable interest arises as soon as the offer is made. In this case there was no contract, as s2 Law of Property (Miscellaneous Provisions) Act 1989 was not satisfied. The right of pre-emption was not converted into an option by the letter of 28 October 1997, and the letter of 18 November 1997 did not exercise an option. It did not accept the offer, but rather made a counter-offer.

In *Freund* v *Charles Scott Developments (South Devon) Ltd* [2002] 2 P & CR 31 the effect of a conditional contract was considered. There, T entered into an agreement to purchase land from F; F's obligation to sell was conditional upon planning permission being granted, but the agreement also provided that at any time F could serve a notice on T requiring completion. F agreed not to oppose any planning application. In the agreement, T was defined as the purchaser and planning permission was defined as a permission following an application made by the purchaser. T assigned the benefit of the contract to C Ltd, who applied for and obtained planning permission. F was not told of the assignment of the contract for a long period. F brought proceedings for a declaration that he was not bound by the agreement, as the agreement was personal to T. The court held that the agreement meant what it said. It was not possible to read the definition of the purchaser as meaning T and its assignees. The planning permission had to be obtained by T and not an assignee. F could not be under an obligation not to oppose a planning application made by someone whose identity he did not know. The identity of the purchaser was important, not only because F agreed not to oppose any planning application, but also because F could serve a notice on the purchaser at any time requiring completion. The fact that the parties were named did not prevent an assignment, but following the assignment of the benefit the parties remained the same and T remained the purchaser for the purposes of the planning application.

In *Hallam Land Management Ltd* v *UK Coal Mining Ltd* [2002] 2 EGLR 80 the Court of Appeal had to deal with the effects of the terms of an option. In 1996 V granted an option to S to purchase 45 acres. The land was in an area identified for development in the local plan. The price to be paid was £100,000 per developable acre, defined as each acre of the site in respect of which planning permission was granted following an application by the purchaser, excluding open space. The purchaser undertook to submit a planning application by a specified date and pursue it. In 1998 S assigned the benefit of the option to H, the appellant. By that time the local authority was opposed to the original development and the appellant submitted an application in respect of 45 acres, of which 2.5 acres were an office and 42.5 acres were open space, of which about 40 per cent would be landscaped. Outline permission was granted and the appellant then purported to exercise the option, contending that the purchase price was £250,000. V contended that the exercise was not valid and sold the land to the second respondent. The appellant claimed specific performance. The Court held that the claim failed. The property was identified in the agreement as 45 acres or substantially the whole. The appellant could not apply for permission in respect of only part. That would involve re-writing the agreement, which was not possible. The agreement was initially reached against the background of the local plan, and it had not been envisaged that the local authority would not permit the development of the whole site. It was significant that a relatively small sum had been paid for the option, and the purchaser was therefore to bear the risk. It was a question of fact as to whether the planning application was for substantially the whole site, and 2.5 acres was not. The landscaping was not development in the ordinary sense of the word, and it was not appropriate to apply a technical planning definition. Even if landscaping was development, 40 per cent, in any event, was not substantially the whole site.

In *Midwood* v *Morgan* [2001] 3 EGLR 127, the precise extent of an option was dealt with. In 1987 M, who owned three pieces of land, transferred some to the defendants, Mr and Mrs Morgan, as co-owners. In relation to part of the land, which he retained, he granted the transferee a right of pre-emption if he decided to sell so long as the transferee was the beneficial owner. The clause made several references to the transferee in the singular. In 1990 by a deed of gift, Mr Morgan transferred his legal and beneficial interest to Mrs Morgan, who became the sole owner. M issued proceedings for a declaration that the right of pre-emption had expired. The court held that it had. In the 1987 transfer there was reference in the pre-emption clause to the transferee in the singular. Other clauses of the transfer referred to the transferees in the plural. The transferee in the pre-emption clause meant both transferees jointly. The obligations relating to the giving of notice and the paying of a deposit referred to both defendants, and the clause that there was a right of pre-emption so long as the transferee remained the owner meant as long as the transferees together were the owners. Both the defendants had to be beneficial owners at the time the clause came to be implemented.

OBP Textbook page 41, section 4.3.

Pre-contract Searches and Inquiries

Searches

One of the searches which has to be carried out is the local search and inquiries of the local authority. This is designed to elicit a variety of information, including planning matters and details about roads, drains and sewers. Inquiries in relation to water, drains and sewers were in the past made of local authorities, although under the Water Act 1989 responsibility for drainage and water was given to the water service companies. In 2002 a new procedure was introduced, under which inquiries about water, sewage and drainage are now to be made direct to water companies and no longer to local authorities.

Local authorities have to record various matters under the Local Land Charges Act (LLCA) 1975, including planning charges. Under s10 LLCA 1975, a person who suffers loss because of an error in an official search is entitled to compensation. In *Smith* v *South Gloucestershire Council* [2002] 38 EGLR 206 the Court of Appeal considered the computation of compensation following an incorrect search. In that case, in 1995 the claimants purchased a derelict farmhouse intending to use it for home, business and investment. In November 1998, after spending £220,000, they discovered that the property was subject to an agricultural occupancy restriction imposed under town and country planning legislation, the effect of which was that house could only be occupied by a person employed in agriculture. When the local search had been carried out in 1995, the council had failed to disclose this condition. The claimants claimed compensation. In September 2001 at first instance, it was held that the compensation was to be assessed in the sum of £197,500, being the difference between the value of the property with the condition and without it in November 1998 when the problem was discovered. The claimant appealed and the Court of Appeal allowed the appeal. It held that the appellants had acted reasonably in not selling the property before receiving compensation. They were entitled to have the compensation assessed by reference to value not at the date the breach of duty was discovered, but at the date of the hearing, September 2001, and the compensation was increased to £292,500.

In *Gooden* v *Northamptonshire County Council* [2002] 1 EGLR 137 the effect of incorrect information given by a local authority was considered. The appellants were purchasing a property to develop. In front of the property was a public highway called the Banks, and between the Banks and the property was a path known as the Slope. The appellant's solicitor made the usual inquiries as to the status of the roads, and was told that the Banks was maintainable at the public expense, but that a shared private access was not. No specific mention was made of the Slope in the question or the reply. The appellant, having purchased, proceeded to develop, and was then informed by the council that the Slope was not part of the maintained public highway. An adjoining owner brought proceedings in respect of interference with the Slope. The appellants claimed damages. By a majority the Court of Appeal found for the council. They found that on the facts the council had not been negligent. The fact that the reply was incorrect did not of itself mean that the council was negligent. In order to found a claim for negligent misstatement the appellant had to establish that the reply given was specific to the inquirer (which it was), it had to be purpose specific as it related to the decision whether to purchase (which it was), and it also had to be transaction specific. As the council did not know of the appellant's development plans, the reply would have failed to satisfy this last requirement. If the council had been negligent, it would have been liable insofar as the information led to the decision to purchase, but no further. In order to recover development losses it would have had to have been shown that the council was aware of the plans.

OBP Textbook page 46, section 5.2.

Investigating and Deducing Title – Particular Problems

Co-owners

It is said that a joint tenancy cannot be severed by a will, but in *Re Woolnough* [2002] WTLR 595 wills were effective to effect a severance. In that case, E and L were joint tenants of a house. In 1981 they made identical wills, providing that the survivor should have the house for life, and on the survivor's death the house should pass to a niece. There was no notice of severance. E died and L made a new will leaving all property to charity. The court held that the wills in which each gave the other a life interest were sufficient to amount to an agreement to sever. The reference in the wills to each person's half share indicated that they were treating the share as being disposed of by the will, which could only occur if there was a beneficial tenancy in common.

OBP Textbook page 74, section 9.2.

Attorneys

The case *Re W* [2001] 4 All ER 88 dealt with the burden of proof in relation to objecting to an enduring power of attorney. In 1996 W granted an enduring power of attorney to her eldest child, X, and two years later X applied for the power to be registered. She gave notice to two of W's other children, who objected to the registration. It was argued that at the time the power was created, W did not have the necessary capacity and understanding. The Court of Appeal held that under s6(6) Enduring Powers of Attorney Act 1985, the burden of proving lack of capacity was on the objectors. The burden was not shifted by the production of some evidence tending to show that the donor of the power lacked capacity, but remained throughout with the objectors.

OBP Textbook page 83, section 9.7.

Completion

In *Twinsectra Ltd* v *Yardley* [2002] 2 WLR 802 the position of a solicitor receiving money was considered. S1 was a solicitor who was acting for a client negotiating for the purchase of a property. A lender was found to finance the purchase, but required a solicitor's undertaking that the money would be repaid, which S1 was not prepared to give. The client then approached a second solicitor, S2, who was prepared to give the relevant undertaking. S2 gave an undertaking that the loan would be retained until it was needed to be used to acquire property, and the money would be used solely for that purpose. S2 also undertook to repay the loan. S1 assured S2 that the money would be used to purchase the property, and the money was paid by S2 to S1, who released it to the client: a large proportion of the money was used otherwise than in the property purchase. The House of Lords held that the undertaking given by S2 made it clear that the money was not at the free disposal of the client, and that S2 was only to part with the money for the specified purpose. The purpose of acquisition of property was sufficiently certain to create a trust, and the fact that the lender had not intended to create a trust was irrelevant. S2 therefore held the money on trust for the lender, subject to a power to apply it by way of a loan in accordance with the undertaking. The money remained the lender's until it was so applied. When S2 paid the money to S1, it was therefore in breach of trust, but S1, although he knew the background, had not behaved dishonestly. To be liable as an accessory to a breach of trust a person has to act dishonestly, and he had not.

OBP Textbook page 99, section 11.5.

Late Completion

Completion notice

In *Aero Properties Ltd* v *Citycrest Properties Ltd* [2002] 2 P & CR 21 the issue of when a completion notice can be served was addressed. The claimants entered into seven related contracts with the defendants. Five contracts were for the purchase of the leases of five flats in a block, one contract was for the purchase of the share capital of D Ltd (which owned the freehold) and one contract was for the purchase of the share capital of I Ltd (which owned the leases of 12 of the flats). Each of the five flat purchase contracts contained a provision that completion was conditional on completion taking place in respect of the other four flat purchase contracts and the two share purchase contracts. Each flat was to be sold free of mortgage, and the contracts incorporated the National Conditions of Sale, except that a completion notice, if served, had to be completed within 16, not ten, days. The contract provided for a 10 per cent deposit, and if less than 10 per cent was paid and the vendor became entitled to forfeit the deposit, the full 10 per cent was payable. Completion date passed and the vendor served a notice to complete. The purchaser contended that the vendor was not ready and willing to complete as the vendor did not have the charge certificates relating to the head lease belonging to I Ltd in its possession, although the whereabouts were known. The vendor contended that the contracts were rescinded, whereas the purchaser claimed that the contracts were still subsisting and claimed specific performance. The court held that the mere fact that charge certificates were not in the possession of the vendor at the time the completion notice was served did not mean the vendor was not able and willing to complete. It was accepted that a seller was entitled to set up the necessary administrative arrangements concerning completion. For a purchaser to show that a completion notice was invalid because a vendor was not ready and willing to perform his outstanding obligations, a purchaser would have to show either that the vendor was in breach of some obligation, or that the vendor would not have been able within the time required to set up the administrative arrangements for completion.

In *Hanson* v *SWEB Property Developments Ltd* [2002] 1 P & CR 35 there was a contract for the sale of a property. The seller agreed to carry out certain work. Under the contract, which incorporated the National Conditions of Sale, while the seller was carrying out the work it was to pay for alternative accommodation for the purchaser. Completion date was ten days after the seller served notice on the purchaser confirming that the works had been completed. The seller served notice on the buyer, but completion did not take place. The buyer claimed that the work had not been satisfactorily carried out, and also disputed how much had to be paid to complete. The buyer wrote offering to pay what he considered was due, which was not agreed by the seller. The seller served a completion notice. The buyer applied for a declaration that the completion notice was invalid, as the works had not been satisfactorily completed, and also that his offering to pay what he considered due was performance of his obligations at completion. The Court of Appeal held that there was an implied term that the work would be properly carried out, and the fact that there was work remaining to be done meant that that obligation had been breached and gave rise to a claim for damages. This was not, however, an obligation such as to prevent the seller from serving a notice to complete. Also, it was not open to the buyer to say that he had performed his obligations by offering to pay what he though was due, when that was not agreed and was wrong.

OBP Textbook page 102, section 12.2.

Remedies

Other remedies

In *Holaw (470) Ltd* v *Stockton Estates Ltd* (2001) 81 P & CR 29 the court considered a variety of problems, including rectification. The facts were complicated, but can be summarised for present purposes as follows. L was the fee simple owner of two pieces of land, A and P. Long leases of both properties had been granted, and C was the lessee of both. A 21-year underlease from 1968 of P was granted to X, and in the lease X was granted a right of way over part of A to enable access to be gained to a car park. In 1989 C contracted to sell the head lease of A to K, who in turn contracted to sell the lease to S, the defendants. The contract between C and K was subject to the Law Society Conditions of Sale, under which there was a clause that the transfer 'shall' contain such reservations and grants of rights over land sold and land retained as would have been implied had both pieces been sold simultaneously. The contract between K and S was, however, subject to the National Conditions of Sale, which contained a clause to the effect that the vendor could require that the transfer reserve or grant such rights. C transferred the head lease of A direct to S, and the transfer stated that it was subject to the rights contained in the 1968 underlease, but there was no reference to other rights. S applied for and obtained first registration. The 1968 underlease expired and in 1990 a new lease of P was granted on the same terms as the 1968 lease, but only including a right of way over A insofar as C was able to grant it. The claimant in due course acquired the head lease of P from C and issued proceedings, claiming that there was a right of way over A in favour of P.

The court held that the claim failed for a variety of reasons. The crucial transaction was the sale of the head lease of A to S in 1989. This was a sale of part, as at that time C owned the head lease to both A and P. This was a sale of the servient tenement and a retention of the dominant tenement. It was held first that C could have required that the transfer to S contain the relevant reservation, but it did not. The contractual provisions relating to the reservation of rights merged in the conveyance on completion and could no longer be enforced, with the result that the issue of rectification had to be considered. The court held that had the sale been from C to K, then C could have obtained rectification, as the relevant contractual condition stated that the transfer 'shall' contain appropriate reservations. C could not, however, claim rectification against the defendants. The contract between K and S merely gave the vendor a right to have the relevant right reserved, which right was not exercised. A right of rectification is an equity which can be binding on successors who acquire with notice, but on the facts as found in this case S did not have sufficient notice of the position to be a purchaser with notice. It was also held that the right was not an overriding interest under the Land Registration Act 1925. A right of rectification can be an overriding interest, but C was not in occupation or in receipt of the rents and profits. The right to rectify arose immediately after completion, by which time C had divested itself of all interest in the property and was no longer in receipt of the rents and profits. The court did not follow *Abbey National Building Society* v *Cann* [1991] AC 56, which held that a sale and mortgage were contemporaneous, but held that in this situation there was a scintilla temporis which had this effect. Finally, this was a sale of a servient tenement, and under the rule in *Wheeldon* v *Burrows* (1879) 12 Ch D 31 there are very limited implied reservations on such a sale. In *Peckham* v *Ellison* (1999) 70 P & CR 439 there had been an exception, but the court held that in this case the facts were not such as to render this an exceptional transaction, so that there would be an implied reservation of an easement in favour of the retained land.

OBP Textbook page 112, section 13.6.

Leases

The grant of a lease

The question of the enforceability of restrictive covenants normally comes up for consideration in relation to freehold properties, but the issue can also be relevant in leasehold conveyancing. In *Willams* v *Kiley T/A CK Supermarkets Ltd* [2002] NPC 149 the local authority had granted leases of a number of shops in a small parade. The claimant was a newsagent, confectioner and tobacconist at number four. The defendant carried on business at numbers six and eight. In the lease of number four there was a covenant restricting the use of the premises to those carried on by the claimant. The use of number six in the lease was as a meat purveyor, but this had been waived, and the lease of number eight specified the use of that unit as a grocery and general store. In the leases of both six and eight covenants prohibited use as a newsagent, confectioner and tobacconist. The defendant operated a small supermarket selling a wide range of products, including tobacco, stationery and confectionery. The claimant contended that this use was in breach of the terms of the leases of six and eight and that there was a letting scheme which enabled him to enforce the covenants directly.

The Court of Appeal indicated that the principles applicable to a letting scheme were similar to those for the existence of a building scheme when dealing with freehold covenants. It is not normally necessary, however, to establish a scheme, because the landlord retains the right to enforce each individual lease. The simple fact that leases contain similar restrictive covenants does not of itself infer a scheme. The Court here, however, found that there was a letting scheme. The leases here were all in similar terms, and the restrictions were originally imposed by the council to establish an overall scheme for the shopping parade. There was a defined area and the restrictions were clearly set out. The leases contained no provision for the uses to be varied, and also contained no express obligation on the council to enforce the covenants. There was reciprocity of obligation, in that each lessee was under an obligation to carry on a particular trade and was protected against competition in that trade from the other lessees. The fact that the council had allowed a change in the use of one unit did not prevent a scheme from arising. This was a straightforward conflict between two lessees, and whether there was a breach was essentially a question of fact. Although the business carried on by the defendant was not exclusively in the conflicting trade, occupying only some 12 per cent of its display area, once the activity was sufficiently large to constitute a separate trade the defendant was in breach. The fact that it was not a dominant activity on the part of the defendant did not lessen the impact on the claimant. The defendant was in breach of the restrictive covenant, and as there was a letting scheme the claimant was entitled to enforce it directly against the defendant.

OBP Textbook page 118, section 14.2.

Statutory intervention

In *J S Bloor (Measham) Ltd* v *Calcott* [2002] 1 EGLR 222 the court held that a tenant of agricultural property protected under the Agricultural Holdings Act 1986 could lose that protection where the landlord could assert a claim to possession based upon proprietary estoppel because of the tenant's conduct, and there was no rule that proprietary estoppel had no operation where statutory protection was involved.

OBP Textbook page 121, section 14.4.

Leasehold covenants

In *BHP Petroleum Great Britain Ltd* v *Chesterfield Properties Ltd* [2002] 1 All ER 821 the effect of the Landlord and Tenant (Covenants) Act 1995 was considered. Under that Act, on an assignment of a reversion a landlord can serve a notice under s8 requesting that that he be released from the landlord covenants. If the tenant does not object, the landlord will be released. If the tenant objects, the landlord can apply to the court for an order for release. This procedure applies to 'landlord covenants', which are covenants to be observed by the landlord, defined as the person for the time being entitled to the reversion. The release provisions do not apply to covenants which are personal to a particular party. In this case, there was an agreement by C to grant a lease to the claimant following building works being completed. In the agreement, C agreed to remedy any building defects arising within six years, and that obligation was expressed to be personal to C. The lease was granted and in due course C transferred its interest in the property to another company and served a notice under s8 of the 1995 Act requesting release. The tenant did not serve a counternotice objecting. In due course defects became apparent in the building works. C contended that it had been released by operation of law, as the tenant had not objected. It was held that a covenant which was personal to the landlord could not be a landlord covenant, and would not therefore be released by a notice served under s8. There was no distinction of principle between a covenant which was personal and one which touched and concerned the land. A covenant which related to the land could, as a matter of contract, be made personal; whether it was was a matter for the contracting parties.

In *Wallis Fashion Group Ltd* v *CGU Life Assurance Ltd* (2001) 81 P & CR 393 the court considered the issue of authorised guarantee agreements under the Landlord and Tenant (Covenants) Act 1995. The defendant was the landlord of a shopping centre in which all the units were let. The lease required the landlord's consent to assign, which was not to be unreasonably withheld. The lease was coming to an end and the plaintiff applied for a new lease under the Landlord and Tenant Act 1954. All matters were agreed except the provision dealing with assignments. The Landlord and Tenant (Covenants) Act 1995 would apply to the new lease, and therefore on an assignment by the tenant the tenant would be released from its obligations under the lease. The landlord, under s16 of the 1995 Act, could, however, on an assignment require the outgoing tenant to enter into an authorised guarantee agreement as a condition of giving consent. The landlord wished to have included in the new lease a clause whereby, in the event of an assignment, the tenant would have to enter into an authorised guarantee agreement. The tenant disagreed and wished for the clause to read that the landlord could require an authorised guarantee agreement only 'where reasonable'. The court found for the tenant. The scheme of the 1995 Act was that a landlord could require an authorised guarantee agreement as a condition of giving consent to an assignment. A landlord could not, however, insist on an authorised guarantee agreement as of right in all cases, but only where it was reasonable to do so.

OBP Textbook page 122, section 14.5.

Consent to assignment

The case *Aubergine Enterprises Ltd* v *Lakewood International Ltd* [2002] 1 WLR 2149 involved the issue of a landlord's consent to an assignment. By a contract, the buyer agreed to buy a leasehold property, with a completion date of 30 September 1999, and the sale was subject to the Standard Conditions of Sale. Under Condition eight, where a landlord's consent to assign was necessary, if consent had not been given or had only been given subject to conditions to which the buyer could reasonably object within three days of completion, the buyer could withdraw. Under the lease the landlord's consent to an assignment was necessary, such consent not to be unreasonably withheld. On 21 September 1999 the landlord wrote to the seller's solicitors in a letter headed 'subject to licence', confirming that the landlord would agree in principle to the assignment and setting out various requirements which would have to be complied with. An engrossed copy of the licence was sent to the landlord for execution. On 30 September 1999 the purchaser purported to withdraw from the contract and requested the return of the deposit. The Court of Appeal held that the consent required under Standard Condition eight was not limited to prior written consent, unconditional consent, consent in a deed or other document, nor did it mean that a conditional consent had to be satisfied by completion date. The fact that the landlord headed letters 'subject to licence' and stated conditions to be performed did not qualify the indication of consent so as to make it equivocal or uncertain. The letter of 21 September 1999 was a consent well outside the three-day period. The letter contained reasonable terms on which the licence could be completed and the buyer was therefore not entitled to withdraw.

OBP Textbook page 124, section 14.6.

Sub-leases

In *Allied Dunbar Assurance plc* v *Homebase Ltd* [2002] 2 EGLR 23 the issue was consent to sub-letting. T had a 25-year lease, which included a covenant not to assign or sublet without the landlord's consent, such consent not to be unreasonably withheld. The lease contained provisions that on any sub-letting the rent was to be not less than the market rent, was to include repairing covenants in similar terms to those in the head lease and was to provide for upwards only rent reviews on the same dates as the review dates in the head lease. T found a prospective sub-tenant who was not prepared to pay the full rent or accept the full repairing liability. A draft agreement was prepared recording a fixed rent from 2005 and the draft underlease contained terms reflecting the head lease. There was also to be a collateral deed, expressed to be personal to the proposed sub-lessee, in which T agreed to indemnify the sub-tenant in respect of the difference between the rent in the agreement and in the head lease, and also the cost of complying in full with the repairing obligations. The landlord refused consent. The court held that the agreement and draft lease and the collateral deed were to be construed as a single document. The rent was as set out in the agreement and did not accord with the terms in the lease. The agreement as to repairs was not in the same form as the lease, as the effect was that repairs were to be carried out by T and the sub-lessee jointly, whereas under the lease the repairs were the tenant's sole responsibility. The proposed underletting did not comply with the requirements as set out in the lease, and therefore no question as to reasonableness arose to be determined. The landlord had an interest in controlling who was sub-tenant and who was in occupation, and wished the person in occupation to be responsible. It made no difference that the indemnity was to be personal to the sub-tenant.

OBP Textbook page 124, section 14.7.

Mortgages

Introduction

In *Raja* v *Lloyds TSB Bank plc* (2001) 82 P & CR 16 the Court of Appeal had to consider the effect of a sale by a mortgagee in possession. The mortgagee, under a legal charge, had taken possession and sold property on 17 October 1991. On 20 October 1997 the mortgagor issued proceedings claiming breach of duty, in that the mortgagee had not obtained the best price and the expenses incurred were unreasonable. The issue was whether the claim was statute barred. The limitation period under the Limitation Act 1980 is 12 years for an action on a specialty, but six years for others. The Court of Appeal held that the duties of a mortgagee in possession arose in equity and not in contract or tort. The duties did not depend on an enforceable contract between the parties, but were owed also to subsequent mortgagees and sureties. The duties did not arise out of an implied contractual obligation. The claim by the mortgagor was therefore not an action on a specialty, and the claim was therefore statute barred, the normal six-year period being applicable to it.

In *Frost* v *James Finlay Bank Ltd* [2002] Lloyd's Rep IR 503 the Court of Appeal considered the responsibility of a mortgagee when it required the borrower to change insurers and use its own subsidiary insurance company to arrange insurance. The Court held that the mere fact that a bank required a borrower to change insurers, and used a subsidiary to process the application, was not the same as giving advice or providing services and, on the facts, the bank had not assumed the duties of an insurance broker and accordingly owed no duty to the borrower.

There continue to be problems regarding undue influence in relation to mortgages. In *Alliance and Leicester plc* v *Slayford* [2001] 1 All ER 1 the consequences of such a finding were examined. A bank advanced money to a husband on the security of his solely-owned house. His wife consented to the transaction in writing, and agreed not to assert any rights she may have against the bank. When the husband defaulted, the bank took possession proceedings and the court refused the application, finding that the wife had been misled and had not had adequate advice, and therefore had an equitable interest not binding on the bank. The bank then instituted proceedings against the husband on the personal covenant to repay, the intention being to obtain a money judgement, bankrupt him and then apply for possession and sale in the insolvency proceedings as an unsecured creditor. The Court of Appeal held that this was not an abuse of process. A mortgagee had a variety of remedies available which could be pursued concurrently until payment in full was made. The wife's equitable interest would not be affected by the proceedings, and she could raise any defence available to her in the future proceedings.

OBP Textbook page 126, section 15.1.

Undue influence

This subject arises in the context of mortgages, but it can arise in many transactions. In *Hammond* v *Osborn* [2002] 2 P & CR 20 the issue was a gift. The donor was an elderly bachelor who was dependent on the donee. After a period in hospital, and without receiving professional advice, he realised assets and transferred £297,000 to the donee. He died intestate and his personal representative applied to have the gift set aside. The court held that there had been a relationship of trust and confidence between the donor and donee. The gift was so large that it gave rise to a presumption of undue influence. In order to rebut the presumption, there had to be proof that the gift was made after full, free and informed consideration by the donor. As he had not had the benefit of independent advice, the presumption was not rebutted. In *Padgham* v *Rochelle* [2002] 99 (38) LSG 36 a father owned a farm.

By his will made in 1982, he appointed his son executor and left property to his grandchildren. In 1995, without the benefit of professional advice, the father signed an agreement drawn up by the son, giving the son a tenancy of the land and buildings which had been left to the grandchildren in the will. The son also claimed that there was an agreement between him and his father that he would run the farm on his own. The father died and the grandchildren challenged the transactions. It was argued that any agreement was merely an informal family arrangement dealing with occupation, and there had been no intention to create legal relations. There was no defined figure for rent, no evidence of change of ownership of stock, and the father would not have given a tenancy in return for a vague obligation by the son to look after animals. After the agreement, the father continued to graze animals on the land and did not tell members of the family of the agreement. However, the agreement had been drawn up without professional advice and had to be interpreted reasonably. There was a start date and it could have taken effect as a binding agreement under the principle in *Walsh* v *Lonsdale* (1882) 21 Ch D 9. However, as the father had had no professional advice, the agreement had been drawn up by the son, who was the main beneficiary, and the father had put trust and confidence in his son, the son had to prove that there was no undue influence. He could not do so and the transactions were set aside.

OBP Textbook page 129, section 15.4.

9

Criminal Law

Mens Rea

Recklessness

R v *Gemmell and Richards* [2002] Crim LR 926 Court of Appeal (Criminal Division) (Dyson LJ, Silber J and Judge Beaumont QC)

Criminal damage – direction on recklessness where young defendants involved – whether *Caldwell* modified

Facts
The appellants were boys aged 11 and 12. They admitted setting fire to some newspapers underneath a 'wheelie-bin'. The bin caught fire and the blaze spread to nearby shops and buildings causing over £1 million worth of damage. At their trial on criminal damage charges it was contended on behalf of the appellants that the *Caldwell* direction on recklessness (*Commissioner of Police of the Metropolis* v *Caldwell* [1982] AC 341) should be modified to take account of their ages, in particular that the objective test based on the foresight of the reasonable prudent adult bystander should not be used. It was further contended that to apply the objective *Caldwell* direction would result in a denial of the right to a fair trial under art 6 of the European Convention on Human Rights (ECHR). The appellants were convicted of criminal damage, following a direction on recklessness derived from *Caldwell*, and appealed.

Held
The appeal was dismissed. The Court of Appeal was bound by *Caldwell* and it was clear that the model direction formulated by Lord Diplock was not designed to take into account the age of the defendants. Article 6 ECHR was not engaged as regards the content of substantive domestic criminal law, where such substantive law did not touch upon issues of access to the court, conduct of proceedings or the constitution of the court.

Comment
In *Elliot* v *C* [1983] 1 WLR 939 the Divisional Court (reluctantly) held that the objective *Caldwell* approach had to be applied to a case where the defendant was an educationally subnormal 14-year-old schoolgirl. Robert Goff LJ acknowledged the obvious unfairness in judging such a defendant by the standard of the reasonable adult, but felt constrained to follow the House of Lords' decision. The House of

Lords subsequently refused a petition for leave to appeal in that case and the present appeal seems indistinguishable as far as the substantive law issues are concerned. The European Convention on Human Rights art 6 argument was never likely to succeed, that article being concerned primarily with procedural issues.

OBP Textbook page 60, section 3.3.

The Protection of Life

Abortion and child destruction

R (On the Application of Smeaton) v *Secretary of State for Health* (2002) The Times 3 May Administrative Court (Munby J)

'Morning after' pill – whether in breach of ss58 and 59 Offences Against the Person Act 1861

Facts

The applicant sought judicial review of a statutory instrument permitting pharmacists to prescribe the 'morning after' pill. The basis of the challenge was that dispensing the drug would be an offence contrary to ss58 and 59 Offences Against the Person Act (OAPA) 1861, and that the conditions laid down in the Abortion Act 1967 specifying when an abortion might be lawful were not satisfied.

Held

The application was dismissed. There was no breach of ss58 and 59 OAPA 1861 in dispensing the drug. The 'morning after' pill prevented fertilisation of the ovum, or the successful implantation of the fertilised ovum. It did not cause the de-implantation of a fertilised ovum. Explaining why the drug would not be regarded as inducing a miscarriage, Munby J observed:

> 'Pregnancy began once the blastocyst had implanted in the endometrium. More particularly, miscarriage was the termination of such a post-implantation pregnancy. Current medical understanding of "miscarriage" plainly excluded results brought about by inter-uterine devices, the pill, the mini-pill and the morning-after pill.'

The court therefore rejected the contention that the term miscarriage could encompass causing a fertilised ovum not to implant. Whatever the word might have been understood to mean in 1861, its meaning was not frozen in time. It had to be construed in the modern context.

Comment

The court is effectively ruling that the 'morning after' pill should be viewed as a contraceptive and not an abortifacient. The ruling is only persuasive as regards the criminal law, as it was a decision of the Administrative Court.

OBP Textbook page 88, section 4.1.

Causation: novus actus interveniens

R v *Dias* [2002] Crim LR 490 Court of Appeal (Criminal Division) (Keene LJ, Sir Richard Tucker and Madison J)

Acts by deceased – whether novus actus interveniens

Facts

D purchased heroin with P. D prepared the syringe. P injected himself with the solution and died shortly afterwards from the resulting overdose. D was convicted of manslaughter on the basis that he had assisted and encouraged P in the act of consuming the heroin. The trial judge ruled that the self-administration by P was an unlawful act. D appealed against conviction on the basis that the self-administration was not an unlawful act, hence he had not acted unlawfully in encouraging the act of self-administration. The trial judge granted a certificate in the following terms: 'Was I correct as a matter of law to direct the jury that it is unlawful for a man to inject heroin into himself?'

Held

The appeal was allowed.

Possession of heroin by P was an unlawful act, but that unlawful act did not cause P's death. Self-administration of heroin by P was not a criminal act contrary to the Misuse of Drugs Act 1971. The unlawful supply of heroin by D was an unlawful act, but the trial judge should have directed the jury to consider: (a) was the supply a substantial cause of death?; and (b) was the supply 'dangerous'?

The trial judge's direction indicated that P's actions broke the chain of causation. As Keene LJ observed:

'That supply of heroin was undoubtedly unlawful, but the difficulty about relying on it as a basis for manslaughter would have been one of causation. [The deceased] was an adult and able to decide for himself whether or not to inject the heroin. His own action in injecting himself might well have been seen as an intervening act between the supply of the drug by the appellant and the death of [the deceased]. The chain of causation was probably broken by that intervening act. That was the interpretation placed on the case of *R* v *Dalby* [1982] 1 All ER 916, (1982) 74 Cr App R 348 in the subsequent decision of this court in *R* v *Goodfellow* [1986] Crim LR 468, (1986) 83 Cr App R 23 at p27 of the latter report. It accords with a passage from Professor Glanville Williams' *Textbook of Criminal Law* (2nd ed), p39, which was cited in argument. ...

"What a person does if he has reached adult years, is of sound mind and is not acting under mistake, intimidation or other similar pressure, is his own responsibility and is not regarded as having been caused by other people. An intervening act of this kind, therefore, breaks the causal connection that would otherwise have been perceived between previous acts and the forbidden consequence." '

Keene LJ continued:

'We accept that there may be situations where a jury could find manslaughter in cases such as this, so long as they were satisfied so as to be sure that the chain of causation was not broken. That is not this case because causation here was not left to the jury ... Assistance and encouragement is not to be automatically equated with causation. Causation raises questions of fact and degree. The recipient does not have to inject the drug which he is encouraged and assisted to take. He has a choice. It may be that in some circumstances the causative chain will still remain. That is a matter for the jury to decide. The Crown's current approach as argued on this appeal hearing, namely that the supply of heroin is unlawful and can be a dangerous act causing death, is sound. The most obvious case is where the supply takes the form of one person injecting the other who then dies. The position is more difficult where the victim injects himself, but there may possibly be situations where the chain of causation could be established. It is, however, important that that issue be left to the jury to determine, as happened at the trial in *Kennedy* [1999] Crim LR 65 ... It may seem to some that there is morally not a great deal between this situation where A hands B a syringe containing a drug such as heroin, with death resulting, and that where A injects B with his consent with the contents of the syringe. But the vital difference (and this is why causation cannot be assumed) is that the former situation involves an act of B's taken voluntarily and leading to his death. We do not wish to suggest that there may not sometimes be cases where, on somewhat different facts, manslaughter by way of gross negligence may arise if a duty of care can be established, or where s23 [of the Offences Against the Person Act 1861] may be relied on so long as the chain of causation is not broken.'

Comment
Suicide has not been a crime since the enactment of the Suicide Act 1961, hence self-manslaughter is not a crime. The result is that P's actions in the present case were not unlawful and, as a result, there was no unlawful activity in relation to which D could be a secondary party.

OBP Textbook page 97, section 4.2.

Diminished responsibility and intoxication

R v Dietschmann [2002] Crim LR 132 Court of Appeal (Criminal Division) (Rose LJ, Bell and Stanley Burnton JJ)

Diminished responsibility – relationship with intoxication – relevance of drug taking

Facts
D was taking anti-depressants and sleeping tablets following the death of his aunt with whom he had been having a sexual relationship. D attended a party where he drank alcohol, although there was no evidence that he had thereby become intoxicated. P allegedly damaged a watch that D's aunt had given to D. D responded by repeatedly punching P in the face. P died from these blows. D was charged with P's murder and, whilst admitting that he had caused P's death, sought to rely on the defence of diminished responsibility. D was convicted of murder and appealed on the basis that the trial judge had misdirected the jury by not explaining that diminished responsibility could be made out not only in cases where D had an

inability to exercise self-control, but also in cases where D had difficulty in exercising self-control.

Held

The appeal was dismissed. Confirming *R* v *Fenton* (1975) 62 Cr App R 261, the Court held that consuming intoxicants did not per se give rise to the abnormality of the mind that was a precondition of establishing diminished responsibility: see further *R* v *Tandy* (1988) 87 Cr App R 45. For the defence of diminished responsibility to be established, the effect of consuming intoxicants had to be permanent brain damage or an irresistible craving for intoxicants that resulted in involuntary consumption.

Comment

If D seeks to rely on diminished responsibility the onus is on him to show that it substantially impaired his responsibility for his actions in respect of the acts that caused the victim's death, ie there must be causation between the diminished responsibility and the killing.

OBP Textbook page 129, section 4.5.

Involuntary manslaughter: killing by gross negligence

R v *Wacker* [2002] Crim LR 839 Court of Appeal (Criminal Division) (Kay LJ, Colman and Ouseley JJ)

Killing by gross negligence – whether one participant in a criminal enterprise owes any duty of care to another

Facts

The appellant was a Dutch lorry driver. His vehicle was intercepted by Customs and Excise Officers at Dover. The officers opened the vehicle's container and discovered the bodies of 58 illegal immigrants of Chinese origin and two other such immigrants who were still alive. The immigrants had been loaded into the lorry at a place near Rotterdam. The lorry's container had been adapted so that there was a wooden framework partitioning it into two distinct areas. The immigrants hid behind the partition. The container was then filled with a consignment of tomatoes to conceal the fact that there were illegal immigrants on board. Because the container was designed as a refrigerated compartment there was insufficient ventilation. The immigrants died due to the lack of air in the container. The appellant was, in due course, convicted of conspiracy to facilitate the entry into the United Kingdom of illegal immigrants and of 58 offences of gross negligence manslaughter. Relying on the doctrine of ex turpi causa non oritur actio (ie that the law of negligence did not recognise the relationship between those involved in a criminal enterprise as giving rise to a duty of care owed by one participant to another) the appellant contended that, following *R* v *Adamako* [1995] 1 AC 171, he had not owed the immigrants any duty of care because they too had been involved in the illegal enterprise. In the absence of a duty of care no liability for killing by gross negligence could be established.

Held

The appeal was dismissed.

Kay LJ:

> 'The concept that one person could be responsible for the death of another in circumstances such as these without the criminal law being able to hold him to account for that death even if he had shown not the slightest regard for the welfare and life of the other is one that would be unacceptable in civilised society. Taking this perspective of the case causes one immediately to question whether the whole approach adopted by both counsel and the judge in the court below can be correct, and we must, therefore, examine this matter. ...
>
> The first question that it is pertinent to ask is why it is that the civil law has introduced the concept of ex turpi causa. The answer is ... that as a matter of public policy the courts will not "promote or countenance a nefarious object or bargain which it is bound to condemn".
>
> In other situations, it is clear that the criminal law adopts a different approach to the civil law in this regard. A person who sold a harmless substance to another pretending that it was an unlawful dangerous drug could not be the subject of a successful civil claim by the purchasers for the return of the purchase price. However the criminal law would, arising of out of the same transaction, hold that he was guilty of the offence of obtaining property by deception. Many other similar examples readily come to mind.
>
> Why ... then ... this distinction between the approach of the civil law and the criminal law? The answer is that the very same public policy that causes the civil courts to refuse the claim points in a quite different direction in considering a criminal offence. The criminal law has as its function the protection of citizens and gives effect to the state's duty to try those who have deprived citizens of their rights of life, limb or property. It may very well step in at the precise moment when civil courts withdraw because of this very different function. The withdrawal of a civil remedy has nothing to do with whether as a matter of public policy the criminal law applies. The criminal law should not be disapplied just because the civil law is disapplied. It has its own public policy aim which may require a different approach to the involvement of the law.
>
> Further the criminal law will not hesitate to act to prevent serious injury or death even when the persons subjected to such injury or death may have consented to or willingly accepted the risk of actual injury or death. By way of illustration, the criminal law makes the assisting another to commit suicide a criminal offence and denies a defence of consent where significant injury is deliberately caused to another in a sexual context. ...The state in such circumstances has a overriding duty to act to prevent such consequences.
>
> Thus looked at as a matter of pure public policy, we can see no justification for concluding that the criminal law should decline to hold a person as criminally responsible for the death of another simply because the two were engaged in some joint unlawful activity at the time or, indeed, because there may have been an element of acceptance of a degree of risk by the victim in order to further the joint unlawful enterprise. Public policy, in our judgment, manifestly points in totally the opposite direction.
>
> The next question that we are bound to ask ourselves is whether in any way we are

required by authority to take a different view. The foundation for the contention that ex turpi causa is as much a part of the law of manslaughter as it is a part of the law of negligence. ... Insofar as Lord Mackay [in *Adomako*] referred to "ordinary principles of the laws of negligence" we do not accept for one moment that he was intending to decide that the rules relating to ex turpi causa were part of those ordinary principles. He was doing no more than holding that in an "ordinary" case of negligence, the question whether there was a duty of care was to be judged by the same legal criteria as governed whether there was a duty of care in the law of negligence. That was the only issue relevant to that case and to give the passage the more extensive meaning accepted in the court below was in our judgment wrong.

The next question which is posed is whether it is right to say in this case that no duty of care can arise because it is impossible or inappropriate to determine the extent of that duty. We do not accept this proposition. If at the moment when the vent was shut, one of the Chinese had said "you will make sure that we have enough air to survive", the appellant would have had no difficulty understanding the proposition and clearly by continuing with the unlawful enterprise in the way that he did, he would have been shouldering the duty to take care for their safety in this regard. The question was such an obvious one that it did not need to be posed and we have no difficulty in concluding that in these circumstances the appellant did voluntarily assume the duty of care for the Chinese in this regard. He was aware that no one's actions other than his own could realistically prevent the Chinese from suffocating to death and if he failed to act reasonably in fulfilling this duty to an extent that could be characterised as criminal, he was guilty of manslaughter if death resulted.

One further issue merits consideration, namely is it any answer to a charge of manslaughter for a defendant to say "we were jointly engaged in a criminal enterprise and weighing the risk of injury or death against our joint desire to achieve our unlawful objective, we collectively thought that it was a risk worth taking". In our judgment it is not. The duty to take care cannot, as a matter of public policy, be permitted to be affected the by countervailing demands of the criminal enterprise. Thus, in this case, the fact that keeping the vent shut increased the chances of the Chinese succeeding in entering the United Kingdom without detection was not a factor to be taken into account in deciding whether the appellant had acted reasonably or not.

[Counsel for the appellant contended that] ... the time when the duty arose cannot be established in the circumstances. With respect to him that is not right. The duty arose from the moment the vent was shut but it was a continuing duty, which continued until air was allowed into the container. At the moment when the duty first arose, the appellant was outside the jurisdiction in Holland. However the duty continued once the ferry had sailed and it is quite clear on the evidence that if the vent had been opened at that stage, the deaths would not have resulted. Thus we can see no difficulty in this regard.

In our judgment ... It is, therefore, wholly unnecessary to examine whether the distinction between matters for which the Chinese were responsible and those incidental to their illegality was a proper distinction or not. Whichever way they might have been characterised in a civil claim had no relevance to the issue that the jury had to decide.

In every other respect we are satisfied that the necessary ingredients of the offences of manslaughter were properly left to the jury. Once the jury had concluded that the appellant was lying when he said that he did not know about the Chinese in the container, this was, in our judgment, as plain a case on the manslaughter charges as one could encounter.'

Comment

In *Lewin* v *Crown Prosecution Service* [2002] EWHC 1049 the Divisional Court considered the position of K who had left the deceased L to sleep in K's car on a very hot day. L had spent the previous evening drinking with K. Once L had fallen asleep in K's car K had been unable to move L. The evidence was that L had been alive at 8.00 am when K had left him in the car, but had died from the effect of the heat by approximately 1.00 pm. The Crown Prosecution Service decided not to prosecute K in respect of the death. L's father unsuccessfully applied for judicial review of the decision not to prosecute. Ruling that liability for killing by gross negligence could not be made out on the facts, Kennedy LJ observed that establishing the duty of care required for the imposition of liability for manslaughter by gross negligence should be undertaken by reference to the ordinary principles of the law of negligence. He explained that a defendant would be regarded as assuming a duty of care towards a passenger in his car for as long as the vehicle was in motion, but he expressed the view that the duty of care would:

'... normally have come to an end as soon as the vehicle was properly parked in a safe place at the end of its journey. It could only persist in a way which would be relevant to the offence of manslaughter if a reasonable person would have foreseen that by leaving the deceased in the vehicle parked in that position [the deceased] was being exposed to the risk "not merely of injury or even of serious injury but of death" (*R* v *Singh (Gurphal)* [1999] Crim LR 582). In this case ... there was, as it seems to me, no realistic possibility of demonstrating beyond reasonable doubt that a reasonable person in the position of [the appellant] would have foreseen the risk of death. The young man who was left in the unlocked car was an adult, not a small child or a dog. Anyone leaving him and knowing that his comatosed state was due to an excessive intake of alcohol would probably have envisaged that in due course he would rouse himself and make his way to bed. The idea that he might suffer significant injury, as opposed to discomfort, as a result of being over heated in the car would be unlikely to cross the mind of anyone not medically trained.'

See further *R* v *Khan* [1998] Crim LR 830.

OBP Textbook page 143, section 4.10.

Non-fatal Offences Against the Person

Stalking

Caurti v *Director of Public Prosecutions* [2002] Crim LR 131 Queen's Bench Divisional Court (Pill LJ and Cresswell J)

Harassment – course of conduct involving two victims

Facts

D threatened to stab N. S, who lived with N, feared for N's safety. D later spoke to N making threats that led N to fear for the safety of S. D was in due course convicted under s4 of the Protection from Harassment Act 1997 in that he was found to have engaged in a course of conduct that caused another to fear, on at least two occasions, that violence would be used against him.

D appealed by way of case stated contending that the trial judge had erred in his view that the phrase 'caused another to fear' in s4 could, by reference to the Interpretation Act 1978, be read as meaning 'causing others to fear'.

Held

The appeal was allowed. Section 4 of the 1997 Act created a serious offence, hence it was appropriate for the court to construe its terms narrowly. The offence was only made out if D caused P, on two or more occasions, to fear that violence would be used against himself. It was not enough (on the basis of the facts giving rise to this appeal) that on the first occasion S feared for N's safety, and on the second occasion that N feared for S's safety.

Comment

The decision of the court is to be contrasted with that in *Director of Public Prosecutions* v *Dunn* [2001] Crim LR 130, where it was held, in relation to the less serious offence under s2 of the 1997 Act, that the Interpretation Act 1978 could be called into aid to support the argument that words such as 'another' and 'the other' could be taken to include the plural form. Under s2 more than one complainant can be included in an information provided those complainants form part of a 'close knit' group, eg husband and wife, and the course of conduct complained of is clearly directed at both parties.

OBP Textbook page 163, section 5.2.

Sexual Offences and Consent

Unlawful sexual intercourse

R v *Kirk* [2002] Crim LR 756 Court of Appeal (Criminal Division) (Judge LJ, Hunt and Keith JJ)

Unlawful sexual intercourse – 'young man's defence' – whether compatible with European Convention on Human Rights

Facts

D, aged 29, had consensual sexual intercourse with a girl who was below the age of 16 at the time. D was charged with having unlawful sexual intercourse contrary to s6(1) of the Sexual Offences Act 1956. At an interlocutory appeal arising from a preliminary hearing held pursuant to the Criminal Procedure and Investigations Act 1996, D contended that s6(3) of the 1956 Act, whereby a male defendant under the age of 24 could establish a defence if he honestly and reasonable believed the complainant to have been over the age of 16, was inconsistent with arts 6 and 14 of the European Convention on Human Rights. This argument rested on the propositions that the s6(3) defence should be available to any male defendant regardless of age, and that it operate so as to prevent a defendant from having a fair trial.

Held

The appeal was dismissed. The restriction of the s6(3) defence to males under the age of 24 was not discriminatory. A woman could not commit the offence under s6(1) as a principal offender, although she could be charged as an accomplice, in which case she too would be able to rely on the s6(3) defence if under the age of 24. A woman having sexual intercourse with a male below the age of 16 could be charged with indecent assault. Although a woman charged with that offence would be able to rely on her honest belief that the male was over the age of 16, the offence carried with it the risk of a higher sentence upon conviction than was the case with the offence under s6(1). The court also noted a number of policy considerations that had to borne in mind. First, if the appellant's submission was correct, girls under the age of 16 who appeared to be older would receive much less protection from the law as regards the offence of unlawful sexual intercourse. Second, even if the law was discriminatory in its operation (which the court did not accept) the fact that pregnancy could result from an act of unlawful sexual intercourse performed by a male defendant was a distinguishing feature of such activity. On balance, therefore, the court rejected the argument that s6(3) operated as a disproportionate fetter on the defence arguments available to a male defendant charged under s6(1) of the 1956 Act.

Comment

The decision underlines that fact that the European Convention on Human Rights impacts far more on the procedural aspects of criminal law than it does on the content of the substantive law. Once the court concluded that s6(3) did not prevent D from having a fair trial (the procedural issue) it had to be conceded that the choice of 24 as the age limit for the young man's defence was a matter for Parliament to determine. The court seems to have assumed that a woman charged as an accomplice to an act of unlawful sexual intercourse would only have been able to avail herself of the s6(3) defence if under the age of 24. This seems doubtful in the light of a long-standing authority such as *Johnson* v *Youden* [1950] 1 KB 544, to the effect that an accomplice must have mens rea (ie know of the facts that constitute the offence) even if the offence committed by the principal offender is one of strict liability.

OBP Textbook page 199, section 6.2.

Theft

Property belonging to another

R v *Sullivan and Ballion* [2002] Crim LR 758 Maidstone Crown Court
(Aitkens J)

Theft – property belonging to another – whether theft from a corpse possible – form
of indictment

Facts

P was a drugs dealer operating on behalf of a criminal syndicate known locally as
'The Firm'. P arrived at premises occupied by the appellants in possession of
£50,000 that he had collected on behalf of 'The Firm'. P took drugs whilst with the
appellants and died of an overdose. The appellants took the £50,000 and were
subsequently charged with theft of the money. At a pre-trial hearing held pursuant
to s40 of the Criminal Procedure and Investigations Act 1996 the appellants
contended that the prosecution had failed to adduce any evidence that the money
had been property belonging to another at the time of the alleged appropriation.

Held

The judge ruled that a verdict of not guilty be entered. The Crown had not
advanced its case on the basis that the property belonged to persons unknown
(although it could have done so). The Crown had also, correctly, chosen not to
advance its case on the basis that the £50,000 was property belonging to 'The Firm',
since the criminal syndicate would have acquired the money through illegal
transactions. *R* v *Kelly* [1998] 3 All ER 741 was authority for the proposition that
property could be regarded as 'belonging to another' for the purposes of s5(1) of the
Theft Act 1968 even where the other's possession of the property was unlawful. In
the present case, however, the appellants had not taken possession of the £50,000
until P had died. A corpse could not be said to be in possession of property. The
judge further rejected submissions: (i) that the £50,000 could be regarded as
belonging to P's estate where P had never been the owner of the money and had
derived possession of it through illegal transactions, and (ii) that the money was
property belonging to the Crown as bona vacantia.

Comment

Presumably the difficulties encountered by the prosecution in this case could have
been avoided if the appellants had simply been charged with theft of property
belonging to persons unknown as the property clearly did not belong to the
appellants at the time they appropriated it. It had not become abandoned property
disposed of with animus revocandi. Neither is it clear why the judge should have
been unwilling to accept the Crown's argument based on the concept of bona
vacantia. Criminal law is not unduly concerned with the lawfulness of P's possession
of property when assessing whether or not D has stolen it (as evidenced by the fact

that D can steal from a thief property stolen by that thief). A further point to consider in cases such as this is that even if D does take property from a corpse and the court finds that it remains property belonging to another for the purposes of theft, D may still have an argument under s2(1)(a) of the Theft Act 1968 to the effect that he honestly believed he had the legal right to take the property.

OBP Textbook page 233, section 7.5.

R v *Dyke and Munroe* [2002] Crim LR 153 Court of Appeal (Criminal Division) (Henry LJ, Douglas Brown and Astill JJ)

Theft of charitable donations – property belonging to another – form of indictment

Facts
The appellants were trustees of a children's cancer charity. They were convicted of theft of sums collected from members of the public who had donated money to the charity. The indictment alleged theft of property belonging to persons unknown, on the basis that the individual donors could not be identified. The appellants were convicted of theft and appealed on the basis that the trial judge had not dealt properly with the issue of whether the property belonged to another as against the appellants.

Held
The appeal was allowed. Ownership of the money donated by members of the public had passed to the charity once it was deposited in the collecting tins used by those collecting on behalf of the charity. Any appropriation of the funds thus collected should have been charged as theft of property belonging to the charity.

Comment
It is not clear why the prosecution encountered such difficulties with the wording of the indictment in this case. Section 5(2) of the Theft Act 1968 makes it clear that property held on trust can be regarded as belonging to those who have the right to enforce the trust. Normally this will be the beneficiaries, but in the case of a charitable trust the Attorney-General has the right to enforce the trust. The indictment could, therefore, have alleged theft of property belonging to the Attorney-General.

OBP Textbook page 235, section 7.5.

Accessorial and Vicarious Liability

Joint enterprise

R v *Concannon* [2002] Crim LR 213 Court of Appeal (Criminal Division) (Judge LJ, Hallett and Stanley Burnton JJ)

Mens rea for joint enterprise – murder – whether in breach of European Convention on Human Rights

Facts
D, along with his co-accused, visited P's home. D attacked P. D's co-accused then stabbed P to death. D denied being present when P was fatally stabbed and denied any knowledge that his co-accused had been in possession of a knife. D was convicted of murder following a direction from the trial judge on joint enterprise that accorded with the ruling of the House of Lords in *R* v *Powell and English* [1991] 1 AC 1. D appealed on the basis that the disparity in mens rea required between a defendant charged with murder as a principal offender and one charged with murder as an accomplice in cases of joint enterprise was unfair and thus the common law did not comply with the requirements of art 6 of the European Convention on Human Rights (ECHR).

Held
The appeal was dismissed. Article 6 ECHR was concerned with procedural fairness, not the fairness of the substantive law of signatory states. It was open to Parliament to amend the law relating to joint enterprise if it saw fit to do so. The Court rejected the notion that an appellant could achieve significant reform of the substantive law by a side route.

Comment
The decision confirms the view that the real impact of the ECHR is as regards the rules of criminal evidence and procedure, rather than the substantive law. Only where the substantive law fails to safeguard fundamental freedoms, such as the right to life or the right not to be subjected to torture etc, will the Convention be successfully invoked: see further *R* v *H* (2001) The Times 17 May.

OBP Textbook pages 14 and 380, sections 1.3 and 13.4.

General Defences: True Defences – Compulsion and Justification

Compulsion: duress of circumstances

R v *Harmer* [2002] Crim LR 401 Court of Appeal (Criminal Division) (May LJ, Goldring and Gross JJ)

Duress – availability where D puts himself at risk of threats

Facts
D was stopped by customs officers and found to be in possession of cocaine. At his trial D sought to rely on the defence of duress. Following the trial judge's ruling regarding the availability of the defence where D had voluntarily become involved with a drugs dealer and thereby exposed himself to the risk of being subjected to violence if he did not comply with demands made by the drugs dealer, D pleaded guilty and subsequently appealed against conviction.

Held
The appeal was dismissed. The defence of duress was not available where D voluntarily became involved with others and he could foresee that they might threaten him with unlawful violence. There was no need for the prosecution to show that D had foreseen that he would be forced to commit particular crimes.

Comment
The decision closely follows the earlier decision of the court in *R* v *Heath* (1999) The Times 15 October. It is clearly a policy decision based on the rationale that D cannot be allowed the defence of duress where he is, so some extent, the author of his own misfortune. Against this it can be argued that the courts ought to distinguish between the defendant who foresees that a criminal organisation may force him to commit crimes if he fails to act as they require, and one who simply foresees that a criminal organisation may subject him to threats of death or grievous bodily harm if he fails to repay debts or return other property.

OBP Textbook page 434, section 15.1.

Justification: self-defence

Shaw (Norman) v *R* [2002] Crim LR 140 Privy Council (Lords Bingham of Cornhill, Hoffmann, Cooke of Thorndon and Scott of Foscote and Sir Patrick Russell)

Self-defence – relevance of defendant's perception of degree of danger

Facts
D confronted M and B who had sold D a substance on the basis that it was cocaine.

M, who was sitting in a van with B, pulled a gun and threatened D. D seized the gun and used it to kill M and B. D, giving unsworn evidence, alleged that he had fired in self-defence believing there were others in the van with M and B who were armed and about to fire at D. D was convicted of murder and appealed.

Held
The appeal was allowed. In such cases a proper direction to the jury on self-defence would be: (a) did D honestly believe that it was necessary to defend himself?; if so, (b) on the basis of the facts and the danger perceived by D, was the force used reasonable.

Comment
Although only persuasive the ruling of the Privy Council is an eminently sensible one. If the defendant who pleads self-defence is to be entitled to rely on the facts as he perceived them to be, that perception must extend not only to whether he thought it was necessary to act in self-defence, but also to the degree of danger he thought he was faced with. Only recently, in *R* v *Martin* [2002] Crim LR 136, the Court of Appeal (Criminal Division) ruled that, whilst a jury would be entitled to take the physical characteristics of D into account when assessing the reasonableness of the force used by way of self-defence, a jury would not normally be permitted to take account of D's mental characteristics. The Privy Council's ruling, if adopted for domestic law, would clearly assist a defendant who, through some degree of mental impairment, perceived a risk to his safety to be greater than it was in reality.

OBP Textbook page 453, section 15.6.

The Anti-terrorism, Crime and Security Act 2001

The Anti-terrorism, Crime and Security Act 2001 was enacted as part of the government's response to the increased threat from international terrorism in the wake of the attacks in New York City on 11 September 2001. The government's original intention had been to create a new offence of incitement to religious hatred, along the lines of the existing incitement to racial hatred offence. These proposals were rejected during the passage of the Bill, however, and the compromise agreed upon was to extend the scope of Pt 2 of the Crime and Disorder Act 1998 by making the offences covered by that provision (ie s29 (assaults); s30 (criminal damage); s31 (public order offences); s32 (harassment etc)) 'racially or religiously aggravated'. For these purposes a religious group means 'a group of persons defined by reference to religious belief or lack of religious belief': see s39(4) of the Anti-terrorism, Crime and Security Act 2001.

Section 113 of the Act introduces a new offence of using a noxious substance to cause harm or intimidate. The offence is made out where D uses a noxious substance or other noxious thing in a manner that is likely to: (a) cause serious damage to real or personal property anywhere in the world; (b) endanger human life or creates a serious risk to the health or safety of the public or a section of the public; or (c) induce in members of the public the fear that the action is likely to endanger their lives or create a serious risk to their health or safety. For these purposes any effect on the person taking the action is to be disregarded. In addition, the prosecution must show that the action in question was designed to influence the government (of the UK) or to intimidate the public or a section of the public (of any country). Threatening to take such action is also made an offence by s113(3). A sentence of up to 14 years' imprisonment can be imposed where D is convicted following trial on indictment.

OBP Textbook pages 162, 165, 170, 179 and 323, sections 5.1, 5.2, 5.4, 5.6 and 11.1.

10

Criminology

Sources of Data

Official statistics

Criminal Statistics 2000 *(2001) Cmnd 5696, London: Home Office*

An indication of the amount of crime during the year is the figure of 5.2 million notifiable offences recorded by the police in 2000. This was a reduction of 2.5 per cent in comparison with the year before. The current rate amounts to 9,800 offences per 100,000 of the population. In comparison the rate was as low as 1,100 per 100,000 in 1950. Whilst there have been changes in the way data was collected over that period, that does not amount to an explanation of the increase in the rate of crime. Property crime made up 82 per cent of the total in 2000 amounting to 4.3 million crimes. Between 1999 and 2000 the burglary rate fell by 8 per cent, having also fallen by 5 per cent in the two previous years. Violent crime rose by 4 per cent in 2000, a much smaller rise than that of 16 per cent in 1999. There were 846 homicides initially recorded in 2000. The recorded crime statistics do not tell the whole story. Figures from the British Crime Survey suggest that the number of offences committed is more than four times the number reported to the police, and even if reported it seems that many are not recorded by the police.

The detection or clear up rate was 24 per cent in 2000, having been 25 per cent in the previous year. The rate was as high as 45 per cent in the 1960s. There were 1.3 million arrests in 2000. Of those arrested 25 per cent were under the age of 18. Where arrest was resorted to, in 57 per cent of cases this was for property offences. The number of people found guilty or cautioned was 1.7 million, this being a 7 per cent decrease on the year before in the figure for indictable offences, whilst for all offences, the rate of decrease was much lower at 1 per cent. In total 1,461,000 were found guilty, whilst 239,000 were cautioned – a figure that includes reprimands and warnings. There was a 10 per cent reduction in the cautioning rate, compared to the previous year. There had also been an 8 per cent reduction in the previous year. Between police force areas, there were big differences in cautioning rates for indictable offences, with Dyfed Powys at 46 per cent, Surrey at 45 per cent and Gloucestershire at 44 per cent having the highest rates. In contrast, Lincolnshire had a rate of 21 per cent, and South Yorkshire was even lower at 15 per cent. A total of 53,210 juveniles were given reprimands or final warnings in the last seven months of 2000, this being the period in which the use of this system was extended to the whole country.

In relation to court proceedings 1.9 million people were proceeded against at magistrates' courts, a 1 per cent increase on the previous year. Inclusive of guilty pleas, convictions remained almost unchanged between 1992 and 2000 at 98 per cent of cases proceeding to a hearing in magistrates' courts. Convictions in the Crown Court remained unchanged in comparison with the previous year at 88 per cent, inclusive of guilty pleas. Convictions following a plea of not guilty rose gradually from 56 per cent of contested hearings in 1992 to 60 per cent in 1997, but went back down in later years, being 55 per cent in 2000. In the Crown Court 77,300 cases were tried, a reduction from the figure of 91,000 three years earlier. Of the 77,300, 60 per cent pleaded guilty. For the remainder who pleaded not guilty as many as 65 per cent of them were acquitted.

A summary of some of the main statistics for notifiable offences (thousands)

	1981	2000
Offences recorded by the police	2,794	5,171
Offences detected	1,056	1,264
Defendants proceeded against	2,373	1,905
Offenders found guilty and cautioned	2,259	1,700
Found guilty	2,105	1,461
Cautioned	144	239

Persons aged 18 and over proceeded against at the Crown Court in 2000 (thousands)

	Male	Female
Violence against the person	57.2	6.3
Sexual offences	6.2	0.1
Burglary	29.3	1.6
Robbery	6.2	0.6
Theft and handling stolen goods	107.2	27.4
Fraud and forgery	18.5	6.9
Criminal damage	11.7	1.2
Drug offences	41.5	5.4
Motoring offences	9.0	0.6
Other offences	63.0	9.0
Totals	349.8	58.9

Sentences and orders 1999 and 2000 (thousands)

	1999	2000
Absolute discharge	15.9	15.7
Conditional discharge	114.1	106.1
Fine	993.3	1,017.1
Probation order	58.4	56.7
Supervision order	12.7	11.6
Community service order	49.6	50.2
Curfew order	1.6	2.6
Attendance centre order	8.7	7.1
Combination order	20.8	19.3
Secure training order	0.2	0.1
Detention and training order	–	5.1
Young offender institution	24.9	20.2
Immediate prison	79.7	80.6
Suspended sentence	3.2	3.1
Sections 90–92 Powers of the Criminal Courts (Sentencing) Act 2000	0.6	0.6

Motoring Offences, England and Wales, 2000 *(2001)*, *Ayres M and Hayward P, London: Home Office*

The data provided in this report concerns the most common form of criminal behaviour. Given the huge amount of people with whom it deals, it is clear that being an offender is a very common occurrence: there were ten million offences in 2000, a 6 per cent increase on 1999 and the highest figure ever recorded. The number of speed limit offences was 1,202,000 in 2000, a considerable change from 761,000 cases in 1996.

Proceedings for motoring offences 2000 (millions)

Type of order	
Fixed penalty notices	3.1
Court proceedings	2.1
Penalty charge notices	4.7
Written warnings	0.1
Vehicle Defect Rectification Scheme notices	0.1
Total	10.0
Number of vehicles licensed	26.2

The penalty charge notices are issued by local authority parking attendants. The fixed penalty notices are issued by the police and traffic wardens. Written warnings are issued by the police. More than six million of the offences, well over half of all offences, are obstruction, waiting and parking offences. Speeding accounted for over 20 per cent of offences, as did licence, insurance and record-keeping offences. Roadside cameras provided evidence for 802,000 offences (a large increase from 319,000 in 1996), which included 61 per cent of speeding offences.

Statistics on Women and the Criminal Justice System *(2001)*, *London: Home Office*

One of the issues, for researchers, is the position of women in the criminal justice system. The data in this report relates to 2000. This publication brings together the key results from recent research and statistics that focus on the treatment of women by the criminal justice system. Criminal statistics show that, in 2000, only 19 per cent of known offenders were women – the figure had been 17 per cent a year earlier. Over the age of 17, male offenders outnumber female offenders by a ratio of around three to one. Women 'grow out of crime' – they are most likely to desist from offending in their late teens. The peak age of reported offending for girls was 14. Of those arrested, 16 per cent are women, but the proportion is higher for fraud and forgery (27 per cent) and theft and handling (21 per cent). Research suggests that following arrest, women are more likely than men to be cautioned and are less likely to have no further action taken or be charged. This partly reflects that women are more likely than men to admit their offences and to be arrested for less serious offences. According to official statistics, female offenders are also more likely to be cautioned for indictable offences.

Although women are less likely than men to be remanded in custody or committed for trial, this mainly reflects differences in offending history and type of offence. Women on remand make up a fifth of the female prison population. Women remanded in custody spend less time in custody than men. In relation to sentencing, women are more likely than men to be discharged or given a community sentence for indictable offences, and are less likely to be fined or sentenced to custody. The top seven offences for women sentenced to custody in 2000 were: theft from shops (2,350 women sentenced to custody), wounding (480), fraud (460), production, supply and possession with intent to supply a class A controlled drug (410), summary motoring (400), burglary (340) and handling stolen goods (300). In terms of community penalties, women accounted for 12 per cent of those supervised by the Probation Service in 2000. Women were less likely than men starting community orders to have previous convictions or to have served a custodial sentence.

There were, on average, 3,350 women in prison in 2000. They made up only 5.2 per cent of the total prison population. Between 1993 and 2000 the average population of women in prison rose by 115 per cent as against 42 per cent for men. Theft and handling accounted for 42 per cent of sentenced receptions of women in 2000, drug offences for 13 per cent and violence against the person for 13 per cent.

Among the population of sentenced female offenders, the main offence groups are drug offences (37 per cent at June 2000), theft and handling (20 per cent) and violence against the person (16 per cent). Some 150 women were sent to prison for fine default in 2000, but as the average stay is only five days, the average number of fine defaulters in the prison population was just three. In mid-2000, ethnic minority groups made up 25 per cent of the female prison population, compared to 19 per cent of the male prison population. An estimated 55 per cent of all women in prison have a child under 16, and over a third of mothers in prison have a child under five. An estimated 20 per cent of women in prison had experienced some time in care. Over 40 per cent of sentenced women prisoners and over 50 per cent of women on remand have reported being dependent on drugs in the year before coming to prison.

International Comparisons of Criminal Justice Statistics *(2002), Barclay G and Tavares C, London: Home Office*

Whilst it is difficult to make comparisons of crime rates across jurisdictions, some guidance is provided by the following material in relation to homicide.

Number of homicides and homicides per 100,000 of the population in urban areas 1998–2000

City	Number of homicides	Homicides per 100,000 population
Canberra	5	0.54
Ottawa	23	0.98
Tokyo	440	1.22
Rome	98	1.24
Athens	53	0.55
Paris	181	2.85
London	538	2.38
Belfast	50	5.85
New York	1,977	8.77
Copenhagen	25	1.68
Moscow	3,863	18.2
Pretoria	1,512	41.12
Washington	733	45.79

OBP Textbook page 17, section 2.2.

Supplementing the official statistics

Victim surveys

The 2001 British Crime Survey (First Results), London: Home Office

This is the ninth survey of people's experiences and perceptions of crime carried out on behalf of the Home Office: it measured crime that occurred in 2000. The first survey was carried out in 1982. The survey is now carried out annually, having previously been biannual. In this latest survey, a representative national sample of 37,000 people over the age of 16, plus an ethnic boost of 3,000, were selected for interview. The ethnic boost was used to remedy perceived gaps in the data for such groups. The sample is double that of the previous survey. The survey is now conducted throughout the year rather than just occurring in the first quarter. These changes are designed to improve the quality of the data. The information from the British Crime Survey provides important insights into criminal behaviour. They certainly tell us that the official statistics do not portray anything like the whole story; though they may well reveal similar trends, as with the recorded fall in crime. The findings at this stage are interim. The survey estimated that 12.9 million offences were committed against individuals and their property in 2000: the figure had been 12 per cent higher in 1999. Where comparisons can be made with categories used in the official statistics, the survey reported more than four times the amount of crime than is the case with the official statistics.

For 2000, the amount of crime recorded is 52 per cent greater than in 1981, but the trend has been downwards in recent years. There was a fall recorded for nearly every offence that is measured, with the exceptions being theft from the person (a 2 per cent increase) and theft of a vehicle (a 1 per cent increase). Of the decreases, burglary saw a 17 per cent reduction and wounding a 34 per cent reduction. On the issue of violence it is still the case that the source of this is likely to be an acquaintance, or because of a domestic dispute, rather than a stranger. Having said that the trend is for the significance of this to reduce, in statistical terms: for example, there were 34 per cent less reported cases of domestic violence in 2000 than there had been in 1999.

Where comparisons can be made only 25 per cent of the British Crime Survey crimes ended up in police records. This is because only 45 per cent were reported to the police, and of these only about 56 per cent of those that were reported ended up being recorded as a crime. The British Crime Survey asked victims why they did not report incidents to the police. The most common set of reasons was that the incident was not serious enough or involved no loss, or that the police would be unable to do much about it (72 per cent). Vandalism and attempted thefts from vehicles were most likely not to be reported.

These surveys are also very valuable as a source of information on the risk of being a victim of crime. The British Crime Survey estimates that 27 per cent of adults in 2000 were victims of at least one of the crimes that the survey records.

This is a fall from 39 per cent in 1995 and 34 per cent in 1997, and indeed it was the lowest ever level of victimisation measured by the survey. Risks of crime are highest for certain groups, such as youngsters, unemployed people, single parents, private renters, inner city dwellers and those living in areas of high physical disorder. Specifically on violence: 3.7 per cent had been victims, with a higher rate of 19 per cent for 16–24-year-old males. Recent sweeps of the British Crime Survey included questions to try to assess to what extent fear of crime had an impact on people's quality of life. The policy aim is to reduce such fear. The trend is for fear of crime to decrease, though this has not been constant and there are variations across offences and types of person. The following groups were most likely to say fear greatly affected their quality of life: women aged 60 plus; Asians; those in poor health; people in low income households; people living in council or Housing Association accommodation; and those living in areas with high levels of physical disorder.

OBP Textbook page 28, section 2.8.

The Criminal Justice System

Developments in penal policy

Justice for All *(2002), London: Home Office*

The process of reform of the criminal justice system is never-ending and this White Paper contains the latest proposals. The main themes are: a better deal for victims and witnesses; getting the process right from the start; fairer and more effective trials; putting sense back into sentencing; more effective punishment and rehabilitation; measures to engage the public; and a more focussed and joined up criminal justice system.

Victims and witnesses
Victims and witnesses, who are often the same person, can be left feeling ill-informed and badly treated by the criminal justice system. Proposals in the White Paper address this so as to aim for a fair balance between defence and prosecution, and also to ensure that the needs of victims and witnesses are considered at every stage. The following are some of the ideas being considered.

1. A national strategy for victims and witnesses.
2. A Victims Code of Practice setting out what victims can expect from the criminal justice agencies.
3. Every service that comes into contact with victims should have a responsibility under the new Code to provide protection, support and information.
4. A right of complaint to the Parliamentary Ombudsman for victims and witnesses.

5. A new Independent Commissioner for victims and witnesses supported by a National Victims Advisory Panel to champion their interests.
6. The introduction of more measures for vulnerable and intimidated witnesses, including pre-recorded video evidence and screens around the witness box.
7. Adopting some of the ideas being developed as part of the Street Crime Initiative, for example victim volunteers being available to accompany victims when giving statements.
8. The extension of specialised support to victims of road traffic incidents and their families.
9. The appointment of victim liaison officers to join Youth Offending Teams as resources become available.

Getting the process right from the start

The aim here is to take some of the delay out of the start of the criminal justice process. This would, for example, help to deal with the problem of defendants who commit offences whilst on bail awaiting trial.

The White Paper has the following proposals to improve the initial stages of the justice process.

1. Give the Crown Prosecution Service responsibility for charging in all but routine cases.
2. Improve case preparation by, for example, further improving the interaction of the police and the Crown Prosecution Service.
3. Give the police power to impose conditions on bail before charge, coupled with measures to prevent offending while on bail.
4. Provide incentives and sanctions to promote effective and focused case preparation.
5. Radically improve the disclosure of information, with both the prosecution and defence obliged to disclose all information necessary to ensure the trial addresses the real issues.
6. Make better use of technology and forensic and technological expertise to enable the police to obtain the evidence to make an effective case.

Fairer and more effective trials

The concerns here are not immediately apparent from the title. It is thought that there are too many cases in which tactical manoeuvres disrupt the process, so a verdict is not reached and justice not done. Courts are deliberately over-booked on the basis that some cases will not go ahead as scheduled. This means that over 40 per cent of victims and witnesses who attend to give evidence are not called to do so on the day. The proposed answers, so as to ensure swifter, fairer and more efficient trials that balance the rights of victims and the accused, include the following.

1. A unified administration, as part of the Lord Chancellor's Department, for the Crown Court and the magistrates' court.
2. An increase in magistrates' sentencing powers from six to 12 months.

3. Reform of the youth courts to enable them to deal with young offenders accused of serious crimes.
4. More use of preparatory hearings so that issues can be raised and clarified in advance.
5. Allowing trial by judge alone in serious fraud and jury intimidation cases.
6. Encouraging early guilty pleas by introducing a clearer tariff of sentence discount for pleading guilty, and arrangements where defendants could seek advance indication of what the discounted sentence would be if they pleaded guilty.
7. Ensuring appropriate safeguards so that innocent defendants are not put under pressure to plead guilty.
8. An overhaul of the rules of evidence, including making available to judges and juries information on previous convictions and conduct where it is relevant, and extending the reported evidence available to magistrates, judges and juries. Evidence of previous convictions is very controversial – a person with a dozen previous convictions for burglary may find it difficult to find a jury that will give him a fair trial if the charge is burglary.
9. Another controversial proposal is that the rule against double jeopardy would not operate in grave cases where compelling new evidence has come to light. This would mean that a person who has already been tried and acquitted could be tried for a second time for the same offence. To make matters worse, this will operate with retrospective effect.

Putting sense back into sentencing
One of the key purposes of custody is to reduce crime once offenders are released, yet half of all convicted criminals are reconvicted within two years. Prison can break up families, impede resettlement and have a devastating effect on children. At the same time there is no consistency in approach to sentencing, with extreme cases of variation in sentencing for similar crimes across the country. The Government wants to put the sense back into sentencing and ensure sentences work to protect the public and punish and rehabilitate offenders. To these ends the following proposals are made.

1. Sentences to be based on what has been shown to work in reducing re-offending.
2. Create a sentencing framework and establish a Sentencing Guidelines Council, chaired by the Lord Chief Justice, to achieve greater consistency.
3. Introduce a new graded framework to tailor sentences to the offender and the offence.
4. Introduce within this framework a series of new and innovative sentences ranging from:

   a) a new suspended sentence called Custody Minus, reform of short custodial sentences and the introduction of Custody Plus;
   b) a new intermittent custody sentence that denies liberty, for example, at the weekend, but allows the offender to continue working and maintain family ties, to a new special sentence for dangerous sexual or violent offenders;

c) introduce an extended version of the Intensive Supervision and Surveillance Programme, so there is a greater opportunity for rehabilitation coupled with a reduced chance of re-offending;

d) ensure that, like adults, young offenders sentenced for serious offences will be released at the halfway point of the sentence and supervised all the way until the end of sentence.

More effective punishment and rehabilitation

The prison population is at record levels. Many prisoners receive short sentences that do not help with effective rehabilitation and resettlement, and often increase the chances of re-offending. The White Paper sets out the challenges faced by the correctional services and how, by more collaborative working with other statutory agencies and the voluntary and community sectors, they can deliver a sentence that reduces crime and helps build safer, more cohesive communities. In the light of this there are proposals:

1. to give greater flexibility to probation officers to drug test offenders on release from custody;
2. to pilot the 'Going Straight' contract, a new rehabilitation programme for 18–20-year-olds including reparation to victims and incentives to participate;
3. to review reception and release procedures for all prisoners to ensure departing prisoners have the appropriate help to resettle;
4. to embark on a modernisation programme to expand capacity in existing prisons, to build new multi-functional community prisons and to close prisons that are not fit for their purpose;
5. to benchmark public sector prisons and close or contract out those that do not meet the necessary standards;
6. to review the categorisation of prisoners to ensure that we balance the needs of security with effective resettlement: this must be a good idea, as we have had a security obsession for far too long;
7. to extend the remit of Multi-Agency Public Protection Panels, appointing independent lay members to the Panels and including a statutory requirement to include a wider range of agencies and local bodies.

Measures to engage the public

The criminal justice system relies on the participation of members of the public, as jurors, magistrates, witnesses and the thousands of individuals and community organisations who work to reduce crime and bring offenders to justice. Yet the system is seen as complex, intimidating and inaccessible to the public, and less than half of those summoned for jury service actually serve. The Government aims to assist this public participation by the following means.

1. Improved channels of communication between criminal justice agencies and the public.

2. By continuing to implement the findings of the Stephen Lawrence Inquiry in order to reduce racism in the criminal justice system, increase diversity and build the confidence of all sections of the community.
3. Helping people to understand the criminal law by bringing it together into accessible documents available via the Internet.
4. Making jury service an important part of citizenship and ensuring that juries better reflect all sections of society and are better supported.
5. By implementing a national strategy to raise the profile of the lay magistracy and encouraging more people to apply from as wide a cross-section of the community as possible.
6. Introducing more restorative justice schemes in addition to the present use of referral orders.

Focusing the criminal justice system on fighting and reducing crime and delivering justice
While the overall crime rate has been falling and has now stabilised, street crime, anti-social behaviour and the fear of crime remains unacceptably high. Also, under-reporting and under-recording remains a concern for crimes such as domestic violence and racist crimes. The following are proposed to tackle these problems.

1. Extend the range of restraining orders.
2. Put domestic violence murder reviews on a statutory footing.
3. Make a breach of a non-molestation order a criminal offence.
4. Provide anonymity for victims of domestic violence.
5. Improve liaison between the civil and criminal courts and the family and criminal courts.
6. Extend existing drug testing provisions to the under 18s, with parental or appropriate adult consent.
7. Arrange referral to treatment services for young people with substance misuse problems, who currently either receive a reprimand or for whom the police take no further action.

Joining up the system
Each criminal justice agency still has its own methods of recording defendants, offenders, charges and cases. This makes cross-referencing, case management and tracking virtually impossible and may lead to inappropriate decisions. Getting the whole system to work together is essential to bring more offenders to justice, improve the service offered to victims and promote confidence in the work of all criminal justice agencies. To these ends the following are proposed in the White Paper.

1. Deliver a strategic approach to information technology integration across the criminal justice system.

2. Strengthen the criminal justice system management framework by setting up 42 local Criminal Justice Boards reporting to a new national Criminal Justice Board.
3. Legislation to integrate the management of the courts within a single courts organisation to replace existing magistrates' courts committees and the court service.
4. Establish a new independent courts inspectorate that will have jurisdiction, for the first time, over the administration of the Crown Court.
5. Strengthen current performance measures by introducing a new information system and appoint Performance Officers to all criminal justice areas.

Sentencing guidelines

In *R* v *Kefford* (2002) The Times 7 March (a Court of Appeal case), the facts of the case were concerned with a series of thefts and offences of false accounting by a building society employee. The offences, which were more than 30 in number and totalled over £11,000, led to the imposition of sentences of 12 months per offence to operate consecutively. The Court was of the view that the appropriate period would have been four months. The main point of interest in the case is the impact of the overcrowding of prisons upon sentencing decisions. Great emphasis was placed upon the importance of only using prison where it was appropriate, and for a period no longer than was necessary. It is only in this way that the prison population will remain at anything like manageable levels. This call by the higher judiciary for restraint on the part of sentencers in the lower courts echoes similar sentiments that have been expressed in the past. Whether the message is being delivered by the appellate judiciary or by legislators it is difficult to influence the punitive obsession that is at work in the United Kingdom.

The Court was keen to establish, as a context for sentencing decisions, the problem of increases in the prison population. The prison system should not have to operate so close to its overcrowded capacity. The stage had now been reached where it would be highly undesirable if the prison population were to continue to rise. The overcrowding situation was not only a matter of grave concern for the prison system, but also for the criminal justice system as a whole. The ability to tackle a prisoner's offending behaviour, and so reduce re-offending, was adversely affected if a prison was overcrowded. Those responsible for imposing sentences had to take into account the impact on the prison system of the number of prisoners the service was being required to accommodate at the present time. The aim was not to deter courts from sending those who committed offences involving violence or intimidation, or other grave crimes, to prison for the appropriate period. However, there were other categories of offences where community punishment or fines were more appropriate. Prison was not necessarily the only appropriate form of punishment for economic crimes, particularly where the offender was of previous good character.

OBP Textbook page 171, section 11.4.

Imprisonment

The role of imprisonment

Prison Population Brief England and Wales: September 2002 *(2002)*, *Simes J and Goodman M, London: Home Office*

The prison population fell unexpectedly in the autumn of 2000, but has increased steadily since and reached a record level in September 2002. The prison population in England and Wales in September 2002 was 72,315, a 7 per cent increase on the number in September 2001 (67,465). There were 67,912 male prisoners in September 2002, an increase of 7 per cent over the year. There were 4,403 female prisoners in September 2002, an increase of 11 per cent over the year. Young prisoners (mainly aged 15 to 20) increased by 6 per cent, from 10,999 in September 2001 to 11,683 in September 2002. Juvenile prisoners aged 15 to 17 increased by 11 per cent over the year to 2,633. Remand prisoners increased by 14 per cent from 11,697 to 13,339. Sentenced prisoners increased by 6 per cent over the year from 54,721 to 58,002. Seven per cent were serving sentences of less than six months, 8 per cent were serving from six months to less than 12 months, 38 per cent were serving from 12 months to less than four years, and 39 per cent were serving sentences of four years and over (excluding life sentence prisoners). There were 5,234 life sentence prisoners in September 2002 (9 per cent of all sentenced prisoners). One hundred and sixty two of these were young persons. There were 5,068 males and 166 females serving life sentences. In September 2002, the ethnic breakdown of the prison population was as follows: 77 per cent white; 16 per cent black; 3 per cent South Asian; and 4 per cent Chinese and other ethnicities. The prison population was 7,855 (12 per cent) higher than the certified normal accommodation of 64,242. The numbers of prisoners held was 1,727 below the operational capacity of the prisons.

Prison population as at 30 September 2002

	Male	Female	Total
Aged 15–17	2,527	106	2,633
On remand	538	13	551
Sentenced	1,989	93	2,082
Civil prisoners	–	–	–
Aged 18–20	8,539	511	9,050
On remand	1,973	142	2,115
Sentenced	6,498	366	6,864
Civil prisoners	68	3	71
Adult	56,846	3,786	60,632
On remand	9,843	830	10,673
Sentenced	46,166	2,910	49,076
Civil prisoners	837	46	883
Total	67,912	4,403	72,315
All remand	12,354	985	13,339
All sentenced	54,653	3,369	58,002
All civil prisoners	905	49	954

OBP Textbook page 180, section 12.1.

Early Release, Suspended Sentences and Community Penalties

Community orders

Implementing Anti-social Behaviour Orders: Messages for Practitioners *(2002), Campbell S, London: Home Office*

Anti-social behaviour orders were introduced under the Crime and Disorder Act 1998. They have been available to the police and local authorities since April 1999 and may be used against any person aged ten or over who has acted in an anti-social manner. Currently, anti-social behaviour orders are not being used consistently between agencies and areas, some finding them effective and efficient, whereas others finding them problematic and too difficult to use. This is a summary of the key practical messages from the Home Office review of anti-social behaviour orders, and details the processes whereby agencies are successfully using them.

For the orders to work, areas should draw up simple, streamlined protocols designed with their local area in mind. This should be designed to help practitioners on the ground deal with anti-social behaviour problems quickly, easily and successfully. Some form of partnership working is desirable and can result in real benefits, such as improved relationships, spreading costs and producing creative solutions. However, it should not be allowed to delay the process. Strategic support and commitment from within the lead agency are essential for anti-social behaviour orders to work successfully. The work of agencies' solicitors is often crucial, as they develop experience over time and can give detailed advice on the process, evidence and legal matters. Problem-solving can target the causes of anti-social behaviour and is often effective without the final step of applying for an anti-social behaviour order being necessary. Fostering a good working relationship with the courts, through consultation and training, can help mutual understanding. After an order is granted, continued close working with partner agencies and the community is essential to sustain public confidence and ensure the problem behaviour does not escalate. There is evidence of fear and intimidation amongst witnesses. To combat this, strategies must be developed to minimise intimidation and support witnesses. Ultimately, the measure of success will be whether the anti-social behaviour stops. This focus should be maintained throughout the process.

Probation Statistics, England and Wales 2000 *(2002), London: Home Office*

In 2000 community sentences were imposed in 30 per cent of sentences for indictable offences, a similar percentage to the 29 per cent in 1999. However, the two types of court experienced different trends. In the Crown Court, the proportion has fallen from 30 per cent in 1995 to 27 per cent in 1996, and then risen to 28 per cent in 1997–1998 before falling to 27 per cent in 1999 and to 26 per cent in 2000. But, in magistrates' courts, the proportion was steady at 27–28 per cent during 1994 and 1995, before increasing slightly to 29 per cent in 1996–1999 and to 31 per cent in 2000. Magistrates' courts imposed 87 per cent of all community sentences in 2000. In 2000, magistrates' courts passed 44 per cent of all new prison sentences for indictable offences. The proportion sentenced to community punishment orders (formerly a Community Service Order) or a community rehabilitation order (formerly probation) for indictable violence against the person offences has nearly doubled between 1990 and 2000. For community rehabilitation orders, the proportion rose from 7 per cent to 12 per cent, and for community punishment orders from 8 per cent to 15 per cent.

Reports prepared for the courts
The number of pre-sentence reports (PSRs) written in 2000 (241,300) was similar to the number written in both 1999 (237,500) and 1998 (236,800). Pre-sentence reports written for adult magistrates' courts rose 8 per cent in 2000 to 178,400. Those written for the Youth Court fell very markedly as Youth Offending Teams took over responsibility for this work. In the Crown Court, the number of pre-sentence reports fell 3 per cent to 56,800.

Criminal court orders

The total number of people starting community sentences in 2000 was 3.5 per cent lower than in 1999 at 122,000. However, the types of orders given are changing, with a continuing increase in the use of community punishment orders and falls in the number of community rehabilitation orders, combination orders and money payment supervision orders.

Persons starting criminal supervision by the probation service (thousands)

Court orders	1996	2000
Community rehabilitation order	49.1	53.7
Community punishment order	46.5	52.2
Community punishment and rehabilitation order	17.0	18.5
Children & Young Persons Act 1969	2.9	0.4
Suspended sentence supervision order	0.5	0.5
Money payment supervision order	6.4	1.6
All court orders	115.4	122.0

Community punishment and rehabilitation orders

These orders were first introduced as combination orders in October 1992 by the Criminal Justice Act 1991, and the number of people starting these orders increased steadily between 1993 and 1998, rising by at least 2,000 each year to peak at 21,200 in 1998. However, the numbers fell for the first time in 1999, and they fell a further 10 per cent in 2000 to 18,500.

Money payment supervision orders

The number of people starting a money payment supervision order rose by 94 per cent in 1996 to 6,400, having fallen each year between 1989 and 1995. The 1996 figure was the highest ever reached, apart from 1989 (6,500). A judgement by the High Court in January 1996 means the courts must now consider all other methods of enforcing the payment of fines before sentencing to prison for default. In spite of this judgement, the numbers fell back in 1998 and 1999. In 2000 there was a further fall to just 1,600 orders. The number of fines has also fallen back.

Gender

There was an average of 17 men with a community punishment order for each woman with a community punishment order in 1990. This ratio has fallen to eight men for each woman with a community punishment order in 2000. Sentencers have become more willing to give a community punishment order to a woman over the period 1990–2000.

Offences

Of those commencing probation orders in 2000, theft and handling stolen goods represented the largest specific offence group at 28 per cent. This was also true of those commencing community punishment orders and community punishment and rehabilitation orders (18 per cent and 17 per cent respectively). However, since 1995 the proportion of those commencing community rehabilitation orders for theft and handling offences has decreased significantly (from 33 per cent to 28 per cent), whereas the proportion of those committing violent offences has increased from 7 per cent to 9 per cent. This pattern is also repeated across the other two main orders.

Previous criminal history

When community punishment and rehabilitation orders were first introduced, the courts used almost half of them (49 per cent in 1993) for offenders who had previously served a prison sentence. However, the 1996 – 2000 figures suggest that there is now little difference between community rehabilitation orders and community punishment and rehabilitation orders in terms of the offender's previous criminal history. For both orders in 2000, about a third had a previous prison sentence and about a quarter had no previous convictions. The courts more often give community rehabilitation orders or community punishment and rehabilitation orders, rather than a community punishment order, to an offender with a previous prison sentence. In 2000, 19 per cent of community punishment orders had previous custody and 47 per cent had no previous convictions. Over the last seven years the proportions of the three main orders that have gone to those with no previous convictions have grown considerably. This is part of a general trend towards more severe sentencing.

Orders – additional requirements

In 1991, 24 per cent of new community rehabilitation orders had an additional requirement. This proportion rose to 33 per cent in 1997 and has remained around this level since then. The requirement to participate in a specified activity has shown steady growth for a number of years. There were 9 per cent of all community rehabilitation orders with such a requirement in 1989, and 20 per cent in 2000. The proportion of all additional requirements that had a residential element declined from 20 per cent in 1989 to 6 per cent in 2000. Up to 1994 some 17 per cent of those beginning a community punishment and rehabilitation order had an additional requirement. This proportion rose to 26 per cent in 1998, but has decreased to 23 per cent in 2000.

Caseloads
Persons supervised by the probation service by type of supervision (thousands)

Court orders	1992	2000
Community rehabilitation order	49.7	57.8
Community punishment order	31.6	43.8
Community punishment and rehabilitation order	1.4	26.1
Children & Young Persons Act 1969	2.2	0.3
Money payment supervision order	7.4	7.0
All court orders	88.5	128.3

Average workload per maingrade officer

These figures give only a rough measure of workload. The actual workload depends not only on the number and length of orders, but also on their complexity and the amount of supervision provided. Over time, national standards, for example, will have changed the work involved in preparing pre-sentence reports and supervising offenders on community sentences. Also, probation service officers are increasingly being used for some work which would traditionally have been done by maingrade officers. The average number of people supervised per maingrade officer has risen each year since 1992 from 20.7 to 36.2 in 2000. This shows the rising caseloads and falling or stable numbers of fully trained maingrade officers. Total reports completed per officer continued to rise from 51.8 in 1993 to 69.3 in 2000. The average court order caseload per officer rose each year between 1992 and 1998 from 11.3 to 18.3. This reflected the growth in caseloads and the fact that numbers of maingrade officers have fallen or remained stable. The average remained unchanged in 1999 at 18.3, but fell for the first time since 1992 to 17.7 at the end of 2000. This fall reflects the fact that a large number of 16–17-year-olds who were formerly the responsibility of the probation service were under the supervision of Youth Offending Teams at the end of 2000. There were some 550 trainee probation officers in post at 31 December 2000.

OBP Textbook page 205, section 13.6.

Police Organisation, the Decision to Prosecute and Cautioning of Offenders

The organisation of police forces in England and Wales

Police Service Strength England and Wales, as at 31 March 2002
(2002), Smith C, Rundle S and Hosking R, London: Home Office

There were 129,603 police officers as at 31 March 2002, which was 3.1 per cent more than the year before. This is the largest figure ever for police strength. Of these, 127,267 were on ordinary duty in the 43 police force areas, and 2,336 officers were on secondment to bodies such as the National Criminal Intelligence Service. Within the service, 22,784 police officers were female, which was 18 per cent of the total. Further, 3,386 or 2.6 per cent of officers were from an ethnic minority group: this is a raise of 14 per cent over the last year. In the year, 10,215 officers were recruited, which was 38 per cent more than in the previous year. The number leaving the police service was 6,420 officers.

Police strength by rank and gender

Rank	Male	Female	Total	% Female
Chief Constable	47	6	53	11
Assistant Chief Constable	141	10	151	7
Superintendent	1,173	83	1,256	7
Chief Inspector	1,443	117	1,550	8
Inspector	5,717	479	6,195	8
Sergeant	16,621	1,953	18,574	11
Constable	79,351	20,137	99,487	20
All ranks	104,483	22,784	127,267	18

OBP Textbook page 212, section 14.1.

Police accountability

Police Complaints and Discipline, 12 months to March 2001 *(2001)*, *Povey D and Cotton J, London: Home Office*

There were 10 per cent fewer complaints than in the previous year. This reversed a downward trend, as there had been 3 per cent, 8 per cent, 2 per cent and 4 per cent fewer complaints in the four previous years. Of the 18,911 complainants, 903 were substantiated – a year-on-year increase of 26 per cent. About a quarter of these were for oppressive behaviour and more than half involved a failure in duty. Disciplinary/misconduct charges against 1,202 officers were proven, and this led to 125 officers being dismissed or required to resign. Of complaints investigated 9 per cent are substantiated. More than a third (34 per cent) of the complaints were informally resolved and a further 34 per cent were withdrawn or dispensed with. The informal resolution system is designed to provide a quick and simple system and the complainant has to agree to this. It is appropriate where an explanation of the behaviour or an apology will suffice. The figure for police officers convicted of criminal offences was 240, and of these 53 were for non-traffic offences.

Provisional Figures to 31 August 2002 *(2002), Criminal Cases Review Commission (website press release)*

Since 31 March 1997, the Commission has received over 5,228 applications and 4,499 cases have been completed. Convictions are referred to the appellate courts if the Commission believes that there is a real possibility that they will be found to be unsafe. A high proportion of applications involve only simple points of fact or law, and can be reviewed within a month or two. Where there are complex issues to investigate, the review may take a year or more. There have been 173 referrals, of which the Court of Appeal have made decisions in 108 cases – in 71 of these cases the sentence was quashed.

OBP Textbook page 214, section 14.2.

Policing by consent: myth or reality?

Policing for London *(2002), FitzGerald M and Hough M, Uffculme, Devon: Willan*

This was a major study of policing in London which gathered data primarily by means of interviews so as to get a representative sample of the London population over the age of 15. Additional interviews were carried out amongst ethnic minorities and further interviews were used in relation to the police. Secondary data and focus groups were also utilised. The study was undertaken in 2000–2001. It is the first major independent study of policing in London since that mounted by the Policy Studies Institute 20 years ago. It found that Londoners did not simply want more patrol officers on the beat, but called for a style of policing that was more responsive to local problems and local needs. Though Londoners were no more fearful of crime than 20 years ago, there were rising concerns about disorderly teenagers, litter, graffiti and drug dealing.

Over a third of the public sought police help in the previous 12 months, and a quarter were approached by the police as suspects. Though two-thirds of those who sought police help were satisfied with the response, levels of satisfaction were lower than in 1981. The majority of those who were stopped as suspects were satisfied with the way they were treated; but dissatisfaction was greatest amongst the young, amongst black suspects and those who lived in poor areas. Confidence in police effectiveness in London fell between 1982 and 2000 – and markedly between the mid-1990s and 2000 – but not as steeply as in other police forces. The falls in public satisfaction and confidence can be attributed, at least in part, to reductions in the capacity of uniformed officers to respond to everyday demands on the police and falls in staff morale. Rising public expectations may also be a factor. The failure of the service to be more responsive to local needs and the fall in staff morale can both be traced in part to performance management regimes that emphasise quantified performance targets, and as a result ignore the complexities of police work. The researchers concluded that the Metropolitan Police needs to achieve a better balance between 'crime fighting' objectives and the equally important ones of 'peacekeeping' and 'order maintenance' if it is to retain the consent of Londoners. The Force also needs to be able to develop ways of managing performance that place greater emphasis on achieving professional standards and less emphasis on hitting numerical targets. The current emphasis on quantitative measures is distorting performance and reducing the quality of service. The legacy of discrimination and over-policing continues to overshadow relations between the police and black people, and there is a danger of similar tensions arising with other groups; but improving police relations with minority groups cannot be achieved in isolation.

OBP Textbook page 223, section 14.3.

Introducing change into policing

Police Reform Act 2002

The Act, which received the Royal Assent on 24 July 2002, introduces a wide variety of changes for police forces of various types within the United Kingdom. The main measures that need to be noted are the introduction of further methods of control of the local forces by central government, the alteration of methods for handling complaints by citizens and the disciplining of individual police officers. The background to this was that the government published the White Paper *Policing a New Century: A Blueprint for Reform* (2001). That set out the government's intentions for the future of policing in England and Wales and followed the normal consultation process. The key principles of the reform programme are: to continue the reduction in crime; to tackle persistent offenders more effectively; to improve detection and conviction rates; to tackle anti-social behaviour; to reduce the fear of crime; to provide support to victims of crime; and to rebuild public confidence in key aspects of the police service. A comment that could be made about these so-called principles is that they sound more like platitudes than principles of a criminal justice system. In the Act, additional systems are introduced for the control of police forces. As part of this the Secretary of State will produce an annual National Policing Plan and present it to parliament. There will also be various systems for giving directions to police forces, including the use of codes of practice. The National Policing Plan will set out the government's priorities for policing and how they are to be delivered, and the indicators by which performance will be measured. Provision is also made for further measures that will allow the Secretary of State to intervene in a force where Her Majesty's Inspectorate of Constabulary is satisfied the force is not efficient or effective. In particular, the Act introduces a new power enabling the Secretary of State to direct a police authority to produce, in conjunction with the relevant chief officer, an action plan to address the poor performance highlighted by Her Majesty's Inspectorate of Constabulary. The Act also allows the Secretary of State to require that Her Majesty's Inspectorate of Constabulary inspects a force or part of a force.

As regards complaints and misconduct, the background to the new provisions was a consultation paper in May 2000: *Complaints against the Police: A Consultation Document* (London: Home Office) which was partly based on earlier investigations into the system of complaints against the police. The Police Complaints Authority will be replaced by a new body: the Independent Police Complaints Commission. As regards the removal, suspension and disciplining of police officers, the Act broadens the circumstances in which senior officers can be removed in the interests of the efficiency or effectiveness of the force, provides for the issue of regulations regarding the procedure for removing senior officers and makes provision for the suspension of senior officers. The Police Reform Act 2002 aims to ensure that the most effective policing methods are used by all police forces, thus tackling the variations in performance between forces. The powers enabling the Home Secretary to issue Codes of Practice to chief officers and make regulations governing the use of police equipment, or requiring forces to adopt particular procedures or practices, are intended to spread good practice throughout the police service and to help raise the standards of all forces to the level of the best.

The Act also contains provisions in relation to numerous other matters, some of which can be noted briefly. It attempts to facilitate the more effective use of police support staff, and provides for community safety accreditation schemes. It also adds to the list of offences for which someone can be arrested without a warrant and places the system of independent custody visiting, to police stations, on a statutory footing. It contains provisions regarding the taking of blood samples from those involved in road traffic incidents. It makes provision for powers for constables in relation to vehicles used in a manner causing alarm, distress or annoyance. Finally, it makes several changes to legislation regarding anti-social behaviour orders and sex offender orders. Anti-social behaviour orders, for example, will be more flexible and widely available.

OBP Textbook page 229, section 14.4.

The decision to prosecute

Cautions, Court Proceedings and Sentencing England and Wales 2000 (2001), Johnson K et al, London: Home Office

This report provides details of how the Crown Prosecution Service (CPS) deals with cases. Not all proceedings go to a verdict at a trial. The number of proceedings discontinued, as a proportion of all cases finalised, was 13 per cent. Discontinued proceedings include cases where witnesses fail to appear, refuse to give evidence or change their story, or evidence is excluded because of material irregularity in its collection. A further reason is that defendants may wait until the day of the hearing to produce driving documents showing that no offence has been committed. They also include cases discontinued on public interest grounds. The CPS can proceed only where sufficient evidence exists to provide a realistic prospect of conviction. The CPS also writes off from its record of current cases a number of proceedings where it is not possible to proceed directly. The most common reason is that the defendant cannot be found. The proportion of cases written off by the CPS was 6 per cent in 2000. This publication also provides statistics on court proceedings and related matters. For example, the number of completed cases at magistrates' courts was 1,911,600 (1 per cent more than the year before). This increase was a result of a 12 per cent increase in the amount of summary non-motoring offences, such as not having a television licence. For the Crown Courts there were 95,300 proceedings completed: this was 2 per cent less than the previous year. The new system of plea before venue has meant both that there are now more people being sentenced in the Crown Court after summary trial, and that less cases are being sent for trial in the Crown Court. There has also been a 2 per cent decrease in the guilty plea rate in the Crown Court, and the acquittal rate in the Crown Court increased by 1 per cent to 65 per cent. Immediate custody has been used more by the courts: this increase was a result of more custodial sentencing in both the magistrates' court (a 1.4 per cent increase to 141 of cases) and the Crown Court (a 1.5 per cent increase to 64 per cent of cases).

OBP Textbook page 233, section 14.5.

Cautioning policy

Cautions, reprimands and final warnings

Excluding motoring offences, there were 239,000 cautions, which was 10 per cent less than the previous year: the change was greater for males with an 11 per cent reduction than for females, where the decrease was 7 per cent. For indictable offences, 151,000 received cautions, a rate 12 per cent lower than the previous year. The cautioning rate was 32 per cent (this being the percentage of those found guilty or cautioned who are cautioned). This rate has been declining over the years – it was 40 per cent in 1995. Cautioning for drug offences fell by as much as 17 per cent in the last year. The cautioning rate for indictable only offences remained the same at 12 per cent. The Crime and Disorder Act 1998 provided for reprimands and warnings instead of cautions for those under the age of 18. These have been used nationally since June 2000: they were being used in only some areas on a pilot basis before that. The figures for 2000 in the table below thus contain data on both the old and the new systems.

Use of reprimands, final warnings and cautions for young offenders in 2000

Indictable offences	
Reprimands	28,400
Final warnings	2,200
Cautions	3,800
Total	64,300
Summary non-motoring offences	
Reprimands	14,400
Final warnings	5,800
Cautions	13,000
Total	33,200
Indictable and summary non-motoring offences	
Reprimands	42,800
Final warnings	18,000
Cautions	36,800
Total	97,500

OBP Textbook page 240, section 14.6.

11

Employment Law

The Concept of Employment

Employee or self-employed

The factors to be taken into consideration in determining when a worker will be regarded as an employee were considered yet again in the following case.

Hewlett Packard Ltd v *O'Murphy* [2002] IRLR 4 Employment Appeal Tribunal (Douglas Brown J, Ms N Amin and Mr B V Fitzgerald MBE)

Contracts of employment – meaning of employee – unfair dismissal

Facts

Mr O'Murphy, a computer specialist, set up a company to provide IT services. The company entered into a contract with an agency to provide IT services to clients of the agency, although it was generally acknowledged that the client was Hewlett Packard (HP). Mr O'Murphy, as the only employee of the company, commenced work at HP in June 1994 and continued until HP informed the agency that they no longer wished Mr O'Murphy to continue because he was unable to carry out the work they required to be done to a sufficiently high standard. Mr O'Murphy presented a claim to the tribunal alleging that he had been unfairly dismissed by HP. As a preliminary question, the tribunal had to consider whether in fact HP was to be regarded as being Mr O'Murphy's employer. The tribunal considered that, because of the amount of control that HP had over Mr O'Murphy and the mutuality of obligations, the reality was that he was an employee. HP appealed to the Employment Appeal Tribunal (EAT).

Held

It was held by the EAT that the tribunal had erred in their finding. There was no contract at all between Mr O'Murphy and HP, and the lack of a contractual nexus between the parties meant that no claim arising out of an alleged contract of employment could succeed. The EAT took into account the fact that there were two parties between the applicant and the respondent – the company set up by Mr O'Murphy and the agency.

OBP Textbook Chapter 2.

The Contract of Employment

Implied terms

On 1 October 2002 new Regulations came into effect giving new rights to more than one million contract workers in the UK. The Fixed-term Employees (Prevention of Less Favourable Treatment) Regulations 2002, which transpose the EC Directive on Fixed-term Work into UK legislation, aim to protect those on fixed-term contracts from discrimination in respect of terms and conditions in comparison to permanent employees. The Regulations will cover persons engaged in seasonal or casual work who have contracts for short periods of time. Employees who are engaged to cover for maternity or paternity leave, or who have been hired to cover for peaks in demand, will also be covered, as will those who are taken on to undertake a particular task and whose contract will expire upon the completion of that particular task.

The Regulations also repeal s197 Employment Rights Act 1996 under which employees on fixed-term contracts could waive their right to a redundancy payment. Any waiver in a fixed-term contract which is renewed or extended after 1 October 2002 will be void. The following is a brief summary of the main Regulations.

Reg 1   Defines a permanent employee as an employee who is not employed under a fixed-term contract.

Reg 2   Defines a comparable employee as an employee who is employed by the same employer as the fixed-term employee who is engaged in the same or broadly similar work, having regard to levels of skill and qualification.

Reg 3   Provides that a fixed-term employee has the right not to be treated less favourably than a comparable employee with respect to the terms of his contract or by being subject to any other detriment unless such treatment can be objectively justified by the employer.

Reg 4   Provides that where a fixed-term employee is treated less favourably than a permanent employee with respect to any term of his contract there may be a defence of objective justification if the employer can show that overall the terms of the contract are at least as favourable as those of the comparator.

Reg 5   Provides that where an employee considers that he may have been treated less favourably he may request from his employer a written statement giving reasons for the treatment: any such statement should be provided within 21 days of the request.

Reg 6   States that an employee who is dismissed by an employer, where one of the principal reasons for the dismissal relates to bringing proceedings under the Regulations or asserting a right or assisting another in asserting a right under the Regulations, shall be regarded as having been dismissed unfairly.

Reg 7   Provides that any employee, who considers that a right conferred by reg 3 has been breached by his employer, may present a complaint to the employment tribunal within three months of the alleged breach.

Reg 8   Provides that if a fixed-term contract has been renewed, or the employee is engaged on a new fixed-term contract, and that the employee has been continuously employed for a period of four years or more, the renewal or new contract takes effect as a permanent contract unless a fixed-term contract can be objectively justified. Any employment prior to 10 July 2002 does not count towards the four-year period.

OBP Textbook page 23, section 3.4.

Dismissal

Introduction

Miller Bros and F P Butler Ltd v *Johnston* (2002) The Times 18 April Employment Appeal Tribunal (Mr Recorder Longstaff QC, Mrs A Gallico and Mr A D Tuffin)

Breach of contract – termination of tribunal – jurisdiction of tribunal

Facts
The question for consideration was whether a tribunal had been correct in awarding damages for breach of contract, or whether the issue was outside the jurisdiction of the tribunal. The applicant and the respondent had entered into financial negotiations prior to the termination of the employment contract. However, such negotiations were not concluded until after the employment relationship had come to an end. Article 3 of the Employment Tribunals Extension of Jurisdiction (England and Wales) Order 1994 provides that proceedings may be brought before an employment tribunal if 'the claim arises or is outstanding on the termination of the employee's employment'. The employment tribunal awarded the applicant £25,000 and the respondents appealed on the grounds that the tribunal did not have jurisdiction to hear the claim.

Held
It was held by the Employment Appeal Tribunal that the termination of the employment contract is the moment when the employee ceases to work for the employer, and that art 3(c) of the 1994 Order requires any claim to be outstanding at the time of termination or to arise as a result of the termination. In this case art 3(c) was not satisfied, and therefore the tribunal did not have jurisdiction to hear the claim. The only option for the applicant was to pursue his claim in the courts.

OBP Textbook page 45, section 4.1.

Constructive dismissal

When an employee resigns on the grounds that the behaviour of the employer was such that there is a fundamental breach of contract on the part of the employer, he will generally face an uphill struggle to prove constructive dismissal. The issue of when an alleged breach of the implied term of mutual trust and confidence would entitle an employee to resign and claim constructive dismissal has recently been considered in a number of cases.

Cantor Fitzgerald International v *Bird and Others* [2002] IRLR 867
Queen's Bench Divisional Court (McCombe J)

Contracts of employment – termination – duty of mutual trust and confidence

Facts

Three employees worked for the claimants as brokers. Their contracts of employment provided that they would receive a fixed annual salary plus a discretionary bonus, which was to be of a minimum fixed percentage of their commission revenue. In 2001 the claimants decided to change the way in which the employees were to be paid, so that they were to be remunerated on a commission only basis. The employees were advised of the proposed change and senior executives tried to persuade the employees to accept the new arrangement. One of the employees was advised of the new scheme by a senior executive, who although friendly, nevertheless gave information which was thought to be misleading. The other two employees were dealt with in a much more aggressive manner and were threatened with the non-payment of their bonus. All the employees decided to reject the new proposals and advised the company accordingly. Another competing company approached the employees with an offer of employment which, despite a restrictive covenant, the employees decided to accept. The employees claimed that the action of the employers amounted to a breach of the implied term of trust and confidence that entitled them to treat the contract as being repudiated by the employer. The claimants sought an injunction restraining the employees from working for the new company.

Held

It was held by the High Court that the two employees who had been treated in an aggressive manner were entitled to treat the behaviour of the employer as a breach of the implied term of trust and confidence. The manner in which they had been advised of the new contractual arrangements was misleading, and the use of swearing and other obscenities was so unacceptable that it was likely to damage or destroy the employment relationship. On the other hand, the third employee was not treated in such a manner that entitled him to resign, and therefore he was in repudiatory breach of his contract of employment. The distinction lay in the manner in which the first two employees and the third employee were dealt with: it was only where an employer behaved in such a way that his conduct was so serious that the inevitable conclusion was that the employment relationship had broken down where the implied term of trust and confidence could be said to have been breached. The court considered that the loss of confidence in management was not sufficient in itself to lead to a breach of the implied term.

Morrow v *Safeway Stores plc* [2002] IRLR 9 Employment Appeal Tribunal (Ms Recorder Cox QC, Mr P R A Jacques CBE and Mr J R Rivers)

Contracts of employment – termination – duty of mutual trust and confidence

Facts
The applicant, a bakery production controller, claimed that she had been unfairly and constructively dismissed following an incident when her store manager had seriously rebuked her in front of other members of staff and at least one customer for failing to have sufficient bread on the supermarket shelves. The tribunal held that although there had been a breach of the implied term of trust and confidence, it was not sufficiently serious as to amount to a repudiatory breach, and therefore did not give rise to a claim of constructive dismissal. The applicant appealed against the decision of the tribunal.

Held
The Employment Appeal Tribunal (EAT) considered that the approach of the tribunal had been incorrect and that a finding of a breach of the implied term of mutual trust and confidence will almost certainly give rise to a repudiatory breach. The EAT remitted the case to a freshly constituted tribunal to determine whether the conduct of the store manager, both in terms of what was said and the circumstances giving rise to the rebuke, did amount to a breach of the implied term of trust and confidence.

OBP Textbook page 53, section 4.5.

Excluded categories

Age limit

There has, over the last few years, been considerable discussion over the age limit with respect to bringing a claim for unfair dismissal. Section 94(1) Employment Rights Act (ERA) 1996 states that: 'An employee has the right not to be unfairly dismissed by his employer'. However, s109(1)(b) ERA 1996 provides that s94 does not apply to a person who has reached the age of 65. The effect of this has been to prevent those persons over the age of 65 from pursuing a claim for unfair dismissal. In *Nash* v *Mash Roe Group plc* [1998] IRLR 168 an employment tribunal held that the cut off provision preventing those over 65 from bringing a claim was incompatible with European law. The argument that was successfully advanced in that case was that, because more men over the age of 65 were economically active, s109 was discriminatory. Similar issues have recently arisen in the cases *Rutherford* v *Town Circle Ltd (T/A Harvest) and Secretary of State for Trade and Industry; Bentley* v *Secretary of State for Trade and Industry* [2002] IRLR 768.

In these joined cases the tribunal had to consider whether ss109 and 156 ERA 1996 were contrary to European law. Section 135 states that:

'An employer shall pay a redundancy payment to any employee of his if the employee:
(a) is dismissed by reason of redundancy, or
(b) is eligible for a redundancy payment by reason of being laid off or kept on short-time.'

Section 156 ERA 1996 provides that an employee does not have any right to a redundancy payment if he has attained the age of 65. In this case, Mr Rutherford brought proceedings claiming compensation for unfair dismissal and redundancy, while Mr Bentley claimed redundancy.

The tribunal held that the exclusion of employees over the age of 65 from the right to bring a claim for unfair dismissal or a redundancy payment is contrary to European law. The evidence presented to the tribunal showed that ss109 and 156 ERA 1996 have a disparate effect on males and females and, in the view of the tribunal, the respondent had failed to show that the discrimination was objectively justified.

The cases will be going to the Employment Appeal Tribunal, and therefore it is too early to assess whether inroads will be made into age discrimination before proposed legislation in 2006.

OBP Textbook page 67, section 4.9.

Reasonableness and the importance of procedure

Asda Stores Ltd v *Thompson and Others* [2002] IRLR 245 Employment Appeal Tribunal (Wall J, Miss C Holroyd and Mr G H Wright MBE)

Unfair dismissal – sufficiency of reason for dismissal – application for discovery of statements obtained during employers' investigation

Facts
The applicants were dismissed following an investigation into illegal drug taking at company events. The respondents had carried out an investigation into the allegations, but statements that were taken from other employees were not disclosed to the applicants prior to their dismissal, on the grounds that it would breach a promise of confidentiality made to those employees who had made the statements. The applicants applied for discovery of the documents and, at a preliminary hearing, the tribunal found that the documents were both relevant and necessary and should therefore be disclosed in totality. The respondents appealed against the order for disclosure.

Held

The Employment Appeal Tribunal held that whilst the tribunal had erred in ordering the documents to be disclosed in full, a tribunal does have the power to order disclosure of documents in anonymised or edited form, which will then preserve the identity of the maker of the statement. Furthermore, the applicants did not need to know the identities of those persons who had made statements with respect to the allegations in order for there to be a fair hearing.

Bournemouth Borough Council v *Meredith* Judgment of 24 July 2002 (not yet reported) Employment Appeal Tribunal (Maurice Kay J, Ms N Amin and Mr D J Hodgkins CB)

Dismissal – conduct amounting to gross misconduct

Facts

Mr Meredith was employed as a music teacher by Bournemouth Borough Council. He was dismissed for gross misconduct following an incident when he took a disruptive 12-year-old girl by the wrist and dragged her outside the classroom during an examination. The girl had refused several instructions to leave the examination room. Mr Meredith appeared before a disciplinary panel, who concluded that he was guilty of gross misconduct, stating, inter alia, 'that as an experienced professional person it was incumbent upon you to keep yourself abreast of the legislation and published guidance on classroom management including that relating to disruptive students'. Mr Meredith was dismissed and claimed that the dismissal was unfair. He was successful at the employment tribunal and the employers appealed.

Held

The appeal was dismissed. The conclusion of the tribunal that the disciplinary panel 'had no reasonable basis upon which to conclude that [Mr Meredith] knew or ought reasonably to have known that what he did amounted to misconduct' was correct, and because the contract of employment did not define 'misconduct' or 'gross misconduct', it was incumbent upon the employers to satisfy the disciplinary panel that Mr Meredith knew, or ought reasonably to have known, that his conduct was prohibited. The conduct of the employers was not within the band of reasonable responses, taking into account the slightness of the injury to the student, the fact that Mr Meredith had nine years' service, the quality of his teaching, the absence of any previous incident of this nature, the lack of clear guidance and the lack of any definition of gross misconduct.

Thomas v *Hillingdon London Borough Council* (2002) The Times 4 October Employment Appeal Tribunal (Ms Recorder Slade QC, Mr Robert Thomson and Mr Peter Wickens)

Dismissal – whether dismissal unfair

Facts

The applicant was dismissed for gross misconduct after using an office computer to visit hard core pornographic websites. The tribunal held that the applicant had been unfairly dismissed because, after holding that the dismissal was within the band of reasonable responses, the tribunal considered that the conduct of the applicant was no more than misconduct and the dismissal was unfair. The respondent's appealed to the Employment Appeal Tribunal (EAT).

Held

It was held by the EAT that, having come to the conclusion that the response of the employer was within the band of reasonable responses, the decision of the tribunal that the dismissal was unfair was perverse and the applicants' complaint was dismissed.

OBP Textbook page 69, section 4.10.

Remedies

Paggetti v *Cobb* (2002) The Times 12 April Employment Appeal Tribunal (Peter Clarke J, Ms J Drake and Mr K M Young CBE)

Unfair dismissal – compensation – national minimum wage

Facts

Mr Paggetti, a groom, was dismissed from his employment by the respondent. He presented a claim of unfair dismissal, which was successful. In determining compensation, the tribunal took into consideration the weekly wage received by the applicant, which was below the national minimum wage. Mr Paggetti appealed to the Employment Appeal Tribunal on the grounds that the tribunal, in determining a week's pay, should have taken the national minimum wage into account.

Held

In a case of unfair dismissal, an employment tribunal is under a duty to consider the national minimum wage when determining a week's pay for the purpose of calculating the basic award and when calculating the net rate of pay for the loss of earnings element of a compensatory award, even if the applicant has not raised the matter.

OBP Textbook page 75, section 4.13.

Reform

Employment Act 2002, Part 3: dispute resolution

Sections 29–41 of the Employment Act 2002 aim to avoid the need for litigation by providing for better workplace communication and improved conciliation between the parties to a dispute. Draft proposals aim to promote the resolution of a dispute in the workplace without the need for recourse to the tribunals. Employers will be required to have minimum statutory dismissal and disciplinary procedures. It is anticipated that any failure on the part of either an employer or employee to comply with the appropriate procedure may result in either an increase or reduction in damages awarded, as appropriate. These sections are due to be implemented in the latter part of 2003.

OBP Textbook page 77.

Redundancy

Redundancy payments

Curr v *Marks & Spencer plc* (2003) The Times 30 January Court of Appeal (Civil Division) (Peter Gibson, Scott Baker and Clarke LJJ)

Contract of employment – redundancy payment – continuity of employment

Facts
The employer operated a 'child break' scheme which, rather than allowing employees a break from their children, provided that an employee could resign at the end of maternity leave but would be allowed to return to a similar post upon her return. The scheme also provided that any employees who took advantage of it would be required to work for a minimum of two weeks per year. The applicant resigned at the end of her maternity leave and took her child break. She returned, but five years later was made redundant. The employer calculated her redundancy pay from the date upon which she returned to work following her child break. The applicant argued that this was an unlawful deduction from her wages, because her earlier period of employment should have been taken into account. The Employment Appeal Tribunal held that the applicant had continued in her employment during the child break, and that this continuity of employment should have been considered when calculating her redundancy payment. The employer appealed.

Held
It was held by the Court of Appeal that the child break scheme did not fall within s212(3)(c) Employment Rights Act 1996, as the terms and conditions of the scheme clearly stated that there was a possibility that the applicant would be re-employed at

the end of the child break. It was clear from the facts that the applicant was not regarded as continuing her employment during the child break.

OBP Textbook page 87, section 5.7.

Consultation

Compensation

A new approach has recently been taken by the Employment Appeal Tribunal (EAT) in determining how much compensation should be paid to an employee who has been unfairly made redundant because of a failure to engage in consultation. The approach that has generally been taken is that an employee who has been made redundant would be entitled to a sum which represents any additional time he would have been employed if consultation had taken place. However, the EAT has adopted a more broad approach in the following case.

Elkouil v *Coney Island* [2002] IRLR 174 Employment Appeal Tribunal (Judge J R Reid QC, Mr P R A Jacques CBE and Mr J C Shrigley)

Unfair dismissal – redundancy – sufficiency of consultation

Facts
The applicant was made redundant without any warning or consultation, even though the employers had known for some weeks that he would be dismissed. At the employment tribunal it was held that the dismissal was unfair, although the tribunal accepted that the employee would have been dismissed even if consultation had taken place. In determining compensation, the tribunal adopted the conventional method of awarding compensation for the period of time that the employee would have been employed if consultation had taken place. The tribunal awarded the applicant two weeks' pay, which represented the additional time the applicant would have had in work if consultation had taken place. The applicant appealed on the grounds that he was entitled to more than two weeks' pay.

Held
The EAT held that the tribunal had failed to take into account the fact that the employers knew of the applicant's impending redundancy about ten weeks before he was dismissed. If the employers had warned the applicant at an earlier stage, he would have had more opportunity to find alternative employment. The EAT considered that, because the applicant had lost the chance of being re-employed earlier than he was, he should be awarded ten weeks' pay rather than the two awarded by the tribunal.

OBP Textbook page 89, section 5.8.

Transfer of undertakings

Duty of care

Hagen v *ICI Chemicals and Polymers Ltd* [2002] IRLR 31 Queen's Bench Divisional Court (Elias J)

Transfer of undertakings – terms of employment – pension rights

Facts

The claimants worked for ICI at a central engineering resource centre. As part of a restructuring it was decided that engineering resources should be transferred to Redpath Engineering Services (RES). The claimants were concerned about the transfer, not least because they feared a loss of benefits, including pensions. The company was aware that without the support of the workforce the transfer was unlikely to proceed, and therefore efforts were made to keep employees informed on the way the transfer was progressing. Representations were made to the employees by the defendants to the effect that their terms and conditions would be the same following transfer, and that they would be offered a broadly similar pension scheme. It was also made clear that if the transfer did not go ahead there would be job losses. The claimants reluctantly accepted the transfer, but then discovered that the representations that had been made with respect to the pension scheme were false. The claimants brought a claim alleging negligent misrepresentation and a breach of the implied terms of mutual trust and confidence.

Held

It was held by the court that the first defendants owed a duty of care to their employees to ensure the accuracy of the information given to them. The court further held that the representations made by the first defendants with respect to pension provisions were false, and therefore there was a breach of the duty of care. However, because the incorrect information that had been given related to pension benefits, liability would not pass to the second defendants, because reg 7 Transfer of Undertakings (Protection of Employment) Regulations 1981 provides that no liabilities transfer to the transferee when they are in connection with occupational pensions.

OBP Textbook page 105, section 5.11.

Discrimination in Employment

Sex discrimination

Lawrence v *Regent Office Care Ltd* [2002] IRLR 822 European Court of Justice

Equal pay – comparator

Facts
The rates of pay of female catering and cleaning staff working for North Yorkshire county council were increased following a job evaluation scheme which had rated the work of the female employees of equal value to the work of men engaged in activities such as gardening and refuse collection. The work of the catering and cleaning staff was contracted out to a private contractor and their pay was cut. The female employees claimed equal pay, using as their comparators the male employees who were still employed by the council. The employment tribunal held as a preliminary issue that the applicants could not compare themselves with the men, because the men were working for a different employer. The matter was subsequently referred to the European Court of Justice by the Court of Appeal.

Held
Whilst there was nothing in the wording of art 141(1) EC to limit the scope of that provision to situations in which men and women worked for the same employer, where the work of both the applicant and the comparator could not be attributed to a single source, art 141(1) EC would not apply. There was no single entity that could remedy the alleged inequality in pay and therefore the application failed.

Morton v *South Ayrshire Council* [2002] IRLR 256 Court of Session (Clerk LJ, Lords MacLean and Caplan)

Equal pay – statutory scheme – comparator

Facts
Female head teachers of primary schools claimed equal pay with secondary school head teachers. The applicants claimed that 75 per cent of primary school head teachers were female, whilst 75 per cent of secondary school head teachers were male. The salary scale for primary school heads was lower than that for secondary school heads. The applicants claimed that there was discrimination contrary to the Equal Pay Act 1970 because they were engaged in the same 'service' within the meaning of art 141 EC. The respondents argued that the applicants could not use as their comparator head teachers who were employed by a different education authority.

Held

The Court of Session, having regard to the case of *Defrenne* v *Sabena (No 2)* Case 43/75 [1976] ECR 455, held that in determining whether there was inequality of pay, the scope of enquiry was not always confined to the applicant's own workplace or indeed to his own employer. In this case pay scales were negotiated by the Scottish Joint Negotiating Committee and any settlement was to be regarded as a national settlement to be implemented by each education authority. The court therefore concluded that a comparator employed by another education authority was permissible. The case was remitted to a tribunal for a full hearing on the facts.

Royal National Orthopaedic Hospital Trust* v *Howard Judgment of 26 July 2002 (not yet reported) Employment Appeal Tribunal (Reid J, Mr I Ezekiel and Mr G H Wright MBE)

Sex discrimination – victimisation – effect of compromise agreement

Facts

Mrs Howard had worked for the National Orthopaedic Hospital Trust for 18 years. She brought an unfair dismissal and sex discrimination claim against her employers, and in 1998 the claims were compromised in a COT3 agreement which stated: 'these proceedings and all claims which the applicant has or may have against the respondent'. Two years later, she was asked by a surgeon to assist at an operation for one day, but the hospital refused to authorise a temporary appointment: she claimed that this was because of her previous sex discrimination claim. Mrs Howard submitted a claim for victimisation to the employment tribunal. The hospital applied to have her claim dismissed on the grounds that the COT3 agreement precluded Mrs Howard's further claim for victimisation. However, the tribunal found for the applicant.

Held

The Employment Appeal Tribunal upheld the decision of the employment tribunal. The compromise agreement did not prevent Mrs Howard from bringing the later claim of victimisation.

OBP Textbook page 108, section 6.1.

Disability discrimination

British Gas Services Ltd* v *McCaull [2001] IRLR 60 Employment Appeal Tribunal (Keene J, Mr B R Gibbs and Professsor P D Wickens)

Unfair dismissal – disability discrimination – reasonable adjustments

Facts

The applicant was a service engineer who was employed to service central heating systems. In order to travel to customers' houses, driving was a necessary part of the job. Whilst driving, the applicant had an epileptic fit which caused him to black out and have an accident. The applicant was off work for some time after the accident and, after a medical examination, the employers' occupational health service advised him that he could no longer drive. The respondents advised him that he could not return to his previous position: however, he could be employed as a customer service adviser. The applicant rejected the offer of the alternative job, because it meant a reduction in salary of up to 30 per cent, and claimed that he had been discriminated against contrary to the Disability Discrimination Act 1995.

Held

The Employment Appeal Tribunal held that the employers had complied with their duty under s6 Disability Discrimination Act 1995 to make reasonable adjustments, even though the employer was unaware of that duty. The question is: what steps did the employer actually take, and in this case the employer had in fact taken steps to accommodate the applicant. The EAT also held that the tribunal had erred in finding that the offer of an alternative position at a much lower salary was unfair: given the circumstances the employer had done all that it could reasonably be expected to do.

Cruickshank v *Vaw Motorcast Ltd* [2002] IRLR 24 Employment Appeal Tribunal (Altman J, Mrs T A Marsland and Mr R N Straker)

Unfair dismissal – disability discrimination – meaning of normal day-to-day activities

Facts

Mr Cruickshank was employed in a foundry and suffered breathing difficulties which were caused by the fumes in the factory. The company's medical advisor stated in a report that he should not continue to work in an area where he would be exposed to fumes, and so the respondents moved Mr Cruickshank to another department. Following a reorganisation, the applicant was again working near to the fumes and as a result he had a considerable amount of time off work due to sickness. The medical advisor advised the company that when Mr Cruickshank was away from the fumes his condition improved, but worsened when he returned to work. The respondents concluded that there were no other suitable vacancies in areas that were unaffected by the fumes and therefore dismissed Mr Cruickshank. He claimed that his dismissal was unfair and contrary to the Disability Discrimination Act (DDA) 1995. The employment tribunal found for the employers on the grounds that the applicant did not suffer from a disability within the meaning of the DDA 1995, and that the dismissal was fair because there were no other suitable vacancies. The applicant appealed to the Employment Appeal Tribunal.

Held

The correct approach in determining whether an employee's illness has a substantial effect on his normal day-to-day activities is to consider the medical condition of the applicant at the time of the alleged discriminatory act, and not his condition at the time of the tribunal hearing. Furthermore, when considering whether an illness is to be regarded as a disability, and the effect on the employee's day-to-day activities, it is necessary to take into account whether there was a substantial and long-term effect whilst the employee was at work. The case was remitted to a freshly constituted tribunal.

Kirkton v *Tetrosyl* [2002] IRLR 840 Employment Appeal Tribunal (Judge J R Reid QC, Ms N Amin and Mr D J Hodgkins CB)

Disability discrimination – meaning of disability

Facts

Mr Kirkton had suffered from prostate cancer, and as a result of surgery he had mild incontinence: he wore one or two incontinence pads a day, had occasional urinary leakage and needed to go the toilet about eight times a day.

Held

The Employment Appeal Tribunal (EAT) upheld the decision of the tribunal that Mr Kirkton did not have a disability within the meaning of the Disability Discrimination Act 1995. The EAT accepted that the tribunal was entitled to take into account the experience of two of the three people sitting on the tribunal, who also suffered from incontinence, and were in a position to judge the severity of Mr Kirkton's symptoms.

Morgan v *Staffordshire University* [2002] IRLR 190 Employment Appeal Tribunal (Lindsay J, Mr P Dawson OBE and Mr J R Rivers)

Disability – meaning of disability – tribunal procedure

Facts

The applicant, who was engaged by the respondents as a catering worker, was assaulted by a supervisor. She was offered alternative positions, but the respondents could not guarantee that she would not come into contact with the supervisor who had assaulted her. The applicant resigned, claiming in her IT 1 form that she had been constructively dismissed and mentioning that she had suffered stress and anxiety. Her claim was later amended to include a specific claim of disability discrimination. The question for determination was whether the stress and anxiety of the applicant amounted to a mental impairment, and therefore a disability, for the purposes of s1 Disability Discrimination Act 1995. At a preliminary hearing, the applicant produced some medical notes but offered no other medical evidence to support her claim. The tribunal held that the applicant was not suffering from a mental disability within the meaning of the 1995 Act. The applicant appealed to the Employment Appeal Tribunal (EAT).

Held

The EAT set out guidelines for determining when an applicant is suffering from a mental impairment. The Disability Discrimination Act 1995 states that: 'mental impairment includes an impairment resulting from or consisting of a mental illness only if the illness is a clinically well-recognised illness'. The EAT said that a mental illness could be established in the following ways.

1. Proof of a mental illness as specified in the World Health Organisation's International Classification of Diseases.
2. Proof of a mental illness, as would be specified in a respected medical publication.
3. Proof by other means of a medical illness recognised by a respected body of medical opinion.

The applicant in this case had therefore failed to establish that she was suffering from a mental impairment within the meaning of the 1995 Act.

OBP Textbook page 127, section 6.2.

Equal Pay

Equal Pay Act 1970

Employment Act 2002, Part 4: miscellaneous

Section 42 of the 2002 Act (implementation date April 2003) provides for the use of questionnaires by employees who are considering bringing an equal pay claim. Questionnaires are already used in race and sex discrimination claims, and it is expected that equal pay questionnaires will allow for a potential applicant to be given information on pay schemes operated by the employer to enable him/her to decide whether or not to commence proceedings.

OBP Textbook page 140, section 7.2.

Employment Law and the Family

Maternity rights

The Employment Act 2002 received Royal Assent on 8 July 2001; however, the Act will be implemented piecemeal over the course of the next two years. The Act further implements the 'family friendly' policies of the government and provides statutory rights to paternity and adoption leave and pay. The Act will also amend the law relating to statutory maternity leave and pay. Provision is also made for flexible working and the use of questionnaires in equal pay claims.

Employment Act 2002, Part 1: maternity/paternity/adoption leave and pay

Sections 1–21 will be implemented by means of Regulations from 6 April 2003.

Maternity leave

Ordinary maternity leave will be increased to 26 weeks regardless of the length of service of an employee. Maternity leave will be triggered automatically if an employee is absent from work with a pregnancy-related illness during a four-week period up to the expected date of confinement.

Any woman with 26 weeks' continuous service with her employer at 15 weeks prior to the expected date of confinement will be entitled to 26 weeks' additional unpaid maternity leave, which will commence immediately after the period of ordinary maternity leave.

Paternity leave

The Regulations will provide that working fathers will be entitled to two weeks' paid paternity leave following the birth of a child after 6 April 2003. Any person entitled to paternity leave will be paid the same rate as statutory maternity pay, which is currently £75 per week but will rise to £100 per week (or 90 per cent of average weekly earnings where these are less than £100) from April 2003.

Adoption leave

Adoptive parents who are newly matched with a child by an approved adoption agency and who have at least 26 weeks' continuous service at the time of the placement will be entitled to 26 weeks' paid leave and a further 26 weeks' unpaid leave. The leave may commence from the date of the placement or up to 14 days before the expected date of placement. Only one of the adoptive parents will be entitled to adoption leave: the other will be entitled to paternity leave. Statutory adoption pay will be paid at the same rate as statutory maternity pay, and those wishing to take such leave must inform their employer within seven days of being notified that they have been matched with a child, unless such notice is not reasonably practicable.

OBP Textbook page 153, section 8.3.

Reform

Section 47 of the Employment Act 2002 provides for the implementation, by means of Regulations, for a provision to enable parents of children under the age of six or, if the child is disabled, under the age of 18, to apply to their employer for more flexible working arrangements. The employer is under no duty to accede to any such request, but must consider the application, hold a meeting with the employee if it intends to refuse, and put its reasons for refusal in writing.

The government published the first draft of the Flexible Working (Procedural Requirements) Regulations 2003 last November and these are intended to come into force on 6 April 2003. The Regulations provide, inter alia:

'(i) When an employer agrees to a request for flexible working he must provide a written note of the contract variation that has been agreed by the parties along with the date on which it is due to take effect;
(ii) if the employer does agree to the request he must hold a meeting with the employee within 28 days of receiving the request;
(iii) when a meeting is held, the result and, if appropriate, any reasons for refusal must be given to the employee in writing within 14 days of the meeting;
(iv) an employee has a right of appeal from an employer's refusal of a request for more flexible working. An employee has the right to be accompanied at any meeting.'

The draft of the Flexible Working (Eligibility, Complaints and Remedies) Regulations 2003 have also been recently published. These Regulations provide:

'(i) A request for flexible working can only be made if the employee has been continuously employed by the employer from whom he is seeking flexible working for six months;
(ii) a penalty if an employer fails to hold a meeting with an employee, or fails to notify an employee of his decision. The penalty will be up to eight weeks' pay.'

OBP Textbook page 160.

Health and Safety

Common law duty

Coxall v *Goodyear Great Britain Ltd* (2002) The Times 5 August Court of Appeal (Civil Division) (Simon Brown and Brooke LJJ)

Health and safety – employer's duty to dismiss

Facts
The claimant, who worked as a paint and line operator at the defendants' factory, suffered from occupational asthma. In 1996 the defendants changed the product which was used to spray the inside of tyres, and following concerns by those engaged in the spraying (including the claimant) the defendants issued the workers with appropriate protective equipment. The claimant had a mild predisposition to asthma which was aggravated by the fumes from the new product. In April 1996 the claimant saw the company doctor who, in a memo, advised the team leader that the claimant should not work with the new paint. The memo did not reach the team

leader and the claimant continued to work with the paint. In May 1996 the claimant was considered unfit to work and was later dismissed. At trial the claimant was awarded damages for the occupational asthma and the defendants appealed.

Held

The appeal was dismissed. The Court of Appeal held that where an employee is at risk, the employer is under a duty to ensure the health and safety of that employee and dismiss the employee if a suitable alternative position cannot be found. Simon Brown LJ said that the principle laid down in the case of *Withers* v *Perry Chain Co* [1961] 1 WLR 1314 that there is no legal duty on an employer to dismiss an employee who wishes to continue to work, even though there may be a risk to the health of the employee, is still relevant today. However, Simon Brown LJ also recognised that there will still be situations where an employer will be under a duty to dismiss an employee because he is in physical danger. The Court of Appeal considered that these two competing principles could only be resolved on a case-by-case basis.

Fairchild v *Glenhaven Funeral Services Ltd and Others* [2002] 3 WLR 89
House of Lords (Lords Bingham of Cornhill, Nicholls of Birkenhead, Hoffmann, Hutton and Rodger of Earlsferry)

Health and safety – employer's liability – causation

Facts

The claimant suffered from mesothelioma, a form of cancer, as a result of negligently being exposed to asbestos by the defendants. The difficulty facing the claimant was that because he had worked for more than one employer, and as each had exposed him to the risk of contracting mesothelioma, it was difficult to prove which of the employers had exposed him to the asbestos fibres which did, in fact, cause his disease. The Court of Appeal, in applying the 'but for' test, rejected the claim because the evidence did not prove which of the defendants had caused the harm. The claimant appealed.

Held

The House of Lords overruled the decision of the Court of Appeal and found for the claimant. The House of Lords said that because each of the defendant employers had negligently exposed the claimant to the risk of a disease which he then contracted, each employer had materially increased the risk of the claimant suffering from that disease.

Sutherland v *Hatton* [2002] IRLR 263 Court of Appeal (Civil Division) (Brooke, Kay and Hale LJJ)

Health and safety – duty to take reasonable care – employer's liability

Facts

Mrs Hatton taught French at a comprehensive school in Liverpool. In October 1995 she was signed off from work because of depression and debility and never returned. She retired on ill health grounds in August 1996. She brought a claim on the grounds that the school authorities had failed to take reasonable steps to protect her from suffering her stress related psychiatric illness. At trial she was awarded the sum of £90,765.83 in damages and the defendants appealed.

Held

The appeal was successful. The Court of Appeal held that the stress caused to Mrs Hatton was not reasonably foreseeable. Mrs Hatton had not brought difficulties that she was facing in school to the attention of the authorities, and her workload was no greater than that of any other teacher in a similar school. Furthermore her stress was also attributable to factors outside the workplace. Hale LJ considered that: 'Her workload and her pattern of absence taken together could not amount to a sufficiently clear indication that she was likely to suffer from psychiatric injury as a result of stress at work such as to trigger a duty to do more than was in fact done'. Hale LJ went on to say:

'This is a classic case where no-one can be blamed for the sad events which brought Mrs Hatton's teaching career to an end. It was sought to meet some of the obvious difficulties in her case by the argument that teaching is such a stressful profession that by 1995 all employers should have had in place systems which would overcome the reluctance of people like Mrs Hatton to reveal their difficulties and seek help. We have already explained why we take the view that, although an employer who does have such a system is unlikely to be found in breach of duty, it is not for this Court to impose such a duty upon all employers, or even upon all employers in a particular profession.'

Comment

This case is of particular importance because it limits the liability of employers for psychiatric injury caused by stress in the workplace. The Court of Appeal laid down important guidelines as to what may or may not amount to workplace stress, which will provide much needed assistance in this difficult area of employment law.

OBP Textbook page 170, section 10.2.

Working Time Regulations

Holiday pay

Blackburn v Gridquest Ltd (T/A Select Employment) [2002] IRLR 604
Court of Appeal (Civil Division) (Pill and Robert Walker LJJ, Sir Martin
Nourse)

Contracts of employment – holiday pay – 'rolled-up' rate

Facts

The employees were employed by different employment agencies who supplied
workers for Ford Motor Company. The claimed that they had not been paid holiday
pay in accordance with the Working Time Regulations 1998. The tribunal found
that holiday pay had been paid but as part of the rolled-up rate of pay: however,
this fact had not been communicated to the workers. The Employment Appeal
Tribunal (EAT) remitted the case to a new tribunal, but the employees appealed to
the Court of Appeal.

Held

The appeal would be allowed and the decision of the EAT in *The College of North
East London* v *Leather* (below) affirmed. Pill LJ said:

> 'A week's pay is the amount payable by the employer under the contract of employment
> for the normal working hours in a week. Only if it is agreed between employer and
> employee that the weekly payment includes an amount for something else, such as holiday
> pay, can it be held to do so. An employer cannot unilaterally decide that the week's pay is
> a payment not only for the hours worked during the week but includes an element of
> holiday pay. The claim that holiday pay was "in fact" paid amounts to an assertion that
> the employer can decide unilaterally what is included in the weekly payment.'

It is clear that the Court of Appeal was concerned with transparency – if an
employee is paid a rolled-up rate, it must be made clear to him that his rate of pay
includes a sum which represents holiday pay. The Scottish EAT has considered the
position of an employee who was advised that his weekly rate of pay included an
element of holiday pay.

MPB Structure Ltd v Munro [2002] IRLR 601 Employment Appeal
Tribunal (Lord Johnston, Mr G R Carter and Dr W M Spiers)

Contracts of employment – holiday pay – 'rolled-up' rate

Facts

Mr Munro complained that a provision in his contract of employment, which
provided that an allowance of 8 per cent in each weekly wage packet was to provide
for holiday pay, was unlawful. His complaint to the employment tribunal was
successful. The employer appealed.

Held

The Employment Appeal Tribunal considered that the effect of the rolled-up rate in this case would be to limit the effect of the Working Time Regulations 1998. Lord Johnston said:

> 'It is clear to us that the basic theme or aim of the Regulations is to ensure that workers obtain appropriate holiday leave and to do so they must have the necessary funds. We consider there is force in the point that by placing the onus of retaining the funds from week to week for holiday purposes on the employee, there may well arise the problem of adequate funding at the time of the holiday leave being taken and this could become compounded if sufficient service in any one year had not been served so as to build up a sufficient entitlement to be the equivalent of a week's wages during the holiday period. We consider that the only way that the provisions of the Regulations and, indeed, their spirit can be met, is for holiday pay to be paid as and when the holiday is taken at the appropriate rate.'

The College of North East London v *Leather* Judgment of 30 November 2001 (not yet reported) Employment Appeal Tribunal (Peter Clark J)

Contract of employment – hourly rate – holiday pay – 'rolled-up' rate

Facts

Ms Leather was employed as a part-time lecturer at the College of North East London. Her contract contained the following term: 'There is no entitlement to paid holiday under this contract'. Ms Leather claimed that reg 13 of the Working Time Regulations 1998 entitled her to holiday pay. The employers claimed that her hourly rate of pay included a sum which represented an element in respect of holiday pay, which amounted pro rata to an equivalent sum received by full-time lecturers.

Held

In upholding the complaint the tribunal concluded that the contract between the parties was for an hourly payment which was solely in respect of hours worked. The respondent could not unilaterally vary the contract to apportion part of the hourly rate to holiday pay, as the Employment Appeal Tribunal considered that would defeat the provisions of the Regulations. The contract specifically stated that there was no entitlement to holiday pay and therefore it followed that no payments were made under the contract for holiday pay. The issue of 'rolled-up' holiday pay has more recently been considered by the Court of Appeal.

OBP Textbook page 183, section 10.4.

Trade Unions

Trade union membership and employers

Wilson and Others v *United Kingdom* (2002) The Times 5 July European Court of Human Rights

Industrial relations – UK violation of right to freedom of association

Facts
Mr Wilson, a journalist, was employed by Associated Newspapers and was a member of the National Union of Journalists (NUJ). In 1989 the employers signalled their intention to de-recognise the NUJ for the purposes of collective bargaining. New contracts were issued which provided for a 4.5 per cent pay increase for journalists who agreed to accept de-recognition. Mr Wilson refused to sign his new contract. However, although his salary was increased, the increase was less than for those journalists who had signed and agreed to the de-recognition. He and others presented claims arguing that the requirement to sign new contracts, and therefore lose their union rights or accept a lower pay rise, was contrary to art 11 European Convention on Human Rights.

Held
The employer had violated art 11 European Convention on Human Rights (the right to freedom and assembly) by using financial incentives to induce employees to give up their rights to trade union representation.

OBP Textbook page 194, section 11.3.

Employment Tribunal Procedure

Introduction

Employment Act 2002, Part 2: tribunal reform

Sections 22–28 Employment Act 2002 provide for tribunal reform. The government set up an Employment Tribunal System Taskforce which was charged with ensuring that the employment tribunal system reflects the needs of its users and the changing environment in which it operates. The Taskforce reported its findings last year and we are currently awaiting a response from the government. It is anticipated that the tribunals will be given increased scope for the use of costs awards, and will possibly allow compensation to be recovered for the time taken for the preparation of a hearing. A date for the implementation of these reforms has yet to be set.

OBP Textbook page 224, section 13.1.

12

English and European Legal Systems

Interpretation of Legislation and Law Reform

Aids to interpretation and construction

Reports of parliamentary debates – Hansard

R v *Secretary of State for the Environment, Transport and Regions, ex parte Spath Holme Ltd* [2001] 1 All ER 195 House of Lords (Lords Bingham of Cornhill, Nicholls of Birkenhead, Cooke of Thorndon, Hope of Craighead and Hutton)

Use of Hansard as a guide to statutory intention

Facts
The case concerned the ability of a minister to use legislation to limit fair rent increases on property.

Held
The legislation was regarded as being clear and unambiguous. The tests for the use of Hansard were not satisfied.

Comment
Lord Bingham makes it clear, in the extract below, that the ability to use Hansard as a guide to statutory intention is a device that is to be used only sparingly. In the case of *Pepper* v *Hart* [1993] 1 All ER 42 the House of Lords (Lord Mackay dissenting) relaxed the general rule which had been understood to preclude reference in the courts of this country to statements made in Parliament for the purpose of construing a statutory provision. In his leading speech, with which all in the majority concurred, Lord Browne-Wilkinson made plain that such reference was permissible only where: (1) legislation was ambiguous or obscure, or led to an absurdity; (2) the material relied on consisted of one or more statements by a minister or other promoter of the Bill together, if necessary, with such other parliamentary material as might be necessary to understand such statements and their effect; and (3) the effect of such statements was clear.

Lord Bingham stated in the present case:

> 'It has been argued that the stringent conditions laid down by the House in *Pepper* v *Hart*
> [[1993] 1 All ER 42] were not satisfied in that very case; see Bennion on *Statutory*

Interpretation (3rd ed, 1997) at pp483–485. That is not a view I could accept; there was a difference of judicial opinion when the matter was first argued in the House and there were very clear statements on the point at issue by the responsible minister. But the case turned on a narrow point, the meaning of "the cost of a benefit" in s63(2) of the Finance Act 1976. The minister gave what was no doubt taken to be a reliable statement on the meaning of that expression. Here the issue turns not on the meaning of a statutory expression but on the scope of a statutory power. In this context a minister might describe the circumstances in which the Government contemplated use of a power, and might be pressed about exercise of the power in other situations which might arise. No doubt the minister would seek to give helpful answers. But it is most unlikely that he would seek to define the legal effect of the draftsman's language, or to predict all the circumstances in which the power might be used, or to bind any successor administration. Only if a minister were, improbably, to give a categorical assurance to Parliament that a power would not be used in a given situation, such that Parliament could be taken to have legislated on that basis, does it seem to me that a parliamentary statement on the scope of a power would be properly admissible.

I think it important that the conditions laid down by the House in *Pepper* v *Hart* should be strictly insisted upon. Otherwise, the cost and inconvenience feared by Lord Mackay, whose objections to relaxation of the exclusionary rule were based on considerations of practice not principle ... will be realised. The worst of all worlds would be achieved if parties routinely combed through Hansard, and the courts dredged through conflicting statements of parliamentary intention ... only to conclude that the statutory provision called for no further elucidation or that no clear and unequivocal statement by a responsible minister could be derived from Hansard. I would further draw attention to the terms of *Practice Direction (Hansard: Citation)* [1995] 1 WLR 192 and *Practice Direction (House of Lords: Supporting Documents)* [1993] 1 WLR 303.

Since, for reasons I have already given, I do not regard the meaning or effect of s11 as ambiguous or obscure or such as to give rise to absurdity, and the unease I felt on reading s31 in isolation has been dispelled by considering s11 in its social and factual context, I do not for my part find that the first threshold test for resorting to Hansard is met. In this, as in most cases, the statute should be treated as "the formal and complete intimation to the citizen of a particular rule of the law which he is enjoined, sometimes under penalty, to obey and by which he is both expected and entitled to regulate his conduct" (per Lord Oliver of Aylmerton, *Pepper* v *Hart*, at 619H). The present case illustrates the dangers of weakening this first threshold test.'

OBP Textbook page 36, section 2.4.

Examples of reform

The Law Commission for England and Wales: Chairman's Newsletter (Summer 2002), London: Law Commission

Details of the work of the Law Commission are provided in this newsletter. The author was the then Chairman of the Law Commission, Carnwath LJ, who was replaced as Chairman by Toulson J in the summer of 2002. Amongst the work in progress that was described in this document was a report on the effective prosecution of multiple offending. That project emerged out of work on the fraud project, in which was considered the problems arising in cases of multiple fraud from the decision in *R* v *Kidd and Others* [1998] 1 WLR 604, to the effect that a defendant convicted only on specimen counts could not be sentenced for other offences. This report does not include a draft Bill, but it is hoped that it will be considered by the government along with other issues arising out of the Auld Report. Also underway is the updating of the General Part of the *Draft Criminal Code*, which was published as Law Com 177 in 1989. They hope to publish a new report in 2004. Work also continues on the report on assisting and encouraging crime. In relation to property and trust law, it was anticipated that a Discussion Paper on work relating to the sharing homes project would be published in 2002. Dr Alison Dunn of the University of Newcastle-upon-Tyne has conducted research on behalf of the Commission and reported to us on the potential socio-economic consequences of the regulation of trustee exemption clauses. The intention again was to publish a consultation paper on this work in 2002. Work also continues on the termination of tenancies project, with the 1994 proposals being amended to take account of changes in the law and responses to the 1998 consultation on physical re-entry. The following are additional examples of recent Law Commission publications.

Criminal law
1. *Consent in Sex Offences* (2000) (A Report to the Home Office Sex Offences Review).
2. *Double Jeopardy and Prosecution Appeals* (2001) Law Com No 267.
3. *Bail and the Human Rights Act 1998* (2001) Law Com No 269.
4. *Evidence of Bad Character in Criminal Proceedings* (2001) Law Com No 273.

Commercial and common law
1. *Third Parties – Rights against Insurers* (2001) Law Com No 272.
2. *Aspects of Defamation Procedure* (A Scoping Study: May 2002).
3. *Limitation of Actions* (2001) Law Com No 270.

Property and trust law
1. *Land Registration for the Twenty-First Century: A Conveyancing Revolution* (2001) Law Com No 271.

OBP Textbook page 39, section 2.8.

The Judiciary and the Magistracy

Appointment to judicial offices

Monthly Judicial Statistics *(September 2002), London: Lord Chancellor's Department*

Information is provided on the judiciary in this publication.

Make up of the judiciary

Lords of Appeal in Ordinary	12
Heads of Divisions	5
Lord Chancellor	1
Lord Chief Justice	1
Master of the Rolls	1
President of Family Division	1
Vice-Chancellor	1
Lords Justices of Appeal	35
High Court Judges	107
Chancery Division	17
Queen's Bench Division	73
Family Division	17
Circuit Judges	617
Technical and Construction	8
Senior Circuit Judges	25
Circuit Judges	584
Recorders	1,325
Barristers	1,187
Solicitors	138
Recorders in Training	116
Barristers	106
Solicitors	10
District Judges	410
Deputy District Judges	752
District Judges (Magistrates' Court)	102
Deputy District Judges (Magistrates' Court)	152

OBP Textbook page 72, section 4.3.

Selection of judges

Ethnic Minority Appointments *(2002), London: Lord Chancellor's Department*

Data is collected in relation to the ethnic background of the judges and the material in this report states the position as at 1 September 2002. The data may be incomplete for a number of reasons. The same report also provides information as to the gender of the judiciary. It appears that we are not quite an equal opportunity society, though there has been a change from the even worse situation that existed in the past. The difficulty is that in order to be appointed as a judge, you need the necessary experience. The root of the problem at the moment is the lack of opportunity to start and develop legal careers. Some further steps are being taken in terms of widening access – by, for example, allowing people to be appointed at an age that is lower than that which was usual in the past. All of the members of the House of Lords, all of the Judges of the Court of Appeal, all of the Heads of Division and indeed all of the High Court judges are white. Women do slightly better as they account for six of the 107 High Court judges, two of the 35 members of the Court of Appeal, and the Head of the Family Division is female. None have made it to the House of Lords. Data for the other courts is presented in tabular form.

Gender and ethnic background of the lower judiciary

	Men	Women	Total	% Ethnic minority
Circuit Judges	559	58	617	1.1
Recorders	1,162	163	1,325	2.9
Recorders in Training	97	19	116	6.0
District Judges	349	80	429	3.5
Deputy District Judges	638	166	804	1.7
District Judges (Magistrates' Courts)	84	18	102	2.9
Deputy District Judges (Magistrates' Courts)	123	29	152	5.9

OBP Textbook page 79, section 4.4.

Lay magistrates (Justices of the Peace)

Judicial Statistics 2002 *(2002), London: Lord Chancellor's Department*

Data is provided on an annual basis in relation to the lay magistracy and the district judges who also sit in the magistrates' courts. The data reveals that fewer magistrates are being appointed, and the proportion of them that are women is declining. From 2001 data was compiled on a financial year basis rather than a calendar year basis. Data is not available for 2000, which was the interim year.

Justices of the Peace appointed since 1990

Year	Total	Men	Women
1990	2,059	996	1,063
1991	2,017	1,008	1,009
1992	2,070	1,080	990
1993	2,062	1,045	1,017
1994	1,593	810	783
1995	1,843	907	936
1996	1,682	830	852
1997	1,573	764	809
1998	1,609	816	793
1999	1,743	884	859
2001	1,618	834	784
2002	1,474	763	711

At 1 April 2002 there was a total of 24,526 Justices of the Peace in England and Wales, nearly 15 per cent fewer than the year previously. Of the total, 12,439 (51 per cent) were men and 12,087 (49 per cent) were women. During 2001/2002, 763 men and 711 women were appointed Justices of the Peace. At the same time, 1,860 magistrates were lost from the bench through resignation and removal (1,272), compulsory retirement (542) or death (46).

Justices of the Peace in England and Wales as at 1 April 2002 and selected previous years

Year	Total	Men	Women
1978	23,483	14,633	8,850
1983	25,934	15,606	10,328
1988	27,926	15,992	11,934
1990	28,667	16,090	12,577
1991	29,062	16,098	12,964
1992	29,441	16,105	13,336
1993	29,686	16,087	13,599
1994	30,054	16,151	13,903
1995	30,088	16,045	14,043
1996	30,326	15,951	14,375
1997	30,374	15,858	14,516
1998	30,361	15,713	14,648
1999	30,260	15,561	14,699
2000	30,308	15,544	14,764
2001	28,735	14,639	14,096
2002	24,526	12,439	12,087

Unification of the stipendiary bench took place in 2000: this created a national jurisdiction throughout England and Wales and a change of title from stipendiary magistrates to district judges (magistrates' courts). There is a single judicial head, the senior district judge (chief magistrate), who is responsible for the administration of the unified bench. There were 95 full-time district judges (magistrates' courts) in post as at 1 January 2002.

OBP Textbook page 89, section 4.8.

The Legal Profession

Solicitors

Legal Services Ombudsman Annual Report for 2001/2002

The report opens with a critique of the manner in which the professional legal bodies are regulated. For example, there are too many agencies with an interest in the regulation of legal services, each with their own approaches and priorities and with too few, if any, co-ordinating influences. The need, it is suggested, is for debate and reform of what is an unacceptable situation.

The Office of the Legal Services Ombudsman completed 1,789 cases in 2001/2002 and this was the third year-on-year increase in cases completed. 1,677 new cases were accepted for investigation, around 200 more than anticipated and provided for. This left 886 cases awaiting investigation at the end of the year, and the average turn around times increased from 4.5 to 6.7 months. The Ombudsman was satisfied with the way in which the Law Society's Office for the Supervision of Solicitors (OSS) handled complaints in only 58 per cent of the 1,629 cases she investigated in 2001/2002 – a slight increase in her overall level of satisfaction from last year's all-time low of 57 per cent. In January 2002 the Ombudsman used her powers under s24(1) Courts and Legal Services Act 1990 to make a number of recommendations to the Law Society in relation to their new Consumer Redress Scheme. The Ombudsman is concerned that the Scheme is disappointingly unambitious and unlikely to deliver the necessary improvement in public confidence. Nor is she currently persuaded that the appointment of a Lay Commissioner will add anything other than symbolic value to the Law Society's complaint-handling arrangements. The Ombudsman investigated 154 allegations concerning the Bar Council's handling of complaints in 2001/2002 and found no cause for criticism or recommendation in 93 per cent of cases. The Bar Council have published comprehensive information on turn around times in 2001, showing that 70 per cent of cases were completed within six months. Published information on compensation awards and fee reductions has shown that the Bar Council are making full use of their powers to award redress for poor service by barristers.

Fifteen per cent of complaints dealt with by the Office for the Supervision of

Solicitors were subsequently referred to the Ombudsman, whereas 33 per cent of complaints dealt with by the Bar Council were subsequently referred. The solicitor's body received 10,585 complaints whilst having 86,603 practitioners. For the Bar the equivalent figures were 12,982 practitioners and 464 complaints. Complaints about solicitors comprised 91 per cent of the Ombudsman's workload; complaints about barristers 8.6 per cent; and complaints about licensed conveyancers 0.3 per cent. One case referred by the Scottish Legal Services Ombudsman represented the remaining 0.1 per cent.

In 61 per cent of cases the Ombudsman was satisfied with the way the complaint had been handled by the professional body and made no formal recommendation or criticism. This is the first time in five years that the Ombudsman's overall level of satisfaction with the handling of complaints by the professional bodies has not diminished. The Ombudsman formally criticised the professional bodies in 11 per cent of cases, an increase in the proportion of cases involving formal criticisms from 6 per cent in 2000/2001. The total number of recommendations made was 561 (in 506 cases) and the Ombudsman's recommendations were complied with in 100 per cent of cases. In terms of compensation this ranged from £50 to £2,000, with the average being £243.

OBP Textbook page 124, section 6.2.

Barristers

Bar Council (2002) 'Bar Council backs reforms in submission to Office of Fair Trading'

As the title indicates the Bar is supporting the idea that its professional rules should be changed so as to broaden the scope for lay clients to have direct access to barristers' services. The ideas under discussion include:

1. the possibility of barristers accepting certain types of criminal cases directly, including police station work, bail applications, appeals, and pleas of guilty dealt with in the magistrates' court;
2. barristers could be free to take proofs of evidence from their lay clients, but not investigate or collect evidence for use in any court;
3. barristers would continue to be prohibited from handling client money;
4. that the Bar's cab rank rule would not apply in direct access cases.

The intention is that the Bar will submit proposals to the Office of Fair Trading in response to the report *Competition in Professions*, which was published in March 2001 and gave professional bodies one year to respond to concerns relating to alleged restrictions on competition. Key proposals to be put to the Office of Fair Trading are: a relaxation of the Bar's rules relating to direct access by lay clients; further liberalisation of rules regarding comparative advertising on fees; a defence of the

Bar's ban on partnerships; a rejection of the suggestion that private practice barristers should be able to conduct litigation; an acceptance that the system for appointing Queen's Counsel should be kept under review; and strong support for upholding legal professional privilege.

OBP Textbook page 128, section 6.3.

Courts, Tribunals and Alternative Dispute Resolution

The main English courts

Judicial Statistics *(2002), London: Lord Chancellor's Department*

County courts
The trend in relation to county courts is that they handle less cases than previously – for example there were 7 per cent less claims made in 2001 than in 2000.

Claims issued and warrants of execution issued in selected years since 1938

Year	Money claims	Claims for the recovery of land	Total	Warrants of execution against goods issued
1938	1,192,777	19,476	1,212,253	458,403
1958	1,273,193	27,749	1,300,942	813,689
1968	1,441,079	40,337	1,481,416	1,621,383
1978	1,356,519	111,026	1,467,545	1,070,533
1988	2,099,805	185,320	2,285,125	1,215,701
1990	3,034,923	276,334	3,311,257	1,344,326
1996	2,145,958	191,595	2,337,553	707,014
1997	2,011,642	197,236	2,208,878	622,408
1998	2,010,606	234,718	2,245,324	543,848
1999	1,760,308	240,029	2,000,337	538,337
2000	1,631,966	239,957	1,871,923	470,270
2001	1,502,879	236,211	1,739,090	394,611

Summary of proceedings started in 2001
Nature of proceedings:

Default actions	1,461,105
Fixed date actions (other than for possession of land)	41,774
Actions for possession of land	236,211
Bankruptcy petitions	21,232
Companies Act winding-up petitions	5,245

Family matters (major areas of work):

Adoption applications (originating)	3,207
Divorce, nullity and judicial separation petitions	208,361

Summary of the enforcement proceedings started in 2001

Nature of proceedings:

Warrants of execution against goods issued	394,611
Warrants of delivery of goods issued	7,799
Warrants of possession of land:	
Issued	133,500
Executed	65,599
Interpleader summonses issued	449
Judgment summonses issued	3,640
Garnishee summonses issued	4,139
Charging order applications issued	22,098

Appellate courts

Appellate courts: appeals entered in selected years since 1938, by court

	1938	1978	1988	2000	2001
Nature of court					
Judicial Committee					
of the Privy Council	107	52	61	90	102
House of Lords					
From courts in					
England & Wales	32	77	75	63	80
Elsewhere	11	6	15	16	4
Court of Appeal					
Civil Division	574	1,401	1,645	1,420	1,358
Criminal Division	–	6,099	7,235	7,740	7,440
High Court					
Chancery Division	–	74	111	147	107
Queen's Bench					
Division	263	510	1,800	4,734	5,293
Family Division	–	247	240	12	13
Total	987	8,466	11,182	14,222	14,397

House of Lords: petitions for leave to appeal presented and disposed of, showing results, 2001

Courts from which appeals were brought	Number of petitions presented	Petitions disposed of				
		Withdrawn	Allowed	Refused	Dismissed as inadmissible	Total
England and Wales						
Court of Appeal						
Civil	196	11	46	135	7	199
Criminal	34	–	13	13	1	27
Court Martial	2	–	2	–	–	2
Attorney General's Reference	–	–	–	1	–	1
Divisional Court	22	2	6	15	–	23
High Court (Leapfrog)	7	–	5	3	–	8
Scotland						
Court of Session	–	–	–	–	–	–
Northern Ireland						
Court of Appeal						
Civil	9	–	1	5	–	6
Criminal	4	–	–	3	–	3
Divisional Court	–	–	–	–	–	–
Total	274	13	73	175	8	269

Note: petitions may be presented in one year but not disposed of until a year later.

Court of Appeal (Criminal Division): results of appeals heard by the full Court, 1992–2001

Year	Conviction		Sentence		Number of retrials
	Allowed	Dismissed	Allowed	Dismissed	
1992	299	370	1,049	439	12
1993	402	524	1,309	600	20
1994	351	577	1,384	643	51
1995	253	521	1,222	38	52
1996	250	469	1,379	603	53
1997	236	367	1,468	602	33
1998	290	403	1,589	609	73
1999	171	380	1,564	614	70
2000	150	333	1,284	522	72
2001	135	313	1,101	561	58

OBP Textbook page 140, section 7.2.

Tribunals and inquiries

Judicial Statistics (2002), London: Lord Chancellor's Department

Data in relation to one of the major tribunals, the Employment Appeal Tribunal, is provided as an illustrative example of the workings of tribunals. The Tribunal hears appeals on a question of law arising from any decisions of, or any proceedings before, an industrial tribunal. For example, it deals with unfair dismissal and redundancy matters and allegations of discriminatory acts. It may also hear applications for compensation from persons unreasonably excluded from unions. The tribunal consists of a High Court judge, who presides, and normally two other members who have special knowledge or experience of industrial relations, either as representatives of employers or of workers, and are appointed on the joint recommendation of the Lord Chancellor and the Secretary of State for Employment.

The Employment Appeal Tribunal: cases received and disposed of showing major areas of jurisdiction, 2001

	Received	Dismissed	Allowed	Remitted	Withdrawn
Unfair dismissal	475	282	37	53	755
Race Relations Act 1976	141	94	20	16	25
Jurisdiction	137	9	4	3	10
Interlocutories	103	62	22	5	23
Employment Tribunal procedures	226	118	16	15	57
Others	407	214	41	40	120
Total	1,489	838	144	148	412

Report of Sir Andrew Leggatt Tribunals for Users: One System One Service (2001), London: Lord Chancellor's Department

The report into tribunals, which was carried out on behalf of the Lord Chancellor's Department, is to be used as a basis for consultation, which in turn may lead to reform. Since the 70 different tribunals deal with over a million cases a year, more than all the civil courts put together, they are clearly an important feature of the legal system. More so since most tribunals deal with cases that involve the rights of private citizens against the state. Many deal with issues that are central to the fight against social exclusion (for example, social security, child support and mental health). The tribunals in England and Wales are administered by ten government departments and by local authorities. They range in size from the Appeals Service, which deals with over 270,000 social security appeals, to the 20 or so regulatory tribunals that rarely, if ever, sit. Tribunals are thus a large and important part of the justice system, and have not in the past received the attention and recognition they deserve. It should be noted, however, that there has been some recent reform. This can be seen in the introduction of the unified Appeals Service, with executive agency status, to deal with social security and child support appeals, and the expanded and reformed Immigration Appellate Authorities which deal with asylum seekers.

The majority of the recommendations in the Leggatt report are aimed at improving the services that tribunal users receive. These include recommendations concerning better access to information and advice, a Customer Charter setting out service standards, improved tribunal procedures, promoting better initial decision-making by departments, and better use of information technology. The report recommends that tribunals should be administered separately from the departments whose policies and decisions they oversee, in order to enhance users' confidence in their independence. Establishing a unified tribunal service is also seen as being necessary. The emphasis of the report, as the title indicates, is to concentrate on what the user needs, not the provider. In particular, the report stresses that 'the distinctive procedures and approach of tribunals should operate so that there are few exceptions to the principle that tribunal users should be able to prepare and present their cases themselves'. The report's recommendations concerning service to users fall into the following main categories.

1. Users should have access to the information they need to understand their rights and the tribunal process, and to enable them, wherever possible, to proceed without representation. These recommendations require both decision–making departments and tribunals to provide appropriate information to users. Similarly, users should have timely access to the independent advice (and, where necessary, the legal representation) they need.

2. Tribunals should publish service standards (including standards for information provision), underpinned by arrangements to spread good practice, a range of administrative performance measures and systems for appraising judicial performance.

3. Tribunals should seek to help the parties participating. Improved training for tribunal judiciary and staff should focus in particular on the skills needed to implement this approach. Procedures should be fair, economic, speedy and proportionate to the issues at stake.

4. Tribunals should actively manage the progress of cases, ensuring that weak cases are weeded out at an early stage. The use of alternative dispute resolution should be encouraged.

5. Finally, it can be noted that the report also stresses the need for tribunals, like the ordinary courts, to be independent and impartial.

OBP Textbook page 147, section 7.4.

Alternative dispute resolution (ADR)

Court-based ADR Initiatives for Non-Family Civil Disputes: the Commercial Court and the Court of Appeal *(2002), Genn H, London: Lord Chancellor's Department*

This report presents an evaluation of the Commercial Court's practice of issuing ADR orders in selected commercial disputes, and a review of the Court of Appeal's mediation scheme established in 1996.

ADR orders in the Commercial Court

Since 1993 the Commercial Court has been identifying cases regarded as appropriate for ADR. The research related to 233 ADR orders made between July 1996 and June 2000. ADR was undertaken in a little over half of the cases in which an ADR order had been issued. However, the figures suggest an increasing use of ADR towards the end of the review period, supporting evidence from elsewhere of a developing interest in the use of ADR among commercial litigants. Of the cases in which ADR was attempted, 52 per cent settled through ADR, 5 per cent proceeded to trial following unsuccessful ADR, 20 per cent settled some time after the conclusion of the ADR procedure, and the case was still live or the outcome unknown in 23 per cent of cases. Among cases in which ADR was not attempted following an ADR order, about 63 per cent eventually settled. About one fifth of these said that the settlement had been as a result of the ADR order being made. However, the rate of trials among the group of cases not attempting ADR following an ADR order was 15 per cent. This compares unfavourably with the 5 per cent of cases proceeding to trial following unsuccessful ADR. The most common reasons given for not trying ADR following an ADR order were: the case was not appropriate for ADR; the parties did not want to try ADR; the timing of the order was wrong (too early or too late); or that there was no faith in ADR as a process in general. ADR orders were generally thought to have had a positive or neutral impact on settlement. Orders can have a positive effect in opening up communication between the parties, and may avoid the fear of one side showing weakness by being the first to suggest settlement.

ADR in the Court of Appeal

The Court of Appeal ADR scheme, established in 1996, is a voluntary scheme in which the Court invites parties to participate. Cases are not individually selected, but, with the exception of certain categories of case, a standard letter of invitation is sent to parties involved in appeals. Since 1999, parties refusing to mediate have been asked to give their reasons for refusal. If both parties agree to mediate, the Court of Appeal arranges mediations and mediators provide their services without charge. Between November 1997 and April 2000, 38 appeal cases were mediated following agreement by both sides. In an additional 99 cases one party was willing to mediate. When the scheme had the benefit of a full-time manager, there was a significant increase in the proportion of cases in which both sides agreed to mediate. The most common reasons given for refusal to mediate were: that a judgement was required for policy reasons; that the appeal turned on a point of law; and the past history or behaviour of the opponent.

About half of the mediated appeal cases settled either at the mediation appointment or shortly afterwards. Among those cases in which the mediation did not achieve a settlement, a high proportion (62 per cent) went on to trial. This suggests that there are special characteristics of appeal cases that need to be considered in selecting cases for mediation. Blanket invitations to mediate, particularly with an implicit threat of penalties for refusal, may not be the most effective approach to the encouragement of ADR at appellate level. Solicitors' experiences of successful mediations in appeal cases were largely positive. However, there were expressions of concern, even among cases that were successfully mediated, about clients' perceptions of being pushed into mediation and sometimes being pressured to settle. Although solicitors generally approved of the Court of Appeal taking the initiative in encouraging the use of ADR in appropriate cases, it was felt that there was a need for the adoption of a more selective approach, such as that being used in the Commercial Court.

Conclusions

Bringing together the results of research on ADR orders in the Commercial Court, the Court of Appeal ADR scheme, and the central London county court mediation scheme, the following conclusions can be drawn.

1. Voluntary take-up of invitations to enter ADR schemes remains at a modest level, even when the mediator's services are provided free or at a nominal cost.
2. Outside of commercial practice, the profession remains very cautious about the use of ADR. Positive experience of ADR does not appear to be producing armies of converts. Explanations may lie in the amount of work involved in preparing for mediation, the incentives and economics of mediation in low value cases, and the impact of the Woolf reforms. More pre-issue settlements and swifter post-issue settlements may diminish the perceived need for ADR in run-of-the-mill civil cases.
3. An individualised approach to the direction of cases toward ADR is likely to be more effective than general invitations at an early stage in the litigation process. This would require the development of clearly articulated selection principles.
4. The timing of invitations or directions to mediate is crucial. The early stages of proceedings may not be the best time, and should not be the only opportunity to consider using ADR.
5. Subjective perceptions of the profession support the view that successful ADR saves the likely cost of proceeding to trial and may save expenditure by promoting earlier settlement that might otherwise have occurred. Unsuccessful ADR can increase the costs for parties.
6. ADR generally results in a high level of customer satisfaction. Mediators with

excellent skills and familiarity with the subject area of the dispute produce the highest levels of satisfaction. The approach of mediators needs to be matched with the expectations of parties and their solicitors.

7. In order to maximise take-up of court-administered schemes there is a need for dedicated administrative support.

OBP Textbook page 150, section 7.6.

Funding of Legal Advice and Representation

Alternative methods of funding: legal expenses insurance and conditional fees

Callery v *Gray (Costs); Russell* v *Pal Pak Corrugated Ltd* [2001] EWCA Civ 1246; [2001] 4 All ER 1 Court of Appeal (Lord Woolf CJ, Lord Phillips MR and Brooke LJ)

Role of conditional fee arrangements

Facts
A conditional fee arrangement and after the event insurance were used in personal injury litigation.

Held
The costs of such arrangements were reasonable in the circumstances and could be recovered.

Comment
The role of conditional fee arrangements has been considered by both the Court of Appeal and the House of Lords in the period since the last issue of *Law Update*. As we will soon see the position that has been reached does not appear to be satisfactory. When legal aid was all but abolished for most civil litigation (family cases being the major exception) these new arrangements were to fill the void, and indeed they offered the potential to be more wide reaching than the system of legal aid had been. These arrangements are also known as 'no win, no fee' arrangements, with the advantage to the claimant being obvious. For the lawyer there would be an uplift or success fee allowing a fee greater than normal costs for the risk that was being taken. The claimant could also hope to recover the amount of the premiums for after the event insurance cover, which is designed to protect the claimant from the costs consequences of losing the case. The issue is: what limits should there be on such arrangements? The Conditional Fee Agreement Regulations 2000 offer obstacles in terms of the procedures to be followed. The early decisions of the courts saw their applicability as being in the area of modest road accident cases. So for claimants there is the clear dilemma that you do not know if you can rely on

such arrangements. *Callery* was such a case. The arrangements for the conditional fee and the insurance were made at an early stage of the litigation and the issue was: is this acceptable? The situation could be one in which the case was not going to be contested. The answer given by Lord Woolf for the Court of Appeal was that in such circumstances it was acceptable for a reasonable success fee and a reasonable insurance premium to be payable as costs by the defendant. For modest motoring personal injury cases, 20 per cent would be the maximum success fee. More difficult cases could permit a higher fee. As to the insurance policy, they allowed the £350 cost in the case but were unsure as to its suitability as a benchmark for other cases.

Callery v *Gray (Nos 1 & 2)* [2002] 1 WLR 2000 House of Lords (Lords Bingham of Cornhill, Nicholls of Birkenhead, Hoffmann, Hope of Craighead and Scott of Foscote)

Conditional fee arrangements – court responsible for developing rules in this area

Facts
The matter of conditional fee arrangements was raised before the House of Lords.

Held
The attitude of their Lordships (by a majority verdict of three to two) was that they were not in a position to intervene in these matters. They saw the Court of Appeal as being the appropriate body to develop rules in this area.

Comment
The reaction to this case was that further guidance was in fact needed, and that further litigation would follow in other cases. The case below is the first example of this.

Halloran v *Delaney* [2002] 1 EWCA Civ 1258 Court of Appeal (Gibson, Brooke and Tuckey LJ)

Costs – payment of a success fee

Facts
The defendant appealed from a decision that provided liability for the claimant's costs, and in particular the payment of a success fee. The claimant had instructed solicitors to act for him in an accident claim under a conditional fee agreement in the Law Society model form.

Held
In claims as simple as the present case that were settled without proceedings, judges should ordinarily allow an uplift of 5 per cent on the claimant's lawyers' costs.

Comment
The merits of leaving the future of conditional fee arrangements to the Court of

Appeal, as espoused in *Callery*, may have to be reconsidered in the light of this decision of the Court of Appeal. The Court imposed a limit of 5 per cent on the success fee for run-of-the-mill personal injury cases that reach a settlement before proceedings are started. The success fee needs to be set at such a level that it will take into account the cases that lawyers lose and for which they will obtain no fee at all. The danger of a figure as low as 5 per cent is that lawyers will not undertake such work and the system will be left without the provision of legal services. It should be noted that the 5 per cent figure is very different to the 20 per cent that was used in the *Callery* case. The result of these appeal cases is more, rather than less, confusion as to the operation of conditional fee arrangements.

OBP Textbook page 161, section 8.6.

Civil Procedure in the High Court

Reactions to the Woolf Report

A Civil Justice Audit *(2002), Shapland J, Sorsby A and Hibbert J, London: Lord Chancellor's Department*

This research had the aim of providing a snapshot of non-family civil justice at the county court and High Court in Sheffield in 1996/1997. It draws together data about cases, costs, people and decisions. This is so as to display the use of the civil courts by different parties, the progress of cases through the stages of civil justice, the key decision points, the costs to different agencies and parties, and the use being made of public civil justice provisions. Given that the research was carried out just before the Woolf reforms, it operates as a baseline for judging the effects of those reforms. The material presented here concentrates on the types of cases and litigants and the progress of the cases.

The cases coming to court

The majority of cases starting in the county court were default summonses, mostly liquidated cases. The vast majority of liquidated plaintiffs were firms (89 per cent). Unliquidated case plaintiffs were more likely to be individuals, as would be expected with personal injury, with defendants also likely to be individuals (63 per cent), though insurance companies will normally be the ultimate controller here.

Possession cases were typically taken by firms or bodies, often the city council, against an individual, with originating applications normally relating to commercial property. Hence the majority of court users were firms. Liquidated cases in the county court were generally of low value, with less than 10 per cent falling above the then small claims limit of £3,000, and a median value of between £201 and £500. The litigant population in the county court contained a very high proportion of litigants in person, both plaintiffs and defendants, many of whom were firms. Unliquidated cases were significantly different, with almost all plaintiffs legally represented and two thirds of actions having both parties represented. At the High Court, the vast majority of cases were liquidated (93 per cent), primarily debts, and almost entirely firms proceeding against other firms. Cases were of remarkably low value, with 65 per cent being up to £3,000. The remainder were unliquidated and showed an entirely different profile, with plaintiffs being individuals (often legally aided) and defendants firms. All plaintiffs at the High Court and the great majority of defendants were legally represented.

The progress of cases

Of our sample of liquidated cases starting in the county court: 23 per cent were withdrawn by the plaintiff or failed prior to judgment; 14 per cent settled prior to the day of a hearing or, if there was no hearing, before judgment; 44 per cent received default judgment; and just 19 per cent had a defence of some sort entered, with 12 per cent having a hearing. In half the cases the plaintiff proved the case through court action. The longest liquidated cases lasted well over a year, but the majority of cases, as far as the court was concerned, ended within two months. For debt recovery in the county court, those specialising in acting for plaintiffs indicated that their aim at issue was to move rapidly to default judgment, since there was normally a considerable history of negotiation between debtor and creditor pre-issue, but that if the case was defended, the aim changed to settlement. High Court cases were very similar in terms of progress. Just 6 per cent had hearings set. Unliquidated cases in the county court showed an equal paucity of trials. Of our sample, 10 per cent were withdrawn by the plaintiff or failed prior to judgment; 48 per cent settled prior to the day of a hearing but often after a defence had been issued; 64 per cent had a defence of some sort entered, but unlike liquidated cases, this did not mean a hearing would occur, and in just 26 per cent was a first hearing held. Unliquidated cases were much slower than liquidated cases, with settlement occurring at all points up to the completion of hearings. Hence a quarter of cases settled over one year from when they began. The range was up to 816 days for settlement. The timescale to settlement ran parallel with the time to the first hearing (suggesting that setting, or having, the first hearing was a real spur to settlement). Unliquidated cases in the High Court showed very similar patterns to those in the county court, though they tended to be slower, to be more likely to have an actual first hearing, and to be even more likely to end in settlement.

Civil Justice Reform Evaluation – Further Findings *(2002), London: Lord Chancellor's Department*

This report continues the process of review in relation to the civil justice reforms which were introduced in April 1999, implementing many of the recommendations in Lord Woolf's final report, *Access to Justice*. Early findings based upon evidence obtained over the first two years were presented in the paper 'Emerging Findings', published in March 2001. The major points in this latest report are as follows. In general, the findings that were included in the previous report are confirmed. As to particular points, first it needs to be noted that overall there has been a drop in the number of claims issued, in particular in the types of claim most affected by the new Civil Procedure Rules 1998 introduced in April 1999. Evidence suggests that the system of pre-action protocols are working well to promote settlement and a culture of openness and co-operation. Part 36 of the Rules, which provides for payments into court and without prejudice offers, has been welcomed by all interested groups as a means of resolving claims more quickly: claims which settle without court proceedings and those where proceedings are issued. There is evidence to show that settlements at the door of the court are now fewer and that settlements before the hearing day have increased. After a substantial rise in the first year following the introduction of the Civil Procedure Rules 1998, there has been a levelling off in the number of cases in which alternative dispute resolution is used. The use of single joint experts appears to have worked well. It is likely that their use has contributed to a less adversarial culture and helped achieve earlier settlements. Case management conferences are a key factor in making litigation less complex, and appear to have been a success. The time between issue and hearing for those cases that go to trial has fallen. The time between issue and hearing for small claims has risen since the introduction of the Civil Procedure Rules 1998, but may now be falling. The number of appeals in the course of proceedings appears to have fallen sharply. It is still too early to provide a definitive view on costs: the picture remains relatively unclear, with statistics difficult to obtain and conflicting anecdotal evidence existing. Where there is evidence of increased costs, the causes are difficult to isolate. The views of litigants in person are difficult to obtain as they tend to use the system only once. Whilst research is currently being undertaken to assess their views, anecdotally it appears that courts are providing the assistance required. Court service user surveys have returned good results.

OBP Textbook page 183, section 9.14.

Bringing proceedings to an end before trial

Payments into Court *(2001), London: The Law Society*

This is the Law Society's response to the Lord Chancellor's Department's consultation paper entitled *Payments into Court in Satisfaction of Claims.* The Law Society expressed its belief that the system whereby the defendant may pay money into court to support an offer to settle the claim should be retained, this being secured under Pt 36 of the Civil Procedure Rules 1998. It was thought that the actual presence of the money is a strong incentive for claimants to accept a defendant's offer. The promotion of settlement was a major aim of the civil justice reforms and, therefore, this function seems to be very supportive of those reforms. Removal of this function may result in satellite enforcement litigation which would otherwise be unnecessary where a claimant has to litigate in order to secure payment of offers accepted under Pt 36 of the Civil Procedure Rules 1998. Such satellite litigation is contrary to the aims of the Civil Procedure Rules 1998. The payment in satisfaction function ensures that defendant's offers are realistic and genuine. It supports the aim of greater settlement of claims. The consultation paper states that about 60 per cent of cases settle before trial generally following acceptance of payments in satisfaction. The removal of this function could undermine the effectiveness of Pt 36, which is proving to be one of the most effective and popular parts of the Civil Procedure Rules 1998. On the use of written offers as a replacement for payments into court, the Law Society is not in favour of this. However, the Law Society supports the idea of a dual system of payments into court and written offers with the advantage of automatic cost protection. Effectively, this is what we have at present. Currently, in order to qualify as a Pt 36 offer and have the benefit of the costs protection offered by Pt 36, an offer must be accompanied by a payment into court once proceedings are issued. However, an offer (written or otherwise) can be made outside the Part 36 provisions and can be drawn to the court's attention when it is considering costs under Pt 44.3. The court can take this into account when exercising its discretion. The Law Society propose that the Rules should offer maximum protection to defendants who make payments in and a more limited protection should be available for defendants who make written offers after issue of proceedings. However, the Rules should provide strong encouragement for offers to be accompanied by payments in for money claims where it is clear that a payment in is a possible option. The general discretion that a court has to consider offers made whether or not under Pt 36 should not be allowed to undermine the Pt 36 procedure itself. The Law Society considers that the court service should retain responsibility for the payments in satisfaction system. Further, it is proposed that a streamlined process for payments in satisfaction be adopted. The Law Society agrees with the conclusion reached in the consultation paper that bankers' orders/guarantees are not appropriate for the following reasons: security issues; loss of interest; inability for the Court Funds Office to recoup running costs; and that it is administratively burdensome. As to escrow accounts, the Law Society does not believe that escrow accounts will provide a suitable alternative arrangement for payments into court. Individual escrow accounts are simply not viable and a single escrow account has too many disadvantages, including complexity, charges, low interest rates, the cost of monitoring and the difficulty for litigants in using the system. Similarly, the Law Society does not believe that credit cards are an appropriate method of settling claims. The fact that authorisation would not be sought until the funds are requested would lead to difficulties retrieving funds when needed. It will be difficult to ensure that, even if sufficient funds were available when the offer was made, that they would continue to be available when payment is required. In addition, there are a number of costs associated with the use of credit cards and with processing the transaction which do not make them attractive for this purpose.

OBP Textbook page 188, section 9.25.

Civil Procedure in the County Court

Jurisdiction and allocation

Lay and Judicial Perspectives on the Expansion of the Small Claims Regime *(2002), Baldwin J, London: Lord Chancellor's Department*

This report investigates the recently extended system of small claims in county courts. Following the recommendations that were made by Lord Woolf in 1995, the financial limit in small claims in England and Wales rose from £1,000 to £3,000 in January 1996 and then to £5,000 in April 1999. This dramatic expansion in the space of only four years has not been paralleled anywhere in the world, and the £5,000 limit is higher than that presently found in almost any other country. Only personal injury and housing repair cases (where the small claims limit is £1,000) have been excluded from this expansion. The aim of such a system is to facilitate citizens' access to the civil courts. It should provide a cheap and simple mechanism by which people who are unfamiliar with legal procedures can bring their disputes to the courts, and enable them to dispense with the services of lawyers if they wish to do so. Even though a dispute may involve only a small sum of money, the small claims procedure, at its best, would give unrepresented litigants a fighting chance of success against a represented and wealthier opponent, without having to run the risk of financial ruin in the process. The present research is from the perspective of two groups of respondents – litigants and district judges. A sample of small claims litigants, including both claimants and defendants, involved in claims in the £3,000–£5,000 band, were interviewed to determine whether they were satisfied with what happened in their cases, comparing their experiences with those of small claims litigants interviewed in two earlier studies. Interviews were also conducted with a sample of district judges to find out what they have made of the continued expansion of small claims.

Evidence from the official statistics shows that the recent rises in the small claims limit have not led, as many feared, to the county courts being inundated with new cases. Indeed, the annual increases in the numbers of small claims being dealt with in the county courts since 1996 have been no more than slight. The main message has to be how little difference the recent developments have made both in terms of numbers and in relation to the actual operation of the courts. Although the results of the study show that most small claims litigants involved in high value claims are well satisfied with the experience, questions still need to be raised about whether the sacrifice in standards of judicial decision-making that the informal small claims procedure inevitably involves can be justified in claims involving sums in excess of £5,000. Professor Baldwin concludes that it would be simplistic to assume that, just because most litigants and district judges feel that the small claims procedure continues to work satisfactorily in dealing with claims of up to £5,000 in value, the limit can safely be raised to greater heights.

OBP Textbook page 198, section 10.11.

Criminal Appeals

Appeals following a trial on indictment

R v *Pendleton (Donald)* [2001] UKHL 66; [2002] 1 All ER 524 House of Lords (Lords Bingham of Cornhill, Mackay of Clashfern, Steyn, Hope of Craighead and Hobhouse of Woodborough)

Fresh evidence – role of the Court of Appeal

Facts
The role of the Court of Appeal in relation to fresh evidence on appeal after conviction had to be considered.

Held
The appeal should be allowed as the conviction was unsafe.

Comment
The proper approach for the Court of Appeal, in cases where there is new evidence that had not been available when the matter was tried by jury, was considered by the House of Lords. Section 23 Criminal Appeal Act 1968 provides for an appeal against conviction in cases where there is fresh evidence. The legal question raised was whether the House of Lords had correctly defined the test to be applied in such cases in *Stafford* v *Director of Public Prosecutions* [1974] AC 878. The House of Lords suggested that the question for the Court of Appeal on an appeal against conviction was whether the conviction was safe, and not whether the accused was guilty. When assessing fresh evidence in a case of any difficulty it would usually be wise for the Court of Appeal to test its own provisional view by asking whether the evidence, if given at trial, might reasonably have affected the decision of the trial jury to convict. If so, the conviction would be unsafe. Trial by jury did not mean trial by jury in the first instance and trial by judges of the Court of Appeal in the second. The Court of Appeal was entrusted with a power of review to guard against the possibility of injustice, but that power had to be exercised with caution, mindful that the Court of Appeal was not privy to the jury's deliberations and should not intrude into territory that properly belonged to the jury. The House of Lords thought that, since the Court of Appeal had directed itself in accordance with the *Stafford* case, its approach had been correct in law. However, given the uncertainties in the case and the fresh psychological evidence, these made it impossible to be sure that the conviction was safe. In holding otherwise, the Court of Appeal had strayed beyond its true function of review and had made findings that had not been open to it in all the circumstances, coming perilously close to considering whether the appellant was, in its judgment, guilty. For these reasons the appeal from the decision of the Court of Appeal should be allowed – the Court of Appeal had refused the appeal from the decision in the Crown Court. The following extract from Lord Bingham states the principles lucidly:

'It is undesirable that exercise of the important judgment entrusted to the Court of Appeal by s2(1) of the 1968 Act should be constrained by words not to be found in the statute and that adherence to a particular thought process should be required by judicial decision. Thus the House in *Stafford* were right to reject the submission of counsel that the Court of Appeal had asked the wrong question by taking as the test the effect of the fresh evidence on their minds and not the effect that that evidence would have had on the mind of the jury ([1974] AC 878 at 880). It would, as the House pointed out, be anomalous for the court to say that the evidence raised no doubt whatever in their minds but might have raised a reasonable doubt in the minds of the jury. I am not persuaded that the House laid down any incorrect principle in *Stafford*, so long as the Court of Appeal bears very clearly in mind that the question for its consideration is whether the conviction is safe and not whether the accused is guilty. But the test advocated by counsel in *Stafford* and by Mr Mansfield in this appeal does have a dual virtue to which the speeches I have quoted perhaps gave somewhat inadequate recognition. First, it reminds the Court of Appeal that it is not and should never become the primary decision-maker. Secondly, it reminds the Court of Appeal that it has an imperfect and incomplete understanding of the full processes which led the jury to convict. The Court of Appeal can make its assessment of the fresh evidence it has heard, but save in a clear case it is at a disadvantage in seeking to relate that evidence to the rest of the evidence which the jury heard. For these reasons it will usually be wise for the Court of Appeal, in a case of any difficulty, to test their own provisional view by asking whether the evidence, if given at the trial, might reasonably have affected the decision of the trial jury to convict. If it might, the conviction must be thought to be unsafe.'

OBP Textbook page 300, section 16.2.

The European Community and the European Union I

Introduction

European Communities (Amendment) Act 2002

The Act, which received Royal Assent on 26 February 2002, provides for the implementation of the provisions in the Treaty of Nice. That Treaty provides for reform of the European Union (the EU) so as to enable the EU to operate effectively after the accession of the applicant Member States. The key institutional changes include:

1. changes to the size and organisation of the College of Commissioners;
2. revision of the current system of weighted votes in the Council;
3. extension of qualified majority voting in the Council and co-decision with the European Parliament;
4. changes to the procedures set out in the Treaty of Amsterdam for authorising a group of Member States to use the EU's institutions to move ahead with activity

in certain areas, even though not all Member States want to take part (enhanced co-operation);

5. changes to the distribution of seats in the European Parliament after enlargement;

6. a package of reforms to alleviate the growing burden on the European Court of Justice and the Court of First Instance.

OBP Textbook page 313, section 17.1.

13

Equity and Trusts

Completely and Incompletely Constituted Trusts

Introduction

Pennington v *Waine* [2002] 4 All ER 214 Court of Appeal (Schiemann, Clarke and Arden LJJ)

Perfecting gifts – an interpretation of *Milroy* v *Lord*

Facts

Mrs Crampton intended to transfer 400 shares, which she owned, to her nephew Harold. To this effect she consulted with a partner of the relevant company's auditors and signed a transfer form. The form was kept on the company's file and was never delivered to the company or to Harold. Mrs Crampton also wanted Harold to be a director of the company, and Harold signed a consent form agreeing to this and she countersigned it. The partner wrote to Harold informing him that nothing further was required. The company's articles required, amongst other provisions, which included a right of pre-emption, that directors were required to hold one share in the company. Subsequently, Mrs Crampton executed a will, which did not include the 400 shares. The issue before the Court after her death was whether the shares were in her residuary estate or whether they were held on trust for Harold absolutely.

Held

The Court of Appeal held that delivery of a share transfer form could be dispensed with in some circumstances. Here, it would have been unconscionable for Mrs Crampton to have recalled what was clearly intended as a gift once Harold had signed the director's consent form. Moreover, the partner's letter to Harold could be construed as meaning that he and Mrs Crampton had become agents for Harold for the purposes of submitting the share transfer form to the company. Mrs Crampton held the legal title in the shares on trust for Harold and thereafter he would have been entitled beneficially to the shares. Arden and Clarke LJJ were strongly influenced by Lord Browne-Wilkinson's observations in *Choithram (T) International SA and Others* v *Pagarani and Others* [2001] 1 WLR 1. Arden LJ proceeded on the basis that a principle which animates the answer to the question whether an apparently incomplete gift is to be treated as completely constituted is that a donor will not be permitted to change his or her mind if it would be unconscionable, in the eyes of equity, vis-à-vis the donee to do so. Clarke LJ took a similar line. He said that he did not think that the conclusion fell foul of the principle that the court will not convert an imperfect gift into a declaration of trust. He said that Lord Browne-Wilkinson:

> '... highlighted the contrast between the maxim that equity will not aid a volunteer and the maxim that it will not strive officiously to defeat a gift. It seems to me that if equity refuses to aid Harold on the facts of this case, it will prefer the former maxim to the latter, whereas all the circumstances of the case lead to the conclusion that it should give effect to the gift, which Ada [Mrs Crampton] intended.'

Comment

It is suggested not only that the *Choithram* case was not open to interpretation in this way, but also that *Pennington* v *Waine* is completely irreconcilable with all the earlier authorities. Indeed it seems that Arden and Clarke LJJ were well aware of this. Arden LJ said that the principle that equity will not assist a volunteer at first sight looks like a hard-edged rule of law not permitting much argument or exception, which led to harsh and seemingly paradoxical results, but that equity had tempered the wind to the shorn lamb. She said that the cases do not reveal any consistent policy consideration behind the rule that equity will not perfect an imperfect gift. She concluded that the objectives of the rule obviously include that donors do not, by acting voluntarily, act unwisely in a way that they would regret. According to her, that policy objective is furthered by permitting donors to change their mind at any time before the transfer becomes completely constituted and is a paternalistic objective, which can outweigh the respect to be given to the donor's original intention as gifts are often held by the courts to be incompletely constituted despite the clearest intention of the donor to make the gift.

Clarke LJ frankly admitted that the circumstances of the case could make bad law. Whilst admitting that the Court of Appeal decision produced a fair outcome, it certainly does make bad law. Not only had Mrs Crampton failed to effect delivery of the shares, but also the company's regulations had not been complied with. The argument in respect of the partner's letter to Harold was, therefore, also irrelevant. The case is entirely inconsistent with the classic statement of authority in *Milroy* v *Lord* (1862) 4 De GF & J 264.

OBP Textbook pages 41–42 and 46–47, sections 4.1 and 4.4.

Resulting Trusts

Failure to exhaust beneficial interest

Twinsectra Ltd v *Yardley* [2002] 2 All ER 377 House of Lords (Lords Slynn of Hadley, Steyn, Hoffmann, Hutton and Millett)

Failure of purpose of loan

Facts

Twinsectra agreed to advance £1,000,000 to Mr Yardley for the acquisition of property. This was subject to a provision that it was advanced to a solicitor on the latter's professional undertaking that the funds would be retained by him until such time as they were applied in the acquisition of property by his client, Mr Yardley, and would in any event be repaid with the interest by the solicitor personally. Mr Yardley's own solicitor, Mr Leach, refused to give such an undertaking. It was given by another solicitor, Mr Sims, who owed Mr Yardley money as a result of some dubious dealings with Nigerian government officials, involving putting up money to bribe the officials to induce the government to pay fees under a completed engineering contract. Mr Yardley obtained the money to acquire the property from another source and Mr Sims simply paid the money away according to Mr Yardley's instructions, mostly to Mr Leach, acting also on behalf of Mr Yardley. The principal issue before the House of Lords was whether Mr Leach was liable to Twinsectra for assisting in a breach of trust. The Court of Appeal held, amongst other things, that the loan had been induced by a fraudulent misrepresentation as to the purposes for which the funds would be used. The funds advanced had been subject to a *Quistclose* trust (see *Barclays Bank Ltd* v *Quistclose Investments Ltd* [1970] AC 567) and that trust had been breached by the utilisation of the funds for purposes other than the acquisition of property. The *Quistclose* trust was analysed as a primary trust in favour of the creditors (characterised as an express 'purpose trust' enforceable by the lender) and, in the event of the failure of that trust, a secondary trust in favour of Quistclose.

Held

The House of Lords agreed that there was a *Quistclose* type of trust but held, as the judge at first instance had found as a finding of fact, that as Mr Leach had not acted dishonestly, he could not be liable for dishonest assistance in breach of trust. Lord Millett reconsidered the operation of a *Quistclose* type of trust to conclude that:

> '[I] hold the *Quistclose* trust to be an entirely orthodox example of the kind of default known as a resulting trust. The lender pays the money to the borrower by way of loan, but he does not part with the entire beneficial interest in the money, and insofar as he does not it is held on a resulting trust for the lender from the outset. Contrary to the opinion of the Court of Appeal, it is the borrower who has a very limited use of the money, being obliged to apply it for the stated purpose or return it. He has no beneficial interest in the money, which remains throughout in the lender, subject only to the borrower's power or duty to apply the money in accordance with the lender's instructions. When the purpose fails, the money is returnable to the lender, not under some new trust in his favour which only comes into being on the failure of the purpose, but because the resulting trust in his favour is no longer subject to any power on the part of the borrower to make use of the money. Whether the borrower is obliged to apply the money for the stated purpose or merely at liberty to do so, and whether the lender can countermand the borrower's mandate while it is still capable of being carried out, must depend upon the circumstances of the particular case.'

Comment

As will be seen in the next section, the decision is an important one on the liabilities of strangers involved in a breach of trust. Lord Millett dissented on this point and, therefore, on the issue of Mr Leach's liability. His analysis of the *Quistclose* type of trust was, however, approved by all of the other members of the House. The analysis by way of pure resulting trust would seem to finally resolve controversy since the *Quistclose* decision as to the precise nature of the trusts where there is a failure of purpose of a loan.

OBP Textbook pages 92–95, section 6.3.

Resulting and Constructive Trusts

Civil Partnerships Bill

Home sharing

The Civil Partnerships Bill is at a very early stage in the parliamentary process. The Bill was put forward in the House of Lords by the Liberal Democrat peer, Lord Lester of Herne Hill. The Bill may be superseded by government legislation as the Deputy Prime Minister's Office has announced that the government hopes to publish a consultation paper about what form a civil partnership should take. At the moment the Bill will constitute wide-sweeping reform of the law relating to the breakdown of a relationship between cohabitants. The Bill will, presumably, 'bite' predominantly at homosexual rather than heterosexual couples. It seems unlikely that heterosexual couples who avoid the legislative implications of marriage will opt for an alternative statutory scheme. Nonetheless the implications of the Bill are enormous.

Once a civil partnership is successfully registered there is either equal sharing of property, as defined in s9, or registration of a property agreement. If the partnership comes to an end, a cessation order will be made and the provisions for distribution of property are quite extensive. Even when a property agreement is registered, Intervention Orders may be granted. Section 36(1) provides that: 'But no order may be made otherwise than in accordance with the terms of any property agreement made by the partners in a civil partnership which is noted in the register *unless the court considers that financial or other hardship would otherwise result to one of the partners*' (emphasis added).

The Civil Partnerships Bill may also be of greater significance as a result of the publication of the long-awaited Law Commission Discussion Paper on Sharing Homes. The Discussion Paper was published on 18 July 2002. As long ago as 1994 the Law Commission launched the Homesharers' Project and the law then, particularly in relation to cohabitants, was described as 'unfair, uncertain and illogical'. The Discussion Paper has, as suggested in an article in *The Times* on

Tuesday 30 July 2002 'Why living together is so risky', caused great disappointment. Stuart Bridge, Law Commissioner for England and Wales, defended the Discussion Paper in a linked article 'Myth of the common law marriage' and in an article entitled 'Fair shares for home sharers' in the New Law Journal on 2 August 2002. The conclusions reached in the Discussion Paper are set out in full below. It does, however, have to be said that this appears to have constituted a lost opportunity to reform an area of the law which is overwhelmingly in need of reform.

'PART VI

CONCLUSIONS

In this Discussion Paper, which concludes the present project, we are not making specific proposals for legislation. It is therefore not a Consultation Paper in the usual format, nor are we seeking responses. The purpose is to provide a legal framework for future public debate and consideration by Government. The main points emerging from the Paper are as follows.

(1) Greater numbers of people are living together in circumstances which are characterised by informality. The present law does not deal adequately with these changing conditions.

(2) Although the trust of land offers a machinery for the establishment of beneficial interests in the shared home which is both coherent and flexible, the current requirements for proving the existence of an interest under a trust are not ideally suited to the typical informality of those sharing a home. To demand proof of an intention to share the beneficial interest can be unrealistic, as people do not tend to think about their home in such legalistic terms. The emphasis on financial input towards the acquisition of the home fails to recognise the realities of most cohabiting relationships. Finally, the uncertainties in the present law can cause lengthy and costly litigation, wasting court time, public funding and the parties' own resources.

(3) It is not possible, however, to devise a statutory scheme for the ascertainment and quantification of beneficial interests in the shared home which can operate fairly and evenly across the diversity of domestic circumstances which are now to be encountered.

(4) It is essential that those who are living together are positively encouraged to investigate the legal consequences of doing so and to make express written arrangements setting out clearly their intentions. Where they purchase property jointly, they will be required to stipulate their beneficial entitlements by Her Majesty's Land Registry. In these and other circumstances, it is essential that the courts continue rigorously to enforce express declarations of trust.

(5) It is difficult to present a convincing case for any more effective criteria than 'common intention' on which an assessment of beneficial entitlement could be based. Intention is clearly important, as it would be wholly unsatisfactory if a person were to obtain a beneficial interest where it was made extremely clear that a particular contribution, by financial or other means, would not be met this way.

(6) In our view, however, the courts have made it too difficult for a person to bring a claim to beneficial entitlement in two respects.

(a) The first is the requirement that the claimant make a direct financial contribution to the acquisition of the shared home. In our view, an indirect contribution to the mortgage (by means of paying the household bills and thereby enabling the other party to pay the mortgage instalments) should be sufficient to enable the courts to infer a common intention that the beneficial entitlement be shared.

(b) The second concerns the quantification of beneficial entitlement. We believe that there is much to be said for adopting a broader approach to quantification, undertaking a survey of the whole course of dealing between the parties and taking account of all conduct which throws light on the question what shares were intended.

Recent reported decisions have indicated that the courts are capable of the flexibility of approach which will be necessary to move the law in the desired direction.

(7) We have however identified, in the course of this project, a wider need for the law to recognise and to respond to the increasing diversity of living arrangements in this country. We believe that further consideration should be given to the adoption, necessarily by legislation, of new legal approaches to personal relationships outside marriage, following the lead given by other jurisdictions (such as France, Australia and New Zealand).

(8) These approaches may include such mechanisms as the formal registration of civil partnerships, or, less formally, a power for the court to adjust the legal rights and obligations of individuals who are or have been living together for a defined period or in defined circumstances. Any status must be clearly and readily identifiable such that all can ascertain whether any such status has been acquired. The consequences of any status must be prescribed so that those involved are fully aware of its legal implications.

(9) The definition of any status conferring legal rights or imposing legal obligations involves broad questions of social policy which fall outside the present project, and which are in any event more appropriate for political debate and decision, rather than for a law reform body. However, the Law Commission would be prepared, if asked, to contribute to any further work in this area which is appropriate given its role as a body concerned with law reform.'

As noted above, it is highly unlikely that heterosexual couples who avoid the legislative implications of marriage will opt for an alternative statutory scheme by way of registration and, if this proves to be the case, the Discussion Paper's fourth conclusion is utterly naïve in respect of such couples.

OBP Textbook pages 96–101 and 141–143, sections 6.4 and 7.10.

Constructive Trusts

Unauthorised profits by fiduciaries

Badfinger Music v *Evans* [2001] 2 WTLR 1 Chancery Division (Lord Goldsmith QC, sitting as a Deputy Judge of the High Court)

Unauthorised profits by fiduciaries – remuneration of trustees

Facts

The claimant, a former member of a pop band 'Badfinger', had, in somewhat dubious circumstances in relation to other interested parties, produced a remixed record album. The pop band had broken up in very acrimonious circumstances. Prior to the break-up, the band had a live concert taped but the tapes, which the claimant had retained throughout, were of too poor quality to be usable. The claimant undertook considerable work in remixing and remastering the tapes with the result that a commercial, successful version was, ultimately, released. Given that the claimant was in a fiduciary relationship with the other interested parties, the question before the court was whether this was an exceptional circumstance entitling him to receive remuneration for the work which he had undertaken.

Held
Lord Goldsmith QC was prepared to utilise the inherent jurisdiction of the court to award remuneration to a fiduciary in the absence of prior authorisation. In doing so he accepted that this was not an occasion where the client had acted honestly and openly in a manner highly beneficial to the other interested parties. Lord Goldsmith QC considered that, although this was an important factor, it was not necessarily a determinative factor. He relied heavily on the undue influence case of *O'Sullivan* v *Management Agency* [1985] 3 All ER 351, where remuneration was awarded by the court to the parties who had actually exercised undue influence. Lord Goldsmith QC added that the existence or absence of conflict of interest was also, although an important factor, again not necessarily determinative. In awarding remuneration, he took two other factors into account. He said that it was relevant that the work done could only realistically have been done by the fiduciary and was of a special character calling for the exercise of a particular kind of professional skill. Lord Goldsmith QC added obiter that, in appropriate circumstances, the court's jurisdiction might extend to awarding a share of profits as part of the remuneration.

Comment
The case constitutes a wide interpretation of the inherent jurisdiction to award remuneration, which, although a first instant decision, may herald a more generous and welcome interpretation in the future for honest fiduciaries, such as in *Regal (Hastings) Ltd* v *Gulliver* [1942] 1 All ER 378 and *Boardman* v *Phipps* [1967] 2 AC 46, who find themselves in breach of the strict interpretation of the conflict of interest and duty rule.

OBP Textbook pages 105–113 and 225–228, sections 7.2 and 13.2.

'Strangers'

Twinsectra Ltd v *Yardley* [2002] 2 All ER 377 House of Lords (Lords Slynn of Hadley, Steyn, Hoffmann, Hutton and Millett)

Strangers – test of liability for assistance in a breach of trust

Facts
As above.

Held
As above, Mr Leach was held not to be liable because the judge had found that he was not dishonest.

Comment

The majority of the House of Lords confirmed that, as per *Royal Brunei Airlines Sdn Bhd* v *Tan (Philip Kok Ming)* [1995] 3 All ER 97, the test of liability for third party assistance in a breach of trust should be dishonesty. On that basis, their Lordships concluded that the Court of Appeal had not been entitled to disturb the judge's decision at first instance that Mr Leach had not been dishonest. It was considered inappropriate to order a retrial so Mr Leach was not liable for dishonest assistance. Lord Hutton's speech contains the main analysis of the test of dishonesty:

'There is a purely subjective standard, whereby a person is only regarded as dishonest if he transgresses his own standard of dishonesty, even if that standard is contrary to that of reasonable and honest people. This has been termed the "Robin Hood test" and has been rejected by the courts as an excuse for liability for dishonesty.

As Sir Christopher Slade stated in *Walker* v *Stones* [2001] QB 902, 939: "… The penniless thief, for example, who picks the pocket of the multi-millionaire is dishonest even though he genuinely considers that theft is morally justified as a fair redistribution of wealth and he is therefore not being dishonest".'

It is now, therefore, tolerably clear that a finding of 'Robin Hood' type of dishonesty will now mean that a claim in accessory liability will succeed. Lord Hutton went on to say:

'Secondly, there is a purely objective standard whereby a person acts dishonestly if his conduct is dishonest by the ordinary standards of reasonable and honest people, even if he does not realise this.

Thirdly, there is a standard which combines an objective test and a subjective test, and which requires that before there can be a finding of dishonesty it must be established that the defendant's conduct was dishonest by the ordinary standards of reasonable and honest people and that he himself realised that by those standards his conduct was dishonest. I will term this the "combined test".'

The new test of dishonesty with which the rest of the majority agreed with is therefore:

'Dishonesty requires knowledge by the defendant that what he was doing would be regarded as dishonest by honest people, although he should not escape a finding of dishonesty because he sets his own standards of honesty and does not regard as dishonest what he knows would offend the normally accepted standards of honest conduct.'

On knowledge of the existence of the trust, Lord Hoffmann said that:

'I do not suggest that one cannot be dishonest without a full appreciation of the legal analysis of the transaction. A person may dishonestly assist in the commission of a breach of trust without any idea of what a trust means. The necessary dishonest state of mind may be found to exist simply on the fact that he knew perfectly well that he was helping to pay away money to which the recipient was not entitled.'

For technical reasons, there was no claim for knowing receipt before the House of Lords. Lord Millett was the only member of the House to comment on this. He commented that: 'The much needed rationalisation of this branch of the law must, therefore, await another occasion'. He went on to suggest (strictly obiter) that there is powerful academic support for the proposition that the liability of the recipient is the same as in other cases of restitution, that is to say strict but subject to a change of position defence.

The decision has, therefore, clarified the law in respect of assistance in breach of trust insofar as it is possible to do so when judges are determining the distinction between honest and dishonest conduct in civil proceedings. It remains open to question as to whether Lord Millett's suggestion in the knowing receipt category of liability will be adopted in some future case.

Dubai Aluminium Co Ltd v *Salaam and Others* (2002) The Times 6 December House of Lords (Lords Slynn of Hadley, Nicholls of Birkenhead, Hutton, Hobhouse of Woodborough and Millett)

Vicarious liability of partners for dishonest assistance

Facts

Dubai Aluminium was defrauded out of US$50 million by several fraudulent participants. An alleged participant by way of dishonest assistance was Mr Amhurst, a senior partner in a firm of solicitors. Dubai Aluminium sued a number of the participants, including both Mr Amhurst and the firm of solicitors (hereafter the Amhurst firm). During the course of the trial all the defendants settled with Dubai Aluminium. The Amhurst firm paid US$10 million and the issue before the House of Lords was whether they could obtain contribution for this amount from two other participants, Mr Salaam and Mr Al Tajir, under the Civil Liability (Contribution) Act 1978. Section 1 of the 1978 Act provides that:

> '(1) Subject to the following provisions of this section, any person liable in respect of any damage suffered by another person may recover contribution from any other person liable in respect of the same damage (whether jointly with him or otherwise). ...
> (4) A person who has made or agreed to make any payment in bona fide settlement or compromise of any claim made against him in respect of any damage (including a payment into court which has been accepted) shall be entitled to recover in accordance with this section without regard to whether or not he himself is or ever was liable in respect of the damage, provided, however, that he would have been liable assuming that the factual basis of the claim against him could have been established.'

The Amhurst firm argued that, had the factual claim against Mr Amhurst been established, it would have been vicariously liable under s10 Partnership Act 1890 and was, therefore, entitled to contribution. The Court of Appeal had held that the Amhurst firm was not vicariously liable because Mr Amhurst's participation in the fraudulent scheme was, at all times, outside the ordinary course of business of the firm.

Held
Section 10 of the Partnership Act 1890 states:

> 'Where, by any wrongful act or omission of any partner acting in the ordinary course of the business of the firm, or with the authority of his co-partners, loss or injury is caused to any person not being a partner in the firm, or any penalty is incurred, the firm is liable therefore to the same extent as the partner so acting or omitting to act.'

The House of Lords held unanimously that equitable wrongs were within that section, that Mr Amhurst was acting in the ordinary course of business and that the Amhurst firm was entitled to the US$10 million contribution.

Comment
Much of the discussion on vicarious liability is not really relevant to an equity and trusts update. The applicable point, made succinctly by Lord Millett, is that vicarious liability for an equitable wrong will lie where the partner is authorised to do acts of the kind in question and does not depend on authority to do the particular acts which constitute the wrong. Dishonest assistance fell squarely within s10 of the 1890 Act but not within ss11 and 13. Section 11 provides:

> 'In the following cases, namely –
> (a) where one partner acting within the scope of his apparent authority receives the money or property of a third party and misapplies it; and
> (b) where a firm in the course of its business receives money or property of a third person, and the money or property so received is misapplied by one or more of the partners while it is in the custody of the firm;
> the firm is liable to make good the loss.'

Section 13 provides:

> 'If a partner, being a trustee, improperly employs trust property in the business or on the account of the partnership, no other partner is liable for the trust property to the persons beneficially entitled therein:
> Provided as follows –
> (1) this section shall not affect any liability incurred by any partner by reason of him having notice of a breach of trust; and
> (2) nothing in this section shall prevent trust money from being followed and recovered from the firm if still in its possession or under its control.'

As Lord Millett points out, ss11 and 13 deal directly with receipt of trust property. Undoubtedly this is correct and equitable wrongs per se fall within s10. Lord Millett made some interesting suggestions as to the nature of so-called 'constructive trusts'. He distinguished between a trust which arose before the occurrence of an impeached transaction and a claim which arose only by reason of that transaction. In the former case, a defendant is trustee even though not expressly appointed as such. For clarity of language, Lord Millett favours substituting dog Latin for bastard French by referring to such cases as de facto trustees rather than 'trustees de son tort'. In the latter case, a defendant is a stranger to the trust at the time of the transaction and, again for clarity of language, Lord Millett favours discarding the words 'accountable as constructive trustee' and substituting 'accountable in equity'. These seem to be eminently sensible suggestions which, it is hoped, the courts adopt in future cases.

OBP Textbook pages 113–130, section 7.3.

Proprietary estoppel

Jennings v *Rice* [2002] WTLR 367 Court of Appeal (Aldous, Mantell and Robert Walker LJJ)

Proprietary estoppel – satisfying the equity

Facts
The case concerned a claim by way of proprietary estoppel, in far from unusual circumstances nowadays, whereby an elderly person had procured services on the faith of informal assurances that the services would, ultimately, be rewarded by generosity in a will. The action in proprietary estoppel was not really in issue in the case, rather it was the equity required to do justice in the case. The deceased, Mrs Royle, died intestate as a childless widow at the age of 93. The claimant had undertaken various services for her, including acting as a principal carer during the latter stages of her life. Mrs Royle had made various vague assurances as to what the claimant would receive under her will, which left the claimant with the expectation that he would receive the house and furniture, valued at £435,000. Mrs Royle's estate was sworn for probate at £1.258 million. At first instance, the claimant had been awarded £200,000 and in his appeal it was contended that he should receive either Mrs Royle's entire estate, or the £435,000 representing the house and furniture. In considering the case the Court of Appeal had to decide whether or not to satisfy the claimant's minimum expectation of £435,000.

Held
The appeal was dismissed. Aldous and Robert Walker LJJ, with both of whom Mantell LJ agreed, reviewed the case law in detail in order to determine the principles which might need to be considered in proprietary estoppel cases. Referring to Lord Scarman in *Crabb* v *Arun District Council* [1976] Ch 179, Robert Walker LJ said that the minimum equity to do justice to the claimant does not require the court to be constitutionally parsimonious, but does recognise that the court must also do justice to the defendant. He went on to explain that the minimum equity arises not from the claimant's expectations alone, but from the combination of expectations, detrimental reliance and the unconscionability of allowing the benefactor or the deceased benefactor's estate to go back on the assurances. On that basis he rejected the notion of a detailed computational approach of what the claimant might have earned in the way of arm's-length remuneration for his services. Although he noted that the going rate for live-in carers can provide a useful cross-check in the exercise of the court's discretion, he considered that the

computational approach placed too much emphasis on detrimental reliance at the expense of the other factors to achieve the minimum to do justice. Having acknowledged that in some circumstances of proprietary estoppel the minimum necessary to do justice will be quite straightforward, he concluded that:

'It would be unwise to attempt any comprehensive enumeration of the factors relevant to the exercise of the court's discretion, or to suggest any hierarchy of factors. In my view they include, but are not limited to … (misconduct of the claimant as in *J Willis & Sons v Willis* [1979] Ch 261 or particularly oppressive conduct on the part of the defendant as in *Crabb* v *Arun District Council* [1976] Ch 179 or *Pascoe* v *Turner* [1979] 1 WLR 431). To these can be safely added the court's recognition that it cannot compel people who have fallen out to live peaceably together, so that there may be a need for a clean break; alterations in the benefactor's assets and circumstances, especially where the benefactor's assurances have been given, and the claimant's detriment has been suffered, over a long period of years; the likely effect of taxation and, (to a limited degree) the other claims (legal or moral) on the benefactor or his or her estate. No doubt there are many other factors, which it may be right for the court to take into account in particular factual situations.'

Comment

As Robert Walker LJ said in this case:

'It cannot be doubted that in this as in every other area of the law, the court must take a principled approach, and cannot exercise an unfettered discretion according to the individual judge's notion of what is fair in any particular case.'

The factors, which were enunciated by the Court of Appeal, followed from a principled analysis by Aldous and Robert Walker LJJ of the circumstances of the previous case law. Previous decisions, such as *Gillett* v *Holt* [2000] 2 All ER 289 and *Sledmore* v *Dalby* (1996) 72 P & CR 196, are now completely justified.

OBP Textbook pages 133–138, section 7.8.

Charitable Trusts

Reform

The government Strategy Review Unit has issued a multi-page consultation document entitled *Private Action, Public Benefit: A Review of Charities and the Wider Not-For-Profit Sector*. Chapter four of this document, 'Reforming The Legal Framework: A Modern Approach To Charities Focusing On Public Benefit' (which can be found, via the Internet, at http:www.cabinet-office.gov.uk/innovation/2002/charity/report/06.htm), recommends a number of reforms.

The Strategy Review Unit recommends a new definition of charity as an organisation which provides public benefit and which has one or more of the following purposes:

1. the prevention and relief of poverty;
2. the advancement of education;
3. the advancement of religion;
4. the advancement of health (including the prevention and relief of sickness, disease or human suffering);
5. social and community advancement (including the care, support and protection of the aged, people with a disability, children and young people);
6. the advancement of culture, arts and heritage;
7. the advancement of amateur sport;
8. the promotion of human rights, conflict resolution and reconciliation;
9. the advancement of environmental protection and improvement;
10 other purposes beneficial to the community.

The stated intention of the Strategy Review Unit is that the reform of charity law will be a one-off change to the parameters that will help secure the position for the future.

Other reforms govern institutions such as independent schools and private hospitals. It is proposed that the Charity Commission would identify charities likely to charge high fees and undertake a rolling programme to check that provision was made for wider access and, in consultation with charities likely to be affected, will issue guidelines as to the level of access appropriate in particular circumstances.

Under the new purpose of 'advancement of religion', it is proposed that the legislation introducing the change clarify that faiths that are multi-deity or non-deity should also qualify.

Charities will be allowed to undertake all trading within the charity, without the need for a trading company but subject to a statutory duty of care. The Charity Commission guidelines on political campaigning should be revised so that the tone is less cautionary and puts greater emphasis on the campaigning and other non-party political activities that charities can undertake.

Suggested administrative reforms include the facilitation of mergers and the introduction of new criteria to enhance the capacity of charities to convert permanent endowment funds into capital. Following the consultation period (which ended on 31 December 2002), the Home Secretary will publish a paper setting out the government's next steps.

OBP Textbook page 171, section 10.4.

Breach of Trusts II: Tracing

Tracing in equity: property in traceable form

Russell-Cooke Trust Company, The v *Prentis* [2002] EWHC 2227; [2002] NLJ 1719 Chancery Division (Lindsay J)

A reconsideration of the rule in *Devaynes* v *Noble: Clayton's Case* (1816) 1 Mer 572

Facts

In 1999 a solicitor, Mr Prentis, advertised an investment scheme offering a fixed return of 15 per cent per annum on sums invested. In the advertisement he pointed out that he and his firm were regulated by the Law Society in the conduct of investment business. The investment scheme attracted over £6 million from over 400 investors. The investment scheme, inevitably, was not a success and the Law Society intervened on 2 June 2000. Trustees were appointed and the issue before Lindsay J concerned what rules should be applied as to beneficial ownership as between investors to funds held in an account.

Held

Lindsay J considered three possible alternatives, *Clayton's Case*, that is first in, first out, the North American Rolling charge and a pari passu division. Following *Vaughan* v *Barlow Clowes International Ltd* [1992] 4 All ER 22, he concluded that there was a counterweight to displace the rule in *Clayton's Case* and that beneficial ownership should be decided on a pari passu basis.

Comment

Lindsay J's observations on the rule in *Clayton's Case* demonstrate a consistent and welcome judicial reaction to its potential to produce entirely unjust results. Lindsay J noted that in other jurisdictions the rule in *Clayton's Case* has been very strongly criticised. He suggested that the modern English approach has been not to challenge the binding nature of the rule, but to permit it to be distinguished by reference to the facts of the particular case. He noted that Leggatt LJ, in *Vaughan* v *Barlow Clowes International Ltd* [1992] 4 All ER 22, had regarded the rule as capricious, arbitrary and inapposite and he went on to follow the Court of Appeal's decision in *Vaughan* to the effect that the rule can be displaced by even a slight counterweight. Indeed Lindsay J went further and said that it might be more accurate to refer to the exception that is, rather than the rule in, *Clayton's Case*. He did not see any reason as to why the North American Rolling charge should apply on the facts of the case but, in any event, considered it to be complicated and expensive to apply.

OBP Textbook page 326, section 20.4.

14

European Union Law

Enforcement Actions against Member States

Breaches of Community law under art 226 EC

Commission v *United Kingdom of Great Britain and Northern Ireland*
Case C–466/98 Judgment of 5 November 2002 (not yet reported) European
Court of Justice

Action for failure by a Member State to fulfil its obligations – art 226 EC – treaties
between Member States and third countries before accession – art 307 EC –
conclusion and application by a Member State of a bilateral agreement with the
United States of America – agreement authorising the USA to revoke, suspend or
limit the traffic rights of air carriers designated by the UK which are not owned by
the latter or its nationals – freedom of establishment – art 43 EC

Facts
Shortly before and after the end of World War II, a number of European States,
including the UK, concluded bilateral agreements on air transport with the USA. In
1946 the UK concluded such an agreement with the USA (the Bermuda I
Agreement) which was replaced by the Bermuda II Agreement of 23 July 1977.
Article 5 of the Bermuda II Agreement provides:

> '1. Each contracting party shall have the right to revoke, suspend, limit or impose
> conditions on the operating authorisations or technical permissions of an airline designated
> by the other contracting party where:
> (a) substantial ownership and effective control of that airline are not vested in the
> contracting party designating the airline or in nationals of such contracting party.'

By virtue of art 3(6), each contracting party was required to grant the appropriate
operating authorisations and technical permissions to an aircraft when, inter alia,
substantial ownership and effective control of that airline was vested in the
contracting party designating the airline or its nationals. Since 1992 the USA has
sought to conclude bilateral 'open skies' agreements with individual European States,
including the Member States of the EU.

In 1994 the Commission sent a letter to Member States warning them against
entering into 'open skies' bilateral agreements with the USA on the ground that
such agreements were likely to have a negative effect on the EU and, in particular,
adversely affect internal Community legislation. Furthermore, the Commission stated

that any negotiations of such agreements could only be carried out at the Community level.

In 1995 the Commission sent a letter to the UK government seeking assurance that the UK would not negotiate or enter into a bilateral agreement with the USA. On 5 June 1995 the UK concluded such an agreement with the USA.

In July 1995, the Commission sent a letter of formal notice to the UK government stating that the UK, by entering into the above agreement, was in breach of art 43 EC, taking into account the fact that the traffic rights accorded to the UK under the agreement were to be granted solely on the basis of the nationality of the carrier, and therefore air carriers which had obtained a licence from the UK in accordance with Council Regulation 2407/92/EEC on the licensing of air carriers (OJ 1992 L240, p1), and those established in the UK which were owned and controlled by nationals of another Member State, would have traffic rights in the USA refused to them, whereas those owned and controlled by UK nationals would be granted those rights.

The UK replied that the offending clause in the Bermuda II Agreement had not been amended by the agreement of 5 June 1995 and that this clause was not in breach of art 43 EC because it did not prohibit the designation by the UK of air carriers which were not owned or controlled by UK nationals, but only gave the USA the opportunity to refuse to accept such a designation whilst allowing the UK to seek consultation in the event of such a refusal.

In response, the Commission issued a reasoned opinion stating that, by concluding the Bermuda II Agreement and applying it, the UK was in breach of art 43 EC. When the UK refused to comply with the reasoned opinion, the Commission commenced proceedings under art 226 EC.

Held
The ECJ held that the UK was in breach of art 43 EC.

Comment
The main argument submitted by the UK government was that art 307 EC was not limited to agreements concluded by Member States before their admission to the EU, but extended to the rights and obligations arising from such agreements, and therefore it was irrelevant whether or not the agreement in question had been amended or replaced since the UK's accession to the Communities. The UK claimed that if a subsequent agreement contained similar rights and obligations as the pre-accession agreement, the situation was outside the scope of art 307 EC. According to the UK, as the rights and obligations conferred in the Bermuda I Agreement had not been substantially changed by the Bermuda II Agreement, the Bermuda II Agreement, although concluded four years after the accession of the UK to the Community, constituted a continuation of the Bermuda I Agreement and therefore could not be considered as a new agreement and was, therefore, not within the scope of art 307 EC.

The Commission argued that, as the Preamble to the Bermuda II Agreement clearly stated that it was concluded 'for the purpose of replacing' the Bermuda I Agreement, it constituted a new agreement. To support this reasoning the Commission submitted that the offending clause was amended when introduced into the Bermuda II Agreement. The Commission argued that art 307 EC, being an exception to the EC Treaty, must be interpreted strictly, and thus even if rights and obligations contained in a pre-accession agreement were repeated in another agreement, that could not support the conclusion that the initial agreement had been in some way perpetuated.

The judgment of the ECJ was not surprising. Article 307 EC is clear. It enshrines the general principle of international law contained in art 30(4) of the Vienna Convention on the Law of Treaties 1969. Article 307(1) provides that:

> 'The rights and obligations arising from agreements concluded before 1 January 1958 or, for acceding States, before the date of their accession, between one or more Member States on the one hand, and one or more third countries on the other, shall not be affected by the provisions of this Treaty.'

Therefore all agreements that the UK concluded before her accession to the Communities have been unaffected by the UK's membership of the EU. However, all subsequent agreements are subject to their compatibility with Community law. In order to avoid, as far as possible, any incompatibility between agreements entered into by the Member States before their accession, para 2 of art 307 EC provides that Member States are required to take all appropriate measures to eliminate such incompatibility, and where necessary assist each other to this end and, where appropriate, adopt a common attitude.

The ECJ rejected the argument submitted by the UK. The Court found that the Bermuda II Agreement was a new agreement, mainly on the basis that its Preamble expressly stated that the Bermuda II Agreement was replacing the Bermuda I Agreement in order to respond to the developments of traffic rights between the USA and the UK. This necessity to adjust the Bermuda I Agreement to new circumstances demonstrated that the Bermuda II Agreement was a new agreement creating new rights and obligations between the contracting parties.

It is also important to note that the Commission enjoys a great measure of discretion in respect of proceedings under art 226 EC. The fact that the Commission did not bring proceedings against the UK for breach of arts 10 and 307 EC until 1997 can be explained by many factors, the most important being that, due to peculiar features of the transport sector, legislative progress at the Community level has been slow and piecemeal and developments have taken place separately in road, rail, inland waterway, air and maritime transport.

In respect of the infringement of art 43 EC, the UK submitted that the activities covered by the Bermuda Agreements, that is air transport outside the EU, were not within the scope of art 43 EC. The Commission argued that art 43 EC applied to all sectors including air transport and, being a basic provision of the EC Treaty, also applied to areas within the competence of Member States.

The ECJ agreed with the Commission. The ECJ held that art 43 EC applied to all undertakings established in a Member State, even if the subject matter of their business in that State consisted of providing services towards non-Member States. Furthermore, even if a Member State had exclusive competence in a specific area, it must exercise its powers in conformity with EC law: *R* v *Secretary of State for Transport, ex parte Factortame Ltd and Others (No 3)* Case C–221/89 [1991] ECR I–3905; *Commission* v *Ireland* Case C–151/96 [1997] ECR I–3327; *Mr & Mrs Robert Gilly* v *Directeur des Services Fiscaux du Bas-Rhin* Case C–336/96 [1998] ECR I–2793; *Criminal Proceedings against Horst Bickel and Ulrich Franz* Case C–274/96 [1998] ECR I–7637 and *Centros Ltd* v *Erhvervs-og Selskabsstyrelsen* Case C–212/97 [1999] ECR I–1459.

Having confirmed that the dispute was within the scope of art 43 EC, the ECJ subsequently examined whether the Bermuda II Agreement, in particular the clause on the ownership and control of airlines, was contrary to art 43 EC. By virtue of this clause the USA was, in principle, under an obligation to grant the rights provided for in the agreement to carriers controlled by the UK, but not to carriers controlled by other Member States or their nationals established in the UK.

The ECJ held that this clause was in breach of art 43 EC, since it was capable of affecting airlines established in the UK where a substantial part of the ownership and the effective control of which was vested either in another Member State or in nationals of such a Member State. The said clause discriminated against air carriers from other Member States by precluding them from the benefit enjoyed with national treatment in the UK. The ECJ emphasised that:

'Contrary to what the United Kingdom maintains, the direct source of that discrimination is not the possible conduct of the United States of America but art 5 of the Bermuda II Agreement, which specifically acknowledges the right of the United States of America to act in that way.'

The ECJ rejected the justification based on the grounds of public order and public safety on the basis that the UK failed to establish the existence of a link between a genuine and serious threat to public order and public safety and the discriminatory measure adopted, that is the offending clause in art 5 of the Bermuda II Agreement: *Bond van Adverteerders* v *Netherlands* Case 352/85 [1988] ECR 2085; *Criminal Proceedings against Donatella Calfa* Case C–348/96 [1999] ECR I–11.

Commission v *Kingdom of Denmark* Case C–467/98 Judgment of 5 November 2002 (not yet reported) European Court of Justice

Commission v *Kingdom of Sweden* Case C–468/98 Judgment of 5 November 2002 (not yet reported) European Court of Justice

Commission v *Republic of Finland* Case C–469/98 Judgment of 5 November 2002 (not yet reported) European Court of Justice

Commission v *Kingdom of Belgium* Case C–471/98 Judgment of 5 November 2002 (not yet reported) European Court of Justice

Commission v *Grand Duchy of Luxembourg* Case C–472/98 Judgment of 5 November 2002 (not yet reported) European Court of Justice

Commission v *Republic of Austria* Case C–475/98 Judgment of 5 November 2002 (not yet reported) European Court of Justice

Commission v *Federal Republic of Germany* Case C–476/98 Judgment of 5 November 2002 (not yet reported) European Court of Justice

Actions for failure by Member States to fulfil their obligations – art 226 EC – conclusion and application by Member States of bilateral 'open skies' agreements with the USA – breach of secondary legislation – external competence of the Community – freedom of establishment – breach of art 43 EC – breach of art 10 EC

Facts

The facts were similar to *Commission* v *United Kingdom of Great Britain and Northern Ireland* Case C–466/98 Judgment of 5 November 2002 (not yet reported), in that the Member States concerned entered into bilateral 'Bermuda type' agreements with the USA shortly before or after the end of World War II. The Member States concerned amended those agreements during the 1950s and 1960s, being, at the relevant time, Members of the European Communities. In the 1990s the agreements were replaced by new 'open skies' agreements, despite opposition from the Commission. The situation of the Member States concerned was slightly different from that of the UK. The Commission challenged the bilateral agreements concluded in the 1990s by the seven Member States concerned, whilst in the case of the UK, the Bermuda II Agreement was seen as infringing, inter alia, art 43 EC (see above).

When the Commission brought proceedings against the seven Member States concerned its principal claim was that they, by having individually entered into 'open skies' agreements with the United States, had failed to fulfil their obligations under the EC Treaty, in particular arts 10 and 43 EC, and also under secondary EC legislation adopted in the area of air transport.

The Commission argued that it had exclusive competence to negotiate relevant agreements with the USA (this claim was not raised against the UK) on the basis that, first, it was 'necessary' within the meaning of the *Rhine Navigation Case* Opinion 1/76 [1977] ECR 741 for such an agreement to be concluded at Community level, and second, that the agreement would 'affect', in the sense contemplated in *Commission* v *Council (Re ERTA)* Case 22/70 [1971] ECR 263, the common rules adopted by the Community in the relevant area.

Held

The ECJ held that the Member States concerned were in breach of arts 10 and 43

EC and had infringed the Community's external competence in respect of the common rules on the establishment of air fares and rates on intra-Community routes and on computerised reservation systems (CRSs).

Comment

The most interesting aspect of the commented cases concerned the issue of the Commission's external competence in the area of air transport, in particular whether or not the Community has exclusive competence in this area. If so, this has important practical implications. If the competence of the Community is exclusive, Member States are prevented from acting unilaterally or collectively in this area, irrespective of whether or not the Community has itself acted. The EC, in internal or external relations, would replace the Member States.

In the above cases it was obvious that the Community could not derive exclusive external competence in the area of air transport from the express terms of the EC Treaty and Acts of Accession. Therefore, the Community had no 'express' external competence in this area. This conclusion is based on the examination of arts 80(1) and 80(2) EC. Under art 80(1) EC the transport provisions apply to rail, road and inland waterways only. Article 80(2) EC provides that the Council may, acting by qualified majority, decide: 'whether, to what extent and by what procedure appropriate provisions may be laid down for sea and air transport'.

Following on from the above situations, and on the basis of the authorisation in art 80(2) EC, but not any express provision of the EC Treaty, the Council, within the framework of the gradual establishment of the internal market in air transport, adopted in 1992 three Regulations:

1. Regulation 2407/92 on the licensing of air carriers;
2. Regulation 2408/92 on access for Community air carriers to intra-Community air routes; and
3. Regulation 2409/92 on fares and rates for air service.

This 'package' has been supplemented by other measures in the field of air transport, of which the most important are: Regulation 2299/89 on a code of conduct for CRSs; and Regulation 95/93 on common rules for the allocation of slots at Community airports.

Since the beginning of the 1990s the Commission had sought to obtain from the Council a mandate to negotiate with the USA a single Europe-wide 'open skies' agreement. A limited mandate was granted by the Council to the Commission in 1996, according to which the Commission was allowed to negotiate in liaison with a special committee appointed by the Council and in areas specified by the Council, such as: competition rules; ownership and control of air carriers; CRSs; code sharing; dispute resolution; leasing; environmental clauses; and transitional measures. However, at the time of writing, the Commission has not been successful in securing a single Europe-wide 'open skies' agreement with the USA.

Having established that the Community had no express external competence in the relevant area, it was necessary to determine whether or not the Community could justify its competence on the doctrine of implied powers. Powers which do not result directly and expressly from a provision or a number of provisions of the EC Treaty, but from global and general objectives laid down by the EC Treaty as interpreted by the ECJ, are known as implied powers. The doctrine of implied powers has been created by the ECJ and mainly applies to the external competences of the EC, although it also has an internal dimension. In the internal sphere it relates to the powers of EC institutions vis-à-vis Member States. The ECJ held in *Germany* v *Commission* Joined Cases 281, 283–285 and 287/85 [1987] ECR 3203 that when the Commission is under an obligation to carry out a specific task assigned to it by the EC Treaty, the latter confers on the Commission the necessary powers to carry out that task.

Implied powers with regard to the external relations of the Community are based on the doctrine of parallelism, according to which the internal competence of the Community should be matched by the external competence – in interno in foro externo, that is, if the EC has a power to make internal law, it should also be entitled to conclude international agreements in that area. Powers may flow from the EC Treaty provisions and from measures adopted, within the framework of those provisions, by the EC institutions. They are not limited to areas in which the internal powers of the Community have already been exercised. An implied power does not become exclusive, however, until the express power on which it is dependent is exercised either internally or externally, and art 308 EC cannot itself vest in the Community an exclusive external competence.

The general principles on implied powers were established in *Commission* v *Council (Re ERTA)* Case 22/70 [1971] ECR 263. In this case the ECJ adopted a radical approach towards the expansion of the Community competences: first, on the attribution of powers to the EC, and second, on their exclusive nature.

In relation to the first question, the ECJ stated that in order to determine in a particular case the EC competence to enter into international agreements, the whole scheme of the EC Treaty no less than its substantive provisions must be taken into account. As a result, the EC power:

'... arises not only from an express conferment by the Treaty – as is the case with arts 113 and 114 [art 133 EC: art 114 was repealed by the Treaty of Amsterdam] for tariff and trade agreements and with art 238 [art 310 EC] for association agreements – but may equally flow from other provisions of the Treaty and from measures adopted, within the framework of those provisions, by the Community institutions.'

As to the second issue, the ECJ stated that where the Community has adopted Community rules within the framework of a common policy, the Member States are not allowed, individually or collectively, to enter into agreements with third States in the areas affected by those rules. The ECJ stated that:

'As and when such common rules come into being, the Community alone is in a position to assume and carry out contractual obligations towards third countries affecting the whole sphere of application of the Community legal system.'

Under the *ERTA* judgment the Community has powers, or 'authority', to enter into international agreements in the context of implied powers based on two sources:

1. on 'other provisions of the Treaty'; and
2. on 'measures adopted, within the framework of those provisions, by the Community institutions'.

The ECJ has previously held that the common commercial policy consisted of interaction between external and internal measures and refused to give priority to either. In the *Rhine Navigation Case* Opinion 1/76 [1977] ECR 741 the Court decided that when EC law had created powers for the institutions of the Community within its internal system in order to attain a specific objective, the EC had authority to enter into the international commitments necessary for the attainment of that objective, even in the absence of an express provision in this respect.

In *Cornelis Kramer & Others* Joined Cases 3, 4–6/76 [1976] ECR 1279 the ECJ confirmed, once again, the existence of an implied external competence of the Community corresponding to its internal competence and susceptible to be extended ratione materiae if analogous competence is conferred to a State under public international law.

However, the extent of the Community implied powers has been limited by the *ILO Case* Opinion 2/91 [1993] ECR I–1061 in which the ECJ held that they arise:

'... whenever Community law created for the institutions of the Community powers within its internal system for the purpose of obtaining a specific objective.'

As a result, the participation of the EC in external relations based on the doctrine of implied powers is conditional upon the necessity to achieve a 'specific objective' of the EC which cannot be attained without the participation of third States: the *WTO Case* Opinion 1/94 [1994] ECR I–5267.

The argument of the Commission based on necessity within the meaning of the Rhine Navigation Case

In the commented cases the ECJ rejected the Commission's argument based on necessity within the meaning of Opinion 1/76 (above). The ECJ emphasised that implied external competence exists not only whenever its internal competence has already been exercised, but also if the internal Community measures are adopted only on the occasion of the conclusion and implementation of the international agreement. The Court stated:

'Thus, the competence to bind the Community in relation to non–Member countries may arise by implication from the Treaty provisions establishing internal competence, provided that participation of the Community in the international agreement is necessary for attaining one of the Community's objectives.'

The ECJ stated that the situation where the internal competence may be effectively exercised only at the same time as the external competence (*WTO Case* Opinion 1/94 [1994] ECR I–5267) did not occur in the commented cases. The conclusion of an international agreement had not been necessary in order to attain objectives of the EC Treaty that could not be attained by establishing autonomous rules, taking into account the fact that the Council was able to adopt the 'third package' without its being necessary to conclude an air transport agreement with the USA.

The argument of the Commission that 'open skies' bilateral agreements would 'affect' in the sense contemplated in the ERTA *judgment, the common rules adopted by the Community in this area*
In this respect the ECJ stated that:

> '... whenever the Community has included in its internal legislative acts provisions relating to the treatment of nationals of non-Member countries or expressly conferred on its institutions powers to negotiate with non-Member countries, it acquired an exclusive external competence in the spheres covered by those acts.
>
> The same applies, even in the absence of any express provisions authorising its institutions to negotiate with non-Member countries, where the Community has achieved complete harmonisation in a given area, because the common rules thus adopted could be affected within the meaning of the *ERTA* judgment if the Member States retained freedom to negotiate with non-Member countries.'

In the light of the above statement, the approach of the ECJ consisted of assessing whether the common rules already adopted were capable of being affected by the 'open skies' agreements entered into by the Member States concerned. The ECJ examined the scope of the relevant Regulations on a case-by-case basis.

In respect of both Regulation 2407/92 (concerning requirements for the granting and maintenance of operating licences by Member States in relation to air carriers established in the Community) and Regulation 2408/92 (relating to access for Community air carriers to intra-Community air routes) the ECJ found that the 'open skies' bilateral agreements did not fall within the area already covered by either of the Regulations, since they contained rules directed to USA air carriers. Therefore, these Regulations did not establish an external competence for the Community.

However, in respect of some provisions of Regulation 2409/92 (concerning fares and rates for air services) the Regulation had, indirectly but definitely, prohibited air carriers from non-Member States from introducing new products or fares lower than the ones existing for identical products where they operated on intra-Community routes. Consequently, the Member States concerned were prohibited from regulating unilaterally in their 'open skies' agreements the issue relating to fares and rates to be charged by carriers from non-Member States on intra-Community routes. Under the above Regulation, the Community has acquired exclusive competence.

In respect of Regulation 2299/89 (on a code of conduct for CRSs) its provisions relating to CRSs offered for use or used in the territory of a Member State are applicable to nationals of non–Member States, and therefore the Community has acquired exclusive competence in these matters.

With regard to Regulation 95/93 (on common rules for the allocation of slots at Community airports), that Regulation applies, subject to reciprocity, to air carriers of non–Member States. Consequently, the Community has exclusive competence to conclude agreements in that area with non–Member States. Notwithstanding this, the Member States concerned were not in breach of Regulation 95/93, because the Bermuda-type Agreements, as subsequently revised, did not apply to the allocation of slots.

In respect of the infringement of the right of establishment by the Member States concerned, the ECJ applied its reasoning in *Commission* v *United Kingdom of Great Britain and Northern Ireland* Case C–466/98 Judgment of 5 November 2002 (not yet reported) to condemn the clause on the ownership and control of airlines contained in the bilateral agreements as being contrary to art 43 EC.

The implications of the ECJ's judgment are that the 'open skies' agreements being in breach of EC law should be terminated, so allowing the Commission to achieve its long sought objective of securing one single, composite agreement with the USA.

OBP Textbook page 82, section 4.4.

Judicial Review in the European Community – Direct Actions against Community Institutions

Article 230 EC actions

Unión de Pequeños Agricultores v *Council of the European Union* Case C–50/00P [2002] 3 CMLR 1 European Court of Justice

Action for annulment – art 230 EC – appeal – Regulation 1638/89 – common organisation of the markets in oils and fats – persons individually concerned – effective judicial protection – admissibility

Facts
On 16 February 2000, the Unión de Pequeños Agricultores (the UPA), a trade association representing small Spanish agricultural businesses, brought an appeal against the judgment of the Court of First Instance (CFI) in *Unión de Pequeños Agricultores* v *Council of the European Union* Case T–173/98 [1999] ECR II–3357 in which the CFI dismissed an application for partial annulment of EC Regulation 1638/89 concerning the establishment of a common market in oils and fats (OJ 1998, L210, p32). The contested Regulation set out schemes in respect of intervention prices, production aid, consumption aid and storage, and imports and exports of olive oil. The CFI held the application inadmissible on the ground that the UPA was not individually concerned by the contested Regulation.

On appeal, the UPA argued that it was individually concerned by the provisions of the contested Regulation because, under national law, it had no legal remedies to review the legality of the Regulation, and therefore had been deprived of the effective judicial protection of its own interests and those of its members.

Held
The ECJ dismissed the appeal as inadmissible.

Comment
The interpretation of requirements relating to individual concern under art 230(4) EC was at issue in the above case. In an Advisory Opinion in the above case, Advocate-General Jacobs submitted that the restrictive interpretation of the concept of individual concern under art 230(4) EC should be relaxed in the situation where the applicant had no legal remedy under national law to challenge an act of general application within the meaning of art 230 EC.

In addition, in *Jégo-Quéré* v *Commission* Case T–177/01 [2002] 2 CMLR 1137 the CFI, in a situation similar to the commented case, decided that the applicant was individually concerned by a measure of general application, that is a measure which did not necessitate any implementing measures at national level, and therefore the applicant could not initiate proceedings before the national courts when the measure in question affected his legal position in a manner which was both definite and immediate, by restricting his rights or by imposing obligations on him. Indeed, the only way in which the applicant in that case could gain access to a national court was to knowingly infringe the contested measure.

The commented case provided the ECJ which the opportunity to review the existing case law and to clarify the requirements relating to individual concern in cases where the applicants wish to challenge a measure of general application on the ground of the absence of any legal remedy before national courts. The more general issue which the ECJ was asked to decide in the commented case was the concept of the EC as a Community based on the rule of law, and the scope of the right to effective judicial protection for any natural or legal person under EC law.

The ECJ sat in plenary session whilst rendering the judgment in the commented case. Its judgment is very disappointing, because the ECJ decided to apply a very restrictive approach to requirements relating to individual concern under art 230(4) EC. The manner in which the ECJ approached the appellant claims shows that the ECJ is not prepared to change its case law on the matter. According to the ECJ, the issue under examination was whether or not the appellant should be allowed to bring an action for annulment of the contested regulation:

'... on the sole ground that, in the alleged absence of any legal remedy before the national courts, [its] right to effective judicial protection requires it.'

The ECJ's formulation of the issue was inferred from the fact that the appellant neither challenged: the finding of the CFI that the contested Regulation was of general application; nor the fact that the specific interests of the appellant (and members of the UPA) were not affected by the contested Regulation; nor that its members were affected by the contested Regulation by reason of certain attributes which were peculiar to them; or by reason of factual circumstances in which they were differentiated from all other persons. Consequently, the appellant recognised that it had no locus standi under art 230(4) EC, as it was not individually concerned by the challenged Regulation.

However, the appellant argued that notwithstanding its lack of individual concern within the meaning of art 230(4) EC, the judgment of the CFI had infringed its fundamental right to effective judicial protection, and for that reason alone the ECJ should examine the circumstances of the case.

The UPA submitted that the contested Regulation did not require any implementing legislation or the taking of any other measures by the Spanish authorities. As a result, the appellant, under national law, could not seek the annulment of a national measure relating to the contested Regulation. This prevented a national court from referring the matter of validity of the contested Regulation to the ECJ under the preliminary ruling procedure. In addition, the appellant and its members could not even infringe the provisions of the contested Regulation so as to be in a position to challenge the validity of any sanction that might, if appropriate, be imposed on them. In this situation, the appellant argued, the right to effective judicial protection required that, where there is no legal remedy under national law, an application for annulment under art 230(4) EC must be held admissible. The appellant relied on the judgment of the ECJ in *Greenpeace Council and Others* v *Commission* Case C–321/95P [1998] ECR I–1651 which, in its submission, confirmed this conclusion.

Advocate-General Jacobs, in his Advisory Opinion on the commented case, stated that, in a situation where there is no legal remedy under national law, the requirements relating to individual concern should be reviewed. The ECJ decided otherwise.

Another interesting aspect of the commented case relates to the ECJ's assessment of the right to effective judicial protection. The Court recognised that individuals are entitled to effective judicial protection of the rights they derive from the Community legal order. This right constitutes one of the general principles of EC law, stemming from the constitutional traditions common to the Member States, and has been enshrined in arts 6 and 13 of the European Convention for the Protection of Human Rights and Fundamental Freedoms. However, the ECJ avoided any reference to art 47 of the Charter of Fundamental Rights, which article was relied upon by the CFI in *Jégo-Quéré* case. This omission probably reflects the ECJ's refusal to enter into any debate on matters related to the EU constitution.

The ECJ avoided the examination of the effectiveness, both for the Community and national systems, of legal remedies available to individuals. The Court's approach consisted of considering the purpose of each of them in general, in that, according to the ECJ, an individual enjoys effective legal protection of his rights stemming from EC law as long as he has access to a court, irrespective of whether it is a national court or a Community court.

In respect of legal remedies available under EC law, the ECJ, in para 40 of its judgment, noted that the EC Treaty provides for two procedures designed to ensure judicial review of the legality of acts of institutions, that is, on the one hand, arts 230 and 241 EC and, on the other, art 234 EC. In the commented case, the appellant had no locus standi under art 230 EC. Also, it could not rely on art 241 EC, taking into account the fact that the plea of illegality can be invoked only against implementing national measures. In the commented case the contested Regulation did not require any national implementing legislation, and did not require the taking of any measure by Spanish authorities. Thus a reference for a preliminary ruling to assess the validity of the challenged Regulation was not available to the appellant, because of the lack of national implementing measures and because, as the appellant stated, neither it or its members could infringe the provisions of the contested measure so as to be in a position to challenge the validity of any sanction that might be imposed upon the UPA or its members.

In this context, it was clear that the appellant did not enjoy effective judicial protection under EC law. The ECJ, however, did not accept that the appellant had no legal remedies (that is, he was suffering from the denial of justice) under Community law. Instead the ECJ stated that there was another way of ensuring the effectiveness of the appellant's right to judicial protection, that is under national law. In para 41 of its judgment, the ECJ stated that:

> '... it is for the Member States to establish a system of legal remedies and procedures which ensure respect for the right to effective judicial protection.'

Indeed, under art 10 EC, Member States are required to implement a complete system of legal remedies and procedures to permit the ECJ to review the legality of measures adopted by the Community institutions: *Les Verts* v *Parliament* Case 294/83 [1986] ECR 1339. This solution is, theoretically, the best to ensure that the right of natural and legal persons to effective judicial protection is respected. In practice, however, the creation of new legal remedies under national law intended to ensure the protection of rights stemming from EC law may be complex and time-consuming, and an expectation of any such thing occurring may therefore be illusory.

Furthermore, the ECJ emphasised that, by virtue of art 10 EC, national courts are required, as far as possible, to interpret and to apply national procedural rules governing the exercise of rights of action in such a way as to enable natural and legal persons to challenge the legality of any decision or other national measure relating to the application to them of a Community measure of general application, by pleading the invalidity of such an act.

The obligation imposed on national courts is, nevertheless, limited, taking into account the fact that the interpretation of national procedural rules is required 'as far as possible'. Therefore, it may occur that a national court will not be able to ensure the right to effective judicial protection for natural and legal persons.

It is also interesting to note that the ECJ refused to examine whether or not the national system of remedies was adequate and appropriate, so as to allow natural and legal persons to bring proceedings before a national court challenging the validity of acts adopted by the EC institutions. In this respect the ECJ stated:

> '... it is not acceptable to adopt an interpretation of the system of remedies, such as that favoured by the appellant, to the effect that a direct action for annulment before the Community Court will be available where it can be shown, following an examination by that Court of the particular procedural rules, that those rules do not allow the individual to bring proceedings to contest the validity of the Community measure at issue. Such an interpretation would require the Community Court, in each individual case, to examine and interpret national procedural law. That would go beyond its jurisdiction when reviewing the legality of Community measures.'

In the light of the above statement, the question arises whether or not such an examination of national procedural rules by the ECJ would actually be impracticable. In the light of the principle of autonomy of national procedural systems, the above statement seems well justified.

Nevertheless, it should be borne in mind that the ECJ has often assessed the effectiveness of national procedural rules within a framework of two procedures under the EC Treaty.

The first procedure concerns actions for damages involving the non-contractual liability of the Community under art 288(2) EC, in particular the ECJ has often verified whether the national remedies have been exhausted in order to decide whether the action should be brought before a national court or before a Community Court: see, for example: *Unifrex* v *Council and Commission* Case 281/82 [1984] ECR 1969; *Krohn* v *Commission* Case 175/82 [1986] ECR 753; *Roquette Frères* v *Commission* Case 20/88 [1989] ECR 1553; *Exporteur in Levende Varkens and Others* v *Commission* Cases T–481 and 484/93 [1995] ECR II–2941. In *Krohn* the ECJ stated that:

> '... the application for compensation provided for by art 178 [art 235 EC] and the second paragraph of art 215 [art 288 EC] of the Treaty was introduced as an autonomous form of action with a particular purpose to fulfill within the system of actions and subject to conditions on its use dictated by its specific nature. None the less, such actions must be examined in the light of the whole system of legal protection for the individual established by the Treaty; the admissibility of such an action may in certain cases be dependent on the exhaustion of national rights of action available to obtain the annulment of the national authority's decision which allegedly caused the damage for which compensation is sought. In order for that to be the case, however, it is necessary that those national rights of action should provide an effective means of protection for the individual concerned and be capable of resulting in compensation for the damage alleged. They do not do so where the annulment of the national authority's decision does not compensate for the damage suffered and therefore does not remove the need for the applicant, if he is to obtain compensation, to bring an action before the court under art 178 and the second paragraph of art 215 of the Treaty.'

The second procedure under which the ECJ often assesses the effectiveness of a national system of remedies in terms of its compatibility with EC law concerns the preliminary ruling procedure under art 234 EC, although it has to be noted that the powers of the ECJ to assess a national system of remedies are of a limited nature, in that in a request for a preliminary ruling the referring court must, inter alia, describe the legal context of the dispute. Thus, the ECJ is relying on the referring court to provide the legal background of the disputed matter.

It follows from the above that any assessment of a national system of remedies is not inconceivable. To the contrary, such an assessment has already been carried out by the ECJ under procedures already existing under EC law. In the commented case, however, the ECJ refused to accept the possibility that in the alleged absence of any legal remedy before the national court allowing the applicant to challenge the validity of an act adopted by an EC institution, the Court would be willing to proceed to such as assessment.

It is also interesting to note that in the commented case the ECJ realised the shortcomings of its restrictive interpretation of art 230(4) EC, as it suggested an alternative method of ensuring wider access to Community Courts; this being the reform of art 230 EC. The Court stated that:

> '... it is for the Member States, if necessary, in accordance with art 48 Treaty on European Union to reform the system currently in force.'

Irrespective of all the discussion on the topics dealt with in this case, the nub of the matter is that the ECJ held that the conditions of admissibility of an action for annulment under art 230 EC brought by a non-privileged applicant to challenge a Community measure of general application have not been changed. The door opened by the judgment of the CFI in *Jégo-Quéré* has been shut (see, for example, *VVG International and Metalsivas* v *Commission* Case T–155/02 Order of 8 August 2002 (not yet reported)).

OBP Textbook page 94, section 5.2.

Free Movement of Persons

Treaty developments

Baumbast v *Secretary of State for the Home Department; R* v *Secretary of State for the Home Department* Case C–423/99 [2002] 3 CMLR 599 European Court of Justice

Free movement of persons – migrant worker – rights of residence of members of the migrants worker's family – rights of children to pursue their studies in the host Member State – arts 10 and 12 of Regulation 1612/68 – citizenship of the European Union right of residence – Directive 90/364/EEC – derogations from the free movement of persons

Facts
Baumbast family
In 1990 Mrs Baumbast, a Colombian national, married Mr Baumbast, a German national, in the UK, where they decided to establish a family home. They have two daughters, the elder, who is a natural daughter of Mrs Baumbast and who possesses Colombian nationality, and the younger, who has dual German and Colombian nationality. The British authority granted a residence permit to the Baumbast family in 1990, valid for five years.

From 1990–1993 Mr Baumbast was employed in the UK, initially as an employed person and subsequently as head of his own company. Following the failure of his company, he had tried to obtain employment in the UK to no avail. Since 1993 he has been employed by German companies in China and Lesotho.

During the relevant period, the Baumbast family owned a house in the UK and the daughters went to school there. The family did not receive any social benefit and was covered by comprehensive medical insurance in Germany, to which country they travelled, when necessary, for medical treatment.

In May 1995 Mrs Baumbast applied for indefinite leave to remain in the UK for her family. In January 1996, the Secretary of State for the Home Department refused to renew a residence permit for the Baumbast family. His decision was challenged by the Baumbast family before the UK Immigration Adjudicator, who decided that:

1. Mr Baumbast had no right to reside in the UK as he was neither a worker nor a person entitled to reside in the UK under Directive 90/364;
2. the daughters had independent rights of residence in the UK under art 12 of Regulation 1612/68;
3. Mrs Baumbast's right to reside in the UK derived from her children's rights, and consequently she was allowed to stay in the UK for a period co-terminous with that during which her daughters were benefitting from the rights of residence under art 12 of Regulation 1612/68.

Mrs Baumbast appealed to the Immigration Tribunal against the Adjudicator's decision.

R family
Mrs R, a national of the United States, her husband Mr R, a French national, and their two children, who have dual French and United States nationality, arrived in the UK in 1990 where they established a family home. R, as a spouse of an EC national, was granted leave to remain in the UK until October 1995.

On the divorce of Mr and Mrs R in 1993, it was decided that the children were to reside with their mother. Since the divorce, Mr R has resided and worked in the UK and has shared responsibility with his former wife for the upbringing of their children. After the divorce, Mrs R established her own business as an interior decorator. She also acquired a house in the UK.

In 1995 Mrs R applied for indefinite leave to remain in the UK for herself and her daughters. In 1996 the children were granted indefinite leave to remain in the UK as members of the family of a migrant worker, but Mrs R's application was refused on the ground that the children were young enough to adjust to life in the United States if they had to accompany their mother.

Mrs R challenged that decision before the UK Immigration Adjudicator. She argued that her children's rights to education under EC law were breached, as well as the right to family life. Her application was dismissed. Mrs R appealed against the decision to the Immigration Tribunal.

The Immigration Tribunal referred to the ECJ the following questions.

1. Whether or not children of a citizen of the European Union who have installed themselves in a host Member State during the exercise of their parent's right of residence as a migrant worker in that Member State are entitled to reside there in order to obtain education under art 12 of Regulation 1612/68. In respect of the Baumbast family, the Immigration Tribunal asked whether or not the fact that only one parent was a citizen of the EU, and that parent had ceased to be a migrant worker in the host Member State, and that the children were not themselves citizens of the EU, affected the rights of the children under the above Regulation. In respect of the R family, the Immigration Tribunal asked whether or not the childrens' rights to residence had been affected by the fact that the parents had meanwhile divorced.

2. Whether or not, where the children have the right to reside under art 12 of Regulation 1612/68 to attend general educational courses in a host Member State, the parent who is the primary carer of those children, irrespective of his/her nationality, is also entitled to reside with the children under art 12 of Regulation 1612/68 in the situation where the parents have meanwhile divorced, or where the parent who is a citizen of the EU has ceased to be a migrant worker in the host Member State.

3. Whether a citizen of the EU who has ceased to be a migrant worker in a host Member State is still entitled to reside there because of his citizenship of the EU, that is, on the basis of art 18(1) EC.

Held

The ECJ made the following observations.

1. Children of a citizen of the EU, who have installed themselves in a host Member State during the exercise of their parent's rights of residence as a migrant worker in that Member State, are entitled to reside there in order to attend general educational courses under art 12 of Regulation 1612/68. This right is neither affected by the fact that the parents of the children have meanwhile divorced, nor by the fact that only one parent is a citizen of the EU and that parent has ceased to be a migrant worker in a host Member State, nor by the fact that the children are not themselves citizens of the EU.

2. Where children are entitled to reside in a host Member State under art 12 of Regulation 1612/68, the parent who is the primary carer of those children, irrespective of his/her nationality, is also entitled to reside with them, notwithstanding the fact that the parents have meanwhile divorced or that the parent who is a citizen of the EU has ceased to be a migrant worker in the host Member State.

3. By virtue of art 18(1) EC a citizen of the EU who has ceased to be a migrant worker in a host Member State is entitled to reside in a host Member State, although the exercise of that right is subject to limitations and restrictions set out in that provision. National authorities of the host Member State must ensure that those limitations and restrictions are applied in conformity with the general principle of EC law, in particular, the principle of proportionality.

Comment

The most interesting aspect of the judgment of the ECJ concerns the Baumbast family, in particular Mr Baumbast, who was refused a residence permit in the UK on the ground that that his comprehensive sickness insurance contracted in Germany could not cover emergency treatment given in the United Kingdom.

In the *Baumbast* case the ECJ, for the first time, has explicitly recognised that art 18(1) EC is directly effective. Until this judgment, it was uncertain whether or not art 18(1) EC was directly effective, although the interpretation of various judgments referring to art 18(1) EC seemed to point towards such recognition: *Maria Martinez Sala v Freistaat Bayern* Case C–85/96 [1998] ECR I–2691; *Arben Kaba v Secretary of State for the Home Department* Case C–356/98 [2000] ECR I–2623. In the commented case, the ECJ removed all doubts in this respect. The Court stated that EU citizenship is destined to be the fundamental status of nationals of the Member States (*Rudy Grzelczyk v Centre d'aide Sociale d'Ottignies-Louvain-la-Neuve* Case C–184/99 [2001] ECR I–6193; *Marie-Nathalie D'Hoop v Office National de l'Emploi* Case C–224/98 Judgment of 11 July 2002 (not yet reported)), and that:

'... in particular, the right to reside within the territory of the Member States under art 18(1) EC, that right is conferred directly on every citizen of the Union by a clear and precise provision of the EC Treaty. Purely, as a national of a Member State, and consequently a citizen of the Union, Mr Baumbast therefore has the right to rely on art 18(1) EC.'

Notwithstanding this it remains that a provision of Community law, in order to produce direct effect, must not only be clear and precise, but must also be unconditional (that is, it must not require the taking of any implementing measures by Community institutions or by Member States). On this point the ECJ admitted that the right granted under art 18(1) EC was conditional on the limitations and conditions laid down by the EC Treaty and by measures adopted to give it effect. Therefore, art 18(1) EC is directly effective notwithstanding the fact that some implementing measures are still necessary, and therefore in their absence art 18(1)

EC is directly effective to some extent. The ECJ tackled this problem in the following manner:

> '... the application of the limitations and conditions acknowledged in art 18(1) EC in respect of the exercise of that right of residence is subject to judicial review. Consequently, any limitations and conditions imposed on that right do not prevent the provisions of art 18(1) EC from conferring on individuals rights which are enforceable by them and which the national courts must protect.'

Consequently, all limitations and conditions must be applied in compliance with EC law and in accordance with the general principles of law, in particular the principle of proportionality. The ECJ, when assessing the situation of Mr Baumbast in the light of the principle of proportionality, took into account the fact that he had sufficient resources within the meaning of Directive 90/364, that he had worked and resided for a number of years in the UK, that his family resided with him during his stay in the UK as a worker and subsequently as a self-employed person and had remained there even after his activities as an employed and self-employed person came to an end, that neither Mr Baumbast nor his family had ever become burdens on the public finances of the host Member State, and that the Baumbast family, including Mr Baumbast, had comprehensive sickness insurance in Germany. In those circumstances, the refusal of the UK to grant Mr Baumbast a residence permit was considered by the ECJ to be disproportionate.

OBP Textbook page 164.

The External Trading Relations of the European Community

The prohibition on discriminatory taxation – art 90 EC

Niels Nygård v *Svineafgifsfonden and Ministeriet for Fødevarer, Landbrug og Fiskeri* Case C–234/99 [2002] ECR I–3657 European Court of Justice

National levy on pigs – arts 25 and 90 EC – charge having an equivalent effect – internal taxation – state aid – levy scheme authorised by the Commission as state aid compatible with arts 87 and 88 EC

Facts
Under Danish law a production levy was charged for every pig, irrespective of whether or not it was intended for a domestic market or for export, bred and slaughtered in Denmark. The same levy was also charged for every pig bred in Denmark and exported live. A part of the revenue generated by the levy was allocated to the financing of the production of pigs in Denmark and so benefitted those exporting pigs. The remainder of the revenue generated by the levy was allocated to the financing of the slaughtering of pigs and of the processing of pig

meat in Denmark and its sale on the domestic and export markets, and so did not bring any benefit to exporters of pigs. The levy scheme was, pursuant to art 88(3) EC, notified and approved by the EU Commission as being lawful state aid.

Mr Nygård, a pig breeder established in Denmark, exported to Germany between 1 August 1992 and 1 July 1993 live pigs intended for slaughter. Under German law he was required to pay a production levy in Germany for each pig supplied to the abattoirs. He paid in Germany the production levy, but refused to do so in Denmark. The Danish Fund commenced proceedings against Mr Nygård before the district court in Skjern (Denmark). The Danish court ordered Mr Nygård to pay the full amount of the production levy in respect of the exported pigs and interest.

Mr Nygård appealed to the Vestre Landsret from the judgment of the district court arguing that:

1. the levy imposed on live pigs for export in Denmark constituted a charge having an equivalent effect to a customs duty on export within the meaning of art 25 EC;
2. in the alternative he claimed that the levy constituted discriminatory taxation prohibited under art 90 EC.

The Vestre Landsret referred to the European Court of Justice (ECJ) for a preliminary ruling the following questions:

1. whether the above production levy was capable of being a charge having an equivalent effect to a customs duty on export, or of constituting discriminatory internal taxation; and
2. whether the fact that a national levy was intended to finance an aid scheme authorised by the Commission in the context of the EC Treaty provisions on state aid precluded a national court from assessing whether such a levy was compatible with other directly effective provisions of the EC Treaty.

Held

The ECJ held that the levy in question should be classified as discriminatory internal taxation prohibited by art 90 EC to the extent to which the advantage deriving from the use made of its revenue compensated in part for the charge imposed on pigs produced for slaughter in Denmark, thereby placing at a disadvantage the production of pigs for live export to other Member States.

In respect of the second question, the ECJ held that the fact that a national levy was intended to finance an aid scheme authorised by the European Commission in the context of the EC Treaty provisions on state aid did not preclude a national court from examining whether such a levy was compatible with other directly effective provisions of the EC Treaty.

Comment

In the above case the ECJ provided important clarifications in respect of three matters:

1. reverse discriminatory taxation under art 90 EC;
2. double taxation under EC law;
3. the jurisdiction of a national court to review the compatibility of state aid approved by the European Commission in the context of directly effective provisions of the EC Treaty other than arts 87 and 88 EC.

Reverse discriminatory taxation

The first step taken by the ECJ consisted of determining whether the national levy in question was a charge under art 25 EC or a discriminatory tax under art 90 EC. In this respect the ECJ referred to the existing case law. The Court repeated that arts 25 and 90 EC are mutually exclusive, and therefore the same charge cannot be classified, at the same time, as a charge having equivalent effect to a customs duty and as an internal discriminatory tax: see, inter alia, *Fazenda Pública* v *União das Cooperatives Abastecedoras de Leite de Lisboa, UCRL (UCAL)* Case C–347/95 [1997] ECR I–4911.

In order to determine whether or not the levy constituted a charge having equivalent effect to a customs duty, the ECJ examined the purpose for which the revenue from the levy was applied. Since the revenue from the levy benefited both domestic products intended for the domestic market and domestic products intended for export, the criteria set out in *Carmine Capolongo* v *Azienda Agricole Maya* Case 77/72 [1973] ECR 611, as further explained in *Fratelli Cucchi* v *Avez SpA* Case 77/76 [1977] ECR 987; *Interzuccheri SpA* v *Societa Rezzano e Cavassa* Case 105/76 [1977] ECR 1029; *Sanders Adour SNC and Guyomarc'h Orthez Nutrition Animale SA* v *Directeur des Services Fiscaux des Pyrenées-Atlantiques* Joined Cases C–149 and 150/91 [1991] ECR I–4337, were not satisfied. Consequently, the levy in question was excluded from the scope of art 25 EC. The ECJ accepted that the levy formed part of a general system of taxation of Danish agricultural products. In the light of the fact that the advantage accruing to the taxed national products processed and marketed on the national market from the use of the revenue generated by the levy had offset only partially the burden borne by those products, the levy in question was in breach of the prohibition of discrimination laid down by art 90 EC.

At first glance, the classification of the levy at issue as a discriminatory internal tax seems perfectly reasonable. However, this is a new and surprising solution in the light of the circumstances of the case. Indeed, the prohibition set out in art 90 EC has always been applied in respect of imported products. Article 90 EC expressly states that:

'... no Member State shall impose, directly or indirectly, on the products of other Member States any internal taxation of any kind in excess of that imposed directly or indirectly on similar domestic products.'

In the above case the situation was that, under Danish law, discriminatory tax had been imposed on domestic products intended for export.

The ECJ justified the extension of the prohibition set out in art 90 EC to exported goods by reference to the *Larsen et Kjerulff Case* Case 142/77 [1978] ECR 1543, a case that stands alone and which provides that art 90 EC 'must be interpreted as also prohibiting any tax discrimination against products intended for export to other Member States'. Probably, this broad interpretation of art 90 EC can be explained by the fact that, notwithstanding the silence of the EC Treaty in this respect, art 90 EC should be interpreted as a separate but complementary provision to art 25 EC, and therefore should also seek to:

> '... fill in any breaches which a fiscal measure might open in the prohibitions laid down, by prohibiting the imposition on imported products of internal taxation in excess of that imposed on domestic products.' (*Sociaal Fonds* v *Brachfeld and Chougol Diamond Co* Cases 2 and 3/69 [1969] ECR 211.)

Notwithstanding this reasoning, it remains that the ECJ's teleological interpretation of art 90 EC, that is based on the objective of the achievement of the common market, is as far away as possible from the literal interpretation of art 90 EC.

Similar considerations must have guided the ECJ when it referred to *Celulose Beira Industrial SA* v *Fazenda Pública* Case C–266/91 [1993] ECR I–4337 in order to assess whether the levy in question was compatible with art 90 EC. In this respect, the ECJ stated that when the advantage accruing to the taxed national products, processed and marketed on the national market, from the use of the revenue generated by the charge offsets only partially the burden borne by those products and thus adversely affects exported domestic products, the charge levied on the exported products, which is in principle lawful, will have to be prohibited to the extent to which it partially compensates the charge borne by the product processed or marketed on the national market, and will have to be reduced proportionally: *Industria Gomma Articoli Vari IGAV* v *Ente Nazionale per la Cellulosa e per la Carta (ENCC)* Case 94/74 [1975] ECR 699.

The ECJ emphasised that it would be the task of the referring court to establish the extent of any discrimination against exported products. For that purpose, the referring court must check the financial equivalence of the total amounts levied on national products processed or marketed on the domestic market in connection with the levy in question, and the advantage afforded exclusively to those products, during the relevant period. Consequently, if:

> '... it appears ... that the production of pigs for slaughter on the domestic market derives from the revenue provided by the Fund, which is the body which receives the levy in issue in the main proceedings, a benefit that is proportionally greater than the production of pigs for live export to another Member State, the levy will have to be considered to constitute discriminatory internal taxation prohibited by art 95 of the Treaty [art 90 EC] insofar as the use made of its revenue compensates in part the charge imposed on pigs bred for slaughter on the domestic market.'

Double taxation under the EC Treaty

The second interesting aspect of the commented case concerns the matter of double taxation. Indeed, Mr Nygård was required to pay a double tax, one in Denmark and the other in Germany, in respect of the same product. He argued that under German law pigs which were imported live to Germany and transferred to primary production in that State were considered as pigs bred in Germany, with the result that, in the event of their being subsequently slaughtered, a levy was imposed on them which corresponded to the Danish levy on pigs intended for slaughter within Denmark. The ECJ answered that in the absence of harmonisation of national tax systems at Community level, double taxation is allowed under the EC Treaty: *Firma Herbert Schabatke GmbH* v *Federal Republic of Germany* Case C–72/92 [1993] ECR I–5509. The ECJ stressed that EC law, as it stands now, does not prohibit the effects of double taxation, even though the elimination of such effects is desirable in the interest of the free movement of goods. This means that unless the double tax constitutes discriminatory internal taxation prohibited by art 90 EC, this provision cannot be relied upon to solve the problem of disparities and discrepancies of national taxation systems. Such a problem can only be resolved in the context of the harmonisation of national taxation systems at Community level: *Commission* v *Denmark* Case 171/78 [1980] ECR 447; *Commission* v *Ireland* Case 55/79 [1980] ECR 481.

The jurisdiction of a national court to review the compatibility of state aid approved by the EC Commission in the context of directly effective provisions of the EC Treaty other than arts 87 and 88 EC

The situation where a tax imposed by a Member State forms, at the same time, part of an aid scheme in that Member State has been previously examined by the ECJ. It has been well established that such a tax can be assessed cumulatively, on the one hand, under arts 25 or 90 EC: that is, it can be classified as a charge having equivalent effect to customs duties or can constitute discriminatory internal tax within the meaning of art 90 EC, and on the other hand, in the context of art 87 EC. In the commented case, however, the referring court found itself in a peculiar situation: the levy scheme was authorised by the European Commission pursuant to art 88(3) EC. Subsequently, the referring court asked the ECJ whether it had jurisdiction to review the compatibility of state aid in the context of directly effective provisions of the EC Treaty, other than arts 87 and 88 EC.

The ECJ has already recognised that discriminatory parafiscal charges are not exempt from the scope of application of art 90 EC merely because, at the same time, they may constitute a means of financing state aid: *Commission* v *Italy* Case 73/77 [1980] ECR 1533; *Pabst et Richarz KG* v *Hauptzollamt Oldenburg* Case 17/81 [1982] ECR 1331. Both arts 88 and 90 EC pursue the same objective and are complementary. However, the difficulty lies in the determination, in concreto, of the extent of control that a national court may exercise in respect of the state aid schemes, taking into account the competence of the European Commission deriving from arts 87 and 88 EC, that is the fact that under those provisions the European Commission has exclusive competence to assess the compatibility of the state aid with the common market. In this respect the ECJ stressed that:

'... the national courts and the Commission fulfil complementary and separate roles within the actual system of supervision of state aid established by the Treaty [EC Treaty], the same applies, a fortiori, where what is in issue is the examination of a parafiscal charge, intended to finance an aid scheme, in the light of Treaty provisions other than those concerning state aid, with a view to remedying, if necessary, infringements of Community law which have not been confirmed in the procedure provided for under art 93 of the Treaty [art 88 EC].'

The ECJ emphasised that national courts are the best placed to gather relevant information and to carry out the assessment required in respect of data which should normally follow from the accounts and other documents relating to the management of the national bodies which collect the levy and allocate subsidies and other benefits. Such assessment by national courts guarantees that individuals' rights deriving from the direct effect of provisions of the EC Treaty prohibiting parafiscal charges (such as arts 25 and 90 EC) are protected. Such assessment, however, should not encroach on the exclusive competences of the European Commission under arts 87 and 88 EC. Consequently, the role of the European Commission is to determine whether an aid scheme is compatible with the common market, taking into account its economic and social nature, which must be assessed within a Community context, whilst national courts must carry out their assessment in the light of the overall domestic taxation system of which that levy forms part.

OBP Textbook page 254, section 13.6.

The Prohibition on Quantitative Restrictions and Equivalent Measures

Justifying QRs and distinctly applied MEQRs

Merck, Sharp & Dohme GmbH v *Paranova Pharmazeutika Handels GmbH* Case C–443/99 [2002] ECR I–3703 European Court of Justice

Boehringer Ingelheim KG, Boehringer Ingelheim Pharma KG (together Boehringer), Glaxo Group Ltd (Glaxo), SmithKline Beecham plc, Beecham Group plc and SmithKline & French Laboratories Ltd (together SmithKline), The Wellcome Foundation Ltd (Wellcome) and Eli Lilly and Co (Eli Lilly) v *Swingward Ltd (Swingward) and Dowelhurst Ltd (Dowelhurst)* Case C–143/00 [2002] ECR I–3759 European Court of Justice

Trade marks – art 7(2) of Directive 89/104/EEC – exhaustion of rights conferred by the trade mark – pharmaceutical products – parallel importations – re-packaging of the trade-marked products

Facts
Merck, Sharp & Dohme GmbH v *Paranova Pharmazeutika Handels GmbH* Case
C–443/99
Merck, the owner of a trade mark for 'Proscar', a pharmaceutical product intended
for the treatment of benign prostatic hyperplasis, had marketed it in Austria.
Paranova Group, taking advantage of the price difference for Proscar (ie it was less
expensive in Spain) intended to import it from Spain and put it on the Austrian
market. Paranova Group obtained authorisation from the Austrian authorities to
proceed. Subsequently, Paranova Group bought Proscar in Spain and had it re-
packaged in Denmark by Paranova-Pack A/S, a company belonging to the Paranova
Group. The re-packaging consisted of giving the product new outer packaging,
namely a new box, and attaching to it new annexes translated into German, setting
out information, precautions for use and requirements for marketing in Austria. The
packaging used in Austria and in Spain contained two blister strips and 14 tablets
each.

On 15 July 1998 Paranova Group notified Merck of its intention to put on the
market in Austria imports of Proscar, together with a sample of the re-packaged
product. Merck opposed the use of the trade mark Proscar in the situation where
the product was packaged in the same manner in the Member State of origin and in
the Member State of export, that is with the same number of strips and tablets.

Paranova Group argued that, inter alia, the Austrian authorities recommended re-
packaging and not mere over-sticking, and that attached labels would have an
appreciable effect on the sale of Proscar in Austria, taking into account that re-
labelled foreign packs engender reactions of mistrust and rejection from both
pharmacists and consumers.

The Commercial Court in Vienna granted an injunction to Merck preventing
Paranova Group from marketing re-packaged Proscar (it held that it was possible for
Paranova Group to put labels on all six sides of the pack without impeding the
marketing of Proscar). Paranova Group appealed to the Oberlandesgericht in Vienna,
which decided to stay proceedings and asked the ECJ to interpret art 7(2) of
Directive 89/104/EEC.

Boehringer Ingelheim KG etc v *Swingward Ltd and Dowelhurst Ltd* Case C–143/00
The facts were similar to the above case, in that Boehringer and others, who had
marketed a number of pharmaceutical products under a trade mark, had tried to
prevent Swingward and others from embarking on the parallel importation of those
products into the UK. The defendants had altered the packaging of the products
concerned and the instruction leaflets going with them in order to market them in
the UK. Depending upon the products, the re-packaging was done in various ways,
such as:

1. in some cases, a label setting out certain essential information, such as the name
   of the parallel importer, etc, had been attached to the original package but the
   trade mark and wording in languages other than English remained visible;

2. in some cases, the product had been re-packaged in boxes designed by the parallel importer on which the trade mark was reproduced;

3. in some cases, the product had been re-packaged in boxes designed by the parallel importer, but the original trade mark, the generic name of the product, the identity of the manufacturer and the parallel importer were inside the box.

Irrespective of the manner of re-packaging, the boxes contained an information leaflet in English which bore the trade mark. The claimants brought proceedings against the defendants for trade mark infringements, arguing that the changes in packaging were contrary to EC law.

The High Court referred a number of questions to the ECJ concerning the interpretation of art 7(2) of Directive 89/104/EEC in respect of the above circumstances, in particular in respect of the requirement of prior notice to the trade mark proprietor by the parallel importer that the re-packaged product is to be put on sale in a Member State of importation in the situation where the intended re-packaging does not prejudice the specific subject matter of the trade mark. Also, the High Court asked the ECJ to provide some clarifications as to the notice itself, and the consequences of failure to give notice.

Held

In *Merck* the ECJ held that the replacement packaging of pharmaceutical products is necessary if, without such re-packaging, effective access to the market concerned, or a substantial part of that market, must be considered to be hindered as a result of strong resistance from a significant proportion of consumers to re-labelled pharmaceutical products.

In *Boehringer* the ECJ held that an owner of a trade-marked product may rely on his trade mark rights in order to prevent a parallel importer from re-packaging products, unless the exercise of those rights contributes to artificial partitioning of the market between Member States. The ECJ confirmed the requirement of prior notice to the owner of a trade mark by the parallel importer in respect of the intended re-packaging. In the event of a dispute, it is the task of a national court to assess, in the light of all relevant circumstances, whether the proprietor had a reasonable time to react to the intended re-packaging. Also, the ECJ confirmed the circumstances in which re-packaging of pharmaceutical products becomes necessary under EC law (see *Merck*, above).

Comment

In both cases the ECJ provided important clarifications concerning the interpretation of art 30 EC and art 7(2) of Directive 89/104/EEC of 21 December 1988 to Approximate the Laws of the Member States Relating to Trade Marks (OJ 1989 L40, p1) as amended by the agreement on the European Economic Area of 2 May 1992 (OJ 1994 L1, p3), in particular in respect of the re-packaging of pharmaceutical products by parallel importers without the consent of a trade mark owner. This matter was previously examined by the ECJ in a number of cases, especially *Bristol-*

Myers Squibb and Others v *Paranova* Cases C–427, 429 and 436/93 [1996] ECR
I–3457 in which the ECJ stated that re-packaging is allowed if:

1. it does not adversely affect the original condition of the product;
2. the new packaging clearly states the name of the manufacturer and the person
   who has re-packaged the product;
3. the re-packaging is not such as to damage the trade mark's reputation; and
4. the re-packager gives notice of its intention to the trade mark owner and supplies
   samples if requested.

In the context of both cases it is important to refer to art 7 of Directive
89/104/ECC, which provides:

> '1. The trade mark shall not entitle the proprietor to prohibit its use in relation to goods
> which have been put on the market in the Community under that trade mark by the
> proprietor or with his consent.
> 2. Paragraph 1 shall not apply where there exist legitimate reasons for the proprietor to
> oppose further commercialisation of the goods, especially where the condition of the goods
> is changed or impaired after they have been put on the market.'

In *Merck* the ECJ was asked to ascertain whether a trade mark owner of a
pharmaceutical product was allowed to prevent the re-packaging by a parallel
importer on the ground that the re-packaging was not necessary for the marketing of
that product in the importing Member State, even though the parallel importer
claimed that without such re-packaging the marketability of the product would be
hindered, taking into account the reluctance of a significant proportion of consumers
of that State to buy a product clearly intended for the market of another Member
State.

Both parties submitted interesting arguments. Merck argued that the matter was
already resolved by the ECJ in *Pharmacia & Upjohn SA* v *Paranova A/S* Case
C–379/97 [1999] ECR I–6927, in which the ECJ stated that a parallel importer
could not justify the re-packaging of an imported product on the ground that some
inconvenience, such as the necessity of overcoming the resistance of consumers to
re-labelled products, required the re-packaging. Paranova Group argued that the
obligation to attach labels constituted an obstacle to the marketing of imported
products and led to an unacceptable partitioning of the common market. Paranova
Group also claimed that, provided the requirements in *Bristol-Myers Squibb and
Others* (above) were met, a parallel importer should be free to re-package the product
concerned, especially in the circumstances where the authorities of the Member
State of importation so required.

The ECJ elucidated the concept of 'necessity' of re-packaging. The Court stated
that such necessity exists, for example, where a parallel importer cannot place
pharmaceutical products on the market in the State of importation because national
law requires their re-packaging, or where national sickness insurance rules make
reimbursement of medical expenses conditional upon certain packaging, or where

well established medical prescription practices are based, inter alia, on standard sizes recommended by professional bodies or sickness insurance institutions. The mere fact that a substantial proportion of consumers in the State of importation will refuse to buy re-labelled foreign packs is not sufficient to re-package pharmaceutical products. It all depends on whether or not such resistance to re-labelled pharmaceutical products constitutes a real impediment to effective access to the market concerned. If so, the re-packaging is necessary. It is the task of the national court to ascertain whether or not strong resistance from a significant proportion of consumers in the State of importation constitutes an impediment to effective market access for the pharmaceutical products concerned. The ECJ emphasised that the trade mark owner may oppose the re-packaging in the situation where the parallel importer, by re-packaging, seeks to secure a commercial advantage.

In *Boehringer* the ECJ confirmed the requirement of prior notice in all circumstances. The ECJ explained that the requirement of prior notice has been set out to fulfil a very important purpose, that is to safeguard the legitimate interests of trade mark owners.

The parallel importer himself must give notice to the trade mark owner of the intended re-packaging. It is not sufficient that the owner is notified by other sources. If the parallel importer fails to give notice, the trade mark owner may oppose the marketing of the re-packaged pharmaceutical products.

As to the period of notice given to the owner to react to the intended re-packaging, the ECJ stated that the proprietor of the trade mark must have a reasonable time to react. What should be considered as a reasonable time depends upon all the relevant circumstances, which the national court should assess in the event of a dispute. Due attention must be paid to the interests of the parallel importer, who will want to put the product concerned on the market in the State of importation as soon as possible after completing the necessary formalities in that State. The ECJ stated that on the basis of evidence before the Court, a period of 15 working days seemed likely to constitute such a reasonable time where the parallel importer gives notice to the trade mark owner together with a sample of the re-packaged pharmaceutical products. The ECJ emphasised that the period of 15 days was purely indicative.

OBP Textbook page 267, section 14.3.

15

Evidence

Introduction

Relevance

Prejudicial effect of irrelevant material

R v Byrne [2002] Crim LR 487 Court of Appeal (Criminal Division)
(Kennedy LJ, Aitkens and Pitchford JJ)

Material that was irrelevant or not sufficiently relevant to the case as put – generally speaking should be excluded, especially if it was likely to prejudice a defendant

Facts

The appellant was convicted of the manslaughter of Terence Bush. The victim's wife witnessed the killing and her evidence was that the appellant and his two brothers all had knives and that all three attacked and stabbed her husband, thereby killing him. The brothers were tried separately, and one was convicted of murder and one of manslaughter. The appellant, however, fled to Ireland and was extradited after his brothers' trials. He was then convicted of manslaughter. That conviction was quashed because of a material misdirection by the trial judge, and a retrial was ordered. At the retrial, the jury failed to reach a verdict and the prosecution proceeded to a second retrial.

At the appellant's first trial the prosecution case had been that all three brothers were engaged in a joint enterprise to murder Mr Bush. But, as a consequence of the appellant's acquittal of murder, at the third trial the prosecution could not, in practice, advance a case that the appellant had a knife and stabbed Mr Bush with it. To do so might suggest that the prosecution was going behind the jury's verdict. Accordingly, the prosecution had to advance a case that the appellant was a secondary party to a joint enterprise of the three brothers to commit an unlawful attack on Terence Bush. The defence put forward by the appellant was that he was present at the time of the attack but he took no part in it. His evidence was that he was trying to restrain his brother Dennis from stabbing Mr Bush, but he was unable to do so. The only person who saw the attack on Mr Bush was his wife, Mrs Maureen Bush. Her evidence at all three trials of the appellant was to the same effect, which was that the appellant had a knife and actually used it on Mr Bush with murderous intent. This was quite contrary to the way that the prosecution was putting its case against the appellant at the second retrial. The prosecution case was that he did not have a knife and did not stab Mr Bush at all, let alone with any intent to kill or to do really serious bodily harm to him. Therefore, the only part of Mrs Bush's evidence that was probative of the prosecution case as put was that the appellant was present at the attack and that he did not restrain his brother Dennis or attempt to do so.

The argument raised by the defence on appeal was as follows: (1) the evidence of Mrs Bush, particularly that concerning the appellant having a knife and stabbing Mr Bush in the stomach, is irrelevant to the way in which the prosecution put its case against the appellant at the second retrial; (2) therefore such evidence is inadmissible; and (3) further, the irrelevant evidence of Mrs Bush is so prejudicial to the appellant that whatever directions the jury was given about its reliability, or the contrary evidence of the pathologist, the jury was bound to be affected by Mrs Bush's evidence, so that the appellant could not have a fair trial.

Held

As a general rule the prosecution is entitled to adduce evidence that is sufficiently relevant to an issue in the case as advanced by the prosecution. But all that is irrelevant, or is not sufficiently relevant to the case as put should, generally speaking, be excluded. The second part of this principle must be particularly observed where the admission of irrelevant evidence (which, by definition, is not probative of the alleged offence) is likely to be prejudicial to the defendant. The evidence of Mrs Bush that the appellant had a knife and used it to stab Mr Bush in the attack was irrelevant to the prosecution case; it was therefore inadmissible and was damaging to the defendant, so that it was mere prejudice. The Court concluded that the admission of that evidence served no purpose in fact other than to incline the jury to think badly of the defendant. As the Court had no idea how the jury reacted to this irrelevant, inadmissible and prejudicial evidence, their Lordships felt bound to conclude that the conviction of manslaughter was unsafe, and accordingly the conviction was therefore quashed.

Comment

Dennis (*The Law of Evidence*, Sweet and Maxwell, 2002) notes that although it is inadmissible, where irrelevant evidence has been admitted for the prosecution, the Court of Appeal is unlikely to find a conviction unsafe unless the evidence is prejudicial to the appellant. In this case, the Court found that the evidence was 'mere prejudice', with the result described above. However, the Court commented that the prosecution was put in a very difficult position given the unique facts of this case.

OBP Textbook page 1, section 1.1.

Corroboration

Problem areas

Lies

R v *Barnett* [2002] Crim LR 489 Court of Appeal (Criminal Division)
(Rose LJ, Jackson and Owen JJ)

Absence of a *Lucas* direction will not necessarily make a conviction unsafe

Facts

The defendant was convicted of handling stolen goods after the police found a painting worth £40,000 under his bed. His explanation for the discovery was that he had found the painting whilst walking his dog. At interview, the defendant said that he was storing the painting for a friend and that he did not know that it was stolen. When the defendant gave evidence at trial, he put forward another version of events. The trial judge summarized the reasons why the prosecution contended that the defendant must have known or believed that the painting was stolen. One of these was that the defendant had told three different stories. The judge did not go on to give a *Lucas* direction (*R* v *Lucas* [1981] QB 720) and the defendant relied on that in his appeal.

Held

The purpose of giving the *Lucas* direction is to avoid the risk that the jury will assume that lying demonstrates, and is consistent only with, a desire to conceal guilt: it intends to prevent the jury from leaping from the conclusion that the defendant has lied to the further conclusion that he must therefore be guilty. Where, however, there is no risk that the jury will follow this forbidden chain of reasoning, there is no need for a *Lucas* direction. No issue of alibi, corroboration or identification arose, and the prosecution had not relied on any of the defendant's specific lies as evidence of guilt.

Comment

The Court commented that in almost every trial where the defendant gives evidence, the prosecution contend that the defendant is telling lies in the witness box. In the great majority of these trials, a *Lucas* direction is inappropriate.

OBP Textbook page 74, section 2.6.

Burden and Standard of Proof

Burden of proof – criminal cases

R v *Drummond* [2002] Crim LR 666 Court of Appeal (Criminal Division) (Longmore LJ, Johnson J and Judge Sir Rhys Davies QC)

Reversal of the burden of proof in s15 Road Traffic Act 1988 – whether this contravenes the European Convention on Human Rights

Facts

The defendant was convicted of causing death by careless driving with excess alcohol contrary to s3A Road Traffic Act 1988. So far as the level of alcohol in his blood was concerned, he asserted that he had had some alcohol prior to the accident, but had also had more alcohol afterwards. He appealed against conviction on the ground that the provision in s15 of the 1988 Act, which placed the burden of proving when the alcohol was taken on the defendant and also required the defendant to show that, but for that drink, his specimen would not have been over the limit, infringed the presumption of innocence in art 6(2) European Convention on Human Rights, which provides that everyone charged with a criminal offence shall be presumed innocent until proven guilty according to law.

Held

It is not the case that all apparently persuasive burdens have to be 'read down' to be evidential burdens. It is necessary to look at the legislation as a whole to see whether Parliament intended to impose a persuasive burden and whether such a burden is justifiable.

Both *R* v *Lambert* [2001] 3 WLR 206 and *R* v *Carass* (Judgment of 19 December 2001, not yet reported) were distinguished on the basis that, for the offence of driving with excess alcohol, it was not necessary to ascertain the defendant's intention. Conviction followed an exact scientific test, and if the accused drank after the event it was he who defeated the aim of the legislature by making the test potentially unreliable. Further, the relevant scientific evidence to set against the specimen result was within the knowledge or means of access of the accused rather than the Crown. This evidence will include:

1. the amount which the accused had to drink after the incident;
2. what is called his 'blood-breath ratio', which is important for calculating the rate at which his body absorbs alcohol;
3. the rate at which his body eliminates alcohol over time; and
4. his body weight.

The legislative interference with the presumption of innocence in s15 of the 1988 Act amounted to an imposition of a persuasive burden on the defendant, and that interference was not only justified but was no greater than necessary: *R* v *Lambert* [2001] 3 WLR 206 applied.

Comment

The Court drew an interesting analogy with the defence of diminished responsibility, which also depends on material to be supplied by the defendant. The Court of Appeal has previously held that the requirement that a defendant has the burden of proving diminished responsibility in a murder case does not infringe art 6(2) of the Convention: *R* v *Lambert, Ali and Jordan* [2001] 2 WLR 211.

OBP Textbook page 79, section 3.2.

Standard of proof – criminal cases

Appropriate direction to the jury

R v *Stephens* (2002) The Times 27 June Court of Appeal (Criminal Division) (Keene LJ, Davis J and the Recorder of Cardiff)

It is not helpful to the jury to draw a distinction between being sure of guilt and being certain of guilt

Facts

The defendant was convicted of wounding with intent after a trial at which the issue had been whether the attack was unprovoked or whether the defendant had acted in self-defence. In his summing up, the judge dealt with the burden and standard of proof, stating that before jurors could convict, they had to be satisfied so that they were sure of guilt, which was the same as being satisfied beyond reasonable doubt. During their deliberations, the jurors sent out a note asking the following questions: (1) what constituted reasonable doubt; and (2) how certain did they have to be? The judge replied as follows: (1) a reasonable doubt was the sort of doubt that might affect the mind of a person dealing with matters of importance in his own affairs; and (2) jurors did not have to be certain, they had to be sure, which was less than being certain.

The sole ground of appeal was that, in ordinary speech, there is no distinction between being sure and being certain, so that the judge's direction might have confused the jury: the judge should have said no more than that jurors had to be satisfied so that they were sure.

Held

It was not helpful to the jury to seek to draw a distinction between being sure of guilt and being certain of guilt. However, the judge had emphasised that the jury had to be sure of guilt before it could convict, and repeated the indication that if the jury concluded that the defendant might not have intentionally caused really serious bodily harm, it should acquit. Nothing emerged from the jury to suggest that it was confused.

Comment

The failure of the judge to direct the jury properly on the issue of the standard of proof is fatal to a conviction; there is no power to remit the case for a retrial and many judges have fallen into error by trying to define what is meant by a reasonable doubt. The Court of Appeal has stressed that judges should not try to define what is meant by reasonable doubt. Lord Goddard CJ expressed concern about the use of the phrase 'reasonable doubt' because that formula often prompts the jury to ask what is a reasonable doubt, in the way that happened here: *R* v *Summers* (1953) 36 Cr App R 14. Lord Goddard went on to say that the better direction is that the jury should be satisfied so that they are sure. Judges often combine the two approved formuli by directing the jury that 'the case must be proved beyond reasonable doubt which means that you must be satisfied so that you are sure before you may convict'. This adopts the dictum from Lord Scarman in *Ferguson* v *R* [1979] 1 WLR 94. It is imperative that the judge gives a clear direction on the incidence of the burden of proof and makes it clear to the jury that they may not convict unless they are sure of guilt. If that is done, there is no need for the judge to use any particular form of words and, on any appeal, the effect of the summing up as a whole will be considered.

OBP Textbook page 94, section 3.4.

Character

Judge's direction as to character

R v *Mauricia* [2002] Crim LR 655 Court of Appeal (Criminal Division) (Longmore LJ, Johnson J and Judge Sir Rhys Davies QC)

Whether preliminary ruling on admissibility of convictions required

Facts

The appellant was convicted of knowingly importing a prohibited Class A drug, namely ecstasy, and sentenced to ten years' imprisonment. A customs officer stopped the appellant when he arrived in England from Holland and found a secret panel in his bag which contained 9,510 ecstasy tablets, worth an estimated £95,100. The issue for the jury was whether the appellant knew the drugs were in his bag. The appellant claimed he had been duped into bringing the drugs into the country. His credibility was central to his defence and he wished to present himself to the jury as a man of good character, saying he had no convictions in Holland for drug offences or any offences of dishonesty. He said he only had driving offences recorded against him.

The Crown served documentation which they said went to prove three convictions recorded against the appellant in 1985 for attempted theft, handling stolen goods and forgery. The appellant disputed the convictions. A number of applications followed and counsel for the appellant asked the judge to rule on whether the convictions would be admitted before the close of the Crown's evidence, so that he could advise the appellant whether to give evidence. The judge ruled that it was inappropriate to decide the issue unless and until it arose at trial. Counsel continued to raise the matter and seek a ruling. He pointed out that the convictions the Crown sought to prove, in an English context, would be regarded as spent convictions and consequently he relied on *R* v *Nye* (1982) 75 Cr App R 247, which held that the best course where spent convictions were in issue was to obtain the judge's ruling at the outset of the case. The judge still postponed his ruling until such time as the appellant put himself forward as a man of good character. He did, however, indicate that if the prosecution were able to prove the convictions, he would not be prepared to give a modified good character direction on the basis of the age of the convictions.

The appellant gave evidence and said he had no convictions in Holland for drug offences or dishonesty. A voir dire then took place as to the admission of the convictions. The Crown sought to prove the convictions by adducing certified certificates of judgment from Holland and fingerprint records, producing forensic analysis confirming that the fingerprints relating to the convictions matched the appellant's. The appellant submitted that proof by fingerprint evidence under s39 Criminal Evidence Act 1948 did not apply where the conviction was a foreign conviction. The judge ruled that counsel for the prosecution could rely on the fingerprint evidence and allowed the evidence of the 16-year-old conviction to be admissible. The appellant admitted the convictions under cross-examination. He submitted on appeal that the judge should have made a ruling at the beginning of the case as to whether he was entitled to be treated as a man of good character, and that a foreign conviction could not be proved by fingerprint evidence.

Held

The judge's ruling not to decide whether the appellant would be treated as a man of good character unless and until the matter arose at trial was the correct way to deal with the situation. It would only have been relevant to prove the appellant's previous convictions if he had put himself forward as a man of good character. The appellant had no business to ask for a ruling, in advance of putting forward good character evidence, as to whether the Crown could prove his previous convictions, since it would only enable him, if a ruling was given in his favour, to go into the witness box and lie about his convictions. Further, it was not for the judge to declare whether the Crown was able to prove or had proved its case. That, if necessary, was a matter for the jury on the totality of evidence. Following *R* v *Dempster* [2001] EWCA Crim 571, it was for the defendant, not the court, to decide how to run his case. The defendant had to decide whether he was going to put himself forward as a man of good character.

Under s7 Evidence Act 1851, the Crown could rely on examined copies of convictions to prove foreign convictions. However, the Crown still had to prove that the examined copies of the convictions related to the appellant. That could be proved by any admissible evidence in the ordinary way. Evidence of fingerprints was easily the most sensible way to proceed, and there was nothing in the 1851 Act or elsewhere to suggest that proceeding by way of fingerprint evidence was in any way inadmissible. Provided that fingerprint evidence was otherwise admissible it could be used to prove the foreign conviction.

Comment
There is now extensive case law surrounding the issue of good character directions.

Failure to mention good character

Sealey v *Trinidad and Tobago; Headley* v *Trinidad and Tobago* (2002) The Times 5 November Privy Council (Lords Hoffmann, Hope of Craighead, Hutton, Rodger of Earlsferry and Sir Philip Otton)

Good character – failure of counsel for the accused to mention good character

Facts
The prosecution case was that the two appellants had stabbed two men during the course of a robbery. One of the men died, and the survivor was one of two principal witnesses for the prosecution at trial. The other principal witness for the prosecution was a policeman, who had known the appellants since childhood and who said that he had seen them during the course of the robbery. Both appellants were convicted of murder and relied on a number of arguments on appeal, including the fact that they had informed their trial counsel that they were of good character before giving evidence, but that no good character evidence was led, so that they were deprived of a good character direction from the judge.

The Court of Appeal rejected this ground of appeal on the basis that it was inconceivable that evidence of good character, backed by a *Vye* direction (*R* v *Vye* [1993] 3 All ER 241) could have resulted in a different verdict, given the strength of the evidence provided by the police officer, which was obviously accepted by the jury.

Held
The crucial matter was that of the credibility of the two appellants and that of the police officer. The appellants were both of previous good character, who said that they were at different places at the time of the robbery and who each produced a witness in support of their alibi. The police officer's evidence made the prosecution's case against the appellants very strong, because his evidence related to his recognition in good light for a reasonable period of time of two young men who were well known to him. The matter for the jury was accordingly whether they were satisfied beyond a reasonable doubt that the police officer was telling the truth and that the appellants were lying. This was the very issue on which a direction as to

credibility and propensity based on good character might have been of considerable importance.

Comment

Delivering the majority judgment, Lord Hutton commented that the importance of credibility may vary according to the factual issue in dispute between a prosecution witness and the accused, but that where the issue in dispute is fundamental to the question of the guilt or innocence of the accused, then whether it relates to non-participation in the offence, or to consent, or to some other defence, the good character direction is an important safeguard to the accused. His Lordship went on to observe that there may be some cases in which the omission of a good character direction does not make a conviction unsafe. The question for the Board in this case was whether the jury would inevitably have convicted had a good character direction been given, and while their Lordships felt that the jury would probably have convicted, that was not enough.

OBP Textbook page 222, section 7.6.

Opinion Evidence

Experts

Attorney-General's Reference (No 2 of 2002) (2002) The Times 17 October Court of Appeal (Criminal Division) (Rose LJ, Pitchers and Treacy JJ)

Interpretation and application of *R* v *Clare; R* v *Peach* [1995] 2 Cr App R 33

Facts

The defendant was tried on indictment for rioting. The Crown sought to prove his identity through two police officers who separately viewed a video film of those involved. As a result of a lengthy viewing of the video, the first officer (D), who became familiar with the appearance of the suspects and was able to recognise the defendant, was presented as a witness with specialist knowledge and no issue was made regarding the admissibility of his evidence. The second officer (P) knew the defendant from previous dealings and recognised him when watching the video. P's evidence was ruled inadmissible by the judge who determined that, as the original evidence had been made available to the jury, they were in a better position than P as they could simultaneously view the film and compare the images with the defendant who was in the dock. Due to the insufficiency of identification evidence against the defendant, the jury were directed to enter a not guilty verdict. The Attorney-General posed three questions for the Court of Appeal.

1. When a suspect was filmed committing an offence, was the evidence of identification by way of recognition from a witness not present at the scene but who knew the defendant and who, having seen the film, identified the suspect as

being the defendant, inadmissible because the film could be played to the jury without calling the witness, and the jury would have the opportunity to compare the defendant in the dock with the suspect on the film and could decide themselves if they were one and the same?

2. For an identification of such a witness to be admissible, was it a requirement of the law that the witness had to have special skills, abilities, experience and knowledge that the jury did not have?

3. If the answer to (2) is 'yes', what should those special skills abilities, experience and knowledge be?

Held

On a review of the authorities there were at least four circumstances in which a jury could be invited to conclude that a defendant committed an offence on the basis of photographic evidence from the scene: (1) where the photographic image was sufficiently clear the jury could compare it with the defendant sitting in the dock (*R v Dodson; R v Williams* [1984] 1 WLR 971); (2) where a witness knew the defendant sufficiently well to recognise him as the offender depicted in the photographic image (*R v Fowden; R v White* [1982] Crim LR 588; *Kajala v Noble* (1982) 75 Cr App R 149; *R v Grimer* [1982] Crim LR 674; *R v Caldwell; R v Dixon* (1993) 99 Cr App R 73; and *R v Blenkinsop* [1995] 1 Cr App R 7), and this might be so even if the photographic image was no longer available for the jury (in *Taylor v Chief Constable of Chester* (1986) 84 Cr App R 191 video film of a thief stealing from a store was accidentally erased after three police officers had viewed it and identified the thief as the defendant); (3) where a witness, who did not know the defendant, spent substantial time viewing and analysing photographic images from the scene, thereby acquiring special knowledge, which the jury did not have, evidence of identification based on comparison between them and a reasonably contemporary photo of the defendant could be given so long as the image and photograph were available to the jury (*R v Clare; R v Peach* [1995] 2 Cr App R 33); (4) a suitably qualified expert with facial mapping skills giving opinion evidence of identification based on a comparison between images from the scene and a reasonably contemporary photo of the defendant could be given, so long as the image and photograph were available to the jury: *R v Stockwell* (1993) 92 Cr App R 260; *R v Clarke* [1995] 2 Cr App R 425; and *R v Hookway* [1999] Crim LR 750.

The answers to the three questions posed by the Attorney-General were: 'no' to the first question; regarding (2) and (3), the answer would need to refer to the knowledge of the witness, which was essentially the basis of the recognition by him. Aside from that knowledge, no special skill, ability or experience was required, save in the situation where the witness did not know the defendant so as to be able to recognise him, but did acquire special skills in relation to those appearing in the video taken at the scene by the frequent playing and analysis of it.

OBP Textbook page 304, section 10.4.

Identification Evidence

Methods of identification

Identification parade

R v *Marrin* (2002) The Times 5 March Court of Appeal (Criminal Division) (Keene LJ, Gage J and Judge Stephens QC)

Identification at a parade – not invalidated because the volunteers wore hats or make-up

Facts

An off duty police officer saw the appellant's co-accused take a cash box from a security man. He chased the co-accused and, while he was struggling with him, felt a vehicle being driven gently into the back of his legs. He later attended an identification parade at which he picked out the appellant as the person driving the vehicle. The case for the prosecution was that the appellant was the getaway driver. At the identification parade, there were eight other men as well as the appellant. In order to reduce disparities in the appearance of the men in terms of their hairline or the appearance of their hair, it was decided by one of the officers that the men should wear baseball caps turned back to front. No objection to this was taken by the appellant or his solicitor. In addition, some form of make-up was used on at least two of the volunteers and possibly as many as four of them. The form that this took was that of colouring or dying of their facial stubble so as to make the hair colouring resemble more closely that of the suspect. The parade took place with all of those taking part being seated. No objection was raised by the appellant or his solicitor to any of the persons paraded or to their appearance.

At trial, objection was taken to the admissibility of evidence of the identification parade, but the judge, having heard evidence on a voir dire, ruled that there had been no breach of Code D, and no substituting by the police of their own procedures instead of the Code, and he ruled also that the parade had been conducted fairly. He therefore allowed the evidence to go before the jury.

In summing up, the judge summarized some of the criticisms of the parade made by the defence, including the placing of caps on all the participants and using make-up on some of the volunteers.

The appellant appealed against conviction on the ground that the constitution and conduct of the parade was flawed, so that evidence of the identification made at the parade should not have been admitted.

Held

Paragraph D.8 of Annex A to the Police and Criminal Evidence Act 1984 provides that: 'The parade shall consist of at least eight people (in addition to the suspect) who so far as possible resemble the suspect in age, height, general appearance and position in life'. The Code and its Annex do not provide in any more detail how that resemblance, 'so far as possible', is to be achieved, but it does not rule out steps being taken to try to achieve that prescribed objective. If steps taken to secure resemblance 'so far as possible' are taken bona fide to achieve that objective, and they are sensible and reasonable steps, then there is no breach.

Comment
The penalty for failing to comply with the many details of the Codes of Practice lies at the discretion of the court to exclude evidence which has been obtained by unfair means.

OBP Textbook page 315, section 11.2.

16

Family Law

Nullity

Transsexuals

Goodwin v *United Kingdom; I* v *United Kingdom* [2002] 2 FLR 487 and 518 European Court of Human Rights

Right of transsexual to marry

Facts
Miss Goodwin (G) was born a male and fathered four children. She went from male to female and lived full time as a woman from 1984 and had irreversible gender re-assignment surgery in 1990. Under English law, she was still male. She claimed that she could not claim a pension or winter fuel allowance at 60, like other women. She faced sexual harassment at work but was unable to sue her employer under English law. She was dismissed on health grounds but insisted that the real reason was because she was a transsexual. When she started work with a new employer she asked for a different NI number so that her new employers could not find out from her previous employers that she had been born male. This request was refused. Her new employers discovered her past and this led to problems at work She was written to by the DSS as a man. She complained that she could not report a theft to the police for fear that a prosecution would reveal her transsexuality. She had to pay higher insurance premiums because she was treated as a man. She also complained about her inability of marry. The UK government submitted that the degree of recognition of G as a female was within the margin of appreciation left to member states under the European Convention on Human Rights.

I was a post-operative male to female transsexual. She complained that she could not find work because she refused to present her birth certificate to a potential employer. She also complained about her inability to marry.

Held
The unsatisfactory situation in which post-operative transsexuals lived in an intermediate zone as not quite one gender or the other was no longer sustainable. That was not to underestimate the difficulties posed and repercussions which any major change in the law would have, not only in the field of birth registration but also for access to records, family law, inheritance, criminal justice, employment and social security. However, these problems were far from insuperable. Society might

reasonably be expected to tolerate a certain inconvenience to enable individuals to live in dignity and worth in accordance with the sexual identity chosen by them at great personal cost.

There was clear and contested evidence of a continuing international trend in favour of not only increased social acceptance of transsexuals but also of legal recognition of the new sexual identity of post-operative transsexuals. Third parties would not would not suffer any material prejudice from any possible changes to the birth register system that might flow from gender re-assignment. The UK government was currently discussing proposals for reform of the registration system in order to allow amendment of civil status data.

The difficulties and anomalies of G and I's situation did not attain the level of daily interference as suffered by the applicant in *B* v *France* [1992] 2 FLR 249. However art 8 of the European Convention on Human Rights emphasised the personal automony of the individual. In the twenty-first century the rights of transsexuals to personal development and to physical and moral security in the full sense judged by others in society could no longer be regarded as a matter of controversy requiring the lapse of time to cast clearer light on the issues involved. Domestic recognition of that evaluation could be found in the report on the Interdepartmental Working Group on Transsexual People and the Court of Appeal's judgment in *Bellinger* v *Bellinger* [2001] 2 FLR 1048.

Despite the Court's reiteration since 1986 and most recently in 1998 of the importance of keeping the need for appropriate legal measures under review having regard to scientific and societal developments, nothing had effectively been done by the UK government. The Court found that the UK government could no longer claim that the matter fell within their margin of appreciation. The fair balance that was inherent in the Convention now tilted decisively in favour of the applicants. There had been a failure to respect G and I's private lives pursuant to art 8.

While art 12 referred in express terms to the right of a man and a woman to marry, the Court was not persuaded that those terms restricted the determination of gender to purely biological criteria. There had been major social changes in the institution of marriage since the adoption of the Convention, as well as dramatic changes brought about by developments in medicine and science in the field of transsexuality. A test of congruent biological factors could no longer be decisive in denying legal recognition to the change of gender of a post-operative transsexual. An inability to conceive or parent a child cannot remove the right to marry. There were other important factors: the acceptance of the condition of gender identity disorder by the medical professions and health authorities within the contracting states; the provision of treatment, including surgery, to assimilate the individual as closely as possible to the gender in which they perceived that they properly belonged; and the assumption by the transsexual of the social role of the assigned gender.

In these cases the applicants lived as women and would only marry men. While it was for the contracting states to determine the conditions under which a person claiming legal recognition as a transsexual established that gender re-assignment had been effected and the form of marriage, the Court found no justification for barring the transsexual from enjoying the right to marry under any circumstances. There had been a breach of art 12.

No compensation was ordered but costs and expenses were awarded.

Comment

Of particular interest is the European Court's decision in relation to the right to marry which was taken despite a lack of consensus amongst European states about whether marriage can include transsexuals. The UK, Ireland, Albania and Andorra currently do not allow transsexuals to change their birth certificates.

In January 2002 leave to appeal to the House of Lords was granted in the case of *Bellinger* v *Bellinger* [2001] 2 FLR 1048. The Interdepartmental Working Group on Transsexual People, set up by the Home Secretary in April 1999, is to be reconvened to give further consideration to the rights of transsexuals. The Working Group originally reported in July 2000 and identified three possible options: retain the status quo; issue birth certificates showing a transsexual's new name and possibly sex; and to grant full recognition of the acquired gender. It made no firm recommendation. The Working Group is due to report later in 2002. The case of *Goodwin* v *United Kingdom; I* v *United Kingdom* will give impetus to their report. In December 2002 the government announced that it will change the law to allow transsexuals to change their birth certificates and to marry in their adopted gender. Such a change in the law is unlikely to come into force until 2004.

OBP Textbook pages 17–20, section 2.2.

Divorce

Divorce statistics

There were 161,580 divorce petitions in 2001 (compared to 657 nullity petitions and 535 judicial separation petitions).

OBP Textbook pages 33–34, section 3.1.

Special provision for Jewish marriages

The Divorce (Religious Marriages) Act 2002 was enacted in July 2002. It inserts s10A into the Matrimonial Causes Act 1973 and applies to Jewish marriages which can only be properly ended by both a divorce under the Matrimonial Causes Act 1973 and a religious divorce according to the usages of Jewish law. Either party petitioning for divorce in such circumstances can ask the court to order that the divorce decree cannot be made absolute until a declaration is produced to the court, made by both parties, that the religious divorce has been obtained. The court can only make such an order if it is satisfied that in all the circumstances of the case it is just and reasonable to do so. The order can be revoked at any time.

OBP Textbook pages 62–63, section 3.12.

The procedure for obtaining a divorce

Please note the Law Society's Family Law Protocol, published in March 2002, which provides for how solicitors should advise clients in the interests of avoiding unnecessary conflict. It advises that petitioners should be encouraged not to name co-respondents in cases of adultery and that respondents should be discouraged from defending divorce petitions or cross-petitioning unless there is good reason to do so.

OBP Textbook pages 63–66, section 3.13.

Jurisdiction and Recognition of Foreign Decrees

Habitual residence

See *Ikimi* v *Ikimi* [2001] 2 FCR 385 in which the Court of Appeal accepted that a woman could be habitually resident under s5(2) Domicile and Matrimonial Proceedings Act 1973 for the purposes of presenting a divorce petition when she was still habitually resident in Nigeria and had only spent 161 days in the UK. 'Ordinary' and 'habitual' were synonymous and a person could have more than one habitual residence at any one time.

OBP Textbook pages 84–86, section 6.1.

Jurisdiction

Brussels II

The Convention on Jurisdiction and the Recognition and Enforcement of Judgments in Matrimonial Matters and in Matters of Parental Responsibility for the Children of Both Spouses (Brussels II) was implemented in March 2001. The Convention deals with jurisdiction and with recognition and enforcement of certain proceedings. These are proceedings relating to divorce, legal separation and annulment and civil proceedings relating to parental responsibility for the children of both spouses on the occasion of divorce, legal separation or annulment. It was signed by all the EU countries apart from Denmark.

In particular Chapter II, art 2 gives uniform jurisdictional rules for the automatic recognition of matrimonial judgments. Jurisdiction is based on the grounds of habitual residence, nationality or domicile in the state in respect of divorce, legal separation or nullity. Jurisdiction in matters of parental responsibility arises where the child is habitually resident in the state: art 3. Generally speaking the country in which proceedings first start has exclusive jurisdiction. If later proceedings are started in another Convention country then that country will refuse jurisdiction. For example, in *A v L (Jurisdiction: Brussels II)* [2002] 1 FLR 1042 F brought proceedings in Spain to appeal against a Spanish order. M brought the child to England and sought to bring fresh proceedings in England. It was held that the English court had no jurisdiction under art 11 of Brussels II (which provides that a second court cannot be seized of an application until the first court's proceedings have been finished).

Chapter III of the Convention deals with recognition and enforcement. Generally UK courts must recognise orders made by other countries who are subject to the Convention.

There will be a Brussels IIB (to come into force in 2003) clarifying and consolidating jurisdictional rules in relation to child contact and residence. Generally the habitual residence of the child will determine jurisdiction.

OBP Textbook pages 88–90, section 6.2.

Recognition of foreign decrees

A bare talaq

In *Sulaiman v Juffali* [2002] 2 FCR 427; [2002] Fam Law 97 H and W were nationals of and domiciled in Saudia Arabia. They were both Muslim and married there in accordance with Sharia law in 1980. In 2001 H pronounced a bare talaq pronounced in England which was then registered in Saudia Arabia. The bare talaq fell foul of s44(1) Family Law Act (FLA) 1986 because it was divorce not obtained through a court. Since the talaq was pronounced in England it could not be an overseas divorce which could otherwise have been recognised under s46 FLA 1986. *Radwan v Radwan (No 2)* [1973] Fam Law 35 and *R v Secretary of State for the Home Department, ex parte Ghulam Fatima* [1986] AC 527 followed.

OBP Textbook pages 92–96, section 6.3.

Ancillary Relief in Divorce, Nullity and Judicial Separation Proceedings

Procedure

The Financial Dispute Resolution (FDR) appointment was discussed by the Court of Appeal in *Rose v Rose* [2002] 1 FLR 978. The Court held that an FDR appointment could narrow the issues and dispel unrealistic expectations but could not be a substitute for a contested trial. The only possible results from an FDR would be an adjournment of the FDR, a consent order or directions to progress the case to a final hearing. In *Rose* v *Rose* the parties disputed the terms of a clean break settlement. At the FDR lengthy submissions were made and the judge indicated what the broad outcome would be if the case was listed for trial. The parties then agreed on an order. Before the order was drawn up H indicated that he was not happy with it and did not consider the agreement to be a final court order. The judge agreed with H. W appealed. The appeal was allowed since the whole purpose and effect of an FDR would be lost or compromised if parties were free to analyse and re-evaluate a crucial decision. The order agreed at the FDR was confirmed.

OBP Textbook pages 102–103, section 7.1.

The impact of *White* v *White*

A number of cases have explained the impact of *White* v *White* [2002] 2 FLR 981. In *Cordle* v *Cordle* [2002] 1 FLR 207 the Court of Appeal explained that there is no rule in *White* v *White* that equality must be achieved unless there are good reasons to justify otherwise. The cross check of equality of outcome is intended to be a safeguard against discrimination. The first duty of the court is to apply the s25 Matrimonial Causes Act (MCA) 1973 criteria in search of a fair outcome. Courts will look first to the housing needs of the parties. Homes are of fundamental importance and there is nothing more awful than homelessness. In the ordinary case the court's first concern will be to provide a home for the primary carer and the children (whose welfare is the first consideration). This may absorb all that is immediately available. Where there is sufficient to go beyond that, the court's concern will be to provide the means for the absent parent to rehouse. Another factor will be buttressing the ability and opportunity to work. One party may need capital provision to enable him or her to get back into the labour market or to retrain or to modernise a skill which, through the years of the marriage, has grown rusty. In the case W received £125,000 of the proceeds of sale of the family home and H £55,000.

In *L* v *L* *(Financial Provision: Contributions)* [2002] 2 FCR 413 W received 37.5 per cent of the assets. This was held to be a fair outcome, which departed from the yardstick of equality in deference to the special contribution of H to the family's wealth. It also recognised in full W's contribution, whose help and support allowed H the freedom to make the most of his skills.

In *B* v *B* [2002] Fam Law 173 the only available asset to H and W were the proceeds of sale of the former family home of £124,000. The eight-year-old daughter lived with W. All the proceeds were transferred to W. W was in receipt of state benefits. H appealed, arguing that applying *White* v *White* he should receive a share of the proceeds either immediately or via a *Mesher* order: *Mesher* v *Mesher* [1980] 1 All ER 126. The appeal was dismissed. First consideration has to be given to the welfare of the child. There was only just enough to house W and the child.

Considering all the factors in s25(2) MCA 1973, the overriding features were s25(2)(f) (the care of the child) and (g) (H's conduct in not disclosing his assets and failing to support his child). There were plainly good reasons for departing from equity.

By contrast in *HJ* v *HJ (Financial Provision: Equality)* [2002] 1 FLR 415 an equal division was ordered in relation to assets of £2.7 million. H's role as breadwinner and W's role as home-maker and parent over 25 years of marriage were of equal standing. There was nothing special or exceptional about H's contribution. There were sufficient resources for an equal division. No account was taken of H's child from his new relationship since that was his choice and his responsibility.

Also in *Lambert* v *Lambert* [2002] 3 FCR 673 a 50 per cent division was ordered. H and W had been married for 23 years and had two financially independent children. The family wealth amounted to £20.2 million. H offered W a 30 per cent share of the family wealth on the basis that he had made a special contribution to the company which provided the family wealth. W claimed a 50 per cent share because of her contribution as a wife and mother, and as a director of the company. The court awarded a 63:37 per cent split in H's favour. W appealed. The Court of Appeal allowed her appeal, holding that it was unacceptable to place greater value on the contribution of the breadwinner than that of the home-maker. The Court criticised disputed and futile evaluation each had made concerning the family wealth. There was a distaste for 'special contributions'. The danger of gender discrimination resulting from special financial contributions was plain, since there would be no equal opportunity for the home-maker to demonstrate the scale of her comparable success. 'Special contribution' remained a legitimate possibility in only exceptional cases.

OBP Textbook pages 107–108, section 7.6.

Section 25(2)(a): a spouse's true earnings

See *Al Khatid* v *Masry* [2002] Fam Law 420 in which the court drew inferences on compelling evidence to judge what the assets of the husband were. The husband was guilty of substantial concealment and deceit. This was also relevant under s25(2)(g) Matrimonial Causes Act 1973 in determining W's award of ancillary relief. Applying *White* v *White* [2002] 2 FLR 981 W was given an award totalling £26 million.

OBP Textbook page 109, section 7.6.

Section 25(2)(g): conduct

In *M* v *M* [2002] Fam Law 177 H and W entered into a pre-nuptial agreement whereby if the marriage ended in divorce W would receive £275,000. After five years of marriage W filed for divorce. They had a child who lived with W. An order was made that W receive £875,000 from H's assets of £7.5 million. The first consideration was the child's welfare under s25(1) Matrimonial Causes Act (MCA) 1973. The pre-nuptial agreement was relevant as part of 'all the circumstances'. It was also relevant under s25(2)(g) MCA 1973. It was unjust to ignore the agreement but also to hold W strictly to it. It did not dictate W's settlement. Given the length of the marriage it was agreed that this not a case for equal division of the assets.

OBP Textbook pages 121–126, section 7.6.

Appealing against an order out of time

It was held in *S* v *S (Ancillary Relief: Consent Order)* [2002] Fam Law 422 that the decision in *White* v *White* [2002] 2 FLR 981 was a supervening event within the meaning of *Barder* v *Barder* [1987] 2 All ER 440 to allow a spouse to appeal against an order out of time. In the case W was awarded the matrimonial home and a lump sum of £800,000. The following month the House of Lords gave its judgment in *White* v *White* and the wife, six months later, applied to have her order set aside and reconsidered.

OBP Textbook pages 149–153, section 7.14.

The Community Legal Service charge

Interest rate

The interest rate from 1 April 2002 is 1 per cent above the Bank of England official rate.

The statutory charge and pension orders

The statutory charge does not apply to any pension sharing or pension attachment orders. It would attach to any lump sum order made to offset pension rights.

OBP Textbook pages 156–161, section 7.16.

Child support

Consequences for existing orders

From April 2002 s4(10) Child Support Act 1991 is amended so that any court order for child maintenance which is in force for a year or more shall not prevent an application for child support from being made. If an application for a child support assessment is then made then the court order ceases to have effect.

There will be a six-year period for phasing in the reforms.

OBP Textbook pages 161–169, section 7.17.

Property Rights and Financial Provision on Death

How the two-stage test is applied – married spouses

Parish v *Sharman* [2001] 2 WTLR 593 Court of Appeal (Jonathan Parker and Thorpe LJJ)

Application for financial relief by spouse

Facts

H and W married in 1967. They separated in 1985 and W petitioned for divorce but the decree was never made absolute and no application for ancillary relief was made. H then lived with S. In 1996 H died leaving his business to a friend and the rest of his property to S. W claimed reasonable financial provision from H's estate. The court dismissed her claim concluding that when H and W separated they had concluded their affairs conclusively and that W had allowed H to arrange his affairs on the basis that he was divorced from her. W appealed.

Held

H and W went their own ways after their separation. The court had exercised its discretion properly and the appeal was dismissed.

Ghandi v *Patel* [2002] Fam Law 262 Chancery Division (Park J)

Application for financial relief by spouse

Facts

P was a prosperous Indian who lived in the UK, married a woman, W, and had two children. P and W then separated but did not divorce. P then purported to marry G through a Hindu ceremony. It was not clear whether P knew he was not divorced. P and G had two children. Their relationship deteriorated. When P died he left G a right of occupation in his property until she remarried or cohabited. G made application under the Inheritance (Provision for Family and Depdendants) Act 1975 as a wife. She argued that under s25(4) any reference to a wife or husband included a reference to a person who in good faith entered into a void marriage with the deceased.

Held

Dismissing the claim, the ceremony was not a marriage at all. Even if there had been a void marriage G had not entered into it in good faith.

OBP Textbook pages 176–180, section 8.6.

Occupation of the Family Home and Property Rights

Proposals for reform to the law of property rights between unmarried couples

The Civil Partnerships Bill was launched in January 2002 as a private member's Bill. The Bill could constitute wide sweeping reforms of the law relating to the property rights of unmarried couples (including same sex couples). There would be a presumption of equal ownership or the registration of a property agreement. If the partnership comes to an end a cessation order could be made and there would then be wide powers to distribute property.

The Relationships (Civil Registration) Bill was also introduced as a private member's bill (in October, 2001). The Bill would allow partners to register their relationship and thereafter have the same rights and responsibilities as married couples in terms of inheritance, housing succession, incapacity, pensions, social security and domestic violence. The partners would be able to lodge any pre-registration agreement about property rights on dissolution. Financial relief could be granted in the same terms as for married persons. This Bill was withdrawn on the government's assurance that it was advancing a cross-departmental review of civil partnerships.

See also two discussion papers published in July 2002. First, the Law Commission published its discussion paper, *Sharing Homes*. The Law Commission attempted to devise a scheme which could provide greater certainty and consistency in evaluating beneficial interests in a shared home. A scheme could encompass direct financial contributions to the purchase of the home and indirect financial contributions such as one party paying for household expenditure to allow the other to pay the mortgage. It considered the difficulties in evaluating non-financial contributions (eg looking after the home and children) and came to the view that a fair scheme was unattainable. It concluded that the existing case-law approach to resulting, implied and constructive trusts offered flexibility, although a more generous attitude to non-financial contributions was recommended. It commended *Midlands Bank* v *Cooke* [1995] 2 FLR 915 in allowing the courts, once a resulting or constructive trust had been established, to take into account all the circumstances in quantifying the beneficial entitlements under the trust. It was considered that codification of the common law would make the law too rigid. It looked at the law in other jurisdictions such as Australia, New Zealand and Canada and found no clear solutions there.

The second discussion paper was published by the Law Reform Board of the Law Society and was called *Cohabitation: The Case for Clear Law*. The paper recommends that the law should permit the registration of same-sex relationships. It was also recommends that unmarried couples (including same sex couples) who have been in a relationship for a continuous period of two years or have a child should have specific rights, including the right to apply to the court for capital provision. It did not recommend a general right to maintenance, confining court orders to lump sum and/or property orders. The case for a clean break can be seen as even stronger where parties have not entered into the commitment of marriage. It did recommend a limited right to maintenance (eg for no more than four years) to allow a partner to retrain for work and to reflect any economic disadvantage caused by the separation which could not be compensated by capital orders. This approach is similar to that advocated by the Scottish Law Commission and to systems adopted in Australia. It recommended that there be a standard definition of cohabitation.

In December 2002 the government confirmed that it would produce a consultation paper in the summer of 2003 to give same-sex couples the chance to register their relationships. Civil partnerships would confer property, pension, inheritance and next-of-kin rights on same sex partners.

How an interest in land may be acquired

By resulting, implied or constructive trust

See *Le Foe* v *Le Foe and Woolwich plc* [2001] 2 FLR 970 in which indirect contributions to the mortgage payments gave rise to a beneficial interest under a resulting trust. W received a 50 per cent share. It seems that *Lloyds Bank* v *Rosset* [1991] AC 107 was not given a strict interpretation. Provided the indirect contribution clearly relates to the house purchase it can give rise to a beneficial interest.

OBP Textbook pages 200–213, section 10.3.

Undue influence

UCB Corporate Services Ltd v *Williams* [2002] 3 FCR 448 Court of Appeal (Peter Gibson, Kay and Jonathan Parker LJJ)

Constructive notice of undue influence

Facts
W and H owned the matrimonial home which was subject to a number of charges. H was a partner in a business in which W played no part. The business obtained a loan from UCB via a further charge on the house. H and W signed the charge attended by all the partners in the business. At the meeting a solicitor gave W brief advice about the effect of the charge but gave no advice as to her obtaining independent legal advice. The business went into difficulties and UCB called in its loan. H and W separated with W still living in the home. W defended the claim by UCB on the basis of H's undue influence and misrepresentations. W believed that the loan was not a new loan but replaced an existing bank loan and provided for no

increase in risk. UCB denied the undue influence and misrepresentation and also argued that it was not fixed with actual or constructive notice of W's claim because she had been advised by a solicitor when she signed the charge. The court found that W would have signed the charge regardless of the undue influence or misrepresentation and that UCB had no actual or constructive notice of W's claim.

Held

Allowing the appeal, W's signing of the charge had been procured by H's fraud. His fraud had deprived W of her right to make a free and informed choice as to whether or not to sign the charge. It mattered not whether W would nevertheless have signed the charge (*CICB Mortgages* v *Pitt* [1993] 3 WLR 802 and *Royal Bank of Scotland* v *Etridge (No 2)* [2001] 4 All ER 449 considered).

UCB could not avoid being fixed with constructive notice of W's claim by merely relying on the honest belief that W was represented by a solicitor at the transaction since it could not be assumed that the solicitor's duty extended to explaining to her the nature and effect of the transaction. UCB had made no enquiry of the solicitor or of the advice he had given to W. The advice given by him to W had been palpably deficient (applying *Royal Bank of Scotland* v *Etridge (No 2)*).

OBP Textbook pages 236–240, section 10.12.

State Benefits

Child benefit

It was confirmed in *R* v *Secretary of State for Work and Pensions* [2002] 2 FLR 1181 that child benefit can only be paid to one parent. In the case a father complained that he was being discriminated against because the child benefit was being paid to the mother (the child spending equal time with both parents). It was held that there was no power to split or rotate the payment of child benefit. The system for paying child benefit was meant to be simple and so it was reasonable for payment to be made to just one parent rather than introduce complexities in trying to share payment.

OBP Textbook page 283, section 12.1.

Separation and Maintenance Agreements

The relationship between separation agreements and the courts

See *X* v *X (Y and Z Intervening)* [2002] 1 FLR 508 in which a couple reached agreement on a clean break settlement. W then sought to resile from the agreement.

It was ordered that the agreement become the court order since it had been a formal agreement properly and fairly arrived at with competent legal advice and there were no grounds for concluding that it would cause any injustice by holding the parties to it (applying *Edgar* v *Edgar* [1980] 1 WLR 1410). In the case H had performed his part of the agreement. The court would not permit parties to depart from an agreement properly and fairly reached between themselves without good and substantial grounds for concluding that an injustice would arise from holding the parties to it.

In *K* v *K (Ancillary Relief: Pre-nuptial Agreement)* [2002] Fam Law 877 H and W, after appropriate advice, made a pre-nuptial agreement whereby H (worth £25 million) would pay W £100,000 (increasing by 10 per cent for each year of the marriage) plus provision for the child. H and W then married but the marriage last 14 months. W claimed a lump sum of £1.6 million. It was held that the agreement was part of the circumstances under s25 Matrimonial Causes Act 1973 and that there would be no injustice in holding the parties to their agreement. The marriage was short. H was ordered to pay a lump sum of £120,000. W was also entitled to periodical payments of £15,000 per annum because of her contribution under s25(2)(f) by caring for the child. To allow the child to be brought up in a home and in a style reflecting his father's wealth a lump sum of £1.2 million was ordered for his benefit.

OBP Textbook pages 302–304, section 14.2.

Parent and Child

Parental responsibility – proposals for reform

Section 111 of the Adoption and Children (ACA) Act 2002 will amend s4 Children Act (CA) 1989 to give an unmarried father parental responsibility if he is registered as the child's father on the birth certificate. The mother would have to consent to him being registered.

There will be a s4A CA 1989 allowing a step-parent to acquire parental responsibility for a child of his or her spouse either by agreement with the spouse or by order of the court. This would provide an alternative to adoption since it would give the step-parent parental responsibility: see s112 ACA 2002.

OBP Textbook page 317, section 15.2.

Child – corporal punishment

In *R* v *Secretary of State for Education and Employment* [2002] 1 FLR 493 (High Court) the claimants were head teachers and parents at certain Christian schools who wished to maintain the right of teachers to administer reasonable chastisement in independent Christian schools. They argued that the restriction on using corporal punishment in s548 Education Act 1996 infringed their human rights. It was held that a religious belief in the correctness of corporal punishment could not attract the protection of art 9 of the European Convention on Human Rights so as to allow a child to benefit from corporal punishment or to allow a teacher to rely on the defence of reasonable chastisement if he/she used corporal punishment.

OBP Textbook pages 318–320, section 15.2.

Child – change of surname

Re R (A Child) [2001] 2 FLR 1358 Court of Appeal (Thorpe and Hale LJJ)

Dispute about child's surname

Facts
F and M were unmarried parents of R. R was registered with F's surname. R lived with M, and F had contact. There was a dispute about contact and F became aware that M had caused R to be known by the surname of her mother's partner, G, and adopted by M as her surname (though she still use her own surname on occasion). M had executed the change of surname by a deed poll but had not registered it. M applied to remove R to Spain to live near G. F and M agreed on the move, that F had parental responsibility and agreed contact arrangements. However they could not agree on R's surname. The judge determined that R's surname should be that of G since that was the name of the rest of the family unit. F appealed.

Held
Any opposed change of surname had to be justified under s1 Children Act 1989. There has to be some evidence that the change of name would lead to some improvement in the child's life: see *Dawson* v *Wearmouth* [1999] 2 AC 308. This included balancing the long term interests of a child in retaining an outward link with the parent with whom he/she was not living against the shorter term benefits of a lack of confusion, convenience, lack of embarrassment and the like.

The surname of G had a relatively insecure foundation. It had been adopted without consultation with F. The better solution would be to combine F and M's surname. This reflected Spanish custom.

Parents and court should be prepared to contemplate the use of both surnames in an appropriate case because it recognises the importance of both parents.

Child's first name

See *Re H (Child's Name: First Name)* [2002] Fam Law 340 (Court of Appeal) which considered a dispute between separated married parents concerning their baby's first name. It was held that first names were less concrete than surnames. Children commonly had more than one first name. The courts could not prevent the parent caring for the child (in this case the mother) from using the first name of her choice at home and with outside bodies, provided she recognised that fact that the child had a fixed series of names on his/her birth certificate.

OBP Textbook pages 320–324, section 15.2.

Child – education

See *Re W (Children) (Education: Choice of School)* [2002] 3 FCR 473 in which parents disputed which schools their three children, aged 12, ten and eight should go to. The Court of Appeal applied in particular s1(2)(c) Children Act 1989 and the effect on them of any change in their current schooling. The court required compelling reasons for making any change which would further disrupt their lives. In this case there were compelling reasons to allow the change (namely the mother moving to a new house too far away from the existing schools and problems with funding the eldest child's private education) and to make specific issues orders authorising a change in each child's schooling.

OBP Textbook pages 333–334, section 15.2.

Shared residence

In *Re A (Children) (Shared Residence)* [2001] EWCA Civ 1795 the Court of Appeal again said that shared residence orders were not necessarily exceptional. However, a shared residence order was not appropriate where a child lived with one parent and had limited contact with the other parent, simply as device to give the parents equal status. A residence order settled where the child should live. In the appeals orders were made that the girls live with their mother and have contact with their father and the boy live with his father and have contact with his mother.

OBP Textbook pages 334–335, section 15.3.

Contact

In 2002 the Children Act Sub-Committee of the Lord Chancellor's Advisory Board on Family Law published *Making Contact Work: A Report to the Lord Chancellor on the Facilitation of Arrangements for Contact between Children and Their Non-residential Parents and the Enforcement of Court Orders for Contact* (Lord Chancellor's Department, 2002). The report looked at the effects of contact on children. It commissioned a report from two clinical psychologists. While contact was deemed to be generally beneficial to children more research was needed. The report also recommended a broadening of the court's powers to enforce contact. It recommended a first step which would be facilitative and non-punitive. This could include parenting programmes. The second step would involve penal sanctions such as being placed on probation or community punishment.

In *Re S (Contact: Children's Views)* [2002] 1 FLR 1156 (High Court) the wishes and feelings of a 16-year-old daughter and a 14-year-old son (both of whom did not wish to have contact with their father) were respected and no orders as to contact were made. The court had to respect the wishes and feelings of the children, even to the extent of allowing them, as occasionally they do, to make mistakes.

By contrast in *Re J-S (A Child) (Contact: Parental Responsibility)* [2002] 3 FCR 433 the Court of Appeal reiterated that there has to be cogent reasons for denying contact to a child from his father. In the case the father had been involved in bringing the child up for the first two years of his life and the child enjoyed his father's company during contact. However, his father behaved deplorably towards the mother, having been violent to her in the past and making unjustified allegations about her and her new partner to social services. The mother was ambivalent about contact. The Court of Appeal allowed an appeal against the refusal of contact because in the medium and long term the child would benefit from contact. The Court of Appeal also allowed the appeal against the refusal to order parental responsibility. Given the father's important role in the child's early life and his continued contact with him the case for parental responsibility was overwhelming (applying *Re H* [1991] 2 All ER 185).

Sahin v *Germany* [2002] 3 FCR 321 European Court of Human Rights

Contact with an unmarried father

Facts
F lived in an unmarried relationship with M. They had a child, C, born in June 1988. F and M separated. F had contact with C until November 1990 when M stopped contact. German law gave M the right to control C's relationship with F but gave F the right to apply to the court for a contact order, if this was in C's interests. A different regime applied to married fathers. The court found that contact with not in C's interests but did not hear evidence from C. F appealed. The appeal court took evidence from an expert who examined C and advised that C (then aged five) should not be asked directly about F because of the risk that C might think her views were decisive. The appeal was dismissed. A further appeal was dismissed. F appealed to the European Court of Human Rights on the ground that the refusal to allow him contact breached art 8 of the European Convention on Human Rights (ECHR) (the right to family life) and art 14 ECHR (because German law discriminated between unmarried and married fathers).

Held
The notion of family life in art 8 ECHR was not confined to married families. The decision to deny F contact with C breached art 8(1). The interference was in accordance with law and had a legitimate aim, the protection of the child in accordance with art 8(2). In order for the denial of contact to be necessary in a democratic society (also in accordance with art 8(2)) there had to be a fair balance

between the rights of the child and those of the parent, with particular importance being attached to the interests of the child which could override those of the parent. In striking that balance the state was afforded a margin of appreciation. In failing to hear evidence from the child the court had failed to have complete information on C's relationship with F. This was an indispensable prerequisite for finding out C's true wishes. The expert's comments about C were too vague. The state had exceeded its margin of appreciation and there had been a violation of art 8.

For the purposes of art 14 a difference in treatment was discriminatory if it had no objective or reasonable justification. For a difference in treatment arising from birth out of wedlock to be compatible with the Convention there had to be very weighty reasons. The aim of the German legislation, namely the protection of the interests of the child and parents, could have been achieved without distinction on the grounds of birth. There had been a breach of art 14.

Comment

The decision appears to encourage courts to either have a child attend to give evidence (currently frowned on by UK courts) or for the children and family reporter to ask the child directly about his/her relationship with his/her father. English courts will have to be careful that the child's views have been sought in reaching conclusions about the child's relationship with his/her father and whether contact should be ordered.

English law and makes no distinction in contact applications between married and unmarried fathers so is unlikely to fall foul of art 14 in the same way as German law.

OBP Textbook pages 354–363, section 15.3.

Adoption

Contact after adoption

See *Re G (Children: Contact)* [2002] 3 FCR 377 (Court of Appeal) which said that current research was in favour of some contact in adoption. One of the possible benefits is that of children simply knowing who the natural parents were. To quote Ward LJ, contact removes 'the sense of the ogre, as they reach adolescence and begin to search for their own identity, with the double crisis not only of adolescence but also of coming to grips with the fact that they are adopted'. The appeal was concerned with children in the process of being adopted having minimal contact with their mother and father (minimal contact being once or twice a year).

OBP Textbook pages 376–378, section 15.8.

Adoption by a sole parent

Re B (A Child) (Sole Adoption by Unmarried Father) [2002] 1 FLR 196
House of Lords (Lords Nicholls of Birkenhead, Mackay of Clashfern, Hoffmann, Millett and Rodger of Earlsferry)

Adoption by unmarried father

Facts
F (the father) and M (the mother) were the parents of B. M showed no interest in B and, without seeing her, put her up for adoption. B was fostered with a view to adoption. F was not aware that M had been pregnant and had given birth to B. Social services contacted F and told him of what had happened. F and M registered the birth and made a parental responsibility agreement giving F parental responsibility. F applied to adopt B. M consented to his application. The Official Solicitor representing B opposed the application on the ground that ending M's relationship with B could not be said to safeguard and promote B's welfare and there was no basis under s15(3)(b) Adoption Act (AA) 1976 (namely 'other reasons justifying the exclusion of the other natural parent') to grant the adoption. M only wanted indirect contact once a year and wanted nothing further to do with B. The judge regarded the circumstances of the case as exceptional because M had rejected B from birth and on account of M's failure to play any part in B's upbringing and that s15(3)(b) was satisfied. The court made the adoption order. The guardian appealed to the Court of Appeal which allowed the appeal. It interpreted s15(3)(b) as dealing with something comparable to death, disappearance or anonymous sperm donation in order to exclude a natural parent. It considered such an interpretation compatible with art 8 of the European Convention on Human Rights (ECHR). F appealed to the House of Lords.

Held
Allowing the appeal, there was sufficient 'other reason justifying the exclusion of the other natural parent' under s15(3)(b) AA 1976 for an adoption order to made in favour of the natural father alone. The Court of Appeal had been wrong to adoption a restrictive interpretation. On its face the permanent exclusion of the child's mother from the life of the child was a drastic step. The court had to be satisfied that the course was in the best interests of the child. Consent of the excluded parent was not itself a sufficient reason, but it was a factor to be taken into account. Its weight would depend on the circumstances. There was no discordance between s15(3)(b) and art 8 ECHR. The balancing exercise required by art 8 did not differ in substance from that undertaken by a court in deciding whether adoption would be in the best interests of the child. The court's conclusion that adoption was in the child's best interests, even though it would exclude the mother from the child's life, identified the pressing social need for adoption and represented the court's considered view on proportionality. The judge could not be said to have misdirected herself.

OBP Textbook pages 379–380, section 15.8.

Adoption and Children Act 2002

In 2001 the Lord Chancellor's Department published *Adoption Proceedings: A New Approach* with the aim of reducing delay and inefficiency in adoption proceedings. It also aimed to increase the number of adoptions. The Adoption and Children Bill was presented to Parliament in March 2001 and became the Adoption and Children Act 2002 in November 2002.

The Act will change the court process for adoption by increasing the number of family judges, concentrating adoption work in specialist adoption centres and looking at ways to improve court rules. It will give clear guidance to local authorities on how to complete Sch 2 reports within the six-week deadline.

The Act will make the welfare of the child paramount in all decisions relating to adoption (as opposed to it being a first consideration). The paramountcy of the child's welfare will apply to dispensing with parental consent. A welfare checklist (similar to that in s1(3) Children Act 1989) will be applied by the courts. The checklist will include extra considerations, eg the relationship between the child and any relatives and how such relatives contribute to the child's welfare and their wishes and feelings. The grounds for dispensing with parental consent will be reduced to three:

1. the parent or guardian cannot be found; or
2. the parent or guardian is incapable of giving consent; or
3. the welfare of the child requires that consent be dispensed with.

There will be an obligation of local authorities to provide post-adoption support. A national adoptions register will be created to allow for a speedier matching of children with prospective adopters (in contrast to the up to two years it can take at present). The child's welfare will be paramount so an adoption could not be denied only because the child and the parents do not share the same racial or cultural background. There will be an independent review mechanism for prospective adopters who feel that they have been turned down unfairly.

There will be a new special guardianship order which will be a halfway house between adoption and no order, giving the applicant parental responsibility but not severing links with the child's natural family. A wider group of people will be able to apply for guardianship than can apply for adoption.

Placement orders will replace freeing orders. Placement orders will last until they are revoked or an adoption order is made or the child marries or becomes 18.

OBP Textbook pages 395–397, section 15.8.

Care proceedings

P, C and S v *United Kingdom* [2002] 2 FLR 631 European Court of Human Rights

Care proceedings and human rights

Facts

While living in the USA P met H and they had a child, B. It was suspected that P suffered from Munchhausen's Syndrome by Proxy and that she deliberately harmed B. P and H separated and it was ordered that B live with H and that contact between P and B be supervised. P was convicted of an offence of harming B. P them met C and they married and came to live in the UK. They had a daughter, S. On the same day that S was born the local authority obtained an emergency protection order and removed S and placed her with foster parents. The local authority applied for a care order. P and C were allowed supervised contact with S and developed an excellent relationship with their child. In the care proceedings P was legally represented but her lawyers then withdrew saying that P was asking them to conduct the case in an unreasonable manner. The court allowed a four-day adjournment for P to get new lawyers. She failed to get new lawyers. The care proceedings were then heard with P unrepresented and lasted 20 days. A care order was made with respect to S, with a finding that P had a personality disorder and that C would not accept that P had harmed her first child, B. The court then adjourned the case for one week to consider freeing S for adoption. P and C attended unrepresented. P applied for an adjournment which was refused. S was freed for adoption. A year later S was adopted and all ties between her and her natural parents severed. P and C were refused leave to appeal. They appealed to the European Court of Human Rights.

Held

The complexity of the case along with the importance of what was at stake and the highly emotive nature of the case required that P should be legally represented. Courts had to strike a balance between the interests of the parents and the welfare of the child. Nevertheless what happened prevented P and C from putting their case in a proper and effective manner. The presence of a lawyer for both the care proceedings and the freeing for adoption application was indispensable. P and C did not have a fair trial and there had been a breach of art 6 of the European Convention on Human Rights (ECHR).

The fact that the emergency protection had been applied for ex parte (without notice to the parents) did not breach art 8 ECHR since P and C were aware that this might happen and there relevant and striking reasons for making such an application. However, the way in which the emergency protection order was implemented, namely the draconian act of removing S shortly after birth was not supported by sufficient and relevant reasons and could not be regarded as necessary in a democratic society for the purpose of safeguarding S. The right to family life under art 8 ECHR had been breached. The local authority should have looked at alternatives for removal, for example the child remaining with the parents under supervision.

P and C argued that the proceedings had put an immense strain on their marriage and prevented them from founding a family. There had been no breach of art 12 ECHR which related to the right to found a family, though there had been a breach of the right not to have family life interfered with under art 8.

The duty to take care proceedings

See *D, P and JC* v *United Kingdom* [2002] 3 FCR 385 (European Court of Human Rights) which followed *Z* v *United Kingdom* [2002] 2 FCR 245 in holding that local authorities who had failed to protect children from sexual abuse should not be immune from being sued for negligence. There was a positive obligation under art 3 of the European Convention on Human Rights (ECHR) to protect children from harm. In the particular circumstances there was no breach of art 3 since there was insufficient information available to the local authority to know about the sexual abuse. However, there was a breach of art 13 ECHR (the right to a remedy) because one of the children had sued the local authority but had the claim struck out because of the House of Lords' decision in *X* v *Bedfordshire County Council* [1995] AC 633. Article 13 required the state to provide a thorough and effective investigation of complaints of sexual abuse and for an individual to establish the liability of the state for acts or omissions involving the breach of Convention rights.

OBP Textbook pages 398–399, section 15.9.

The burden of proof in care proceedings

In *Re O and N (Children) (Non-accidental Injury: Burden of Proof)* [2002] 2 FLR 1167 the Court of Appeal, considering *Re H and R* [1996] 1 FLR 80, said that the burden of proof was on the local authority to establish its case. There was no burden on a parent to disprove the case alleged against him or her. In the particular case the allegations against the mother could not be elevated beyond suspicion that she had harmed her baby. Suspicions and doubts did not establish a risk of future harm by her. The case involved a child who had been seriously injured by either his mother or father. His father admitted causing some injury but not the most serious injuries. A care order was made for that child and the younger sibling on the basis of the father's admitted abuse of one child and because the mother had failed to protect that child from harm. In revised findings the Court said that the mother was to be treated as not having caused harm to one child or be likely to cause harm to either child. In *Re B (Non-accidental Injury: Compelling Medical Evidence)* [2002] 2 FLR 599 a child died while in the care of his mother and her boyfriend. Both denied causing the child any injury. Care proceedings were taken with respect to the child's sibling. The court found that the boyfriend had caused the injuries and that the mother had not failed to protect the child. On appeal the Court of Appeal found that it was not possible to exonerate the mother and that she had clearly failed to protect the dead child. It warned against making positive findings against one party (in this case the boyfriend) when both carers had failed to protect the child.

Comment

There has been criticism of *Re O and N* because of the Court of Appeal's declaration that the mother was not to be treated as presenting a risk to her children despite the injuries to one child while in her and the father's care. It is argued that the evidence was sufficient for there to be a finding that there was a real possibility that she could harm both children in the future. The more flexible approach in *Re B* will be more attractive to local authorities when faced with doubts as to which of two or more carers caused serious injuries to a child.

OBP Textbook pages 399–401, section 15.9.

Care plans

Re S, Re W (Children: Care Plan) [2002] 2 WLR 720 House of Lords (Lords Nicholls of Birkenhead, Mackay of Clashfern, Browne-Wilkinson, Mustill and Hutton)

The local authority's care plan

Facts

In *Re S* three children were made the subject of care orders with care plans that the eldest child live with foster parents and the younger two children be rehabilitated with their mother. There were concerns that the care plans would not be acted upon by the local authority and that this would constitute a major breach of the rights of the mother. The concerns were justified when the local authority failed to implement the care plan due to budgetary problems. In *Re W* two children were made the subject of care orders with care plans that they live with their maternal grandparents (who lived in the USA but who were prepared to come to England) and have contact with their parents. There were uncertainties, including when the grandparents might move to England. Despite the uncertainties the court made care orders. The Court of Appeal made two major adjustments and innovations in the construction and application of the Children Act 1989. First, courts were given a wider discretion to make interim care orders when there were gaps in the care plan or where the passage of a relatively brief period would see some event happening vital to the deciding the future. In *Re W* the care orders were set aside and interim care orders made. Second, courts could identify 'starred' milestones in the care plan when important stages in the plan should be completed. If a starred milestone was not achieved the local authority would be obliged to reactivate the interdisciplinary process which helped create the care plan and inform the children's guardian. Either the guardian or the local authority could apply to the court for directions which could grant relief pursuant to ss7 and 8 Human Rights Act (HRA) 1998. The Secretary of State appealed in both cases as did the mother in *Re S* case and the local authority in *Re W* case.

Held

The introduction of a starred system could not be justified as a legitimate exercise in interpreting the 1989 Act in accordance with s3 HRA 1998. The Court of Appeal went well beyond the boundary of interpretation allowed by s3. The starred system constituted an amendment to the 1989 Act, not an interpretation. Courts were not empowered to intervene in the way local authorities discharged their parental responsibilities under final care orders. Parliament had entrusted to local authorities, not the courts, the responsibility for looking after children under care orders. The starring system departed from that principle. Sections 7 and 8 HRA 1998 did not provide a legal basis for the introduction of the new system.

The failure of the state to provide an effective remedy for a violation of art 8 of the European Convention on Human Rights (ECHR) did not make the Children Act 1989 incompatible with the Convention. The making of the care order involved a process which was compatible with arts 6 and 8 ECHR. Any infringement of rights after a care order had been made flow from the local authority's failure to comply with its obligations under the 1989 Act. A parent could bring proceedings against a local authority under s7 HRA 1998. Alternatively, there are administrative and complaint procedures available to such a parent. There is also the ability to apply to discharge a care order under the 1989 Act.

An interim care order was to enable the court to safeguard the child until the court was in a position to decide whether or not to make a care order. It was a temporary 'holding' measure. An interim care order could not be used to supervise the local authority. Before making a care order the court should have before it a sufficiently firm and particularised care plan so that there was a reasonably clear picture of the foreseeable future of the child. The court had to balance the need to be satisfied about the appropriateness of the care plan and the avoidance of over-zealous investigation into matters which were properly within the administrative discretion of the local authority.

The mother's appeal was dismissed while those of the Secretary of State would be allowed.

The government was asked to give urgent attention to the serious practical and legal problems identified by the Court of Appeal. One of the most urgent questions is whether some degree of court supervision of local authorities' discharge of parental responsibilities would bring about an overall improvement in the quality of child care provided by local authorities. An example of a local authority failing to implement an effective care plan can be found in *Re F* [2002] Fam Law 8 in which the local authority's failure to implement its care plan led to the children being further harmed.

Comment

Courts can affect the implementation of a care plan through applications for contact (s34 Children Act (CA) 1989) and applications to discharge care orders: s39 CA 1989. For example, in *Re B (Minors) (Termination of Contact: Paramount Consideration)* [1993] Fam Law 301 the Court of Appeal held that while the plans of the local authority must command the greatest respect and consideration from the court, Parliament had given to the courts, not the local authority, the duty to decide on contact between child and parent. By allowing rehabilitative contact under s34 the court set the care plan (which was for the child to be permanently placed with another family) in a new direction.

If a supervision order is made the role of the children's guardian continues until the supervision order ends: s12(5)(b) Criminal Justice and Court Services Act 2000. This could allow the guardian to monitor how the local authority operates the supervision order.

The government introduced an amendment to the Adoption and Children Bill to create a looked-after children reviewing officer. The amendment includes the officer reviewing the care plan for children subject to care orders and having a care plan for children voluntarily accommodated.

In *Re B (Interim Care Orders: Directions)* [2002] Fam Law 252 the Court of Appeal (Thorpe and Buxton LJJ) stated that the court had wide powers to make directions under s38(6) CA 1989. This included directing a residential placement for a mother and baby, against the wishes of the local authority. *Re C (Interim Care Order: Residential Assessment)* [1997] 1 FLR 1 is the leading authority which allows the court to make directions where the court needs to obtain information necessary for its own decision, notwithstanding that control over the child rests with the local authority in all other respects.

OBP Textbook pages 398–411, section 15.9.

Status of a child

The presumption of legitimacy

Re H and A (Paternity: Blood Tests) [2002] 1 FLR 1145 Court of Appeal (Dame Elizabeth Butler-Sloss P, Thorpe and Kay LJJ)

Establishing the parentage of a child

Facts

F and M married in 1975. They had a son born in 1975. Then, in 1997, M gave birth to twins, C1 and C2. In 1993 M started a relationship with P which involved sexual intercourse between 1995 and 1999. P said that M had told him that he was the father of the twins, not F. F was unaware of relationship between M and P and considered himself as the father of the twins. The relationship between M and P ended in 1999. P applied for a declaration of parentage under s55A Family Law Act

(FLA) 1986 and for contact and parental responsibility. M challenged his claim to the paternity of C1 and C2. P applied for blood tests under s21 Family Law Reform Act 1969. F stated that if the court ordered a blood test that established P as the father of the children he would abandon them and M. The court dismissed the application for blood tests holding that the possible disastrous disintegrative effects upon F and M's family unit outweighed the need to find the truth. P appealed.

Held

Allowing the appeal, the paternity of a child was to be established by science and not by legal presumption or inference. In the nineteenth century when science had nothing to offer and illegitimacy was a social stigma the presumption of the legitimacy of children born during marriage was a necessary tool. However, with the advances of science and with more children born out of marriage, paternity was to be established by science. Establishing scientific fact allowed for planned management. This could be contrasted with the risk of perpetuating uncertainty that bred rumour and gossip with the risks to the children in the future. Unpalatable truth could be easier to live with than uncertainty.

Comment

P was able to take advantage of the amendments to s21 FLRA 1969 which allowed blood samples to be taken without the consent of the parents if the court considers that it would be in the best interests of each child for the sample to be taken.

OBP Textbook pages 426–433, section 15.12.

Parenting order under s30 Human Fertilisation and Embryology Act (HFEA) 1990

See *Re C (Application by Mr and Mrs X under s30 HFEA 1990)* [2002] Fam Law 351 (High Court) in which H and W could not conceive a child. With the assistance of an organisation called COTS they entered into a surrogacy agreement with M which included a payment of £12,000 covering potential loss of earnings and expenses. M was unemployed. H and W did not wish for her to work during any pregnancy. M conceived a child using H's sperm and a child was born. Application was made to justices for an order under s30 HFEA 1990 giving parental responsibility for the child to H and W. The justices refused to make the order because of the payment of £12,000. On appeal the payment was authorised and the s30 order made. The payment was held not to be disproportionate and entered into in good faith. It was manifestly in the interests of the child that the order be made.

OBP Textbook pages 435–438, section 15.12.

Taxation on Separation and Divorce

Working Families Tax Credit

The Working Families Tax Credit (WFTC) is available to all couples (married or unmarried) or single parents with one or more children under 16 (or under 19 if still in full time education) living with them. One or both of the parents must work 16 hours a week or more. From April 2002 it comprises:

1. a basic tax credit of £60 a week;
2. an extra tax credit of £11.65 a week if one partner works at least 30 hours a week;
3. a tax credit for each child of £26.45 from birth, £27.90 from the September after their 16th birthday until the day before they are 19;
4. a childcare tax credit of up to 70 per cent of eligible child care costs to a maximum of £135 a week for one child, £200 a week for two or more children;
5. extra credits for disabled children.

WFTC is reduced by 55p for each £1 of net income above £94.50 a week. There are reductions if there are savings above £3,000, and the person is not eligible if there are savings over £8,000. Payments of child maintenance or child support are disregarded as income.

As an example Zoe, a single parent, works 27 hours a week and earns £200 a week net. She has a child aged seven and pays £60 a week childcare. She will receive:

1. a basic tax credit of £60;
2. a tax credit for her child of £26.45;
3. a childcare tax credit of £42 (ie 70 per cent of £60).

Total tax credit = £128.45
Less 55 per cent of £105.50 (income above £94.50) = £70.52.

This is then used to reduce the amount of tax owed or as an extra payment.

Once granted WFTC lasts for six months when it is reassessed.

OBP Textbook pages 440, section 16.2.

17

Jurisprudence

Utilitarianism

Criticisms of utilitarianism

Simmonds N E (2002) **Central Issues in Jurisprudence,** *London: Sweet and Maxwell*

Simmonds provides a useful account of some of the advantages and disadvantages of utilitarianism. These come out quite clearly in the extract below. Within the sphere of jurisprudence there are a number of different strategies for deciding how decisions should be made. Utilitarianism has the advantage of offering just the one principle, that of utility, but in reality it is avoiding the hard question. That, of course, is: how should choices as to what is to be regarded as having utility be made? To leave it to each individual to make their own choice or to take the aggregate of such choices may well produce consequences that we would wish to declare as unacceptable:

'Some critics of utilitarianism have resisted the idea that the betterment of the human condition can be treated as the maximisation of some single value such as "welfare": they have argued for a plurality of values, and have claimed that such plurality undercuts the aggregative structure of utilitarian theory. Others have pointed out that one cannot move from the claim that morality is intended to have good consequences to the conclusion that we should maximise such consequences in aggregate, because this ignores the importance of how the good consequences are distributed amongst persons: perhaps equalising welfare is more important than maximising it, for example. Finally, some distinguished philosophers have resisted the very idea that morality might have a "point" in any straightforward sense: for such thinkers (Kant and Kierkegaard are examples) morality represents a wholly autonomous and self-contained perspective upon life, that is irreducible to other terms (such as "happiness" or "welfare").

Utilitarianism may be thought to be a suitable principle to guide the decisions of those who exercise public power (including judges and legislators) even if it is not the fundamental principle of morality as a whole. It may be said, for example, that utilitarianism possesses two virtues that are highly desirable in public decision-making. In the first place, utilitarianism seems to make each issue turn upon a question of fact: in each case we will be asking what will actually serve to maximise welfare. Thus the theory seems to offer the attractive prospect of decisions based upon hard evidence and firm criteria (an appearance that may well be misleading). Secondly, utilitarianism can claim to treat conflicting interests with absolute equality: everyone's interests are taken into account and are given equal weight; the decisions that result simply reflect the neutral results of the calculus of losses and gains in utility.

Since we expect public officials to act upon the basis of evidence and objective criteria that treat everyone's interests equally, we may feel that the principle of utility is the appropriate guide for their decisions. Here, the principle of utility is not being offered as a philosophical explication of the basis of morality, but as a public conception of justice that is recommended by some of our specific moral beliefs regarding the proper role and responsibilities of public officials.

The idea that utilitarianism is recommended by its egalitarian character is sometimes invoked as a basis for amending or rejecting the doctrine. Ronald Dworkin has argued that utilitarianism attempts to implement a basic value of "equal concern and respect", but does so in an inadequate or misguided way. Equal concern and respect finds a more adequate expression, Dworkin holds, in a theory of individual rights': at 20–21.

OBP Textbook page 52, section 6.3.

Continental Legal Positivism: Kelsen's Theory

The Pure Theory

Ross H 'Hans Kelsen and the Utopia of Theoretical Purism' (2001) Kings College Law Journal 174

Kelsen wanted to explain law of all types and to this end attempted to produce a pure theory of law, a science of law free of metaphysical elements. To do this it was necessary to isolate the key elements necessary for such an endeavour. He was concerned with what the law was, and not what it perhaps ought to be. As part of this he would certainly want to exclude the social sciences. A number of writers have suggested that Kelsen, in various ways, had failed in his search for purity. Sawer and Tur, for example, thought the attempt to explain whole systems and their component parts were endeavours that Kelsen shared with sociologists. Most particularly, Weber's science of social action and Kelsen's approach can be shown to have had common intellectual origins. Ross in his article explores both those and other reasons to suggest that Kelsen may have been a sociologist. As the extract below shows, whilst it may not be possible to arrive at a definitive answer in relation to that issue, it does allow certain conclusions to be drawn. These are that the purity that Kelsen sought is probably neither attainable or desirable, that in short his approach is a case of throwing out the baby with the bath water:

'In order to reach a proper understanding of exercises of social legal power in judicial or social contexts as an integral part of sociological enquiry – in other words, to understand the "subjective meaning" of the relevant judicial or social behaviour – an understanding of the underlying normative conceptions is arguably essential, as Weber suggests. Clearly Kelsen's focus on matters such as the analysis of legal concepts, the notion of validity and efficacy of laws, the ideas of structure and hierarchy and similar analytical tasks assists sociological enquiry ...

In this essay I have sought to highlight ways in which Kelsen might perhaps more convincingly be regarded as having been "engaging in sociology" in writing the Pure

Theory of Law. I have identified where Kelsen's pure theory and Weber's sociology shared significant areas of commonality. I argued that common philosophical under-pinnings (German Idealist philosophy and Southwest German Neo-Kantianism) lent support to the view that aspects of the Pure Theory of Law could be regarded as being strikingly "sociological" in a Weberian sense ... I noted in passing Richard Tur's contention that the Pure Theory of Law had a "collectivist Verstehende" orientation, arguing that an idea of legal meaning could be ascribed to an institutional actor such as a judge. I observed that Kelsen's pure theory was at points "sociological" in the Weberian sense in terms of its field of enquiry in that it explored aspects of human behaviour – or more specifically, social action – which embody specific processes that are, at least in part, conceptual in nature. Despite Kelsen's denial, the pure theory also quite clearly explored "mental processes" and "physical events".

But I believe that none of this actually "made" Kelsen a sociologist or "made" the Pure Theory of Law a conscious exercise in Weberian sociology. What it did, however, is call into question the sustainability of Kelsen's grand design to "purify" his theoretical enterprise by eliminating sociology and related human sciences – the study of social action, behaviours, activities, motivations, attitudes, assumptions or their influence from its domain. Kelsen's Pure Theory of Law thus failed to establish that "purity" was an achievable objective. In fact Kelsen made a better case for establishing the very opposite: that "purity" in the sense that Kelsen conceived this was probably unattainable. One might even suggest that, post-Weber, it was, and remains, an entirely Utopian aspiration': at 194.

Weyland I 'The Application of Kelsen's Theory of the Legal System To European Community Law – The Supremacy Puzzle Resolved' (2001) Law and Philosophy 1

Within Kelsen's system the validity of a law is to be tested in terms of other higher laws from which it is derived. There is a hierarchy of laws or norms, at the top of which is a grundnorm or basic norm. Such a hierarchical system would explain a system of delegated legislation. The norms themselves become more concrete as you descend the hierarchy – this is the concretisation of norms. The basic norm is the norm that performs the task of validating all other norms within a legal system. It is not validated itself and each legal system will have a basic norm. Within England and Wales in the pre-European Union era it may have been appropriate to think of the authority of the Queen in Parliament as supplying the basic norm. Now, of course, the situation is more complex. Where there is a written constitution then the hierarchy of norms may be based upon its propositions.

Kelsen's work has proved to be disappointing when applied to the real world. I've already suggested that a basic norm for the constitution in England and Wales is elusive at the present time. Attempts to apply his work to revolutionary situations have also been of limited success. It might be that such situations are so unsettled that it is difficult to know if you have a legal system at all. For Kelsen, a legal system was characterised by a settled system. The norms of the legal order have to be by and large effective – this is the principle of effectiveness. What is certain is that there is a legal system in England and Wales with an elusive basic norm. What

Weyland attempts, in the extract below, is to use Kelsen's theory to solve the difficulties that membership of the European Union has given rise to. I will leave him to speak for himself in a moment, but a few introductory points can be made. The core of his approach is that the European Communities Act (ECA) 1972 was a special type of statute, and as such can have a position higher in the hierarchy than other statutes and thus can prevail over them – even if they pre-date them. The argument seems convincing on its own terms, but some doubts can be raised. Kelsen sought purity and the device of excluding the actual workings of the legal system can be objected to. Constitutions are what happens, and you should, in my view, develop your theory so that it fits with such practices – rather than attempting to make the events of the world correspond with a theory that has been developed in a highly abstract fashion. Any special status that the 1972 Act may have now was neither intended nor apparent in 1972. Weyland presents his argument as follows:

'Once Kelsen's theory is applied to conflicts between norms emanating from domestic and European sources, both the principles of the supremacy of Acts of Parliament and of Community law, properly understood, can be accommodated. This is because, as stated above, Parliament may act either as an ordinary legislature or as a constitutional organ. The constitutional nature of a British statute is determined by its contents and the ECA is undoubtedly such a statute.

Parliament's authority as a constitutional organ derives directly from the basic norm, whereas its legal powers as an ordinary legislature stem from constitutional norms, some of which, as stated above, have been created by Parliament itself acting as a constitutional body. Constitutional norms enacted by Parliament are on a higher level than enacted norms of an ordinary character, and, in case of conflict, the former override the latter. The rule of conflict derived from the Treaty [EC] and the ECA, which establishes the supremacy of Community legislation, is of a constitutional nature and by virtue of the principle "lex superior" renders invalid an ordinary statute which is incompatible with Community law, regardless of whether the latter was enacted at a later date or preceded it. The application of the principle of "lex posterior" is in this case subject to and qualified by the principle of "lex superior", as it only authorizes the repeal of ordinary Acts of Parliament by EC legislation, but not vice-versa. Furthermore as the principle of "lex posterior" only applies to norms on the same level of the hierarchy, an ordinary Act of Parliament can neither impliedly nor expressly repeal a constitutional statute.

The doctrine of implied repeal has now been discarded by constitutional and European Law writers on account of its rejection both by the national courts and the ECJ. Although it has never arisen in practice and it is highly unlikely to occur in future, academic writers have also addressed the issue of whether a statute that expressly repealed Community law provisions would be valid. They have either taken the view that the doctrine of sovereignty requires an affirmative answer or that the issue will have to be resolved by the courts if and when the situation arises ...

Given that Parliament has the power ... to repeal its own laws, the ECA may, as most constitutional lawyers believe, be repealed by another constitutional Act of Parliament. In the next section I shall attempt to show that Parliament may bind itself even on the constitutional level, although in respect of the repealability of the ECA it did not do so ...

The main logical argument relied on by writers like Wade in support of the traditional view, namely that Parliament cannot change the rules from which its authority derives, rules which the judiciary has created and only the judiciary can change, loses its cogency once it becomes clear that Parliament operating on the level of the constitution has been given by the basic norm the legal power to amend rules that determine its authority both as a constitutional and an ordinary legislator. It is of course true that even within Kelsen's theory, legal ideology, in particular as reflected in the judgements of the appellate courts in our system, is crucial to the content (though not the validity) of the basic norm. Thus judicial recognition of the validity of Acts of Parliament, regardless of their nature, has led to the acceptance of Parliament's authority to create statutes both on the level of constitutional and general norms ...

Kelsen's theory also provides a rational justification for judicial declarations of the unconstitutionality of ordinary Acts of Parliament that conflict with Community law. This is now acknowledged by the judiciary, although only in respect of the effect of invalidity in the particular case. Therefore euphemisms like "the disapplication" of an Act of Parliament have been used ...

As the supremacy doctrine only leads to what amounts to a declaration of invalidity of legislation that conflicts with Community law in the particular case it does not have the effect of repealing the statute. However in practice once national provisions have been deemed incompatible with Community law it is unlikely that the state would seek to enforce them. A much more logical solution would be to give the courts the power to render them invalid': at 14–18.

OBP Textbook page 94, section 9.2.

Modern Positivism

The rule of recognition

Coleman J 'Methodology' (p311) in Coles J and Shapiro S (2002) **The Oxford Handbook of Jurisprudence,** *Oxford: Oxford University Press*

In the extract below Coleman examines and comments upon Dworkin's attack upon Hart's methodology and the attempt at what Hart called 'descriptive jurisprudence'. In this, Hart was involved in a search for the meaning of certain words and concepts that could be used to explain a legal system. This would involve finding concepts such as law about which there were shared understandings. Dworkin's suggestion is that these ideas will prove to be elusive, in that ideas such as law will have multiple, rather than universal, meanings:

'Dworkin is the most important proponent of normative jurisprudence, and his most famous argument for the claim that jurisprudence is normative is the semantic sting. According to Dworkin, positivism is not only a substantive view of the kind of thing law is, it is underwritten by a certain semantics of concepts, and related accounts of both what it is to understand a concept's meaning and to retrieve its content. He labels that web of commitments "criterial semantics". According to his formulation of criterial semantics, we follow shared rules in using any word: these rules set out criteria that supply the word's meaning. Knowing the meaning of a concept is evidenced by a certain kind of understanding. Because the meaning of concepts is given by the shared criteria of their application, to understand the meaning is to know what those criteria are. So understood, the point of the jurisprudential project is to identify the shared criteria for properly applying the concept law.

Law, however is an "essentially contested" concept in the sense that competent language users disagree not only about whether this or that scheme of governance (for example Nazi Germany) is an instance of law, and about what the criteria for applying the concept of law ought to be; they disagree also about what the criteria for applying the concept of law are. If competent language users can intelligibly disagree about the criteria for applying a concept that they share, then the meaning of the concept cannot be fixed by shared criteria for applying it; and the project of jurisprudence cannot consist in identifying what those shared criteria are.

The semantic sting thus undermines a criterial semantics of concepts generally, of the concept of law, in particular, and the substantive legal positivism that it underwrites. In this way, the semantic sting argument paves the way for the view that law is an interpretive concept. In determining what law is we do not identify shared criteria for the application of the term. Instead we defend certain substantive normative premises and orient our analysis of what law is according to them': at 414–415.

OBP Textbook page 113, section 10.2.

Morality and law

Honore T 'The Necessary Connection between Law and Morality' (2002) Oxford Journal of Legal Studies 489

On of the great issues in jurisprudence is the relationship between law and morality, and it has given rise to a number of debates. As a leading positivist, Hart's position is that the fact that a rule may be the product of a legal system and thus a law does not provide an answer to the question of whether or not, at the moral level, we should in fact obey that rule. Thus he advocated a strict divorce of the question of the identification of what is valid law from the question of obedience of the law. Hart utilised the device of a rule of recognition as a means of supplying the ultimate criterion of legal validity. Law in such a system is that which is identified by whoever has official power or authority to perform this role. Hart thought that the point of distinguishing questions of legal validity from the question of what is morally right is to drive a wedge between personal conscience and what the State demands in the name of law. That is, a citizen of a State should always be able to say, 'Yes, this is the law, but it is too evil to be obeyed'. What the State demands must always be subject to scrutiny. This then is one version of the positivist's desire to separate law from morality. There are, of course, other views as espoused both by other positivists and natural lawyers. Fuller, as a natural lawyer, suggests that legal systems necessarily have a moral content, brought about by the attention paid to the eight principles of the inner morality of law. This is that the eight principles assert implicitly the principle of procedural fairness that rulers should proceed carefully with those they rule; they should be general, prospective, open, fair, stable, not require the impossible and so on. The rulers command obedience in Fuller's legal system but they must do it in a fair way, one which recognises individual moral divergences in its citizens. What Honore suggests in the extract below is that the desire of positivists to divorce law from morality is a problematic one in the following sense. His argument that moral issues are clearly used in the actual practice of legal systems is a compelling one. Whether as legislators, judges, reformers, students or lecturers in or of the law, we make use of moral arguments. Hart's point about the recognition of law as such can still stand because we can use these moral considerations in relation to decisions as to whether or not to obey the law. These ideas seem to allow us to make progress in understanding legal systems, but we still have the million dollar question – how do we justify our moral assertions? Honore puts his argument on the connection between law and morality as follows:

'The connection between law and critical morality is necessary in that it is not contingent. It applies to every law and every legal system. The proposed interpretation of every law in every legal system can legally be challenged on the ground that it is not morally defensible, whether the challenge succeeds or fails in a particular instance.

It is also a connection that does, in my view, enhance the claims of law to our respect. The positivist doctrine is something of a prison. How is the law to escape from received ideas, including received ideas about morality? It is because of the necessary connection with morality that judges, officials, writers and teachers whose function it is to interpret the law have been able over the centuries to mould it so as to take account of moral considerations. The same connection, arising from the claim of law to be morally in order, has served to inspire reformers and promote law reform. Hence the values of fairness, equity, justice, honesty, humanity, dignity, prudence, abstention from violence and a host of other values that conduce to co-operation and co-existence play a prominent role in the law even when they are not incorporated in any formal source of law. The interpreter's mandate is to apply the law as an item that purports to be morally in order. The requirement that a judge should do justice according to law expresses this mandate though obliquely.

I have argued that the view here advocated derives from positive law, since the positive law of societies with legal systems, unlike the theory of positivism, makes arguments addressed to critical morality admissible in the interpretation and application of law. But is this true only of the law of certain societies? It is, in the sense that it applies fully only to those societies in which the interpretation of law is a serious intellectual discipline, so that a legal culture exists which in which there are recognized experts, often professionally organized. It would not apply to a society, if there has even been one, in which law was regarded merely as a system of threats. Nor would it apply to one what was not institutionally advanced enough to possess a legal culture': at 494.

OBP Textbook page 118, section 10.5.

Natural Law

Finnis

Bix B 'Natural Law: The Modern Tradition' (p82) in Coles J and Shapiro S (2002) **The Oxford Handbook of Jurisprudence,** *Oxford: Oxford University Press*

Bix offers valuable insight into the work of Finnis, who is an important recent writer in the natural law field. The difference between the work of Hart and Finnis is articulated and this work is a further example of the importance of moral issues and the sterility and aridity of positivist endeavours that seek to exclude or marginalise them:

'Law plays a role within Finnis's moral theory, in that there are certain common goods that are best obtained through the specific kind of social coordination that law offers, and there is a sense in which participation in the community and in the common good of building a (political) community is an integral part of living a good life. Finnis also discusses legal theory in the narrower sense of the term. In analyzing the concept of law, he agrees with the general approach of H L A Hart: that one should look at "law" (or "legal system") in its fullest or highest form, rather than in some lowest common denominator of all systems we might consider "legal" and that such an approach must incorporate the perspective of participants. However, Finnis narrows and strengthens Hart's "internal perspective": it is the viewpoint of those who not only appeal to practical reasonableness but also are practically reasonable. According to Finnis, one must select the "internal viewpoint" according to the idea of "central case" (the concept in its fullest sense), and that this will direct one away from a morally neutral perspective: "If there is a point of view in which legal obligation is treated as at least presumptively a moral obligation … a viewpoint in which the establishment and maintenance of legal as distinct from discretionary or statically customary order is regarded as a moral ideal if not a compelling demand of justice, then such viewpoint will constitute the central case of the legal viewpoint". This may seem a minor modification, to Hart's approach, but it is one sufficient to move a theorist across the border, from legal positivism (law conceptually separated from morality) to natural law theory (moral evaluation central to understanding law).

Finnis's criticism of legal positivism, implicit in his views on "internal perspectives" and express in other writings, is that a proper theory of law will require moral evaluation. The basic claim is the same sort of teleological argument discussed earlier in relation to Fuller's work: one cannot fully understand a reason – giving activity like law without the (moral) evaluation of what it would mean for the official statements and enactments to give citizens a good reason for action': at 88–89.

OBP Textbook page 165, section 11.13.

American Realism

Patterns of American jurisprudence

Kelley P 'Holmes, Langdell and Formalism' (2002) Ratio Juris 26

The extract by Kelley focuses on one issue in relation to the American realist movement, that being its role as a revolt against formalism. American realism was a diverse approach, for example having an emphasis on the courts, an emphasis upon the judges, an interest in prediction and also an interest in law in action. Holmes was one of the leading advocates of American realism. It sought a science of law based on a study of law in action – a very empirical approach. It engaged in a revolt against formalism as seen in abstract thinking – a desire to get to the facts. It was a reaction to black letter law approaches in which you apply legal principles to hypothetical fact situations, ie answering problem questions. It is Langdell that is commonly set up as the advocate of formalism, the traditional approach to legal education and the expectation that judges will rigidly follow precedents. Holmes and Langdell are supposed to be arch foes, with Holmes by way of contrast being aware of the potential for creativity on the part of the judiciary. The theme in the extract is that these differences and contrasts are overdone. Whilst Holmes pointed to the flexibility in rules and listed 64 techniques of precedent that provide for much uncertainty, he still recognised that legal rules are the dominant factor in decision-making. If the actual facts of two cases are the same, usually the decisions in those cases will be identical. It can also be noted that his own career as a judge was much more conservative than might have been expected:

'We can see, then, that in their prescriptions for judicial decision-making, the theories of Holmes and Langdell converge. The point of convergence is at what we might call extreme legalism: the position that judges ought to decide a current case based on the rules established by past precedent, without appeals to special claims of justice in an individual case, and without appeals to any higher order normative principles beyond or in back of the prior precedent.

Holmes arrived at this extreme legalism by the following route. All laws are scientifically reducible to laws of antecedence and consequence: if you do X and Y happens, judges will order that Z be done. Moreover, laws are only justified by their consequences. Law has only practical ends: its social consequences for the community or policy. But there is no scientific basis for choosing among policies, even with scientific studies of the social consequences of alternative laws. The judge's role is not, therefore, to choose among different policies but to root out misguided metaphysical or theological reasoning, relate each law to the social consequences that alone justify it, and make the law more effective in achieving that policy by making the law more clear, definite, and certain, and therefore more effective in influencing human behaviour.

Langdell arrived at this extreme legalism by a different route. If law is separate and distinct from morality, any scientific understanding of law must clearly separate the law from normative justifications for the law. The best way to do that is to isolate the true or correct legal meaning of legal doctrines. A scientific judge, then, should decide cases objectively, by logical application of these purified legal doctrines to the facts of the case. This would keep the judge's own personal moral judgments, which may differ from judge to judge, out of the law. The law will then be more even-handed, predictable, and knowable.

For both Holmes and Langdell, then, appeals to justice in the individual case and to higher order normative principles related to justice were not persuasive. For Holmes, this was because justice was a metaphysical fiction, and an individual case is simply an occasion to set out a rule that will influence human behaviour in a certain way in the future. For Langdell, this was because there are always equally plausible arguments about what justice requires in an individual case, there is no scientific way to determine the uniquely just result, and objective, predictable results are achievable if we focus simply on the logical application of purified legal doctrine.

For Langdell, then, and to a large extent for Holmes, judicial decision-making in a common law system is appropriately legalistic. Courts should simply apply pre-existing rules and doctrines – purified by Langdell or reduced by Holmes – to make the legal system predictable, consistent, and knowable': at 48–49.

OBP Textbook page 210, section 13.7.

Feminist Jurisprudence

Feminism in perspective

Naffine N 'In Praise of Legal Feminism' (2002) Legal Studies 71

Naffine's article is very useful as an account of the various endeavours that make up the legal feminists endeavours, the difficulties that they have faced, the sources of these difficulties and the impact that their work has had. Some of these difficulties are perhaps of their own making. For example, whilst there remains a common sensical, matter-of-fact view of the category of 'man' as legal actor and citizen, by contrast the concept of woman – the subject of feminism – has been endlessly turned over and inspected. This anxiety has grown to the point that some feminists now wonder whether their most basic working term, 'woman', has any integrity, whether their very subject matter has imploded.

The basic themes of the article are as follows. It suggests that the general purpose of legal feminism is to make sense of the many ways gender shapes law, to reveal the many ways that law, as a consequence, harms women, and to try to change law so that women are helped. It observes that legal feminists remain at the margins of the legal academy, but that they participate nevertheless in the legal community and so can render its ideas intelligible and thus gain some intellectual purchase. It characterises the methods and approaches of legal feminists as ecumenical and pragmatic. The second and third parts of the article are about the intellectual and political problems which, in the view of the author, have caused the greatest concern to feminist theorists. Finally, in the fourth part there is a consideration of the response of the legal academy to feminist scholarship. It is noted that whilst feminists have convincingly demonstrated laws failure to make sense of many aspects of women's lives, legal institutions have proven remarkably resistant to feminism and its findings. The extract below states well two of the more interesting issues. First, that perhaps the idea of women as an oppressed group has been overstated; women do have a voice, they can make a difference and this can be achieved within existing social structures. Also, the point is made that those who espouse a new master plan for women are in danger of becoming the new dictators:

'Certainly, law has been unwelcoming to women. Until recently women were denied (for many purposes) personhood, married women were denied property and all women had a very limited public life. The charges levelled at law have been stated in strong terms. Catharine MacKinnon has perhaps put them in their most extreme form, charging the institutions of law with the utter silencing of women. "Take your foot of our necks", she says, "then we will hear in what tongue we speak". In MacKinnon's account, it would seem that women are fully determined by oppressive masculine institutions; they have no autonomy to speak of. But how then does MacKinnon herself express her concerns and what is the point of her speaking at all, if female autonomy has been so thoroughly extinguished? Why isn't the game up for women and, further, why does MacKinnon engage with law at all and propose particular legislative change, as she does with sexual harassment?

It seems that feminists are trying to have it both ways. Some, like MacKinnon, appear to be saying that women are determined by a patriarchal culture, in which law plays a defining role, and that there is little point in searching for a free and articulate female voice within that culture. Certainly, this is how some of her critics have interpreted MacKinnon's work. At the same time, it seems that feminists are making claims for the autonomy of women; after all, that is surely the point of the entire feminist enterprise. And as lawyers, many like MacKinnon seem paradoxically to be looking to a masculinist law to defend the freedoms of women. The presupposition is necessarily that female agency has not been extinguished, notwithstanding the misogyny of law, and that it is even possible to employ such law to enhance the autonomy of women. What are we to make of all this? At face value, it appears that feminists are caught in a contradiction. However, feminists such as MacKinnon are not operating at a superficial level: their work is reflective and philosophical and they are well aware of the apparent paradoxes thrown up by their work. So we need to delve deeper into their thinking to discover the reasons for this apparent discrepancy between their theory and method ...

Feminists who claimed the authority of the authentic woman, it was said, were likely to reproduce their own way of being female, their own particular axis of identities. The authentic female would therefore be a feminist clone: probably white, middle class, heterosexual and educated. The concerns of this type of woman would then dominate the feminist agenda, as it seems they have, and yet again, the less educated, the less powerful, would be rendered inarticulate. Feminists would be just as bad as misogynists. They might even be worse because they would also be hypocrites. And thus it would not in fact be an arbitrary grouping of cultural understandings of femaleness that determined the meaning of woman, but a quite particular one: the cluster of characteristics which described the woman of privilege. It was therefore important for feminists not to speak with too much generality. They must neither suggest nor imply that their experience was universal, for this would be to eclipse the views of differently placed women': at 81–82 and 88–89.

Munro V 'Legal Feminism and Foucault – A Critique of the Expulsion of Law' (2001) Journal of Law and Society 546

Whilst this article raises difficult issues, most centrally the utility of Foucault's thought in the enterprises of feminist legal critique, it still has much to offer the reader. In particular the insights that his work offers into power, oppression and resistance seem to have much to offer. Another central theme of the article is the possibility of achieving legal reform, an upbeat message is delivered as regards that point. The extract offers some conclusions as regards these themes:

'In presenting a pathway for the re-evaluation of the Foucaultian approach to legal theory more generally, the arguments of Ewald and Tadros also present a pathway for a re-evaluation of the Foucaultian approach to feminist legal theory. We have seen over preceding sections that feminist theorists generally have good cause to listen to the arguments of Foucault and in light of this emerging interpretation of his approach to law, it seems also that feminist legal theorists should be paying his thesis more serious attention.

While Smart and others have done so, they have done so primarily by using Foucaultian methodology to highlight the power regimes behind law, thereby presenting a case for reform outwith the legal arena. However, the emerging revaluation discussed within the confines of this article permits a more engaged application of Foucaultian theory within feminist legal critique. The possibility that Foucault's crucial distinction lies between juridical and disciplinary rather than between legal and non-legal has been consistently highlighted. Amongst the most significant implications of that possible interpretation is the realization that Foucaultian theories of disciplinary power and subversive resistance can be applied accurately within the legal sphere. Furthermore, they can be employed not only to highlight the existence of power struggles as Smart's alleged modification of Foucault suggests, but also to present the immanent possibility of resistance through legal channels.

This offers a spectrum of possibilities to legal feminists who have become dissatisfied with the determinism of the radical feminist critique but have been reluctant to disassociate themselves from legal reform in the way that Smart's prescriptive thesis demands. Several feminist legal theorists have recognized the merits of the Foucaultian approach, embodied in Smart's descriptive thesis, which highlights the constructive aspects of social power and their effects upon the micro levels of personal and communal experience. Like Smart, many such theorists have sought to illustrate the extent to which these constructive aspects of social power originate from and are manifest within the normative expectations encapsulated within prevailing legal doctrines. In the fields of medical law and rape, for example, the extent to which cultural norms pertaining to the body and to the appropriate standard of conduct for the "proper" woman are embodied within the law has increasingly been recognized within contemporary analysis. Likewise, the extent to which cultural norms pertaining to the imperatives of the man as sexual aggressor are embodied within the law have also been highlighted. Regardless of the legitimacy or otherwise of its claims to modification of Foucault, the descriptive thesis presented by Carol Smart has doubtless provided much of the impetus and inspiration behind these emerging conceptual pursuits. However, theorists engaging in this kind of analysis have equally been curtailed by the limitations of Smart's prescriptive thesis which, immersed within the assumption of synthesis between the legal and the juridical, denounces the possibility of reform through legal mechanisms. According to Sandland, Smart's prescriptive stance on the deconstruction of law and legal reform seems to be saying to these subsequent feminist theorists that the substance of the law is irrelevant, or not worth bothering with because engagement with law on its own terms is inevitably counterproductive.

As a consequence of this stance, contemporary feminist theorists have been led to doubt the legitimacy of their instincts to embark upon legal reform and legal challenge in the shadow of this thesis': at 563–564.

OBP Textbook page 271, section 19.5.

The Common Law Tradition

The three rules of statutory construction

Goldsworthy J 'Legislative Intentions, Legislative Supremacy and Legislative Positivism' (p45) in Goldsworthy J and Campbell T (2002) **Legal Interpretation in Democratic States,** *Aldershot: Dartmouth Press*

Goldsworthy provides a number of good examples of why the literal rule will not suffice – thus providing room for judicial activism in the sphere of statutory interpretation:

'(1) The Highway Act 1835 included a long section (s78) dealing mainly with improper driving of horse-drawn vehicles. In the middle of the section, the improper riding of any horse or beast was prohibited. But the provisions at the end of the section, imposing penalties, referred only to drivers, not riders. When the prohibition of improper riding was inserted in Parliament as an amendment, the consequential need to amend the penalty provision was apparently overlooked. The court decided that a literal construction would lead to an absurd result that Parliament could not have intended – namely, the creation of an offence not subject to any penalty. It adopted a non-literal construction to give effect to Parliament's apparent intention.

(2) Section 8(1) of the Road Traffic Act 1972 (UK) provided that in certain circumstances any person "driving or attempting to drive" a vehicle could be required to take a breath test. The defendant drove through a red light, stopped, and changed seats with his passenger. He was then asked to take a breath test, although by then he was clearly not "driving or attempting to drive" the vehicle. (Indeed, that might have been true even if he had remained in the driver's seat.) The court held that he was nevertheless required to take the test.

(3) Section 8(1) of the Food and Drugs Act 1955 prohibited the sale of "any food intended for, but unfit for, human consumption". Some children asked for lemonade, were given corrosive caustic soda, and drank some of it. Read literally, s8(1) did not apply: the vendor had not sold the children food unfit for human consumption, because caustic soda is not food. But the apparent purpose of the provision was to protect the public from harmful products being sold as food, and it was interpreted accordingly.

(4) Rule 14(2) of the Magistrates' Courts Rules 1968 (UK) states that at the conclusion of the evidence for the complainant, "the defendant may address the court". It does not

provide that the court must listen to the defendant's address. Nevertheless, this is surely implied.

(5) An Alberta by-law required that "all drug stores shall be closed at 10pm on each and every night of the week". It would be consistent with a literal interpretation of these words for a drug store to close promptly at 10pm, and then re-open a few minutes later. But the Supreme Court of Alberta properly rejected an argument to that effect on the ground that only a lawyer could have suggested it': at 47.

OBP Textbook page 338, section 24.7.

18

Land Law

Easements and Profits

Introduction: examples of easements

Mobil Oil Co Ltd v *Birmingham City Council* [2002] 2 P & CR 14 Court of Appeal (Civil Division) (Aldous, Sedley and Arden LJJ)

Petrol station separated from highway by adjoining land – owner of station claimed right of way over adjoining land under deed of exchange – construction of deed – commercial efficacy – whether words in a contract could be ignored – whether an easement of way had been granted

Facts

M owned a petrol station which was separated from the highway by adjoining land owned by Birmingham City Council (BCC). Part of the adjoining land was leased to M by BCC as additional forecourt space under a lease made in 1987. In the first rent review under that lease, BCC contended that M was dependent upon the 1987 lease for rights of access to the petrol station and that this should be recognised in a 'ransom' rent. M disputed this and claimed that it was entitled to rights of way over the adjoining land quite apart from the lease. The rent review arbitration was stayed while M sought determination of its claim by the court. M relied upon a deed of exchange dated 1959 and a grant of a 14-year lease of part of the adjoining land of the same date (the 1987 lease was a second renewal of that lease). By virtue of the deed of exchange, the freehold of the land upon which the petrol station was to be built was conveyed to NB (a predecessor in title of M), who built and operated the petrol station. The lease related to part of the adjoining land and was renewed several times, with the 1987 lease being the current one. Clause 3 of the deed of exchange imposed an obligation upon BCC to '(a) make and incorporate the [adjoining land] fronting the [freehold land] hereby conveyed to [NB] into the public highway' as and when practicable and '(b) provide such crossings as are reasonably necessary to give such access to the filling and/or service station to be constructed on the adjoining land belonging to [NB] so that access shall be available for the purposes of [NB's] trade and/or business and customers by the time the said filling and/or service station is completed and open for trading'. Although the adjoining land had been designated to form part of a road widening scheme (which, if carried into effect, would have resulted in M's freehold abutting directly onto the highway and thus obviating the need for any right of way), there was no immediate prospect

360

of such road widening taking place. M contended that Clause 3 had the effect of conferring a grant (either expressly, impliedly or by virtue of s62 Law of Property Act 1925) of a right of way over BCC's adjoining land. However, at first instance the deputy judge ruled that M did not possess such a right of way, since he took the view that the words of Clause 3 were meaningless in the context of the deed and should be ignored. M appealed, contending that a right of way over BCC's adjoining land was essential to give commercial efficacy to the deed, especially since both in 1959 and at present the relevant parties knew that the aforementioned road widening would not take place in the immediate future.

Held

The view of the deputy judge that words in a contract should be ignored was 'only acceptable in extreme circumstances'. It was not appropriate to ignore the words here since they appeared in two places in Clause 3, albeit changed to an extent. The effect of the deputy judge's ruling was to remove an obligation on BCC because 'he was unable to resolve the tension imposed by the words' (per Aldous LJ). Rather, the words were likely to have been intended by the parties to carry a meaning, and the Court should give effect to that meaning if it could be ascertained. The only conclusion that was consistent with the wording of Clause 3, and the commercial reality as evidenced by the context in which the 1959 deed was concluded, was that put forward by M (ie there was an implied right of way). However, M's easement of way would determine if the anticipated road widening scheme took place. It was not established that NB were in occupation of the freehold land prior to the deed of exchange and therefore the factual basis for a grant under s62 Law of Property Act 1925 was not made out. Accordingly, the appeal would be allowed (Sedley LJ dissenting).

Comment

The case demonstrates the importance the courts attach to commercial efficacy when construing legal documents in respect of commercial land transactions. Here there could be no doubt that the parties intended and expected that the freehold land should be used as a garage, for which it was a commercial necessity that NB and its successors should have rights of access over the adjoining land. The case also makes clear that words used by parties in a legal document are likely to be intended to have a meaning, and the court should give effect to that meaning if it can be ascertained (in this regard the Court applied *Investors Compensation Scheme Ltd* v *West Bromwich Building Society (No 1)* [1998] 1 WLR 896). The case represents one of those classic situations where the majority agreed as to the result, but not as to the reasoning to be used to achieve that result.

OBP Textbook pages 235–237, section 12.1.

Saeed v *Plustrade Ltd* [2001] EWCA Civ 2011 Court of Appeal (Civil Division) (Auld and Walker LJJ, Sir Christopher Slade)

Landlord of flat block granted tenants right to park on the forecourt of premises – new landlord when refurbishing the block prevented tenants from parking for three years – reduction in car parking spaces from 13 to four – whether right to park could amount to an easement – whether reduction in spaces constituted a substantial interference with the right to park

Facts

S (the claimant) held a long lease of a flat in a mansion block which was registered land. The lease was granted in 1977 by the then landlord C together with a right to park a private motor car in common with other persons so entitled in a defined area of land retained by the landlord 'when space is available'. S acquired her lease and flat in 1985, by which time there was a designated parking area for 13 cars on the forecourt of the mansion block. Between 1987–2001 additional long leases were granted, but without parking rights. P Ltd (the defendants) purchased the mansion block. Between 1997–2000 they carried out conversion and refurbishment work and prevented tenants from parking on the forecourt by erecting posts thereon. Under P Ltd's new parking arrangements there would only be four car parking spaces (reduced from 13), which they wanted to sell to their new tenants. S contended that she had a right to park in the nature of an easement and that P Ltd had interfered with the same. She claimed compensation for the loss of her proprietary right and a declaration as to that right. P Ltd argued that S had no right to park, only a licence which was not binding upon them (ie there was no breach of S's lease). At first instance the judge held that S had an easement to park, there was no express right which empowered P Ltd to determine that right and that there had been a substantial interference with S's right to park for some three years, for which she was awarded £6,300 damages. P Ltd appealed.

Held

It was not necessary to determine whether a right to park was in the nature of an easement because S's rights were binding upon P Ltd as an overriding interest under s70(1)(g) Land Registration Act (LRA) 1925. Although the lease gave P Ltd the right to specify where parking was to take place, that right did not allow the landlord to withdraw that specification, or not to specify at all, since that would constitute a breach of the principle that a landlord should not derogate from its grant. The fact that S was prevented between 1997–2000 from parking was a clear derogation from the right to park given to her in the lease. The reduction in car parking spaces from 13 to four constituted a substantial interference with the right to park. Accordingly, the appeal would be dismissed and the award of damages affirmed.

Comment

Following the decision in *Copeland* v *Greenhalf* [1952] Ch 488 – which laid down the principle that for a right to be an easement it must be a right against other land and not a right to possession of the other (ie servient) land – the view emerged that there could not be an easement of car parking. However, in the unreported decision of *Newman* v *Jones* (22 March 1982) Megarry V-C held that a right to park a car on the forecourt of a block of flats passed as an easement under s62 Law of Property Act (LPA) 1925. Further, in *London and Blenheim Estates Ltd* v *Ladbroke Retail Parks Ltd* [1993] 4 All ER 157 an easement of car parking was recognised subject to certain qualifications (it must not be a right to park in a defined space and the use must not leave the servient owner without any reasonable use of his land). In the light of these case developments it is somewhat surprising that the Court of Appeal in *Saeed* 'left open' the question whether a right to park could amount to an easement. Further, the Court's reason for doing so – S had an overriding interest under s70(1)(g) LRA 1925 – is open to serious doubt. For a right to be such an overriding interest it must be a proprietary right, like an easement. Since the Court made no finding as to whether S had an easement, the only remaining basis for the right to park would have been a contractual right, which is not a proprietary right.

OBP Textbook page 237, section 12.1.

Mortgages

The rights of the mortgagor

Paragon Finance plc v *Nash and Another; Paragon Finance plc* v *Staunton and Another* (2001) The Times 25 October Court of Appeal (Civil Division) (Thorpe and Dyson LJJ, Astill J)

Mortgagors in arrears – variable interest clause in mortgage – mortgagee charging interest above prevailing market rates – whether lender's discretion to vary interest rates subject to an implied term to vary rates fairly – whether subsequent interest rate changes could be taken into account in deciding if a mortgage agreement was an extortionate credit bargain?

Facts
PF (the claimants) brought possession proceedings as mortgagee in two actions against N and his wife and S and his wife (the defendants) on the ground that they were in arrears with their mortgage interest repayments. Both mortgage agreements contained a variable interest clause. The defendants admitted the arrears of interest but contended by way of defence and counterclaim that the mortgage agreements had become extortionate credit bargains within s138 Consumer Credit Act 1974. They did not contend that the loan agreements were extortionate credit bargains at the outset. Rather, that they (the loan agreements) had become such subsequently because of the rates of interest that they were required to pay (PF had not reduced

its interest rates in line with the Bank of England or prevailing market rates). The defendants sought to have the loan agreements reopened under s139 of the 1974 Act and sought to plead an implied term that PF was bound to exercise its discretion to vary interest rates fairly, honestly and in good faith and not arbitrarily, capriciously or unreasonably, having regard to all relevant matters and ignoring irrelevant matters. PF applied to have the defendants' counterclaim struck out on the ground that they had no real chance of succeeding at trial. The Recorder struck out the defendants' pleadings and refused them permission to amend. The defendants appealed.

Held

The discretion to vary interest rates during the mortgage term given to a mortgagee in a mortgage agreement was not completely unfettered but was subject to an implied term that it was not to be exercised for an improper purpose, dishonestly, capriciously, arbitrarily or in a way in which no reasonable lender would reasonably do. However, the fact that PF had set interest rates without reference to the prevailing market rates did not show that PF was in breach of that implied term. Here the crux of the borrowers' complaint was that the gap between PF's rates and those charged by the Halifax Building Society had widened from 1995 onwards from about 2 per cent points to 4–5 per cent points. A reason why PF charged interest rates above prevailing market rates was because it was in serious financial difficulties because many of its borrowers had defaulted, and this in turn resulted in the money markets charging PF higher rates because it was deemed to be a greater risk than other mortgage lenders: PF had passed those higher costs onto its borrowers. Accordingly, it could not be said that PF's discretion to set interest rates was being exercised capriciously, arbitrarily, unreasonably or for an improper purpose. The borrowers' argument that the rates of interest were exorbitant so as to bring the agreements within s138 of the 1974 Act had 'no real prospect of success'. This was because only charges existing at the time of the bargain were to be taken into account in deciding whether a credit bargain was extortionate for the purposes of s138 – subsequent changes in interest rates had to be excluded from the calculation. Further, since the setting of interest rates by the mortgagee was not 'contractual performance' within s3(2)(b) Unfair Contract Terms Act 1977, the defendants could not establish a breach of that provision by arguing that PF had defeated their reasonable expectation that in performing its side of the bargain, the lender would not apply rates of interest significantly out of line with those 'applied by comparable lenders to borrowers in comparable situations' (per Dyson LJ). Accordingly, the appeal would be dismissed.

Comment

The case establishes that a mortgagee's discretion to vary interest rates is subject to an implied term that rates are to be varied fairly. It further establishes that in deciding whether a credit bargain is extortionate for the purposes of s138 of the 1974 Act, only charges existing at the time the agreement was entered into could be taken into account (ie subsequent variations in interest rates were excluded). The Court made clear that it could only intervene if a credit bargain had been grossly unfair to the borrower, and this could be established if either the payments required to be made were grossly exorbitant or it had grossly contravened the principles of fair dealing. In essence, the 1974 Act only provides borrowers with limited protection from the operation of the market place.

OBP Textbook pages 281–285, section 14.5.

The remedies of the legal mortgagee

Freeguard v *Royal Bank of Scotland plc* (2002) The Times 25 April Chancery Division (Simon Berry QC)

Property charged to bank by previous owner – mortgagee sold the property in exercise of its power of sale – legal owner claimed property sold at an undervalue – whether mortgagee owed a duty of care to the legal owner, even though owner not the mortgagor

Facts
F (the claimant) acquired an option to purchase land but the option was never registered. Subsequently, the owners of the land charged it to RBS (the defendant) but the charge was never registered. F's option and RBS's charge were competing equities and proceedings to determine which had priority were resolved in favour of RBS. Notwithstanding this determination, F purchased the land subject to the charge even though she was not the mortgagor. Thereafter RBS sold the land in exercise of its power of sale as mortgagee. F issued proceedings contending that RBS had sold the land at an undervalue and that in so doing it had breached its duty of care towards her, the legal owner of the land (in essence she argued that there was such a duty even though she was not the borrower). The Deputy Master struck out F's claim on the basis that RBS did not owe her a duty of care. F appealed.

Held
A mortgagee owed a duty of care in equity not only to the mortgagor or any subsequent incumbrancer, but also to the legal owner of land even if the owner was not the mortgagor. This was because F, like a subsequent incumbrancer, had an interest which was subject only to a prior right (here the legal charge), and she would therefore suffer loss if RBS breached its duty of care. RBS owed F a duty of care and the Deputy Master had been wrong to strike out F's claim. Accordingly, the appeal would be allowed.

Comment
The decision constitutes a logical extension of the duty of care owed by a mortgagee when exercising its power of sale and is consistent with case developments in this

field over the last decade. In *Downsview Nominees Ltd* v *First City Corporation Ltd* [1993] AC 295 it was held that a mortgagee owed a duty of care not just to the mortgagor but also to any subsequent incumbrancer. In *Medforth* v *Blake* [2000] Ch 86 it was held that a receiver owed a duty of care not just to the mortgagor, but also to any other person who had an interest in the equity of redemption.

OBP Textbook pages 288–293, section 14.8.

Bristol & West plc v *Bartlett; Paragon Finance plc* v *Banks; Halifax plc* v *Grant* (2002) The Times 9 September Court of Appeal (Civil Division) (Schiemann, Buxton and Longmore LJJ)

Mortgagor defaulted on mortgage – mortgagee took possession and sold property at a price that produced a significant shortfall on the mortgage debt – mortgagee brought an action to recover the shortfall – mortgagor raised the defence of limitation – effect of sale on mortgagor's liability for the shortfall – whether a limitation period of 12 years or six years applied

Facts

In each of the three cases the mortgagors had defaulted on their mortgage repayments. Thereafter the mortgagees sold the properties charged as security, but for prices that left a significant shortfall in the amounts due under the mortgages at the dates of sale. The mortgagees brought proceedings to recover the shortfalls after six years but before 12 years had elapsed. Under s20 Limitation Act 1980 (which governs claims for a mortgage debt) the limitation period in respect of the principal claimed was 12 years from the time the cause of action accrued, but only six years in respect of claims for interest. Under s5 of the 1980 Act (which governs claims under a simple contract) the limitation period was six years. In the lead case, B (the mortgagor) raised a defence of limitation to the action of BW (the mortgagee) for the shortfall, claiming that the effect of the sale was to discharge the liability arising under the covenant to pay in the mortgage deed. Accordingly, he contended that his only obligation to pay the outstanding mortgage debt arose as an implied term under a simple contract, that the matter was governed by s5 of the 1980 Act and that, on the facts, BW's action was time barred as being outside the relevant six-year period. The issue was whether a limitation period of six or 12 years applied to the claims of the mortgagees. The Court heard the cases as conjoined appeals.

Held

The right to sue for a mortgage debt arose at the time the debt became payable, ie when the borrower failed to pay a third monthly instalment. The fact that at some subsequent time the mortgagee exercised its power of sale and discharged the mortgage did not mean that the debt arising under the covenant to pay contained in the mortgage deed ceased to be payable by the mortgagor. Even where there was an express provision in the mortgage deed that the borrower would pay the amount of any shortfall between the mortgage debt and the sale price to the lender, the cause of action was still that for the mortgage debt arising on default under the terms of the deed. No separate cause of action arose when the shortfall was ascertained. Since BW's action concerned the recovery of money secured by a mortgage, the appropriate limitation period was that laid down in s20 of the 1980 Act (ie 12 years). Further, the 12-year limitation period continued to apply to claims for any principal sum, even though the mortgage had been discharged where the lender had exercised its power of sale. It followed that claims for interest were subject to a six-year limitation period. BW was entitled to judgment for the principal of their loan but B was given permission to advance arguments concerning interest at trial. Accordingly, B's appeal was allowed in part.

Comment

The case establishes that s20 Limitation Act 1980 and a 12-year limitation period applies to any action to recover any principal sum secured by way of mortgage in existence when the right to recover accrued, and that it is not necessary for the principal sum to be still secured by the mortgage when the action is brought. The argument that the effect of a sale by a lender is to discharge the liability arising under the covenant to pay in the mortgage deed was rejected.

OBP Textbook pages 288–293 and 328, sections 14.8 and 15.3.

Possession and the question of undue influence

National Westminster Bank plc v *Amin* [2002] 1 FLR 735 House of Lords (Lords Nicholls of Birkenhead, Hoffmann, Hope of Craighead, Scott of Foscote and Rodger of Earlsferry)

Parents agreed to mortgage home as security for a loan for their son – parents spoke Urdu but did not speak or read English – confirmation from solicitor that the charge was properly explained – solicitor spoke no Urdu – subsequently son found himself in financial difficulties – mortgagee commenced possession proceedings – whether mother's defence of undue influence should be struck out – whether solicitor's confirmation sufficient given the communicational problems

Facts

In 1972 Mr and Mrs A emigrated from Uganda to the UK. They spoke Urdu. In 1988 their son, who had been educated in the UK, sought a loan from the National Westminster Bank offering as security for the same a charge over his parents' home. Although Mr and Mrs A had lived in the UK for a number of years significantly neither of them spoke, read or wrote English. The bank wrote to a solicitor enclosing the mortgage document and asking him to ensure that Mr and Mrs A were aware of the terms and conditions contained therein, and to obtain and witness their signatures to the mortgage. For this purpose, the solicitor convened a meeting attended by Mr and Mrs A and their son which culminated in the parents signing the mortgage. The meeting was conducted in English and there was no request that Urdu should be spoken on that occasion. After the meeting, the solicitor confirmed to the National Westminster Bank that he had explained the terms and conditions of the mortgage to Mr and Mrs A. Subsequently, the son found himself in financial difficulties and the National Westminster Bank (the claimant) brought possession proceedings against Mrs A (the defendant), her husband having died.

Mrs A raised the defence of undue influence, submitting that the mortgage should be avoided because of undue influence exerted upon her by her son (the debtor), for whose benefit the mortgage had been entered into. She further submitted that the National Westminster Bank had failed to advise her, in the absence of her son, of the amount of her potential liability under the mortgage, of the risks she was undertaking and that she had not been advised to obtain independent legal advice. The bank applied to have Mrs A's defence struck out, arguing that it could not be fixed with constructive notice of the son's alleged undue influence as it had acted in reliance on the solicitor's confirmation that he had explained the charge to Mrs A and her late husband. The deputy district judge and the appeal judge decided that Mrs A's defence should not be struck out. However, the Court of Appeal found in favour of the bank and struck out the defence. In essence it concluded that Mrs A had no reasonable prospects of defending the possession proceedings. Mrs A appealed, contending that the solicitor who had secured her signature to the mortgage document was not her solicitor.

Held

It was appropriate that the case should be remitted to the county court for trial. There was a serious question as to the status of the solicitor which would have to be determined at trial – whether he was acting for Mr and Mrs A or for the National Westminster Bank, and whether he had in fact given a proper or sufficient explanation of the transaction in question. While the bank might be able to rely upon an inaccurate confirmation supplied by a solicitor engaged by the client, it was not entitled to rely on an inaccurate confirmation supplied by a solicitor acting on its own behalf. There was nothing to suggest that Mr or Mrs A had instructed the solicitor in question, whereas the National Westminster Bank had given him instructions. Even if it was established that the solicitor acted for Mrs A, he would not be able to inform the National Westminster Bank of the outcome of any meeting with Mrs A without her authorisation and she had not given any such authorisation.

Further, even if it was established that the solicitor was acting for Mrs A, it was not inevitable that her defence of undue influence would be struck out. That was because there were several features present in the case that raised the issue of whether something more might be required of the National Westminster Bank before it could claim to be free of constructive notice of the son's undue influence. These features included the following:

1. National Westminster Bank was aware that Mr and Mrs A could not speak English and therefore knew that they were especially vulnerable to exploitation;
2. the letter from National Westminster Bank to the solicitor had not indicated that special care was needed when advising Mr and Mrs A and had not stressed the importance of them receiving proper advice about the consequences of the proposed transaction; and
3. the letter from the solicitor to National Westminster Bank had not stated that Mr and Mrs A had understood what had been explained to them about the mortgage document.

Accordingly, the appeal would be allowed.

Comment

This decision is a compelling example of the willingness of the courts to take special steps to ensure that people especially vulnerable to exploitation in financial situations are protected. While the understanding of a mortgage transaction by a borrower could be inferred in ordinary cases, that was not the situation here where the solicitor explaining the mortgage document to the chargor spoke no Urdu, and the chargor neither spoke nor read English, and these communicational difficulties were known to the mortgagee. In such circumstances there was a clear possibility that the bank knew, or ought to have known, that the advice given by the solicitor would be defective.

OBP Textbook pages 296–306, section 14.8.

Adverse Possession

Running of time

J A Pye (Oxford) Ltd v *Graham* [2002] 3 WLR 221 House of Lords
(Lords Bingham of Cornhill, Mackay of Clashfern, Browne-Wilkinson, Hope of Craighead and Hutton)

Licensee remained in occupation of farmland after expiration of grazing licence – landowner refused request for a new licence – occupant continued limited use (grazing) of land – occupant willing to pay to occupy land if requested – whether in such circumstances occupant had shown intention to possess the land – whether landowner's title extinguished by adverse possession

Facts

P (the paper owner) purchased in 1977 a large estate. Thereafter, he sold the greater part of it, including Manor Farm, but retained 57 acres of farmland because of its development potential. In respect of this retained land he granted a grazing licence to the owners of Manor Farm. Subsequently, G became the registered proprietor of

Manor Farm and when his written grazing licence expired in December 1983 he requested a renewal, which was refused because of the possibility of P making a planning permission application in respect of the 'grazing land'. Nevertheless, G continued to use the land and in August 1984 he completed a cut of hay which, on payment, he was allowed to take. In 1985 a further request by G for a renewal of the agreement, and to take a cut of hay, were not answered. G remained in occupation of the relevant land, which he maintained and farmed as a unit with his own adjoining land.

In June 1997, G registered cautions at the Land Registry against P's title to the land on the basis that he had obtained title by adverse possession. In August 1997, P applied to the Land Registry to warn off these cautions and in April 1998 issued an originating summons seeking their cancellation. In 1998, G died. In January 1999, P (the claimant) commenced proceedings against G's widow and personal representatives (the defendants) for possession of the 'grazing land', contending that the requisite 12 years had not elapsed. In support of this contention, P argued that G's oral request to P for a further licence demonstrated an intention to submit to P's right of possession, which was at variance with an intention to possess required for the purposes of s15(1) and paras 1 and 8(1) of Sch 1 to the Limitation Act 1980 (in a written statement prepared for the trial, G made clear that he would have accepted a new licence and paid for the same). The judge dismissed the summons and action, finding that G had enjoyed factual possession of the land from January 1984, that his intention to possess and adverse possession took effect from September 1984 and that P's title had been extinguished. On P's appeal the Court of Appeal held that G had not manifested an intention to possess the land. When the licence expired, G's intention had been to continue that limited permissive use of the disputed land given under the terms of the licence (ie to use it solely for grazing purposes), and that fact coupled with his statement that he would have accepted another licence if offered demonstrated a lack of intention to possess the land to the exclusion of the owner. There was no evidence that G had ever changed his intention concerning the use of the land. P had therefore not been dispossessed of the land and the limitation period had never begun to run against him. The defendants appealed to the House of Lords.

Held

The question to be posed was whether the squatter (G) had dispossessed the paper owner of the land (P) by ordinary possession of the land in question for the relevant time in the absence of consent from the owner. Two requirements had to be satisfied in order to establish adverse possession. First, a squatter had to exercise a sufficient degree of physical custody and control (ie factual possession). In order to establish such possession, a squatter had to show absence of the paper owner's consent, a single and exclusive possession that he had been treating the land in the manner of an occupying owner and that no other individual had done so. Second, the squatter had to have an intention to possess the land. It was not necessary for him to demonstrate an intention to own or acquire ownership of the land. Rather, the requisite intention was to possess on his own behalf and to exclude the world at large, including the paper title owner, so far as was reasonably practicable. Accordingly, it was immaterial that the squatter would have been willing to pay the paper title owner to occupy the land if requested to do so. Given that G had been in factual possession of the land from January 1984 onwards (the licence expired in December 1983), and from September 1984 onwards had used it as his own, and since P had done nothing on the land and was effectively excluded from it throughout the relevant period, G had manifested an intention to possess the land. The judge had correctly concluded that G had established a possessory title. Accordingly, the appeal would be allowed.

Comment

This is an important decision on adverse possession for at least four reasons. First, the thrust of their Lordships' judgment was to move away from an emphasis upon 'adverse' possession. Lord Browne-Wilkinson put the matter thus: 'In my judgment much confusion and complication would be avoided if reference to adverse possession were to be avoided so far as possible and effect given to the clear words of the [Limitation] Acts. The question is simply whether the defendant squatter has dispossessed the paper owner by going into ordinary possession of the land for the requisite period without the consent of the owner' (at pp232–233). Secondly, establishing a sufficient degree of custody and control depends upon the circumstances of each case, and in particular the nature of the land and the manner of its usage. Thirdly, their Lordships emphasised a possessory justification for acquiring title by limitation – factual possession plus intention to possess. Finally, at first instance, Neuberger J concluded that the word 'action' in s15(1) Limitation Act 1980 only applied to proceedings brought in a court by an owner seeking to recover disputed land. It did not extend to an application to the Land Registry to warn off cautions, nor to an application by originating summons to remove cautions because neither application was an action to recover [the disputed] land.

OBP Textbook pages 323–326, section 15.3.

19

Law of International Trade

Sale of Goods

Conditions and warranties – fob contracts: the obligations of the parties

Veba Oil Supply and Trading GmbH v *Petrotrade Inc* [2002] 1 Lloyd's Rep 295 Court of Appeal (Simon Brown, Tuckey and Dyson LJJ)

Using a test method other than that specified in the contract – material departure from instructions – determination not binding?

Facts

The defendants sold a cargo of 25,000 plus tonnes of gasoil to the claimant buyers, fob Antwerp. A clause in the contract provided:

'Product/Quality Gasoil meeting the following guaranteed specifications:
Test Limit Method ASTM
Density at 15 deg. C + 0.876kg/l. max D1298'

A further clause provided for quantity and quality to be determined by a mutually agreed independent inspector at the loading installation. The determination was to be final and binding for both parties 'save fraud or manifest error'.

Thirty-four thousand tonnes of gasoil were loaded at Antwerp and CB, the appointed inspectors, produced a report stating that the density was 0.8750 kg/l (which was within the contractual specification). The inspectors used the test method D4052 rather than the specified D1298. The gasoil was sold on to the Lebanese Ministry of Oil, but when tested on arrival it was found that the density of the gasoil exceeded the contractual maximum.

The buyers contended that as the inspectors had not used the specified test, the determination was not binding on them and they claimed damages in respect of the breach. The defendants argued that the use of a test other than that specified was not a material departure rendering the determination invalid. It was argued by the defendants that the test used had a lower margin of error and was widely used in calculating the density of gasoil; in addition to which it was customary at Antwerp.

Morrison J found for the claimants. The defendants appealed.

Held

Dismissing the appeal, the Court of Appeal held that the inspectors had departed from their instructions and the determination was therefore not binding. Simon

Brown LJ (at p300) in setting out his position referred to Lord Denning's judgment in *Campbell* v *Edwards* [1976] 1 Lloyd's Rep 522, where he stated that:

'... if an expert makes a mistake while carrying out his instructions, the parties are nevertheless bound by it for the very good reason that they have agreed to be bound by it. Where, however, the expert departs from his instructions, the position is very different: in those circumstances the parties have not agreed to be bound.'

Once a material departure from instructions is established, the determination is not binding on the parties: see *Shell UK Ltd* v *Entrerprise Oil plc* [1999] 2 Lloyd's Rep 456.

Simon Brown LJ agreed with Morrison J when, in referring to the judgment of Dillon LJ in *Jones* v *Sherwood Services Ltd* [1992] 1 WLR 277, he concluded:

'I cannot think that the Court of Appeal meant more by the word material than "not de minimis." It is not the business of the Court to weigh the importance of a stipulation in a contract. If the requirement to use the method specified ... was contractual that is an end of the matter, whether or not the Court thinks it was important or would have made a difference' (p301).

Comment

This case clearly states that the courts will not be concerned with why a party to a contract asks for a particular test. It is for the parties to the contract 'to define their rights and obligations according to their own needs' (per Simon Brown LJ at p301).

OBP Textbook pages 5 and 72, sections 1.4 and 2.7.

International Sale Contracts

The obligations of the cif seller: the bill of lading – application of the COGSA 1971 and the Hague-Visby Rules: documents

Parsons Corporation and Others v *CV Scheepvaartonderneming Happy Ranger, The Happy Ranger* [2002] 2 All ER (Comm) 24 Court of Appeal (Aldous, Tuckey and Rix LJJ)

'Straight' bills of lading – documents of title?

Facts

Parsons Corporation entered into a contract of carriage with the defendant shipowners for the carriage of three reactors from Porto Marghera in Italy to Jubail in Saudi Arabia. During loading, one of the hooks on the vessel's crane broke and a reactor was damaged when it fell to the ground.

The contract was contained in three documents: a signed printed front page headed 'Contract of Carriage', a six-page printed rider and an attached specimen form of bill of lading.

The rider contained a clause providing for English law to apply in the event of any dispute arising under the contract of carriage and bill of lading. The specimen bill of lading contained a General Paramount Clause providing for:

> 'The Hague Rules ... as enacted in the country of shipment shall apply to this contract. When no such enactment is in force in the country of shipment, Articles I to VIII of the Hague Rules shall apply. In such case liability of the Carrier shall be limited to £100 sterling per package.
>
> In trades where the ... Hague-Visby rules – apply compulsorily, the provisions of the respective legislation shall be considered incorporated in this Bill of Lading.'

The claimants sought damages in the sum of approximately US$2.4 million. The defendants argued that as Italy had not enacted the Hague Rules and a bill of lading had not been issued at the time the reactor was dropped, neither the Hague nor the Hague-Visby Rules applied and therefore their liability was limited to £100 per package. The claimants appealed against the judge's finding for the defendants.

The questions for the Court included: did the Hague-Visby Rules apply to the contract of carriage and, if not, could the carriers rely on the £100 per package liability limitation clause?

Held: (Rix LJ dissenting)

The appeal was allowed. The Hague Rules are not enacted in Italy and under Art I(b) the Hague-Visby Rules apply only to contracts of carriage 'covered by a bill of lading or any similar document of title'.

Tuckey LJ stated that the Hague-Visby rules applied compulsorily to the contract of carriage. If a bill of lading is to be issued the contract comes within the definitions of Art I(b) and s1(4) of the Carriage of Goods by Sea Act (COGSA) 1971.

The words 'in any event' in Art IV r5(a) of the Hague-Visby Rules should be given their natural meaning and therefore the defendants' liability was limited as provided for in art IV r5.

Comment

The judgments included a discussion on 'straight' bills of lading. One of the defendants' arguments as to why the Hague-Visby Rules did not apply to the contract of carriage, centred on the submission that such bills were not documents of title within the meaning of Art I(b) of the Hague-Visby rules and s1(4) COGSA 1971. This submission was accepted by Tomlinson J ([2002] 1 All ER (Comm) 176). Tuckey LJ in the Court of Appeal concluded that the bills issued by the defendant shipowners for cargo were not 'straight' bills, and therefore it was not necessary to decide this point. As to whether a 'straight' bill would be a bill of lading or similar document of title within the meaning of the Hague-Visby Rules, Tuckey LJ stated that *CP Henderson & Co v Comptoir d'Escompte de Paris* (1873) LR 5 PC 253 'is only authority for the proposition that a bill naming a consignee which does not contain the words "or order or assigns" is not negotiable (transferable)': at p33. Rix LJ, in his dissenting judgment, concluded that he 'would merely underline Tuckey LJ's comment that it would be unwise to assume that all of the statements in the textbooks regarding "straight" bills are correct.'

The case is under appeal to the House of Lords.

OBP Textbook pages 54 and 226, sections 2.3 and 8.3.

Article

Malcolm Clarke 'Transport Documents: Their Transferability as Documents of Title; Electronic Documents' *[2002] LMCLQ 356*

This article considers the obstacles facing Bolero (electronic bills of lading) and possible solutions put forward by UNCITRAL. In doing so, the article gives a useful account of the nature and role of a bill of lading; the concept of negotiability and transferability in dealing with a bill of lading; and the nature of relationships with regard to the parties to a Bolero bill of lading. Students may find this a useful article if they are undertaking research into bills of lading.

OBP Textbook page 58, section 2.3.

Fas

Transpacific Eternity SA v Kanematsu Corporation and Another, The Antares III [2002] 1 Lloyd's Rep 233 Queen's Bench Division (Commercial Court) (David Steel J)

The passing of property – conflicting claims

Facts

The first defendant, KC, agreed to buy a quantity of soya bean extraction meal and flake from S. The first defendant opened a letter of credit and payment was made. NT Co, a company which had a course of dealing with S, agreed to sell 4,500 tonnes of soya bean meal to S, on fas terms. Payment was to be made under a letter of credit. Subsequently, the second defendant, VF Ltd, was substituted as a seller in place of NT Co.

The claimant owners chartered their vessel, *The Antares III*, to M & S Shipping for a voyage from India to Singapore. M & S had authority to issue bills of lading on the owner's behalf.

Approximately 10,450 tonnes of soya bean extraction were loaded on *The Antares III*, with loading completed on 19 May. Various bills of lading were issued, one of which was made out to the order of the second defendant, VF Ltd. However, the letter of credit provided for shipment up to 30 April, and although it was extended to 8 May, a replacement bill was required. The bank rejected the replacement bill and therefore a further bill, the 'switch bill', was issued. In the switch bill, S was named as the shipper and KC as the notifying company.

When *The Antares III* arrived in Japan, KC presented the switch bill and discharge of the cargo commenced. The carriers then learned of VF Ltd's claim to part of the cargo and sufficient tonnage was left on board to cover the disputed part.

The issue for the court was whether KC or VF Ltd were the owners of the cargo.

VF Ltd contended that it was the owner of the cargo because property had not passed to S under the sale agreement and therefore KC could not obtain title. VF Ltd submitted that property was intended to pass when payment was made by S and this was clear from the bills of lading which were made out to the order of VF Ltd, thus preserving the right of disposal.

KC argued that the presumption of preserving a right of disposal was displaced in the context of an fas contract under which the mate's receipts had named S as consignee. KC submitted that the intention of the parties was that property would pass at the ship's rail.

Held

The second defendants, VF Ltd, were the owners of the disputed part cargo.

The presumption under s19 of the Sale of Goods Act 1979 remains valid for an fob contract and there was no justification for treating an fas contract differently. The terms of the mate's receipts did not alter the construction of the contracts. In dealing with the passing of property and payment by letter of credit issue, David Steel J quoted from the judgment of Staughton LJ in the Court of Appeal in *Mitsui & Co Ltd* v *Flota Mercante Grancolombiana SA* [1988] 2 Lloyd's Rep 208:

> 'Nor can I attach much weight to the fact that the balance of the price was ... payable by letter of credit. Even the most copper-bottomed letter of credit sometimes fails to produce payment for one reason or another; and the seller who has a letter of credit for 100 per cent of the price will nevertheless often retain the property in his goods until he has presented the documents and obtained payment. If only 20 per cent is outstanding his worries will be less, but they may not have disappeared altogether.'

OBP Textbook page 84, section 2.9.

Methods of Financing: Documentary Credits

Developments – letters of credit

In 2002 the ICC published the eUCP 500/2, which adds e-commerce rules to the old UCP500. The eUCPs govern electronic equivalents of paper documents presented under letters of credit.

OBP Textbook page 128, section 4.2.

Carriage of Goods: Carriage of Goods by Sea Act 1971 and the Hague-Visby Rules

Seaworthiness: Art III r1

Papera Traders Co Ltd and Others v *Hyundai Merchant Marine Co Ltd and Another, The Eurasian Dream* [2002] 1 Lloyd's Rep 719 Queen's Bench Division (Commercial Court) (Cresswell J)

The meaning of unseaworthiness

Facts

A fire broke out on *The Eurasian Dream*, a car carrier, whilst the vessel was in port. The master and crew did not extinguish the fire and the cargo, consisting of new and second-hand cars, was destroyed or damaged, resulting in a constructive total loss.

The claimant cargo owners claimed against the defendant carriers for loss or damage to the cargo. The claimants argued that *The Eurasian Dream* was unseaworthy and there was a failure on the part of the managers of the vessel to exercise due diligence before and at the beginning of the voyage and therefore there was a breach of art III r1 of the Hague/Hague-Visby Rules. Alternatively, there was a breach of art III r2.

Held

The Eurasian Dream was unseaworthy in that it was 'not in a suitable condition and suitably manned and equipped' (per Cresswell J at p742). The vessel had an inadequate number of walkie-talkies which resulted in a lack of communication between the bunkering team and other members of the crew. Some of the fire extinguishers were defective; a main valve was corroded; at least two fire hydrants were tied with rope which affected their utility; and generally this 'reflected the poor fire-fighting training and incompetence of the master and crew' (p742). In addition to the poor state of the equipment, the master was new to the vessel and to car carriers in general. The master and crew were ignorant of the fire hazards involved in carrying vehicles on a car carrier. Also a large amount of the documentation provided for the vessel did not relate to car carriers and was therefore potentially misleading. As the finding was that the ship was unseaworthy and the defendants had failed to exercise due diligence, there was no need to look at the alternative claim of a breach of art III r2.

Comment

Cresswell J in his judgment (p736) referred to 'the classic definition of seaworthiness' contained in the judgment of Scrutton LJ in *FC Bradley & Sons Ltd* v *Federal Steam Navigation Co* (1926) 24 Ll LR 446 at p454, approving a statement from *Carver on Carriage by Sea*:

'The ship must have that degree of fitness which an ordinary careful owner would require his vessel to have at the commencement of her voyage having regard to all the probable circumstances of it. Would a prudent owner have required that it (sc the defect) be made good before sending his ship to sea, had he known of it?'

Cresswell J then lists the components of the duty to exercise due diligence in providing a seaworthy ship.

Apart from giving good examples of what amounts to unseaworthiness, the judgment in this case usefully sets out the burden of proof when dealing with Art III rr1 and 2. The burden of proof is on the cargo owner to prove that the vessel was unseaworthy and that the loss or damage was caused by that unseaworthiness: *The Europa* [1908] P 84. If the claimant cargo owner is able to discharge that burden, the burden passes to the defendant carriers/shipowners to prove that they exercised due diligence to make the ship seaworthy: *The Toledo* [1995] 1 Lloyd's Rep 40.

OBP Textbook page 232, section 8.5.

Marine Insurance: Institute Cargo Clauses, Loss and Indemnity

Institute cargo clauses: duration of the cover; the exclusions

Bayview Motors Ltd v *Mitsui Marine and Fire Insurance Co Ltd and Others* [2002] 1 Lloyd's Rep 652 Queen's Bench Division (Commercial Court) (David Steel J)

ICC cover – 'final place of storage'? – withholding by customs – within the excepted peril of seizure?

Facts
The claimants purchased two consignments of motor vehicles, on cif terms. Both consignments were shipped from Japan to Santo Domingo (Dominican Republic) under all risks, warehouse to warehouse, marine cargo policies. Although the motor vehicles were sold cif Santo Domingo, the contracts of sale referred to the Turks and Caicos Islands as being the destination of the goods.

The consignments arrived at Santo Domingo but were not released by the customs staff for transhipment on to the Turks and Caicos Islands.

The claimants alleged that the vehicles had been stolen or taken without legal justification by the customs' employees, and claimed under the insurance policies for the loss of the vehicles.

The defendant insurers argued that (1) the vehicles had been 'confiscated' by the customs authority because they had not been declared for transhipment at the landing ports and, therefore, the loss came within the excepted peril of 'seizure'; and

(2) the loss was proximately caused by the claimants' failure to avert or minimise the loss by failing to seek legal advice to preserve rights against the Dominican customs. A further issue for the court was whether the loss had occurred after cover had ceased, ie because the goods had been landed at Santo Domingo.

Held (inter alia)

1. The area within the port where the motor vehicles were placed was in effect a bonded store to which the customs controlled access. It was therefore not the final place of storage and cover under the insurance policies extended to 60 days after completion of discharge from the vessel. Hence the loss occurred during cover.
2. A partial loss, which later became an actual total loss, occurred when the customs improperly refused to release the vehicles. In effect there had been conversion which was an insured peril under the all risks policy.
3. The excepted peril of seizure was not applicable because the customs officials were not acting lawfully as organs of the state. There was therefore no taking by lawful authority;
4. The failure to take legal advice was not a proximate cause of the loss.

OBP Textbook pages 289 and 297, sections 11.2 and 11.5.

Article

Baris Soyer 'Defences Available to a Marine Insurer' [2002] LMCLQ 199

This article considers the defences available to a marine insurer, particularly in the light of *The Milasan* [2000] 2 Lloyd's Rep 458, a case where a yacht sank in calm weather. The burden of proof and proximate causation is discussed, with references to cases such as *Rhesa Shipping Co SA* v *Edmunds, The Popi M* [1985] 1 WLR 918 and *Leyland Shipping Co Ltd* v *Norwich Union Fire Insurance Society Ltd* [1918] AC 350.

OBP Textbook pages 292 and 293, sections 11.4 and 11.5.

Arbitration

Enforcement of the award – appealing against an arbitral award on a point of law

Mousaka Inc v *Golden Seagull Maritime Inc and Another* [2002] 1 All ER 726 Queen's Bench Division (Commercial Court) (David Steel J)

North Range Shipping Ltd v *Seatrans Shipping Corp* [2002] 4 All ER 390 Court of Appeal (Peter Gibson, Aldous and Tuckey LJJ)

Interpretation of s69 Arbitration Act 1996 in light of the Human Rights Act 1998 Sch 1, Pt 1, art 6

Facts
In both cases the courts were dealing with, inter alia, the question of whether a judge was obliged to give reasons for refusing leave of appeal under the Arbitration Act 1996, s69, and the Human Rights Act 1998, Sch 1, Pt 1, art 6.

Held
In *Mousaka Inc* the judge summarised (at p734) the relevant Strasbourg jurisprudence:

'... Article 6 obliges courts to give reasons. The extent of this duty varies according to the nature of the decision and the circumstances of the case. ... Full reasons should be given for a decision on the merits ... art 6 ... does not guarantee a right of appeal. ... If a right of appeal is rejected, the applicant must be made aware of the grounds on which the decision was reached: in many cases this may take the form of an endorsement of the lower court's decision. ... Where there are legitimate restraints on a right of appeal ... it is sufficient for the court to refer to these limitations.'

In *North Range Shipping* Tuckey LJ in the Court of Appeal expressed the view that the trend of the law has been towards an increased recognition of the duty to give reasons. Article 6 does not state that reasons have to be given. However, it does state that 'in the determination of his civil rights ... everyone is entitled to a fair and public hearing'. Tuckey LJ also stated (pp396–397) that 'it is common ground that the right to a fair hearing generally carries with it an obligation to give reasons.'

Permission to appeal was granted, but the appeal was dismissed.

Comment
These two cases deal with s69 of the Arbitration Act 1996 in light of art 6 of Sch 1 of the Human Rights Act 1998. Cases referred to in the judgments include: *Antaios Cia Naviera SA* v *Salen Rederierna AB, The Antaios* [1984] 3 All ER 229 (HL); *Henry Boot Construction (UK) Ltd* v *Malmaison Hotel (Manchester) Ltd* [2001] 1 All ER 257 (CA); and *Webb* v *United Kingdom* (1997) 24 EHRR CD 73 (E Com HR).

OBP Textbook page 348, section 13.9.

20

Public International Law

Immunity from Jurisdiction

State immunity

Arrest Warrant of 11 April 2000 (Democratic Republic of the Congo v *Belgium)* Judgment of 14 February 2002 (not yet reported) International Court of Justice

State immunity – international warrant in absentia – international crimes

Facts
Under a Belgian law of 1993, Belgian courts have universal jurisdiction in respect of grave breaches of the 1949 Geneva Conventions and Additional Protocols I and II and crimes against humanity. The above law applies irrespective of whether or not the alleged offender has acted in an official capacity. On the basis of the above law the Belgian investigating judge issued on 11 April 2000 an international arrest warrant in absentia against the then Minister for Foreign Affairs of Congo, Mr Abdulaye Yerodia Ndombasi, for serious violations of international humanitarian law and crimes against humanity. On 17 October 2000 the Congo filed an application before the International Court of Justice (ICJ) against Belgium, challenging the arrest warrant. The government of Congo argued that the arrest warrant violated, inter alia, the principle that 'a state may not exercise its authority on the territory of another state', the principle of sovereign equality among member states of the United Nations (laid down in art 2(1) of the UN Charter) and the diplomatic immunity of the Minister for Foreign Affairs of a sovereign state (as recognised by art 41(2) of the Vienna Convention on Diplomatic Relations 1961). The government of Belgium, being less revolutionary than its judiciary, tried to remove the case from the ICJ agenda, arguing that Mr Yerodia no longer had ministerial responsibility and that Belgium was undertaking a review of the relevant legislation. The ICJ rejected both arguments. On 14 February 2002 the ICJ rendered its judgment.

Held
The ICJ held that the arrest warrant was issued in violation of customary international law concerning the absolute inviolability and immunity from criminal proceedings of the incumbent foreign minister, and was therefore in breach of the principle of sovereign equality among states (held by 13 votes to three). Those acts engaged Belgium's international responsibility. The ICJ stated that its findings in

this case constituted a form of satisfaction which would make good the moral injury complained of by the Congo. Further, the ICJ held that Belgium must, by means of its own choosing, cancel the unlawful arrest warrant and inform all concerned parties of its cancellation (held by ten votes to six).

Comment

This is a very disappointing decision from the point of view of the development of international human rights. The ICJ clearly stated that the incumbent foreign minister enjoyed absolute immunity from criminal proceedings, even though he was accused of having committed crimes under international law. The Court, however, emphasised that the immunity does not mean impunity, since the immunity from jurisdiction does not affect individual criminal responsibility. Accordingly, there are circumstances where an individual can be held responsible:

1. before the courts of his own country; or
2. his state may waive immunity and allow another state to bring him to justice; or
3. after he ceases to hold public office he may be tried by any state which has jurisdiction under international law to do so; or
4. in the future he may be brought before the International Criminal Court.

The above judgment, nevertheless, confirms that political power means protection and immunity. While in office, notorious abusers of human rights, instead of being prosecuted, are protected by international law!

In the light of this judgment it seems that the removal of immunity in respect of former heads of state is unlikely to be extended in practice to heads of state while in office. A federal court of the US upheld sovereign immunity in respect of a serving head of state, Jean-Bertrand Aristide, for his alleged involvement in a political assassination: *Lafontant* v *Aristide* 844 F Supp 128 (Eastern Dist NY 1994). In the context of the *Arrest Warrant* case, the proceedings against the Libyan head of state, Muammar Qadhafi, in France should not be allowed to proceed.

The ICJ agreed with the contentions of the Congo that, under international customary law, serving foreign ministers when abroad enjoy absolute immunity from criminal jurisdiction and inviolability. They are protected from 'any act of authority' by another state irrespective of whether they are in foreign territory in an 'official' or 'private' capacity, whether the acts were performed before or during the period of office and whether or not they were performed in an official or private capacity. This rule also applies in the situation when a Minister for Foreign Affairs is accused of having committed international crimes.

The implications of the above judgment are far-reaching. Notwithstanding the fact that the judgment of the ICJ applies only to the case at issue, and therefore is binding only between the parties to the proceedings, it is unlikely that the ICJ will change its approach in the future. Therefore, not only Belgium, but also other states (for example the USA in respect of the US Alien Tort Claims Act) will have to review their national legislation in the light of the above judgment, taking into account the statement of the ICJ that persons enjoying immunity must be protected from 'any act of authority' by another state that would prevent them from exercising the functions of their office.

It is also important to note that in the above judgment the ICJ did not examine the matter of whether or not Belgium was entitled to enact national legislation under which municipal courts have universal jurisdiction in respect of international crimes. The Congo decided to withdraw its original argument, which challenged the legality of the Belgian law under international law. Consequently, the ICJ assumed for the purposes of the case that Belgium had jurisdiction under international law to issue the arrest warrant.

OBP Textbook page 150, section 9.2.

Al-Adsani v *United Kingdom (No 2)* (2002) 34 EHRR 11 European Court of Human Rights

Sovereign immunity preventing the claimant from pursuing domestic cases – prohibition of torture – human rights – no breach of the right to fair hearing under art 6(1) of the European Convention on Human Rights

Facts
Mr Al-Adsani, a British passport holder and Kuwaiti citizen, served in the Kuwaiti Air Force during the Gulf war and after the Iraqi invasion became a member of the Kuwaiti resistance movement. At that time he came into possession of sexual videotapes involving Sheikh Jaber al-Saud al-Sabah, who was related to the Emir of Kuwait. By some means the tapes entered into general circulation. Sheikh Jaber blamed Mr Al-Adsani for this. Mr Al-Adsani alleged that he was kidnapped by Sheikh Jaber al-Saud al-Sabah, taken to prison in Kuwait and beaten by security guards. After his release from prison he was tortured by the Sheikh and his servants. The claimant spent six weeks in hospital in England and was treated for burns covering 25 per cent of his body. In August 1992 he brought an action against Sheikh Jaber al-Saud al-Sabah and the government of Kuwait. At first instance it was held that the government was entitled to state immunity under the State Immunity Act 1978. On appeal it was argued that:

1. immunity did not apply to acts prohibited by international law;
2. torture was contrary to international law, and in particular to the 1984 Torture Convention and other human rights treaties;
3. torture is a criminal offence by virtue of the Criminal Justice Act 1988.

The Court of Appeal rejected the appeal in March 1996. In December 1996 the House of Lords refused leave to appeal.

In March 1997 the claimant, having exhausted domestic remedies, lodged an application to the European Commission of Human Rights under the European Convention on Human Rights (ECHR) (Application No 35763/97).

Held

The European Court of Human Rights held:

1. unanimously that there had been no violation of art 3 of the Convention;
2. by nine votes to eight that there had been no violation of art 6(1) of the Convention.

Comment

The right of access to courts constitutes an inherent part of the right to a fair trial guaranteed under art 6(1) ECHR. Its objective is to avoid the denial of justice, for example a situation where a person has no access to national courts in a contracting state: *Golder* v *United Kingdom* (1994) 18 EHRR 393. The European Court of Human Rights confirmed that this right is not, however, absolute. Some limitations are allowed, provided that they do not restrict or reduce access to a national court in such a manner, or to such an extent, as to impair the very essence of the right: *Waite and Kennedy* v *Germany* (2000) 30 EHRR 261. Those limitations must pursue a legitimate aim, and must be proportionate to the objective sought to be attained by the contracting state. In the commented case, the Court had to determine whether or not the limitation was justified on the basis of the doctrine of sovereign immunity.

The Court accepted that the application of the doctrine of sovereign immunity, under which a state grants sovereign immunity to another state in respect of civil proceedings, had pursued the legitimate aim of complying with international law to promote comity and good relations between states.

The issue of proportionality was, however, more controversial. The starting point in the deliberations of the European Court of Human Rights was that the ECHR must be interpreted in accordance with international law, in particular art 31(3) of the Vienna Convention on the Law of Treaties 1969 which provides that in the interpretation of a treaty, account must be taken of: 'any relevant rules of international law applicable in the relations between the parties'. Consequently, the Court had to take into consideration relevant rules of international law, in particular those relating to the grant of state immunity. The Court stated that generally recognised rules of public international law on state immunity could not, in principle, be considered as imposing a disproportionate restriction on the right to access to court. Nevertheless, this case was unusual, taking into account the fact that the applicant's claim was related to torture, the prohibition of which has acquired the status of ius cogens in international law, and as such prevails over treaty law and other rules of international law.

The prohibition of torture has been recognised by the International Criminal Tribunal for the Former Yugoslavia as having the status of ius cogens. In *Furundzija* IT–95–17/1 'Lasva Valley' (1999) 38 ILM 317 (Trial Chamber II) the International Criminal Tribunal for the Former Yugoslavia stated that:

'Because of the importance of the values it protects, [the prohibition of torture] has evolved into a peremptory norm or ius cogens, that is, a norm that enjoys a higher rank in the international hierarchy than treaty law and even "ordinary" customary rules. The most conspicuous consequence of this higher rank is that the principle at issue cannot be derogated from by states through international treaties or local or special customs or even general customary rules not endowed with the same normative force ... Clearly, the ius cogens nature of the prohibition against torture articulates the notion that the prohibition has now become one of the most fundamental standards of the international community. Furthermore, this prohibition is designed to produce a deterrent effect, in that it signals to all members of the international community and the individuals over whom they wield authority that the prohibition of torture is an absolute value from which nobody must deviate.'

The United Nations General Assembly has adopted a large number of resolutions recognising torture as a crime under international law. Lord Browne-Wilkinson in *R v Bow Street Metropolitan Stipendiary Magistrate, ex parte Pinochet Ugarte (No 3)* [1999] 2 WLR 827 stated that torture was 'an international crime in the highest sense' long before the 1984 Torture Convention recognised it as such. Also, under art 3 ECHR the right not be subjected to torture or to inhuman or degrading treatment or punishment is an absolute right, suffering no exception under any circumstances.

The European Court of Human Rights examined in depth the new developments in international law in respect of the prohibition of torture as a norm of ius cogens, but nevertheless stated that:

'... the Court, while noting the growing recognition of the overriding importance of the prohibition of torture, does not accordingly find it established that there is yet acceptance in international law of the proposition that states are not entitled to immunity in respect of civil claims for damages for alleged torture committed outside the forum state. The 1978 [State Immunity] Act, which grants immunity to states in respect of personal injury claims unless the damage was caused within the United Kingdom, is not inconsistent with those limitations generally accepted by the community of nations as part of the doctrine of state immunity.'

Consequently the European Court of Human Rights held that there was no violation of art 6(1) ECHR by the UK, and that the UK was entitled, under the State Immunity Act 1978, to grant immunity to a foreign state in respect of personal injury claims when the damage occurred outside the forum state.

OBP Textbook page 152, section 9.2.

21

Succession

Animus Testandi

Undue influence

Re Good (Deceased); Carapeto v ***Good and Others*** (2002) The Times
22 May Chancery Division (Rimer J)

Disabled testatrix named housekeeper as executor and principal beneficiary under
her will – on the testatrix's death her family alleged undue influence – burden of
proof in respect of undue influence – factors applicable to the award of costs in a
probate action

Facts
The deceased, who had suffered from physical disabilities, engaged C (the claimant)
as her housekeeper and invited her to live in her house. After she died, the
deceased's final will showed that C and her family had been named as executors and
were the principal beneficiaries under it. G and others (the defendants) were all
members of the deceased's family and they argued that although she had had
testamentary capacity when the will was drawn up, it was invalid because undue
influence had been exercised over the deceased by C and her family. C sought to
prove the will in solemn form. It was accepted that C's family had been sufficiently
implicated in the events preceeding the will being drawn up to raise a suspicion as
to whether the deceased knew and approved its contents.

Held
The party propounding a will (ie C) had the burden of proving that the testatrix
knew and approved of its contents. Such a burden would usually be discharged by
establishing that the will had been duly executed and that the testator had
testamentary capacity. In cases which, like the instant one, gave rise to suspicion, the
necessary proof of knowledge and approval could only be met by demonstrating that
the testatrix not only understood the nature of the testamentary provision, but also
its effect. On the evidence, C had demonstrated that the deceased knew and
approved of the contents of her will. Accordingly, C could successfully defend the
allegation of undue influence and the will was valid.

As to the award of costs in a probate action, the usual order under r44.3 Civil
Procedure Rules 1998 was that the unsuccessful party would pay the costs. To
depart from this usual order a judge could, when taking into account all the

circumstances (for the purposes of r44.3), have regard to the principles set out in *Spiers* v *English* [1907] P 122 – that it might be appropriate to make an alternative costs order where the testatrix or those interested in the residue had caused the litigation, or if the circumstances led reasonably to an investigation. Here there were grounds for suspecting undue influence and the defendants were entitled to test their case. Nevertheless, C had to go through the unpleasantness of defending a charge of undue influence. In all the circumstances, it was appropriate for the defendants to pay half of C's costs.

Comment
The case is noteworthy for two main reasons. First, it makes clear that in the particular context of the case (disabled testatrix naming housekeeper and family as principal beneficiaries of her will), undue influence was to be construed as coercion and it was for the defendants to prove that C's family so overbore the deceased that she had been induced to execute the will. It was not enough to demonstrate that they had simply persuaded her to make generous provision for them. Here the defendants could not prove coercion. Second, it identified factors to be applied when considering a departure from the usual rule as to costs in a probate action.

OBP Textbook pages 72–74, section 5.4.

Family Provision

Who can apply under the 1975 Act?

Gandhi v *Patel* [2002] 1 FLR 603 Chancery Division (Park J)

Woman went through Hindu marriage ceremony with the deceased – man already married – woman claimed under the Inheritance (Provision for Family and Dependants) Act 1975 against the deceased's estate arguing that for the purposes of the Act she should be regarded as the deceased's wife – whether ceremony a void marriage for the purposes of s25(4) of the 1975 Act – whether claimant entered ceremony in good faith

Facts
HG (the claimant) had gone through a Hindu marriage ceremony in an Indian restaurant with JG (the deceased) which had been presided over by a Brahmin priest. After the ceremony, which did not comply with the requirements of the Marriage Act 1949, HG lived with JG at one of his properties and had two children with him. No attempt was made to go through an English marriage ceremony. Further, at the time of the Hindu marriage ceremony, JG had been married to another woman whom he never divorced. The relationship between HG and JG was a stormy one and, some time after the birth of their second child, they began leading separate lives, albeit that they continued to reside in the same house. The

relationship between the parties further deteriorated, culminating in HG bringing domestic violence proceedings against JG, which he strongly disputed and which were settled on the basis of mutual non-molestation undertakings. Shortly before JG died, HG instituted proceedings against him for the transfer of one of his properties to her. In those proceedings she stated that she was not married to JG. Under the terms of JG's will, HG was allowed to live in a house which JG had left to their son until she died, remarried or cohabited. This was the only reference to HG in the will. HG brought proceedings under the Inheritance (Provision for Family and Dependants) Act 1975, contending that the will did not make reasonable financial provision for her and maintaining that, despite the fact that she had not been married to the deceased, she should in the circumstances be regarded for the purposes of the Act as 'the wife of the deceased'. The issue to be determined was whether HG was 'a person who in good faith [had] entered into a void marriage' within the meaning of s25(4) of the 1975 Act.

Held

For a ceremony to create a void marriage it had, at the very least, to purport to be a marriage of the kind contemplated by the Marriage Act 1949. Here the Hindu marriage ceremony had not complied with the requirements of English law and did not purport to do so. Further, no attempt had been made by the participants to comply with those requirements. In such circumstances, it could not be said that the marriage was a void one. Rather, it had amounted to a 'non-marriage'. Even if the Hindu ceremony had amounted to a void marriage, it was clear on the evidence that HG had not entered into it in good faith. On the balance of probabilities, HG knew that the 'marriage' was not valid at the time she entered into it. She knew that JG was married to someone else at the time of the ceremony. Even if the Hindu ceremony had created a void marriage, HG's claim against JG's estate would have failed on the ground that she did not enter the marriage in good faith. Accordingly, judgment was given for JG's executors.

Comment

The court made clear that the meaning of 'void marriage' in s25(4) of the 1975 Act was the same as in s11 Matrimonial Causes Act 1973. Interestingly the court stated, per incuriam, that if the claim had succeeded in principle, it would have found that JG's will had not made reasonable provision for HG, but that her reasonable provision would probably have been reduced because of the allegations of unsatisfactory conduct by her in her relationship with the deceased: see s3(1)(g) of the 1975 Act.

OBP Textbook pages 188–189, section 12.2.

Dispositions intended to defeat applications

Nathan v *Leonard* (2002) The Times 4 June Chancery Division (John Martin QC)

Codicil to will provided that if certain beneficiaries challenged the will they would lose their interest under it – one such beneficiary made an application under the Inheritance (Provision for Family and Dependants) Act 1975 thus triggering the condition – whether the condition was void as contrary to public policy

Facts

The testatrix (DN) owned a beneficial half share in a property. The other half belonged to the defendants (SL and PL), her friends. DN made a will leaving her estate between a number of beneficiaries. Her residuary estate was to be divided between her son (AN) and the defendants. After the will had been drawn up, DN prepared a codicil which contained a condition providing that her entire estate would go to SL and PL in the event of any other beneficiary contesting her will. After DN died, her son made a claim under the Inheritance (Provision for Family and Dependants) Act 1975 for further provision from his mother's estate. The court considered as a preliminary issue whether the condition subsequent was void as being contrary to public policy, because it had the effect of deterring a beneficiary from making a claim under the 1975 Act for fear of losing his benefit under the will.

Held

The fact that the condition subsequent to the will would deter a beneficiary from challenging the will for fear of losing his benefit under it did not of itself render the condition void as contrary to public policy. The condition did not prevent a beneficiary from making a claim under the 1975 Act. The loss of benefit under the will resulting from a challenge to it by way of an application for financial provision under the 1975 Act was a matter which the court could have regard to when considering the application. The court would decide whether reasonable provision had been made for the applicant, and in so doing it would have regard to the fact that, because of the condition, AN had received nothing from his mother's estate. However, since here the condition subsequent was void for uncertainty, it was unenforceable and the dispositions under DN's will were unaffected by it. Accordingly, the preliminary issue was determined in favour of AN.

Comment

The case establishes that a condition subsequent to a will which would have the effect of deterring a beneficiary from making a claim under the 1975 Act (because he could lose a benefit under the will by challenging it) was not in itself void for being contrary to public policy. The reality was that such a condition would be an additional factor which a potential applicant would have to consider before issuing proceedings under the 1975 Act. The court made it clear that the validity or otherwise of the condition did not turn on assessing how much of a deterrent it was in any particular case. The reason the testatrix drafted the codicil was to protect her disposition.

OBP Textbook pages 225–227, section 12.14.

Taxation of Estates

General powers of appointment – discretionary trusts

Melville v *Inland Revenue Commissioners* [2001] STC 1271 Court of Appeal (Civil Division) (Peter Gibson, Arden and Kay LJJ)

Inheritance tax – discretionary trusts – general power of appointment – meaning of 'property' within s272 Inheritance Tax Act (IHTA) 1984

Facts

The settlor had transferred property into a discretionary settlement subject to a right to require the trustees to revest all or part of the settled property in him at any time during his lifetime after the expiry of 90 days. The trustees were given various powers which were in theory capable of affecting the value of the taxpayer's general power of appointment. These powers of the trustees were, however, only exercisable with the settlor's consent during the lifetime of the settlor.

The purpose of the scheme was to produce a saving of capital gains tax at very little cost in inheritance tax (IHT). Capital gains tax holdover relief would be available, because the transfer was immediately chargeable to IHT. However, the value of the assets transferred to the trust would be heavily discounted because the settlor could reclaim them, so there would be little IHT.

The Inland Revenue argued that the general power was not property comprised in his estate for inheritance tax purposes. Therefore, he had made a chargeable transfer of the entirety of the property transferred into the discretionary settlement.

Mr Justice Lightman found for the taxpayer. He held that the general power of appointment was a valuable right in the taxpayer's estate.

Held

The Court of Appeal agreed with Mr Justice Lightman that the right to require the revesting of the assets was 'property' within the meaning of s272 Inheritance Tax Act 1984. That section defines property to include 'rights and interests of any description'. The Court held that the holder of a general power of appointment unquestionably had a valuable right, the value of which had to be taken into account in the value of the holder's estate under s5(1) IHTA 1984, unless excluded by some other provision of the IHTA 1984.

Comment

The decision that a general power of appointment is to be regarded as property worked in the taxpayer's favour in this case. However, there may be cases where the existence of a general power of appointment will mean that a taxpayer will face a charge to IHT which would not have arisen had the Inland Revenue's contention that it is not property been accepted.

It should be noted that an important change resulting from this year's Budget is that the effect of the decision in *Melville* v *Inland Revenue Commissioners* [2001] STC 1271 has been reversed. Powers over trust property (for example, powers of revocation or general powers of appointment) will not be treated as part of the power holder's free estate. This is a welcome change and will prevent what could have been some significant unfairness and complexity.

Reservation of benefit

Inland Revenue Commissioners v *Eversden* [2002] STC 1109 Chancery Division (Lightman J)

Inheritance tax – reservation of benefit – transfers between spouses

Facts
Ms Greenstock (the settlor) created a settlement in 1988. Her husband was the life tenant and after his death the property was to be held for a class of discretionary beneficiaries, which included the settlor, for 80 years. Thereafter, it was to be held on trust for the settlor's daughter and her issue. The trustees had power to acquire property for the use and enjoyment of the beneficiaries. The settlor also transferred the matrimonial home to the trustees to hold as to 95 per cent on the trusts of the settlement and as to 5 per cent for her.

The husband occupied the matrimonial home, as life tenant of the trust, with the settlor until he died in 1992. The trustees then sold the matrimonial home and used the proceeds to acquire a replacement property and an investment bond. The settlor had a 5 per cent interest in the replacement property and the bond. From the date of the purchases until her death in 1998, the settlor was in sole occupation of the replacement property but had no benefit from the bond.

The Inland Revenue argued that, as a result of the reservation of benefit rules, the whole of the trust fund was included in the settlor's estate. This was because she was included in the class of discretionary beneficiaries and had occupied the replacement property.

Held
The issues for the court were: was the inclusion of the settlor in the class of discretionary beneficiaries a reservation of benefit; was the occupation of the replacement property a reservation of benefit; and did the transfer of the property to the husband for life exempt the trust fund from the reservation of benefit rules for all time or only for so long as the life interest continued?

Lightman J found as follows: it was clear that the inclusion of the settlor in a class of discretionary beneficiaries was a reservation of benefit. The trustees must be presumed to have given the settlor a right to occupy the replacement property rent free and to the exclusion of the other beneficiaries in return for the settlor allowing the full proceeds of sale to be used in the purchase. However, the transfer by the settlor had to be looked at with regard to the date it was made. The transfer was, at that date, an exempt transfer between spouses. It therefore completely excluded the reservation of benefit rules for all time.

Comment
The last point is obviously valuable when trying to arrange the affairs of spouses in an inheritance tax efficient manner.

Faulkner v *Inland Revenue Commissioners* [2001] STC (SCD) 112 Special Commissioners (Nuala Brice J)

Inheritance tax – right to occupy property after death – creation of interests in possession for inheritance tax purposes

Facts
The testator (T) directed in his will that H and his wife, or the survivor of them, should be permitted to live in a house which formed part of T's estate for as long as they so wished. T died in March 1981, after which H and his wife moved into the property. H survived his wife and died in August 1998. The Inland Revenue contended that at the date of his death, H had an interest in possession in settled property within s49(1) Inheritance Tax Act 1984. The surviving trustee of T's will (F) contended that the will created neither a settlement nor an interest in possession. It merely gave directions to allow H and his wife a licence to occupy the property. He also argued that if H had had any beneficial interest, it was shared with the three residuary beneficiaries under the will, and so any interest in possession enjoyed by H amounted to one quarter only of the value of the property.

Held
The special commissioners agreed with the Inland Revenue and dismissed F's contentions. The will did not give any dispositive powers to the trustees to decide whether or not H and his wife should occupy the property. The trustees had no discretion to refuse any request by H and his wife that they be permitted to occupy the property. It followed that the will created a settlement in favour of H and his wife, and that H had an interest in possession at the date of his death. That interest was not shared with the residuary beneficiaries, who had no interest at all in the property during H's occupation.

Comment
This case is a good illustration of the significance for inheritance tax purposes of having a right to occupy a property, as opposed to merely being permitted to do so.

OBP Textbook page 356, section 21.1.

22

Tort

Parties to an Action in Tort

Liability

Matthews v *Ministry of Defence* [2002] 3 All ER 513 Court of Appeal
(Lord Phillips MR, Mummery and Hale LJJ)

Injury to serviceman – Crown immunity – human rights

Facts
The claimant alleged that, in the course of his service in the Royal Navy from 1955 to 1968, in various boiler rooms he had been exposed to asbestos fibres and, as a result, that he had developed asbestos-related injuries. Taking a preliminary point, the defendant contended that it was immune from liability by virtue of s10 Crown Proceedings Act 1947. The claimant argued that this provision is incompatible with art 6(1) of, and art 1 of the First Protocol to, the European Convention for the Protection of Human Rights and Fundamental Freedoms.

Held
The defendant's preliminary point was valid: s10 was not incompatible with the Convention; the action would be dismissed.

Comment
Section 10 of the 1947 Act was repealed by the Crown Proceedings (Armed Forces) Act 1987, but only prospectively, although its effect can be revived by the Secretary of State 'by reason of any imminent national danger or of any great emergency'. The prospective repeal of s10 prompted the Court of Appeal to say: 'it does appear to us to be harsh that servicemen who are now discovering that they have sustained injury as a result of tortious conduct prior to 1987 should be treated so less favourably than servicemen who have sustained injury in similar circumstances, but as a result of more recent events'.

OBP Textbook page 10, section 2.2.

Joint and Several Tortfeasors

Contribution between tortfeasors

Royal Brompton Hospital NHS Trust v *Hammond* [2002] 2 All ER 801
House of Lords (Lords Bingham of Cornhill, Mackay of Clashfern, Steyn,
Hope of Craighead and Rodger of Earlsferry)

Contribution – 'the same damage' – s1(1) Civil Liability (Contribution) Act 1978

Facts
Under a building contract in standard form an NHS Trust (the employer) employed
a main contractor (the contractor) for phase one of the construction of a hospital.
Architects (the architect) were engaged under the contract. The work was not
completed on time. The contractor and the employer settled their dispute following
arbitration and the employer now sued the architect, alleging negligence. The
architect sought contribution from the contractor and the contractor applied to strike
out this claim. The contractor succeeded at first instance and the Court of Appeal
upheld this decision. The architect contended that the words 'the same damage' in
s1(1) Civil Liability (Contribution) Act 1978 should be given a broad and purposive
interpretation and therefore that the claim should not have been struck out.

Held
This was not the case: the words should be given their natural and ordinary
meaning and, on the facts, the claim had been rightly struck out.

Lord Bingham of Cornhill:

> 'It would seem to me clear that any liability the employer might prove against the
> contractor and the architect would be independent and not common. The employer's
> claim against the contractor would be based on the contractor's delay in performing the
> contract and the disruption caused by the delay, and the employer's damage would be the
> increased cost it incurred, the sums it overpaid and the liquidated damages to which it
> was entitled. Its claim against the architect, based on negligent advice and certification,
> would not lead to the same damage because it could not be suggested that the architect's
> negligence had led to any delay in performing the contract.'

Comment
Their Lordships rejected the contention (see, eg, *Friends' Provident Life Office* v
Hillier Parker May & Rowden [1995] 4 All ER 260) that the 1978 Act should be
given a wide interpretation.

OBP Textbook page 18, section 3.5.

Vicarious Liability

Partnership

Dubai Aluminium Co Ltd v *Salaam* (2002) The Times 6 December House of Lords (Lords Slynn of Hadley, Nicholls of Birkenhead, Hutton, Hobhouse of Woodborough and Millett)

Firm – partner – 'wrongful act or omission' – contribution

Facts

It was alleged (but never proved) that Mr Amhurst, a partner in a firm of solicitors (the firm), had assisted in an elaborate fraud by drafting certain agreements. The defrauded plaintiff's claim against the firm and Mr Amhurst was settled by a payment of $US10 million. The firm now made contribution claims, based on s1(1) Civil Liability (Contribution) Act 1978, against two of the fraudsters. In order to succeed, the firm had to show that it was liable in respect of the plaintiff's loss.

Held

The firm's claim would be successful. Mr Amhurst's alleged wrongdoing had been a 'wrongful act or omission' which he had carried out while 'acting in the ordinary course of the business of the firm', within s10 Partnership Act 1890. As Lord Nicholls of Birkenhead explained, there was nothing in the language of s10 to suggest that the wrongful act or omission was intended to be confined to common law torts as opposed to the equitable wrong of dishonest participation in a breach of trust. Drafting agreements of such a nature for a proper purpose would be within the ordinary course of the firm's business. Drafting those particular agreements was to be regarded as an act done within the ordinary course of the firm's business, even though they were drafted for a dishonest purpose. Those acts were so closely connected with the acts Mr Amhurst was authorised to do that for the purpose of the firm's liability they could fairly and properly be regarded as done by him while acting in the ordinary course of the firm's business and the firm was accordingly liable. In deciding contribution the personal innocence of the other partners was not a relevant matter to be taken into account. For all relevant purposes the firm stood in the shoes of Mr Amhurst.

OBP Textbook page 37, section 4.8.

The Duty of Care and 'Protected Parties'

The character of the plaintiff

Rees v *Darlington Memorial Hospital NHS Trust* [2002] 2 All ER 177
Court of Appeal (Waller, Robert Walker and Hale LJJ)

Negligent sterilisation – unwanted pregnancy – disabled mother – liability

Facts
The severely visually handicapped claimant had been adamant that she did not want a child: her disability would make difficult its care and upbringing. A sterilisation operation was performed negligently by the defendants: subsequently, she gave birth to a son who was healthy, although there was a low risk that he had inherited the claimant's genetic condition. Could the claimant recover any, and if so which, of the costs of bringing up her child?

Held (Waller LJ dissenting)
The claimant could recover any extra costs which were attributable to her disability.

Hale LJ:

'All of their Lordships' discussion [in *McFarlane* v *Tayside Health Board* [1999] 4 All ER 961] was on the basis that the child was healthy, and therefore that the costs were those of bringing up a healthy child. It did no violence to their reasoning to conclude in *Parkinson* v *St James and Seacroft University Hospital NHS Trust* [2001] 3 All ER 97 that the extra costs of bringing up a disabled child altered the justice of the case. In *McFarlane*'s case the parents were no different from any others in their ability actually to look after the child ... The parents who spend the most on their child may in fact get much less pleasure, let alone much less long-term benefit, from that investment. The parents who have little money to spend but a great deal of love and attention to give may get much more. But who can say? That is why they must be assumed to cancel one another out. That is why the high-flying career woman whose sterilisation fails is in no better position than the hard-pressed single parent. It is probably safe to assume that the ordinary person would be more sympathetic to the hard-pressed single parent than to the high-flying career woman. But they differ from one another only in their financial circumstances and the law does not usually regard this as relevant. There is, however, a crucial difference between them and a seriously disabled parent. These able-bodied parents are both of them able to look after and bring up their child. No doubt they would both benefit from a nanny or other help in doing so. But they do not need it in order to be able to discharge the basic parental responsibility of looking after the child properly and safely, performing those myriad essential but mundane tasks such as feeding, bathing, clothing, training, supervising, playing with, reading to and taking to school which every child needs. They do not need it in order to avoid the risk that the child may have to be taken away to be looked after by the local social services authority or others, to the detriment of the child as well as the parent. That is the distinction between an able-bodied parent and a disabled parent who needs help if she is to be able to discharge the most ordinary tasks involved in the parental responsibility which has been placed upon her as a result of the defendant's negligence. Hence I would conclude that, just as the extra costs involved in discharging that responsibility towards a disabled child can be recovered, so too can the extra costs involved in a disabled parent discharging that responsibility towards a healthy child. Of course we can assume that such a parent benefits, and benefits greatly, from having a child she never thought she would have. We can and must assume that those benefits negative the claim for the ordinary costs of looking after and bringing him up. But we do not have to assume that it goes further than that. She is not being over-compensated by being given recompense for the extra costs of childcare occasioned by her disability. She is being put in the same position as her able-bodied fellows.'

OBP Textbook page 108, section 8.2.

Negligence: Breach of the Duty

Magnitude of the risk

Coxall v *Goodyear Great Britain Ltd* (2002) The Times 5 August Court of Appeal (Simon Brown and Brooke LJJ)

Employee running risk of physical danger – employer's duty to dismiss

Facts
Although the defendant employer's manufacturing process was safe and satisfactory, as both the defendant and the claimant employee were aware, exposure to the fumes involved placed the claimant asthma sufferer at risk of exacerbation of his condition. His condition having deteriorated, he sought damages from the defendant.

Held
His action would be successful. Simon Brown LJ said that counsel for the defendant's central contention had been that an employer was not under a duty to remove an employee from safe work, still less dismiss him, because he was not suited to the work. Rather, he submitted, it was for the employee to decide whether or not to take the risk of continuing in his job. He had relied on *Withers* v *Perry Chain Co Ltd* [1961] 1 WLR 1314. His Lordship thought that this argument went too far. The principal consideration in determining whether any particular case fell within the *Withers* principle was the actual nature and extent of the known risk. Cases would undoubtedly arise when, despite the employee's desire to remain at work notwithstanding his recognition of the risk he ran, the employer would nevertheless be under a duty in law to dismiss him for his own good so as to protect him against physical danger. That duty arose in this case.

Comment
The ordinary principles of employer's liability apply to claims for psychiatric or physical injury or illness arising from the stress of work: *Hatton* v *Sutherland* (2002) The Times 12 February. In her judgment in this case, Hale LJ identified four

categories of claims for psychiatric injury and enunciated 16 propositions in relation to aspects of liability arising from stress at work.

OBP Textbook page 132, section 9.4.

Negligence: Causation

Omissions

Chester v *Afshar* [2002] 3 All ER 552 Court of Appeal (Hale LJ, Sir Christopher Slade and Sir Denis Henry)

Surgery – failure to advise as to risks – liability

Facts

For some years the claimant had suffered severe back pain. As the defendant surgeon was aware, she was anxious to avoid surgery. Nevertheless, he advised her to have an operation, but failed to warn her of the risk of paralysis. The operation was performed without negligence but paralysis ensued. The claimant alleged that, had she been warned, she would have sought further opinions as to her options: she did not contend that she would never, at any time or under any circumstances, have consented to surgery. On appeal, the defendant argued that the claimant was entitled to succeed only if she established that, had she been warned of the risk, she would never have consented to an operation.

Held

This was not the case: the appeal would be dismissed.

Sir Denis Henry:

> 'The law is designed to require doctors properly to inform their patients of the risks attendant on their treatment and to answer questions put to them as to that treatment and its dangers, such answers to be judged in the context of good professional practice ... The object is to enable the patient to decide whether or not to run the risks of having that operation at that time. If the doctor's failure to take that care results in her consenting to an operation to which she would not otherwise have given her consent, the purpose of that rule would be thwarted if he were not to be held responsible when the very risk about which he failed to warn her materialises and causes her an injury which she would not have suffered then and there ... It would in our judgment be unjust to hold that the effective cause of the claimant's injury was the random occurrence of the 1 per cent to 2 per cent risk ... rather than the defendant's failure to bring such risk to her attention.'

OBP Textbook page 146, section 10.4.

Proof of causation

Fairchild v *Glenhaven Funeral Services Ltd* [2002] 3 All ER 305 House of Lords (Lords Bingham of Cornhill, Nicholls of Birkenhead, Hoffmann, Hutton and Rodger of Earlsferry)

Negligence – causation – breach of duty by more than one employer – liability

Facts

Lord Bingham of Cornhill stated the essential question underlying these three appeals as follows:

'If (1) C was employed at different times and for differing periods by both A and B, and (2) A and B were both subject to a duty to take reasonable care or to take all practicable measures to prevent C inhaling asbestos dust because of the known risk that asbestos dust (if inhaled) might cause a mesothelioma, and (3) both A and B were in breach of that duty in relation to C during the periods of C's employment by each of them with the result that during both periods C inhaled excessive quantities of asbestos dust, and (4) C is found to be suffering from a mesothelioma, and (5) any cause of C's mesothelioma other than the inhalation of asbestos dust at work can be effectively discounted, but (6) C cannot (because of the current limits of human science) prove, on the balance of probabilities, that his mesothelioma was the result of his inhaling asbestos dust during his employment by A or during his employment by B or during his employment by A and B taken together, is C entitled to recover damages against either A or B or against both A and B?'

In the Court of Appeal ([2002] 1 WLR 1052) C failed against both A and B.

Held

C could recover damages against both A and B.

Lord Bingham of Cornhill:

'I would answer that where conditions (1)–(6) are satisfied C is entitled to recover against both A and B. That conclusion is in my opinion consistent with principle, and also with authority (properly understood). Where those conditions are satisfied, it seems to me just and in accordance with common sense to treat the conduct of A and B in exposing C to a risk to which he should not have been exposed as making a material contribution to the contracting by C of a condition against which it was the duty of A and B to protect him. I consider that this conclusion is fortified by the wider jurisprudence reviewed above. Policy considerations weigh in favour of such a conclusion. It is a conclusion which follows even if either A or B is not before the court. It was not suggested in argument that C's entitlement against either A or B should be for any sum less than the full compensation to which C is entitled, although A and B could of course seek contribution against each other or any other employer liable in respect of the same damage in the ordinary way. No argument on apportionment was addressed to the House. I would in conclusion emphasise that my opinion is directed to cases in which each of the conditions specified in (1)–(6) … above is satisfied and to no other case. It would be unrealistic to suppose that the principle here affirmed will not over time be the subject of incremental and analogical development. Cases seeking to develop the principle must be decided when and as they arise.'

Comment

Their Lordships applied *McGhee* v *National Coal Board* [1972] 3 All ER 1008, but disapproved of a dictum of Lord Bridge in *Wilsher* v *Essex Area Health Authority* [1986] 3 All ER 801. This dictum is reproduced on p150 of the OBP Textbook.

OBP Textbook page 147, section 10.6.

Loss of a chance

Sharif v *Garrett & Co* [2002] 3 All ER 195 Court of Appeal (Simon Brown, Chadwick and Tuckey LJJ)

Solicitors – negligence – action struck out – assessment of damages

Facts

The appellants' cash and carry warehouse was partially destroyed by fire. Insurance cover had been arranged by brokers (PBL) but the insurers refused to meet the claim. The appellants engaged the respondent solicitors to sue PBL but the claim was struck out for want of prosecution. The respondents admitted that they had been negligent and accepted that, if the claim against PBL had been successful, the appellants would have recovered at least £842,000 plus interest. In their claim against the respondents the appellants were awarded only the premium paid to the insurers (about £12,000) and the costs paid to the respondents (about £11,000) plus interest, the judge having concluded that their prospects of recovering their losses from PBL were negligible. On appeal, the appellants contended that their prospects had been good: the judge should have awarded them substantial damages for loss of a chance.

Held

The appeal would be allowed and, in all the circumstances, the appellants would be awarded £250,000 by way of damages. Their claim against PBL had not been entirely straightforward. Indeed, there had been a substantial risk that they would lose altogether and, if they had won, it was most unlikely that they would recover the full value of their claim.

Comment

For a statement of the principles to be applied to the assessment of damages in cases such as this, see the judgment of Simon Brown LJ in *Mount* v *Baker Austin* [1998] PNLR 493 at 510–511.

OBP Textbook page 151, section 10.7.

Private Nuisance

Who can be sued in nuisance?

Marcic v *Thames Water Utilities Ltd* (2002) The Times 14 February Court of Appeal (Lord Phillips MR, Aldous and Ward LJJ)

Nuisance – frequent flooding of house – remedies

Facts

Like many others in the area, the claimant's house was regularly and seriously affected by flooding and back flow of foul water from the defendant statutory water and sewerage undertaker's sewer system. He sought an injunction to prevent the flooding and damages in respect of the damage which it caused to his property. Judge Richard Harvey QC held that at common law – nuisance, negligence, breach of statutory duty or under the rule in *Rylands* v *Fletcher* (1868) LR 3 HL 330 – his claim could not succeed. However, the defendant's failure to provide a proper drainage system infringed his human rights as provided in the European Convention for the Protection of Human Rights and Fundamental Freedoms and by virtue of s6 of the Human Rights Act 1998, that failure constituted a breach of the duty owed to him by the defendant. The Convention rights in question were contained in art 8 (right to respect for private and family life) and in art 1 of the First Protocol (protection of property). Both parties appealed.

Held

The defendant's appeal (as to liability under the Human Rights Act 1998) would be dismissed but the claimant's cross-appeal (as to liability in nuisance) would be allowed. The Master of the Rolls observed that *Goldman* v *Hargrave* [1967] 1 AC 645 and *Leakey* v *National Trust* [1980] QB 485 marked a significant extension of the law of nuisance, which had already been radically extended by *Sedleigh-Denfield* v *O'Callaghan* [1940] AC 880. Applying the principles in *Goldman* and *Leakey*, the defendant was under a duty to the claimant to take such steps as, in all the circumstances, were reasonable to prevent the discharge of sewerage on to his property. Applying the *Leakey* test of duty to a sewerage undertaking, the reasonableness of the defendant's conduct had to be judged having regard to all the steps open to it to take to abate the nuisance. The defendant had failed to demonstrate by way of defence that it was not reasonably practicable for it to prevent the nuisance.

OBP Textbook page 246, section 18.10.

Fire

The Fires Prevention (Metropolis) Act 1774

Johnson v *BJW Property Developments Ltd* [2002] 3 All ER 574 Queen's Bench Division (Technology and Construction Court) (Judge Thornton QC)

Escape of fire – independent contractor negligent – liability

Facts

The claimant and the defendant owned and occupied adjoining properties, separated by a party wall. In the defendant's premises, a fireplace was built into the party wall: a domestic fire lit there spread into, and caused extensive damage to, the claimant's premises. An independent contractor, employed by the defendant, had been negligent in installing a new fire surround: he had removed fire protection from the fireplace and not replaced it. The claimant maintained that the defendant was strictly liable for the escape of fire from its premises, a view supported, by implication, by s86 Fires Prevention (Metropolis) Act 1774 (the fire which spread into its premises had been lit deliberately, it had not 'accidentally' begun). The defendant also relied on s86 of the 1774 Act, contending that 'accidentally' covered fires started in domestic grates.

Held

The claimant was entitled to succeed. The 1774 Act was of no relevance to the fire in the grate since that fire had been started deliberately. It was the escape of the fire which gave rise to liability and the possible defence of accidental escape. Here the escape had not been accidental: it had resulted from negligence for which the defendant was responsible.

Judge Thornton QC:

'... all the requirements that need to be shown to give rise to an occupier's vicarious liability for the negligence of his independent contractor have been made out. The relevant work was undertaken negligently on and adjacent to a party wall. It involved a special risk to, and by its very nature endangered, the claimant's adjoining premises. I conclude that the claimant is entitled to judgment against the defendant for liability with damages to be assessed. That liability is in both negligence and nuisance, being both a primary liability for the fire damage and also vicarious liability for the negligence of its independent contractor in causing that damage.'

OBP Textbook pages 40 and 279, sections 5.2 and 21.4.

Defamation

Publication

McManus v *Beckham* [2002] 4 All ER 497 Court of Appeal (Waller, Clarke and Laws LJJ)

Slander – publication in press of slanderous words – liability

Facts
The claimant proprietors of an autograph shop alleged that the defendant, Victoria Beckham, had said, in the presence of customers, that the autograph on a photograph of her husband David was a fake. The incident received considerable press coverage. Could the claimants rely on the press coverage in establishing the loss they said they had suffered?

Held
They could, to the extent that it was just to do so.

Waller LJ:

> 'What the law is striving to achieve in this area is a just and reasonable result by reference to the position of a reasonable person in the position of the defendant. If a defendant is actually aware (1) that what she says or does is likely to be reported, and (2) that if she slanders someone that slander is likely to be repeated in whole or in part, there is no injustice in her being held responsible for the damage that the slander causes via that publication. I would suggest further that if a jury were to conclude that a reasonable person in the position of the defendant should have appreciated that there was a significant risk that what she said would be repeated in whole or in part in the press and that that would increase the damage caused by the slander, it is not unjust that the defendant should be liable for it. Thus I would suggest a direction along the above lines rather than by reference to "foreseeability".'

OBP Textbook page 301, section 23.6.

Qualified privilege

Kearns v *General Council of the Bar* [2002] 4 All ER 1075 Queen's Bench Division (Eady J)

Qualified privilege – communication from Bar Council to Bar

Facts
Responding to a request for guidance from a member of the Bar, the Bar Council sent a letter to all heads of chambers and senior clerks/practice managers stating – incorrectly – that the claimants were not solicitors. Two days later the Bar Council sent a letter of correction and apology to those who had received their original letter, a letter of apology having been faxed to the claimants the previous day.

Nevertheless, the claimants sued for libel and the Bar Council sought the summary dismissal of those proceedings on the grounds of qualified privilege. The claimants did not allege malice.

Held
The Bar Council's application would be successful.

Eady J:

> '... it has long been the policy of the law to protect persons in certain kinds of relationship with one another, and indeed to encourage in such cases free and frank communications in what is perceived to be the general interest of society. In those cases, one does not need to assess the interest of society afresh in each case. We all need to know where we stand. In this area the law was thought to be settled, on the basis that the balance would fairly be struck if liability in such situations was confined to those cases where the occasion of communication was abused – in the sense that malice could be established. Nothing short of malice would undermine the law's protection ... I am left in no doubt that this is a classic case of qualified privilege based upon an existing relationship, and on a common and corresponding interest in the subject matter of the letter. Since malice is not alleged the defendants are, in my judgment, entitled to the summary relief sought.'

Comment
His Lordship distinguished *Stuart* v *Bell* [1891] 2 QB 341 since it turned upon duty as opposed – as here – to an established relationship.

There is no rule of practice that courts should direct issues of qualified privilege to be heard in advance of the main trial of defamation, although in exercise of his discretion the judge could direct this course: *Macintyre* v *Phillips* (2002) The Times 30 August.

OBP Textbook page 310, section 23.14.

Justification or truth: remedies

Grobbelaar v *News Group Newspapers Ltd* [2002] 4 All ER 732 House of Lords (Lords Bingham of Cornhill, Steyn, Hobhouse of Woodborough, Millett and Scott of Foscote)

Libel – challenging jury's verdict – substitution of amount of damages

Facts
In a series of articles in the defendants' newspaper (*The Sun*) it was alleged that the claimant, a professional footballer, had taken money to fix matches. He brought an action for libel and the defendants' plea of justification was left to the jury. In the event, the jury awarded the claimant damages of £85,000. The defendants appealed and the Court of Appeal concluded that the jury's verdict represented a miscarriage of justice and would be set aside. The claimant appealed against this decision.

Held

While it was safe to infer that the jury was satisfied that the claimant had made corrupt agreements and corruptly accepted money, since the defendants had failed to prove that the claimant had actually fixed matches or attempted to do so, the first instance finding in the claimant's favour would be restored. Lord Steyn dissented from this decision. However, since it would be an affront of justice to award the claimant substantial damages, the jury's award would be quashed and an award of £1 substituted.

Lord Millett:

'In my view an appellate court ought not to find the verdict of a jury on liability to be perverse unless there is no rational explanation for it ... If the jury found that the sting of the libel lay in the allegations of match-fixing rather than the allegations of the corrupt agreements, they were entitled to find that this had not been established. This is sufficient to uphold their verdict for the appellant on liability. They should not be taken to have reached a perverse finding, in the teeth of overwhelming evidence to the contrary, that the newspaper had also failed to establish the existence of the corrupt agreements. But a finding that the appellant had been a party to either or both corrupt agreements would be enough to deprive him of any right to substantial damages. It would be an affront to justice if a man who accepts bribes to throw matches should obtain damages for the loss of his reputation as a professional sportsman merely because he cannot be shown to have carried out his part of the bargain.'

OBP Textbook pages 303 and 314, sections 23.12 and 23.18.

Remedies

Kiam v *MGN Ltd* [2002] 2 All ER 219 Court of Appeal (Simon Brown, Waller and Sedley LJJ)

Libel – damages – jury's award – power to substitute

Facts

In proceedings for libel, the judge indicated that an award of damages within the range of £40,000–£80,000 might be appropriate. The jury awarded £105,000. The defendant appealed against this award, asking the Court of Appeal to exercise its power under s8 Courts and Legal Services Act 1990 to reduce it.

Held (Sedley LJ dissenting)

The appeal would be dismissed.

Simon Brown LJ:

'This court can only interfere with a jury's award if it is "excessive". (We are not here concerned with the other limb of the power, to vary an "inadequate" award.) The question for the court is whether a reasonable jury could have thought the award necessary to compensate the claimant and to re-establish his reputation. If the answer is "No", the award is to be regarded as excessive and the court will substitute for it a "proper" award. But what is a "proper" award? Is it whatever sum the court thinks appropriate, wholly uninfluenced by the jury's view? Or is it rather the highest award which the jury could reasonably have thought necessary? I take it to be the latter. In *Gorman* v *Mudd* [1992] CA Transcript 1076, for example, where the court substituted an award of £50,000 for the jury's award of £150,000, Neill LJ concluded that "on no possible view could the award of damages exceed £50,000", Rose LJ agreeing "that a proper award cannot exceed £50,000". The Court of Appeal should surely take as much account as it properly can of the jury's attitude to the case and only on this approach would it be doing so. To my mind, therefore, this court should not interfere with the jury's award unless it regards it as substantially exceeding the most that any jury could reasonably have thought appropriate ... the present award ... is not so far removed from my own (or evidently, the trial judge's) view of the true value of the claim as to justify the exercise of the s8 power.'

OBP Textbook page 315, section 23.18.

Passing Off

Made by a trader in the course of a trade

Irvine v *Talksport Ltd* [2002] 2 All ER 414 Chancery Division (Laddie J)

Brochure – false endorsement – applicability of passing off

Facts
Having obtained the rights to broadcast live the Formula One Grand Prix World Championship, the defendant radio station sent a brochure to potential advertisers. On the front cover of the brochure was a photograph of the claimant, a prominent British racing driver, which had been purchased from a photograph agency. As purchased, the photograph showed the claimant holding a mobile telephone: as it appeared in the brochure, he was holding a portable radio bearing the defendant's name. In an action for damages for passing off, the court had to decide whether (1) the law of passing off applied to cases of false endorsement, and (2) it was necessary to show that the claimant and the defendant shared a 'common field of activity'.

Held
Passing off could apply to false endorsement and it was not necessary to show that the parties shared a common field of activity.

Laddie J:

'... to succeed, the burden on the claimant includes a need to prove at least two, interrelated, facts. First that at the time of the acts complained of he had a significant reputation or goodwill. Second that the actions of the defendant gave rise to a false message which would be understood by a not insignificant section of his market that his goods have been endorsed, recommended or are approved of by the claimant ... I have come to the conclusion that Mr Irvine succeeds in this action.'

Comment

The 'common field of activity' requirement was enunciated by Wynn-Parry J in *McCulloch* v *May* [1947] 2 All ER 845. In *Harrods Ltd* v *Harrodian School Ltd* [1996] RPC 697, Millett LJ had observed that this approach was contrary to numerous previous authorities.

OBP Textbook page 358, section 28.3.

Remedies

Loss of pension rights

Needler Financial Services Ltd v *Taber* [2002] 3 All ER 501 Chancery Division (Sir Andrew Morritt V-C)

Transfer of pension – demutualisation – credit against loss?

Facts

Acting on the assumed negligent advice of the claimant financial services company, Mr Taber transferred his deferred benefits under an occupational pension scheme to the Norwich Union. Having retired and found that his Norwich Union pension was less than he would have received under his original scheme, Mr Taber sought compensation. When Norwich Union was demutualised Mr Taber received an appropriate number of shares: should the value of these shares be taken into account when determining the amount that he should receive?

Held

It should not since the demutualisation benefit by way of shares had not been caused by the pension misselling.

Sir Andrew Morritt V-C:

> '... the relevant question is whether the negligence which caused the loss also caused the profit in the sense that the latter was part of a continuous transaction of which the former was the inception ... the demutualisation benefit was not caused by and did not flow, as part of a continuous transaction, from the negligence. In causation terms the breach of duty gave rise to the opportunity to receive the profit, but did not cause it (see ... *Galoo Ltd* v *Bright Grahame Murray* [1994] 1 WLR 1360 at 1375).'

OBP Textbook page 389, section 30.8.

Loss of housekeeping capacity

Lowe v *Guise* [2002] 3 All ER 454 Court of Appeal (Potter and Rix LJJ, Morland J)

Personal injury – damages – reduced ability to provide gratuitous carer services

Facts

The claimant had been injured as a result of the negligent driving of the defendant. The claimant lived with his mother and his severely disabled brother. Prior to the accident the claimant had provided gratuitous carer services for his brother, estimated at some 77 hours per week. For two months following the accident he had been unable to provide any care to his brother at all. Thereafter he had resumed looking after his brother, but he had been limited by his injuries to providing only 35 hours per week, the shortfall being made up by his mother. Could he recover damages for the carer services that he was no longer able to provide?

Held

He was so entitled.

Rix LJ:

'... the disabled brother is part of the household and one whose care had, prior to the accident, been the [claimant's] prime responsibility. That care was not a mere gratuitous favour bestowed on a third party, but was a responsibility of his own, adopted by him and owed to his brother, but also to his mother with whom he shared the household. When he lost the ability to care for his brother for more than 35 hours per week, he lost something of real value to himself (as well as to his brother) which was his contribution to his family's welfare, and his loss imposed a corresponding obligation on his mother to make good by her own care what he was no longer able to provide. In my judgment the [claimant] is entitled to claim in respect of the loss of his ability to look after his brother. Since he will maintain his state [invalid care] allowance, he has suffered no loss so far as that allowance is itself concerned. But he has suffered a loss nevertheless because, even though his care was provided gratuitously, it can and ought as a matter of policy to be measured in money's worth. To the extent that his mother has by her own additional care mitigated the [claimant's] loss, it may be that the [claimant] would hold that recovery in trust for his mother ... The common law should not, and need not, leave the question "am I my brother's keeper?" with the wrong answer.'

Comment

This decision should be compared with the decision of the House of Lords in *Hunt v Severs* [1994] 2 All ER 385 where the defendant tortfeasor was himself the voluntary carer.

A dependency claim by infants under the Fatal Accidents Act 1976 should not include damages related to the value of services provided by their father and step-mother, in place of their deceased mother, if the damages would not reach the service providers because they did not wish to be paid for their service: *H v S* (2002) The Times 3 July.

OBP Textbook page 389, section 30.9.

Loss of expectation of life

The level of bereavement damages has been raised to £10,000 for causes of action accruing on or after 1 April 2002.

OBP Textbook page 398, section 30.16.

Miscellaneous Defences and Limitation

Limitation

Cave v Robinson Jarvis and Rolf [2002] 2 All ER 641 House of Lords (Lords Slynn of Hadley, Mackay of Clashfern, Hobhouse of Woodborough, Millett and Scott of Foscote)

Limitation of action – defendant unaware of breach of duty – s32(2) Limitation Act 1980

Facts

The claimant alleged that the defendant solicitors had been negligent in preparing a document conferring upon him mooring rights. The defendants pleaded, inter alia, that the action was time-barred and the claimant contended that s32(2) Limitation Act 1980 applied since the allegedly negligent drafting was an intentional act and any breach of duty was unlikely to be discovered for some time. The claimant's contention was accepted at first instance and by the Court of Appeal: time had not begun to run until the alleged drafting flaw had come to light. Did s32(2) apply even where (as here) the defendant had not been aware that he had been committing a breach of duty?

Held

It did not: the defendants' appeal would be allowed.

Lord Millett:

'Section 32(2) was … enacted to cover cases where active concealment should not be required. But such cases were limited in two respects: first, the defendant must have been guilty of a deliberate commission of a breach of duty; and secondly, the circumstances must make it unlikely that the breach of duty will be discovered for some time. Given that s32(2) is (or at least may be) required to cover cases of non–disclosure rather than active concealment, the reason for limiting it to the deliberate commission of a breach of duty becomes clear. It is only where the defendant is aware of his own deliberate wrongdoing that it is appropriate to penalise him for failing to disclose it. In my opinion, s32 of the 1980 Act deprives a defendant of a limitation defence in two situations: (i) where he takes active steps to conceal his own breach of duty after he has become aware of it; and (ii) where he is guilty of deliberate wrongdoing and conceals or fails to disclose it in circumstances where it is unlikely to be discovered for some time. But it does not deprive a defendant of a limitation defence where he is charged with negligence if, being unaware of his error or that he has failed to take proper care, there has been nothing for him to disclose.'

Comment

Their Lordships disapproved of the Court of Appeal's decision in *Brocklesby* v *Armitage & Guest* [2001] 1 All ER 172 and overruled Laddie J's decision in *Liverpool Roman Catholic Archdiocese Trustees Incorporated* v *Goldberg* [2001] 1 All ER 182.

OBP Textbook page 413, section 31.5.

Torts to Chattels

Conversion

Kuwait Airways Corp v *Iraqi Airways Co (No 3)* [2002] 3 All ER 209
House of Lords (Lords Nicholls of Birkenhead, Steyn, Hoffmann, Hope of Craighead and Scott of Foscote)

Conversion – 'but for' test – successive conversion – consequential loss

Facts
During the invasion and occupation of Kuwait, the Iraqi forces seized ten of the claimant's (KAC's) aircraft and flew them to Iraq. The Iraq Revolutionary Command Council (RCC) dissolved the claimant and transferred all its property to the state-owned defendant (IAC). Before military action began, the claimant sued for the return of the aircraft, or payment of their value, and damages. In the course of the war, four aircraft ('the Mosul Four') were destroyed by coalition bombing. The other six ('the Iran Six') were evacuated to Iran and eventually returned to Kuwait on payment of a substantial sum by the claimant to the Iran Government for their safekeeping.

Held (Lord Scott of Foscote dissenting)
The claim in respect of the Mosul Four would fail since, on the facts, the claimant had been unable to satisfy the Iraqi law 'but for' test as to loss or damage. However, as to the Iran Six, where the aircraft were recovered largely undamaged, the Iraqi test was no more stringent than the requirements of English law. Accordingly, in principle, the damages awarded should include the amount paid to the Government of Iran, the reasonable costs of overhauling and repairing the aircraft on their return and the reasonable costs of chartering substitute aircraft and making good any loss of profits.

Lord Nicholls of Birkenhead:

'... in the present proceedings the court has to apply the so-called double actionability rule, as generally understood since the decision of the House in *Chaplin* v *Boys* [1969] 2

All ER 1085. The rule is that, in order to be actionable here, the acts done abroad must satisfy both limbs of a dual test. The acts must be such that, if done in England, they would be tortious. Additionally, the acts must be civilly actionable under the law of the country where they occurred ... In general, the basic features of the tort [of conversion] are threefold. First, the defendant's conduct was inconsistent with the rights of the owner (or other person entitled to possession). Second, the conduct was deliberate, not accidental. Third, the conduct was so extensive an encroachment on the rights of the owner as to exclude him from use and possession of the goods. The contrast is with lesser acts of interference. If these cause damage they may give rise to claims for trespass or in negligence, but they do not constitute conversion ... Here, on and after [RCC's dissolution of KAC], IAC was in possession and control of the ten aircraft. This possession was adverse to KAC. IAC believed the aircraft were now its property, just as much as the other aircraft in its fleet, and it acted accordingly. It intended to keep the goods as its own. It treated them as its own. It made such use of them as it could in the prevailing circumstances, although this was very limited because of the hostilities. In so conducting itself IAC was asserting rights inconsistent with KAC's rights as owner ... IAC's acts would have been tortious if done in this country.'

Comment

This decision was applied in *Marcq* v *Christie Manson and Woods Ltd* [2002] 4 All ER 1005, where Jack J held that auctioneers could not be liable in conversion if they had acted in good faith and without notice and that the burden of proving that they had so acted lay on the auctioneers.

OBP Textbook page 418, section 32.4.

Old Bailey Press

The Old Bailey Press integrated student law library is tailor-made to help you at every stage of your studies from the preliminaries of each subject through to the final examination. The series of Textbooks, Revision WorkBooks, 150 Leading Cases and Cracknell's Statutes are interrelated to provide you with a comprehensive set of study materials.

You can buy Old Bailey Press books from your University Bookshop, your local Bookshop, direct using this form, or you can order a free catalogue of our titles from the address shown overleaf.

The following subjects each have a Textbook, 150 Leading Cases/Casebook, Revision WorkBook and Cracknell's Statutes unless otherwise stated.

Administrative Law
Commercial Law
Company Law
Conflict of Laws
Constitutional Law
Conveyancing (Textbook and 150 Leading Cases)
Criminal Law
Criminology (Textbook and Sourcebook)
Employment Law (Textbook and Cracknell's Statutes)
English and European Legal Systems
Equity and Trusts
Evidence
Family Law
Jurisprudence: The Philosophy of Law (Textbook, Sourcebook and
    Revision WorkBook)
Land: The Law of Real Property
Law of International Trade
Law of the European Union
Legal Skills and System
    (Textbook)
Obligations: Contract Law
Obligations: The Law of Tort
Public International Law
Revenue Law (Textbook,
    Revision WorkBook and
    Cracknell's Statutes)
Succession

Mail order prices:	
Textbook	£14.95
150 Leading Cases	£11.95
Revision WorkBook	£9.95
Cracknell's Statutes	£11.95
Suggested Solutions 1998–1999	£6.95
Suggested Solutions 1999–2000	£6.95
Suggested Solutions 2000–2001	£6.95
Law Update 2003	£10.95

Please note details and prices are subject to alteration.

To complete your order, please fill in the form below:

Module	Books required	Quantity	Price	Cost
		Postage		
		TOTAL		

For Europe, add 15% postage and packing (£20 maximum).
For the rest of the world, add 40% for airmail.

ORDERING

By telephone to Mail Order at 020 8317 6039, with your credit card to hand.

By fax to 020 8317 6004 (giving your credit card details).

Website: www.oldbaileypress.co.uk

By post to: Mail Order, Old Bailey Press at Holborn College, Woolwich Road, Charlton, London, SE7 8LN.

When ordering by post, please enclose full payment by cheque or banker's draft, or complete the credit card details below. You may also order a free catalogue of our complete range of titles from this address.

We aim to despatch your books within 3 working days of receiving your order.

Name

Address

Postcode   Telephone

Total value of order, including postage: £

I enclose a cheque/banker's draft for the above sum, or

charge my   ☐ Access/Mastercard   ☐ Visa   ☐ American Express
Card number

☐☐☐☐ ☐☐☐☐ ☐☐☐☐ ☐☐☐☐

Expiry date   ☐☐☐☐

Signature: ....Date: ....